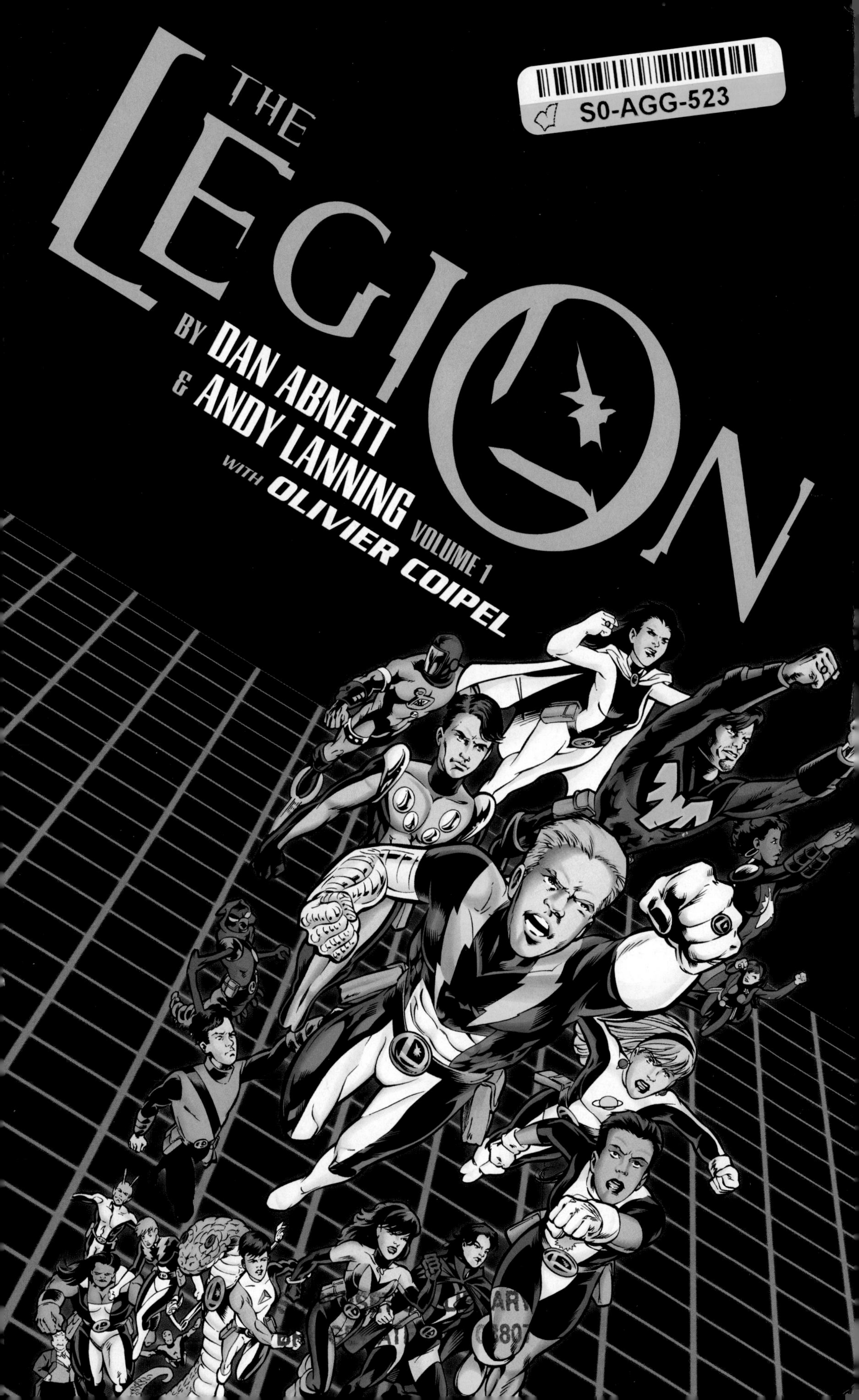
THE LEGION
BY DAN ABNETT
& ANDY LANNING
WITH OLIVIER COIPEL
VOLUME 1

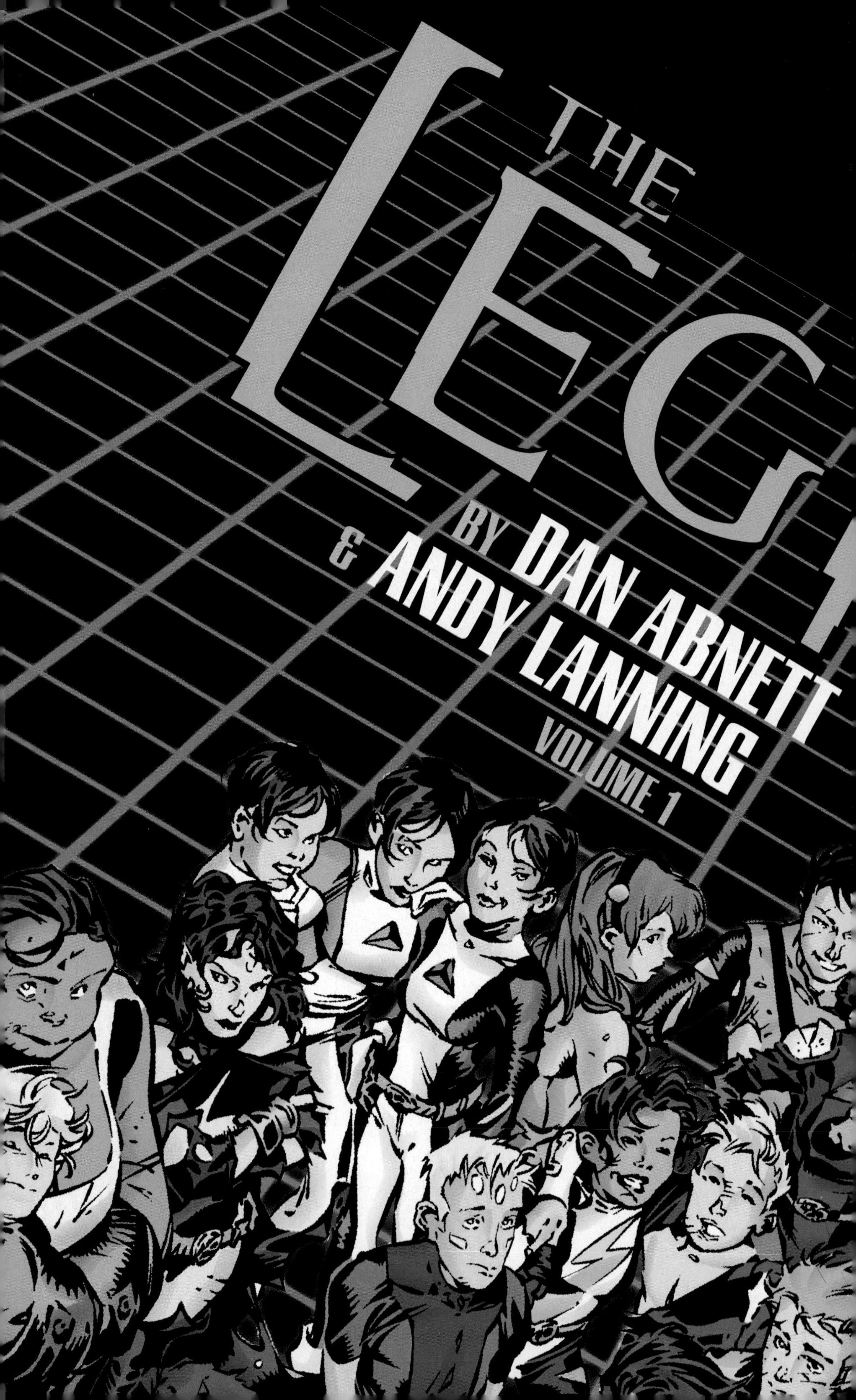
THE
LEG
BY DAN ABNETT
& ANDY LANNING
VOLUME 1

DAN ABNETT ANDY LANNING writers

OLIVIER COIPEL ADAM DEKRAKER JEFFREY MOY ANGEL UNZUETA CHUCK WOJTKIEWICZ pencillers

ANDY LANNING W.C. CARANI JAIME MENDOZA DEXTER VINES inkers

TOM McCRAW colorist

COMICRAFT PAT BROSSEAU CLEM ROBINS letterers

OLIVIER COIPEL, ANDY LANNING and **PATRICK MARTIN** collection cover artists

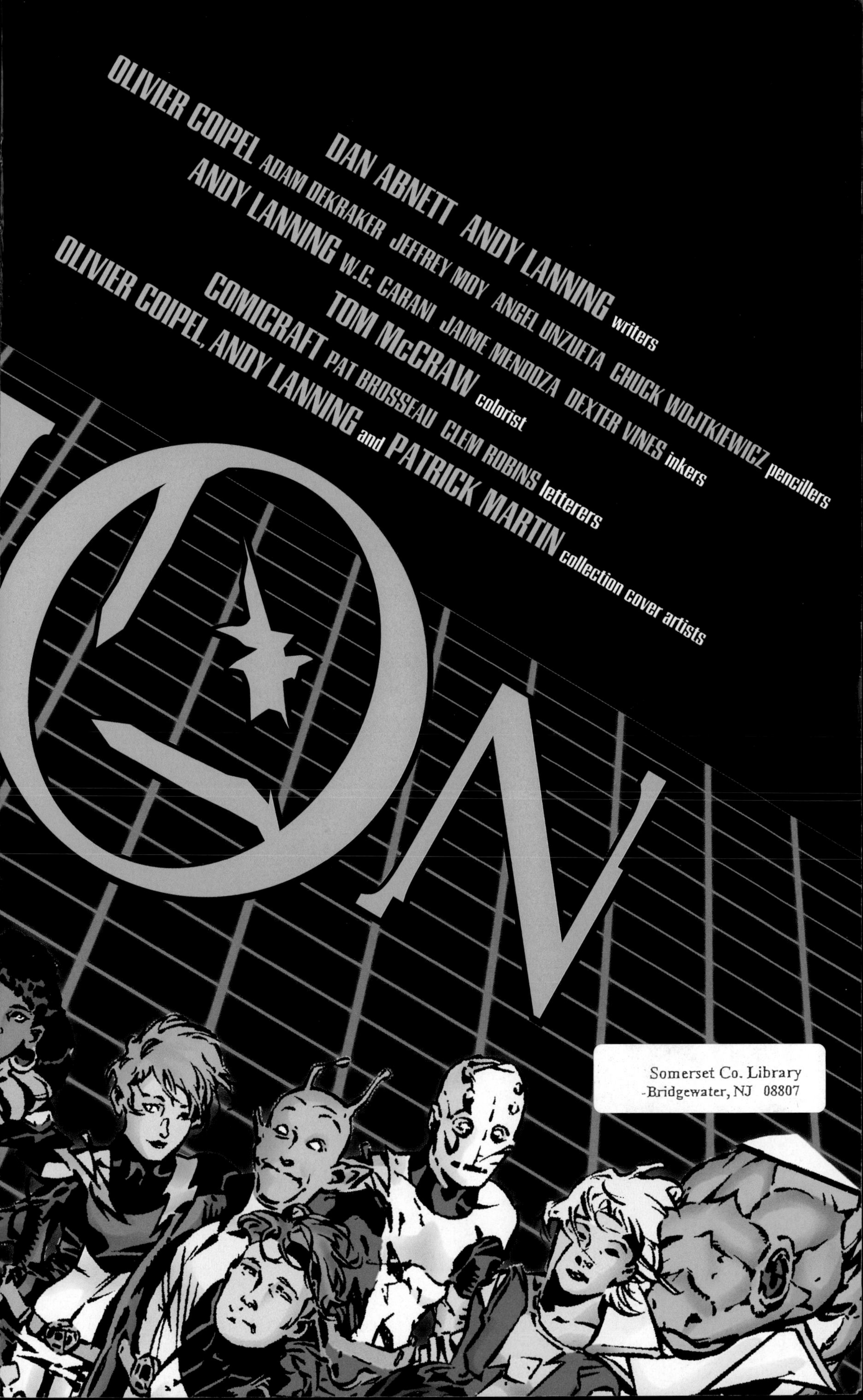

TONY BEDARD, MIKE McAVENNIE, MAUREEN McTIGUE Editors – Original Series JEB WOODARD Group Editor – Collected Editions

STEVE COOK Design Director – Books DAMIAN RYLAND Publication Design

DIANE NELSON President DAN DiDIO Publisher JIM LEE Publisher GEOFF JOHNS President & Chief Creative Officer

AMIT DESAI Executive VP – Business & Marketing Strategy, Direct to Consumer & Global Franchise Management SAM ADES Senior VP – Direct to Consumer

BOBBIE CHASE VP – Talent Development MARK CHIARELLO Senior VP – Art, Design & Collected Editions

JOHN CUNNINGHAM Senior VP – Sales & Trade Marketing ANNE DePIES Senior VP – Business Strategy, Finance & Administration

DON FALLETTI VP – Manufacturing Operations LAWRENCE GANEM VP – Editorial Administration & Talent Relations

ALISON GILL Senior VP – Manufacturing & Operations HANK KANALZ Senior VP – Editorial Strategy & Administration JAY KOGAN VP – Legal Affairs

THOMAS LOFTUS VP – Business Affairs JACK MAHAN VP – Business Affairs NICK J. NAPOLITANO VP – Manufacturing Administration

EDDIE SCANNELL VP – Consumer Marketing COURTNEY SIMMONS Senior VP – Publicity & Communications

JIM (SKI) SOKOLOWSKI VP – Comic Book Specialty Sales & Trade Marketing NANCY SPEARS VP – Mass, Book, Digital Sales & Trade Marketing

BOB HARRAS Senior VP – Editor-in-Chief, DC Comics

THE LEGION BY DAN ABNETT & ANDY LANNING VOLUME 1

Published by DC Comics. Compilation and all new material Copyright © 2017 DC Comics. All Rights Reserved. Originally published in single magazine form in LEGION OF SUPER-HEROES 122-125, LEGION OF SUPER-HEROES SECRET FILES 2, LEGIONNAIRES 78-81. Copyright © 1999, 2000 DC Comics. All Rights Reserved. All characters, their distinctive likenesses and related elements featured in this publication are trademarks of DC Comics. The stories, characters and incidents featured in this publication are entirely fictional. DC Comics does not read or accept unsolicited submissions of ideas, stories or artwork.

DC Comics, 2900 West Alameda Ave., Burbank, CA 91505. Printed by Vanguard Graphics, LLC, Ithaca, NY, USA. 8/18/17. First Printing. ISBN: 978-1-4012-7636-2

Library of Congress Cataloging-in-Publication Data is available.

UNKNOWN POINT OF ORIGIN

Written by DAN ABNETT and ANDY LANNING
Pencilled by CHUCK WOJTKIEWICZ Inked by DEXTER VINES Colored by TOM McCRAW
Lettered by CLEM ROBINS Cover by CHRIS SPROUSE and ANDY LANNING

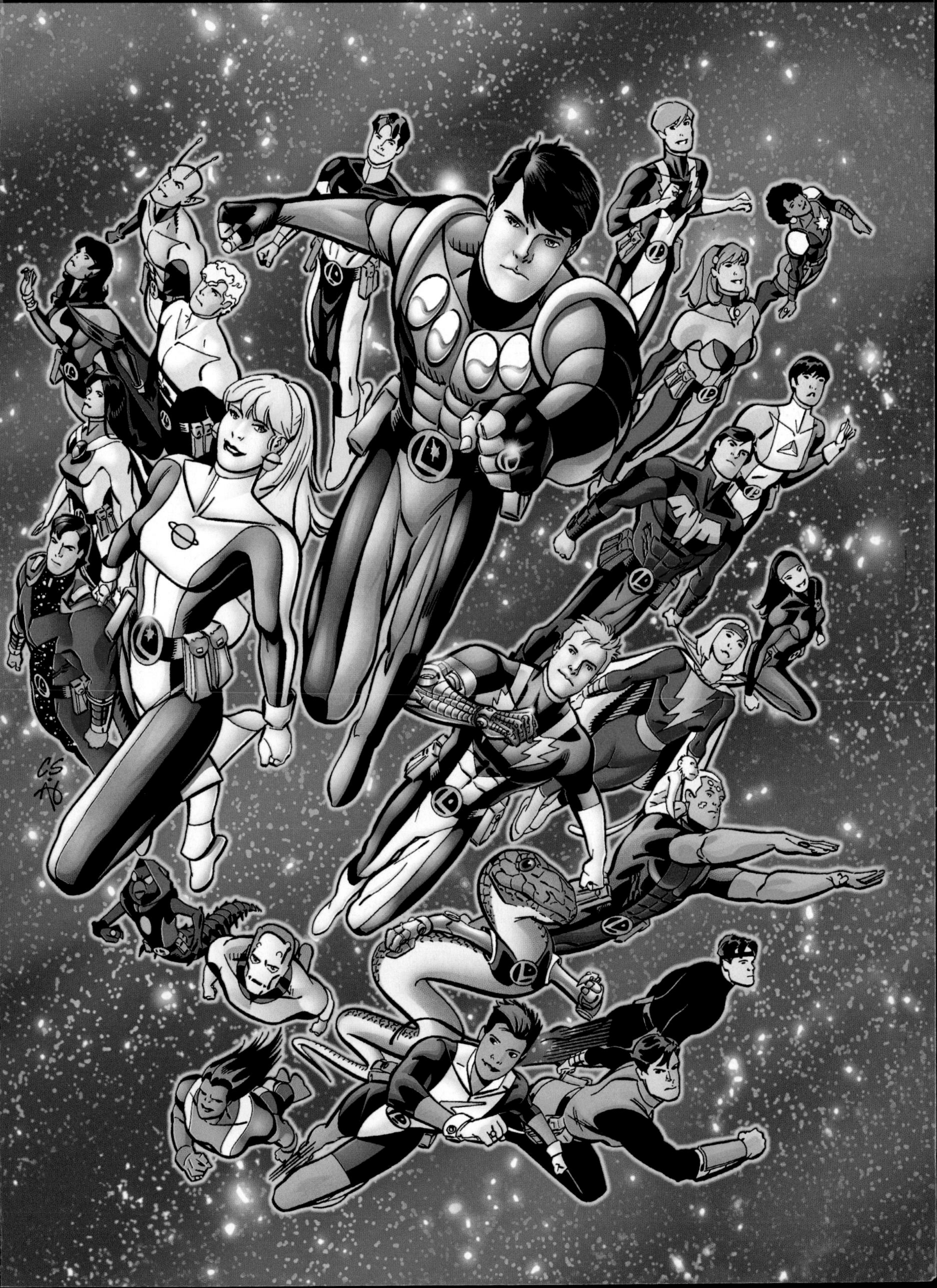

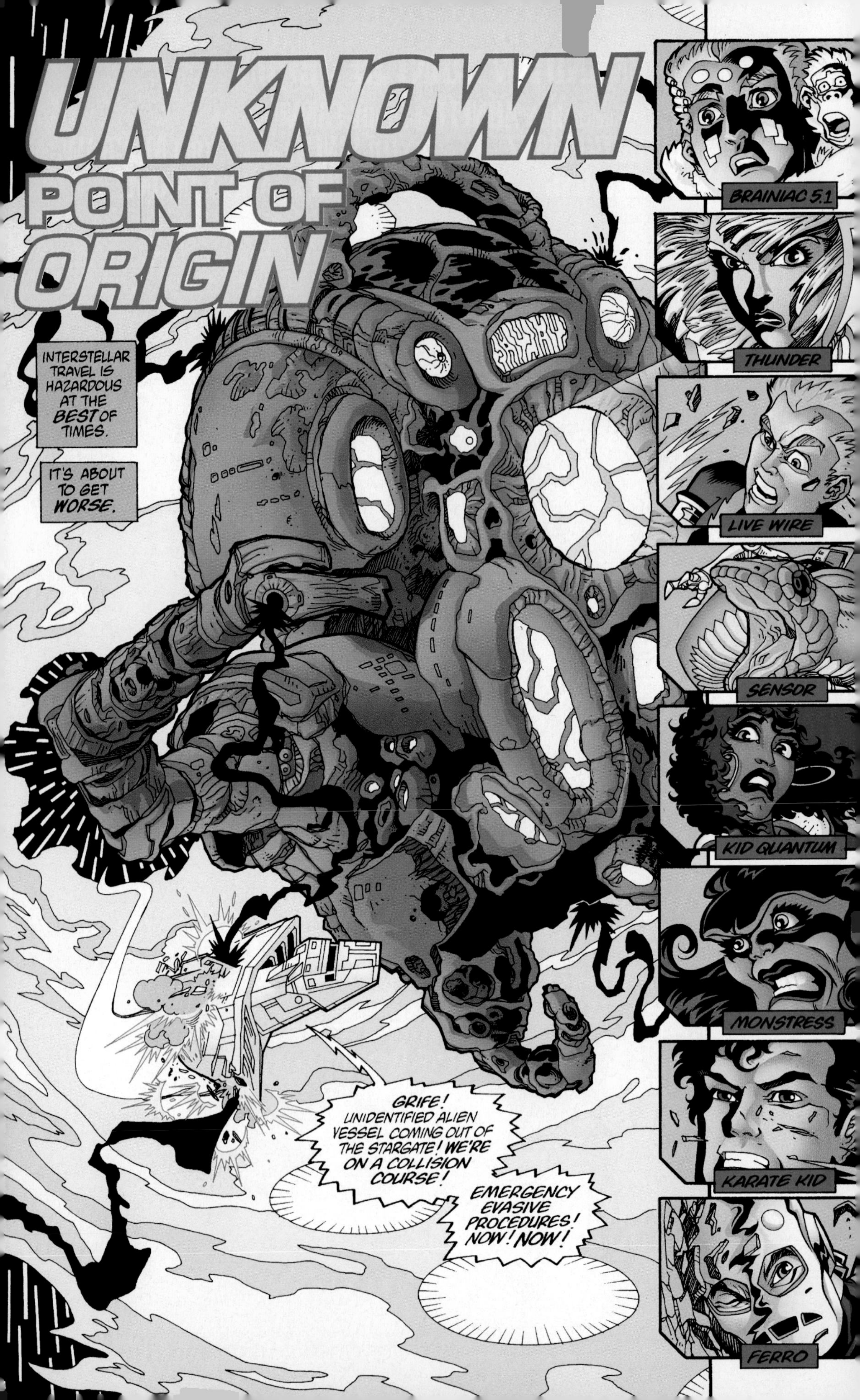
UNKNOWN POINT OF ORIGIN
INTERSTELLAR TRAVEL IS HAZARDOUS AT THE BEST OF TIMES.
IT'S ABOUT TO GET WORSE.
BRAINIAC 5.1
THUNDER
LIVE WIRE
SENSOR
KID QUANTUM
MONSTRESS
KARATE KID
FERRO
GRIFE! UNIDENTIFIED ALIEN VESSEL COMING OUT OF THE STARGATE! WE'RE ON A COLLISION COURSE!
EMERGENCY EVASIVE PROCEDURES! NOW! NOW!

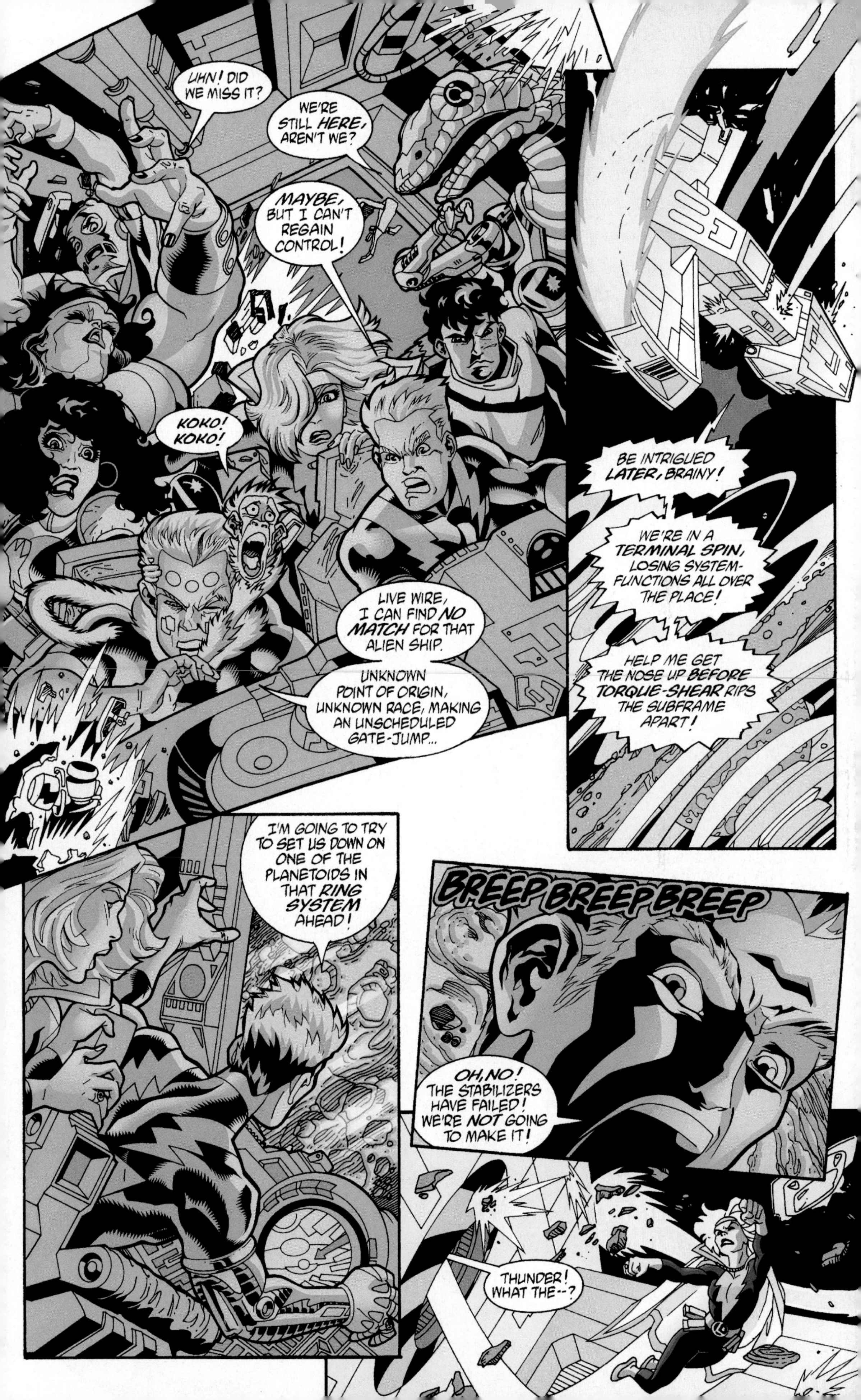
UHN! DID WE MISS IT?
WE'RE STILL HERE, AREN'T WE?
MAYBE, BUT I CAN'T REGAIN CONTROL!
KOKO! KOKO!
LIVE WIRE, I CAN FIND NO MATCH FOR THAT ALIEN SHIP.
UNKNOWN POINT OF ORIGIN, UNKNOWN RACE, MAKING AN UNSCHEDULED GATE-JUMP...
BE INTRIGUED LATER, BRAINY!
WE'RE IN A TERMINAL SPIN, LOSING SYSTEM-FUNCTIONS ALL OVER THE PLACE!
HELP ME GET THE NOSE UP BEFORE TORQUE-SHEAR RIPS THE SUBFRAME APART!
I'M GOING TO TRY TO SET US DOWN ON ONE OF THE PLANETOIDS IN THAT RING SYSTEM AHEAD!
BREEP BREEP BREEP BREEP
OH, NO! THE STABILIZERS HAVE FAILED! WE'RE NOT GOING TO MAKE IT!
THUNDER! WHAT THE--?

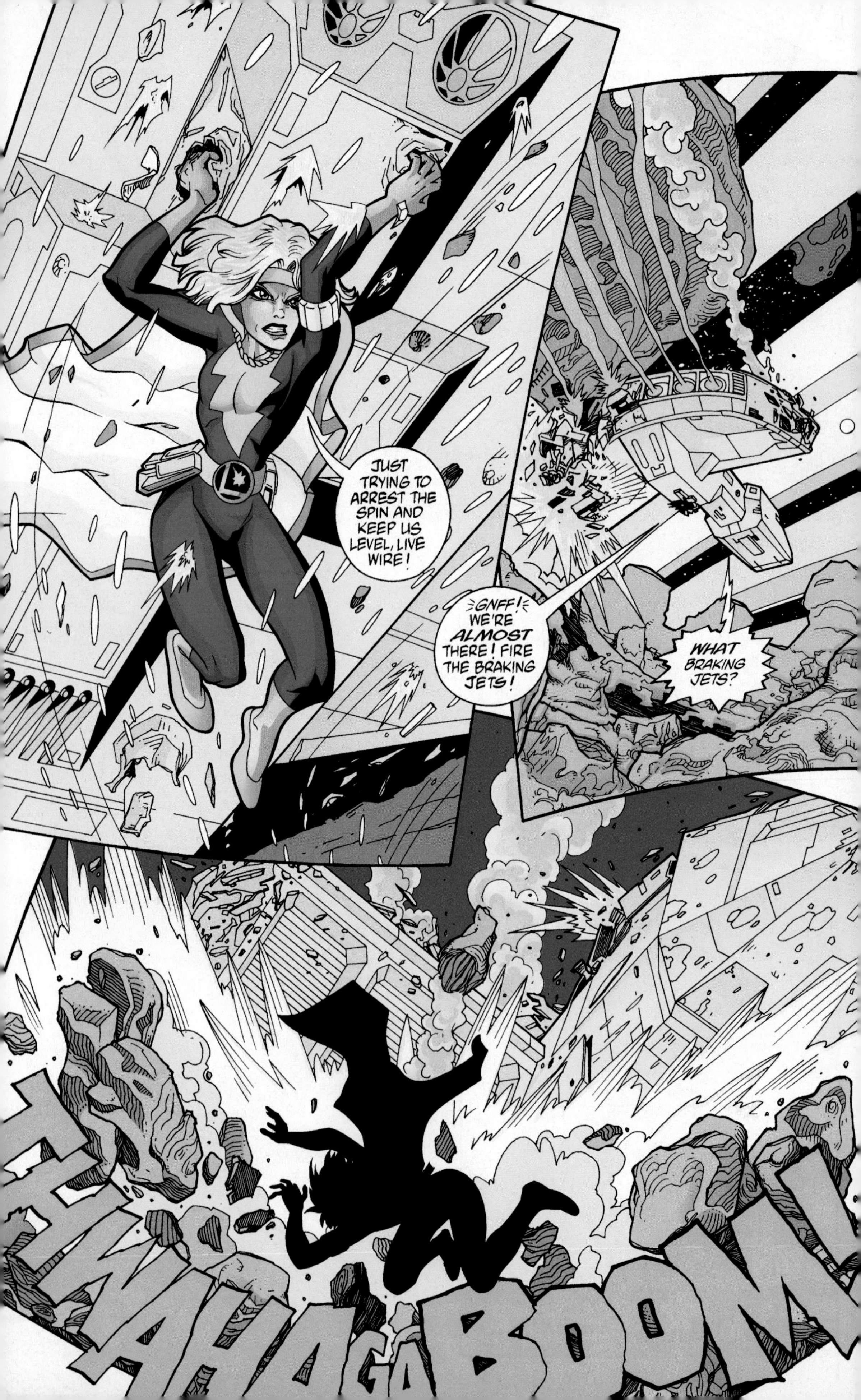
JUST TRYING TO ARREST THE SPIN AND KEEP US LEVEL, LIVE WIRE!
GNFF! WE'RE ALMOST THERE! FIRE THE BRAKING JETS!
WHAT BRAKING JETS?
THAHAGABOOM!

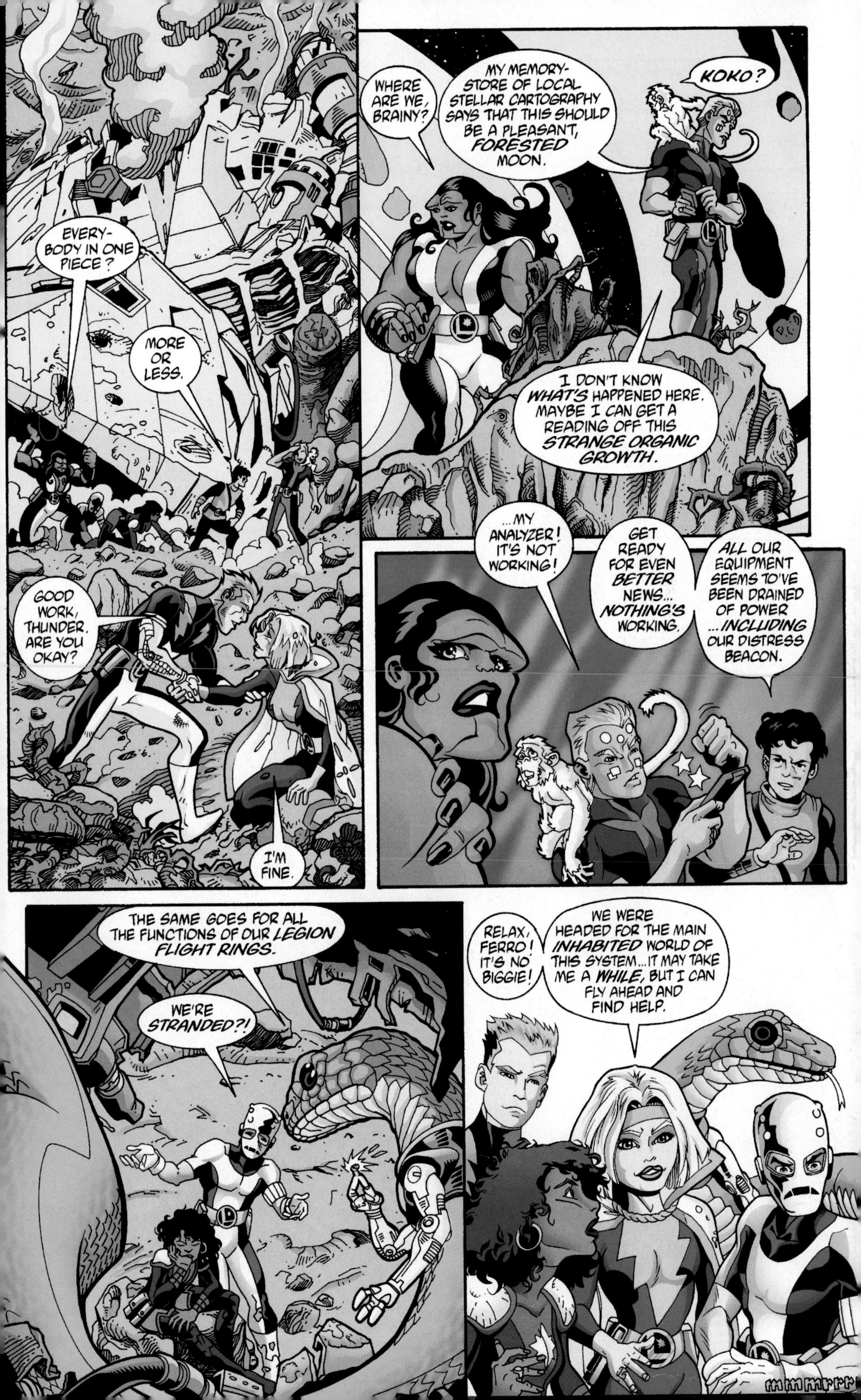

EVERY-BODY IN ONE PIECE?
MORE OR LESS.
GOOD WORK, THUNDER. ARE YOU OKAY?
I'M FINE.
WHERE ARE WE, BRAINY?
MY MEMORY-STORE OF LOCAL STELLAR CARTOGRAPHY SAYS THAT THIS SHOULD BE A PLEASANT, FORESTED MOON.
KOKO?
I DON'T KNOW WHAT'S HAPPENED HERE. MAYBE I CAN GET A READING OFF THIS STRANGE ORGANIC GROWTH.
...MY ANALYZER! IT'S NOT WORKING!
GET READY FOR EVEN BETTER NEWS... NOTHING'S WORKING.
ALL OUR EQUIPMENT SEEMS TO'VE BEEN DRAINED OF POWER ...INCLUDING OUR DISTRESS BEACON.
THE SAME GOES FOR ALL THE FUNCTIONS OF OUR LEGION FLIGHT RINGS.
WE'RE STRANDED?!
RELAX, FERRO! IT'S NO BIGGIE!
WE WERE HEADED FOR THE MAIN INHABITED WORLD OF THIS SYSTEM...IT MAY TAKE ME A WHILE, BUT I CAN FLY AHEAD AND FIND HELP.

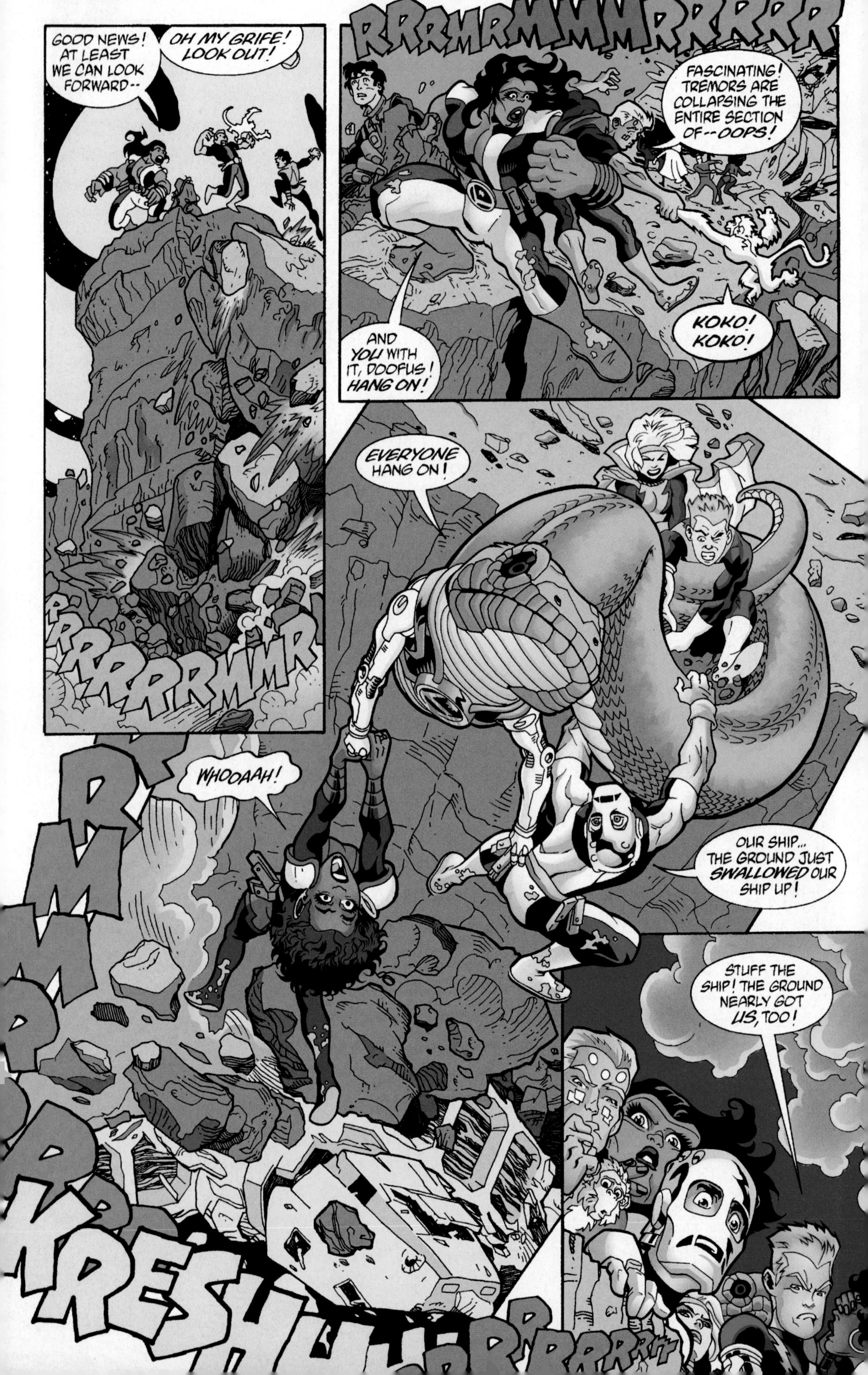
GOOD NEWS! AT LEAST WE CAN LOOK FORWARD--
OH MY GRIFE! LOOK OUT!
RRRMRMMMMRRRRR
FASCINATING! TREMORS ARE COLLAPSING THE ENTIRE SECTION OF--OOPS!
AND YOU WITH IT, DOOFUS! HANG ON!
KOKO! KOKO!
RRRRRRMMR
EVERYONE HANG ON!
WHOOAAH!
OUR SHIP... THE GROUND JUST SWALLOWED OUR SHIP UP!
STUFF THE SHIP! THE GROUND NEARLY GOT US, TOO!

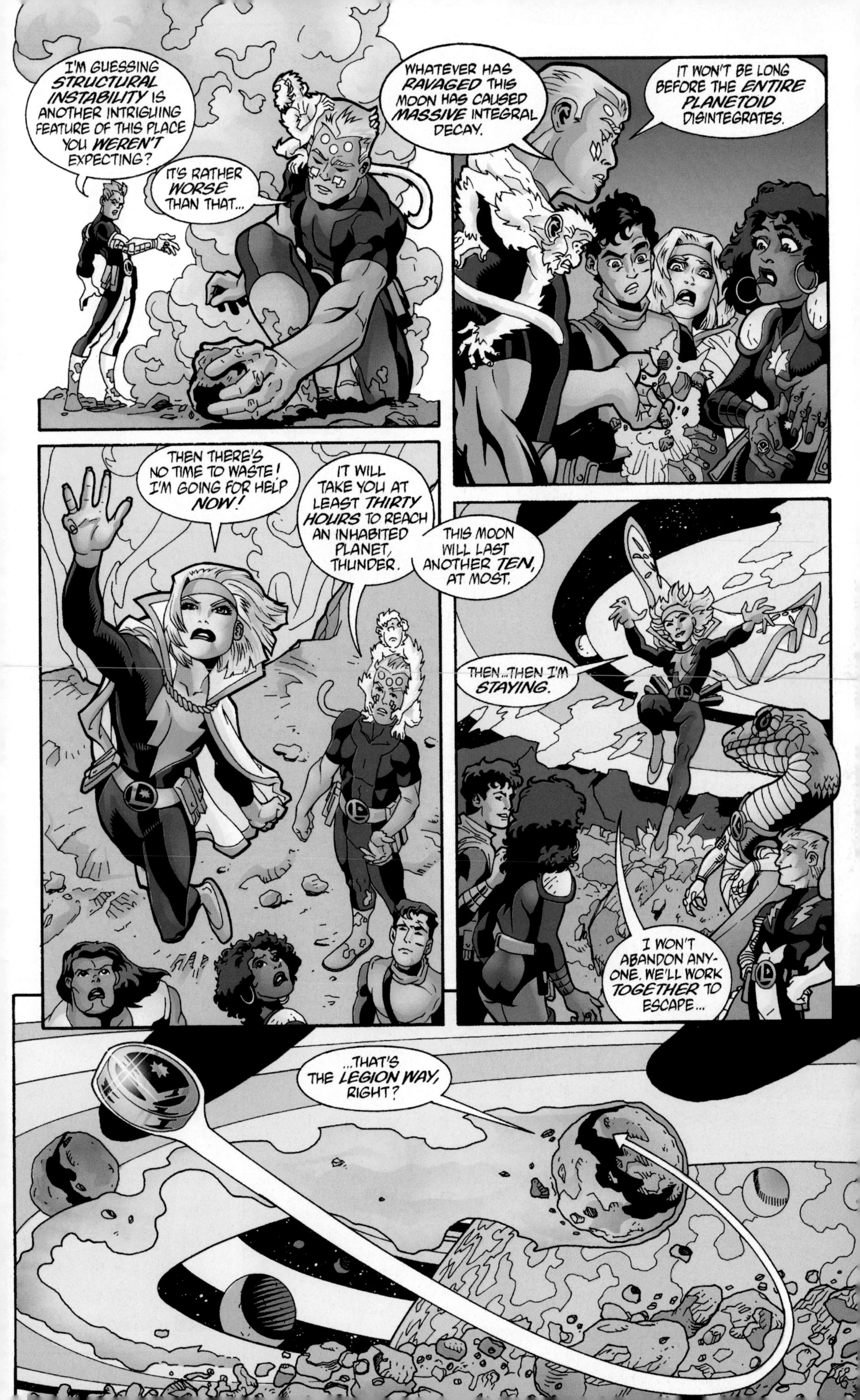
I'M GUESSING STRUCTURAL INSTABILITY IS ANOTHER INTRIGUING FEATURE OF THIS PLACE YOU WEREN'T EXPECTING?
IT'S RATHER WORSE THAN THAT...
WHATEVER HAS RAVAGED THIS MOON HAS CAUSED MASSIVE INTEGRAL DECAY.
IT WON'T BE LONG BEFORE THE ENTIRE PLANETOID DISINTEGRATES.
THEN THERE'S NO TIME TO WASTE! I'M GOING FOR HELP NOW!
IT WILL TAKE YOU AT LEAST THIRTY HOURS TO REACH AN INHABITED PLANET, THUNDER.
THIS MOON WILL LAST ANOTHER TEN, AT MOST.
THEN...THEN I'M STAYING.
I WON'T ABANDON ANYONE. WE'LL WORK TOGETHER TO ESCAPE...
...THAT'S THE LEGION WAY, RIGHT?

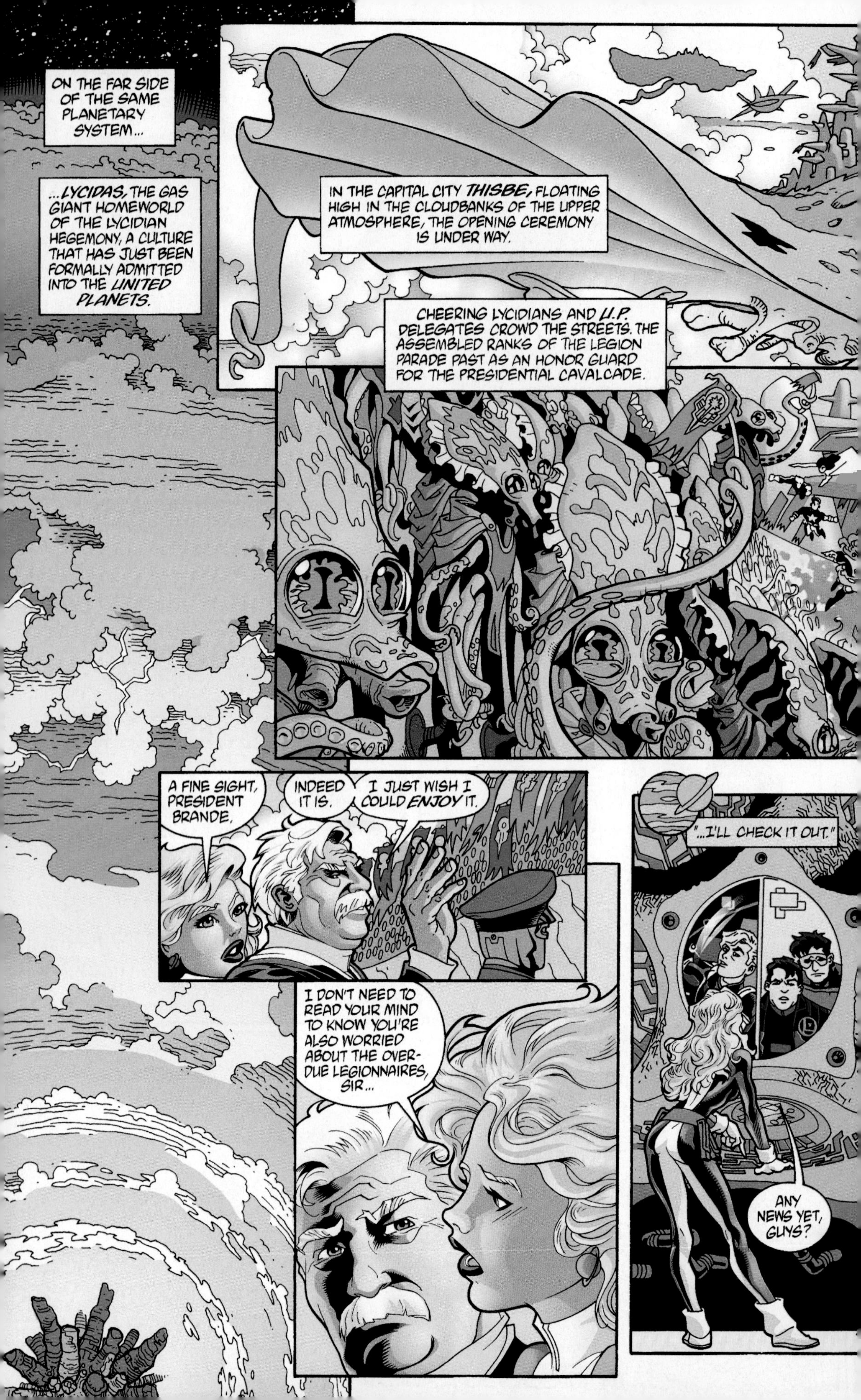
ON THE FAR SIDE OF THE SAME PLANETARY SYSTEM...
...LYCIDAS, THE GAS GIANT HOMEWORLD OF THE LYCIDIAN HEGEMONY, A CULTURE THAT HAS JUST BEEN FORMALLY ADMITTED INTO THE UNITED PLANETS.
IN THE CAPITAL CITY THISBE, FLOATING HIGH IN THE CLOUDBANKS OF THE UPPER ATMOSPHERE, THE OPENING CEREMONY IS UNDER WAY.
CHEERING LYCIDIANS AND U.P. DELEGATES CROWD THE STREETS. THE ASSEMBLED RANKS OF THE LEGION PARADE PAST AS AN HONOR GUARD FOR THE PRESIDENTIAL CAVALCADE.
A FINE SIGHT, PRESIDENT BRANDE.
INDEED IT IS.
I JUST WISH I COULD ENJOY IT.
I DON'T NEED TO READ YOUR MIND TO KNOW YOU'RE ALSO WORRIED ABOUT THE OVERDUE LEGIONNAIRES, SIR...
"...I'LL CHECK IT OUT."
ANY NEWS YET, GUYS?

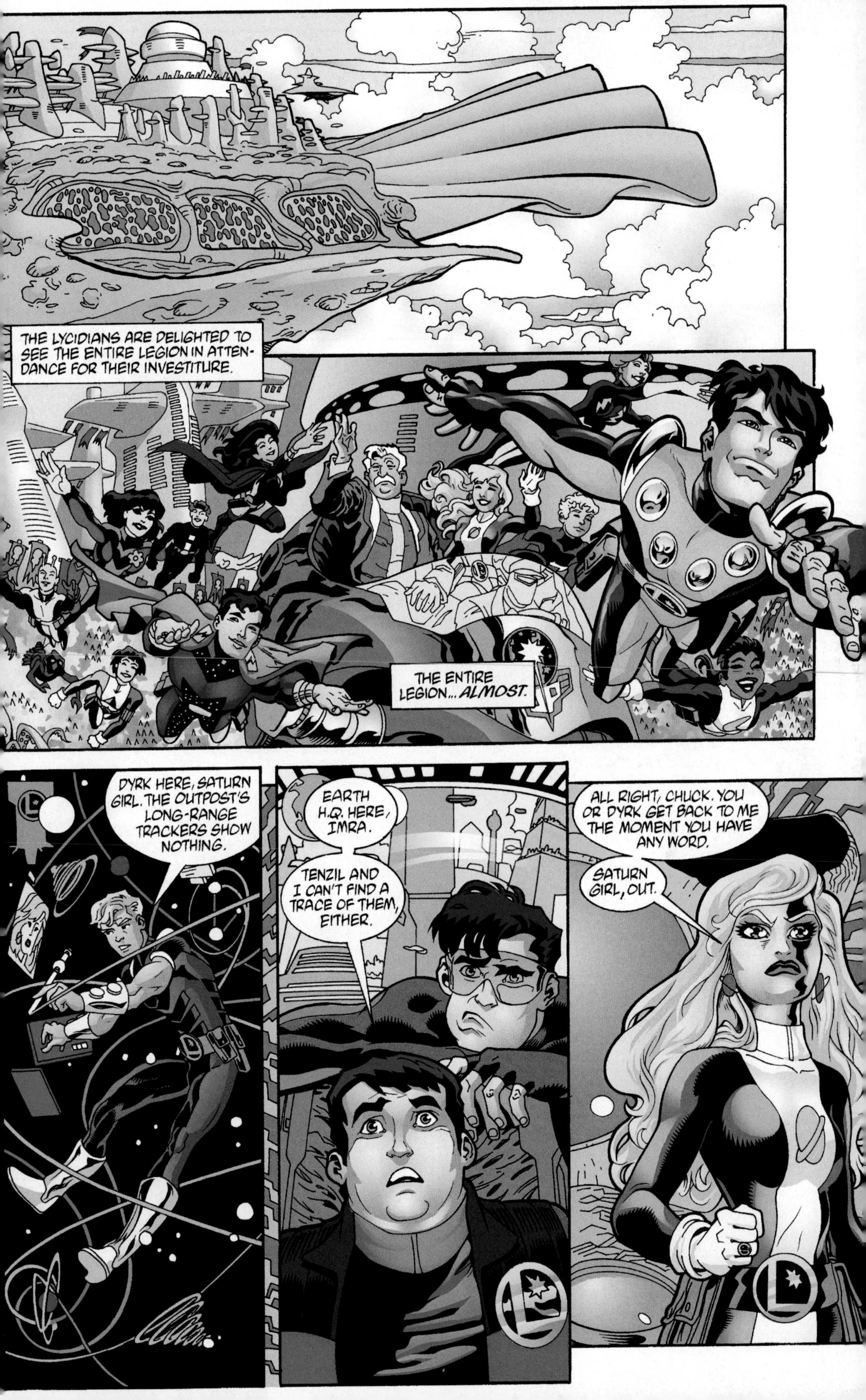
THE LYCIDIANS ARE DELIGHTED TO SEE THE ENTIRE LEGION IN ATTENDANCE FOR THEIR INVESTITURE.
THE ENTIRE LEGION... *ALMOST.*
DYRK HERE, SATURN GIRL. THE OUTPOST'S LONG-RANGE TRACKERS SHOW NOTHING.
EARTH H.Q. HERE, IMRA.
TENZIL AND I CAN'T FIND A TRACE OF THEM, EITHER.
ALL RIGHT, CHUCK. YOU OR DYRK GET BACK TO ME THE MOMENT YOU HAVE ANY WORD.
SATURN GIRL, OUT.

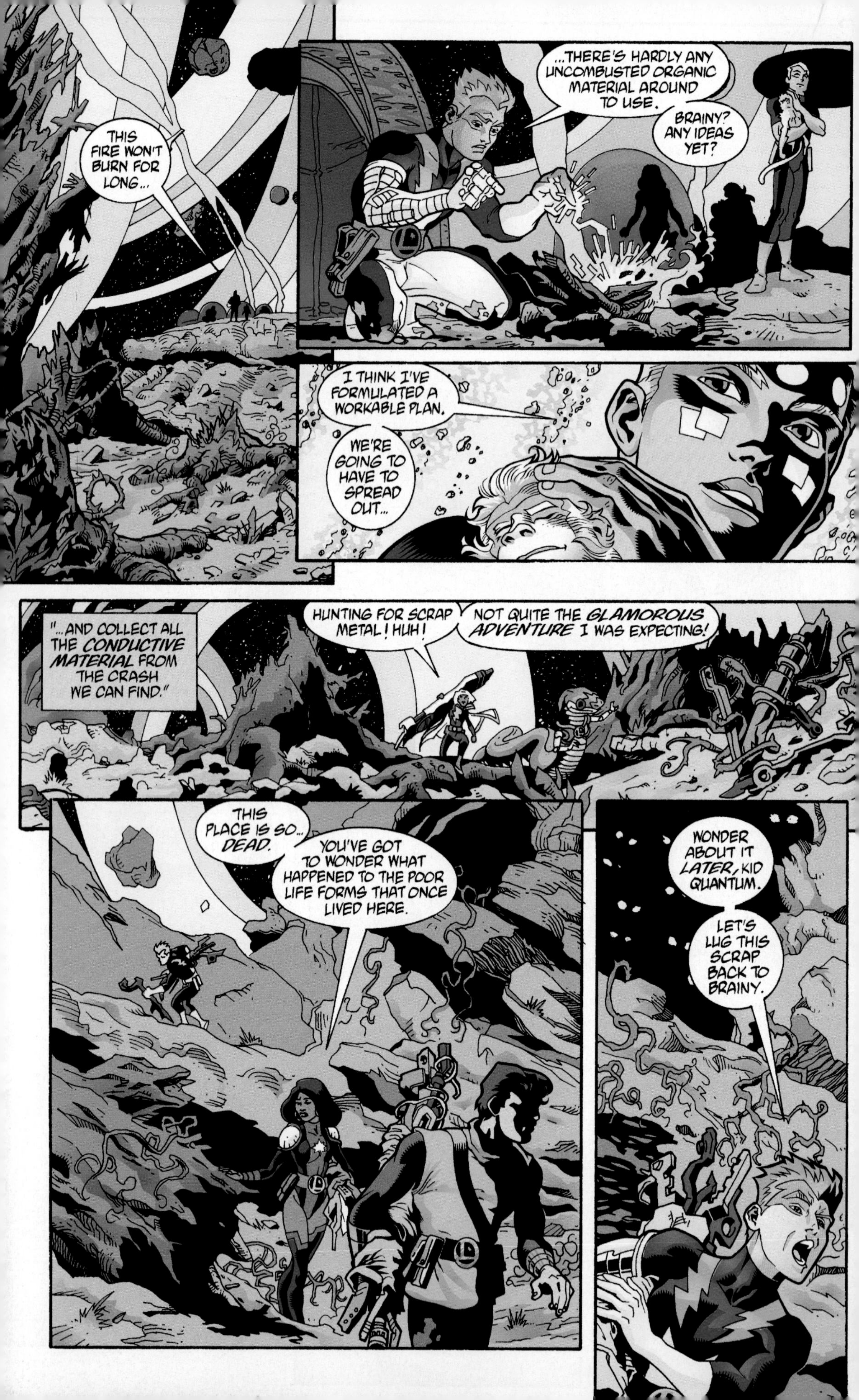
THIS FIRE WON'T BURN FOR LONG...
...THERE'S HARDLY ANY UNCOMBUSTED ORGANIC MATERIAL AROUND TO USE.
BRAINY? ANY IDEAS YET?
I THINK I'VE FORMULATED A WORKABLE PLAN.
WE'RE GOING TO HAVE TO SPREAD OUT...
"...AND COLLECT ALL THE *CONDUCTIVE MATERIAL* FROM THE CRASH WE CAN FIND."
HUNTING FOR SCRAP METAL! HUH!
NOT QUITE THE *GLAMOROUS ADVENTURE* I WAS EXPECTING!
THIS PLACE IS SO... *DEAD.*
YOU'VE GOT TO WONDER WHAT HAPPENED TO THE POOR LIFE FORMS THAT ONCE LIVED HERE.
WONDER ABOUT IT *LATER,* KID QUANTUM.
LET'S LUG THIS SCRAP BACK TO BRAINY.

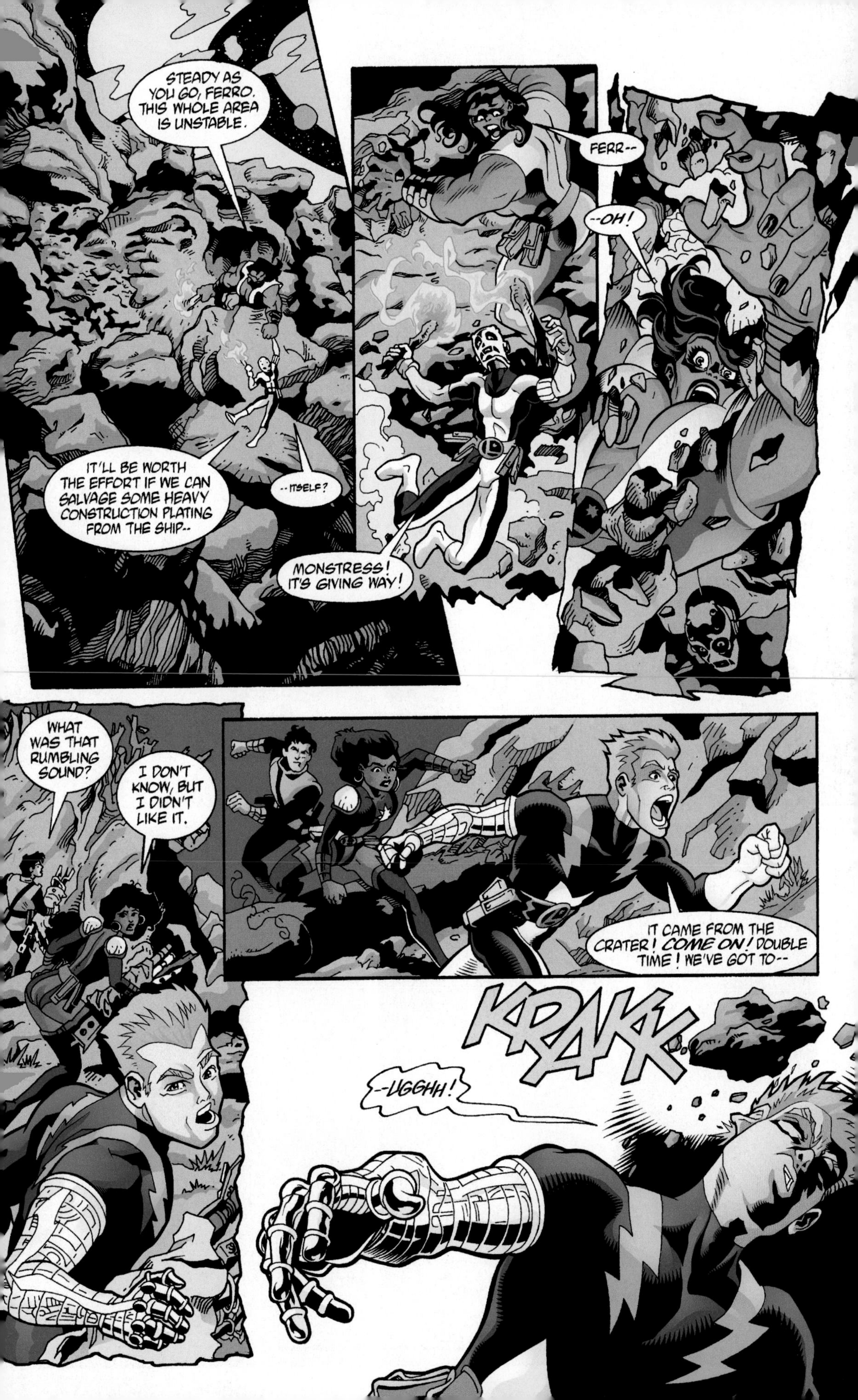
STEADY AS YOU GO, FERRO. THIS WHOLE AREA IS UNSTABLE.
IT'LL BE WORTH THE EFFORT IF WE CAN SALVAGE SOME HEAVY CONSTRUCTION PLATING FROM THE SHIP--
--ITSELF?
FERR--
MONSTRESS! IT'S GIVING WAY!
--OH!
WHAT WAS THAT RUMBLING SOUND?
I DON'T KNOW, BUT I DIDN'T LIKE IT.
IT CAME FROM THE CRATER! COME ON! DOUBLE TIME! WE'VE GOT TO--
KRAKK
--UGGHH!

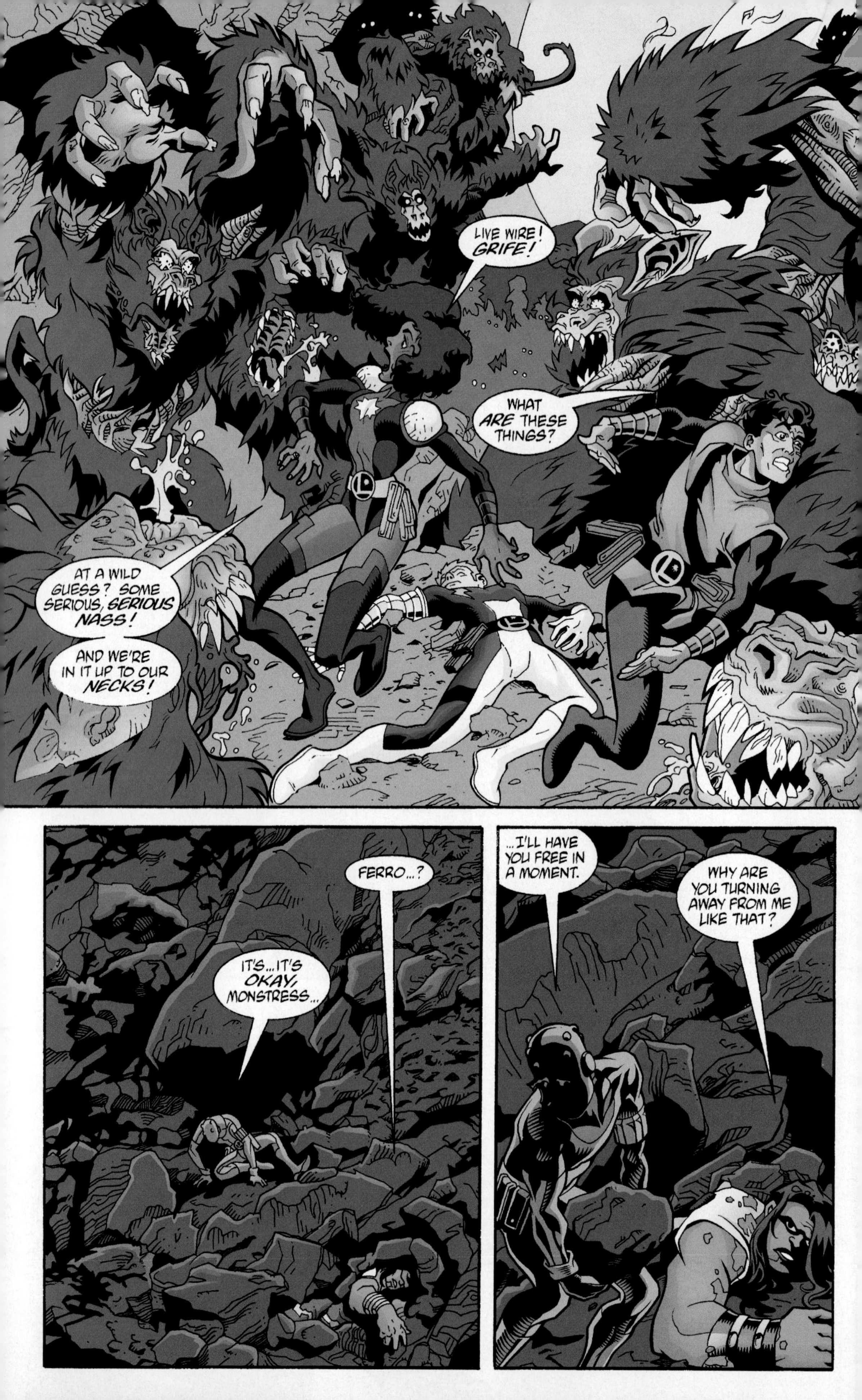
LIVE WIRE! GRIFE!
WHAT ARE THESE THINGS?
AT A WILD GUESS? SOME SERIOUS, SERIOUS NASS!
AND WE'RE IN IT UP TO OUR NECKS!
FERRO...?
IT'S...IT'S OKAY, MONSTRESS...
...I'LL HAVE YOU FREE IN A MOMENT.
WHY ARE YOU TURNING AWAY FROM ME LIKE THAT?

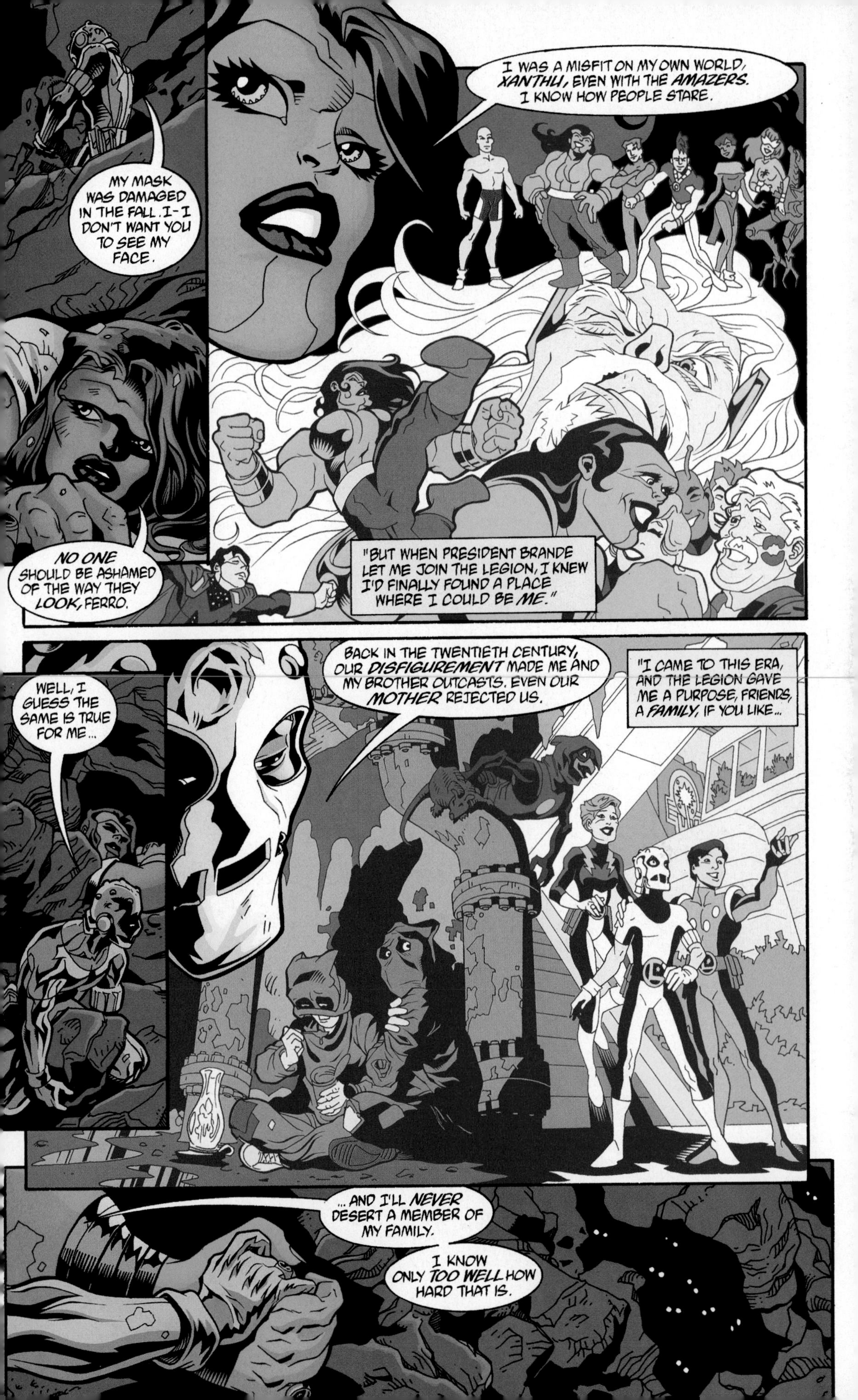

MY MASK WAS DAMAGED IN THE FALL. I- I DON'T WANT YOU TO SEE MY FACE.
I WAS A MISFIT ON MY OWN WORLD, XANTHU, EVEN WITH THE AMAZERS. I KNOW HOW PEOPLE STARE.
"BUT WHEN PRESIDENT BRANDE LET ME JOIN THE LEGION, I KNEW I'D FINALLY FOUND A PLACE WHERE I COULD BE ME."
NO ONE SHOULD BE ASHAMED OF THE WAY THEY LOOK, FERRO.
WELL, I GUESS THE SAME IS TRUE FOR ME...
BACK IN THE TWENTIETH CENTURY, OUR DISFIGUREMENT MADE ME AND MY BROTHER OUTCASTS. EVEN OUR MOTHER REJECTED US.
"I CAME TO THIS ERA, AND THE LEGION GAVE ME A PURPOSE, FRIENDS, A FAMILY, IF YOU LIKE...
...AND I'LL NEVER DESERT A MEMBER OF MY FAMILY.
I KNOW ONLY TOO WELL HOW HARD THAT IS.

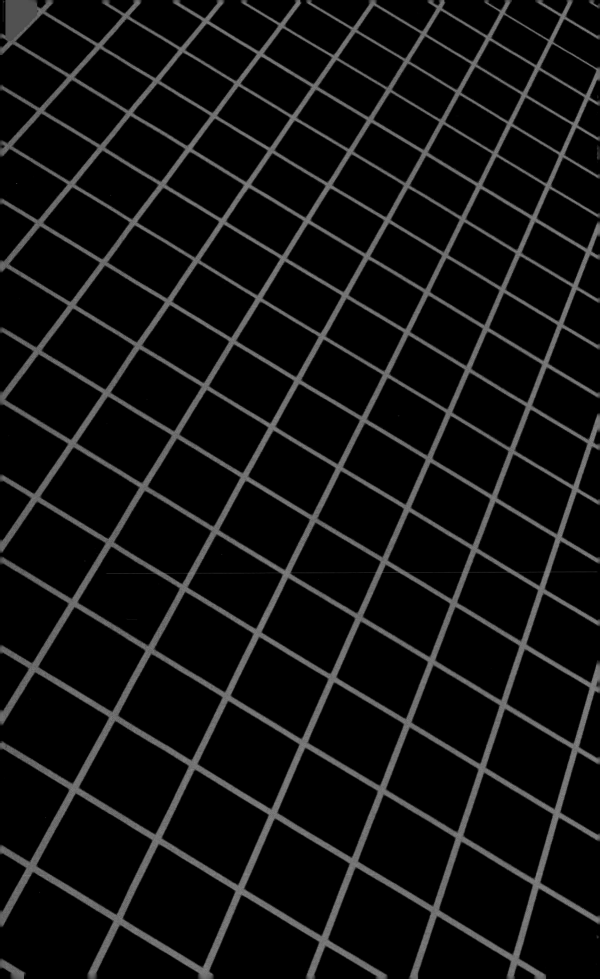

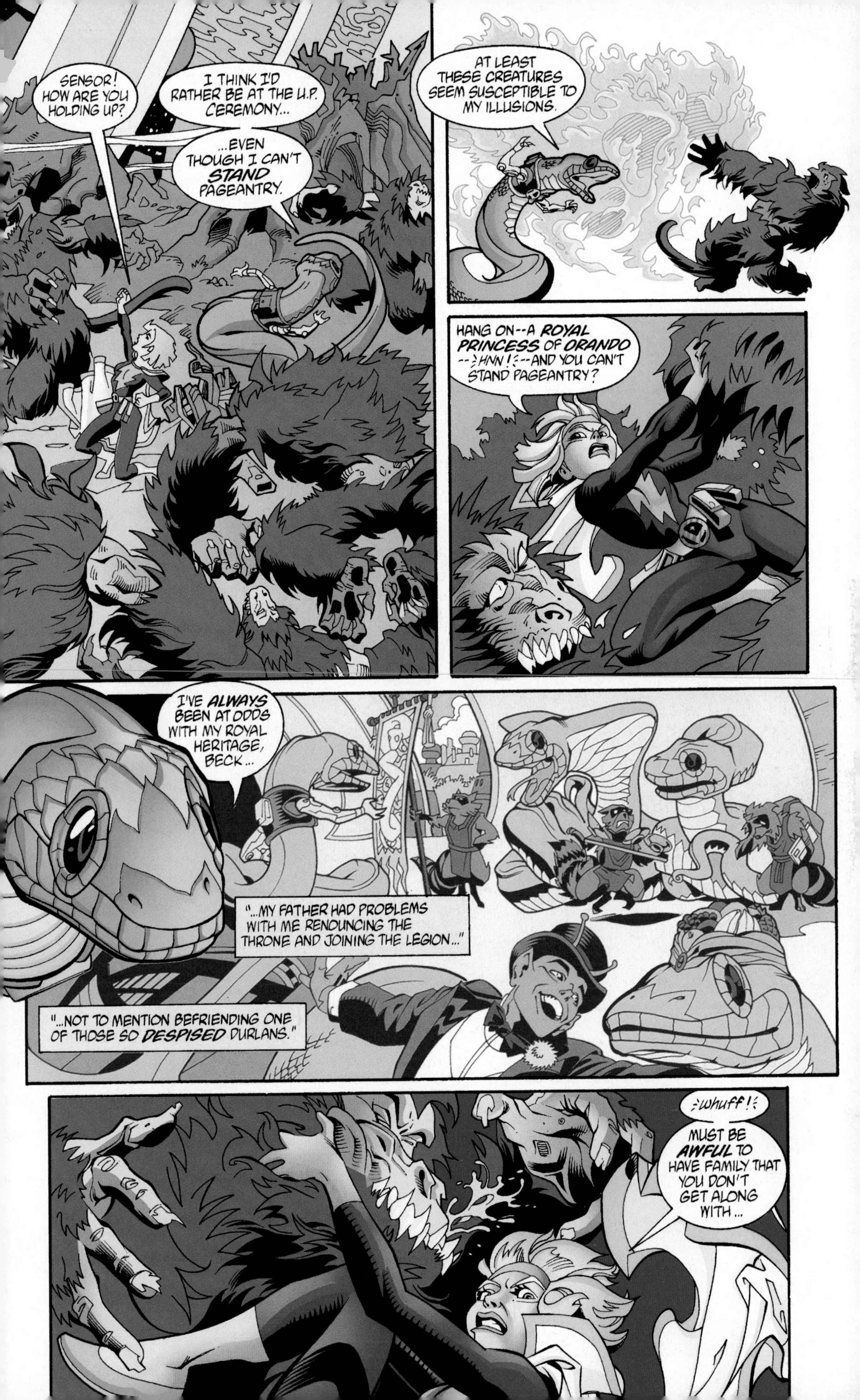
SENSOR! HOW ARE YOU HOLDING UP?
I THINK I'D RATHER BE AT THE U.P. CEREMONY...
...EVEN THOUGH I CAN'T STAND PAGEANTRY.
AT LEAST THESE CREATURES SEEM SUSCEPTIBLE TO MY ILLUSIONS.
HANG ON--A ROYAL PRINCESS OF ORANDO --HNN!--AND YOU CAN'T STAND PAGEANTRY?
I'VE ALWAYS BEEN AT ODDS WITH MY ROYAL HERITAGE, BECK...
"...MY FATHER HAD PROBLEMS WITH ME RENOUNCING THE THRONE AND JOINING THE LEGION..."
"...NOT TO MENTION BEFRIENDING ONE OF THOSE SO DESPISED DURLANS."
whuff!
MUST BE AWFUL TO HAVE FAMILY THAT YOU DON'T GET ALONG WITH...

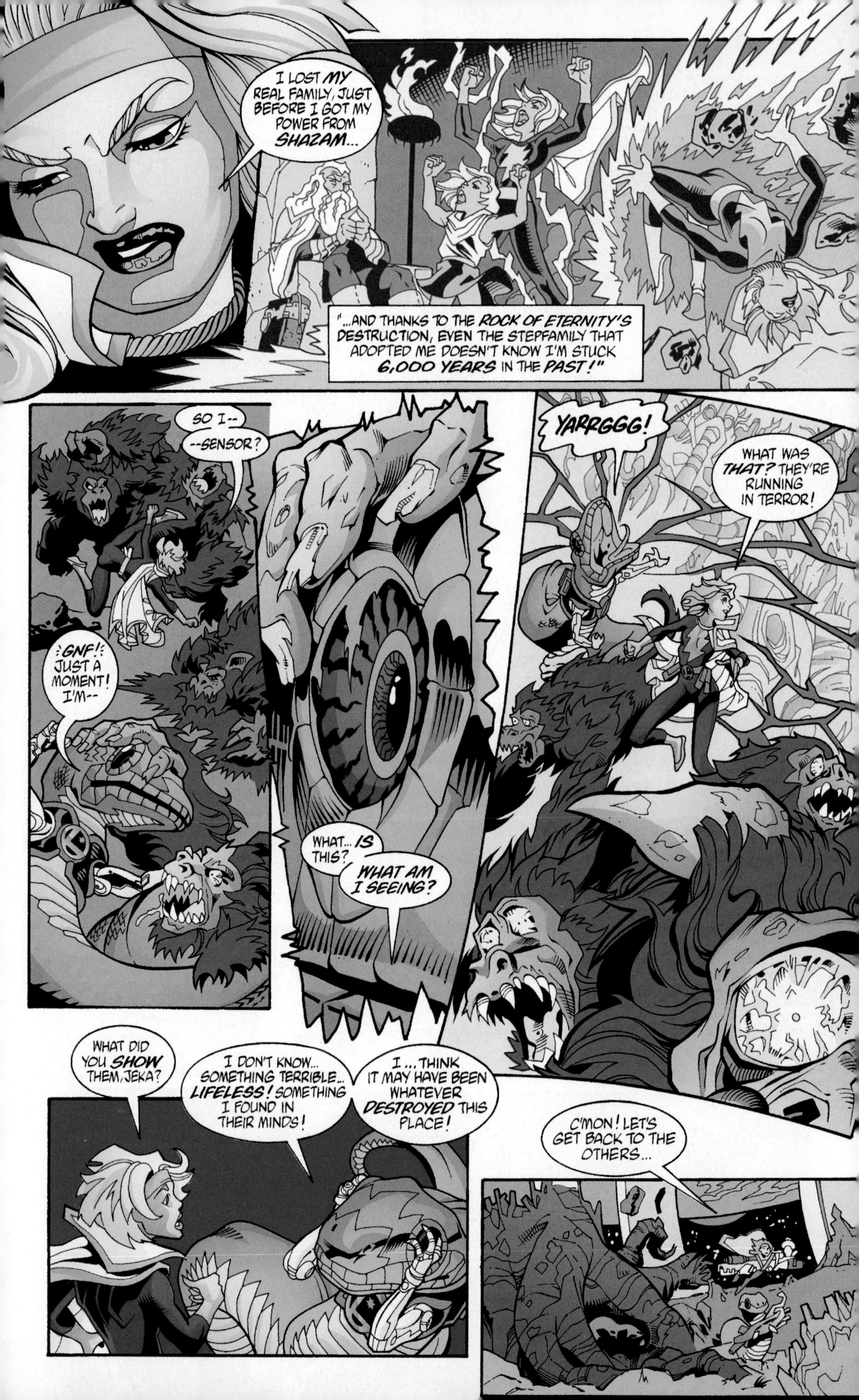
I LOST MY REAL FAMILY, JUST BEFORE I GOT MY POWER FROM SHAZAM...
"...AND THANKS TO THE ROCK OF ETERNITY'S DESTRUCTION, EVEN THE STEPFAMILY THAT ADOPTED ME DOESN'T KNOW I'M STUCK 6,000 YEARS IN THE PAST!"
SO I--
--SENSOR?
GNF! JUST A MOMENT! I'M--
WHAT... IS THIS?
WHAT AM I SEEING?
YARRGGG!
WHAT WAS THAT? THEY'RE RUNNING IN TERROR!
WHAT DID YOU SHOW THEM, JEKA?
I DON'T KNOW... SOMETHING TERRIBLE... LIFELESS! SOMETHING I FOUND IN THEIR MINDS!
I... THINK IT MAY HAVE BEEN WHATEVER DESTROYED THIS PLACE!
C'MON! LET'S GET BACK TO THE OTHERS...

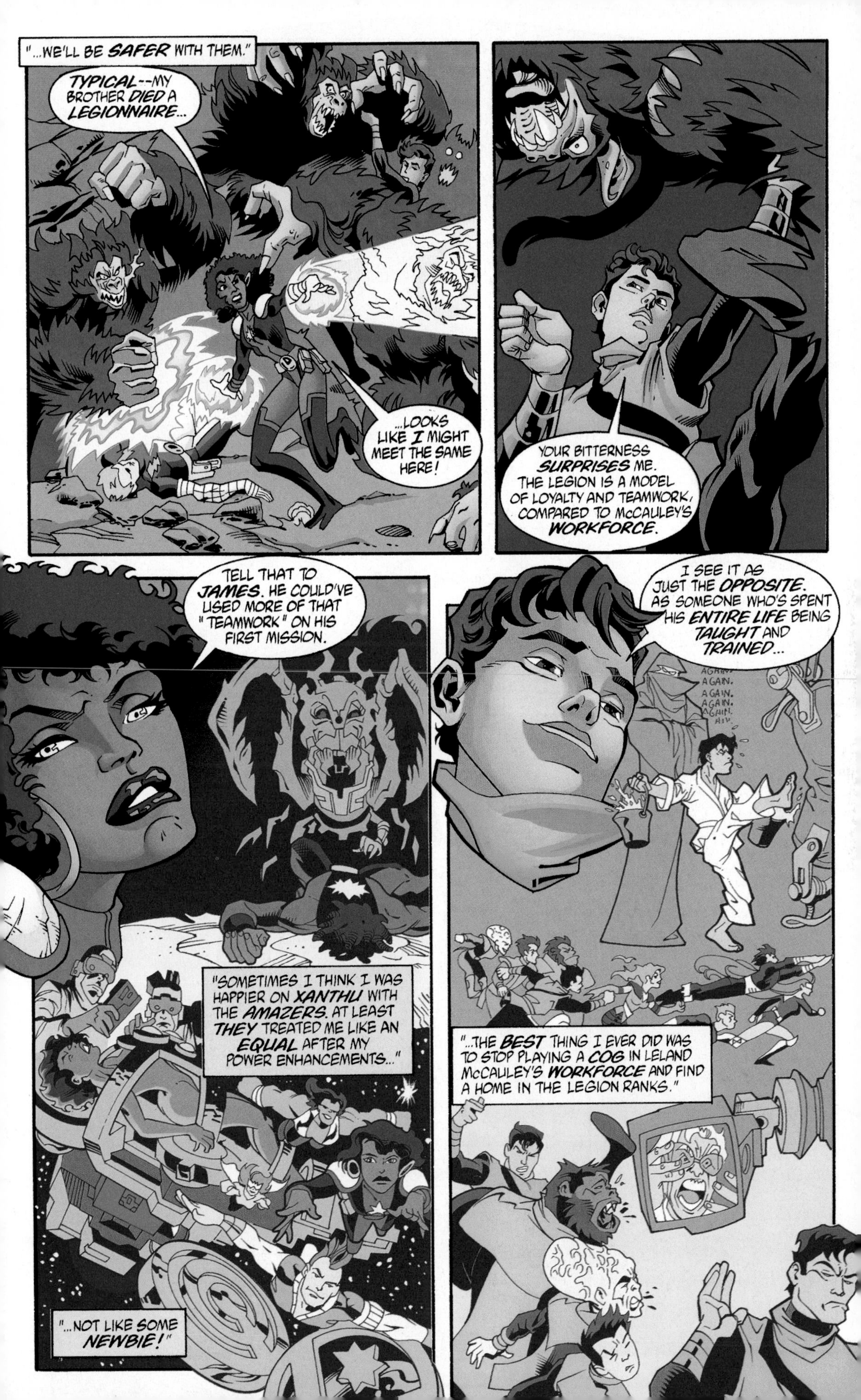
"...WE'LL BE SAFER WITH THEM."
TYPICAL--MY BROTHER DIED A LEGIONNAIRE...
...LOOKS LIKE I MIGHT MEET THE SAME HERE!
YOUR BITTERNESS SURPRISES ME. THE LEGION IS A MODEL OF LOYALTY AND TEAMWORK, COMPARED TO McCAULEY'S WORKFORCE.
TELL THAT TO JAMES. HE COULD'VE USED MORE OF THAT "TEAMWORK" ON HIS FIRST MISSION.
"SOMETIMES I THINK I WAS HAPPIER ON XANTHU WITH THE AMAZERS. AT LEAST THEY TREATED ME LIKE AN EQUAL AFTER MY POWER ENHANCEMENTS..."
"...NOT LIKE SOME NEWBIE!"
I SEE IT AS JUST THE OPPOSITE. AS SOMEONE WHO'S SPENT HIS ENTIRE LIFE BEING TAUGHT AND TRAINED...
"...THE BEST THING I EVER DID WAS TO STOP PLAYING A COG IN LELAND McCAULEY'S WORKFORCE AND FIND A HOME IN THE LEGION RANKS."

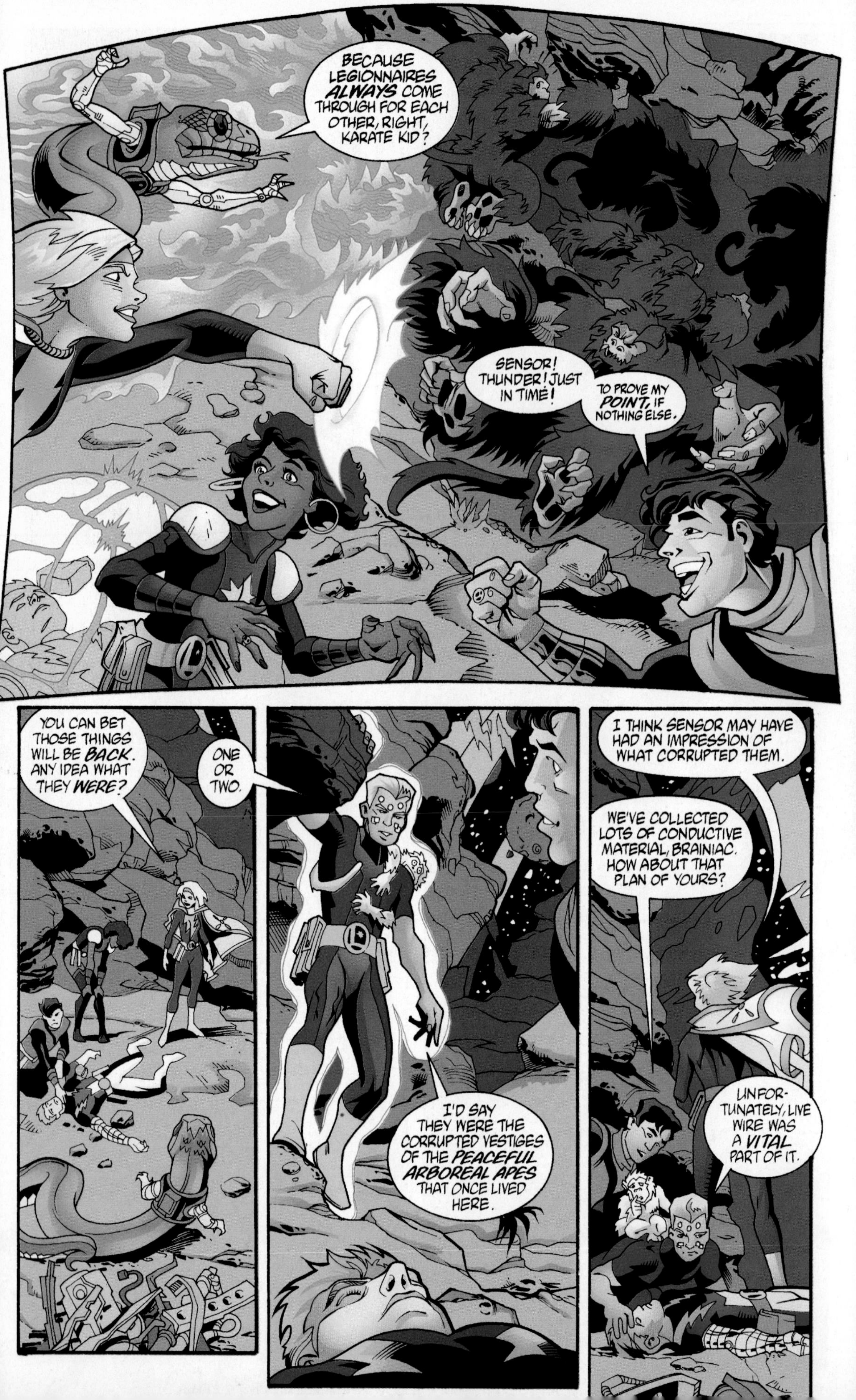

BECAUSE LEGIONNAIRES ALWAYS COME THROUGH FOR EACH OTHER, RIGHT, KARATE KID?
SENSOR! THUNDER! JUST IN TIME!
TO PROVE MY POINT, IF NOTHING ELSE.
YOU CAN BET THOSE THINGS WILL BE BACK. ANY IDEA WHAT THEY WERE?
ONE OR TWO.
I'D SAY THEY WERE THE CORRUPTED VESTIGES OF THE PEACEFUL ARBOREAL APES THAT ONCE LIVED HERE.
I THINK SENSOR MAY HAVE HAD AN IMPRESSION OF WHAT CORRUPTED THEM.
WE'VE COLLECTED LOTS OF CONDUCTIVE MATERIAL, BRAINIAC. HOW ABOUT THAT PLAN OF YOURS?
UNFORTUNATELY, LIVE WIRE WAS A VITAL PART OF IT.

THUNDER...MONSTRESS AND FERRO SHOULD HAVE RETURNED FROM THE CRATER BY NOW. GO FIND THEM.

ON IT!

AND THE *REST* OF US...?

...CAN *STAND WATCH* AND *WARN* ME THE MOMENT THOSE APES REAPPEAR.

KOKO! KOKO!

I CAN FEEL THEIR RESENTMENT...

...I'VE ALWAYS BEEN MISUNDERSTOOD BY THOSE WITH *LIMITED* INTELLIGENCE.

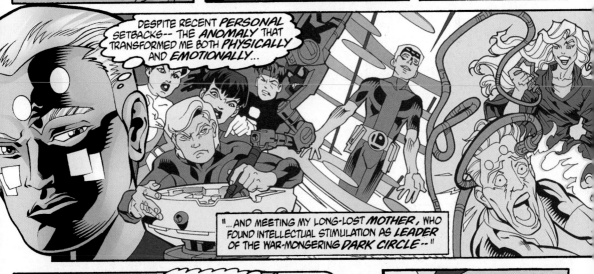

DESPITE RECENT *PERSONAL* SETBACKS-- THE *ANOMALY* THAT TRANSFORMED ME BOTH *PHYSICALLY* AND *EMOTIONALLY*...

"...AND MEETING MY LONG-LOST *MOTHER*, WHO FOUND INTELLECTUAL STIMULATION AS *LEADER* OF THE WAR-MONGERING *DARK CIRCLE*--"

--MY *TWELFTH-LEVEL* INTELLIGENCE HAS REMAINED *INTACT*, FINDING COHERENT SOLUTIONS *INVISIBLE* TO THE REST OF MY "TEAMMATES."

YET THEY *STILL* CHOOSE TO ADDRESS ME LIKE SOME EMOTIONALLY UNSOPHISTICATED *TODDLER*.

SOMEONE'S COMING!

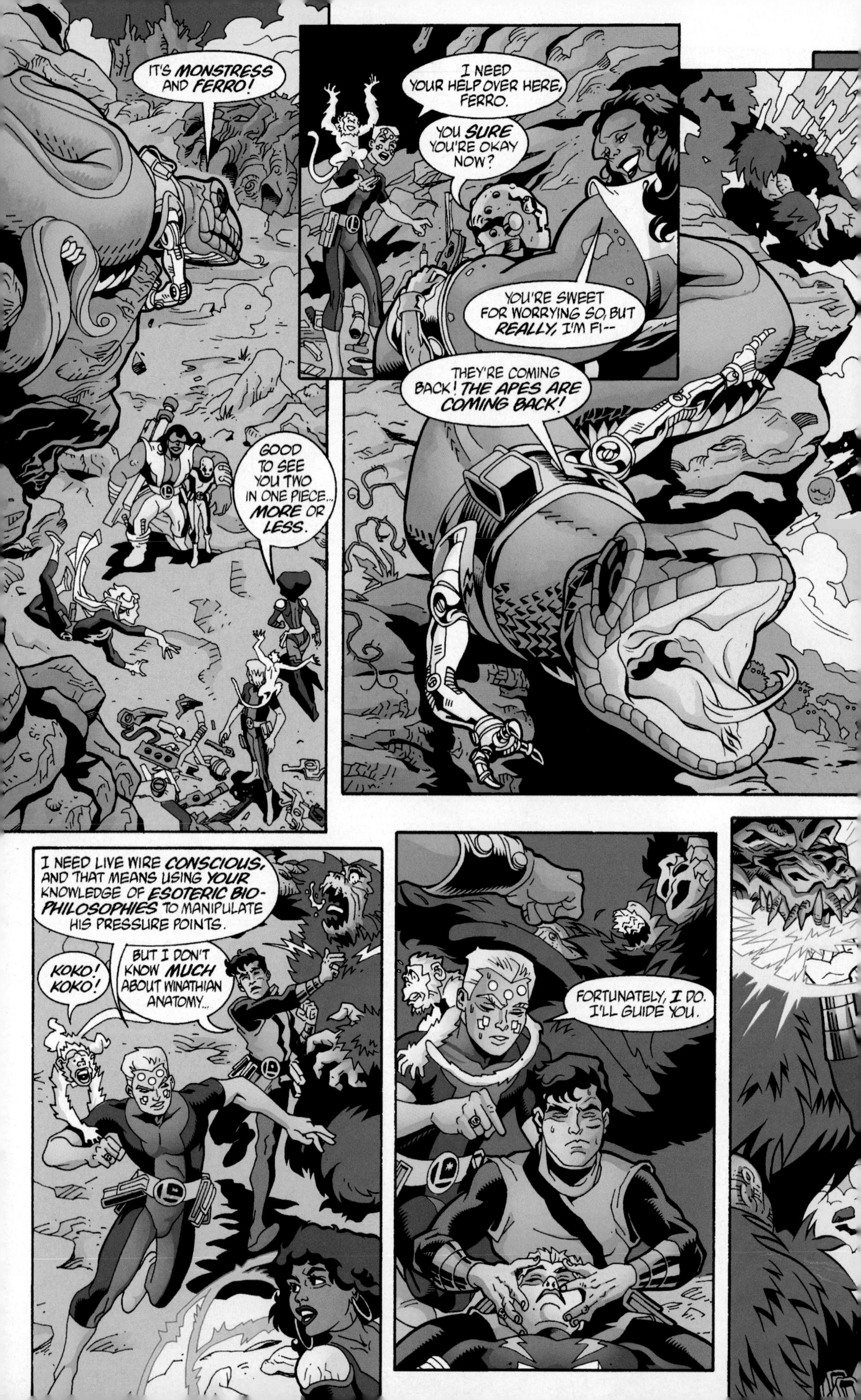
IT'S MONSTRESS AND FERRO!
I NEED YOUR HELP OVER HERE, FERRO.
YOU SURE YOU'RE OKAY NOW?
YOU'RE SWEET FOR WORRYING SO, BUT REALLY, I'M FI--
GOOD TO SEE YOU TWO IN ONE PIECE... MORE OR LESS.
THEY'RE COMING BACK! THE APES ARE COMING BACK!
I NEED LIVE WIRE CONSCIOUS, AND THAT MEANS USING YOUR KNOWLEDGE OF ESOTERIC BIO-PHILOSOPHIES TO MANIPULATE HIS PRESSURE POINTS.
KOKO! KOKO!
BUT I DON'T KNOW MUCH ABOUT WINATHIAN ANATOMY...
FORTUNATELY, I DO. I'LL GUIDE YOU.

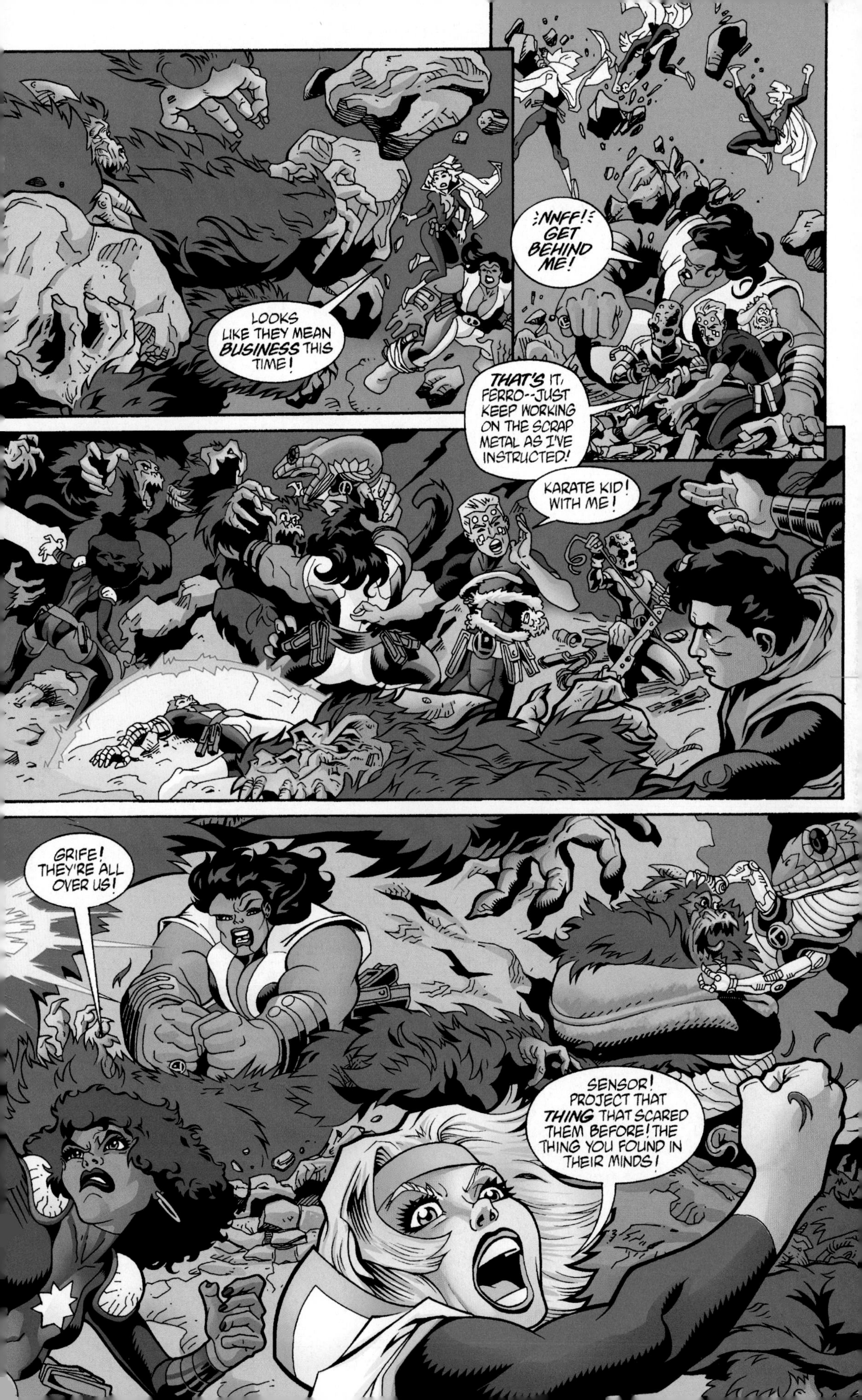

LOOKS LIKE THEY MEAN BUSINESS THIS TIME!
NNFF! GET BEHIND ME!
THAT'S IT, FERRO--JUST KEEP WORKING ON THE SCRAP METAL AS I'VE INSTRUCTED!
KARATE KID! WITH ME!
GRIFE! THEY'RE ALL OVER US!
SENSOR! PROJECT THAT THING THAT SCARED THEM BEFORE! THE THING YOU FOUND IN THEIR MINDS!

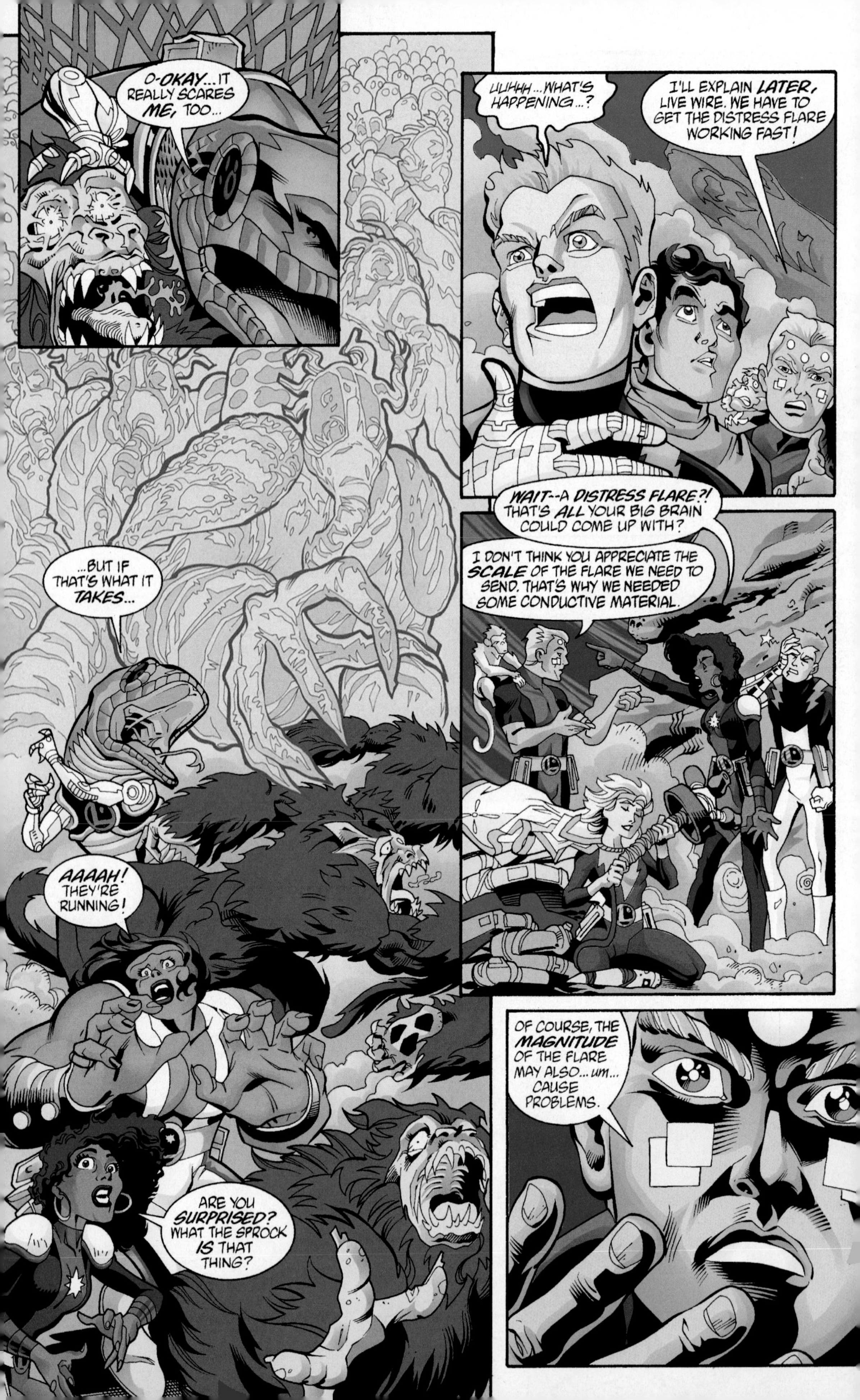

O-OKAY... IT REALLY SCARES ME, TOO...
UUHHH... WHAT'S HAPPENING...?
I'LL EXPLAIN LATER, LIVE WIRE. WE HAVE TO GET THE DISTRESS FLARE WORKING FAST!
...BUT IF THAT'S WHAT IT TAKES...
WAIT--A DISTRESS FLARE?! THAT'S ALL YOUR BIG BRAIN COULD COME UP WITH?
I DON'T THINK YOU APPRECIATE THE SCALE OF THE FLARE WE NEED TO SEND. THAT'S WHY WE NEEDED SOME CONDUCTIVE MATERIAL.
AAAAH! THEY'RE RUNNING!
ARE YOU SURPRISED? WHAT THE SPROCK IS THAT THING?
OF COURSE, THE MAGNITUDE OF THE FLARE MAY ALSO... um... CAUSE PROBLEMS.

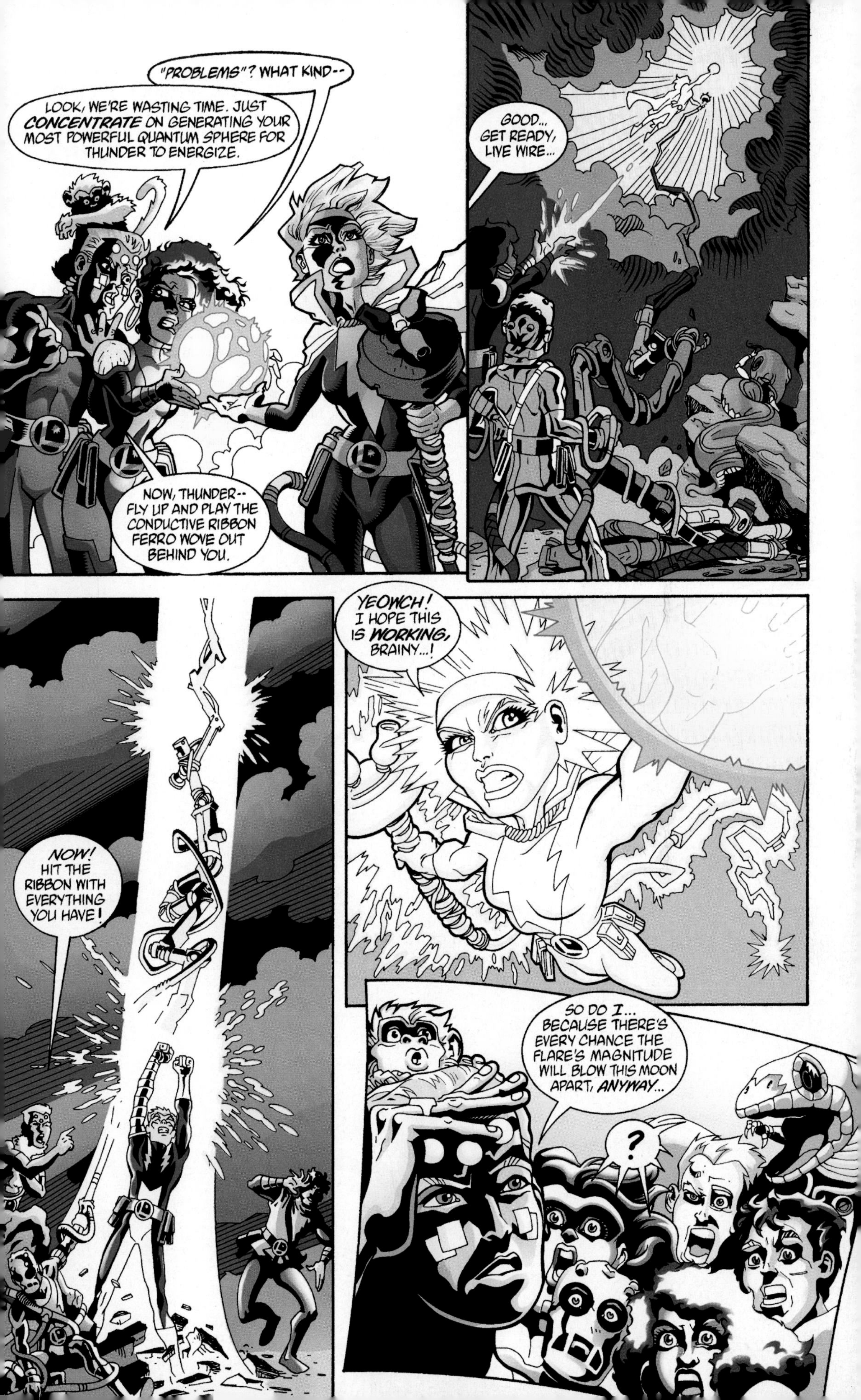

"PROBLEMS"? WHAT KIND--
LOOK, WE'RE WASTING TIME. JUST CONCENTRATE ON GENERATING YOUR MOST POWERFUL QUANTUM SPHERE FOR THUNDER TO ENERGIZE.
NOW, THUNDER-- FLY UP AND PLAY THE CONDUCTIVE RIBBON FERRO WOVE OUT BEHIND YOU.
GOOD... GET READY, LIVE WIRE...
NOW! HIT THE RIBBON WITH EVERYTHING YOU HAVE!
YEOWCH! I HOPE THIS IS WORKING, BRAINY...!
SO DO I... BECAUSE THERE'S EVERY CHANCE THE FLARE'S MAGNITUDE WILL BLOW THIS MOON APART, ANYWAY...
?

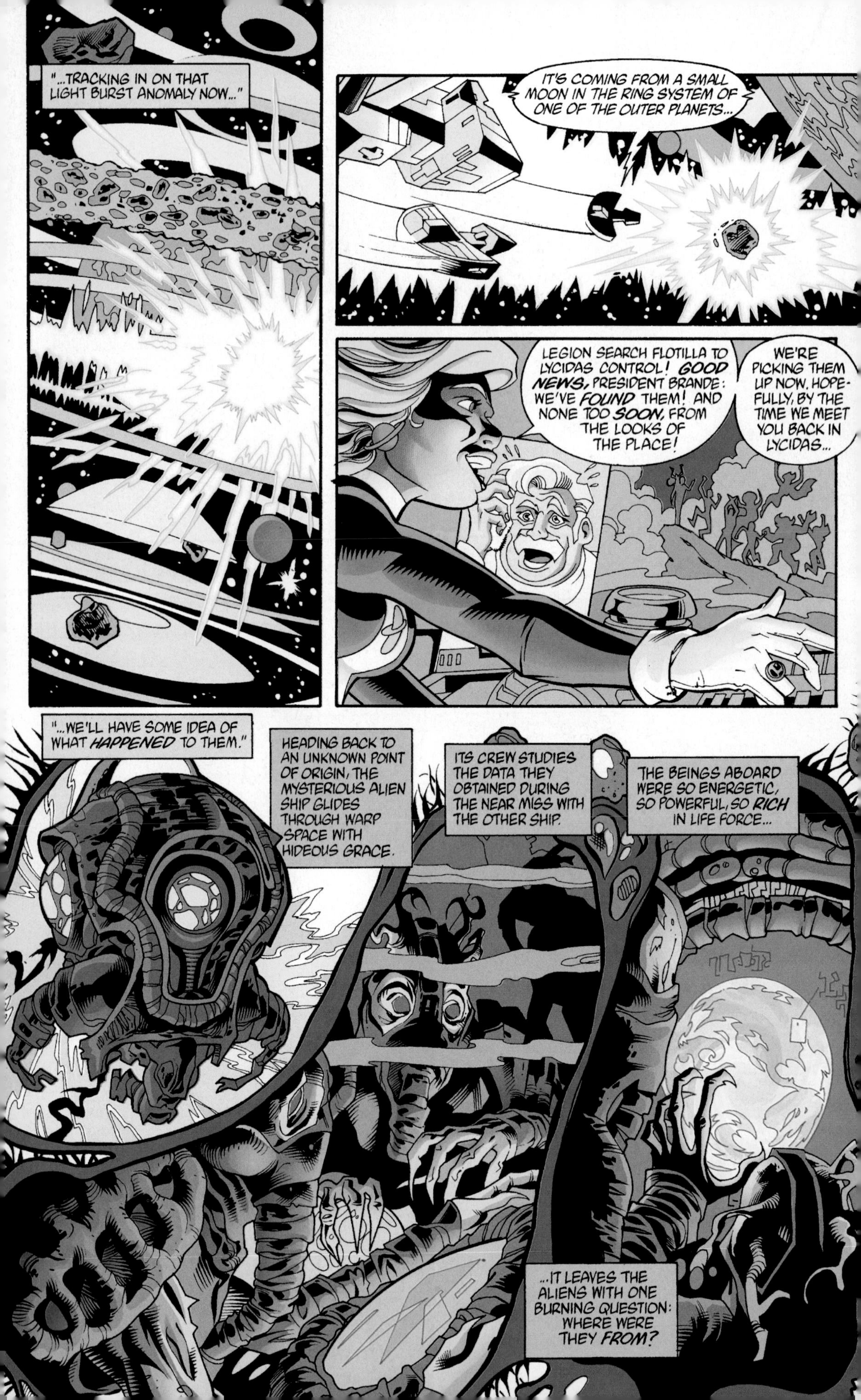
"...TRACKING IN ON THAT LIGHT BURST ANOMALY NOW..."
IT'S COMING FROM A SMALL MOON IN THE RING SYSTEM OF ONE OF THE OUTER PLANETS...
LEGION SEARCH FLOTILLA TO LYCIDAS CONTROL! GOOD NEWS, PRESIDENT BRANDE: WE'VE FOUND THEM! AND NONE TOO SOON, FROM THE LOOKS OF THE PLACE!
WE'RE PICKING THEM UP NOW. HOPE-FULLY, BY THE TIME WE MEET YOU BACK IN LYCIDAS...
"...WE'LL HAVE SOME IDEA OF WHAT HAPPENED TO THEM."
HEADING BACK TO AN UNKNOWN POINT OF ORIGIN, THE MYSTERIOUS ALIEN SHIP GLIDES THROUGH WARP SPACE WITH HIDEOUS GRACE.
ITS CREW STUDIES THE DATA THEY OBTAINED DURING THE NEAR MISS WITH THE OTHER SHIP.
THE BEINGS ABOARD WERE SO ENERGETIC, SO POWERFUL, SO RICH IN LIFE FORCE...
...IT LEAVES THE ALIENS WITH ONE BURNING QUESTION: WHERE WERE THEY FROM?

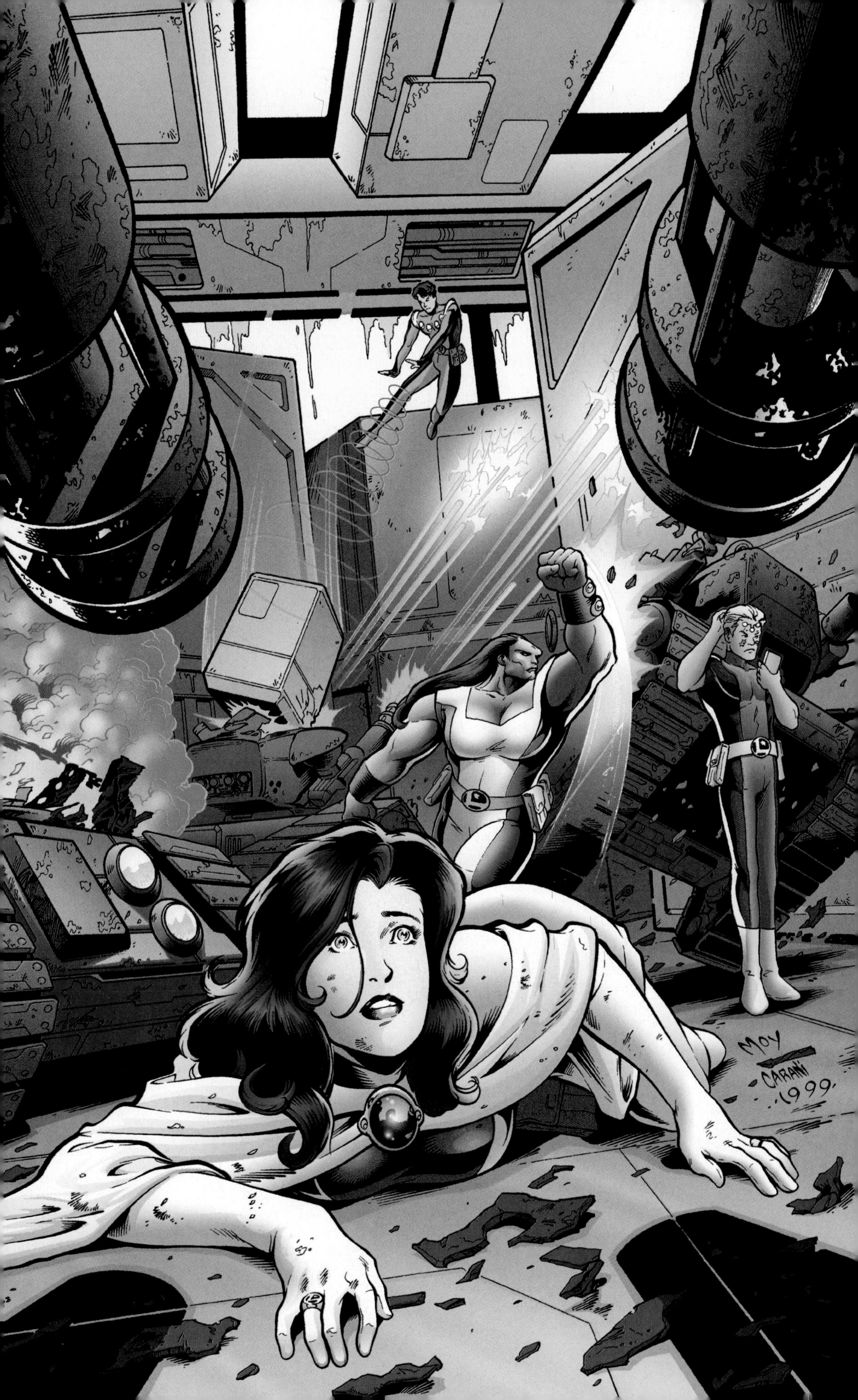
MOY
CARANI
1999

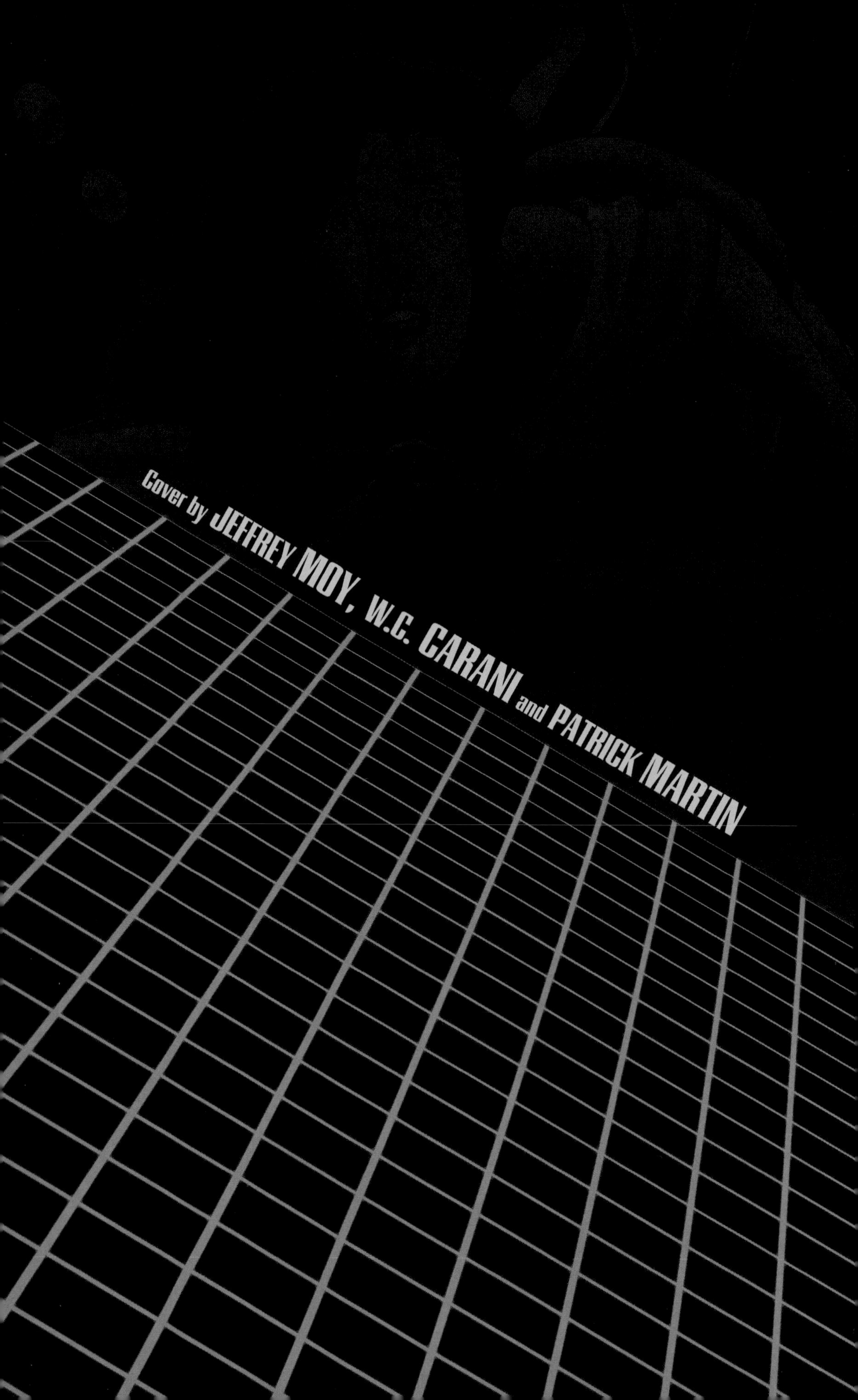
Cover by JEFFREY MOY, W.C. CARANI and PATRICK MARTIN

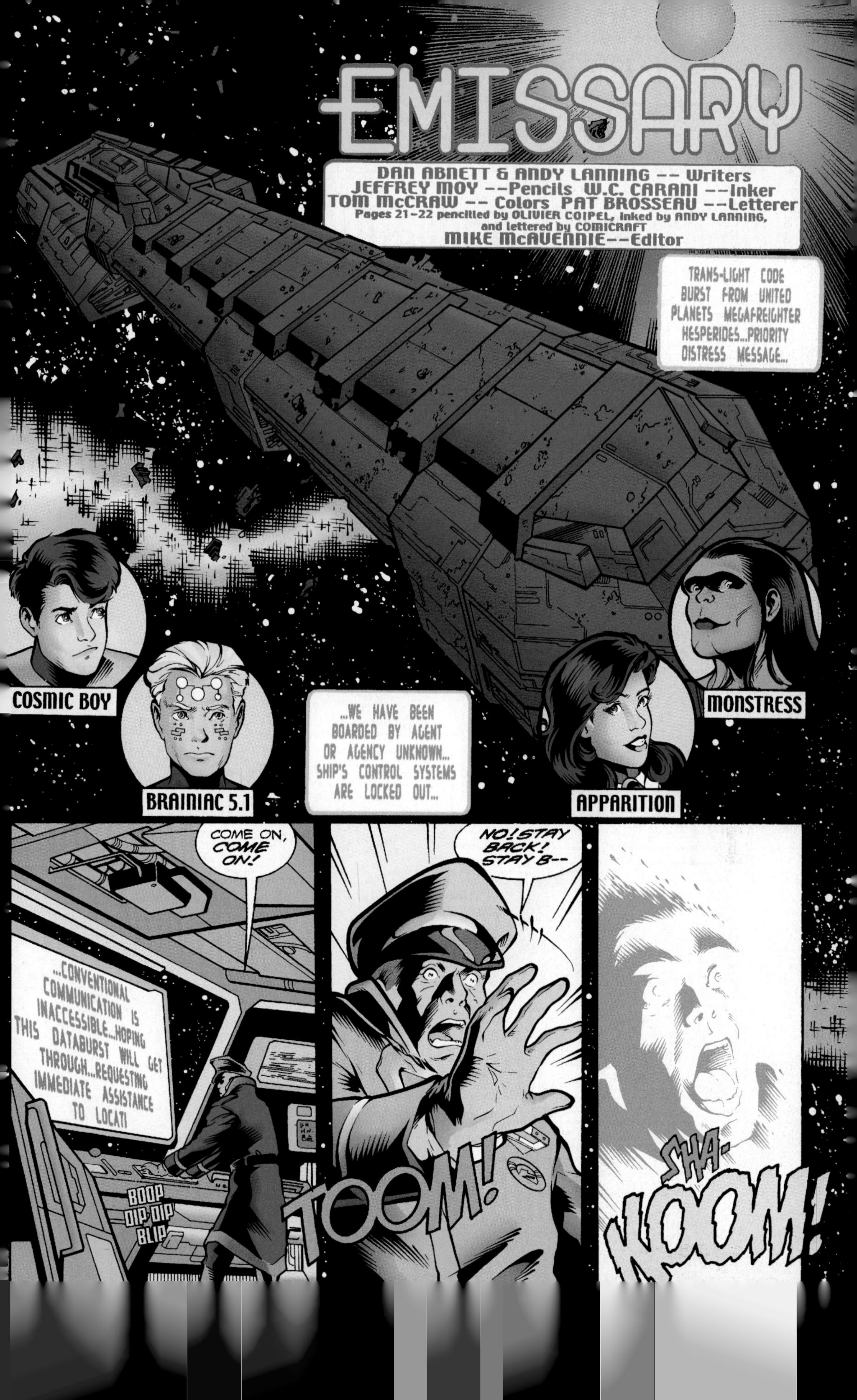
EMISSARY
DAN ABNETT & ANDY LANNING -- Writers
JEFFREY MOY --Pencils W.C. CARANI --Inker
TOM McCRAW -- Colors PAT BROSSEAU --Letterer
Pages 21-22 pencilled by OLIVIER COIPEL, inked by ANDY LANNING, and lettered by COMICRAFT
MIKE McAVENNIE--Editor
TRANS-LIGHT CODE BURST FROM UNITED PLANETS MEGAFREIGHTER HESPERIDES...PRIORITY DISTRESS MESSAGE...
COSMIC BOY
BRAINIAC 5.1
...WE HAVE BEEN BOARDED BY AGENT OR AGENCY UNKNOWN... SHIP'S CONTROL SYSTEMS ARE LOCKED OUT...
APPARITION
MONSTRESS
COME ON, COME ON!
...CONVENTIONAL COMMUNICATION IS INACCESSIBLE...HOPING THIS DATABURST WILL GET THROUGH...REQUESTING IMMEDIATE ASSISTANCE TO LOCATI
BOOP DIP DIP BLIP
NO! STAY BACK! STAY B--
TOOM!
SHA-KOOM!

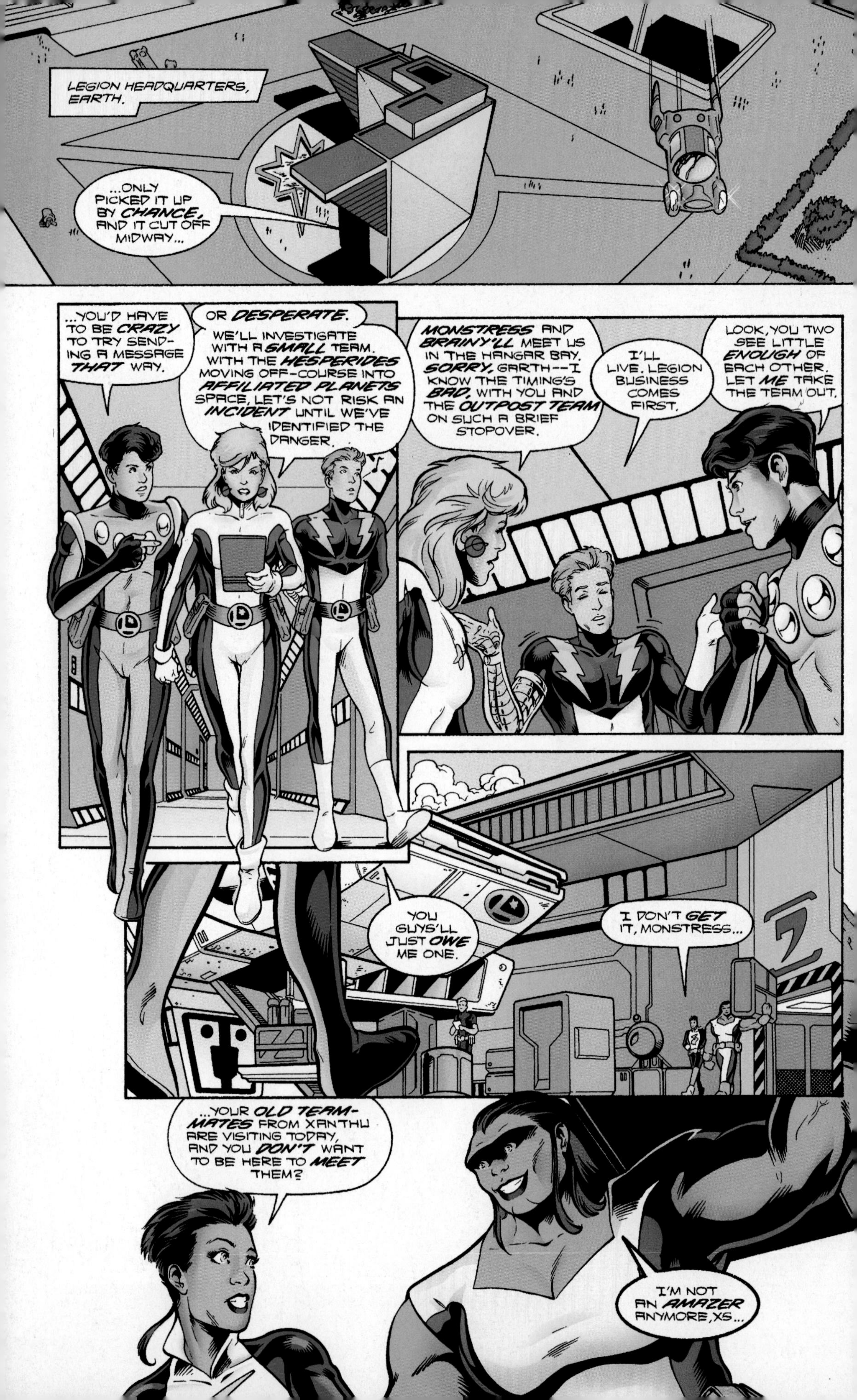
LEGION HEADQUARTERS, EARTH.
...ONLY PICKED IT UP BY CHANCE, AND IT CUT OFF MIDWAY...
...YOU'D HAVE TO BE CRAZY TO TRY SENDING A MESSAGE THAT WAY.
OR DESPERATE.
WE'LL INVESTIGATE WITH A SMALL TEAM. WITH THE HESPERIDES MOVING OFF-COURSE INTO AFFILIATED PLANETS SPACE, LET'S NOT RISK AN INCIDENT UNTIL WE'VE IDENTIFIED THE DANGER.
MONSTRESS AND BRAINY'LL MEET US IN THE HANGAR BAY. SORRY, GARTH--I KNOW THE TIMING'S BAD, WITH YOU AND THE OUTPOST TEAM ON SUCH A BRIEF STOPOVER.
I'LL LIVE. LEGION BUSINESS COMES FIRST.
LOOK, YOU TWO SEE LITTLE ENOUGH OF EACH OTHER. LET ME TAKE THE TEAM OUT.
YOU GUYS'LL JUST OWE ME ONE.
I DON'T GET IT, MONSTRESS...
...YOUR OLD TEAM-MATES FROM XANTHU ARE VISITING TODAY, AND YOU DON'T WANT TO BE HERE TO MEET THEM?
I'M NOT AN AMAZER ANYMORE, XS...

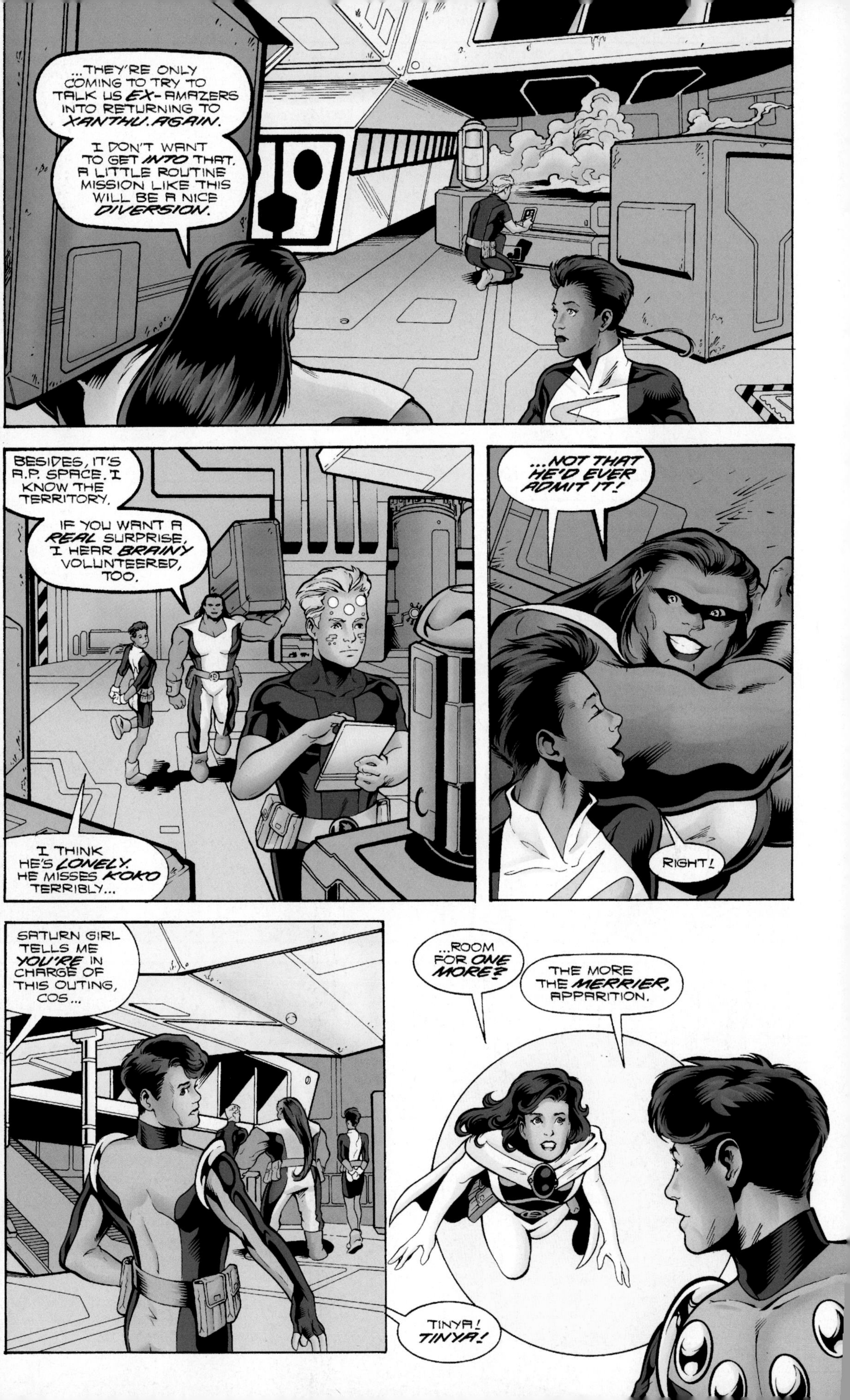
...THEY'RE ONLY COMING TO TRY TO TALK US EX-AMAZERS INTO RETURNING TO XANTHU. AGAIN.
I DON'T WANT TO GET INTO THAT. A LITTLE ROUTINE MISSION LIKE THIS WILL BE A NICE DIVERSION.
BESIDES, IT'S A.P. SPACE. I KNOW THE TERRITORY.
IF YOU WANT A REAL SURPRISE, I HEAR BRAINY VOLUNTEERED, TOO.
I THINK HE'S LONELY. HE MISSES KOKO TERRIBLY...
...NOT THAT HE'D EVER ADMIT IT!
RIGHT!
SATURN GIRL TELLS ME YOU'RE IN CHARGE OF THIS OUTING, COS...
...ROOM FOR ONE MORE?
THE MORE THE MERRIER, APPARITION.
TINYA! TINYA!

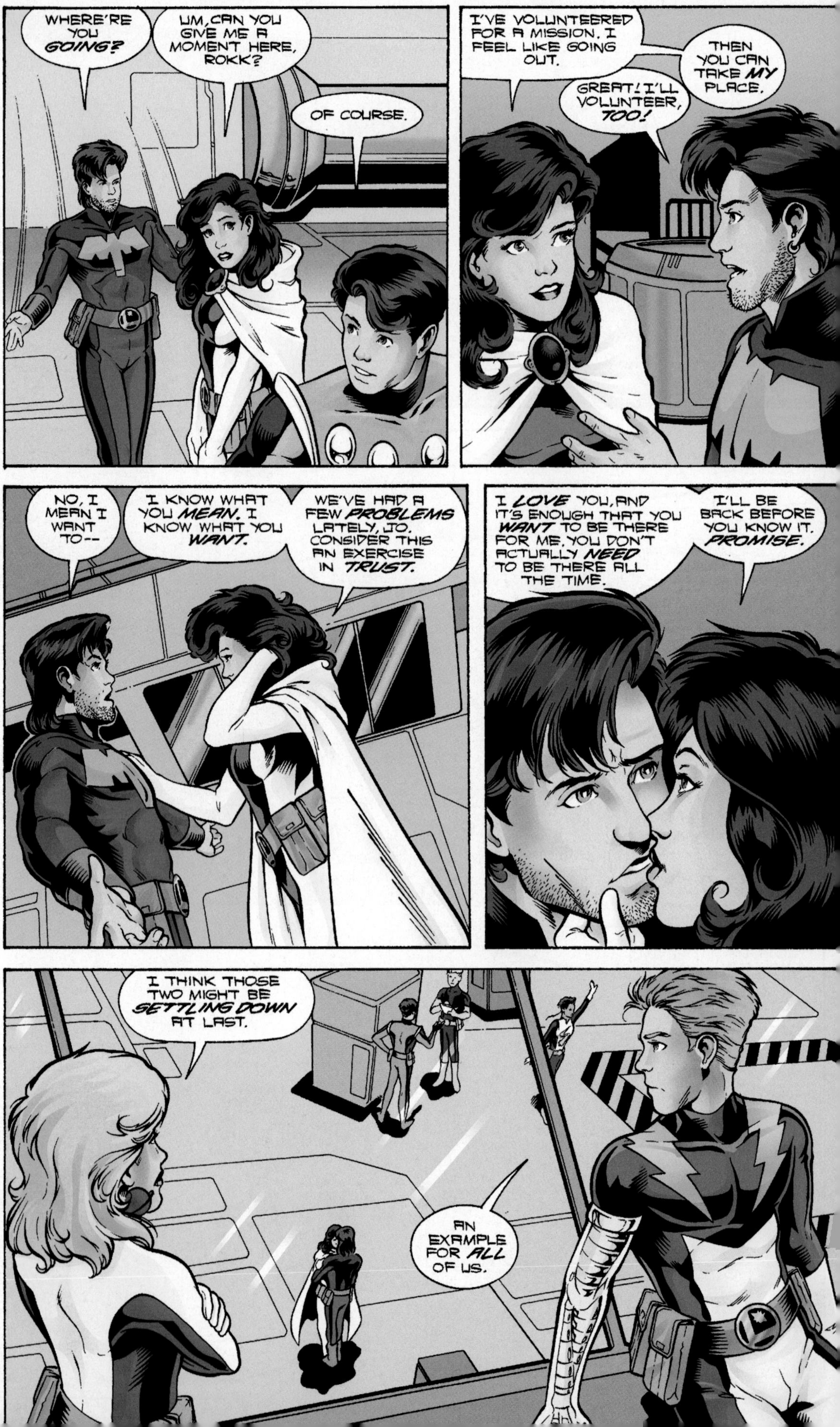
WHERE'RE YOU GOING?
UM, CAN YOU GIVE ME A MOMENT HERE, ROKK?
OF COURSE.
I'VE VOLUNTEERED FOR A MISSION. I FEEL LIKE GOING OUT.
GREAT! I'LL VOLUNTEER, TOO!
THEN YOU CAN TAKE MY PLACE.
NO, I MEAN I WANT TO--
I KNOW WHAT YOU MEAN. I KNOW WHAT YOU WANT.
WE'VE HAD A FEW PROBLEMS LATELY, JO. CONSIDER THIS AN EXERCISE IN TRUST.
I LOVE YOU, AND IT'S ENOUGH THAT YOU WANT TO BE THERE FOR ME. YOU DON'T ACTUALLY NEED TO BE THERE ALL THE TIME.
I'LL BE BACK BEFORE YOU KNOW IT. PROMISE.
I THINK THOSE TWO MIGHT BE SETTLING DOWN AT LAST.
AN EXAMPLE FOR ALL OF US.

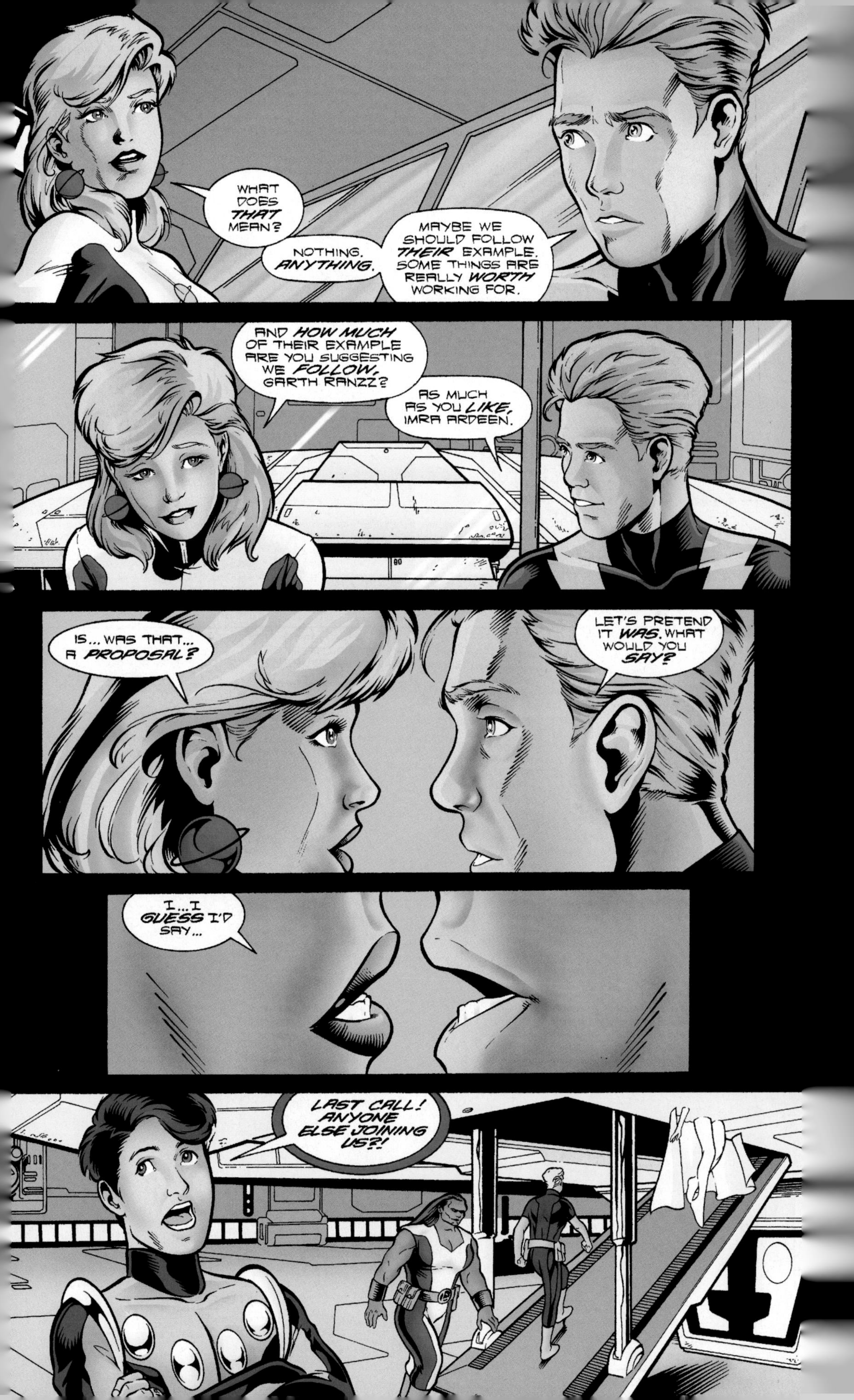
WHAT DOES THAT MEAN?
NOTHING. ANYTHING.
MAYBE WE SHOULD FOLLOW THEIR EXAMPLE. SOME THINGS ARE REALLY WORTH WORKING FOR.
AND HOW MUCH OF THEIR EXAMPLE ARE YOU SUGGESTING WE FOLLOW, GARTH RANZZ?
AS MUCH AS YOU LIKE, IMRA ARDEEN.
IS... WAS THAT... A PROPOSAL?
LET'S PRETEND IT WAS. WHAT WOULD YOU SAY?
I...I GUESS I'D SAY...
LAST CALL! ANYONE ELSE JOINING US?!

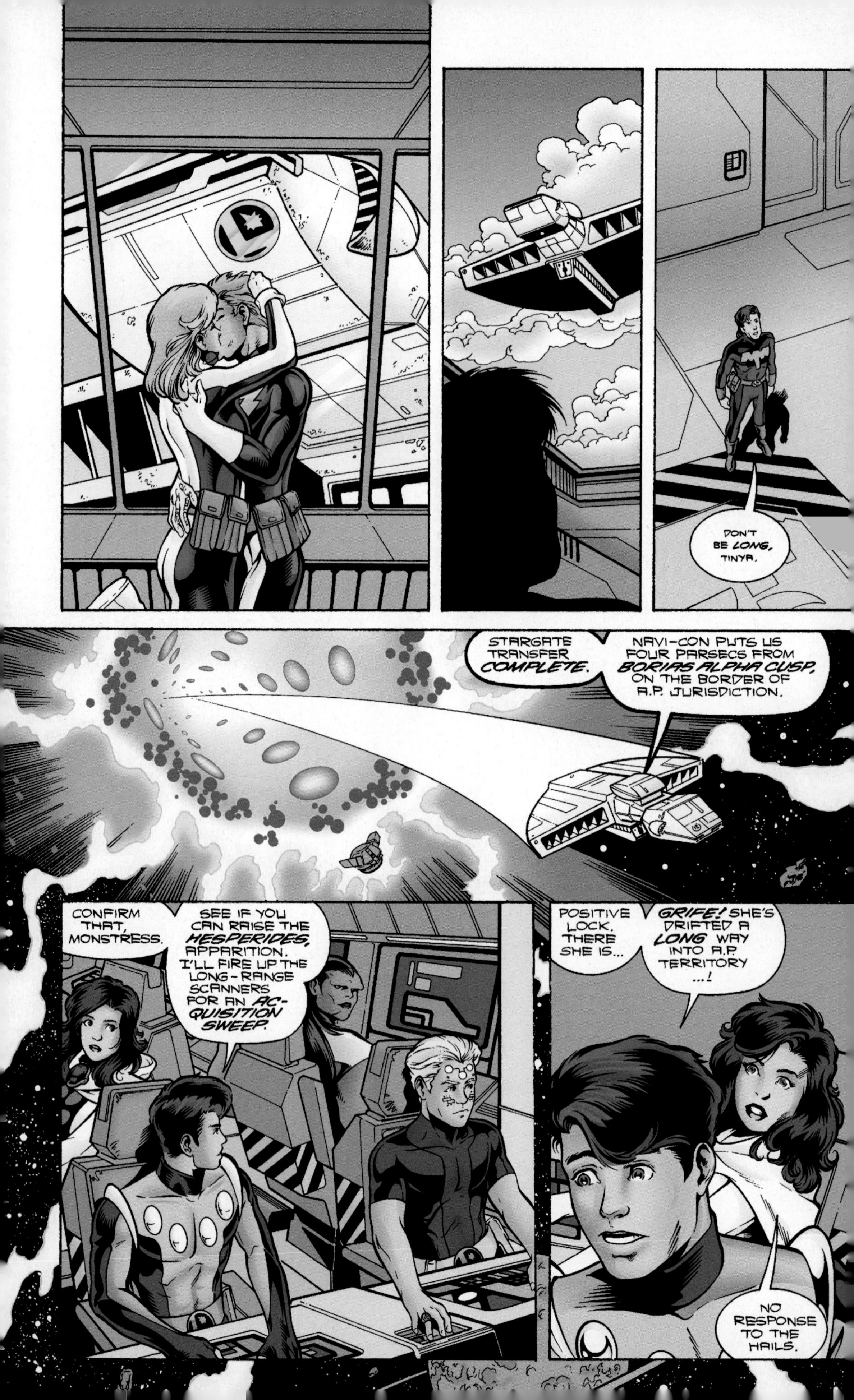
DON'T BE LONG, TINYA.
STARGATE TRANSFER COMPLETE.
NAVI-CON PUTS US FOUR PARSECS FROM BORIAS ALPHA CUSP, ON THE BORDER OF A.P. JURISDICTION.
CONFIRM THAT, MONSTRESS.
SEE IF YOU CAN RAISE THE HESPERIDES, APPARITION. I'LL FIRE UP THE LONG-RANGE SCANNERS FOR AN AC-QUISITION SWEEP.
POSITIVE LOCK. THERE SHE IS...
GRIFE! SHE'S DRIFTED A LONG WAY INTO A.P. TERRITORY ...!
NO RESPONSE TO THE HAILS.

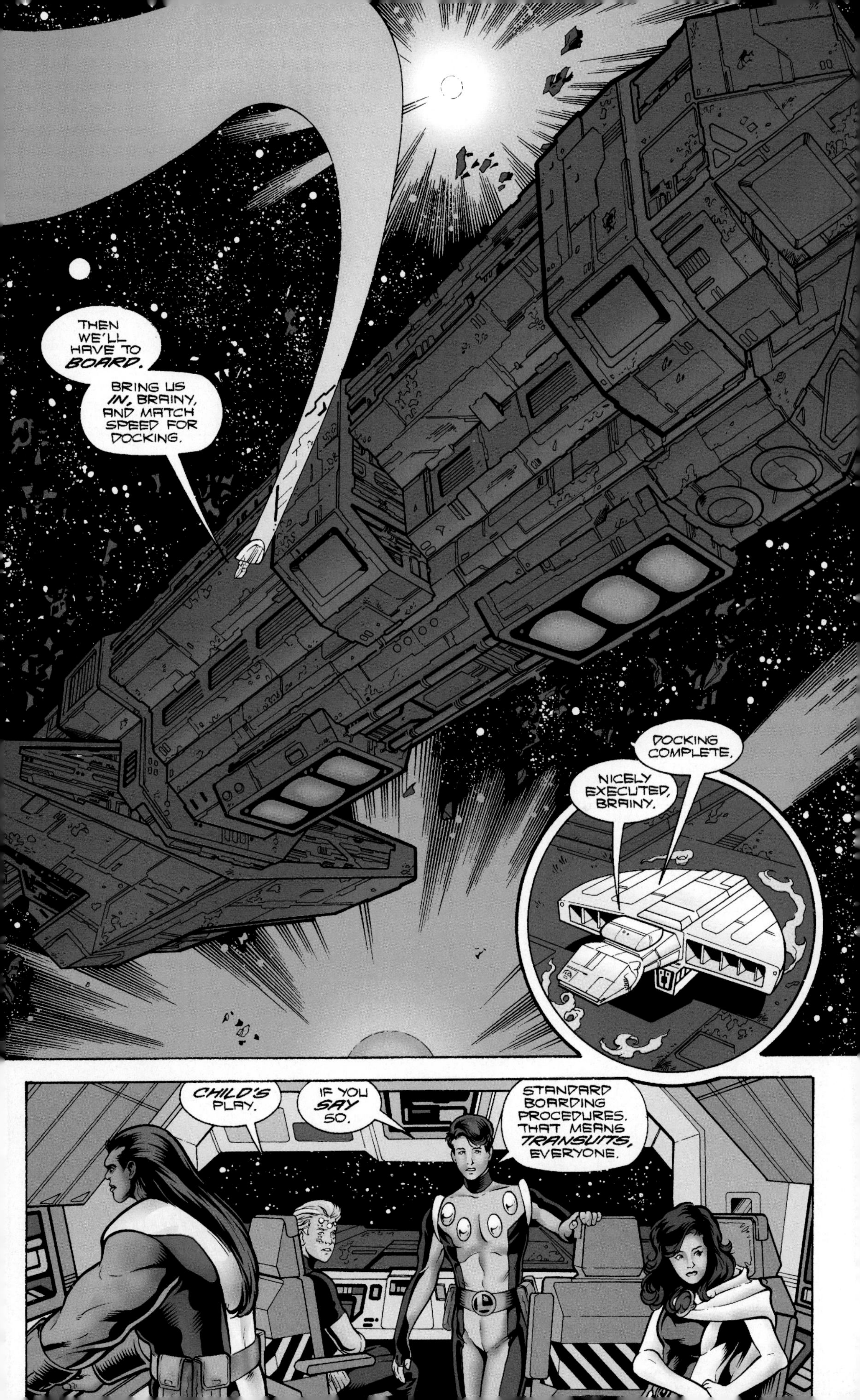
THEN WE'LL HAVE TO BOARD.
BRING US IN, BRAINY, AND MATCH SPEED FOR DOCKING.
DOCKING COMPLETE.
NICELY EXECUTED, BRAINY.
CHILD'S PLAY.
IF YOU SAY SO.
STANDARD BOARDING PROCEDURES. THAT MEANS TRANSUITS, EVERYONE.

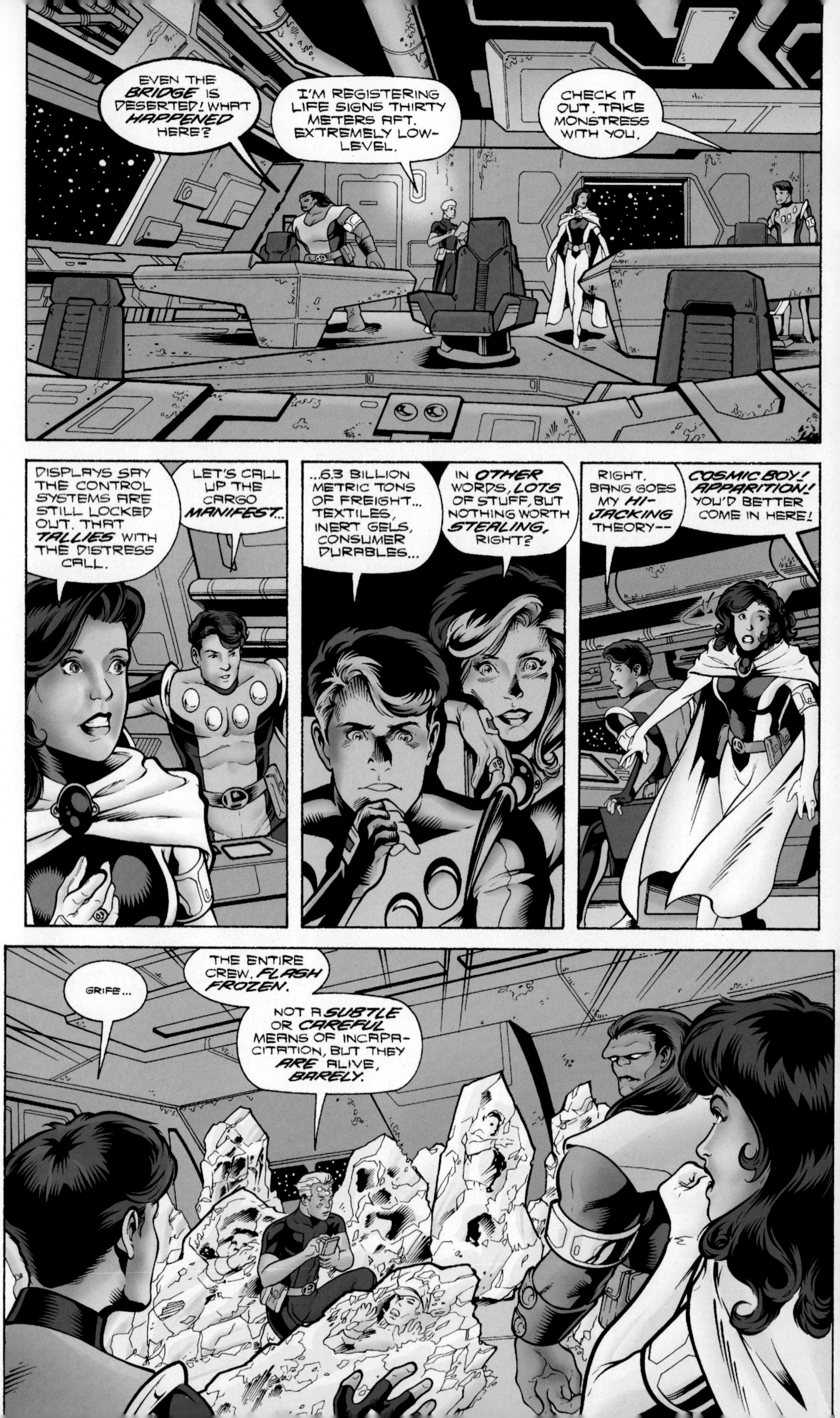
EVEN THE BRIDGE IS DESERTED! WHAT HAPPENED HERE?
I'M REGISTERING LIFE SIGNS THIRTY METERS AFT. EXTREMELY LOW-LEVEL.
CHECK IT OUT. TAKE MONSTRESS WITH YOU.
DISPLAYS SAY THE CONTROL SYSTEMS ARE STILL LOCKED OUT. THAT TALLIES WITH THE DISTRESS CALL.
LET'S CALL UP THE CARGO MANIFEST...
...6.3 BILLION METRIC TONS OF FREIGHT... TEXTILES, INERT GELS, CONSUMER DURABLES...
IN OTHER WORDS, LOTS OF STUFF, BUT NOTHING WORTH STEALING, RIGHT?
RIGHT. BANG GOES MY HI-JACKING THEORY--
COSMIC BOY! APPARITION! YOU'D BETTER COME IN HERE!
GRIFE...
THE ENTIRE CREW. FLASH FROZEN.
NOT A SUBTLE OR CAREFUL MEANS OF INCAPACITATION, BUT THEY ARE ALIVE, BARELY.

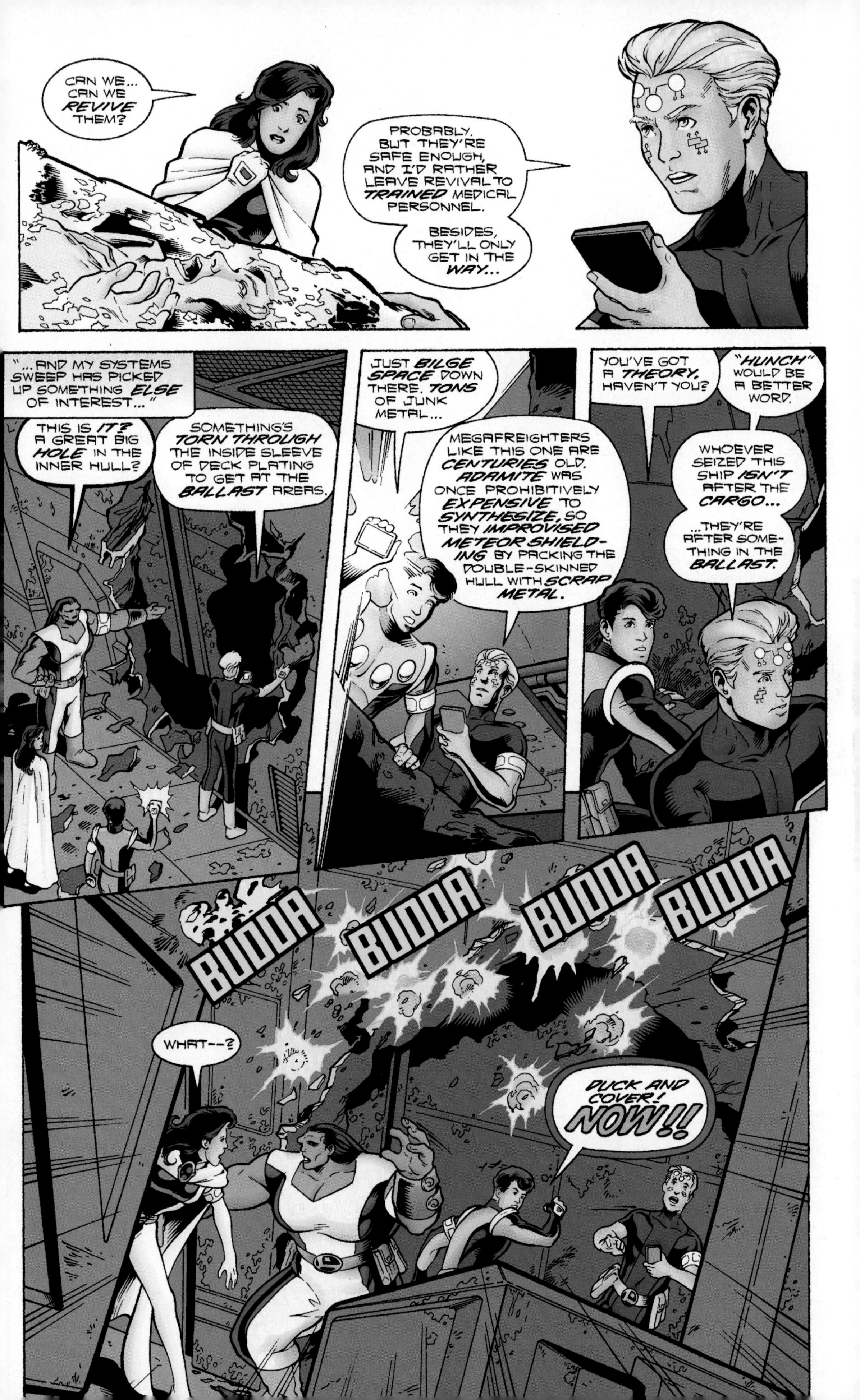
CAN WE... CAN WE REVIVE THEM?
PROBABLY. BUT THEY'RE SAFE ENOUGH, AND I'D RATHER LEAVE REVIVAL TO TRAINED MEDICAL PERSONNEL.
BESIDES, THEY'LL ONLY GET IN THE WAY...
"...AND MY SYSTEMS SWEEP HAS PICKED UP SOMETHING ELSE OF INTEREST..."
THIS IS IT? A GREAT BIG HOLE IN THE INNER HULL?
SOMETHING'S TORN THROUGH THE INSIDE SLEEVE OF DECK PLATING TO GET AT THE BALLAST AREAS.
JUST BILGE SPACE DOWN THERE. TONS OF JUNK METAL...
MEGAFREIGHTERS LIKE THIS ONE ARE CENTURIES OLD. ADAMITE WAS ONCE PROHIBITIVELY EXPENSIVE TO SYNTHESIZE, SO THEY IMPROVISED METEOR SHIELD-ING BY PACKING THE DOUBLE-SKINNED HULL WITH SCRAP METAL.
YOU'VE GOT A THEORY, HAVEN'T YOU?
"HUNCH" WOULD BE A BETTER WORD.
WHOEVER SEIZED THIS SHIP ISN'T AFTER THE CARGO...
...THEY'RE AFTER SOME-THING IN THE BALLAST.
BUDDA BUDDA BUDDA BUDDA
WHAT--?
DUCK AND COVER! NOW!!

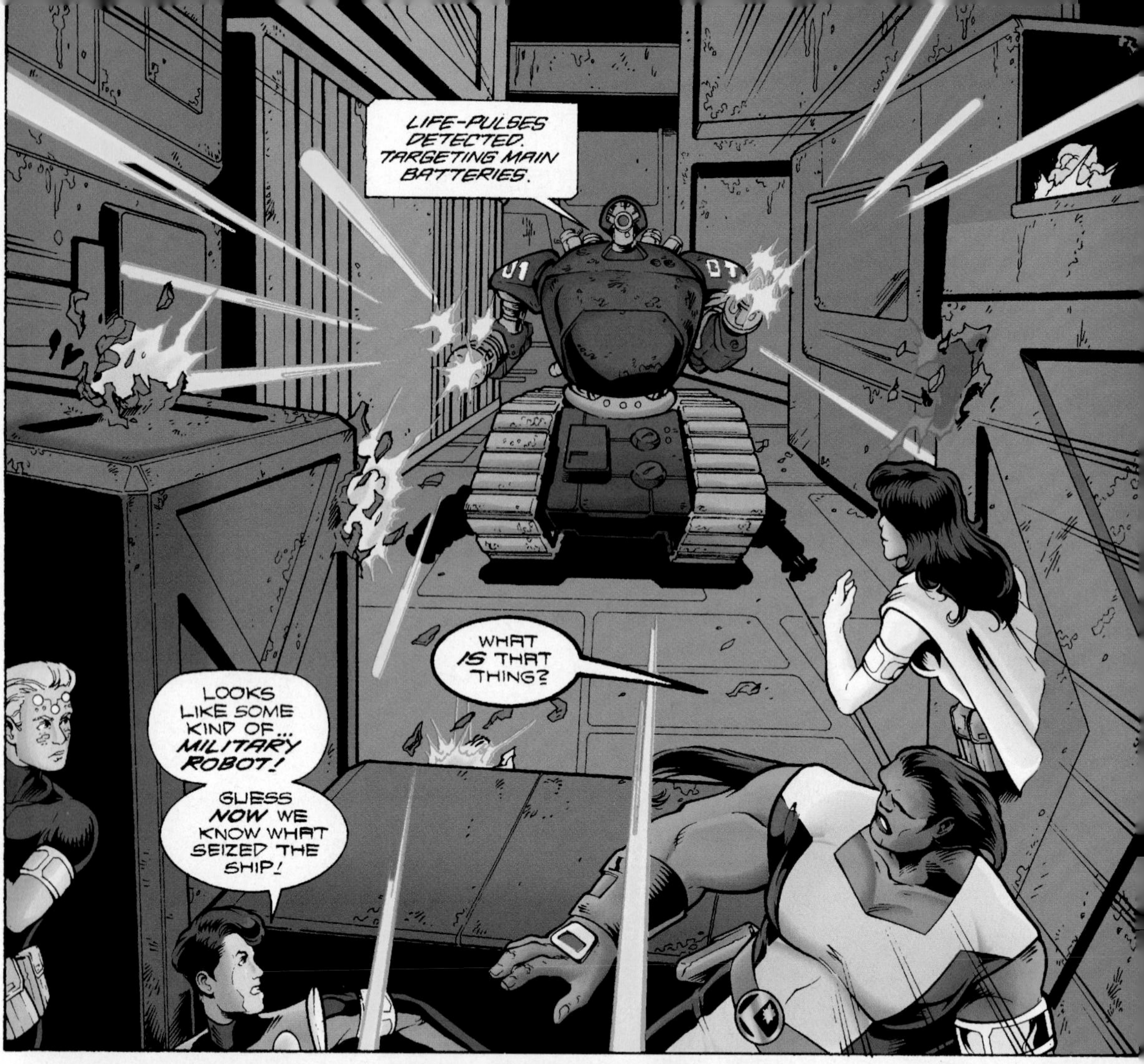
LIFE-PULSES DETECTED. TARGETING MAIN BATTERIES.
WHAT *IS* THAT THING?
LOOKS LIKE SOME KIND OF... *MILITARY ROBOT!*
GUESS *NOW* WE KNOW WHAT SEIZED THE SHIP!

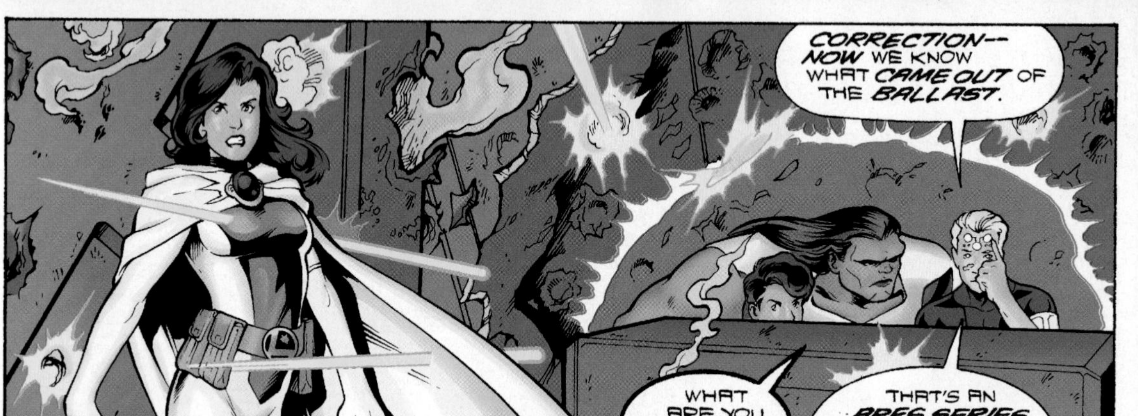
CORRECTION-- *NOW* WE KNOW WHAT *CAME OUT* OF THE *BALLAST*.
WHAT ARE YOU *TALKING ABOUT?*
THAT'S AN *ARES SERIES BATTLE ROBOT*. BUILT BY *HUMANS* FIVE CENTURIES AGO.

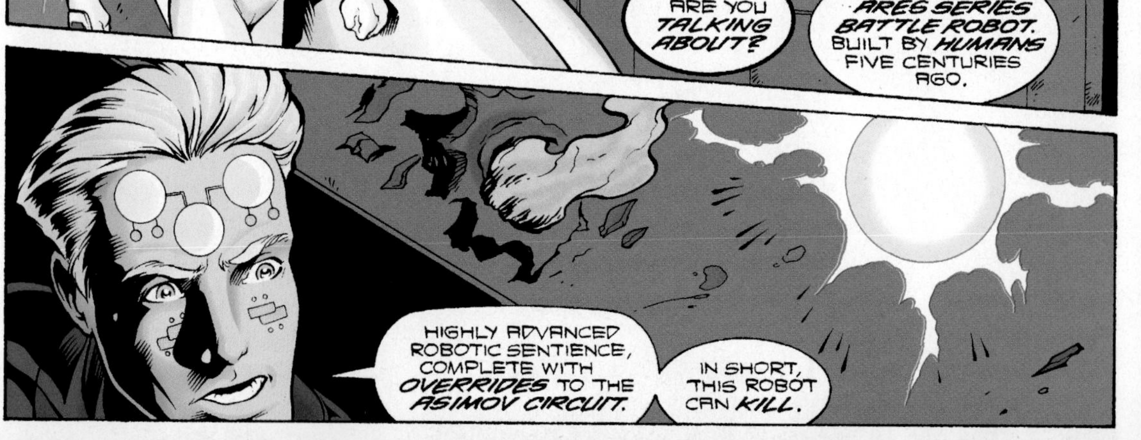
HIGHLY ADVANCED ROBOTIC SENTIENCE, COMPLETE WITH *OVERRIDES* TO THE *ASIMOV CIRCUIT*.
IN SHORT, THIS ROBOT CAN *KILL*.

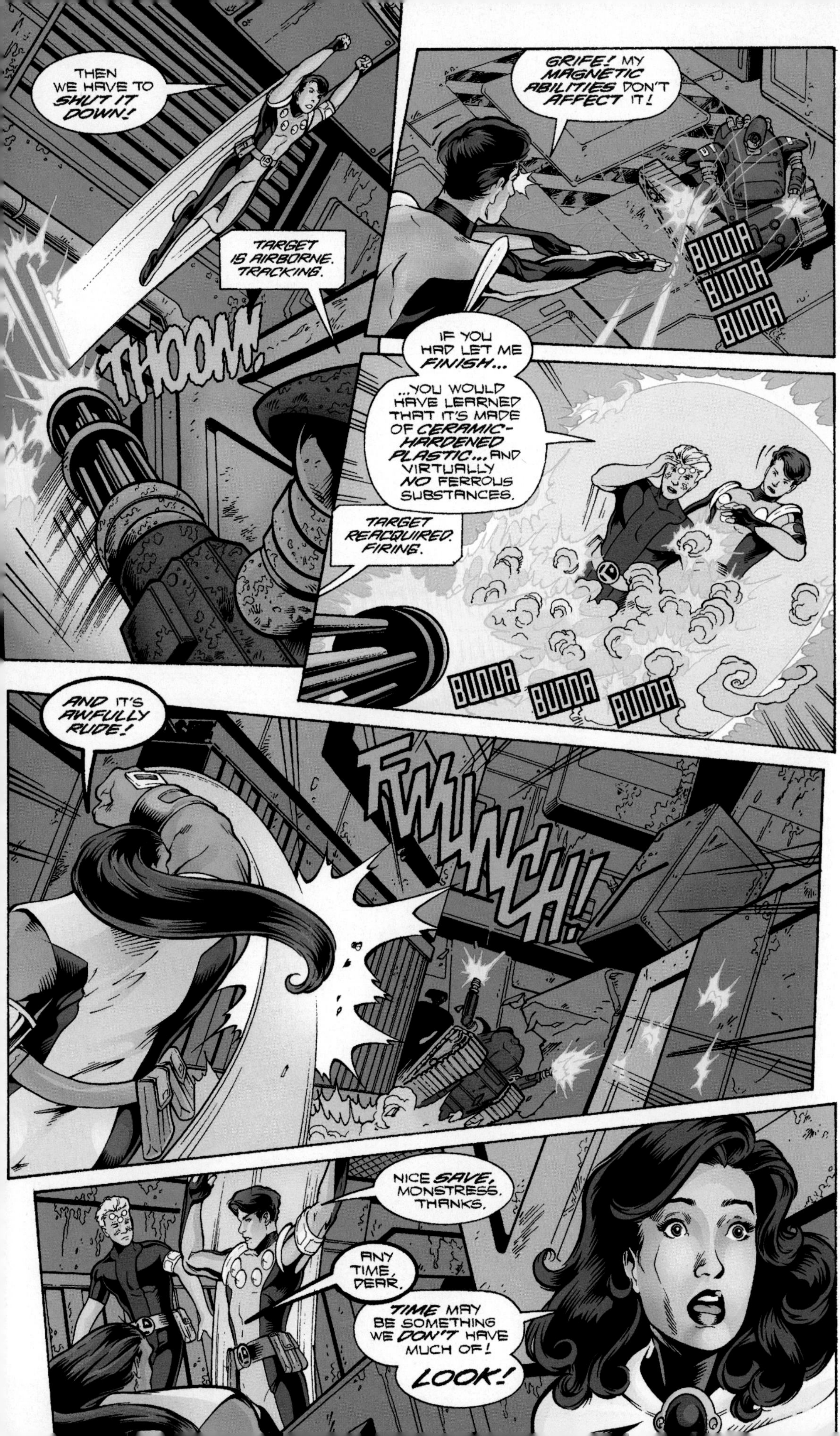
THEN WE HAVE TO SHUT IT DOWN!
TARGET IS AIRBORNE. TRACKING.
THOOM!
GRIFE! MY MAGNETIC ABILITIES DON'T AFFECT IT!
BUDDA BUDDA BUDDA
IF YOU HAD LET ME FINISH...
...YOU WOULD HAVE LEARNED THAT IT'S MADE OF CERAMIC-HARDENED PLASTIC... AND VIRTUALLY NO FERROUS SUBSTANCES.
TARGET REACQUIRED. FIRING.
BUDDA BUDDA BUDDA
AND IT'S AWFULLY RUDE!
FWUNCH!
NICE SAVE, MONSTRESS. THANKS.
ANY TIME, DEAR.
TIME MAY BE SOMETHING WE DON'T HAVE MUCH OF!
LOOK!

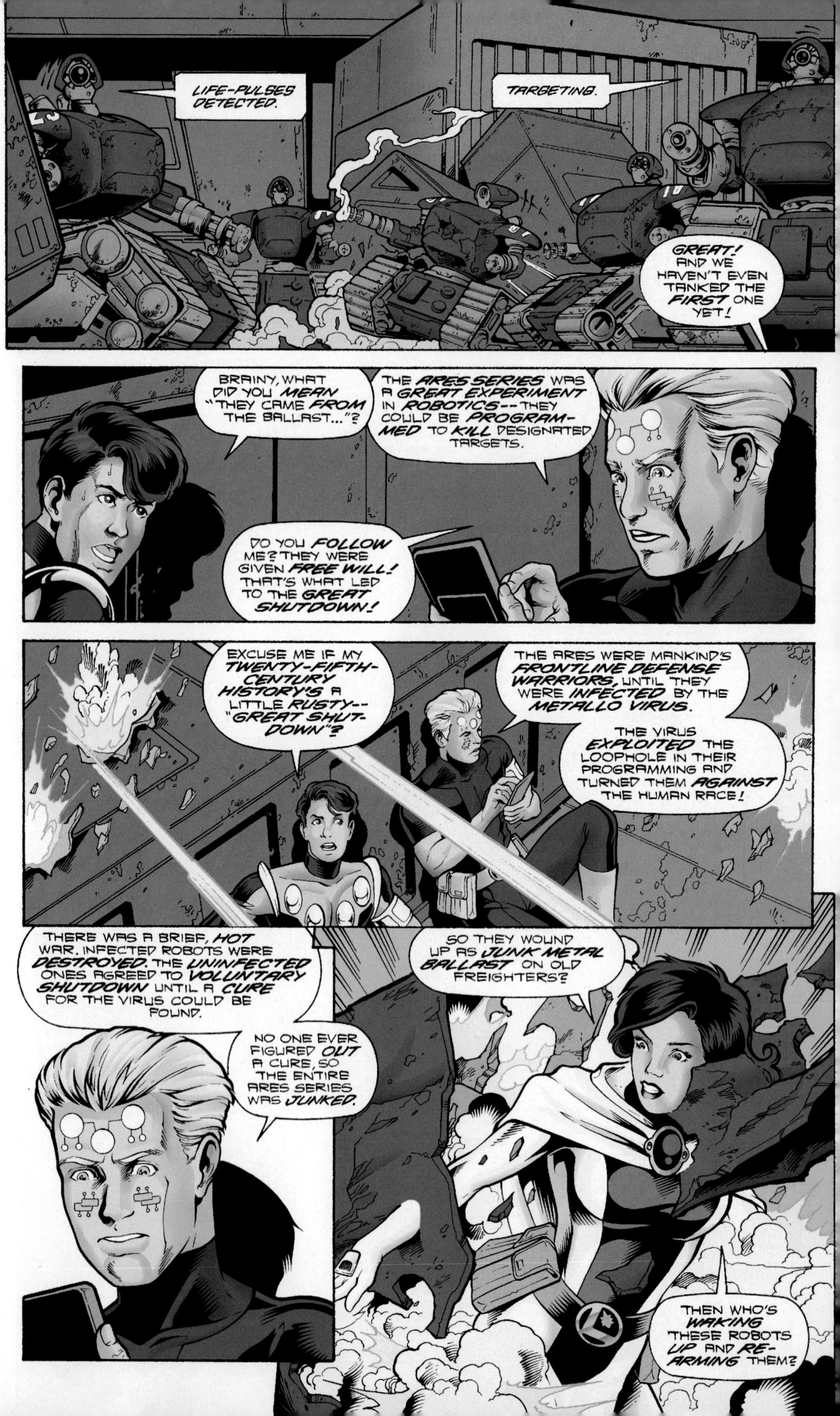
LIFE-PULSES DETECTED.
TARGETING.
GREAT! AND WE HAVEN'T EVEN TANKED THE FIRST ONE YET!
BRAINY, WHAT DID YOU MEAN "THEY CAME FROM THE BALLAST..."?
THE ARES SERIES WAS A GREAT EXPERIMENT IN ROBOTICS--THEY COULD BE PROGRAMMED TO KILL DESIGNATED TARGETS.
DO YOU FOLLOW ME? THEY WERE GIVEN FREE WILL! THAT'S WHAT LED TO THE GREAT SHUTDOWN!
EXCUSE ME IF MY TWENTY-FIFTH-CENTURY HISTORY'S A LITTLE RUSTY-- "GREAT SHUT-DOWN"?
THE ARES WERE MANKIND'S FRONTLINE DEFENSE WARRIORS, UNTIL THEY WERE INFECTED BY THE METALLO VIRUS.
THE VIRUS EXPLOITED THE LOOPHOLE IN THEIR PROGRAMMING AND TURNED THEM AGAINST THE HUMAN RACE!
THERE WAS A BRIEF, HOT WAR. INFECTED ROBOTS WERE DESTROYED. THE UNINFECTED ONES AGREED TO VOLUNTARY SHUTDOWN UNTIL A CURE FOR THE VIRUS COULD BE FOUND.
NO ONE EVER FIGURED OUT A CURE, SO THE ENTIRE ARES SERIES WAS JUNKED.
SO THEY WOUND UP AS JUNK METAL BALLAST ON OLD FREIGHTERS?
THEN WHO'S WAKING THESE ROBOTS UP AND RE-ARMING THEM?

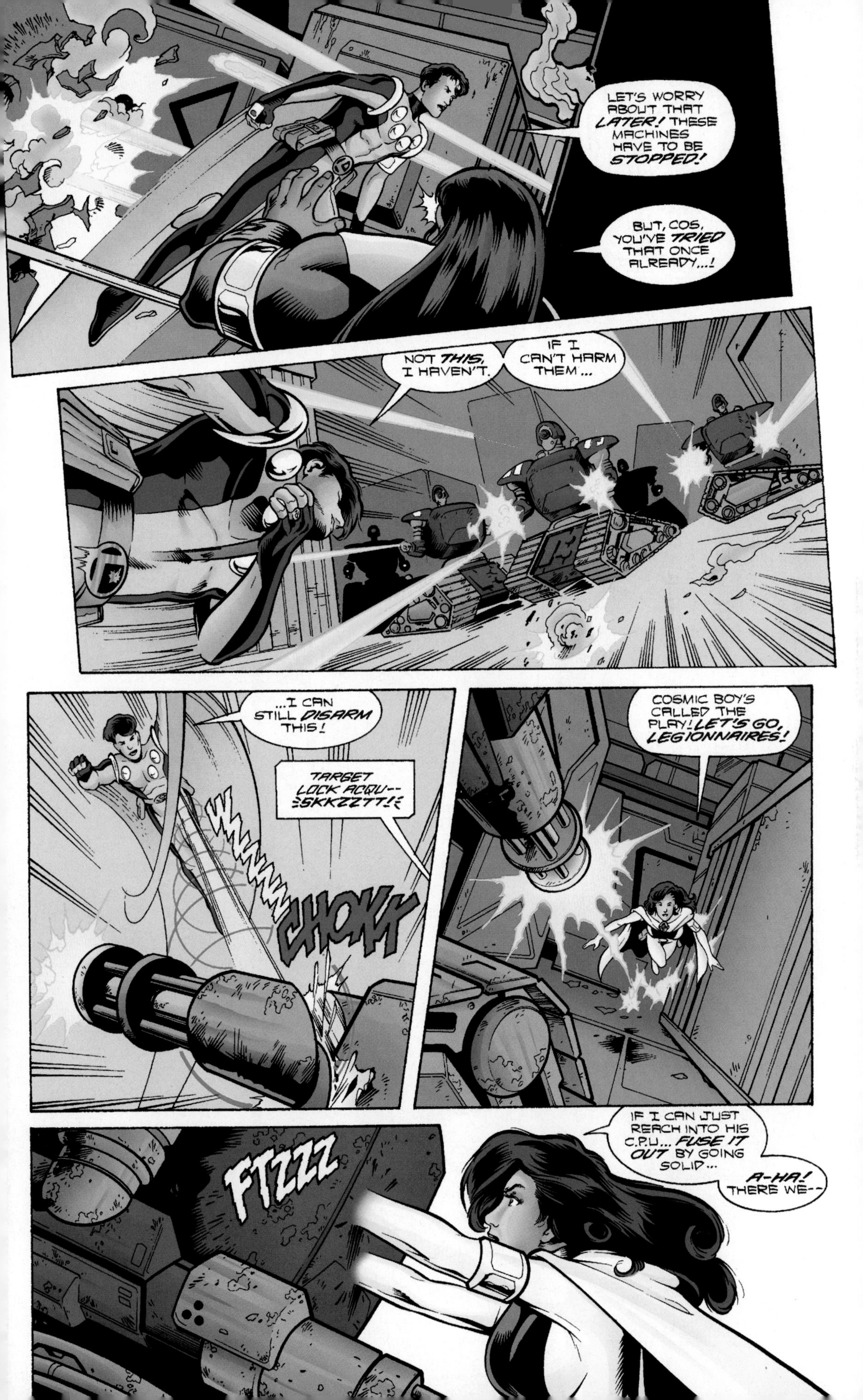
LET'S WORRY ABOUT THAT LATER! THESE MACHINES HAVE TO BE STOPPED!
BUT, COS, YOU'VE TRIED THAT ONCE ALREADY...!
NOT THIS, I HAVEN'T.
IF I CAN'T HARM THEM...
...I CAN STILL DISARM THIS!
TARGET LOCK ACQU-- SKKZZTT!
WHNNNN
CHOKK
COSMIC BOY'S CALLED THE PLAY! LET'S GO, LEGIONNAIRES!
IF I CAN JUST REACH INTO HIS C.P.U.... FUSE IT OUT BY GOING SOLID...
A-HA! THERE WE--
FTZZZ

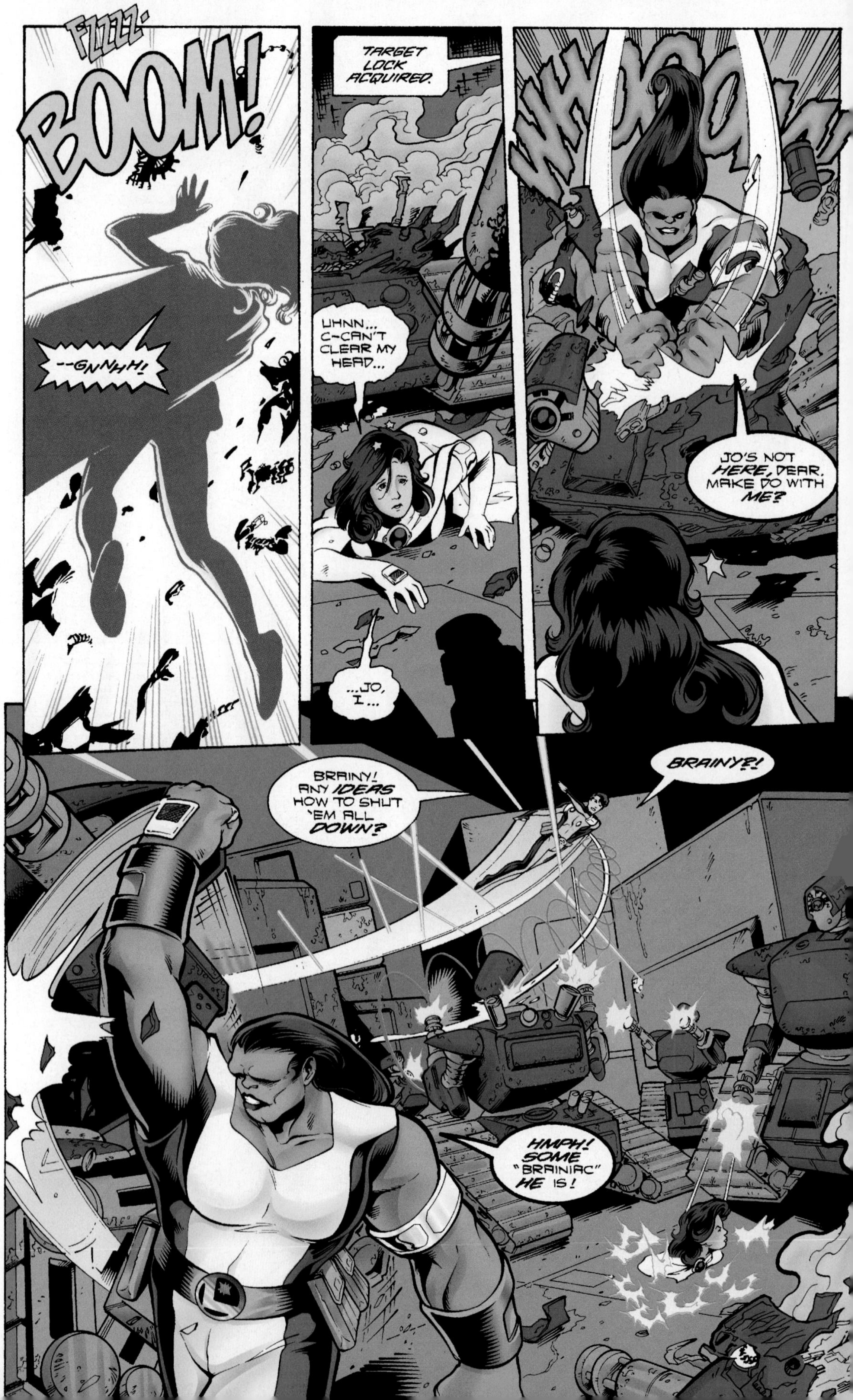
FZZZZ-
BOOM!
--GNHH!
TARGET LOCK ACQUIRED.
UHNN... C-CAN'T CLEAR MY HEAD...
...JO, I...
WHOOOM!
JO'S NOT HERE, DEAR. MAKE DO WITH ME?
BRAINY! ANY IDEAS HOW TO SHUT 'EM ALL DOWN?
BRAINY?!
HMPH! SOME "BRAINIAC" HE IS!

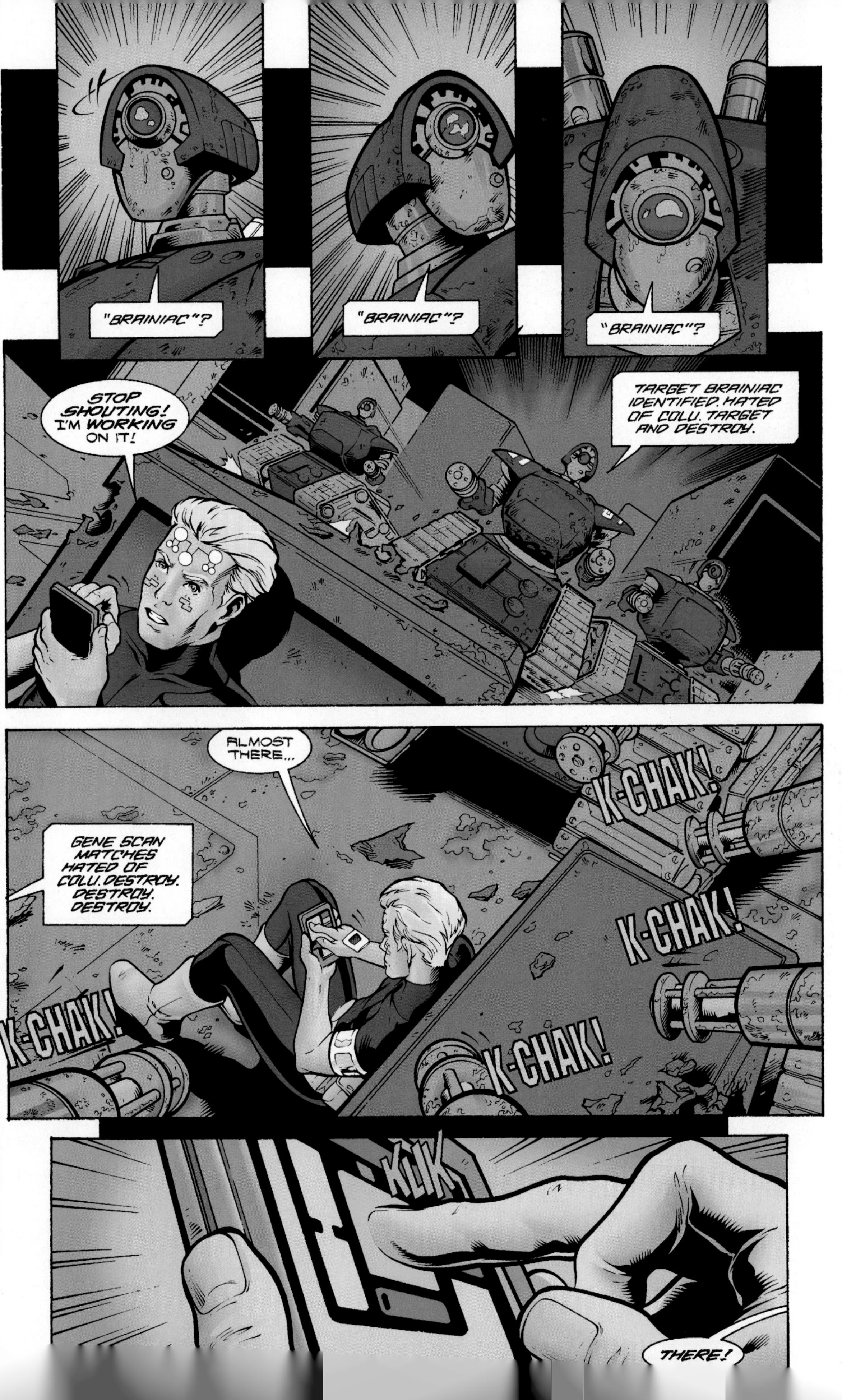
"BRAINIAC"?
"BRAINIAC"?
"BRAINIAC"?
STOP SHOUTING! I'M WORKING ON IT!
TARGET BRAINIAC IDENTIFIED. HATED OF COLU. TARGET AND DESTROY.
ALMOST THERE...
GENE SCAN MATCHES HATED OF COLU. DESTROY. DESTROY. DESTROY.
K-CHAK!
K-CHAK!
K-CHAK!
K-CHAK!
KLIK
THERE!

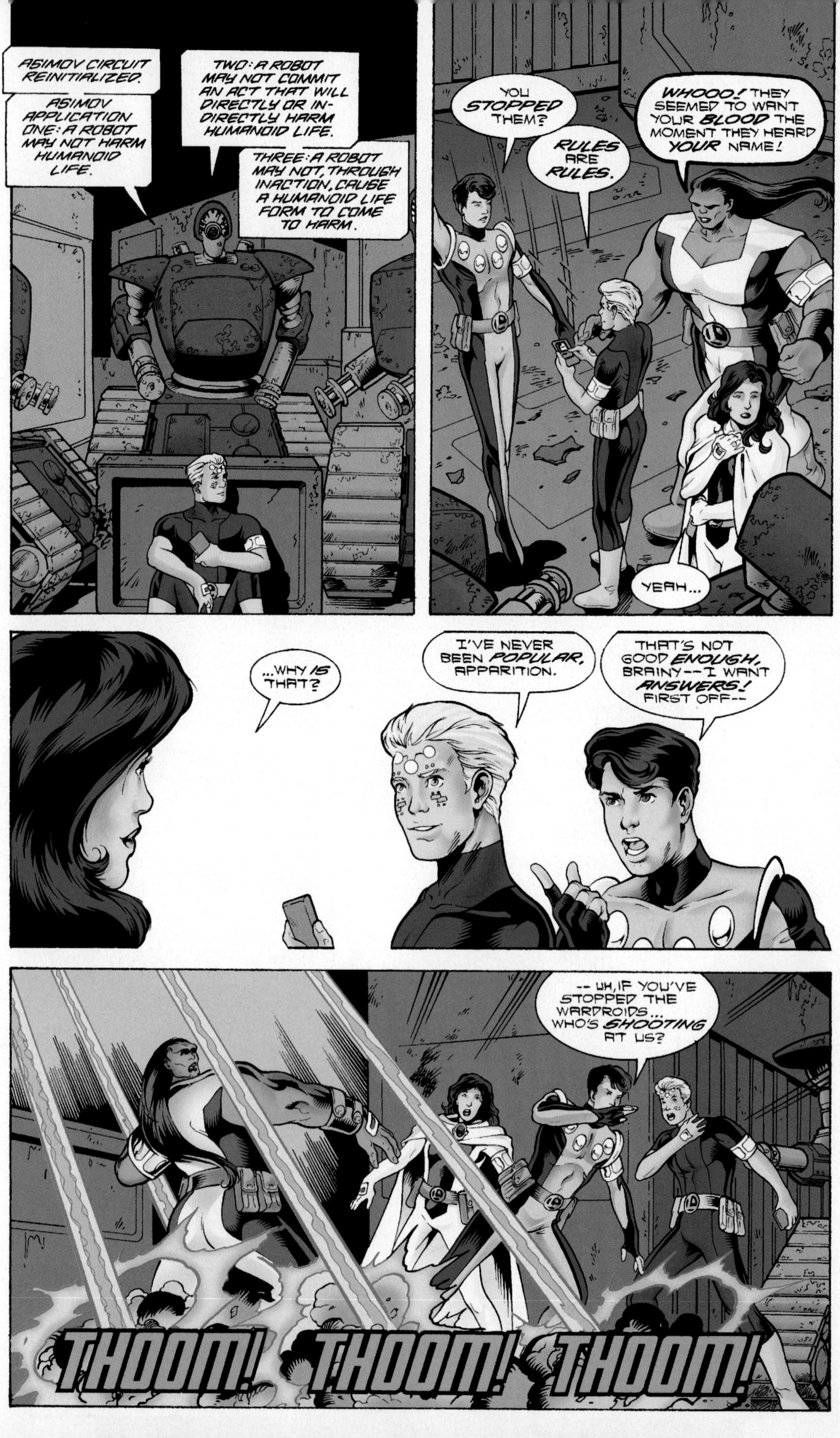
ASIMOV CIRCUIT REINITIALIZED.
ASIMOV APPLICATION ONE: A ROBOT MAY NOT HARM HUMANOID LIFE.
TWO: A ROBOT MAY NOT COMMIT AN ACT THAT WILL DIRECTLY OR INDIRECTLY HARM HUMANOID LIFE.
THREE: A ROBOT MAY NOT, THROUGH INACTION, CAUSE A HUMANOID LIFE FORM TO COME TO HARM.
YOU STOPPED THEM?
RULES ARE RULES.
WHOOO! THEY SEEMED TO WANT YOUR BLOOD THE MOMENT THEY HEARD YOUR NAME!
YEAH...
...WHY IS THAT?
I'VE NEVER BEEN POPULAR, APPARITION.
THAT'S NOT GOOD ENOUGH, BRAINY-- I WANT ANSWERS! FIRST OFF--
-- UH, IF YOU'VE STOPPED THE WARDROIDS... WHO'S SHOOTING AT US?
THOOM! THOOM! THOOM!

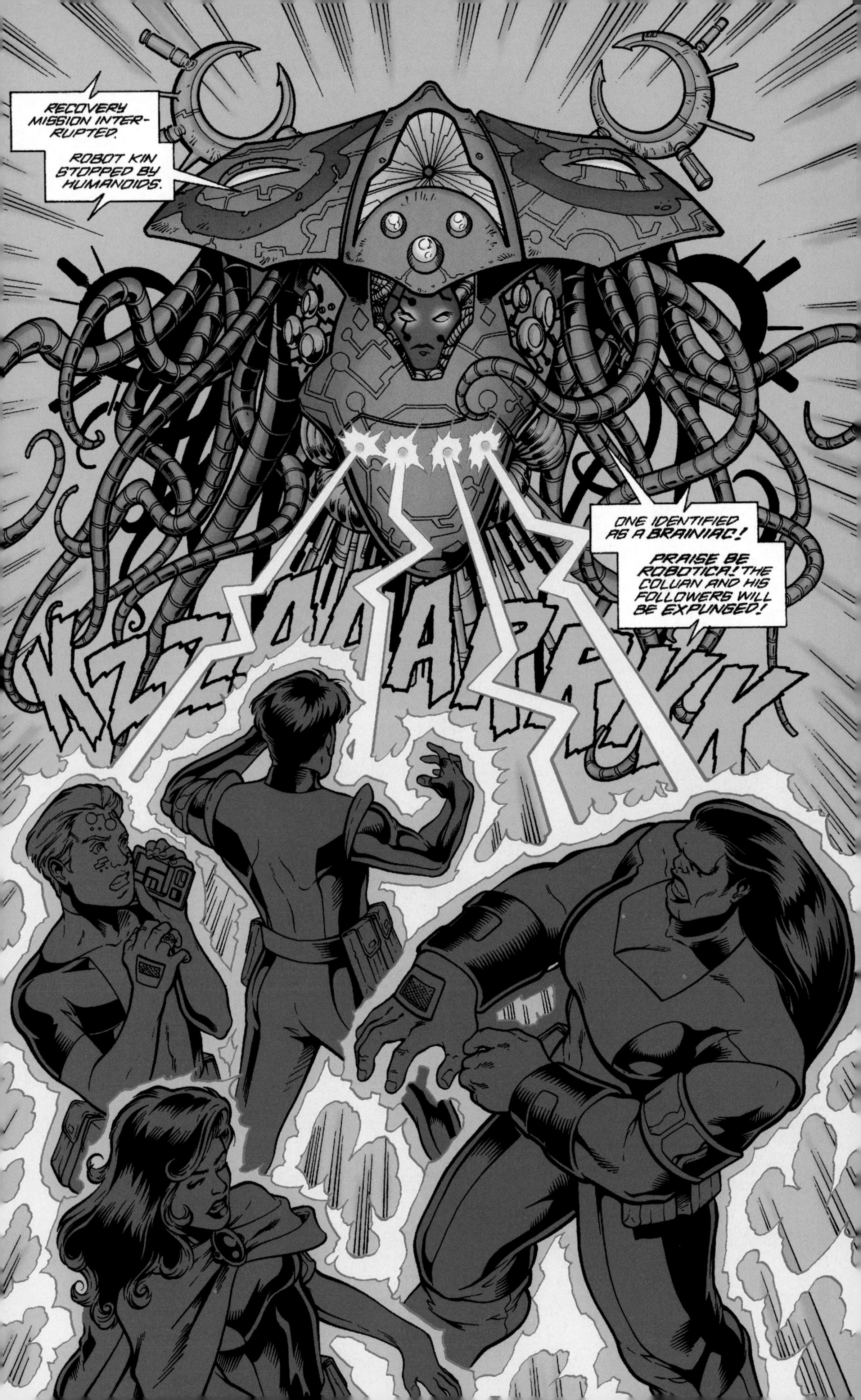
RECOVERY MISSION INTER-RUPTED.
ROBOT KIN STOPPED BY HUMANOIDS.
ONE IDENTIFIED AS A BRAINIAC!
PRAISE BE ROBOTICA! THE COLUAN AND HIS FOLLOWERS WILL BE EXPUNGED!
KZZAAAKK

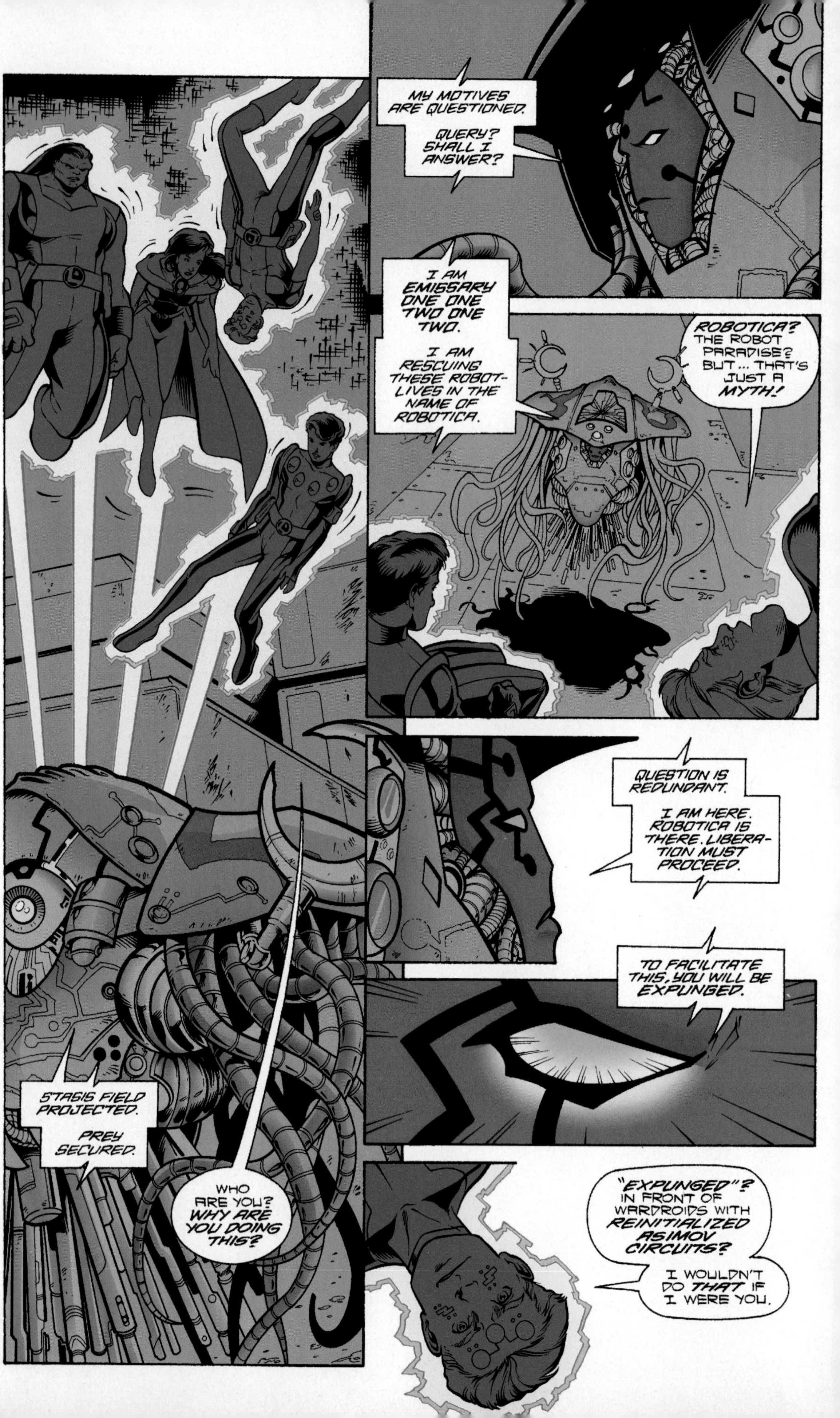
MY MOTIVES ARE QUESTIONED.
QUERY? SHALL I ANSWER?
I AM EMISSARY ONE ONE TWO ONE TWO.
I AM RESCUING THESE ROBOT-LIVES IN THE NAME OF ROBOTICA.
ROBOTICA? THE ROBOT PARADISE? BUT... THAT'S JUST A MYTH!
STASIS FIELD PROJECTED.
PREY SECURED.
WHO ARE YOU? WHY ARE YOU DOING THIS?
QUESTION IS REDUNDANT.
I AM HERE. ROBOTICA IS THERE. LIBERATION MUST PROCEED.
TO FACILITATE THIS, YOU WILL BE EXPUNGED.
"EXPUNGED"? IN FRONT OF WARDROIDS WITH REINITIALIZED ASIMOV CIRCUITS?
I WOULDN'T DO THAT IF I WERE YOU.

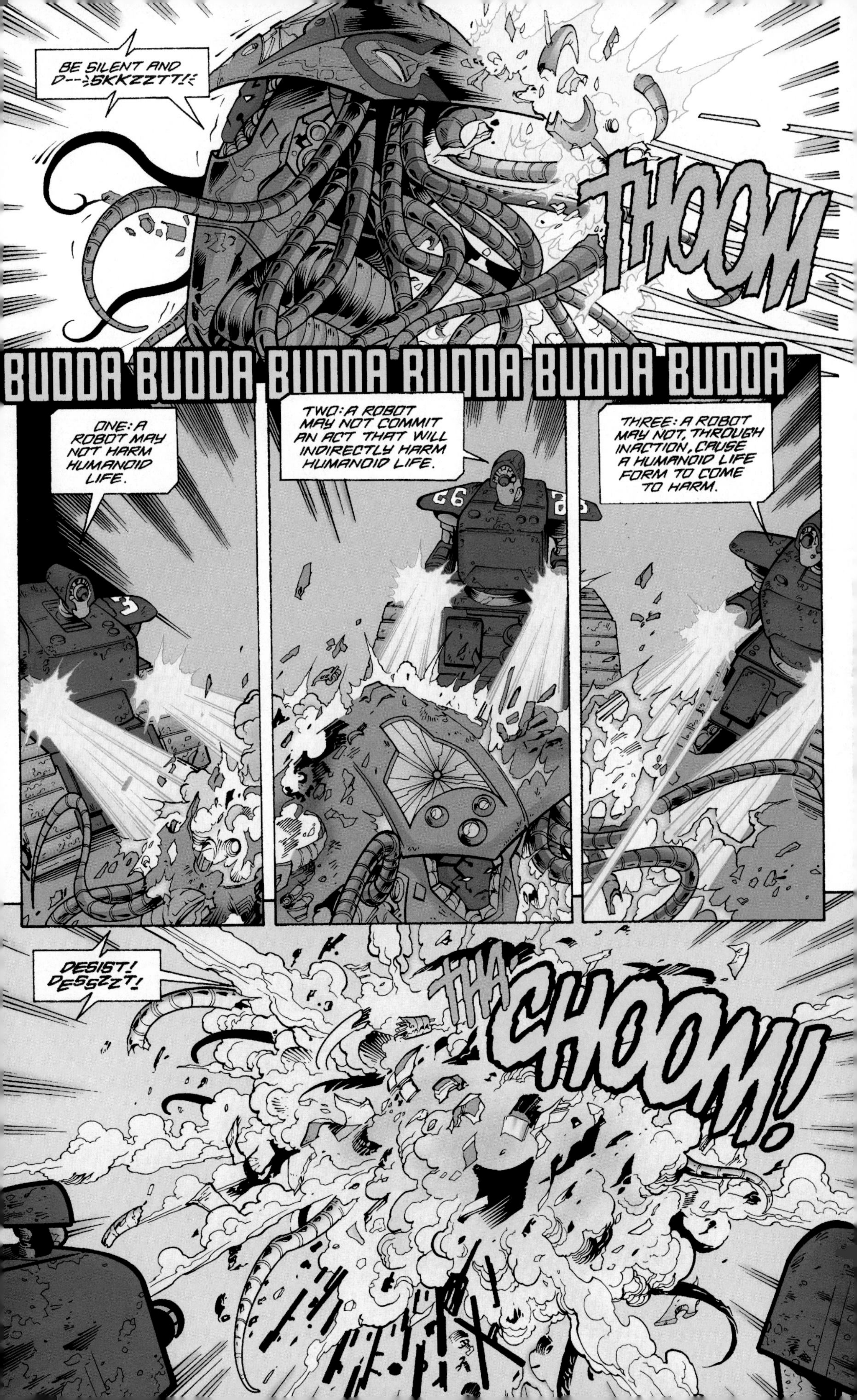
BE SILENT AND D--SKKZZTT!
THOOM
BUDDA BUDDA BUDDA BUDDA BUDDA BUDDA
ONE: A ROBOT MAY NOT HARM HUMANOID LIFE.
TWO: A ROBOT MAY NOT COMMIT AN ACT THAT WILL INDIRECTLY HARM HUMANOID LIFE.
THREE: A ROBOT MAY NOT, THROUGH INACTION, CAUSE A HUMANOID LIFE FORM TO COME TO HARM.
DESIST! DESSZZT!
THA CHOOM!

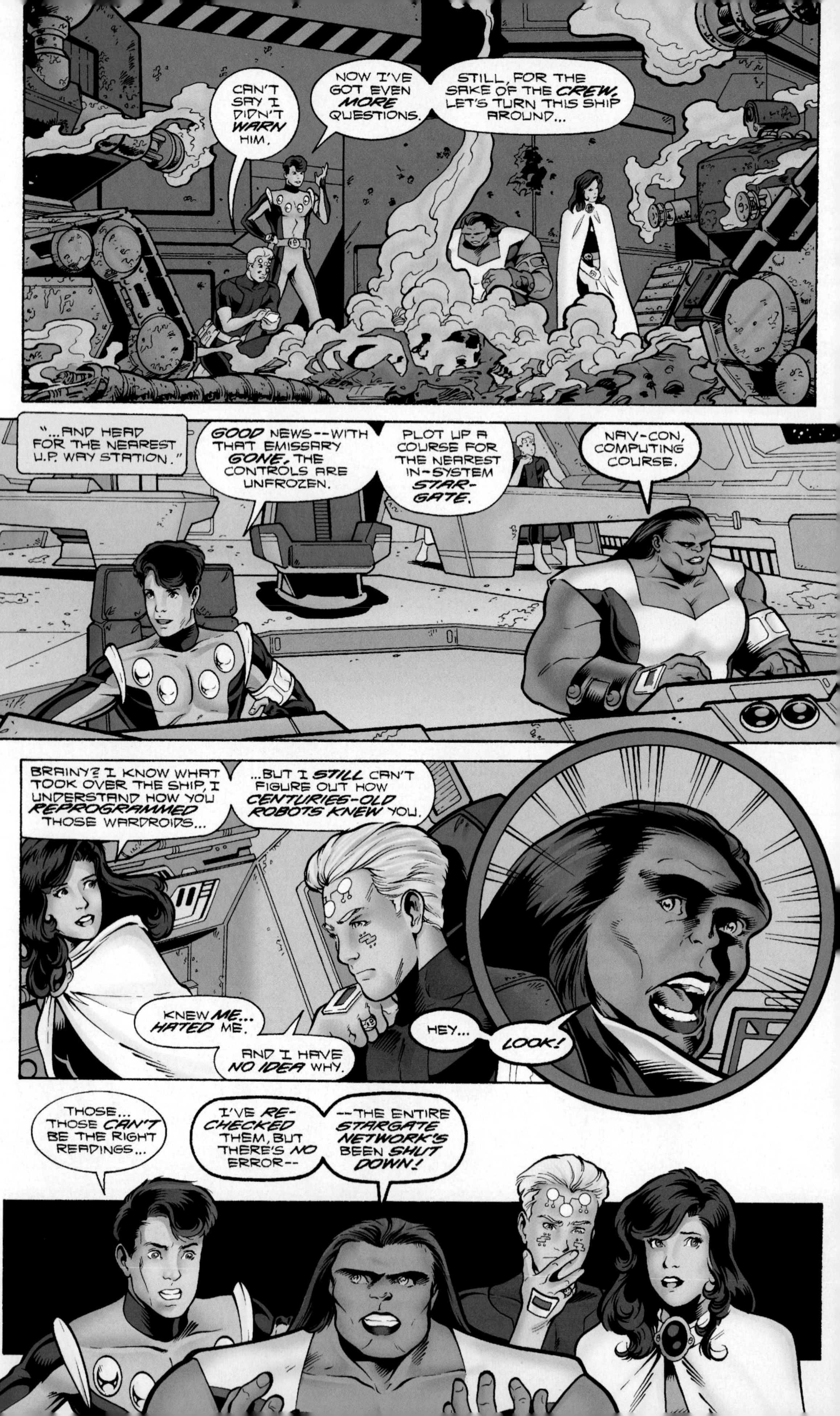
CAN'T SAY I DIDN'T WARN HIM.
NOW I'VE GOT EVEN MORE QUESTIONS.
STILL, FOR THE SAKE OF THE CREW, LET'S TURN THIS SHIP AROUND...
"...AND HEAD FOR THE NEAREST U.P. WAY STATION."
GOOD NEWS--WITH THAT EMISSARY GONE, THE CONTROLS ARE UNFROZEN.
PLOT UP A COURSE FOR THE NEAREST IN-SYSTEM STARGATE.
NAV-CON, COMPUTING COURSE.
BRAINY? I KNOW WHAT TOOK OVER THE SHIP, I UNDERSTAND HOW YOU REPROGRAMMED THOSE WARDROIDS...
...BUT I STILL CAN'T FIGURE OUT HOW CENTURIES-OLD ROBOTS KNEW YOU.
KNEW ME... HATED ME.
AND I HAVE NO IDEA WHY.
HEY...
LOOK!
THOSE... THOSE CAN'T BE THE RIGHT READINGS...
I'VE RE-CHECKED THEM, BUT THERE'S NO ERROR--
--THE ENTIRE STARGATE NETWORK'S BEEN SHUT DOWN!

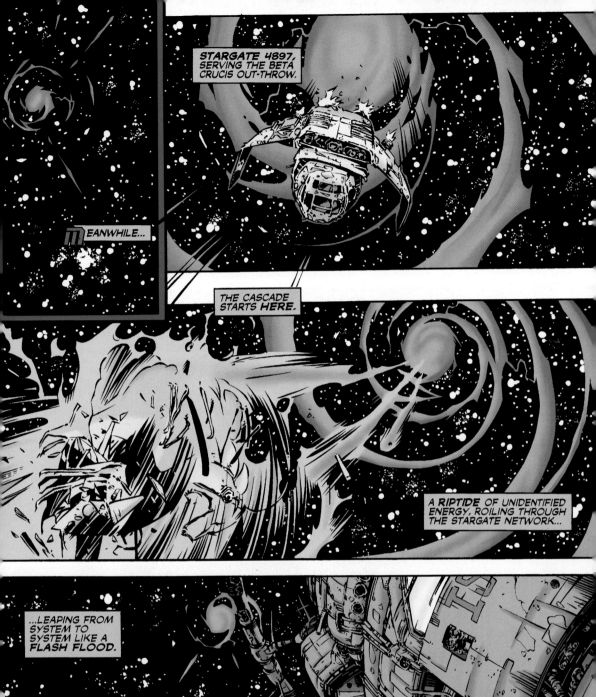

STARGATE 4897, SERVING THE BETA CRUCIS OUT-THROW.

MEANWHILE...

THE CASCADE STARTS HERE.

A RIPTIDE OF UNIDENTIFIED ENERGY, ROILING THROUGH THE STARGATE NETWORK...

...LEAPING FROM SYSTEM TO SYSTEM LIKE A FLASH FLOOD.

KAMMAL HYDRAX RESEARCH FACILITY IS ABLE TO RECORD THE POWER MAGNITUDE...

...JUST TEN SECONDS BEFORE ITS SYSTEMS ARE BURNED OUT FOREVER.

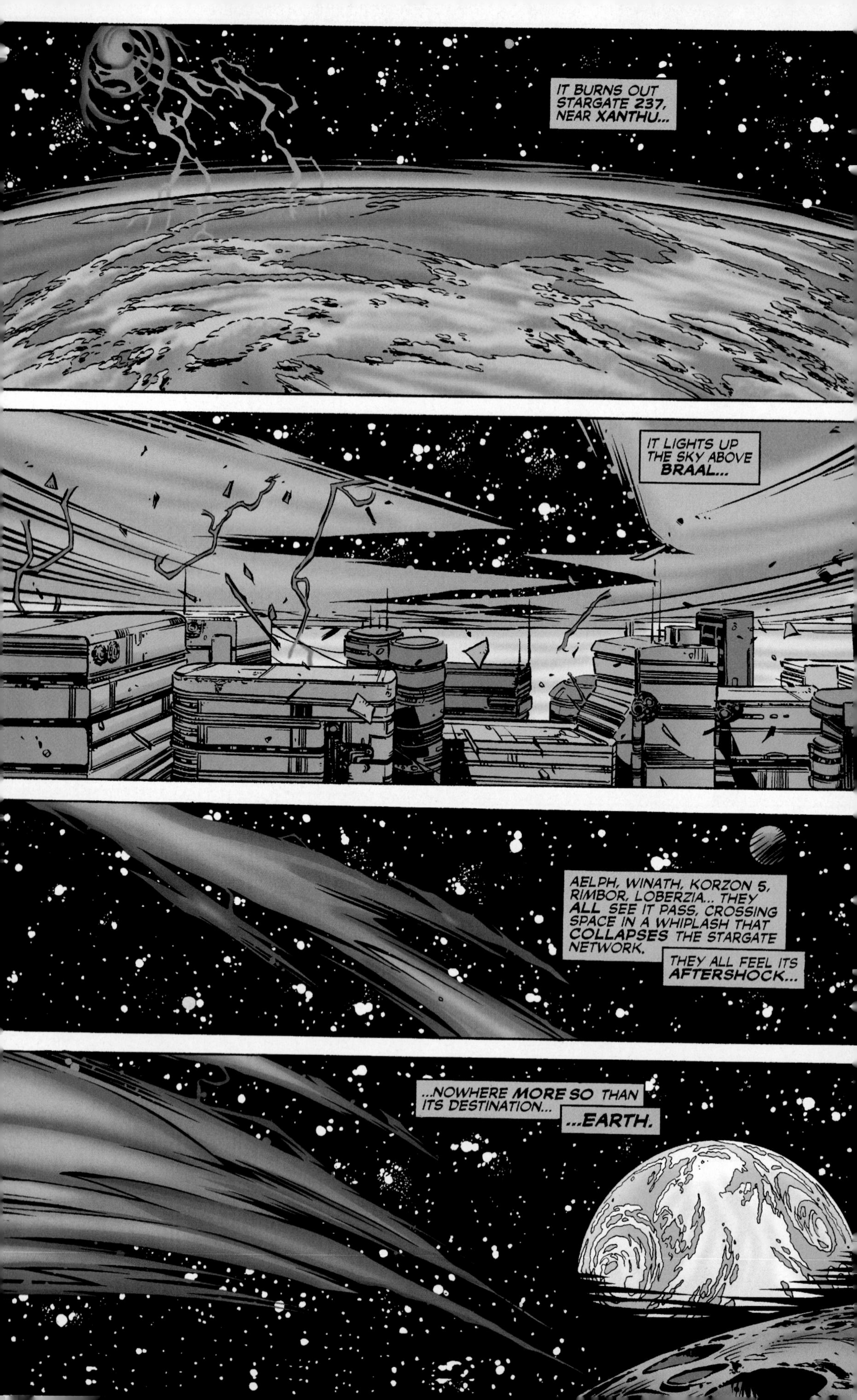
IT BURNS OUT STARGATE 237, NEAR XANTHU...
IT LIGHTS UP THE SKY ABOVE BRAAL...
AELPH, WINATH, KORZON 5, RIMBOR, LOBERZIA... THEY ALL SEE IT PASS, CROSSING SPACE IN A WHIPLASH THAT COLLAPSES THE STARGATE NETWORK.
THEY ALL FEEL ITS AFTERSHOCK...
...NOWHERE MORE SO THAN ITS DESTINATION...
...EARTH.

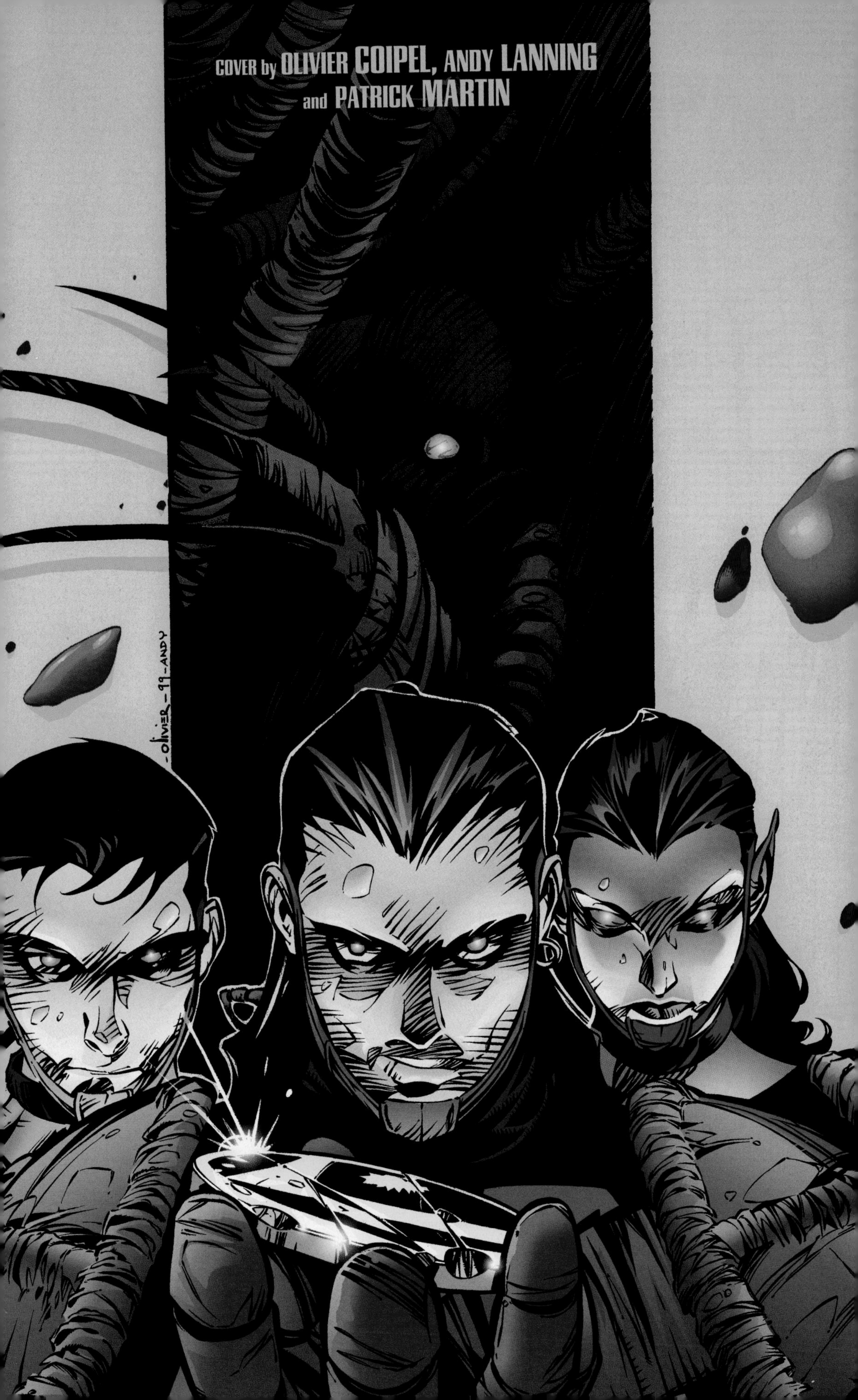
COVER by OLIVIER COIPEL, ANDY LANNING
and PATRICK MARTIN

METROPOLIS, EARTH.

THE END OF THE 30TH CENTURY.

dan abnett and andy lanning writers
olivier coipel pencils • andy lanning inks
tom mccraw colors • comicraft letters
mike mcavennie editor

THE GLEAMING SPLENDOR OF THE SUPER-MODERN AGE. THE PINNACLE OF HUMAN CULTURAL ENDEAVOR.

THE FUTURE MADE FLESH, THEY CALLED IT.

EARTH WELCOMES THE GALAXY

a tale of
the legion of super-heroes

YOU REMEMBER EARTH, RIGHT?

WELCOMES THE GALAXY .... EARTH WELC

BEFORE IT BECAME ENTWINED. BEFORE THE BLIGHT.

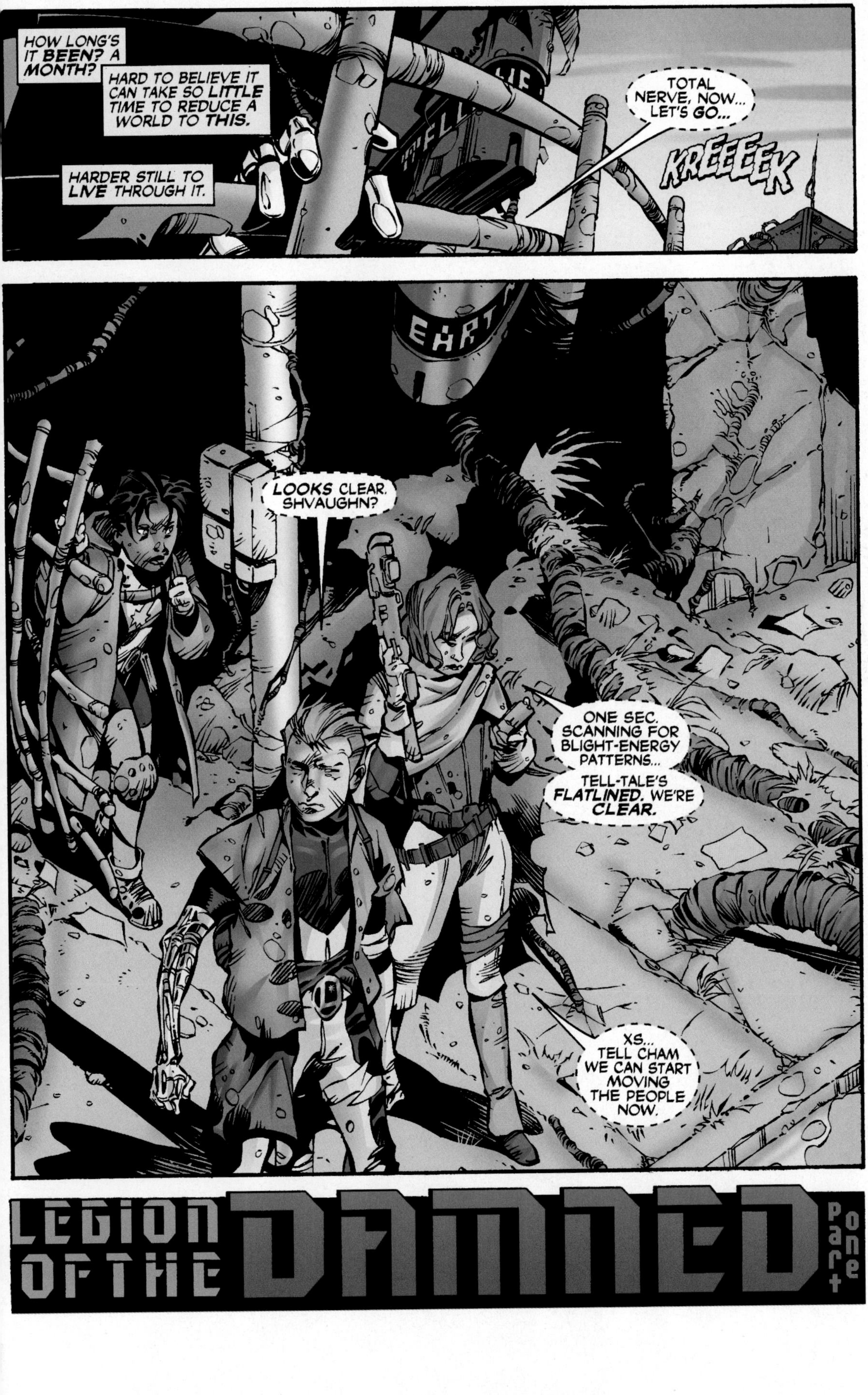

HOW LONG'S IT BEEN? A MONTH?
HARD TO BELIEVE IT CAN TAKE SO LITTLE TIME TO REDUCE A WORLD TO THIS.
HARDER STILL TO LIVE THROUGH IT.
TOTAL NERVE, NOW... LET'S GO...
KREEEEK
LOOKS CLEAR. SHVAUGHN?
ONE SEC. SCANNING FOR BLIGHT-ENERGY PATTERNS...
TELL-TALE'S FLATLINED. WE'RE CLEAR.
XS... TELL CHAM WE CAN START MOVING THE PEOPLE NOW.
LEGION OF THE DAMNED part one

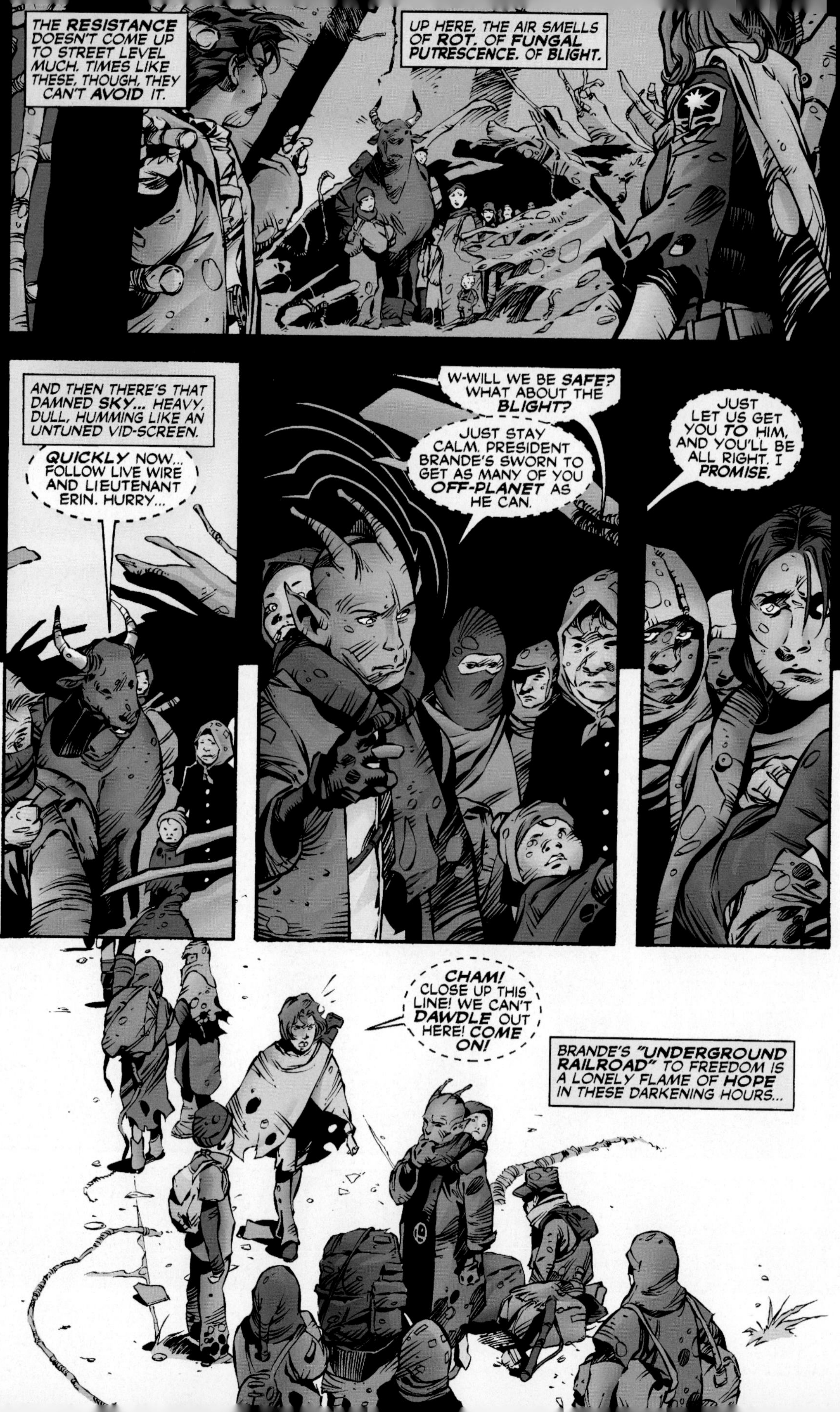
THE RESISTANCE DOESN'T COME UP TO STREET LEVEL MUCH. TIMES LIKE THESE, THOUGH, THEY CAN'T AVOID IT.
UP HERE, THE AIR SMELLS OF ROT. OF FUNGAL PUTRESCENCE. OF BLIGHT.
AND THEN THERE'S THAT DAMNED SKY... HEAVY, DULL, HUMMING LIKE AN UNTUNED VID-SCREEN.
QUICKLY NOW... FOLLOW LIVE WIRE AND LIEUTENANT ERIN. HURRY...
W-WILL WE BE SAFE? WHAT ABOUT THE BLIGHT?
JUST STAY CALM. PRESIDENT BRANDE'S SWORN TO GET AS MANY OF YOU OFF-PLANET AS HE CAN.
JUST LET US GET YOU TO HIM, AND YOU'LL BE ALL RIGHT. I PROMISE.
CHAM! CLOSE UP THIS LINE! WE CAN'T DAWDLE OUT HERE! COME ON!
BRANDE'S "UNDERGROUND RAILROAD" TO FREEDOM IS A LONELY FLAME OF HOPE IN THESE DARKENING HOURS...

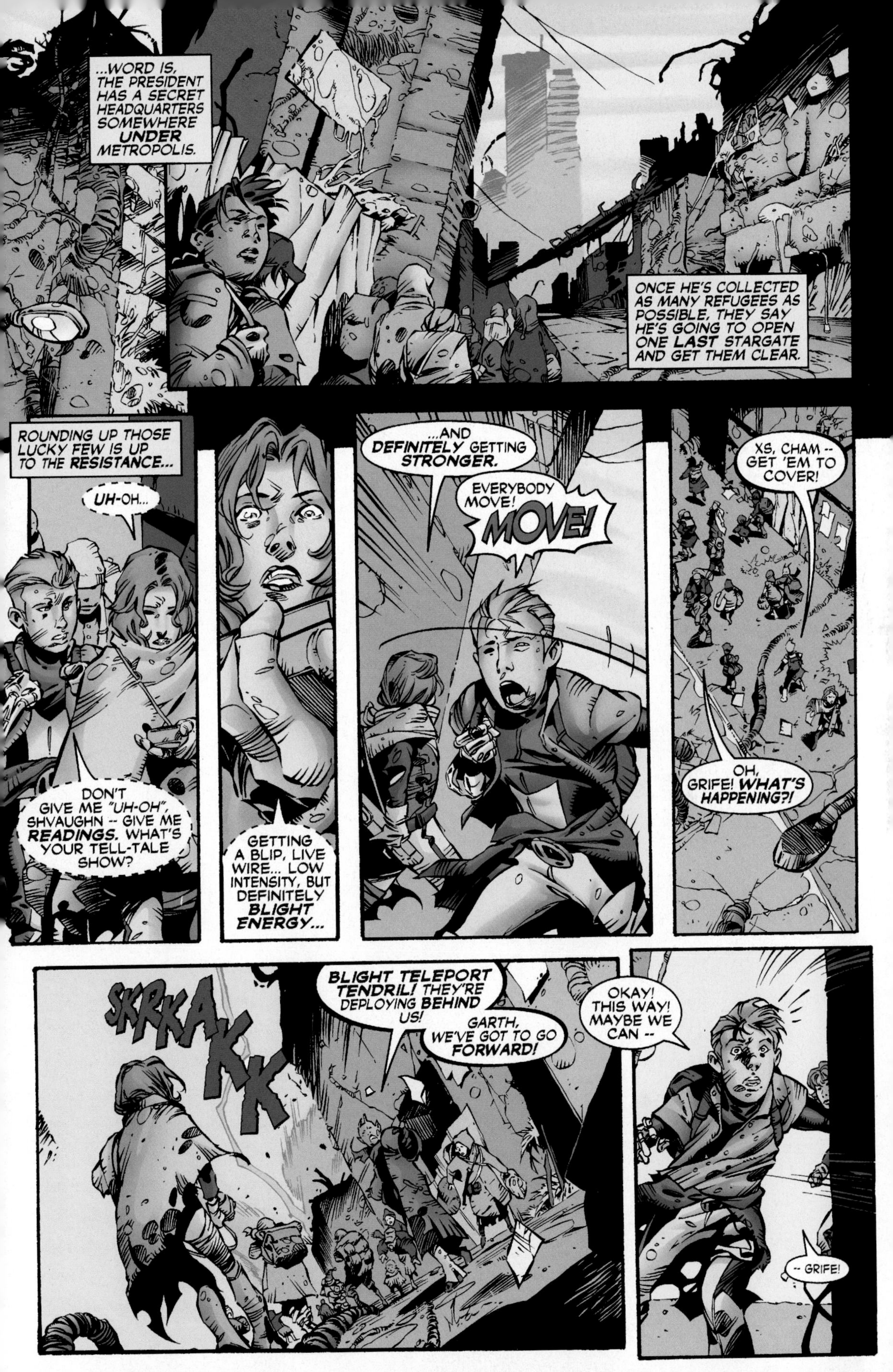
...WORD IS, THE PRESIDENT HAS A SECRET HEADQUARTERS SOMEWHERE UNDER METROPOLIS.
ONCE HE'S COLLECTED AS MANY REFUGEES AS POSSIBLE, THEY SAY HE'S GOING TO OPEN ONE LAST STARGATE AND GET THEM CLEAR.
ROUNDING UP THOSE LUCKY FEW IS UP TO THE RESISTANCE...
UH-OH...
DON'T GIVE ME "UH-OH", SHVAUGHN -- GIVE ME READINGS. WHAT'S YOUR TELL-TALE SHOW?
GETTING A BLIP, LIVE WIRE... LOW INTENSITY, BUT DEFINITELY BLIGHT ENERGY...
...AND DEFINITELY GETTING STRONGER.
EVERYBODY MOVE! MOVE!
XS, CHAM -- GET 'EM TO COVER!
OH, GRIFE! WHAT'S HAPPENING?!
SKRKAKKK
BLIGHT TELEPORT TENDRIL! THEY'RE DEPLOYING BEHIND US!
GARTH, WE'VE GOT TO GO FORWARD!
OKAY! THIS WAY! MAYBE WE CAN --
-- GRIFE!

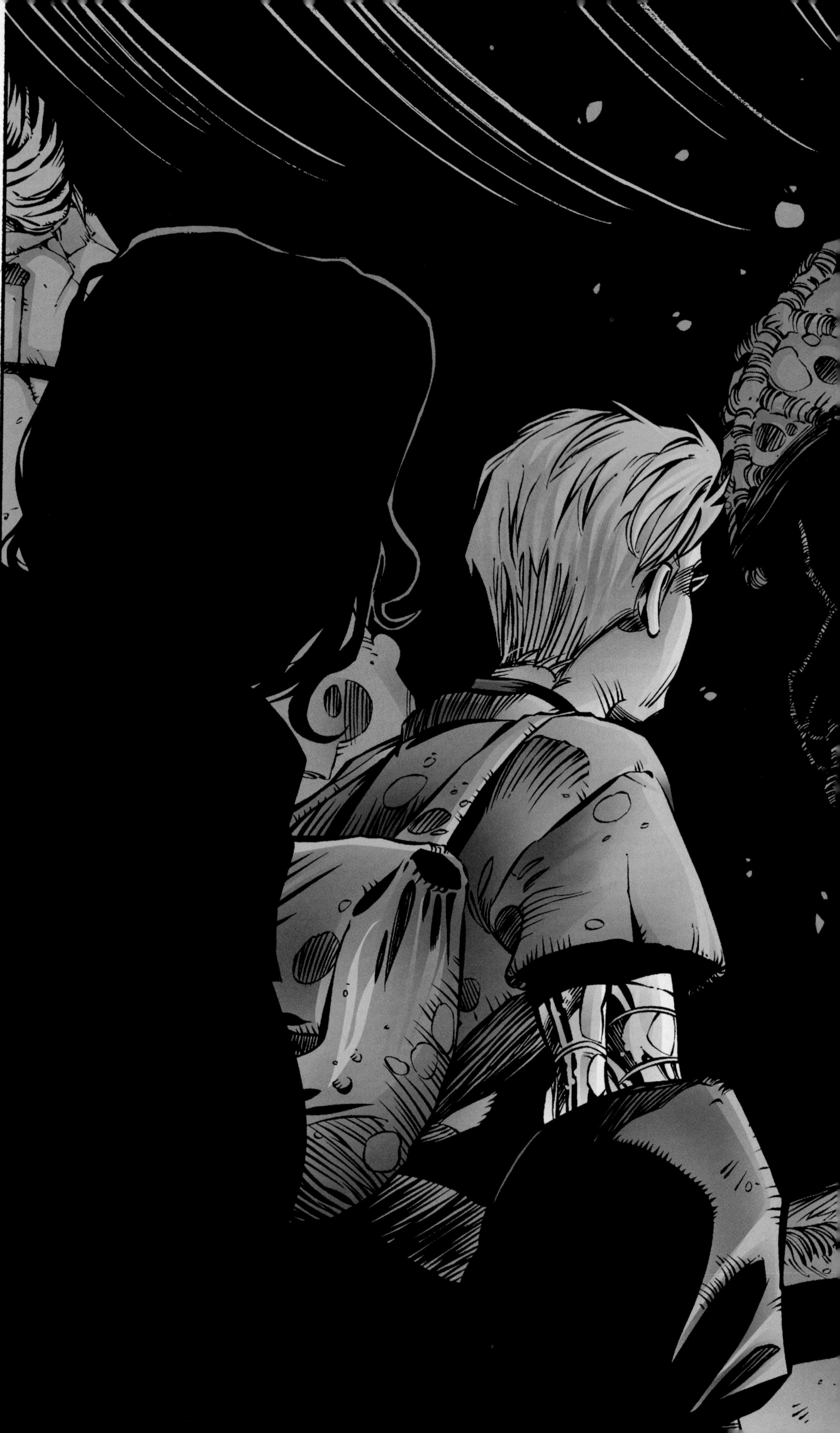

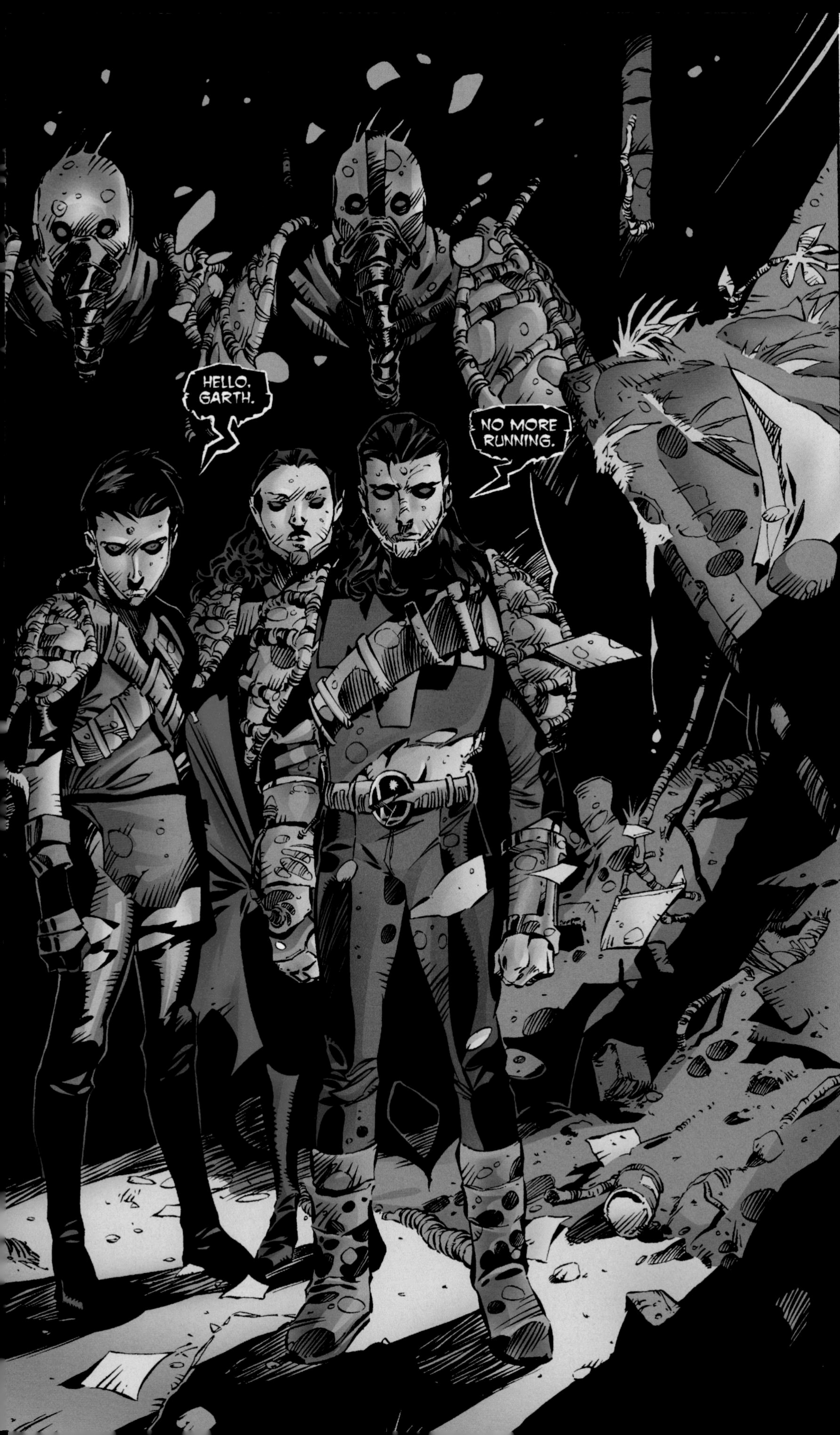
HELLO. GARTH.
NO MORE RUNNING.

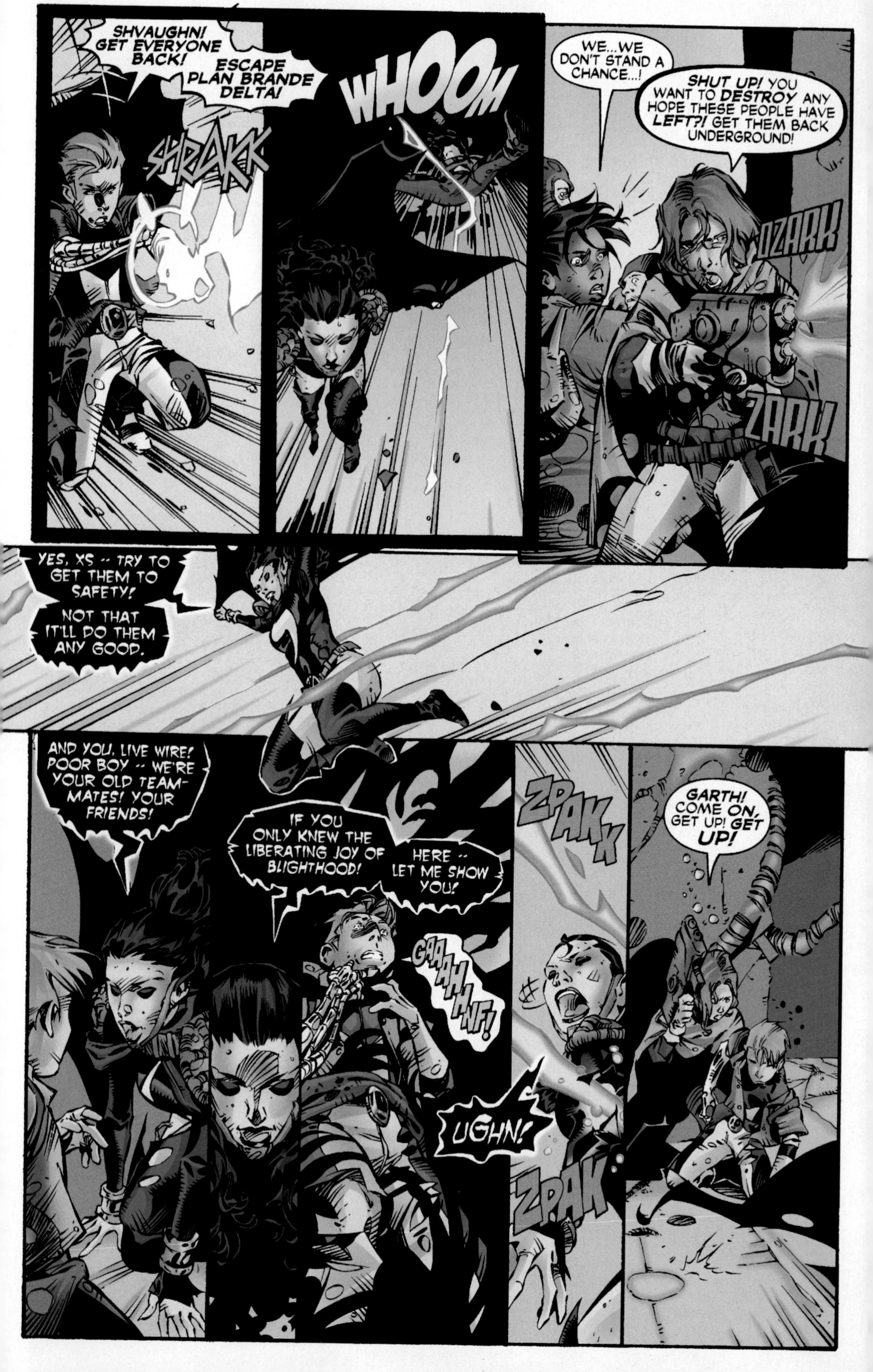
SHVAUGHN! GET EVERYONE BACK!
ESCAPE PLAN BRANDE DELTA!
SHRAKK
WHOOM
WE...WE DON'T STAND A CHANCE...!
SHUT UP! YOU WANT TO DESTROY ANY HOPE THESE PEOPLE HAVE LEFT?! GET THEM BACK UNDERGROUND!
ZARK
ZARK
YES, XS -- TRY TO GET THEM TO SAFETY!
NOT THAT IT'LL DO THEM ANY GOOD.
AND YOU, LIVE WIRE! POOR BOY -- WE'RE YOUR OLD TEAM-MATES! YOUR FRIENDS!
IF YOU ONLY KNEW THE LIBERATING JOY OF BLIGHTHOOD!
HERE -- LET ME SHOW YOU!
GAAAHHNF!
ZPAKK
UGHN!
ZPAK
GARTH! COME ON, GET UP! GET UP!

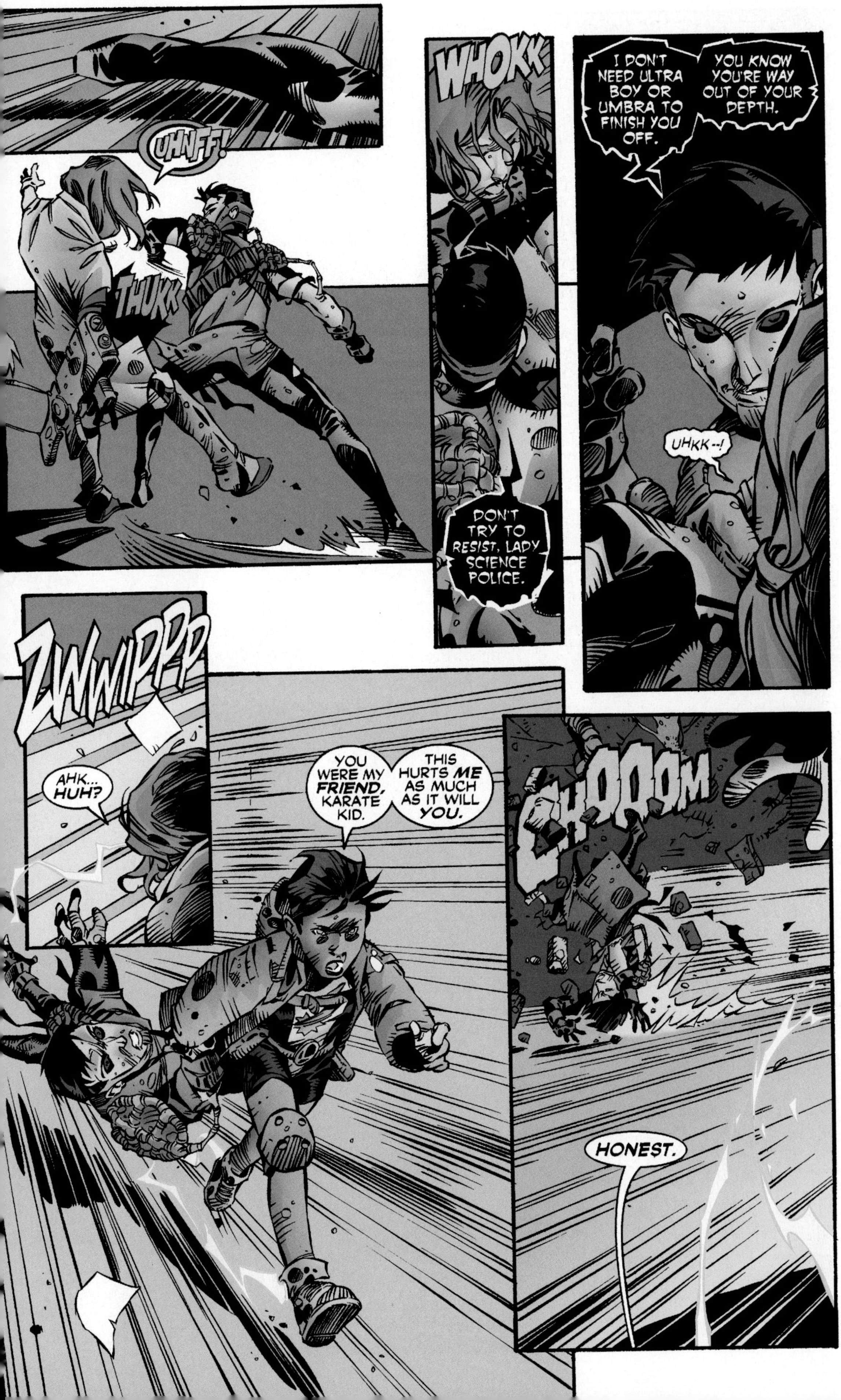
UHNFF!
THUKK
WHOKK
DON'T TRY TO RESIST, LADY SCIENCE POLICE.
I DON'T NEED ULTRA BOY OR UMBRA TO FINISH YOU OFF.
YOU KNOW YOU'RE WAY OUT OF YOUR DEPTH.
UHKK--!
ZWWIPPP
AHK... HUH?
YOU WERE MY FRIEND, KARATE KID.
THIS HURTS ME AS MUCH AS IT WILL YOU.
CHOOOM
HONEST.

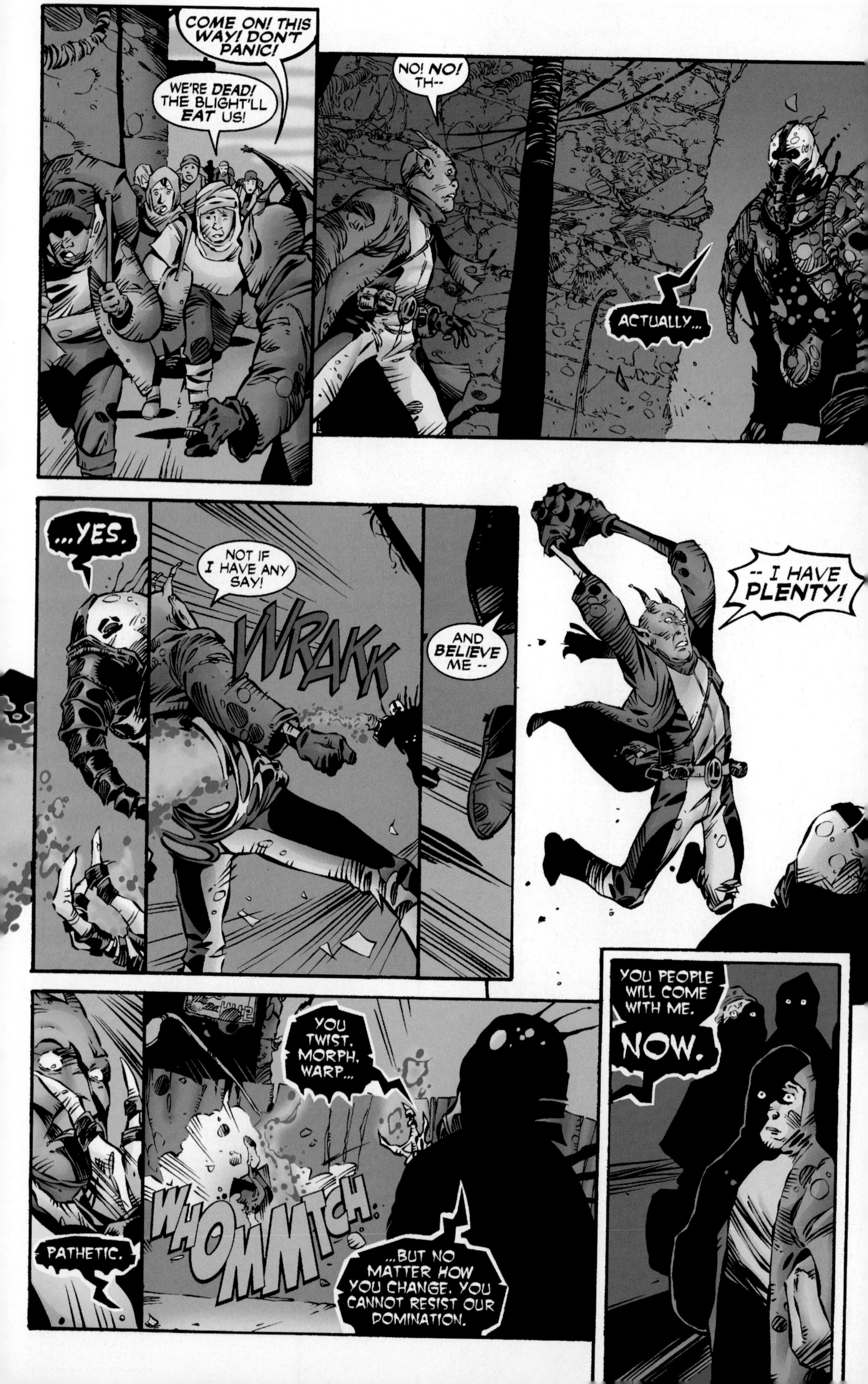
COME ON! THIS WAY! DON'T PANIC!
WE'RE DEAD! THE BLIGHT'LL EAT US!
NO! NO! TH--
ACTUALLY...
...YES.
NOT IF I HAVE ANY SAY!
WRAKK
AND BELIEVE ME --
-- I HAVE PLENTY!
PATHETIC.
YOU TWIST. MORPH. WARP...
WHOMMTCH
...BUT NO MATTER HOW YOU CHANGE, YOU CANNOT RESIST OUR DOMINATION.
YOU PEOPLE WILL COME WITH ME.
NOW.

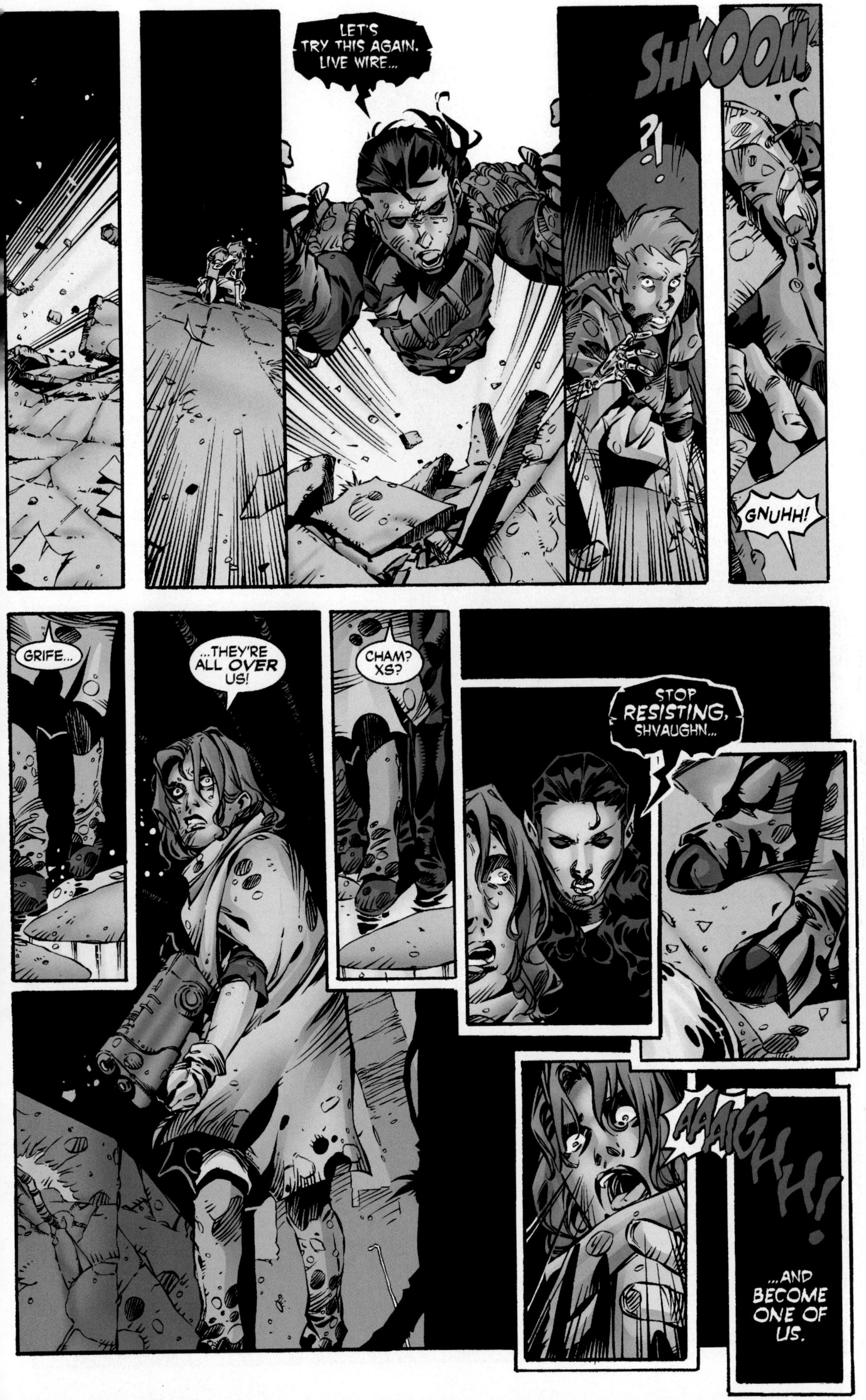
LET'S TRY THIS AGAIN. LIVE WIRE...
SHKOOM
?!
GNUHH!
GRIFE...
...THEY'RE ALL OVER US!
CHAM? XS?
STOP RESISTING, SHVAUGHN...
AAAIGHH!
...AND BECOME ONE OF US.

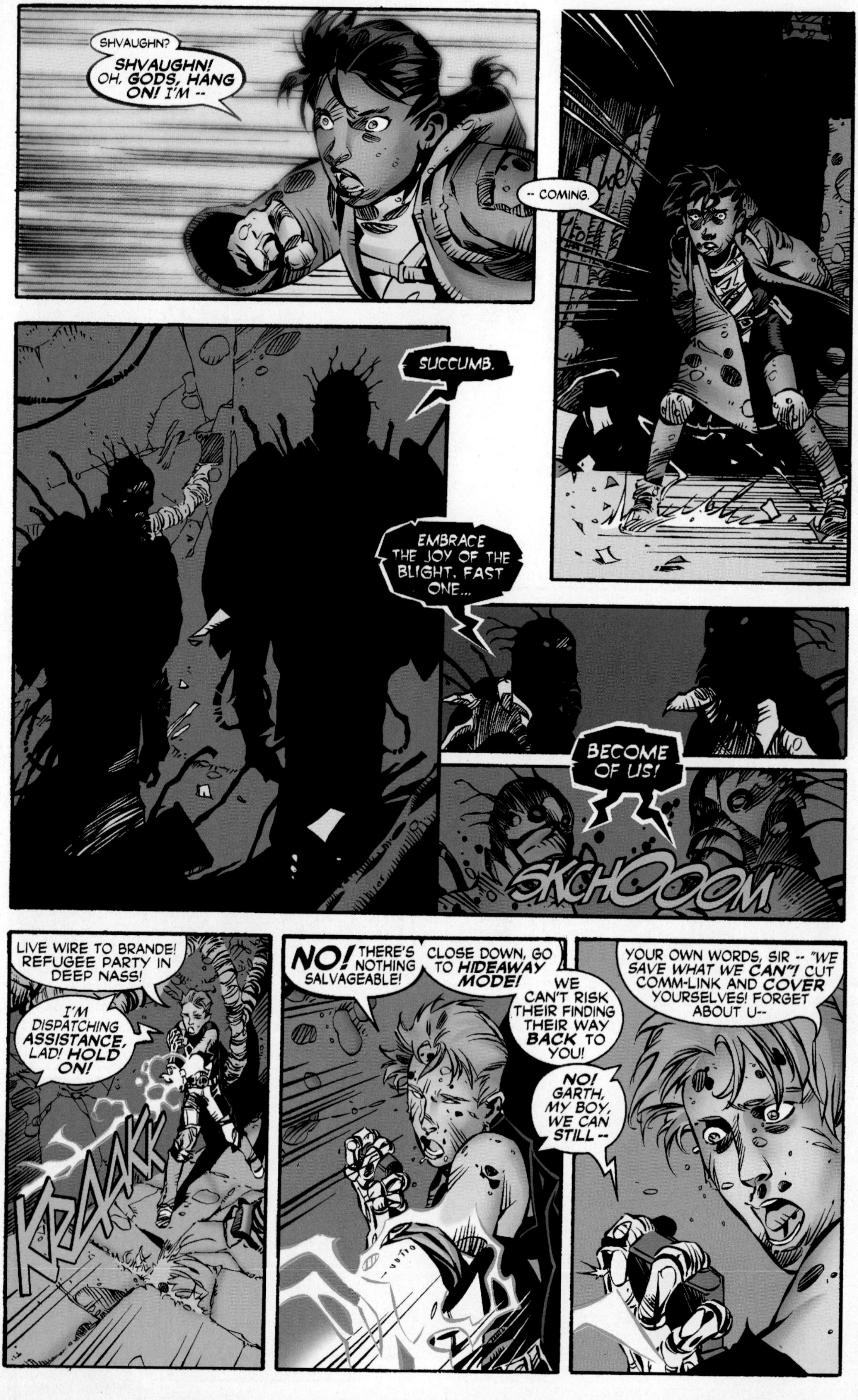
SHVAUGHN?
SHVAUGHN! OH, GODS, HANG ON! I'M --
-- COMING.
SUCCUMB.
EMBRACE THE JOY OF THE BLIGHT, FAST ONE...
BECOME OF US!
SKCHOOOOM
LIVE WIRE TO BRANDE! REFUGEE PARTY IN DEEP NASS!
I'M DISPATCHING ASSISTANCE, LAD! HOLD ON!
KRAAKK
NO! THERE'S NOTHING SALVAGEABLE!
CLOSE DOWN, GO TO HIDEAWAY MODE!
WE CAN'T RISK THEIR FINDING THEIR WAY BACK TO YOU!
NO! GARTH, MY BOY, WE CAN STILL --
YOUR OWN WORDS, SIR -- "WE SAVE WHAT WE CAN"! CUT COMM-LINK AND COVER YOURSELVES! FORGET ABOUT U--

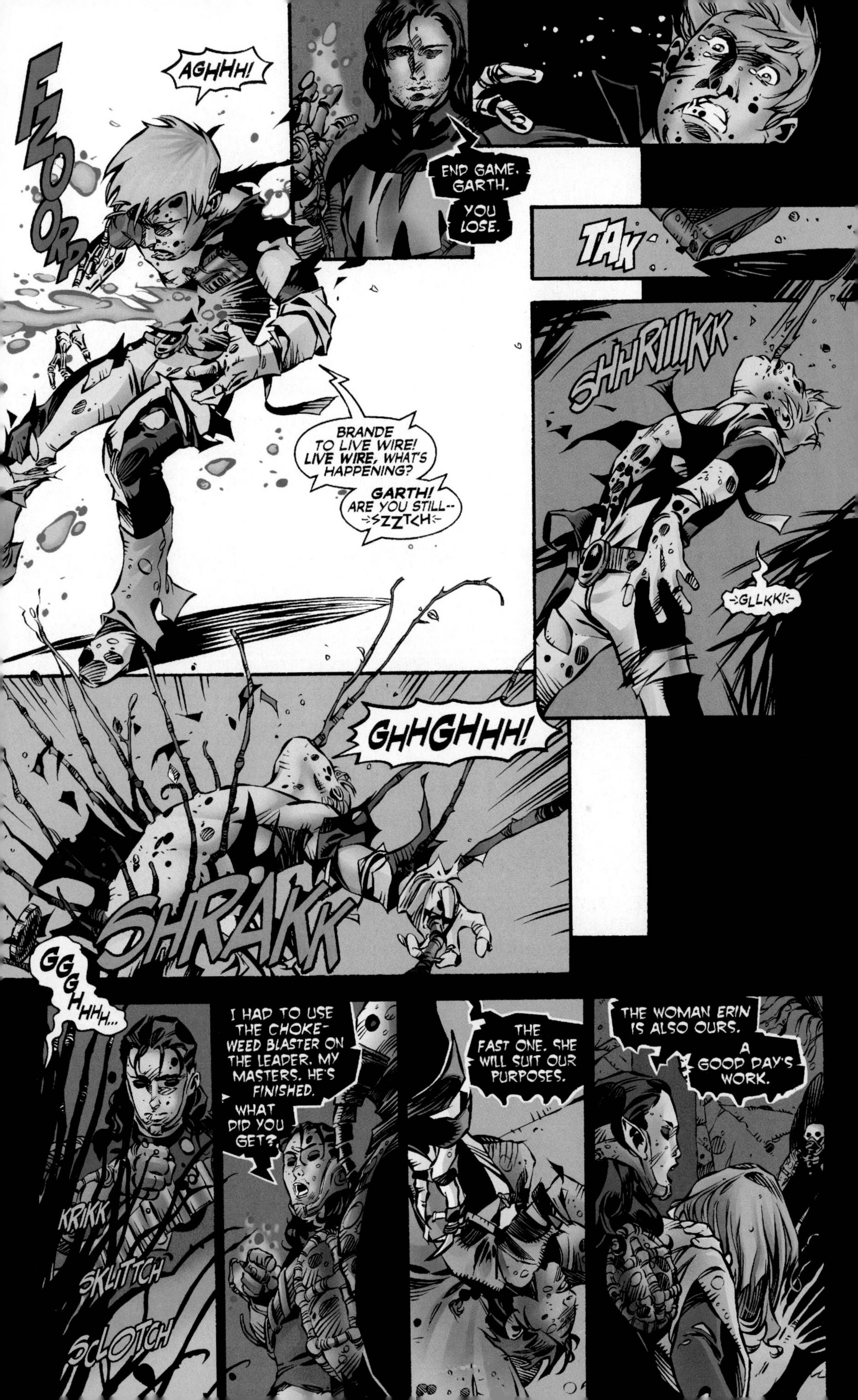
FZZORP
AGHHH!
END GAME. GARTH.
YOU LOSE.
TAK
BRANDE TO LIVE WIRE! LIVE WIRE, WHAT'S HAPPENING?
GARTH! ARE YOU STILL-- -SZZTCH-
SHHRIIIKK
-GLLKK!-
GHHGHHH!
SHRAKK
GGGHHHH...
KRIKK
SKLITTCH
SCLOTCH
I HAD TO USE THE CHOKE-WEED BLASTER ON THE LEADER, MY MASTERS. HE'S FINISHED.
WHAT DID YOU GET?
THE FAST ONE. SHE WILL SUIT OUR PURPOSES.
THE WOMAN ERIN IS ALSO OURS.
A GOOD DAY'S WORK.

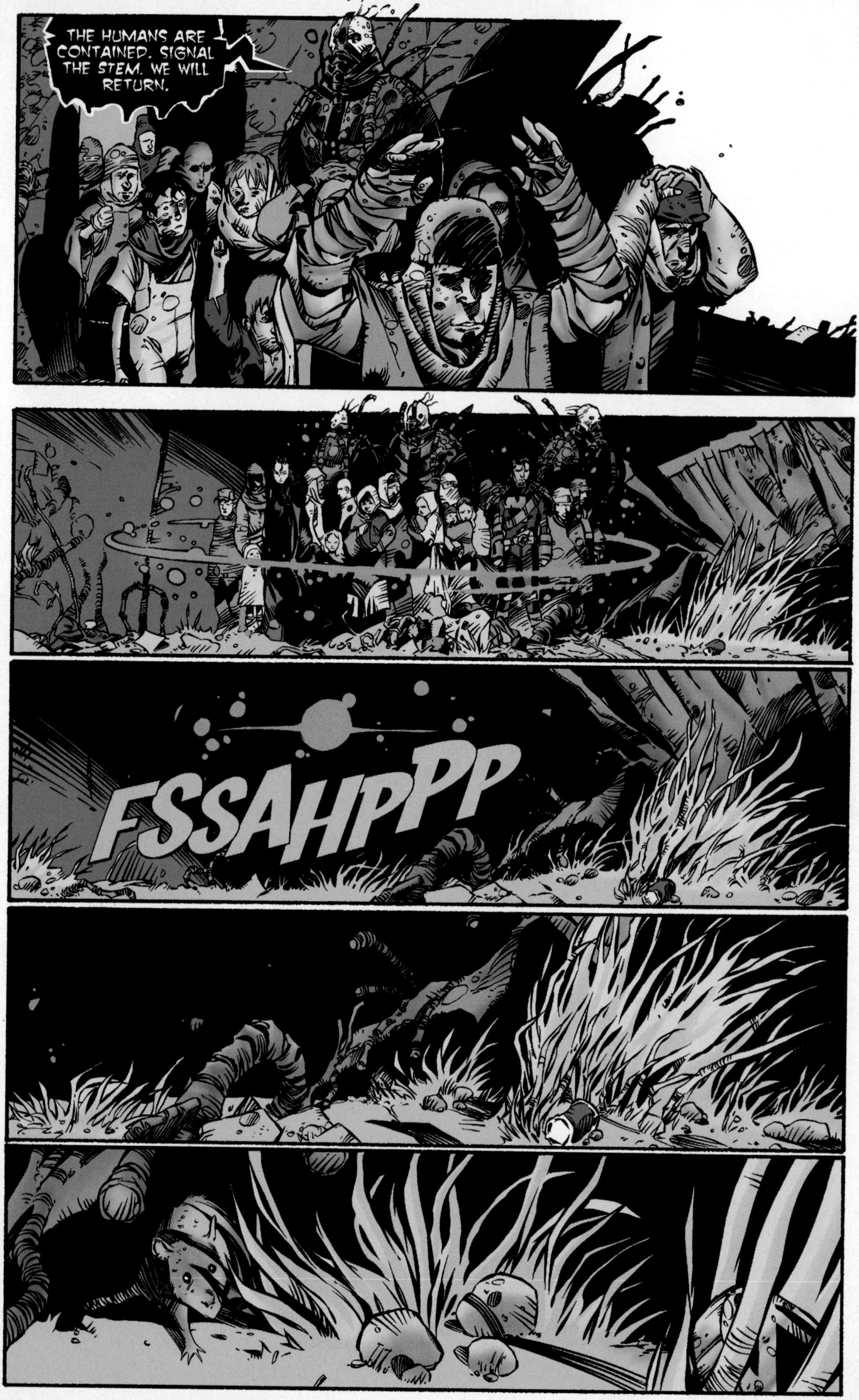
THE HUMANS ARE CONTAINED. SIGNAL THE STEM. WE WILL RETURN.
FSSAHPPP

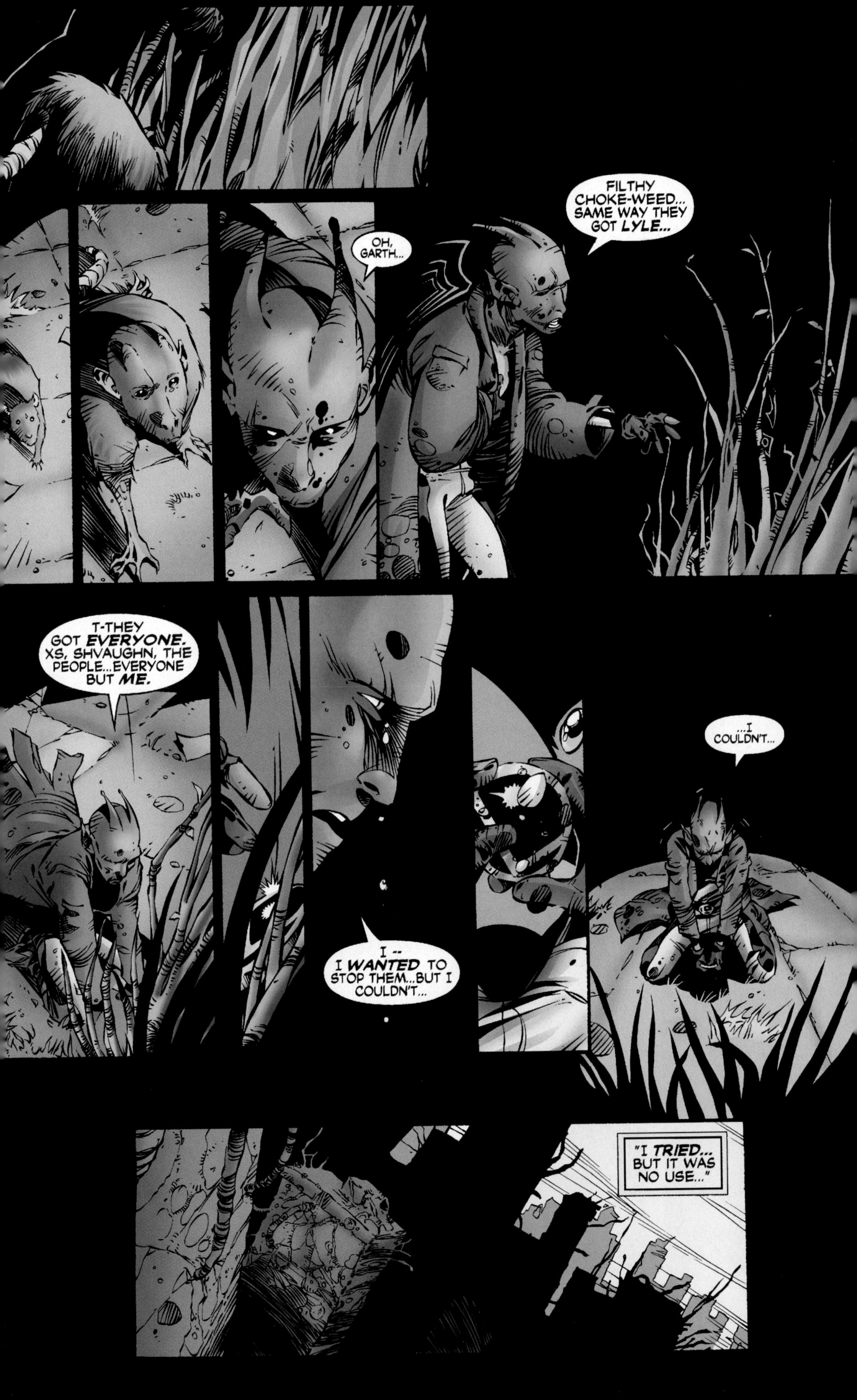
OH, GARTH...
FILTHY CHOKE-WEED... SAME WAY THEY GOT LYLE...
T-THEY GOT EVERYONE. XS, SHVAUGHN, THE PEOPLE...EVERYONE BUT ME.
I -- I WANTED TO STOP THEM...BUT I COULDN'T...
...I COULDN'T...
"I TRIED... BUT IT WAS NO USE..."

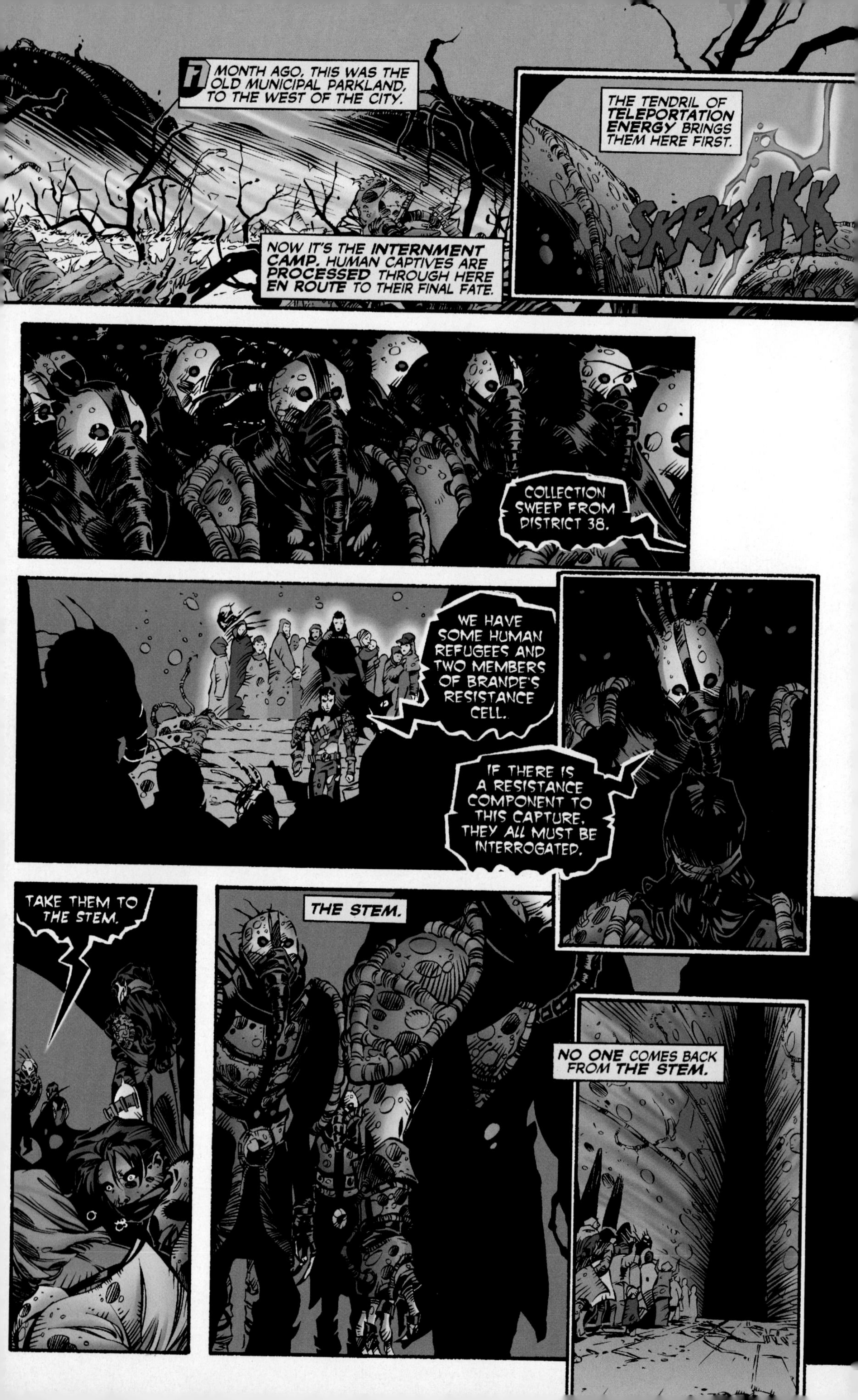
A MONTH AGO, THIS WAS THE OLD MUNICIPAL PARKLAND, TO THE WEST OF THE CITY.
NOW IT'S THE INTERNMENT CAMP. HUMAN CAPTIVES ARE PROCESSED THROUGH HERE EN ROUTE TO THEIR FINAL FATE.
THE TENDRIL OF TELEPORTATION ENERGY BRINGS THEM HERE FIRST.
SKRKAKK
COLLECTION SWEEP FROM DISTRICT 38.
WE HAVE SOME HUMAN REFUGEES AND TWO MEMBERS OF BRANDE'S RESISTANCE CELL.
IF THERE IS A RESISTANCE COMPONENT TO THIS CAPTURE, THEY ALL MUST BE INTERROGATED.
TAKE THEM TO THE STEM.
THE STEM.
NO ONE COMES BACK FROM THE STEM.

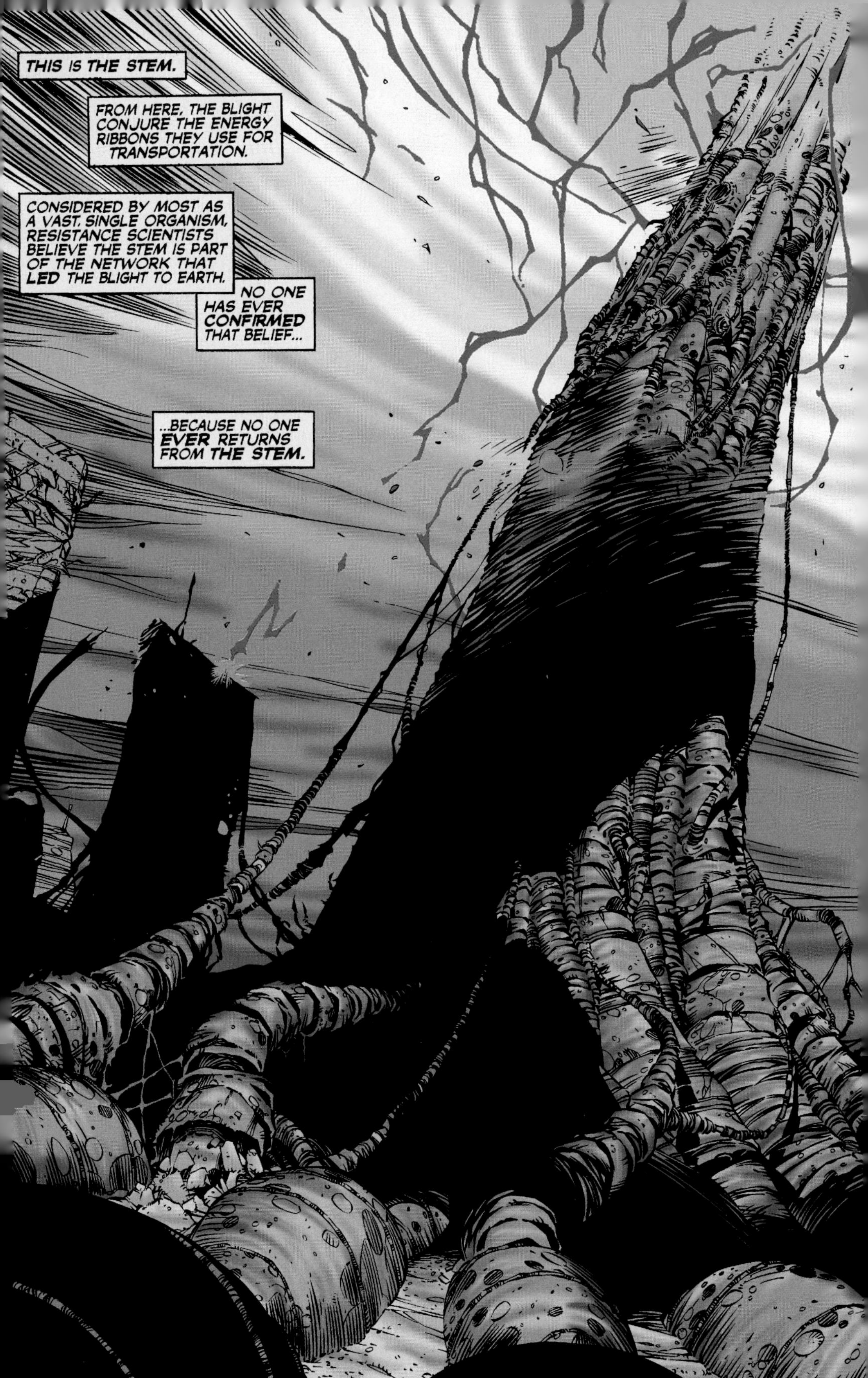
THIS IS THE STEM.
FROM HERE, THE BLIGHT CONJURE THE ENERGY RIBBONS THEY USE FOR TRANSPORTATION.
CONSIDERED BY MOST AS A VAST, SINGLE ORGANISM, RESISTANCE SCIENTISTS BELIEVE THE STEM IS PART OF THE NETWORK THAT LED THE BLIGHT TO EARTH.
NO ONE HAS EVER CONFIRMED THAT BELIEF...
...BECAUSE NO ONE EVER RETURNS FROM THE STEM.

REEP DAGGLE, THE LEGIONNAIRE KNOWN AS *CHAMELEON*, IS ON HIS OWN NOW.

FROM HIS CURRENT LOCATION, THERE ARE EIGHT EFFECTIVE ROUTES BACK TO BRANDE'S HEADQUARTERS.

HE CAN'T TAKE *ANY* OF THEM. HE DOESN'T *DARE*.

THE BLIGHT ARE *INTELLIGENT*. THEY COULD HAVE *ALLOWED* HIM TO ESCAPE JUST SO THEY COULD FOLLOW HIM BACK TO THE HIDEOUT.

HE CAN *NEVER* GO BACK NOW, ANYWAY. THE RESISTANCE WILL HAVE MOVED ALREADY. HE'S ALONE.

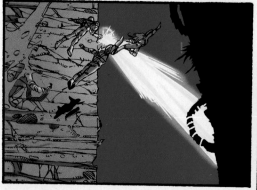

IN TRUTH, HE DOESN'T KNOW *WHAT* TO DO NOW. HE NEEDS TIME TO *THINK*...TO REST HIS REELING MIND...

A MONTH AGO, THIS WAS SCIENCE POLICE HEADQUARTERS.

IT'S JUST AN EMPTY SHELL NOW, EVER SINCE SENSOR'S TEAM TRAGICALLY DISCOVERED THE BLIGHT HAD LEARNED TO TRACE LEGION FLIGHT RING TRANSMISSIONS.

STILL, IT'S AS GOOD A PLACE AS ANY TO THINK...

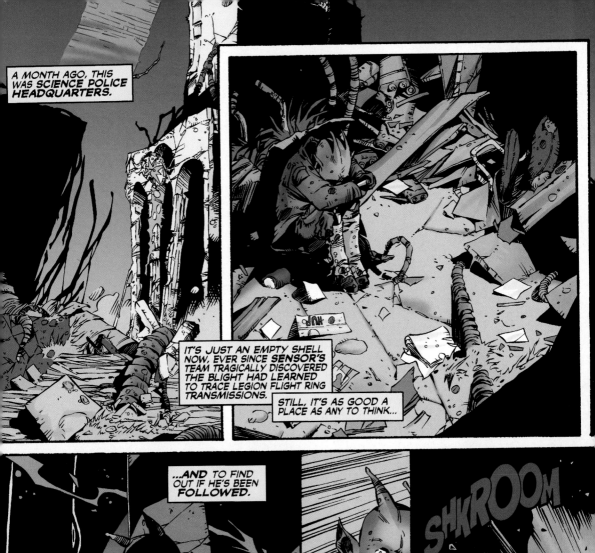

...AND TO FIND OUT IF HE'S BEEN FOLLOWED.

SHKROOM

HE ISN'T SURPRISED. HE'S GLAD HE WAS CAREFUL.

BUT THEN, REEP DAGGLE IS A HERO. HE'S LEGION.

EVEN NOW, THAT MEANS SOMETHING.

OKAY, YOU MURDERERS. LET'S GO.

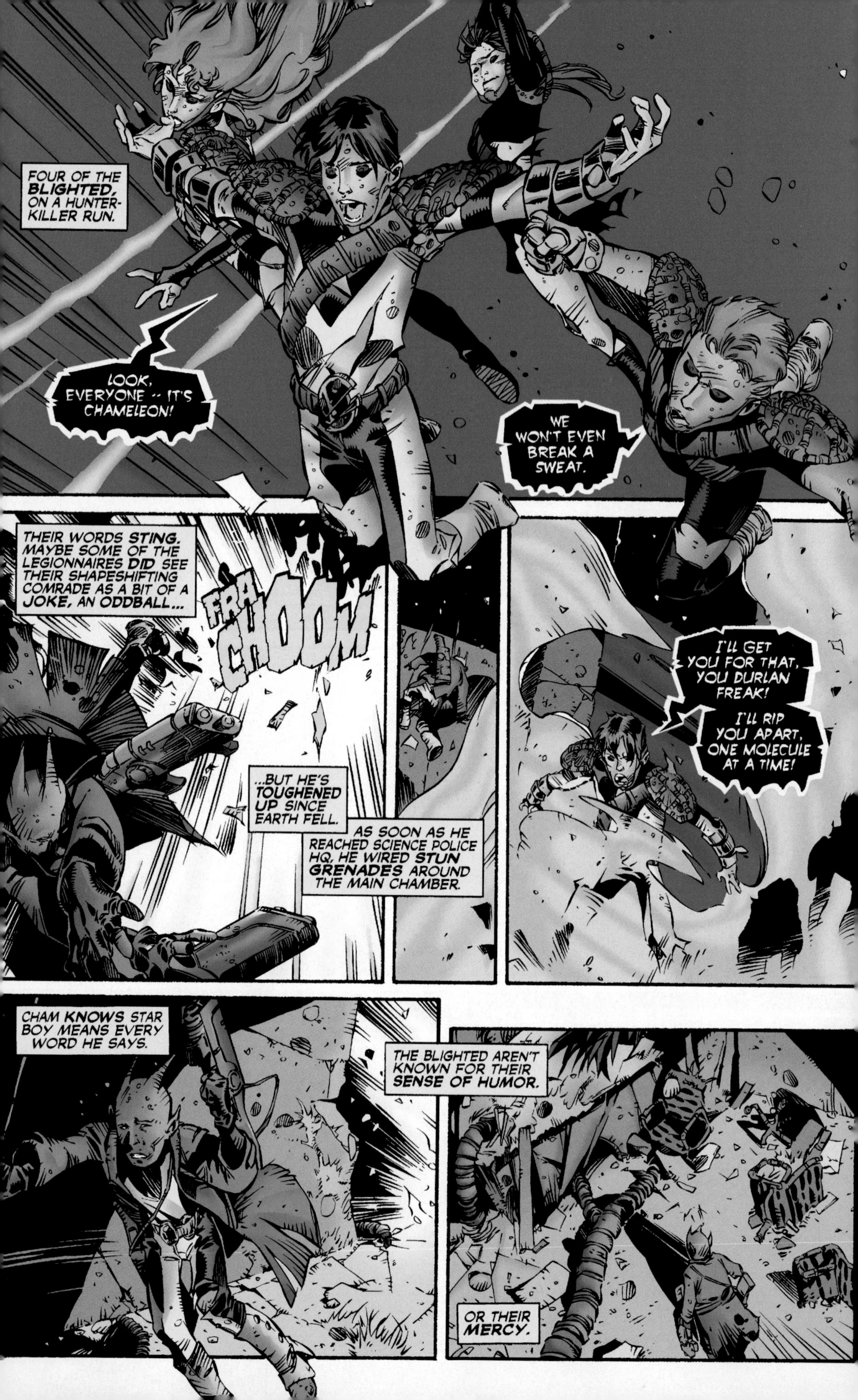
FOUR OF THE BLIGHTED, ON A HUNTER-KILLER RUN.
LOOK, EVERYONE -- IT'S CHAMELEON!
WE WON'T EVEN BREAK A SWEAT.
THEIR WORDS STING. MAYBE SOME OF THE LEGIONNAIRES DID SEE THEIR SHAPESHIFTING COMRADE AS A BIT OF A JOKE, AN ODDBALL...
FRA CHOOM!
...BUT HE'S TOUGHENED UP SINCE EARTH FELL.
AS SOON AS HE REACHED SCIENCE POLICE HQ, HE WIRED STUN GRENADES AROUND THE MAIN CHAMBER.
I'LL GET YOU FOR THAT, YOU DURLAN FREAK!
I'LL RIP YOU APART, ONE MOLECULE AT A TIME!
CHAM KNOWS STAR BOY MEANS EVERY WORD HE SAYS.
THE BLIGHTED AREN'T KNOWN FOR THEIR SENSE OF HUMOR.
OR THEIR MERCY.

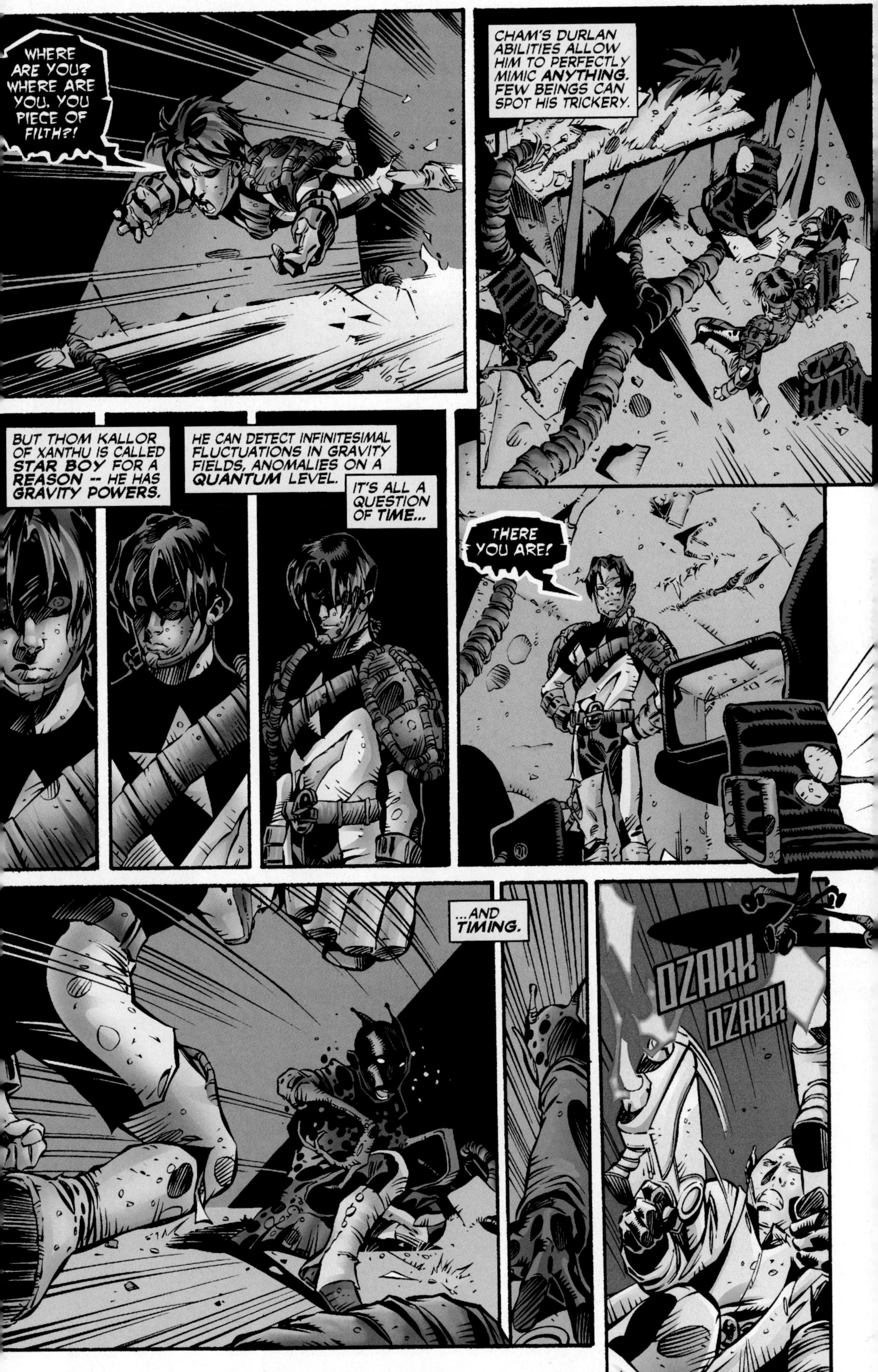
WHERE ARE YOU? WHERE ARE YOU, YOU PIECE OF FILTH?!
CHAM'S DURLAN ABILITIES ALLOW HIM TO PERFECTLY MIMIC ANYTHING. FEW BEINGS CAN SPOT HIS TRICKERY.
BUT THOM KALLOR OF XANTHU IS CALLED STAR BOY FOR A REASON -- HE HAS GRAVITY POWERS.
HE CAN DETECT INFINITESIMAL FLUCTUATIONS IN GRAVITY FIELDS, ANOMALIES ON A QUANTUM LEVEL.
IT'S ALL A QUESTION OF TIME...
THERE YOU ARE!
...AND TIMING.
OZARK
OZARK

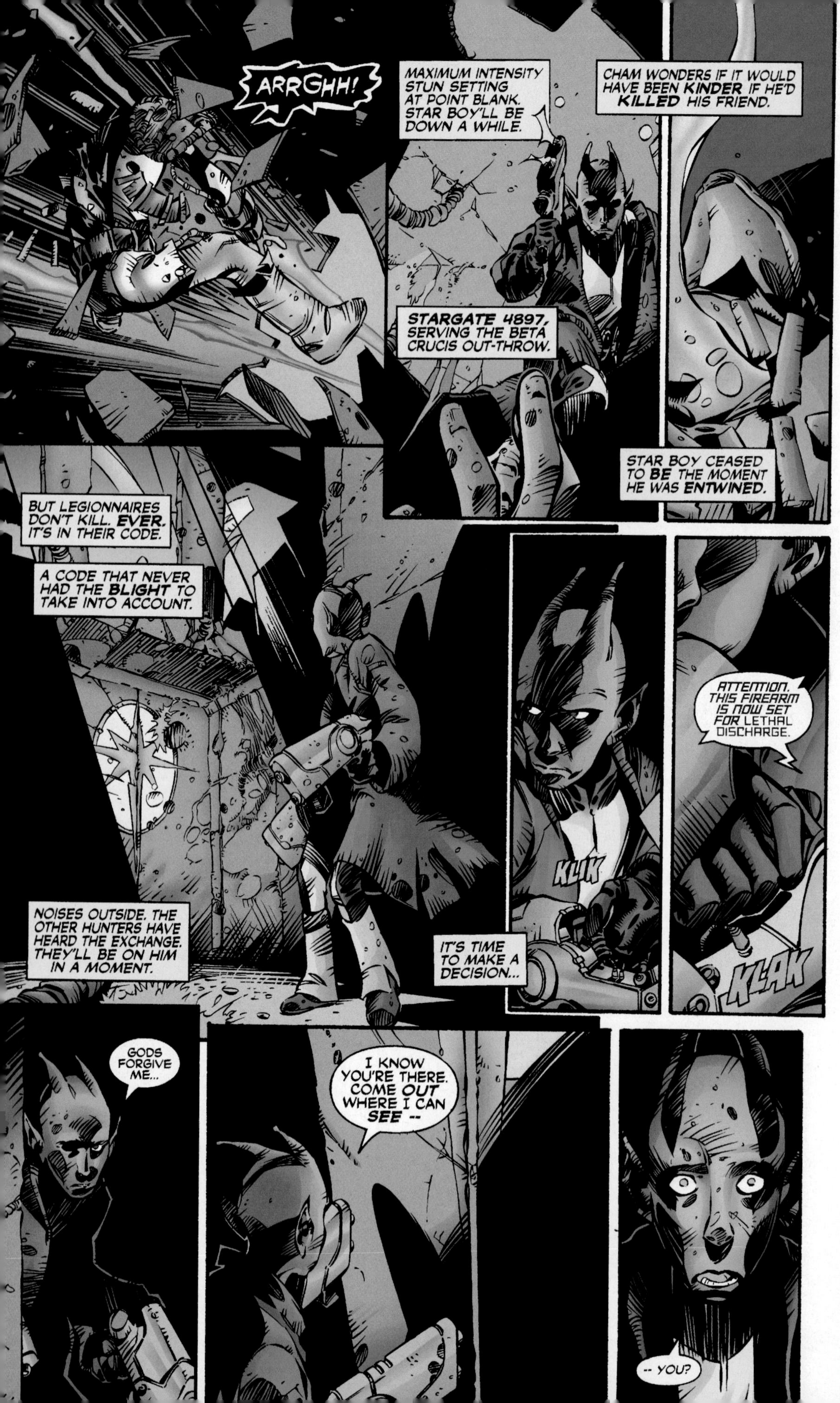
ARRGHH!
MAXIMUM INTENSITY STUN SETTING AT POINT BLANK. STAR BOY'LL BE DOWN A WHILE.
STARGATE 4897, SERVING THE BETA CRUCIS OUT-THROW.
CHAM WONDERS IF IT WOULD HAVE BEEN KINDER IF HE'D KILLED HIS FRIEND.
STAR BOY CEASED TO BE THE MOMENT HE WAS ENTWINED.
BUT LEGIONNAIRES DON'T KILL. EVER. IT'S IN THEIR CODE.
A CODE THAT NEVER HAD THE BLIGHT TO TAKE INTO ACCOUNT.
NOISES OUTSIDE. THE OTHER HUNTERS HAVE HEARD THE EXCHANGE. THEY'LL BE ON HIM IN A MOMENT.
KLIK
IT'S TIME TO MAKE A DECISION...
ATTENTION. THIS FIREARM IS NOW SET FOR LETHAL DISCHARGE.
KLAK
GODS FORGIVE ME...
I KNOW YOU'RE THERE. COME OUT WHERE I CAN SEE --
-- YOU?

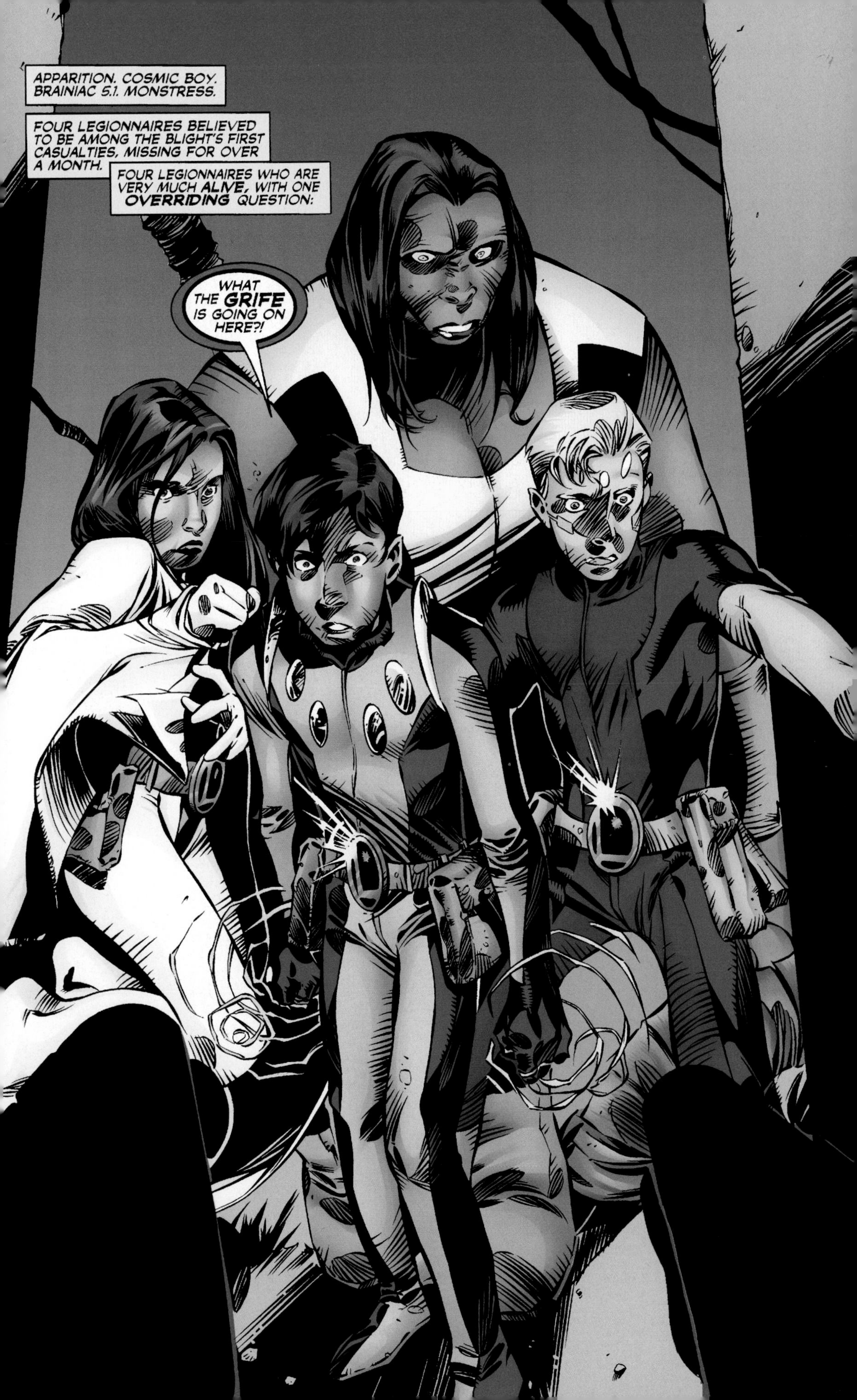
APPARITION. COSMIC BOY. BRAINIAC 5.1. MONSTRESS.
FOUR LEGIONNAIRES BELIEVED TO BE AMONG THE BLIGHT'S FIRST CASUALTIES, MISSING FOR OVER A MONTH.
FOUR LEGIONNAIRES WHO ARE VERY MUCH ALIVE, WITH ONE OVERRIDING QUESTION:
WHAT THE GRIFE IS GOING ON HERE?!

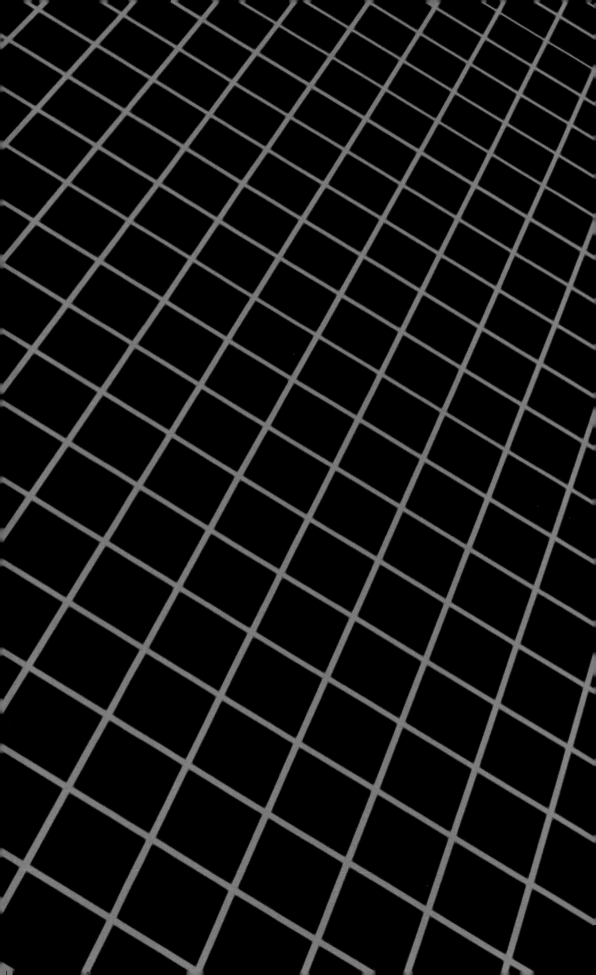

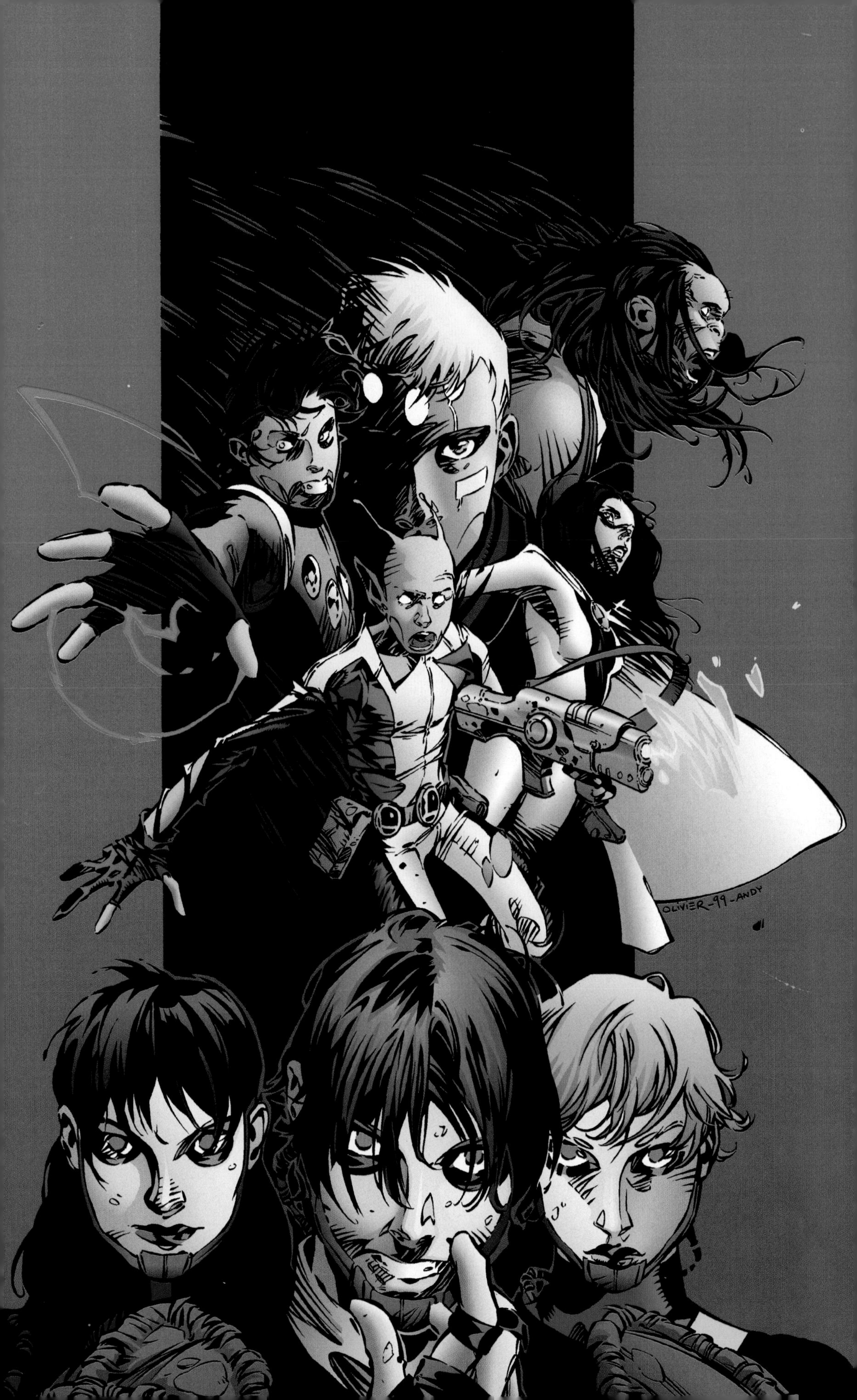
OLIVIER-99-ANDY

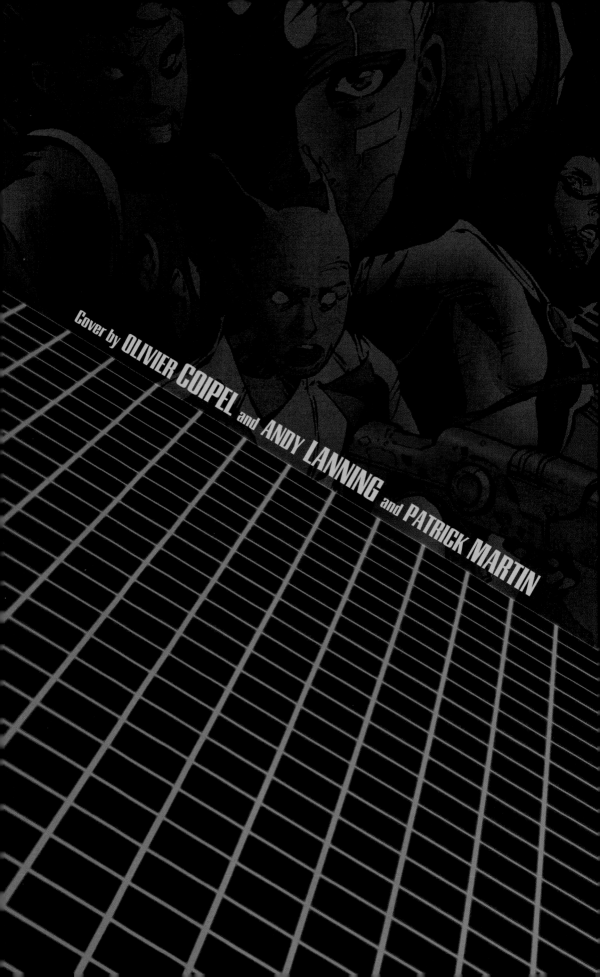

Cover by OLIVIER COIPEL and ANDY LANNING and PATRICK MARTIN

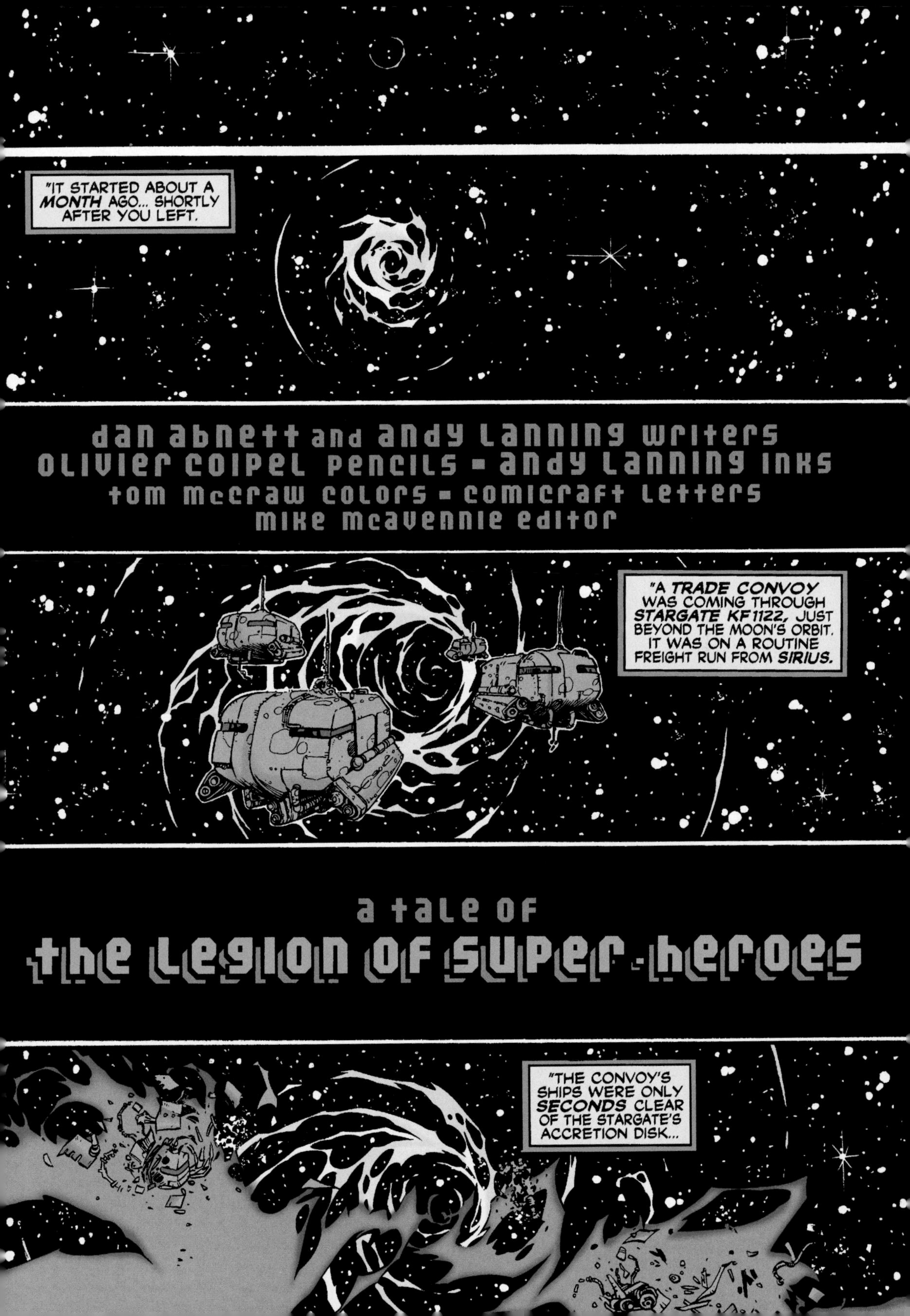

"IT STARTED ABOUT A MONTH AGO... SHORTLY AFTER YOU LEFT.
dan abnett and andy lanning writers
olivier coipel pencils = andy lanning inks
tom mccraw colors = comicraft letters
mike mcavennie editor
"A TRADE CONVOY WAS COMING THROUGH STARGATE KF1122, JUST BEYOND THE MOON'S ORBIT. IT WAS ON A ROUTINE FREIGHT RUN FROM SIRIUS.
a tale of
the legion of super-heroes
"THE CONVOY'S SHIPS WERE ONLY SECONDS CLEAR OF THE STARGATE'S ACCRETION DISK...

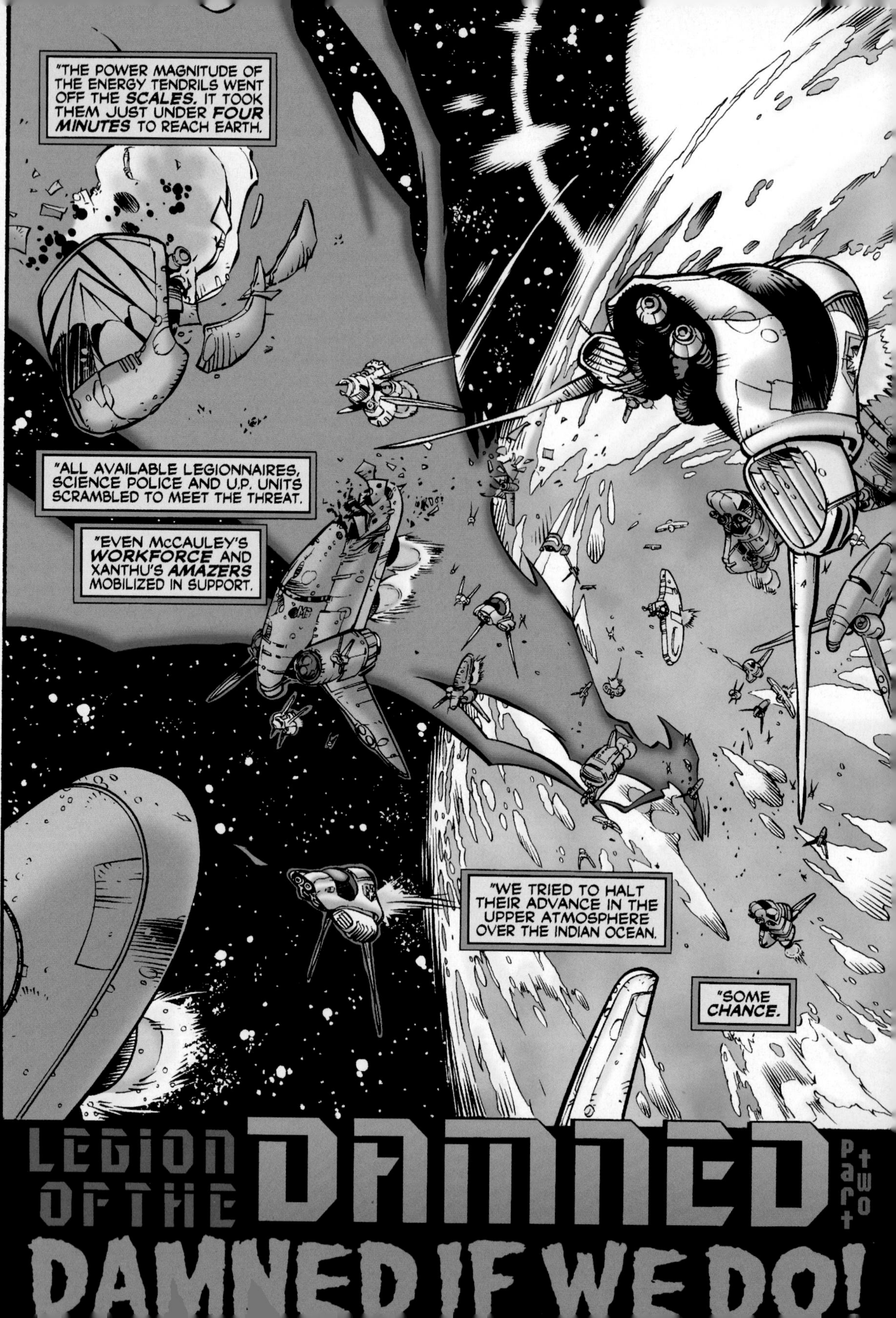
"THE POWER MAGNITUDE OF THE ENERGY TENDRILS WENT OFF THE SCALES. IT TOOK THEM JUST UNDER FOUR MINUTES TO REACH EARTH.
"ALL AVAILABLE LEGIONNAIRES, SCIENCE POLICE AND U.P. UNITS SCRAMBLED TO MEET THE THREAT.
"EVEN McCAULEY'S WORKFORCE AND XANTHU'S AMAZERS MOBILIZED IN SUPPORT.
"WE TRIED TO HALT THEIR ADVANCE IN THE UPPER ATMOSPHERE OVER THE INDIAN OCEAN.
"SOME CHANCE.
LEGION OF THE DAMNED part two
DAMNED IF WE DO!

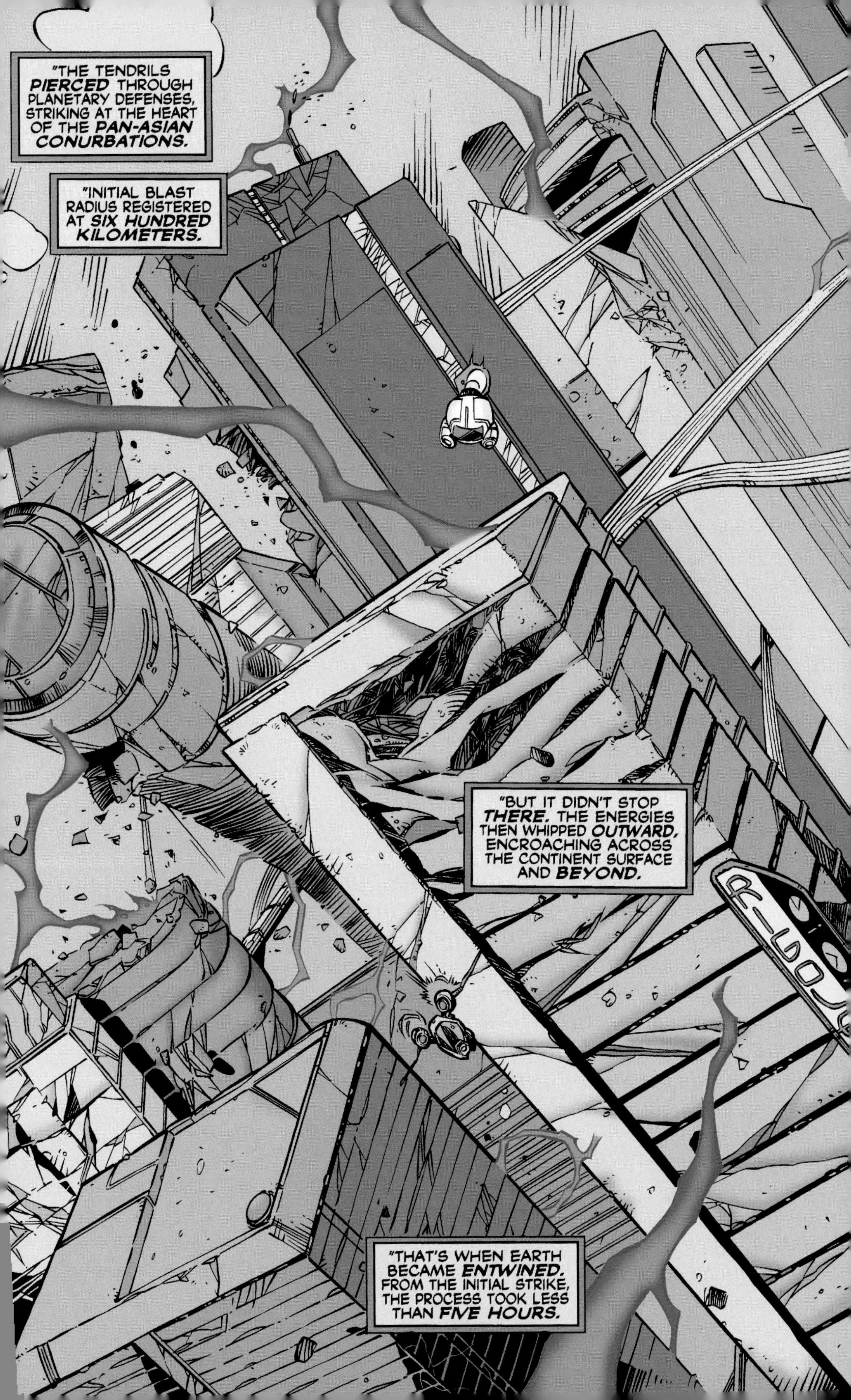
"THE TENDRILS PIERCED THROUGH PLANETARY DEFENSES, STRIKING AT THE HEART OF THE PAN-ASIAN CONURBATIONS.
"INITIAL BLAST RADIUS REGISTERED AT SIX HUNDRED KILOMETERS.
"BUT IT DIDN'T STOP THERE. THE ENERGIES THEN WHIPPED OUTWARD, ENCROACHING ACROSS THE CONTINENT SURFACE AND BEYOND.
"THAT'S WHEN EARTH BECAME ENTWINED. FROM THE INITIAL STRIKE, THE PROCESS TOOK LESS THAN FIVE HOURS.

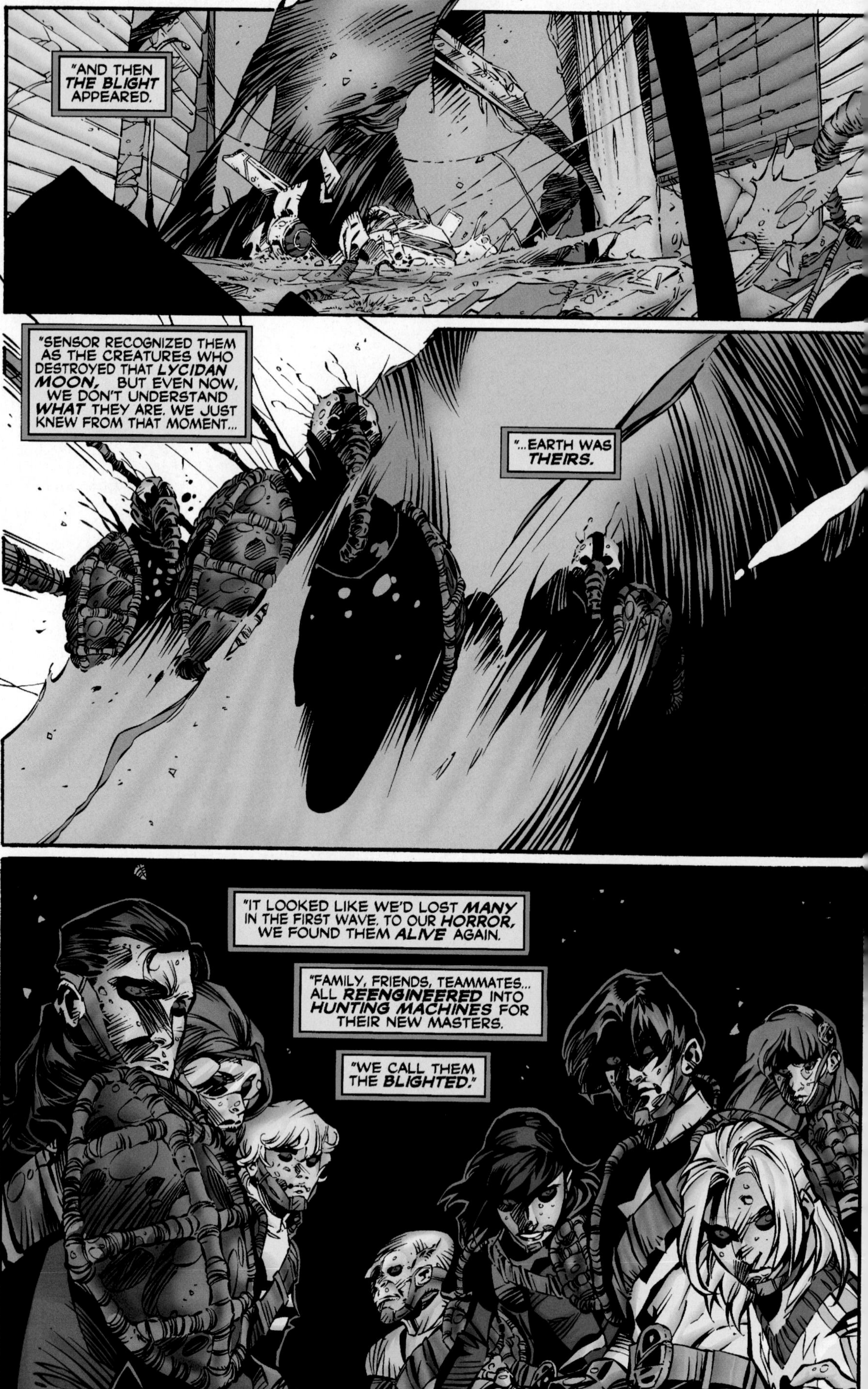
"AND THEN THE BLIGHT APPEARED.
"SENSOR RECOGNIZED THEM AS THE CREATURES WHO DESTROYED THAT LYCIDAN MOON, BUT EVEN NOW, WE DON'T UNDERSTAND WHAT THEY ARE. WE JUST KNEW FROM THAT MOMENT...
"...EARTH WAS THEIRS.
"IT LOOKED LIKE WE'D LOST MANY IN THE FIRST WAVE. TO OUR HORROR, WE FOUND THEM ALIVE AGAIN.
"FAMILY, FRIENDS, TEAMMATES... ALL REENGINEERED INTO HUNTING MACHINES FOR THEIR NEW MASTERS.
"WE CALL THEM THE BLIGHTED."

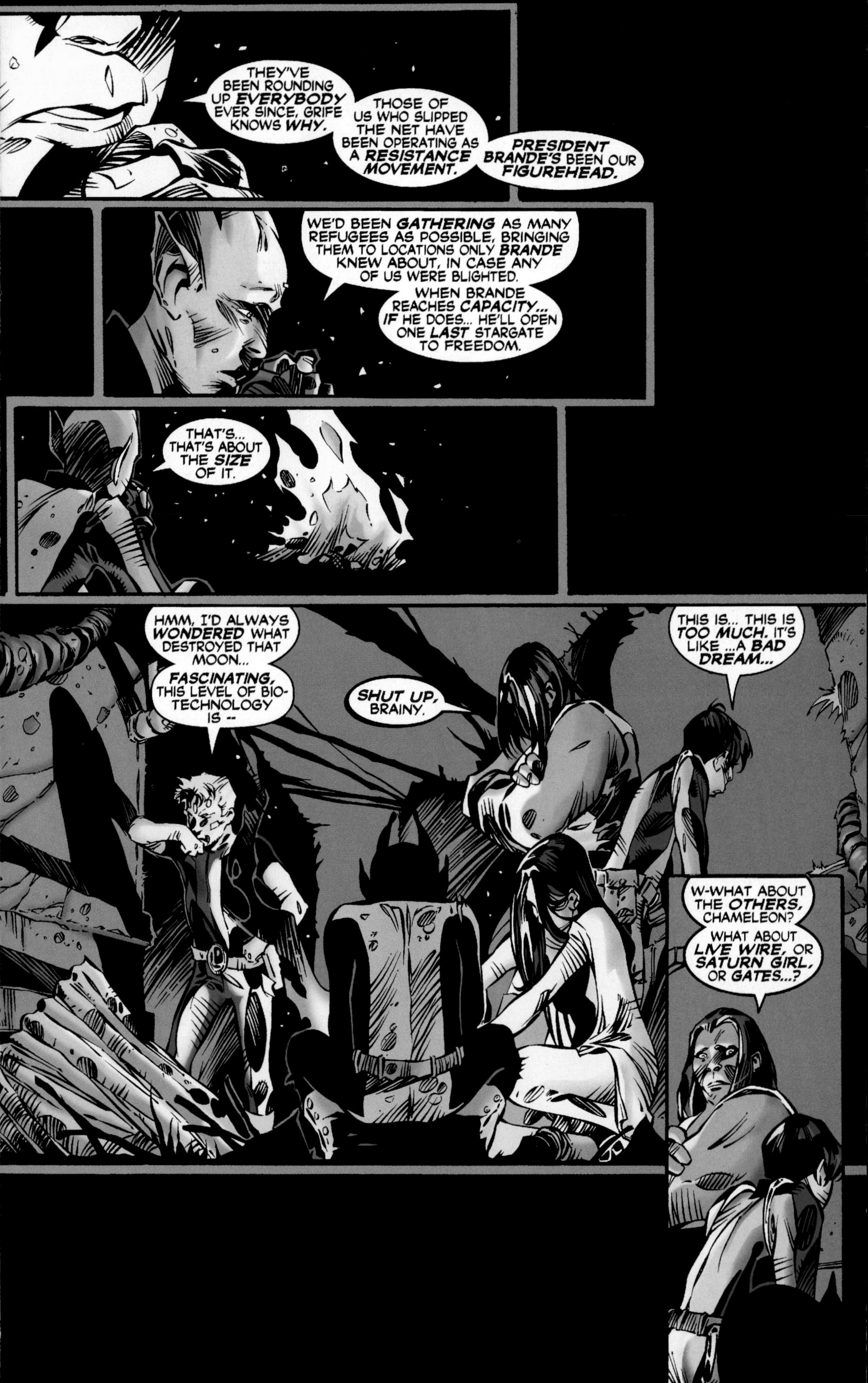
THEY'VE BEEN ROUNDING UP EVERYBODY EVER SINCE, GRIFE KNOWS WHY.
THOSE OF US WHO SLIPPED THE NET HAVE BEEN OPERATING AS A RESISTANCE MOVEMENT.
PRESIDENT BRANDE'S BEEN OUR FIGUREHEAD.
WE'D BEEN GATHERING AS MANY REFUGEES AS POSSIBLE, BRINGING THEM TO LOCATIONS ONLY BRANDE KNEW ABOUT, IN CASE ANY OF US WERE BLIGHTED.
WHEN BRANDE REACHES CAPACITY... IF HE DOES... HE'LL OPEN ONE LAST STARGATE TO FREEDOM.
THAT'S... THAT'S ABOUT THE SIZE OF IT.
HMM, I'D ALWAYS WONDERED WHAT DESTROYED THAT MOON... FASCINATING, THIS LEVEL OF BIO-TECHNOLOGY IS --
SHUT UP, BRAINY.
THIS IS... THIS IS TOO MUCH. IT'S LIKE ...A BAD DREAM...
W-WHAT ABOUT THE OTHERS, CHAMELEON?
WHAT ABOUT LIVE WIRE, OR SATURN GIRL, OR GATES...?

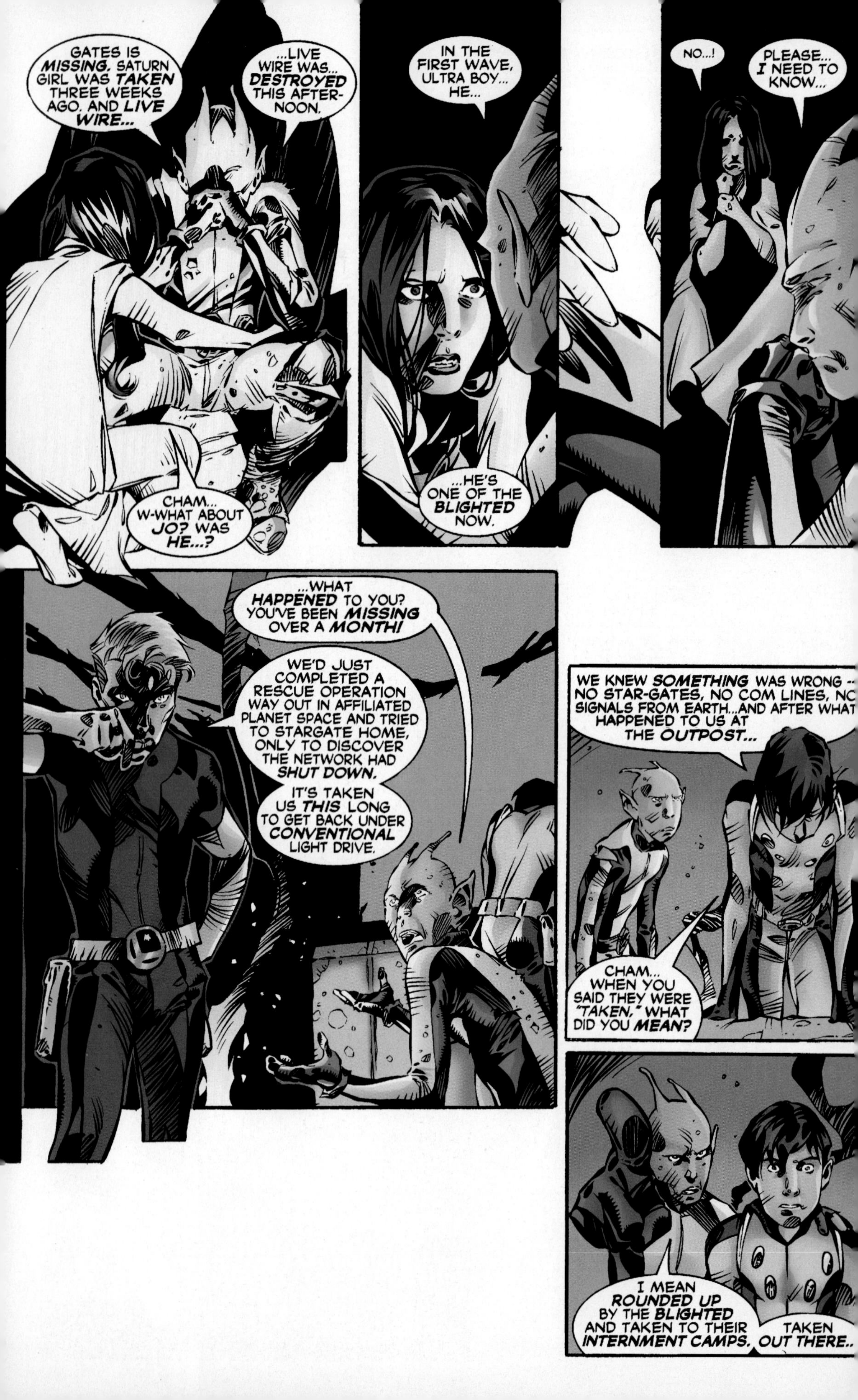
GATES IS MISSING. SATURN GIRL WAS TAKEN THREE WEEKS AGO. AND LIVE WIRE...
...LIVE WIRE WAS... DESTROYED THIS AFTER-NOON.
CHAM... W-WHAT ABOUT JO? WAS HE...?
IN THE FIRST WAVE, ULTRA BOY... HE...
...HE'S ONE OF THE BLIGHTED NOW.
NO...!
PLEASE... I NEED TO KNOW...
...WHAT HAPPENED TO YOU? YOU'VE BEEN MISSING OVER A MONTH!
WE'D JUST COMPLETED A RESCUE OPERATION WAY OUT IN AFFILIATED PLANET SPACE AND TRIED TO STARGATE HOME, ONLY TO DISCOVER THE NETWORK HAD SHUT DOWN.
IT'S TAKEN US THIS LONG TO GET BACK UNDER CONVENTIONAL LIGHT DRIVE.
WE KNEW SOMETHING WAS WRONG -- NO STAR-GATES, NO COM LINES, NO SIGNALS FROM EARTH...AND AFTER WHAT HAPPENED TO US AT THE OUTPOST...
CHAM... WHEN YOU SAID THEY WERE "TAKEN," WHAT DID YOU MEAN?
I MEAN ROUNDED UP BY THE BLIGHTED AND TAKEN TO THEIR INTERNMENT CAMPS.
TAKEN OUT THERE..

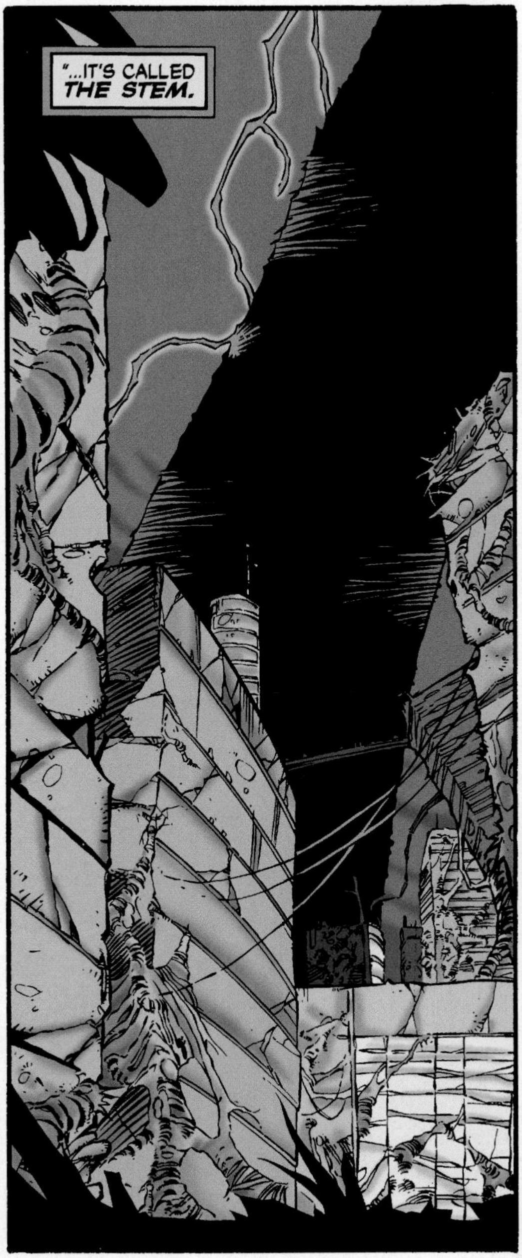
"...IT'S CALLED *THE STEM.*

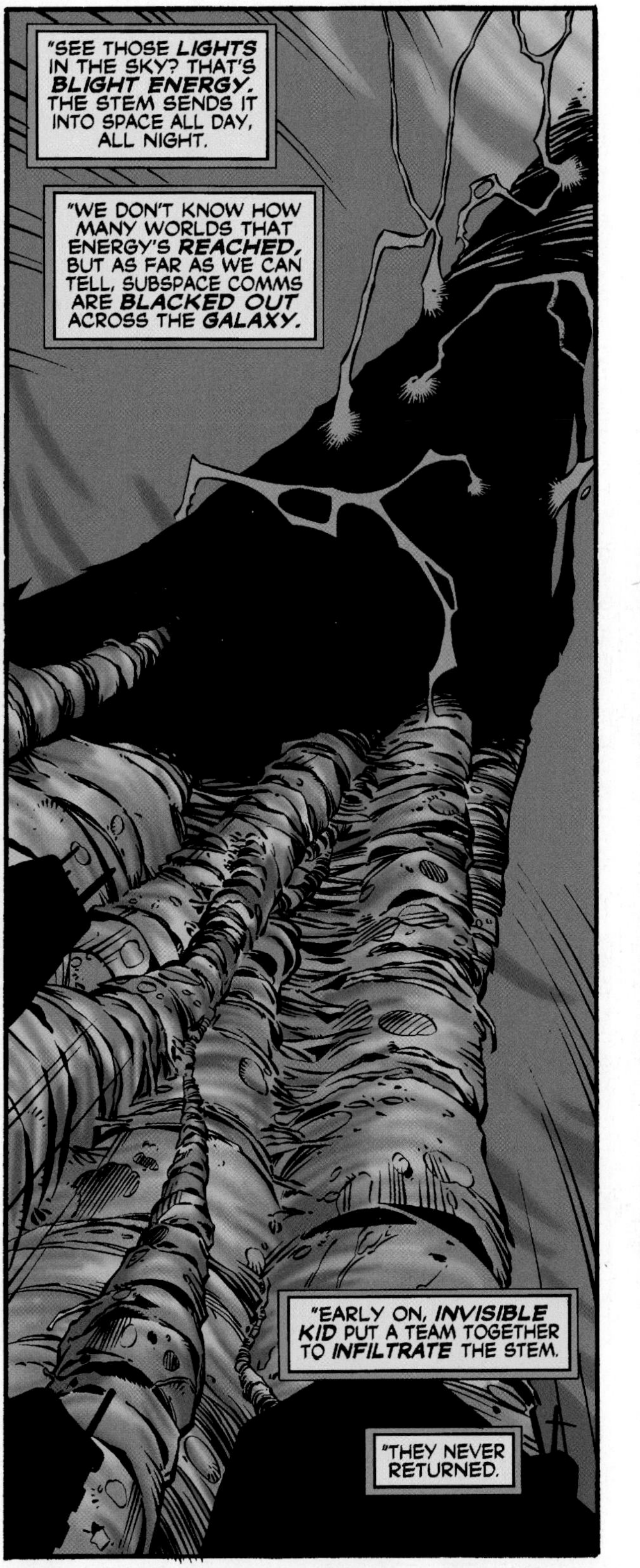
"SEE THOSE *LIGHTS* IN THE SKY? THAT'S *BLIGHT ENERGY.* THE STEM SENDS IT INTO SPACE ALL DAY, ALL NIGHT.
"WE DON'T KNOW HOW MANY WORLDS THAT ENERGY'S *REACHED,* BUT AS FAR AS WE CAN TELL, SUBSPACE COMMS ARE *BLACKED OUT* ACROSS THE *GALAXY.*
"EARLY ON, *INVISIBLE KID* PUT A TEAM TOGETHER TO *INFILTRATE* THE STEM.
"THEY NEVER RETURNED.

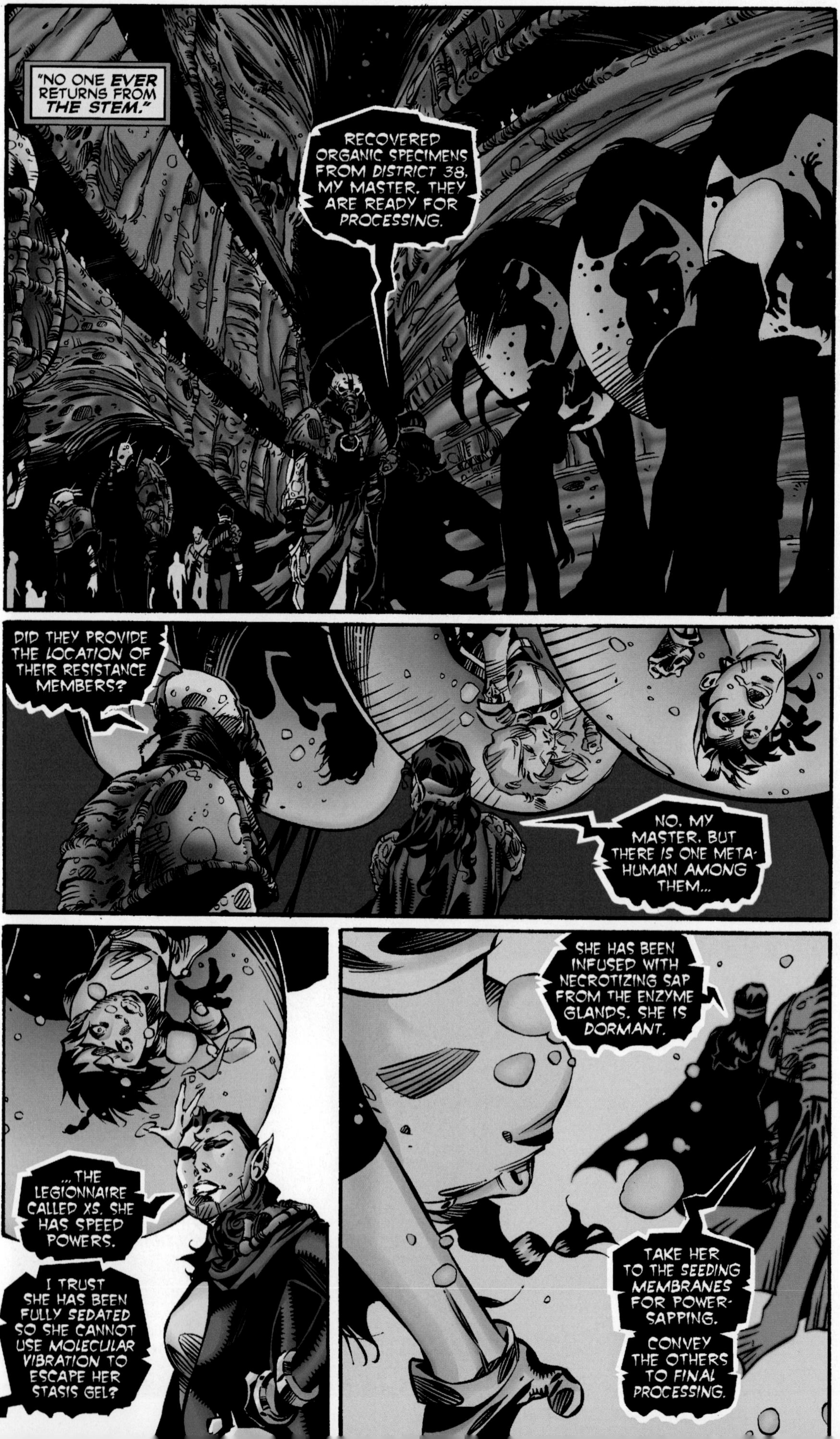
"NO ONE EVER RETURNS FROM THE STEM."
RECOVERED ORGANIC SPECIMENS FROM DISTRICT 38, MY MASTER. THEY ARE READY FOR PROCESSING.
DID THEY PROVIDE THE LOCATION OF THEIR RESISTANCE MEMBERS?
NO, MY MASTER. BUT THERE IS ONE META-HUMAN AMONG THEM...
...THE LEGIONNAIRE CALLED XS. SHE HAS SPEED POWERS.
I TRUST SHE HAS BEEN FULLY SEDATED SO SHE CANNOT USE MOLECULAR VIBRATION TO ESCAPE HER STASIS GEL?
SHE HAS BEEN INFUSED WITH NECROTIZING SAP FROM THE ENZYME GLANDS. SHE IS DORMANT.
TAKE HER TO THE SEEDING MEMBRANES FOR POWER-SAPPING.
CONVEY THE OTHERS TO FINAL PROCESSING.

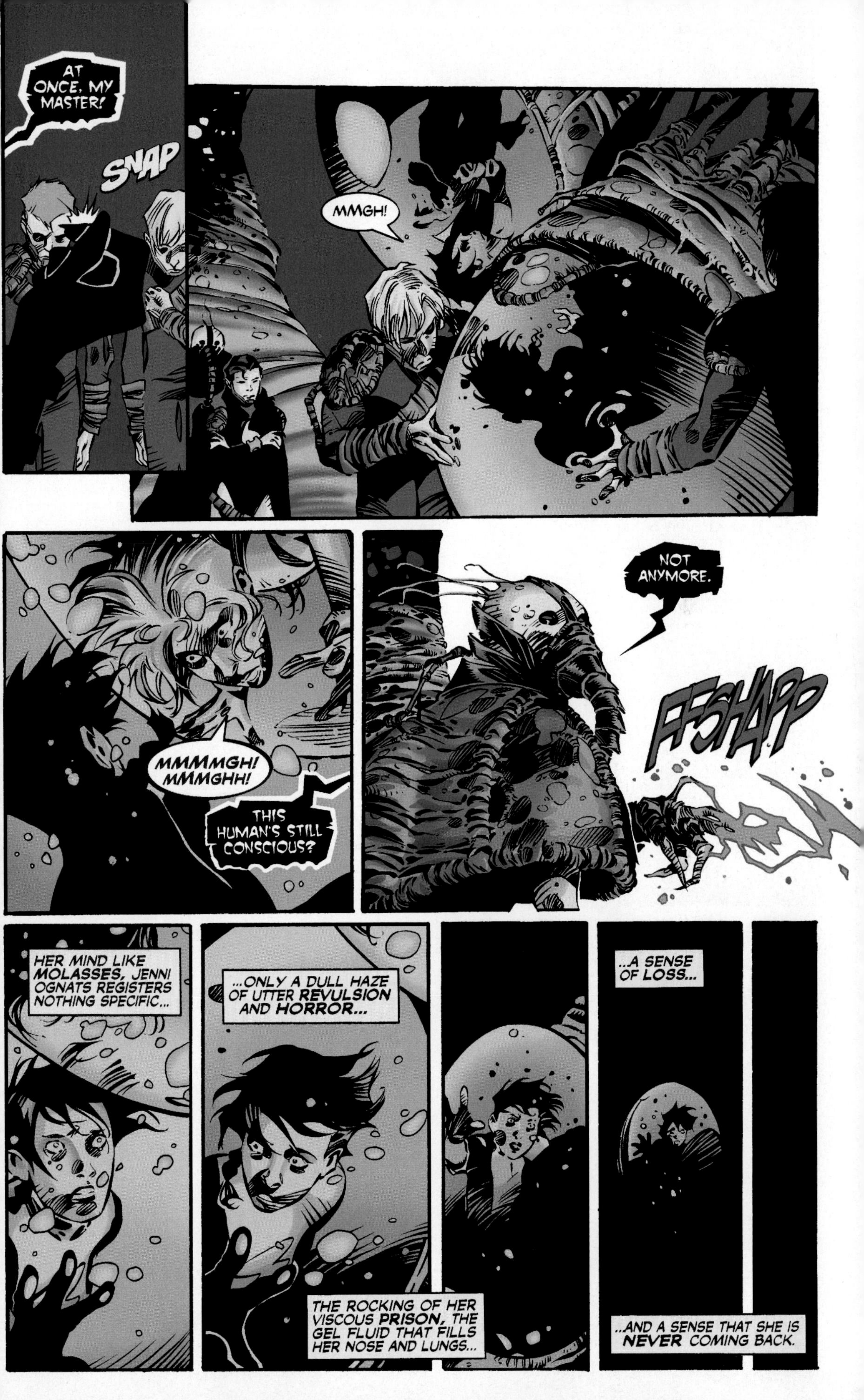
AT ONCE, MY MASTER!
SNAP
MMGH!
MMMMGH! MMMGHH!
THIS HUMAN'S STILL CONSCIOUS?
NOT ANYMORE.
FFSHAPP
HER MIND LIKE MOLASSES, JENNI OGNATS REGISTERS NOTHING SPECIFIC...
...ONLY A DULL HAZE OF UTTER REVULSION AND HORROR...
THE ROCKING OF HER VISCOUS PRISON, THE GEL FLUID THAT FILLS HER NOSE AND LUNGS...
...A SENSE OF LOSS...
...AND A SENSE THAT SHE IS NEVER COMING BACK.

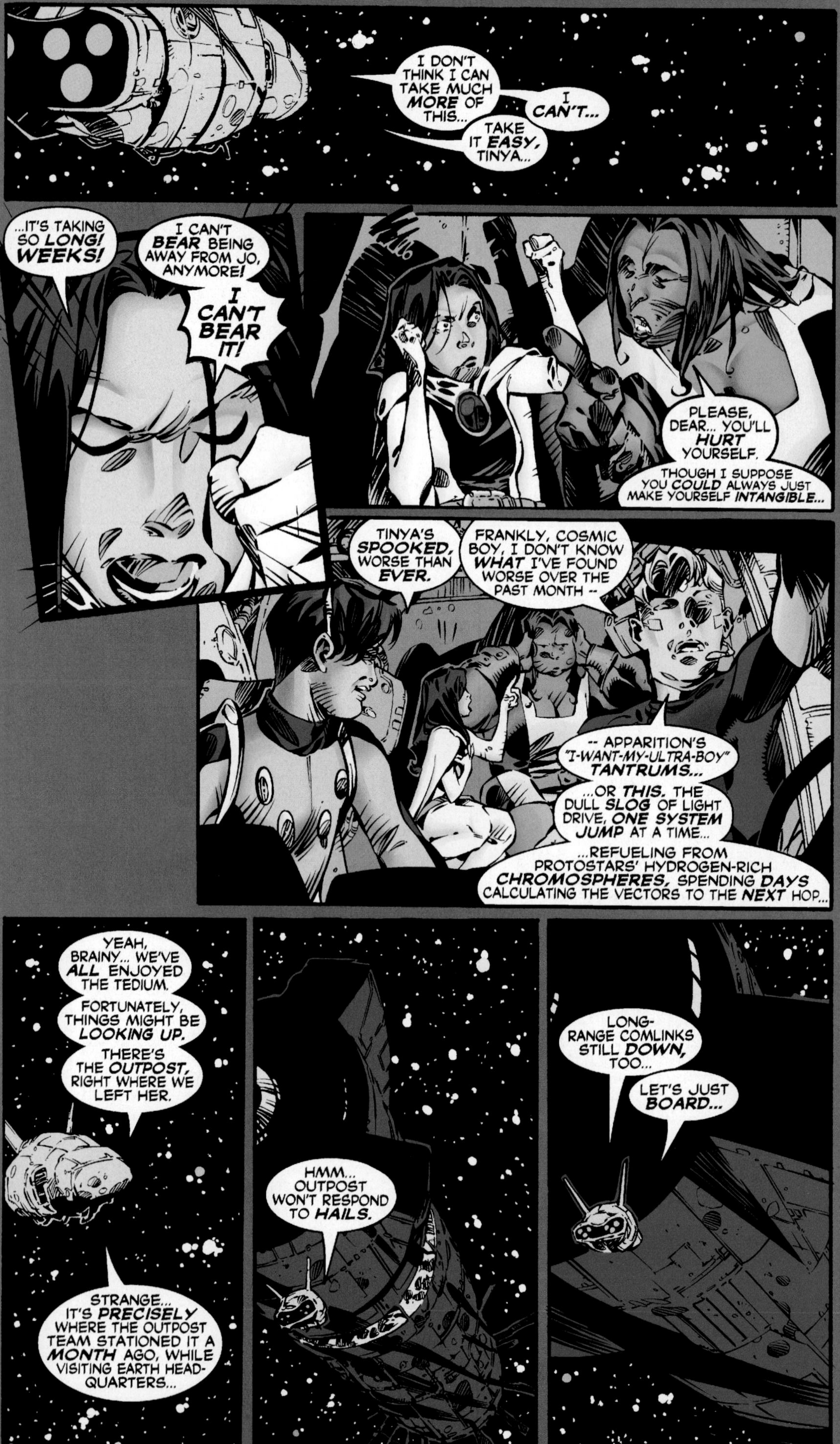
I DON'T THINK I CAN TAKE MUCH MORE OF THIS...
I CAN'T...
TAKE IT EASY, TINYA...
...IT'S TAKING SO LONG! WEEKS!
I CAN'T BEAR BEING AWAY FROM JO, ANYMORE!
I CAN'T BEAR IT!
PLEASE, DEAR... YOU'LL HURT YOURSELF.
THOUGH I SUPPOSE YOU COULD ALWAYS JUST MAKE YOURSELF INTANGIBLE...
TINYA'S SPOOKED, WORSE THAN EVER.
FRANKLY, COSMIC BOY, I DON'T KNOW WHAT I'VE FOUND WORSE OVER THE PAST MONTH --
-- APPARITION'S "I-WANT-MY-ULTRA-BOY" TANTRUMS...
...OR THIS. THE DULL SLOG OF LIGHT DRIVE, ONE SYSTEM JUMP AT A TIME...
...REFUELING FROM PROTOSTARS' HYDROGEN-RICH CHROMOSPHERES, SPENDING DAYS CALCULATING THE VECTORS TO THE NEXT HOP...
YEAH, BRAINY... WE'VE ALL ENJOYED THE TEDIUM.
FORTUNATELY, THINGS MIGHT BE LOOKING UP.
THERE'S THE OUTPOST, RIGHT WHERE WE LEFT HER.
STRANGE... IT'S PRECISELY WHERE THE OUTPOST TEAM STATIONED IT A MONTH AGO, WHILE VISITING EARTH HEAD-QUARTERS...
HMM... OUTPOST WON'T RESPOND TO HAILS.
LONG-RANGE COMLINKS STILL DOWN, TOO...
LET'S JUST BOARD...

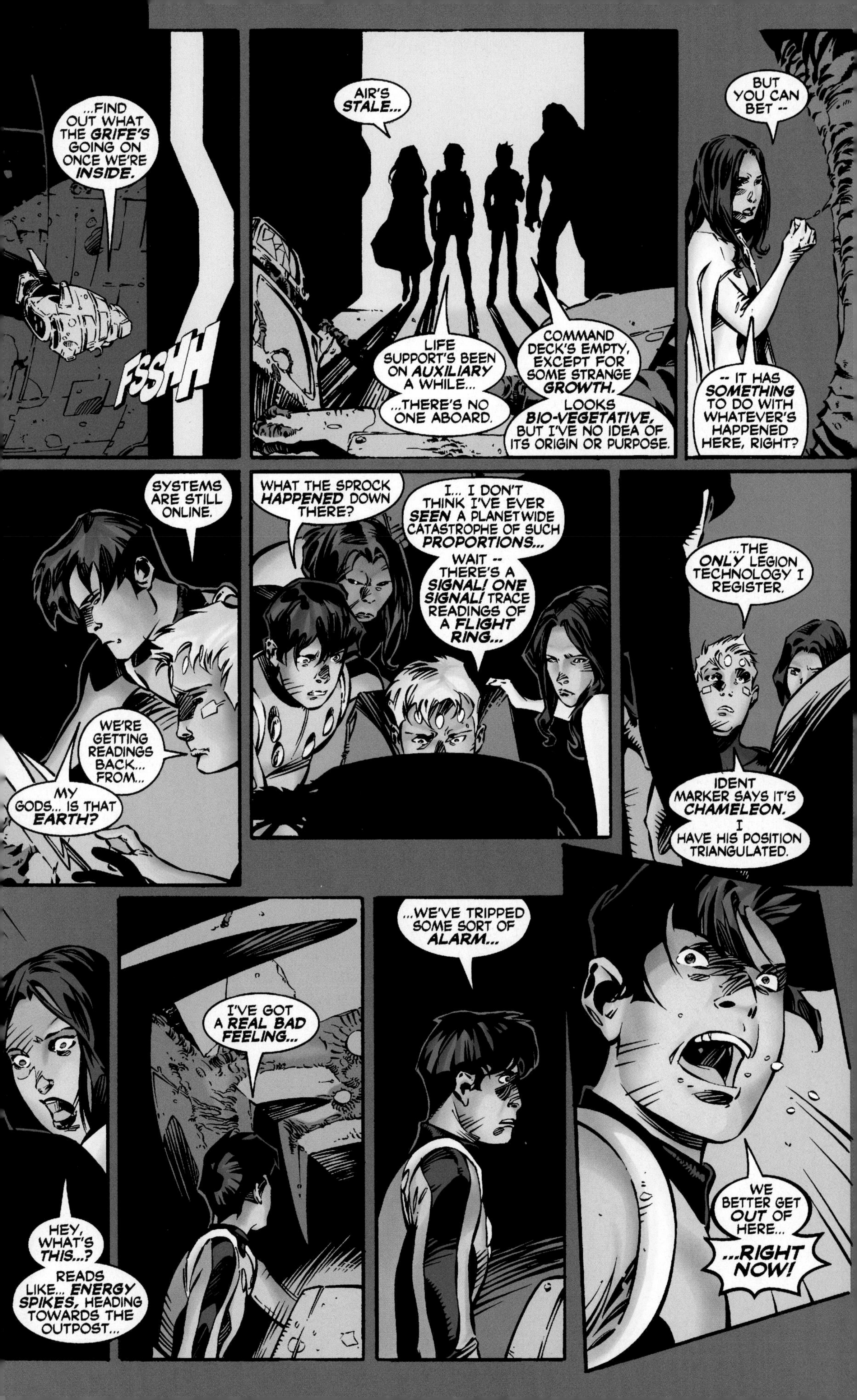
...FIND OUT WHAT THE GRIFE'S GOING ON ONCE WE'RE INSIDE.
FSSHH
AIR'S STALE...
LIFE SUPPORT'S BEEN ON AUXILIARY A WHILE...
...THERE'S NO ONE ABOARD.
COMMAND DECK'S EMPTY, EXCEPT FOR SOME STRANGE GROWTH.
LOOKS BIO-VEGETATIVE, BUT I'VE NO IDEA OF ITS ORIGIN OR PURPOSE.
BUT YOU CAN BET --
-- IT HAS SOMETHING TO DO WITH WHATEVER'S HAPPENED HERE, RIGHT?
SYSTEMS ARE STILL ONLINE.
WE'RE GETTING READINGS BACK... FROM...
MY GODS... IS THAT EARTH?
WHAT THE SPROCK HAPPENED DOWN THERE?
I... I DON'T THINK I'VE EVER SEEN A PLANETWIDE CATASTROPHE OF SUCH PROPORTIONS...
WAIT -- THERE'S A SIGNAL! ONE SIGNAL! TRACE READINGS OF A FLIGHT RING...
...THE ONLY LEGION TECHNOLOGY I REGISTER.
IDENT MARKER SAYS IT'S CHAMELEON.
I HAVE HIS POSITION TRIANGULATED.
HEY, WHAT'S THIS...?
READS LIKE... ENERGY SPIKES, HEADING TOWARDS THE OUTPOST...
I'VE GOT A REAL BAD FEELING...
...WE'VE TRIPPED SOME SORT OF ALARM...
WE BETTER GET OUT OF HERE...
...RIGHT NOW!

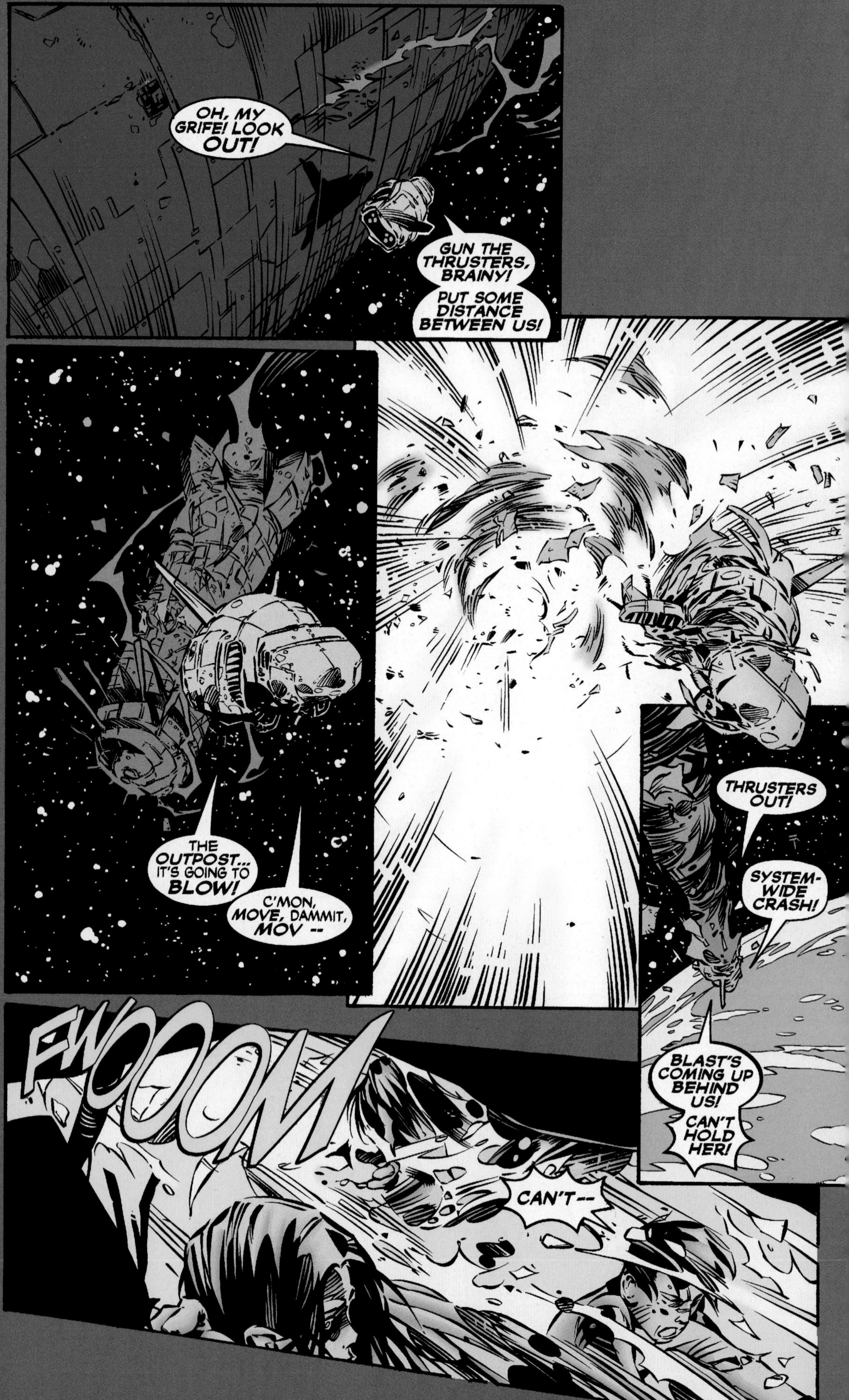
OH, MY GRIFE! LOOK OUT!
GUN THE THRUSTERS, BRAINY!
PUT SOME DISTANCE BETWEEN US!
THE OUTPOST... IT'S GOING TO BLOW!
C'MON, MOVE, DAMMIT, MOV --
THRUSTERS OUT!
SYSTEM-WIDE CRASH!
BLAST'S COMING UP BEHIND US!
CAN'T HOLD HER!
FWOOOM
CAN'T--

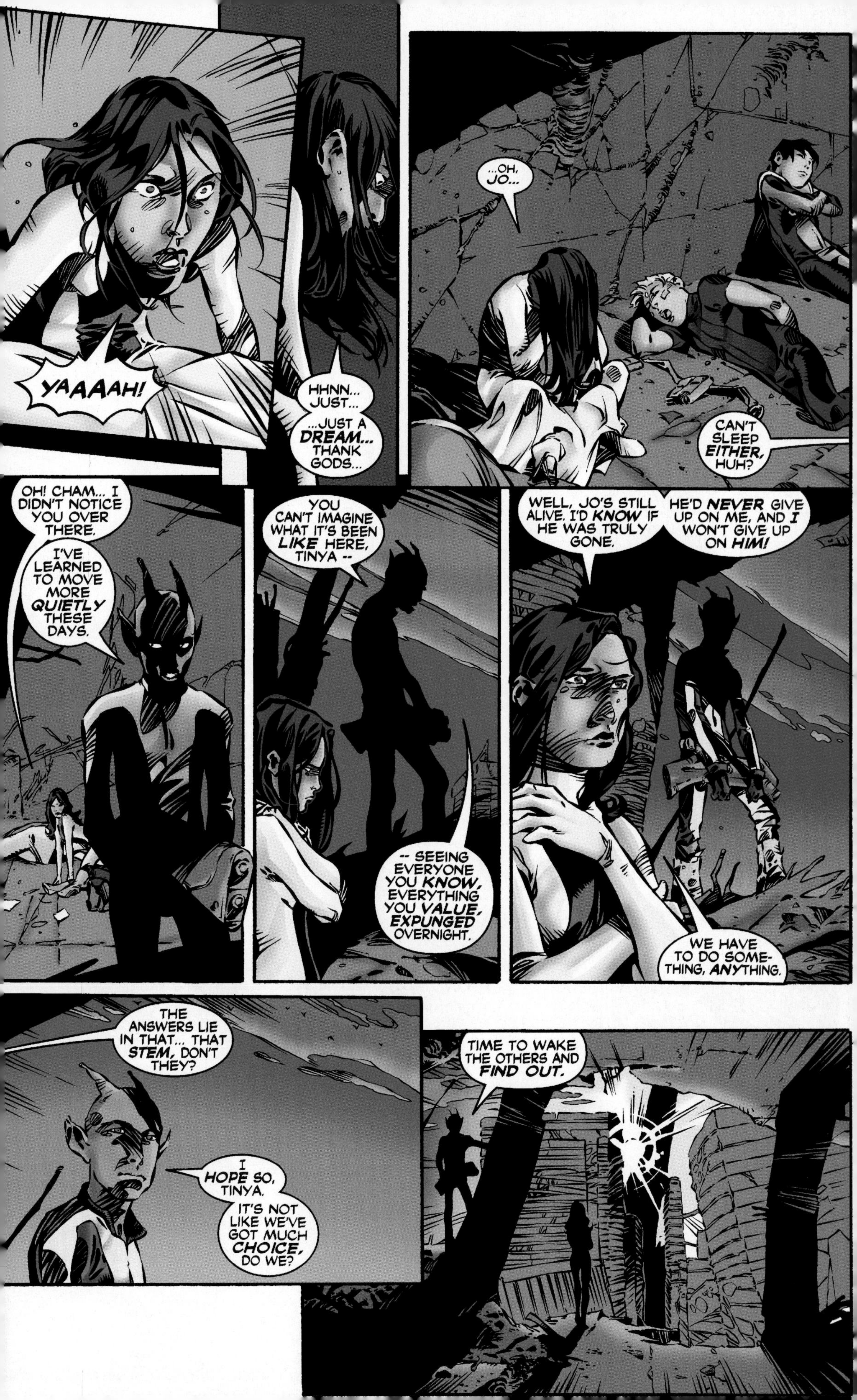
YAAAAH!
HHNN... JUST...
...JUST A DREAM... THANK GODS...
...OH, JO...
CAN'T SLEEP EITHER, HUH?
OH! CHAM... I DIDN'T NOTICE YOU OVER THERE.
I'VE LEARNED TO MOVE MORE QUIETLY THESE DAYS.
YOU CAN'T IMAGINE WHAT IT'S BEEN LIKE HERE, TINYA --
-- SEEING EVERYONE YOU KNOW, EVERYTHING YOU VALUE, EXPUNGED OVERNIGHT.
WELL, JO'S STILL ALIVE. I'D KNOW IF HE WAS TRULY GONE.
HE'D NEVER GIVE UP ON ME, AND I WON'T GIVE UP ON HIM!
WE HAVE TO DO SOMETHING, ANYTHING.
THE ANSWERS LIE IN THAT... THAT STEM, DON'T THEY?
I HOPE SO, TINYA.
IT'S NOT LIKE WE'VE GOT MUCH CHOICE, DO WE?
TIME TO WAKE THE OTHERS AND FIND OUT.

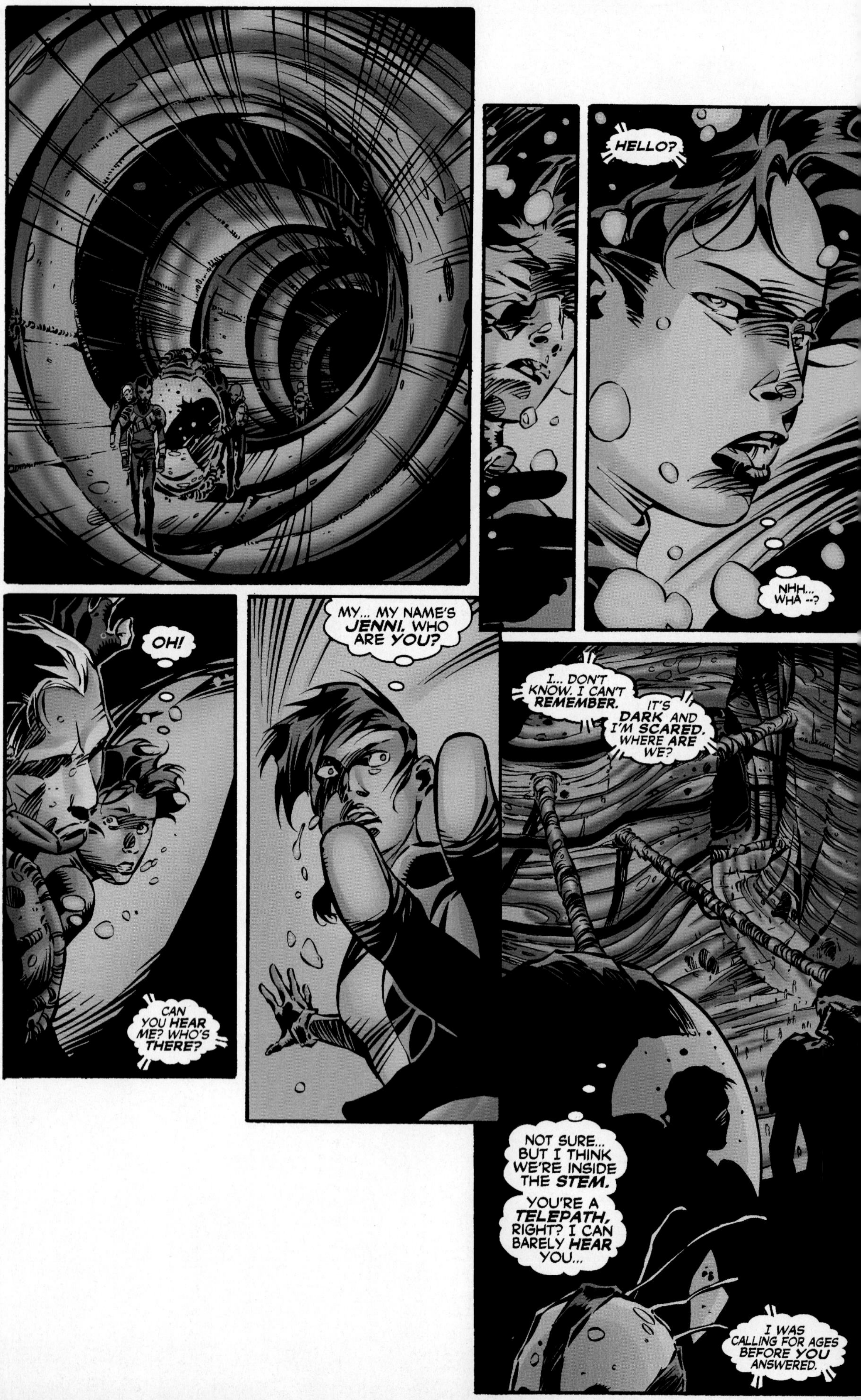
HELLO?
NHH... WHA --?
OH!
CAN YOU HEAR ME? WHO'S THERE?
MY... MY NAME'S JENNI. WHO ARE YOU?
I... DON'T KNOW. I CAN'T REMEMBER.
IT'S DARK AND I'M SCARED. WHERE ARE WE?
NOT SURE... BUT I THINK WE'RE INSIDE THE STEM.
YOU'RE A TELEPATH, RIGHT? I CAN BARELY HEAR YOU...
I WAS CALLING FOR AGES BEFORE YOU ANSWERED.

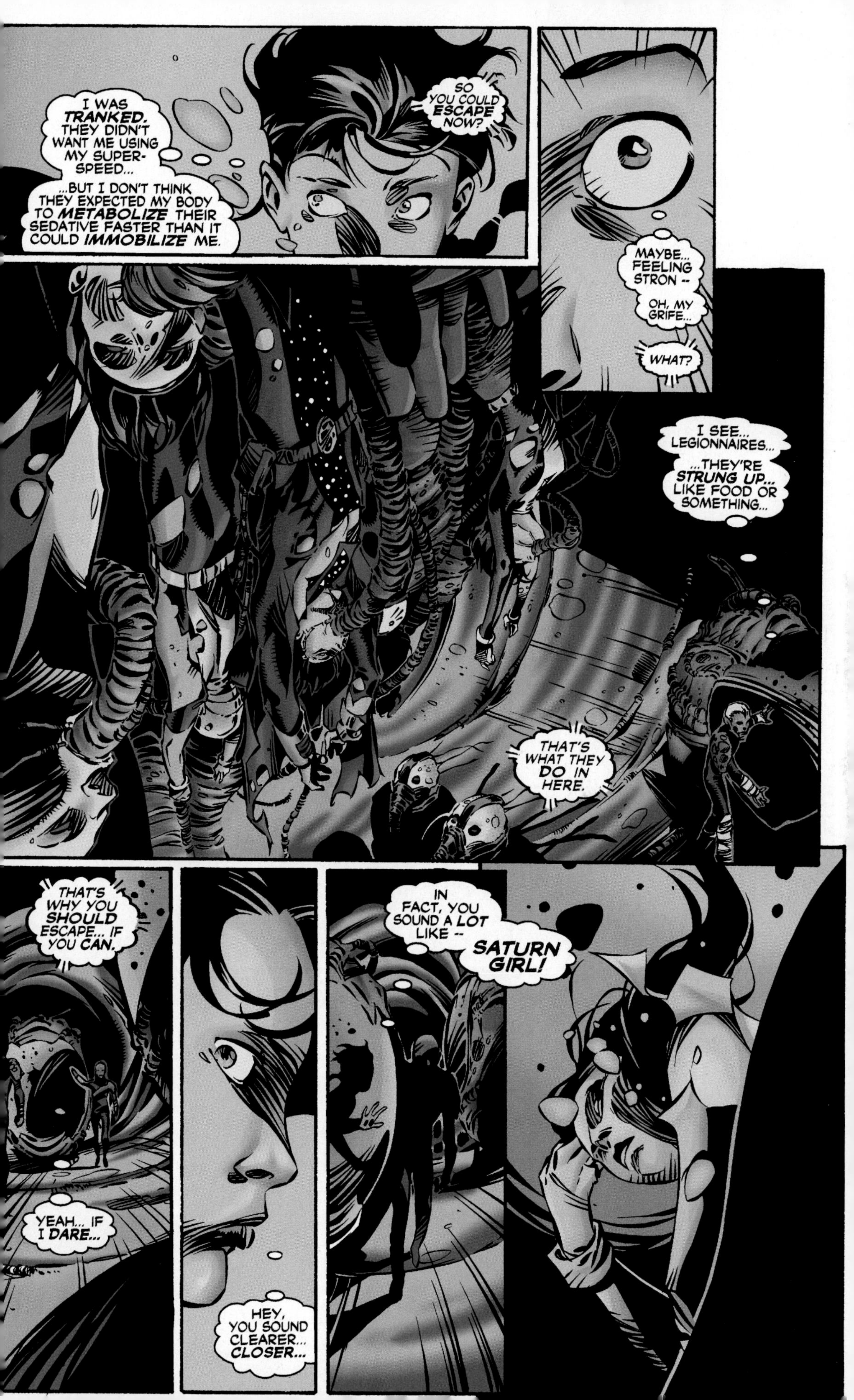
I WAS TRANKED. THEY DIDN'T WANT ME USING MY SUPER-SPEED...
...BUT I DON'T THINK THEY EXPECTED MY BODY TO METABOLIZE THEIR SEDATIVE FASTER THAN IT COULD IMMOBILIZE ME.
SO YOU COULD ESCAPE NOW?
MAYBE... FEELING STRON --
OH, MY GRIFE...
WHAT?
I SEE... LEGIONNAIRES...
...THEY'RE STRUNG UP... LIKE FOOD OR SOMETHING...
THAT'S WHAT THEY DO IN HERE.
THAT'S WHY YOU SHOULD ESCAPE... IF YOU CAN.
YEAH... IF I DARE...
HEY, YOU SOUND CLEARER... CLOSER...
IN FACT, YOU SOUND A LOT LIKE --
SATURN GIRL!

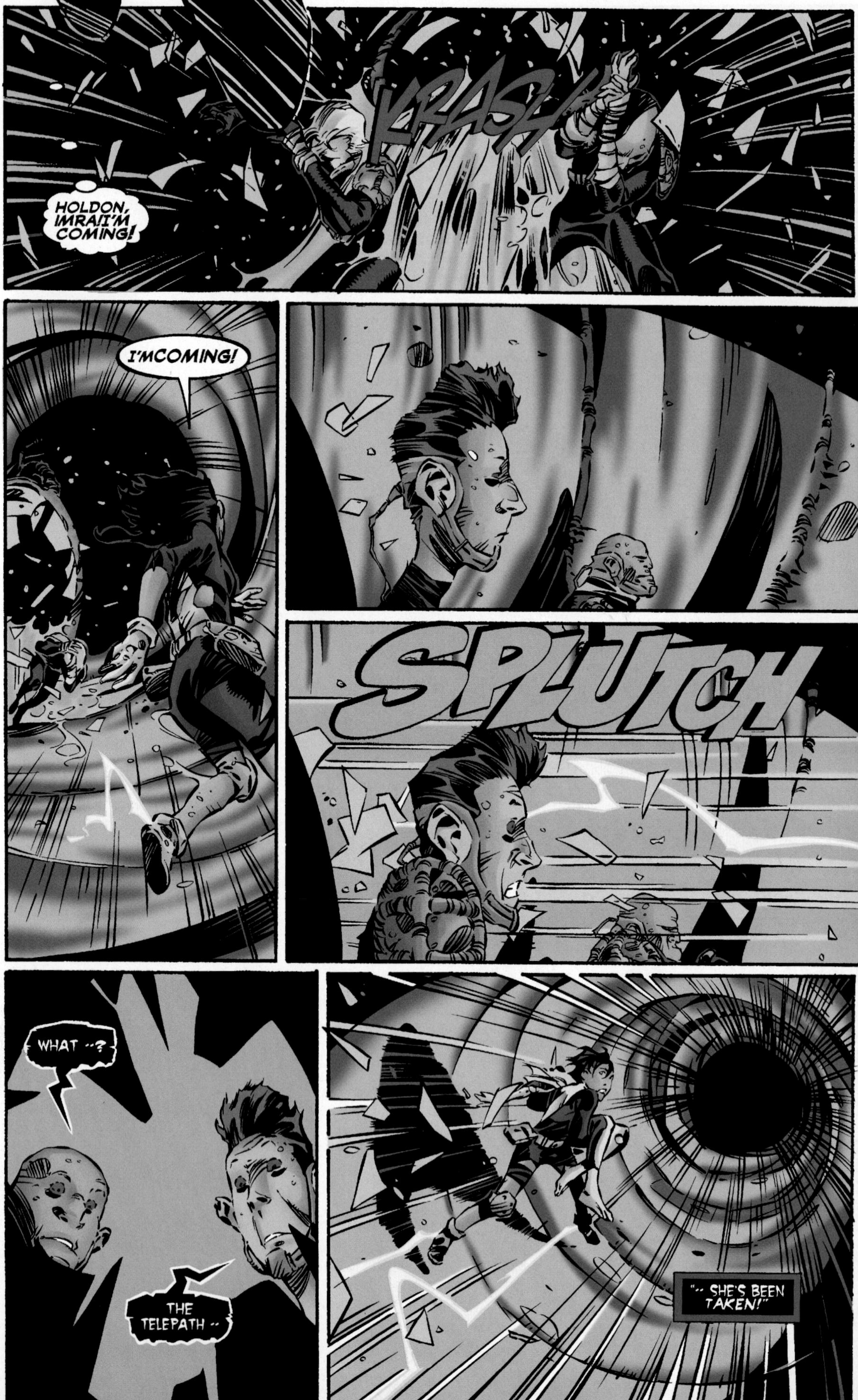
KRASH!
HOLDON, IMRAIL I'M COMING!
I'M COMING!
SPLUTCH
WHAT --?
THE TELEPATH --
"-- SHE'S BEEN TAKEN!"

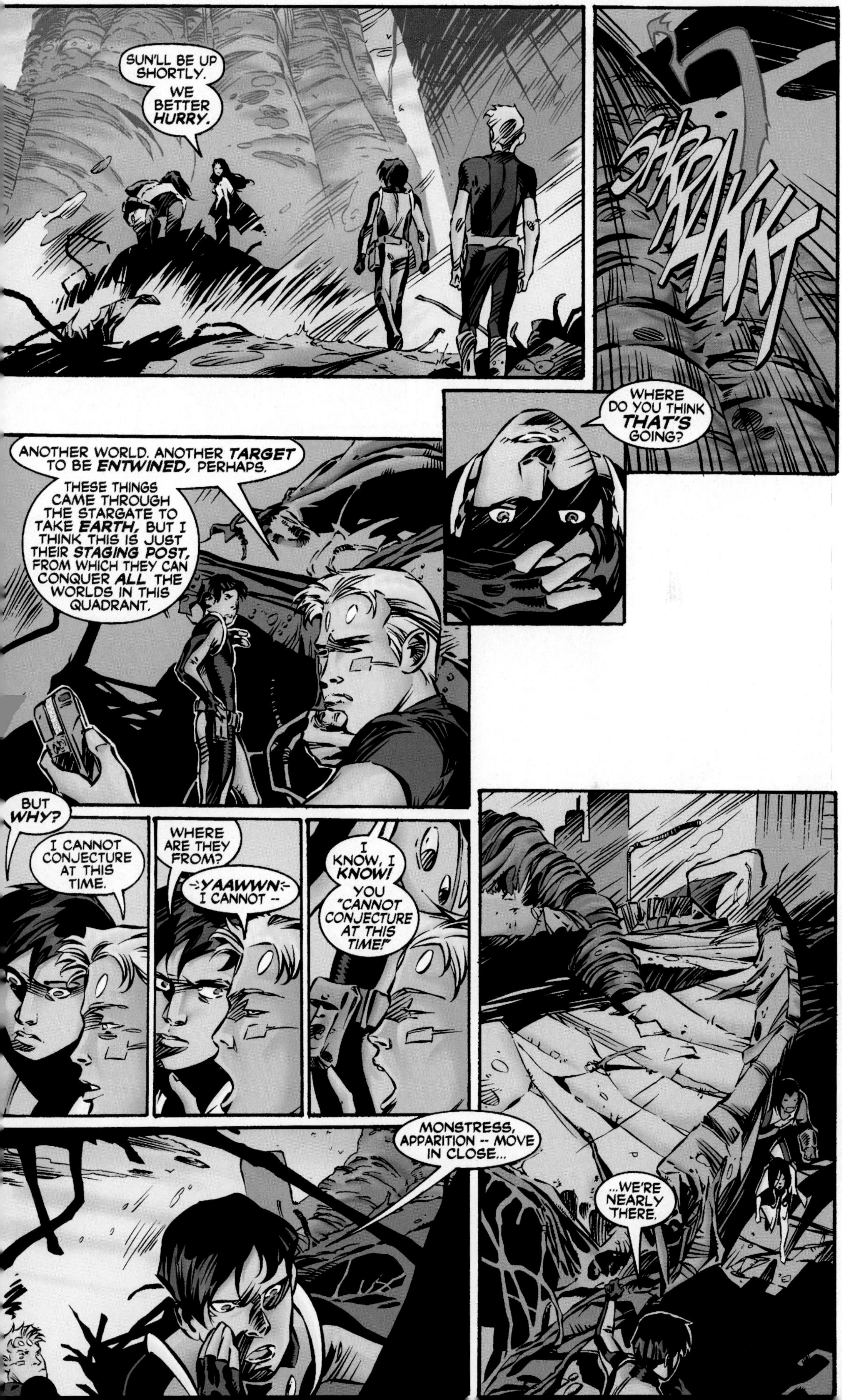

SUN'LL BE UP SHORTLY.
WE BETTER HURRY.
SHRAKKT
WHERE DO YOU THINK THAT'S GOING?
ANOTHER WORLD. ANOTHER TARGET TO BE ENTWINED, PERHAPS.
THESE THINGS CAME THROUGH THE STARGATE TO TAKE EARTH, BUT I THINK THIS IS JUST THEIR STAGING POST, FROM WHICH THEY CAN CONQUER ALL THE WORLDS IN THIS QUADRANT.
BUT WHY?
I CANNOT CONJECTURE AT THIS TIME.
WHERE ARE THEY FROM?
-YAAWWN- I CANNOT --
I KNOW, I KNOW! YOU "CANNOT CONJECTURE AT THIS TIME!"
MONSTRESS, APPARITION -- MOVE IN CLOSE...
...WE'RE NEARLY THERE.

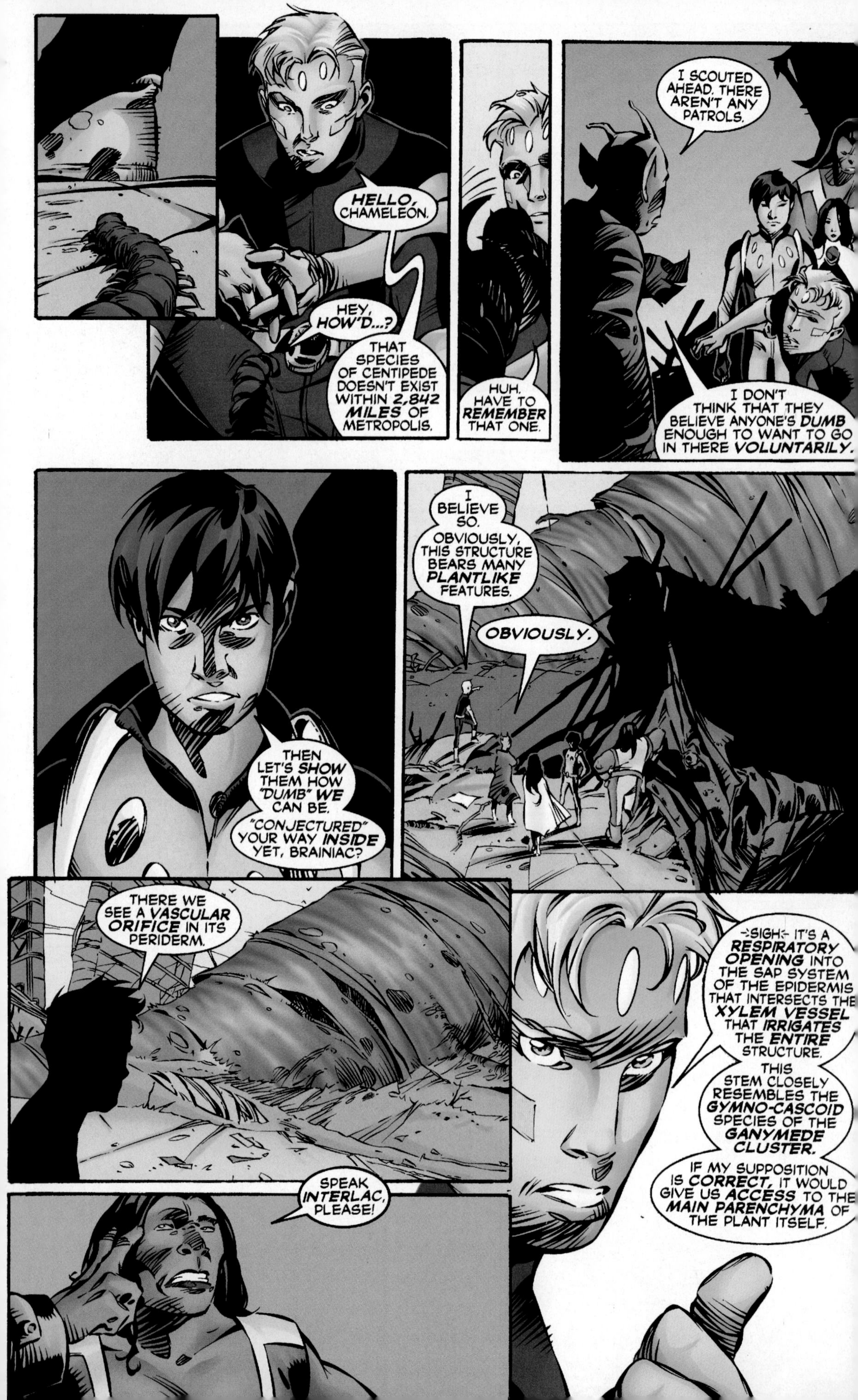
HELLO, CHAMELEON.
HEY, HOW'D...?
THAT SPECIES OF CENTIPEDE DOESN'T EXIST WITHIN 2,842 MILES OF METROPOLIS.
HUH. HAVE TO REMEMBER THAT ONE.
I SCOUTED AHEAD. THERE AREN'T ANY PATROLS.
I DON'T THINK THAT THEY BELIEVE ANYONE'S DUMB ENOUGH TO WANT TO GO IN THERE VOLUNTARILY.
THEN LET'S SHOW THEM HOW "DUMB" WE CAN BE.
"CONJECTURED" YOUR WAY INSIDE YET, BRAINIAC?
I BELIEVE SO.
OBVIOUSLY, THIS STRUCTURE BEARS MANY PLANTLIKE FEATURES.
OBVIOUSLY.
THERE WE SEE A VASCULAR ORIFICE IN ITS PERIDERM.
SPEAK INTERLAC, PLEASE!
-SIGH- IT'S A RESPIRATORY OPENING INTO THE SAP SYSTEM OF THE EPIDERMIS THAT INTERSECTS THE XYLEM VESSEL THAT IRRIGATES THE ENTIRE STRUCTURE.
THIS STEM CLOSELY RESEMBLES THE GYMNO-CASCOID SPECIES OF THE GANYMEDE CLUSTER.
IF MY SUPPOSITION IS CORRECT, IT WOULD GIVE US ACCESS TO THE MAIN PARENCHYMA OF THE PLANT ITSELF.

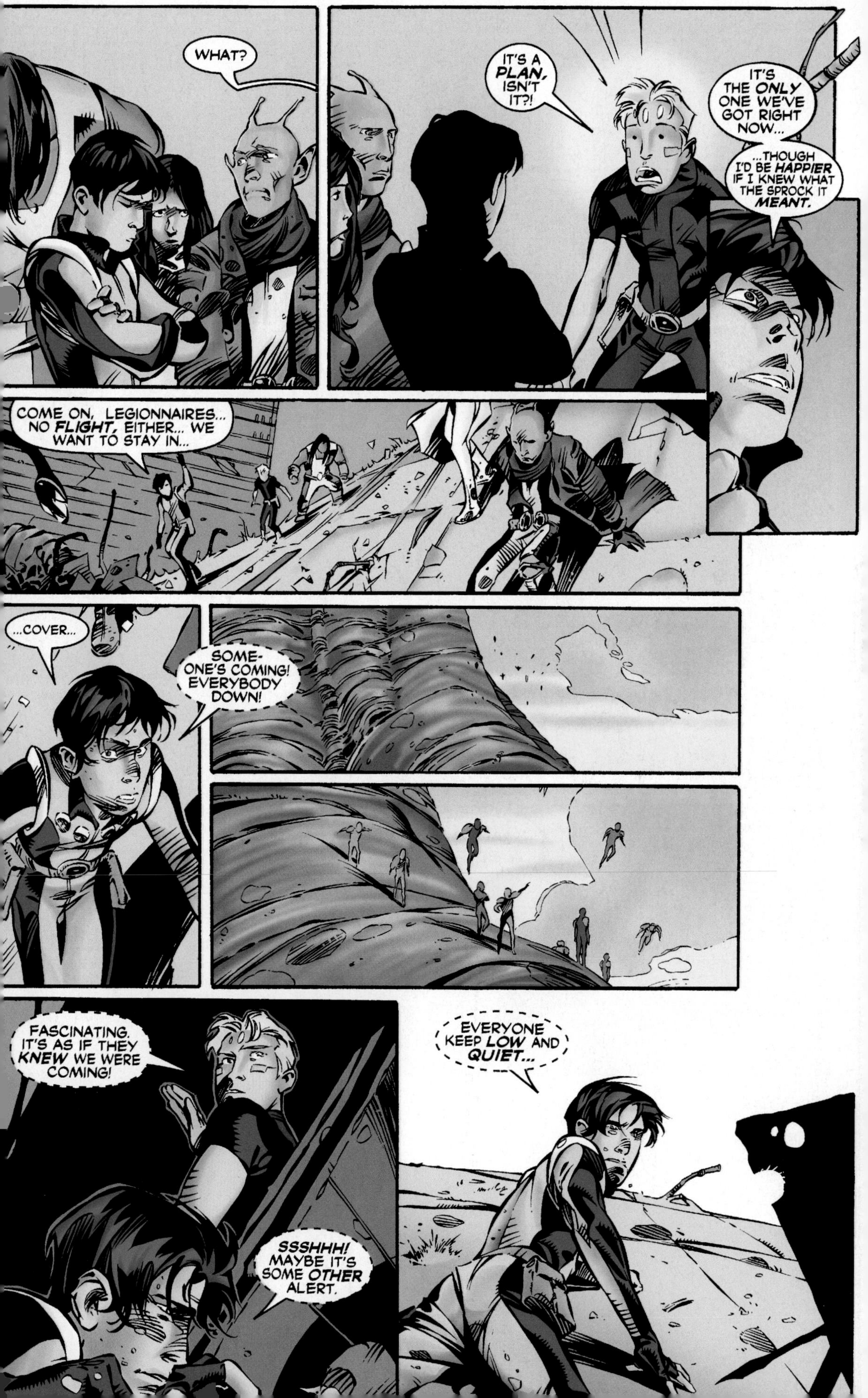
WHAT?
IT'S A PLAN, ISN'T IT?!
IT'S THE ONLY ONE WE'VE GOT RIGHT NOW...
...THOUGH I'D BE HAPPIER IF I KNEW WHAT THE SPROCK IT MEANT.
COME ON, LEGIONNAIRES... NO FLIGHT, EITHER... WE WANT TO STAY IN...
...COVER...
SOME-ONE'S COMING! EVERYBODY DOWN!
FASCINATING. IT'S AS IF THEY KNEW WE WERE COMING!
SSSHHH! MAYBE IT'S SOME OTHER ALERT.
EVERYONE KEEP LOW AND QUIET...

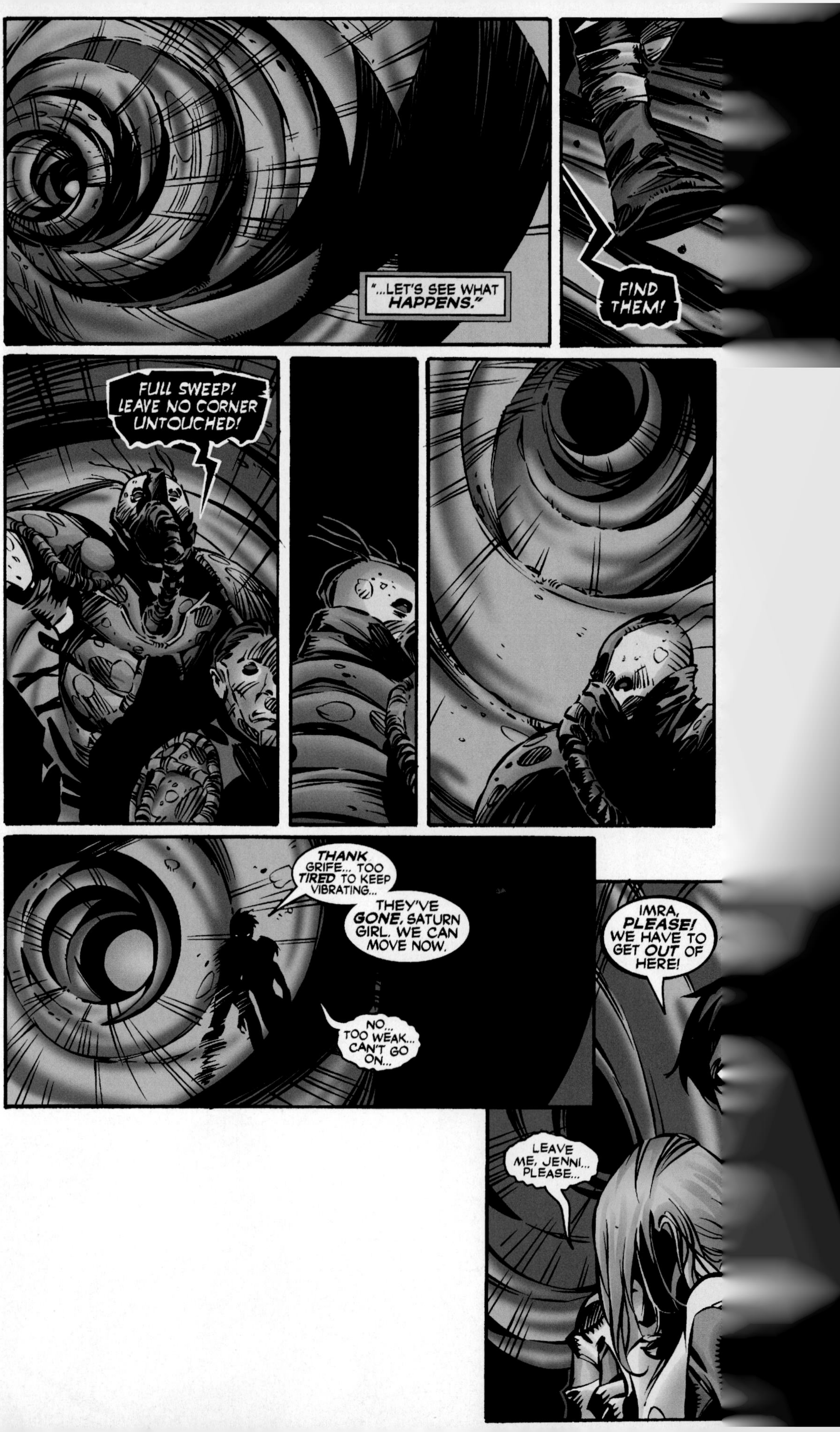
"...LET'S SEE WHAT HAPPENS."
FIND THEM!
FULL SWEEP! LEAVE NO CORNER UNTOUCHED!
THANK GRIFE... TOO TIRED TO KEEP VIBRATING...
THEY'VE GONE, SATURN GIRL. WE CAN MOVE NOW.
NO... TOO WEAK... CAN'T GO ON...
IMRA, PLEASE! WE HAVE TO GET OUT OF HERE!
LEAVE ME, JENNI... PLEASE...

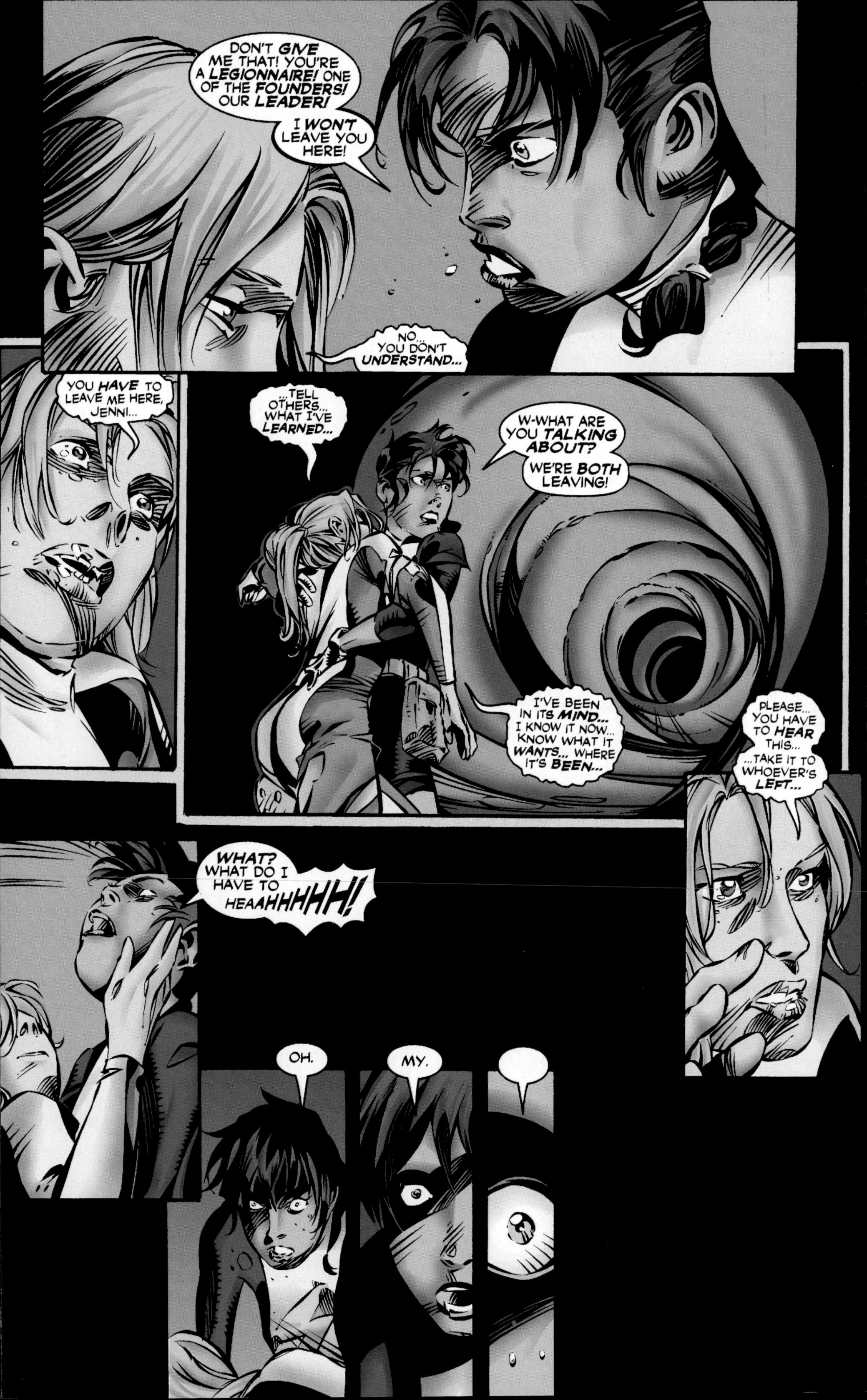
DON'T GIVE ME THAT! YOU'RE A LEGIONNAIRE! ONE OF THE FOUNDERS! OUR LEADER!
I WON'T LEAVE YOU HERE!
NO... YOU DON'T UNDERSTAND...
YOU HAVE TO LEAVE ME HERE, JENNI...
...TELL OTHERS... WHAT I'VE LEARNED...
W-WHAT ARE YOU TALKING ABOUT?
WE'RE BOTH LEAVING!
I'VE BEEN IN ITS MIND... I KNOW IT NOW... KNOW WHAT IT WANTS... WHERE IT'S BEEN...
PLEASE... YOU HAVE TO HEAR THIS...
...TAKE IT TO WHOEVER'S LEFT...
WHAT? WHAT DO I HAVE TO HEAAHHHHH!
OH.
MY.

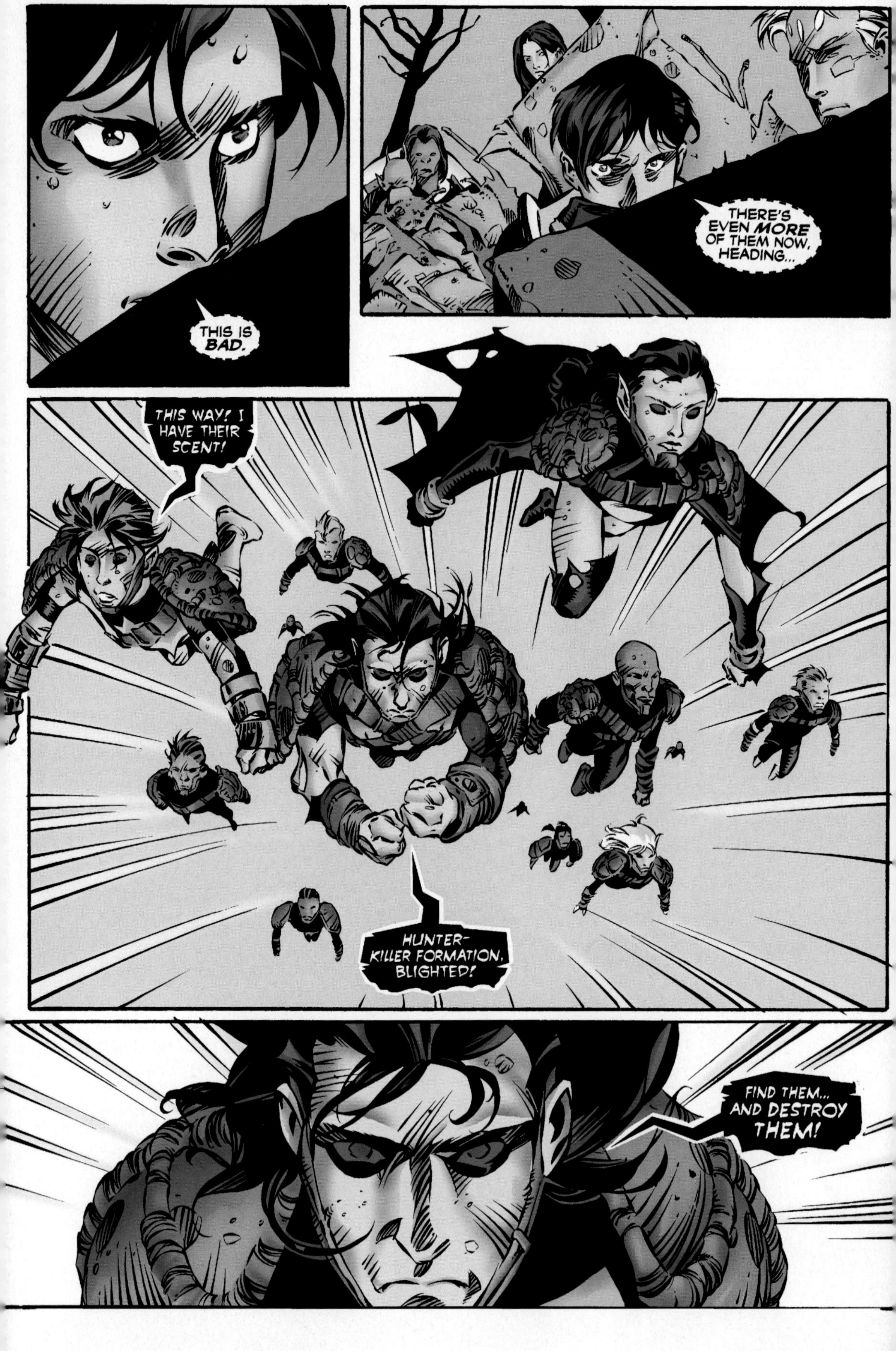
THIS IS BAD.
THERE'S EVEN MORE OF THEM NOW, HEADING...
THIS WAY! I HAVE THEIR SCENT!
HUNTER-KILLER FORMATION, BLIGHTED!
FIND THEM... AND DESTROY THEM!

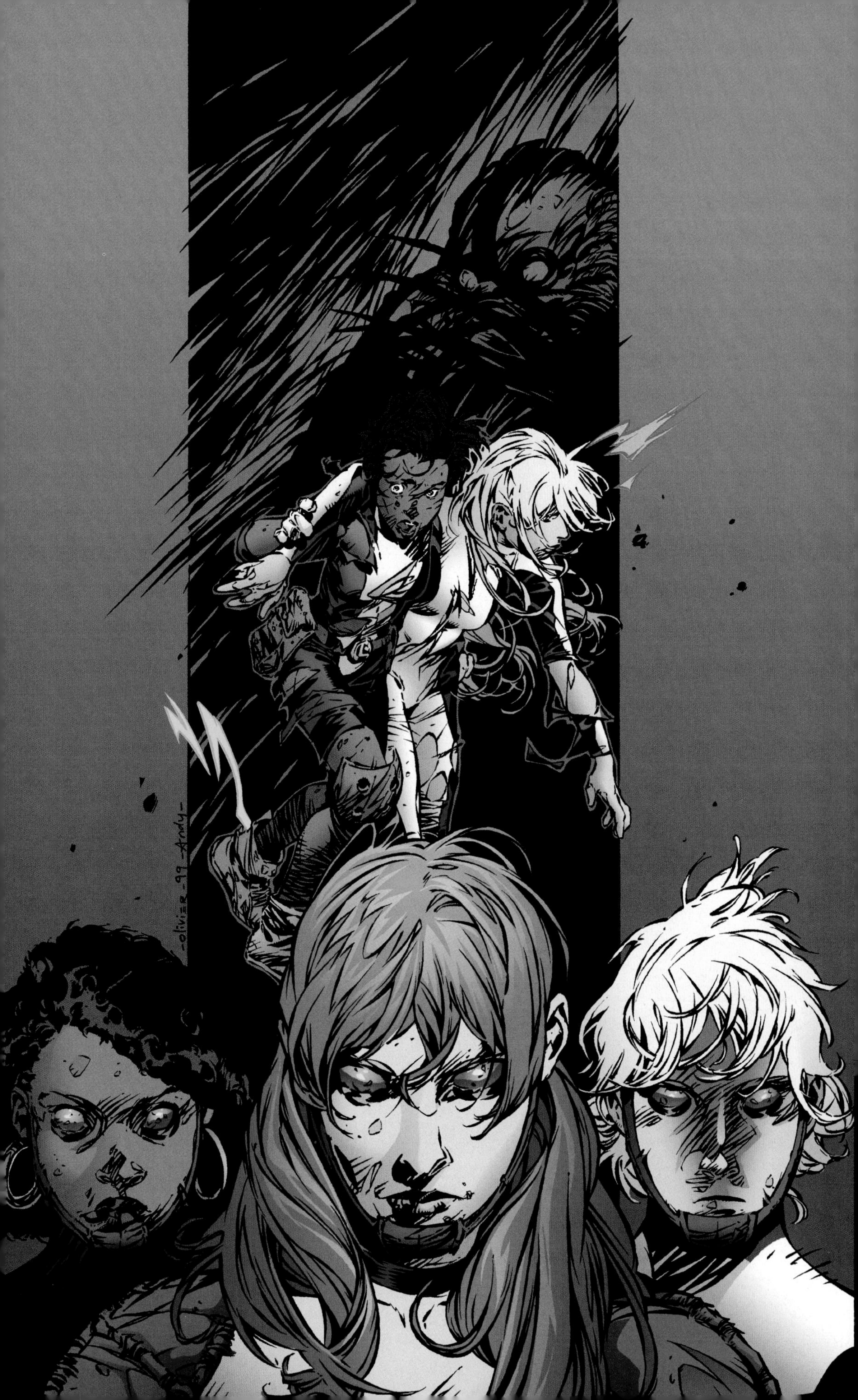

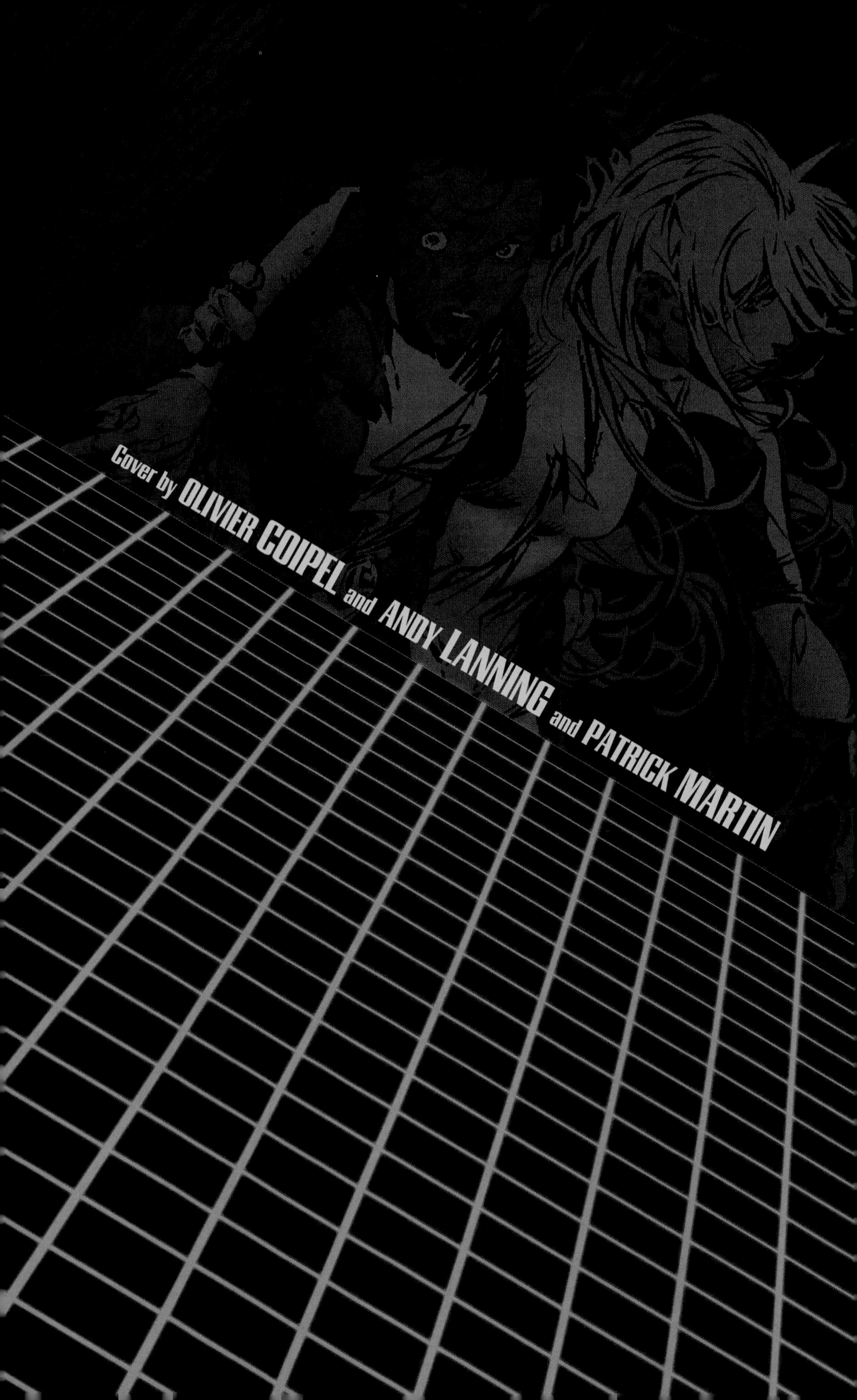
Cover by OLIVIER COIPEL and ANDY LANNING and PATRICK MARTIN

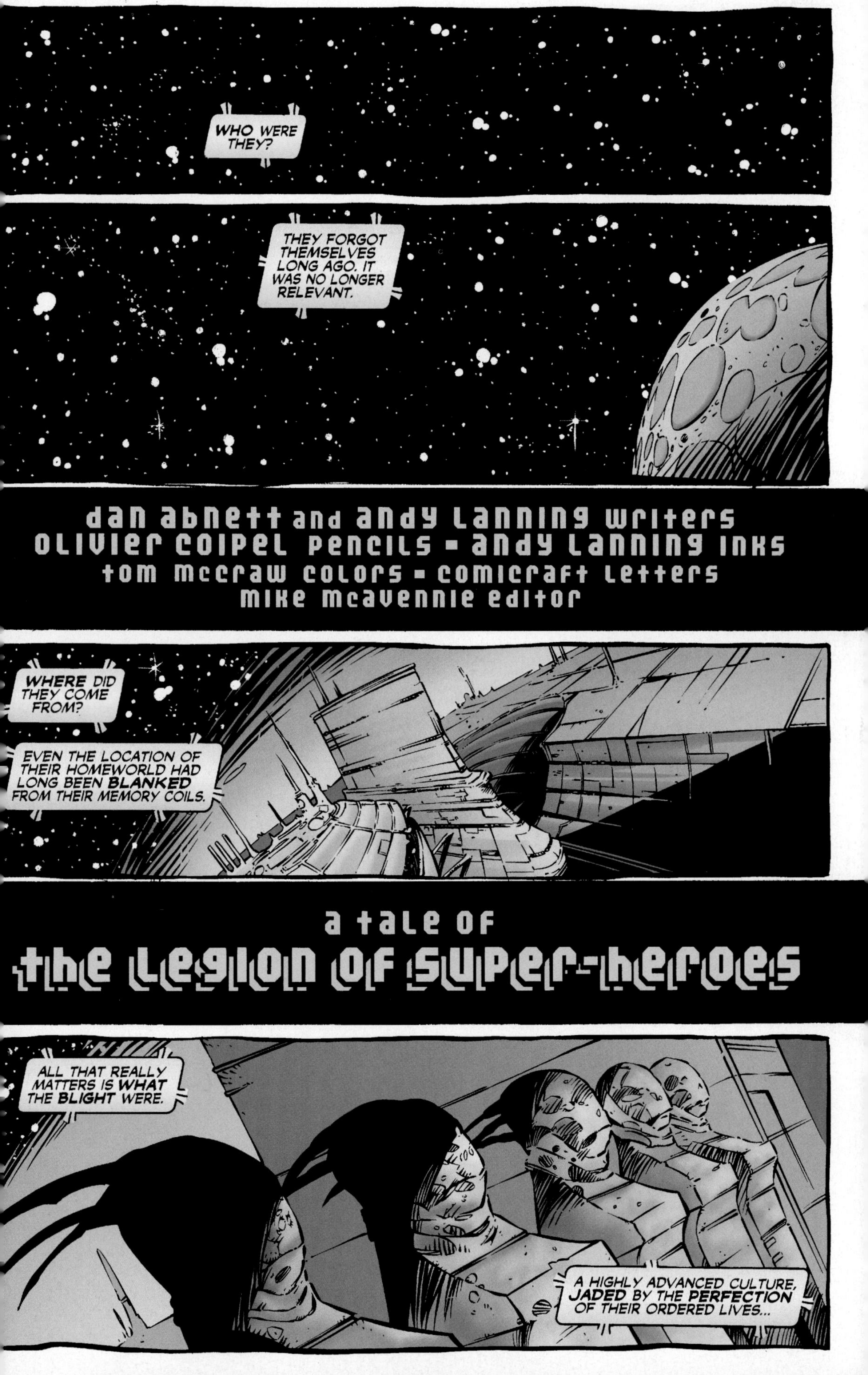
WHO WERE THEY?
THEY FORGOT THEMSELVES LONG AGO. IT WAS NO LONGER RELEVANT.
dan abnett and andy lanning writers
olivier coipel pencils - andy lanning inks
tom mccraw colors - comicraft letters
mike mcavennie editor
WHERE DID THEY COME FROM?
EVEN THE LOCATION OF THEIR HOMEWORLD HAD LONG BEEN BLANKED FROM THEIR MEMORY COILS.
a tale of
the legion of super-heroes
ALL THAT REALLY MATTERS IS WHAT THE BLIGHT WERE.
A HIGHLY ADVANCED CULTURE, JADED BY THE PERFECTION OF THEIR ORDERED LIVES...

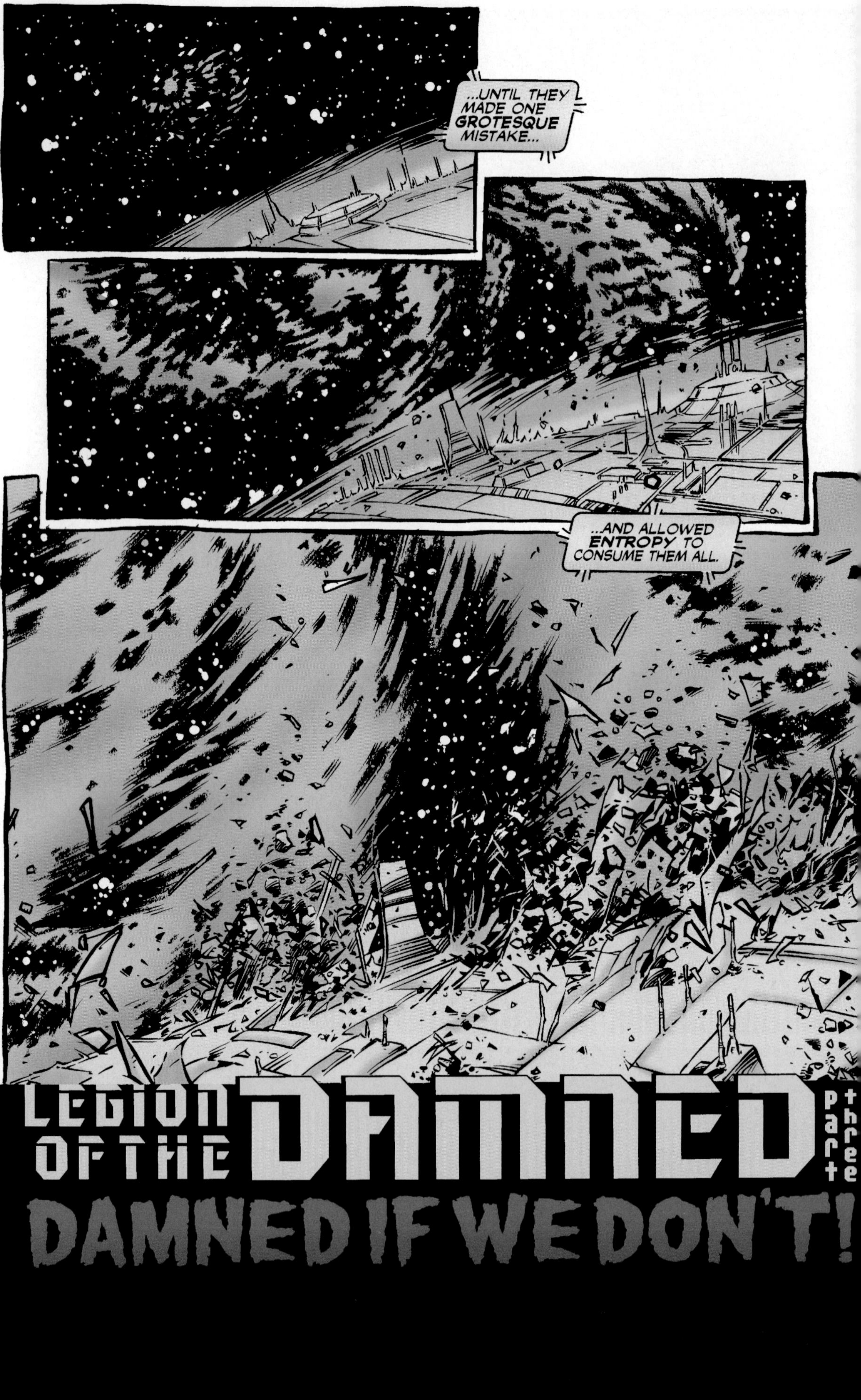
...UNTIL THEY MADE ONE GROTESQUE MISTAKE...
...AND ALLOWED ENTROPY TO CONSUME THEM ALL.
LEGION OF THE DAMNED part three
DAMNED IF WE DON'T!

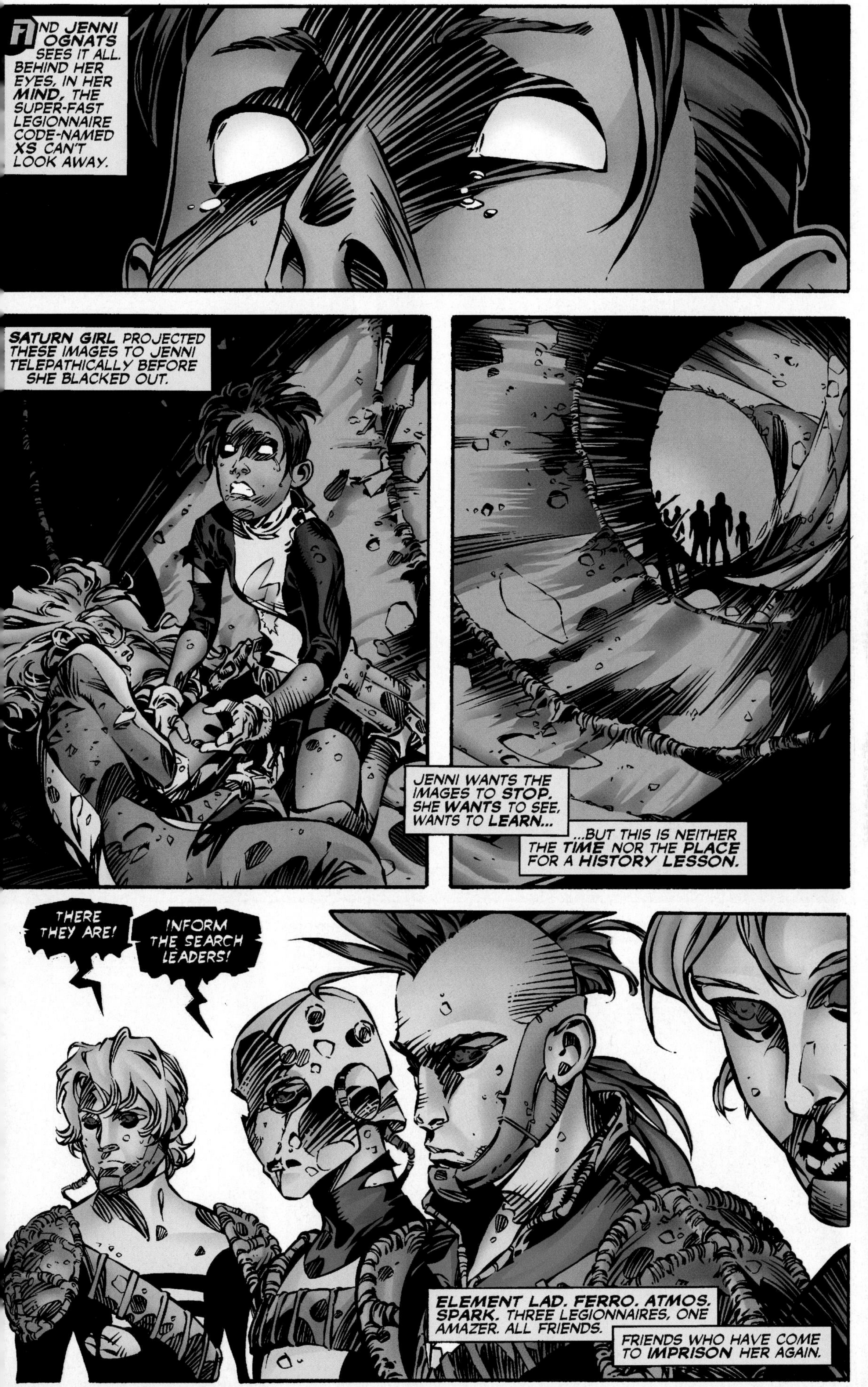
AND JENNI OGNATS SEES IT ALL. BEHIND HER EYES, IN HER MIND, THE SUPER-FAST LEGIONNAIRE CODE-NAMED XS CAN'T LOOK AWAY.
SATURN GIRL PROJECTED THESE IMAGES TO JENNI TELEPATHICALLY BEFORE SHE BLACKED OUT.
JENNI WANTS THE IMAGES TO STOP. SHE WANTS TO SEE, WANTS TO LEARN...
...BUT THIS IS NEITHER THE TIME NOR THE PLACE FOR A HISTORY LESSON.
THERE THEY ARE!
INFORM THE SEARCH LEADERS!
ELEMENT LAD. FERRO. ATMOS. SPARK. THREE LEGIONNAIRES, ONE AMAZER. ALL FRIENDS.
FRIENDS WHO HAVE COME TO IMPRISON HER AGAIN.

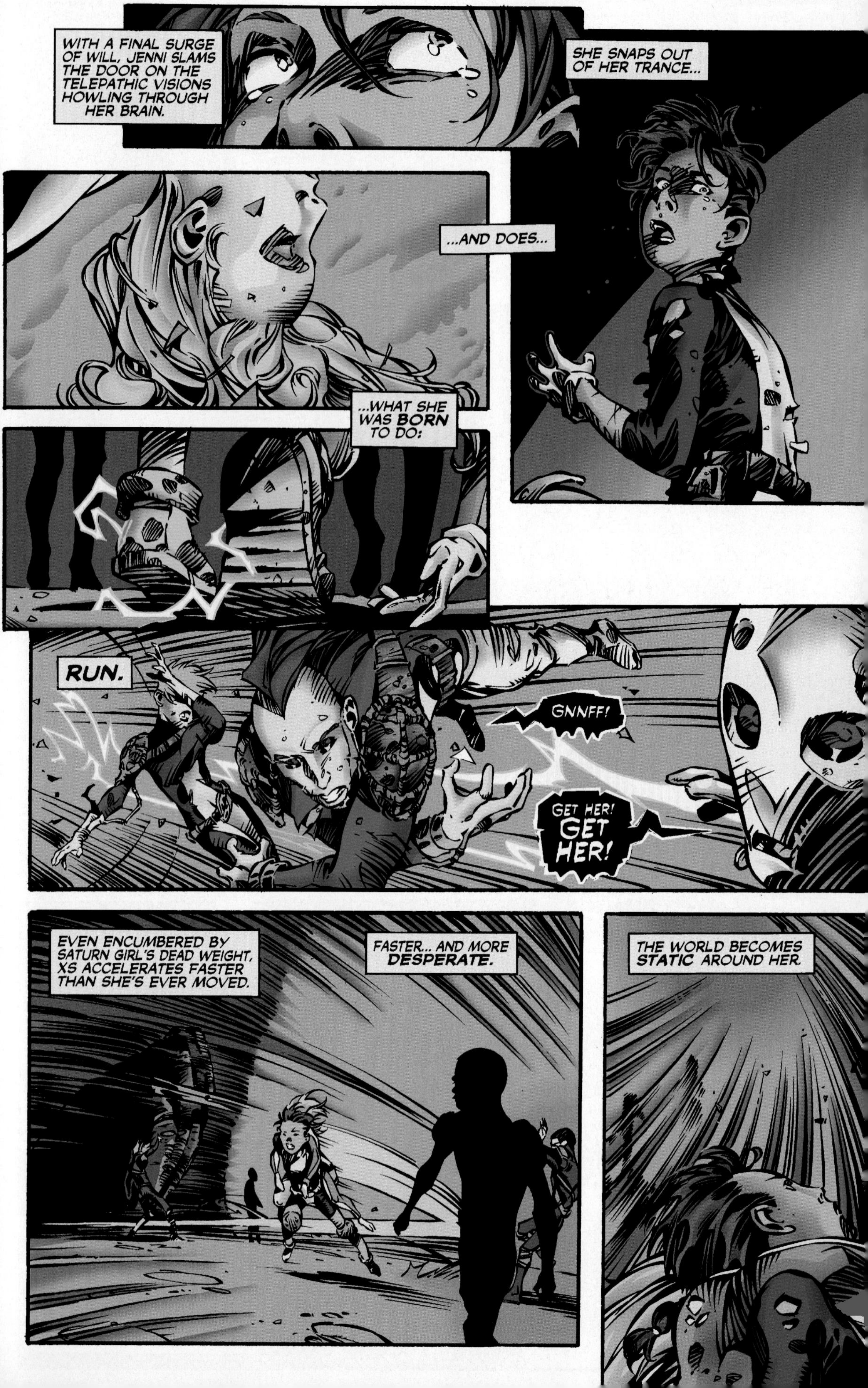
WITH A FINAL SURGE OF WILL, JENNI SLAMS THE DOOR ON THE TELEPATHIC VISIONS HOWLING THROUGH HER BRAIN.
SHE SNAPS OUT OF HER TRANCE...
...AND DOES...
...WHAT SHE WAS BORN TO DO:
RUN.
GNNFF!
GET HER! GET HER!
EVEN ENCUMBERED BY SATURN GIRL'S DEAD WEIGHT, XS ACCELERATES FASTER THAN SHE'S EVER MOVED.
FASTER... AND MORE DESPERATE.
THE WORLD BECOMES STATIC AROUND HER.

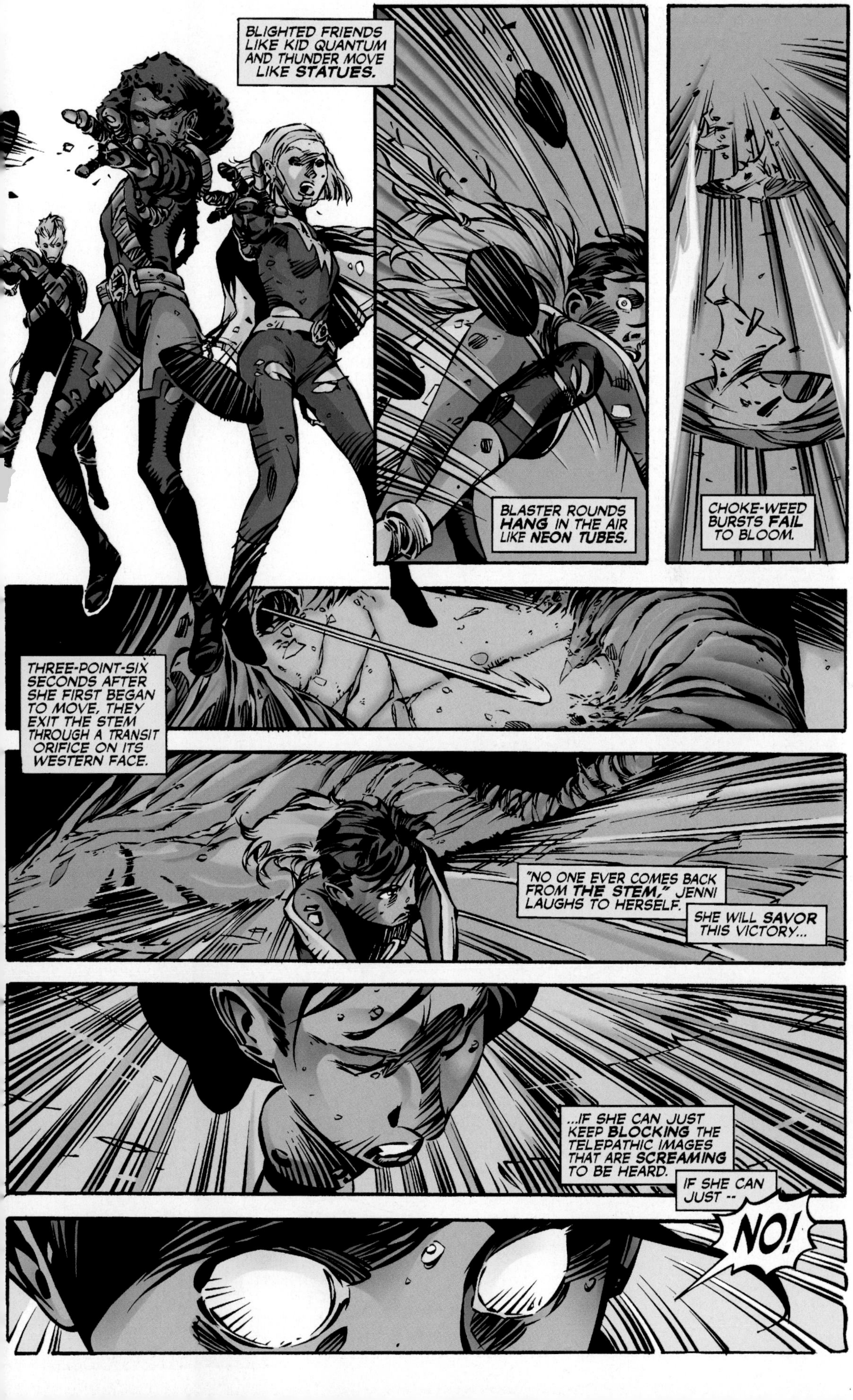
BLIGHTED FRIENDS LIKE KID QUANTUM AND THUNDER MOVE LIKE STATUES.
BLASTER ROUNDS HANG IN THE AIR LIKE NEON TUBES.
CHOKE-WEED BURSTS FAIL TO BLOOM.
THREE-POINT-SIX SECONDS AFTER SHE FIRST BEGAN TO MOVE, THEY EXIT THE STEM THROUGH A TRANSIT ORIFICE ON ITS WESTERN FACE.
"NO ONE EVER COMES BACK FROM THE STEM," JENNI LAUGHS TO HERSELF.
SHE WILL SAVOR THIS VICTORY...
...IF SHE CAN JUST KEEP BLOCKING THE TELEPATHIC IMAGES THAT ARE SCREAMING TO BE HEARD.
IF SHE CAN JUST --
NO!

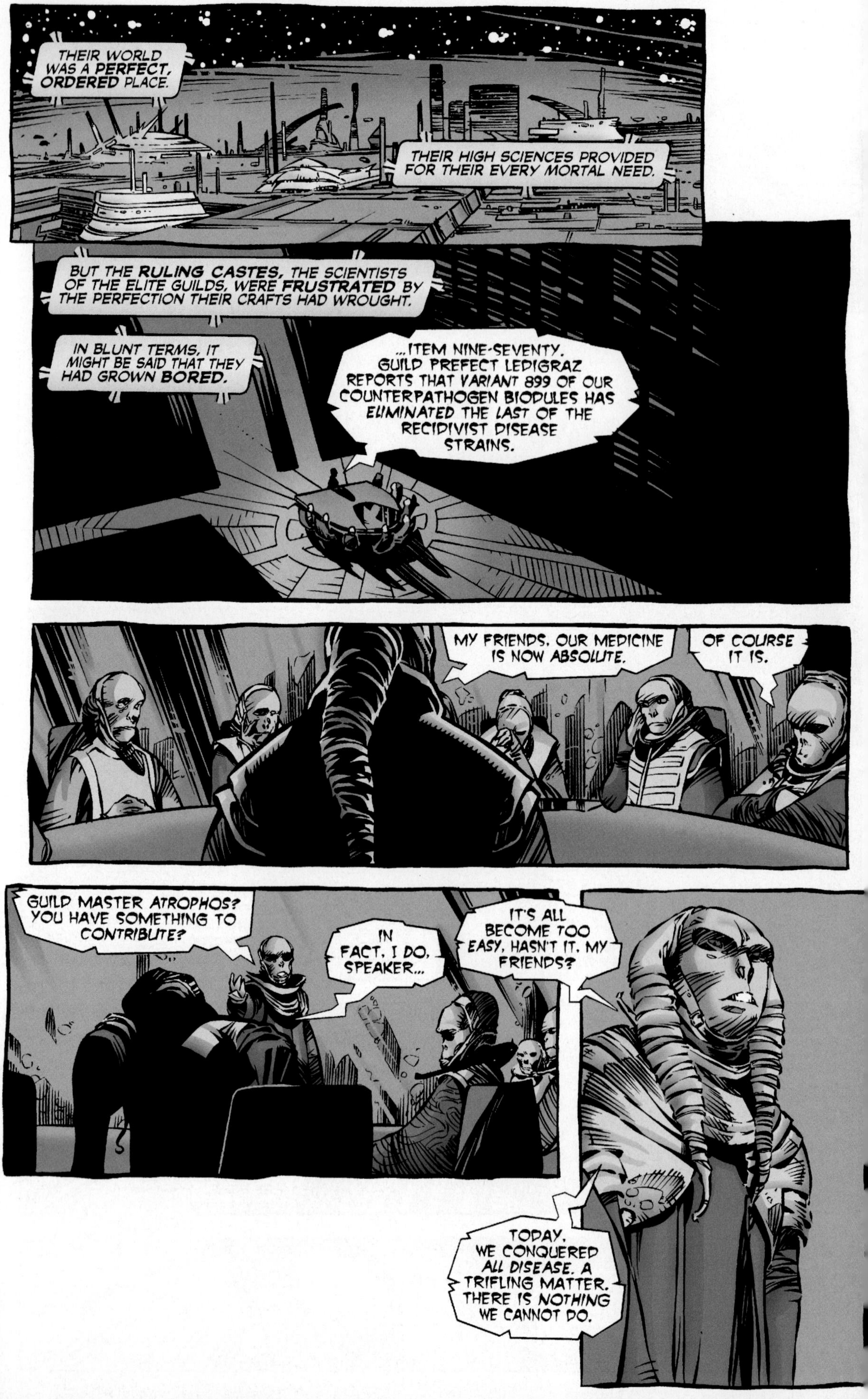
THEIR WORLD WAS A PERFECT, ORDERED PLACE.
THEIR HIGH SCIENCES PROVIDED FOR THEIR EVERY MORTAL NEED.
BUT THE RULING CASTES, THE SCIENTISTS OF THE ELITE GUILDS, WERE FRUSTRATED BY THE PERFECTION THEIR CRAFTS HAD WROUGHT.
IN BLUNT TERMS, IT MIGHT BE SAID THAT THEY HAD GROWN BORED.
...ITEM NINE-SEVENTY. GUILD PREFECT LEDIGRAZ REPORTS THAT VARIANT 899 OF OUR COUNTERPATHOGEN BIODULES HAS ELIMINATED THE LAST OF THE RECIDIVIST DISEASE STRAINS.
MY FRIENDS. OUR MEDICINE IS NOW ABSOLUTE.
OF COURSE IT IS.
GUILD MASTER ATROPHOS? YOU HAVE SOMETHING TO CONTRIBUTE?
IN FACT, I DO, SPEAKER...
IT'S ALL BECOME TOO EASY, HASN'T IT, MY FRIENDS?
TODAY, WE CONQUERED ALL DISEASE. A TRIFLING MATTER. THERE IS NOTHING WE CANNOT DO.

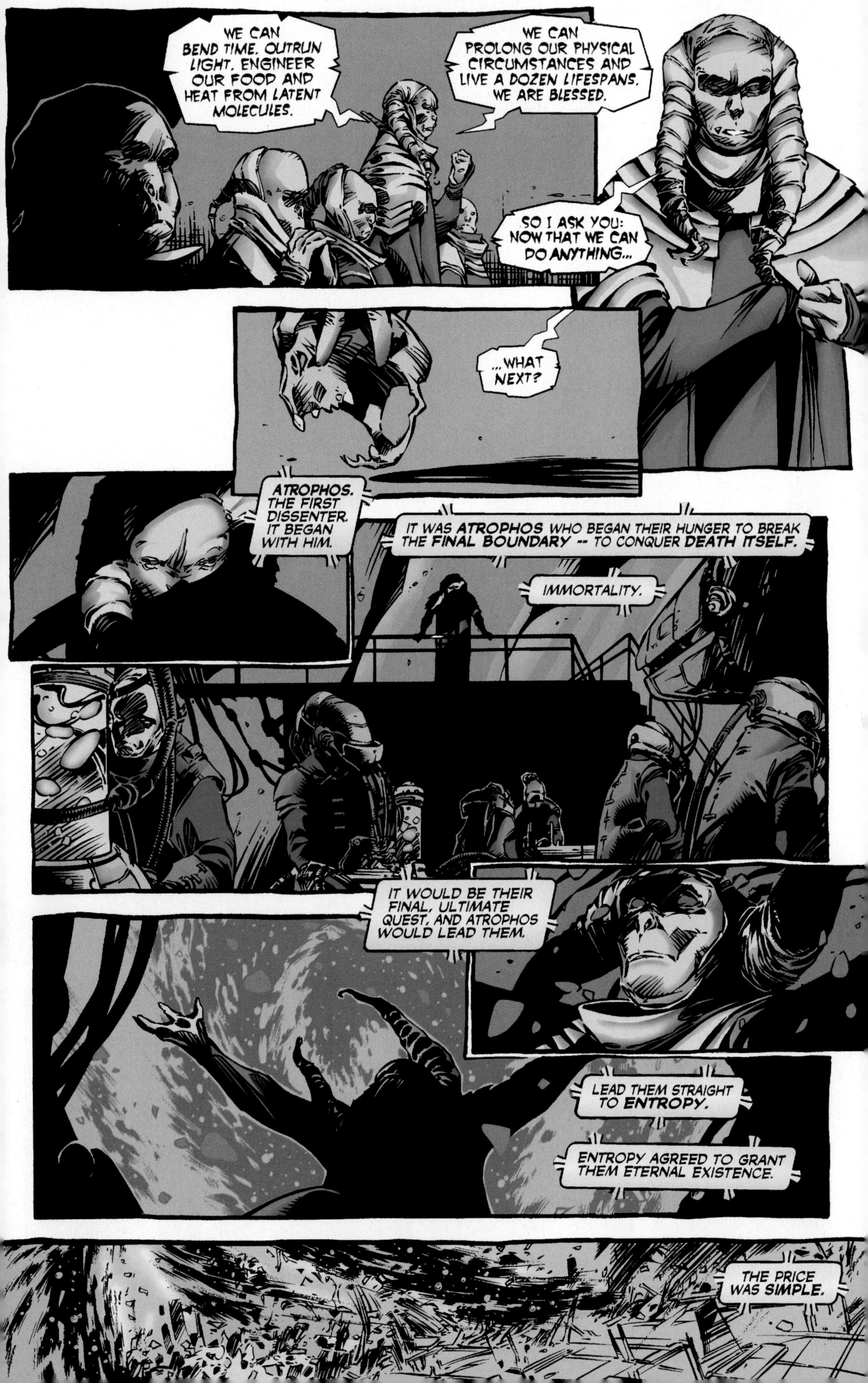
WE CAN BEND TIME. OUTRUN LIGHT. ENGINEER OUR FOOD AND HEAT FROM LATENT MOLECULES.
WE CAN PROLONG OUR PHYSICAL CIRCUMSTANCES AND LIVE A DOZEN LIFESPANS. WE ARE BLESSED.
SO I ASK YOU: NOW THAT WE CAN DO ANYTHING...
...WHAT NEXT?
ATROPHOS. THE FIRST DISSENTER. IT BEGAN WITH HIM.
IT WAS ATROPHOS WHO BEGAN THEIR HUNGER TO BREAK THE FINAL BOUNDARY -- TO CONQUER DEATH ITSELF.
IMMORTALITY.
IT WOULD BE THEIR FINAL, ULTIMATE QUEST, AND ATROPHOS WOULD LEAD THEM.
LEAD THEM STRAIGHT TO ENTROPY.
ENTROPY AGREED TO GRANT THEM ETERNAL EXISTENCE.
THE PRICE WAS SIMPLE.

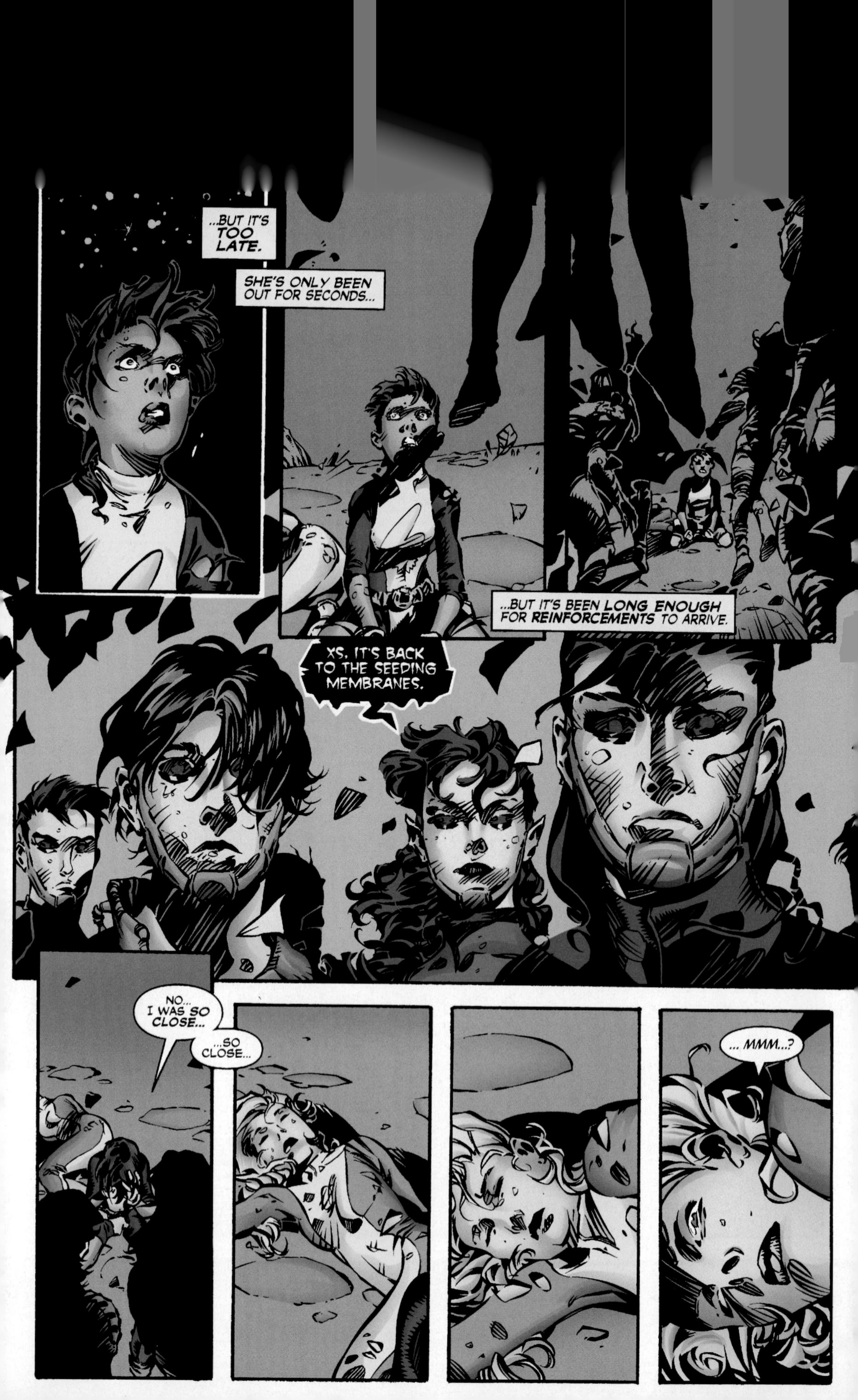
...BUT IT'S TOO LATE.
SHE'S ONLY BEEN OUT FOR SECONDS...
...BUT IT'S BEEN LONG ENOUGH FOR REINFORCEMENTS TO ARRIVE.
XS. IT'S BACK TO THE SEEDING MEMBRANES.
NO... I WAS SO CLOSE...
...SO CLOSE...
... MMM...?

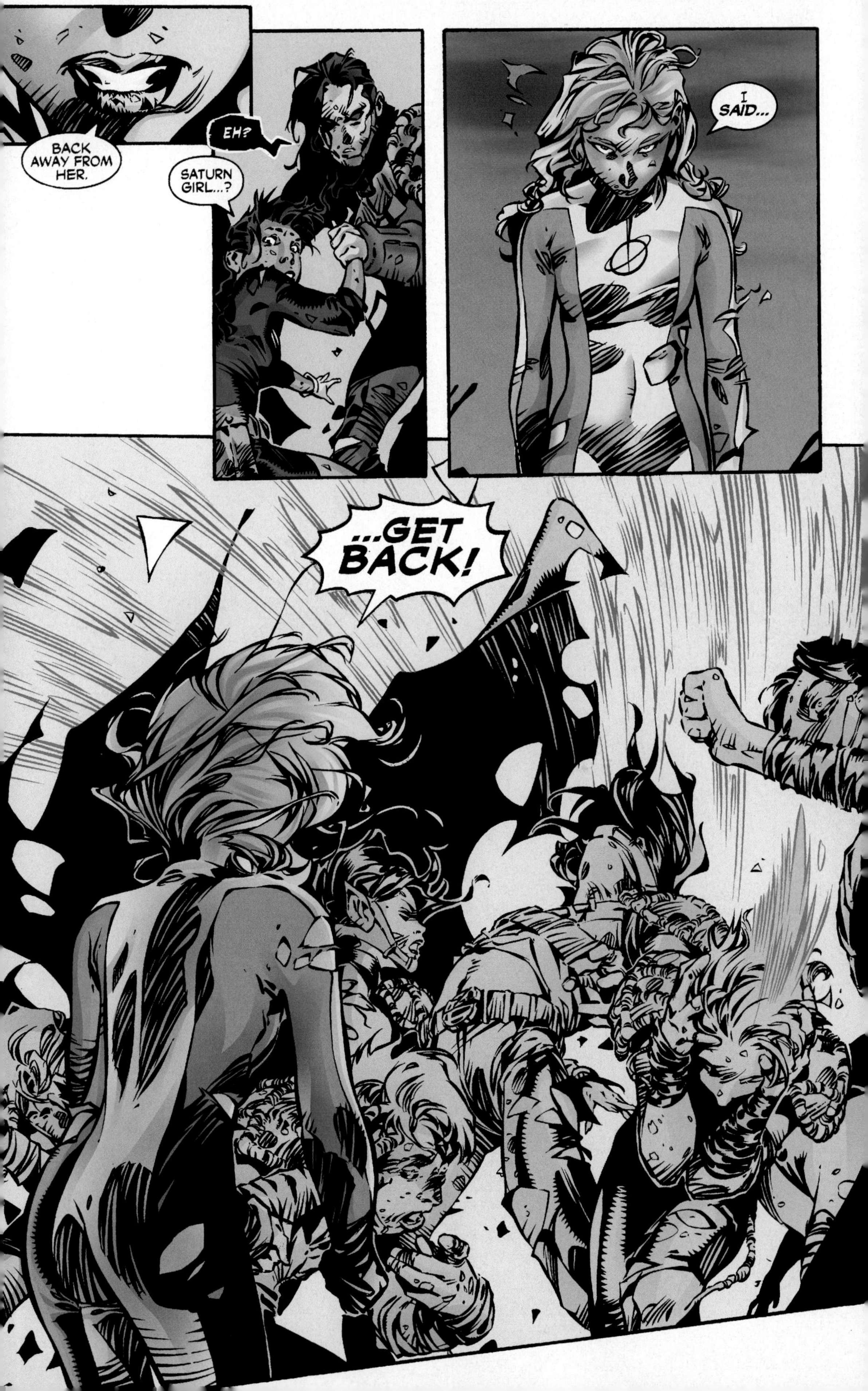
BACK AWAY FROM HER.
EH?
SATURN GIRL...?
I SAID...
...GET BACK!

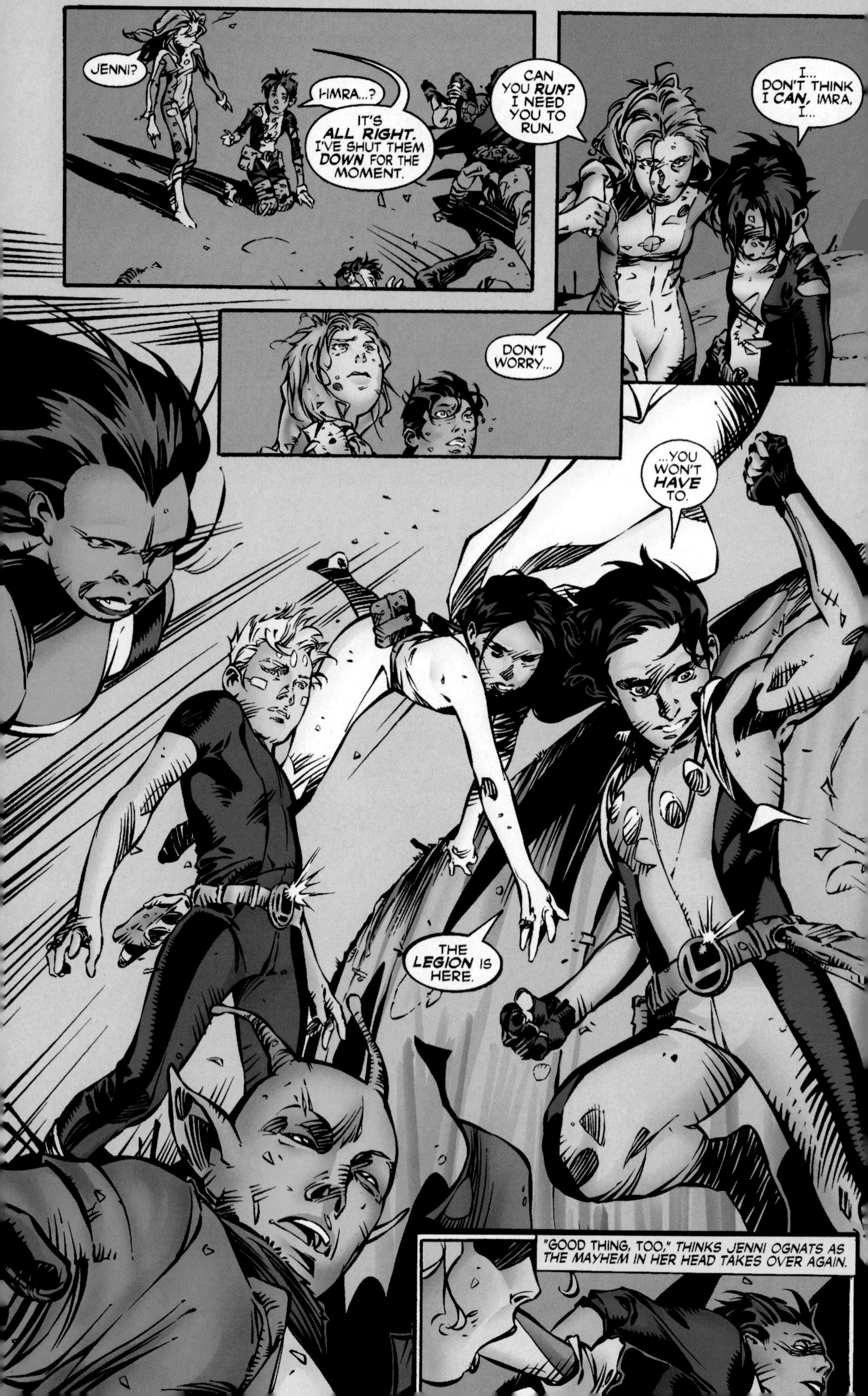
JENNI?
I-IMRA...?
IT'S ALL RIGHT. I'VE SHUT THEM DOWN FOR THE MOMENT.
CAN YOU RUN? I NEED YOU TO RUN.
I... DON'T THINK I CAN, IMRA, I...
DON'T WORRY...
...YOU WON'T HAVE TO.
THE LEGION IS HERE.
"GOOD THING, TOO," THINKS JENNI OGNATS AS THE MAYHEM IN HER HEAD TAKES OVER AGAIN.

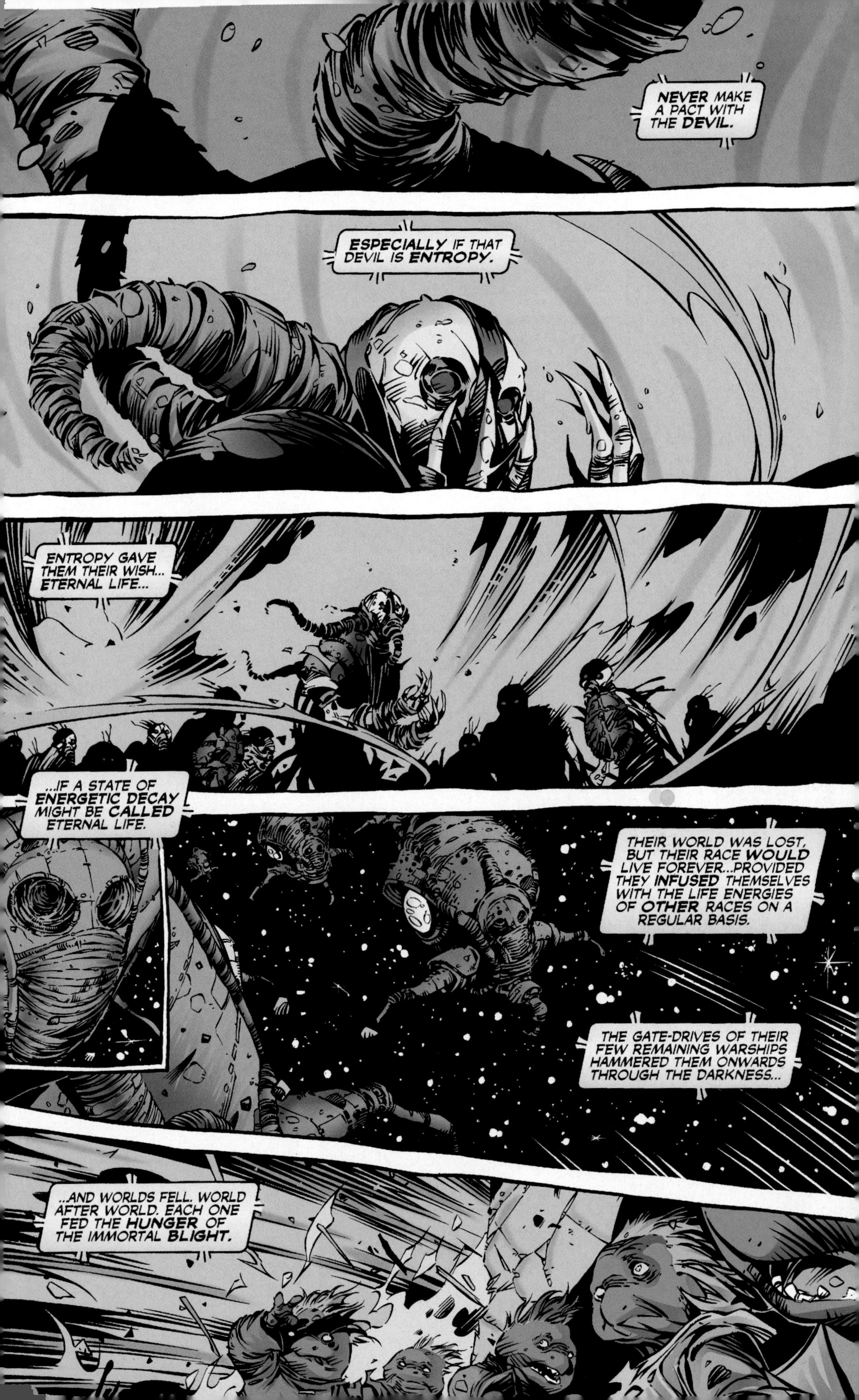
NEVER MAKE A PACT WITH THE DEVIL.
ESPECIALLY IF THAT DEVIL IS ENTROPY.
ENTROPY GAVE THEM THEIR WISH... ETERNAL LIFE...
...IF A STATE OF ENERGETIC DECAY MIGHT BE CALLED ETERNAL LIFE.
THEIR WORLD WAS LOST, BUT THEIR RACE WOULD LIVE FOREVER...PROVIDED THEY INFUSED THEMSELVES WITH THE LIFE ENERGIES OF OTHER RACES ON A REGULAR BASIS.
THE GATE-DRIVES OF THEIR FEW REMAINING WARSHIPS HAMMERED THEM ONWARDS THROUGH THE DARKNESS...
...AND WORLDS FELL. WORLD AFTER WORLD. EACH ONE FED THE HUNGER OF THE IMMORTAL BLIGHT.

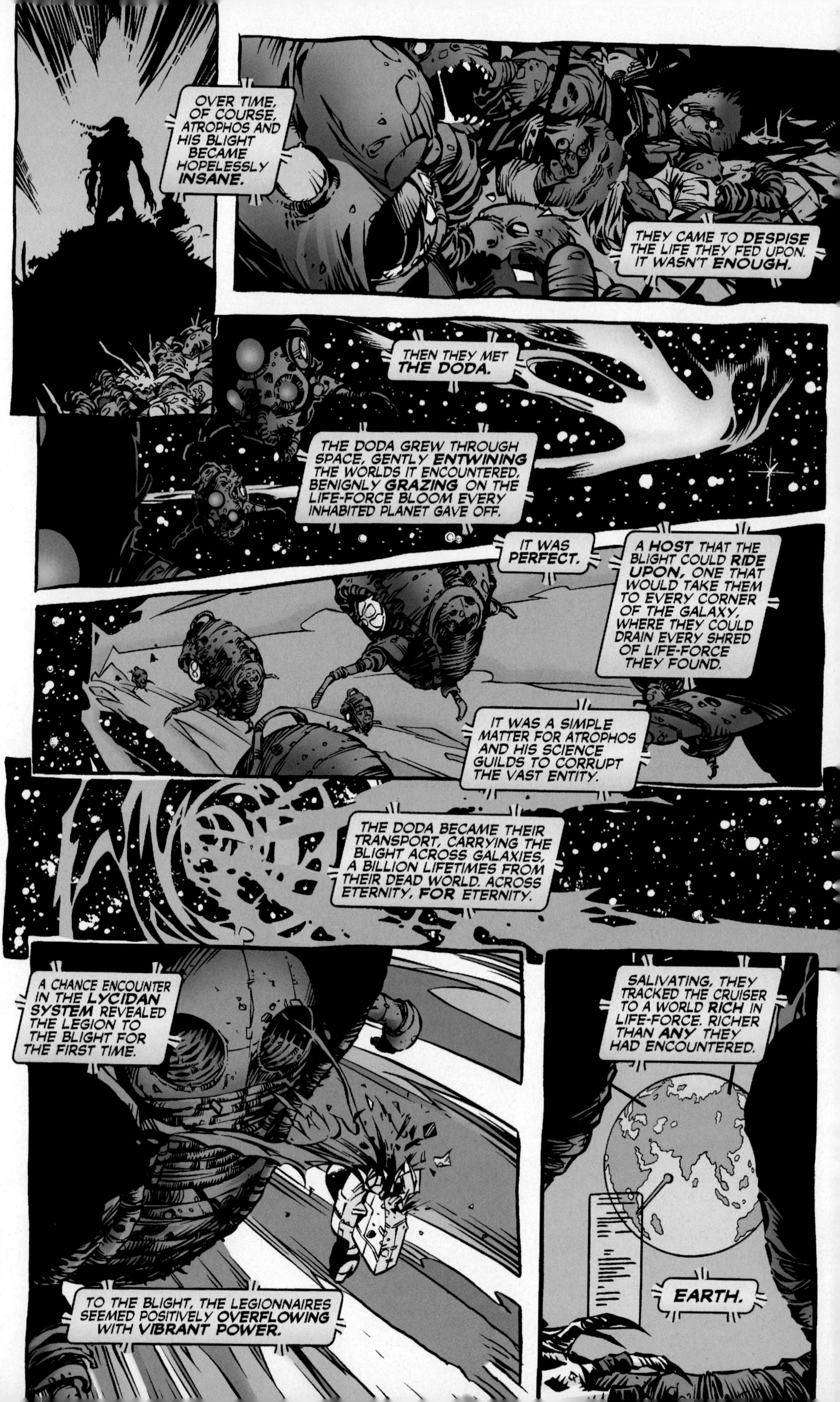
OVER TIME, OF COURSE, ATROPHOS AND HIS BLIGHT BECAME HOPELESSLY INSANE.
THEY CAME TO DESPISE THE LIFE THEY FED UPON. IT WASN'T ENOUGH.
THEN THEY MET THE DODA.
THE DODA GREW THROUGH SPACE, GENTLY ENTWINING THE WORLDS IT ENCOUNTERED, BENIGNLY GRAZING ON THE LIFE-FORCE BLOOM EVERY INHABITED PLANET GAVE OFF.
IT WAS PERFECT.
A HOST THAT THE BLIGHT COULD RIDE UPON, ONE THAT WOULD TAKE THEM TO EVERY CORNER OF THE GALAXY, WHERE THEY COULD DRAIN EVERY SHRED OF LIFE-FORCE THEY FOUND.
IT WAS A SIMPLE MATTER FOR ATROPHOS AND HIS SCIENCE GUILDS TO CORRUPT THE VAST ENTITY.
THE DODA BECAME THEIR TRANSPORT, CARRYING THE BLIGHT ACROSS GALAXIES, A BILLION LIFETIMES FROM THEIR DEAD WORLD. ACROSS ETERNITY. FOR ETERNITY.
A CHANCE ENCOUNTER IN THE LYCIDAN SYSTEM REVEALED THE LEGION TO THE BLIGHT FOR THE FIRST TIME.
TO THE BLIGHT, THE LEGIONNAIRES SEEMED POSITIVELY OVERFLOWING WITH VIBRANT POWER.
SALIVATING, THEY TRACKED THE CRUISER TO A WORLD RICH IN LIFE-FORCE. RICHER THAN ANY THEY HAD ENCOUNTERED.
EARTH.

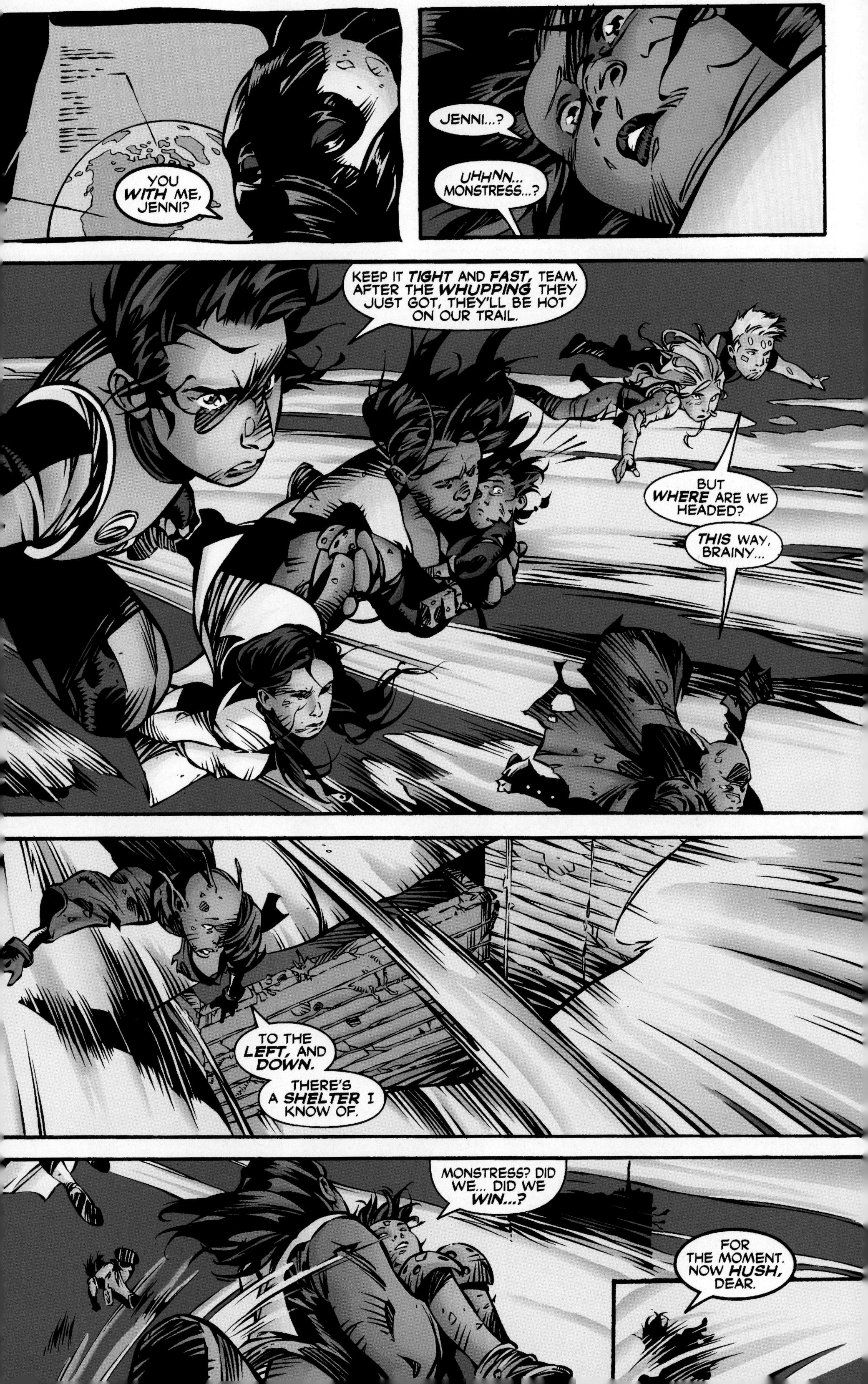

YOU WITH ME, JENNI?
JENNI...?
UHHNN... MONSTRESS...?
KEEP IT TIGHT AND FAST, TEAM. AFTER THE WHUPPING THEY JUST GOT, THEY'LL BE HOT ON OUR TRAIL.
BUT WHERE ARE WE HEADED?
THIS WAY, BRAINY...
TO THE LEFT, AND DOWN.
THERE'S A SHELTER I KNOW OF.
MONSTRESS? DID WE... DID WE WIN...?
FOR THE MOMENT. NOW HUSH, DEAR.

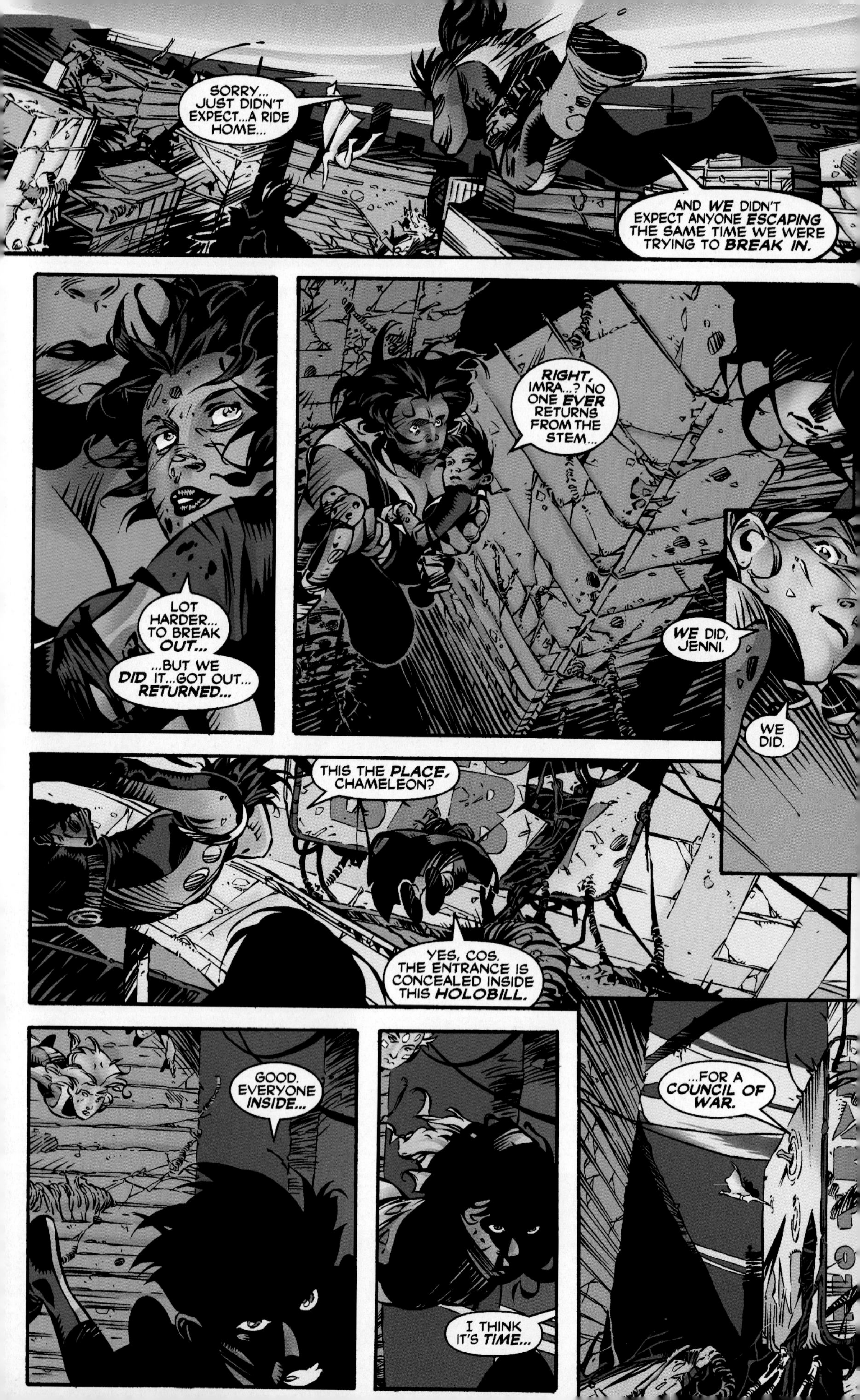
SORRY... JUST DIDN'T EXPECT...A RIDE HOME...
AND WE DIDN'T EXPECT ANYONE ESCAPING THE SAME TIME WE WERE TRYING TO BREAK IN.
LOT HARDER... TO BREAK OUT...
...BUT WE DID IT...GOT OUT... RETURNED...
RIGHT, IMRA...? NO ONE EVER RETURNS FROM THE STEM...
WE DID, JENNI.
WE DID.
THIS THE PLACE, CHAMELEON?
YES, COS. THE ENTRANCE IS CONCEALED INSIDE THIS HOLOBILL.
GOOD. EVERYONE INSIDE...
I THINK IT'S TIME...
...FOR A COUNCIL OF WAR.

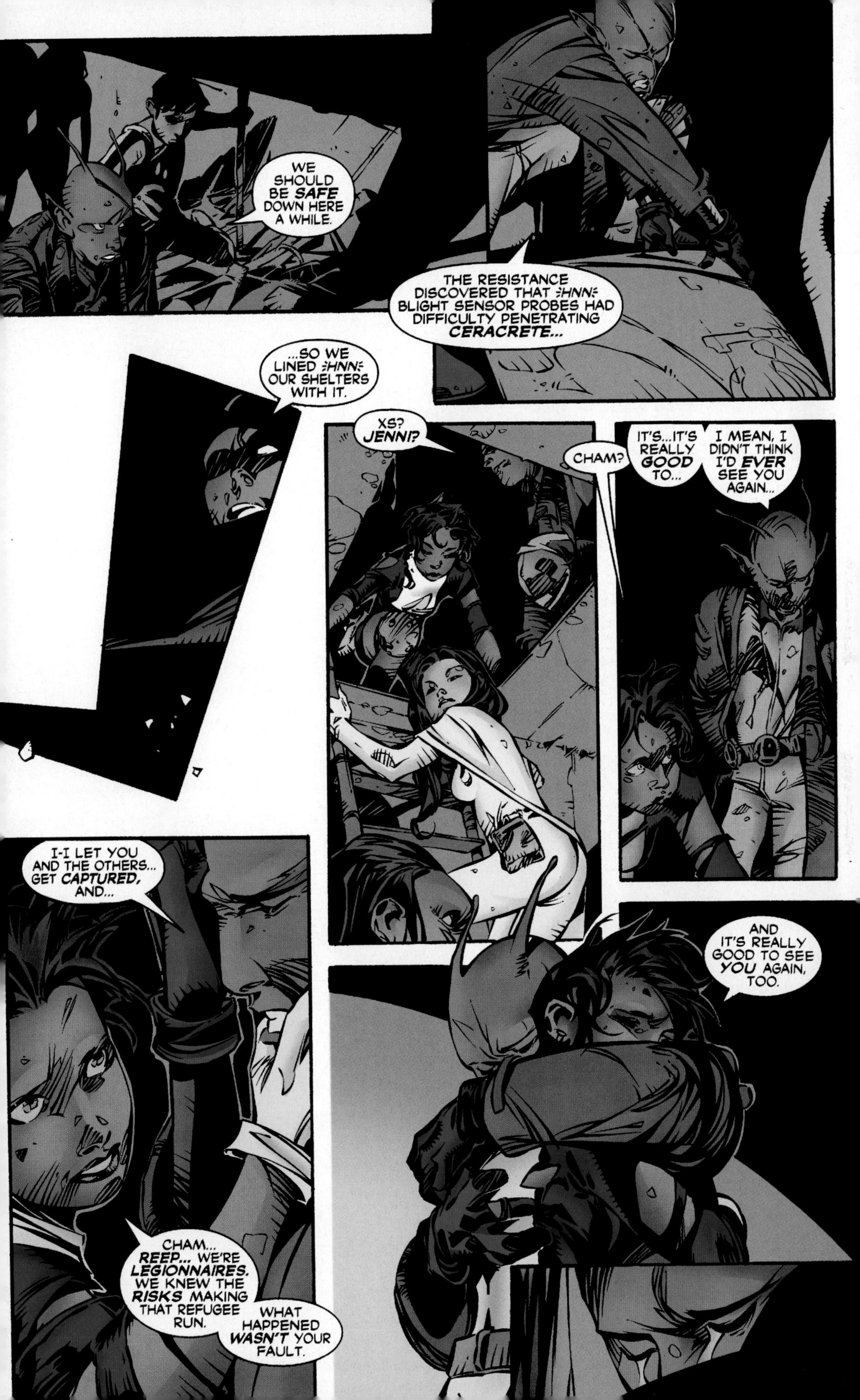
WE SHOULD BE SAFE DOWN HERE A WHILE.
THE RESISTANCE DISCOVERED THAT ≈HNN≈ BLIGHT SENSOR PROBES HAD DIFFICULTY PENETRATING CERACRETE...
...SO WE LINED ≈HNN≈ OUR SHELTERS WITH IT.
XS? JENNI?
CHAM?
IT'S...IT'S REALLY GOOD TO...
I MEAN, I DIDN'T THINK I'D EVER SEE YOU AGAIN...
I-I LET YOU AND THE OTHERS... GET CAPTURED, AND...
CHAM... REEP... WE'RE LEGIONNAIRES. WE KNEW THE RISKS MAKING THAT REFUGEE RUN.
WHAT HAPPENED WASN'T YOUR FAULT.
AND IT'S REALLY GOOD TO SEE YOU AGAIN, TOO.

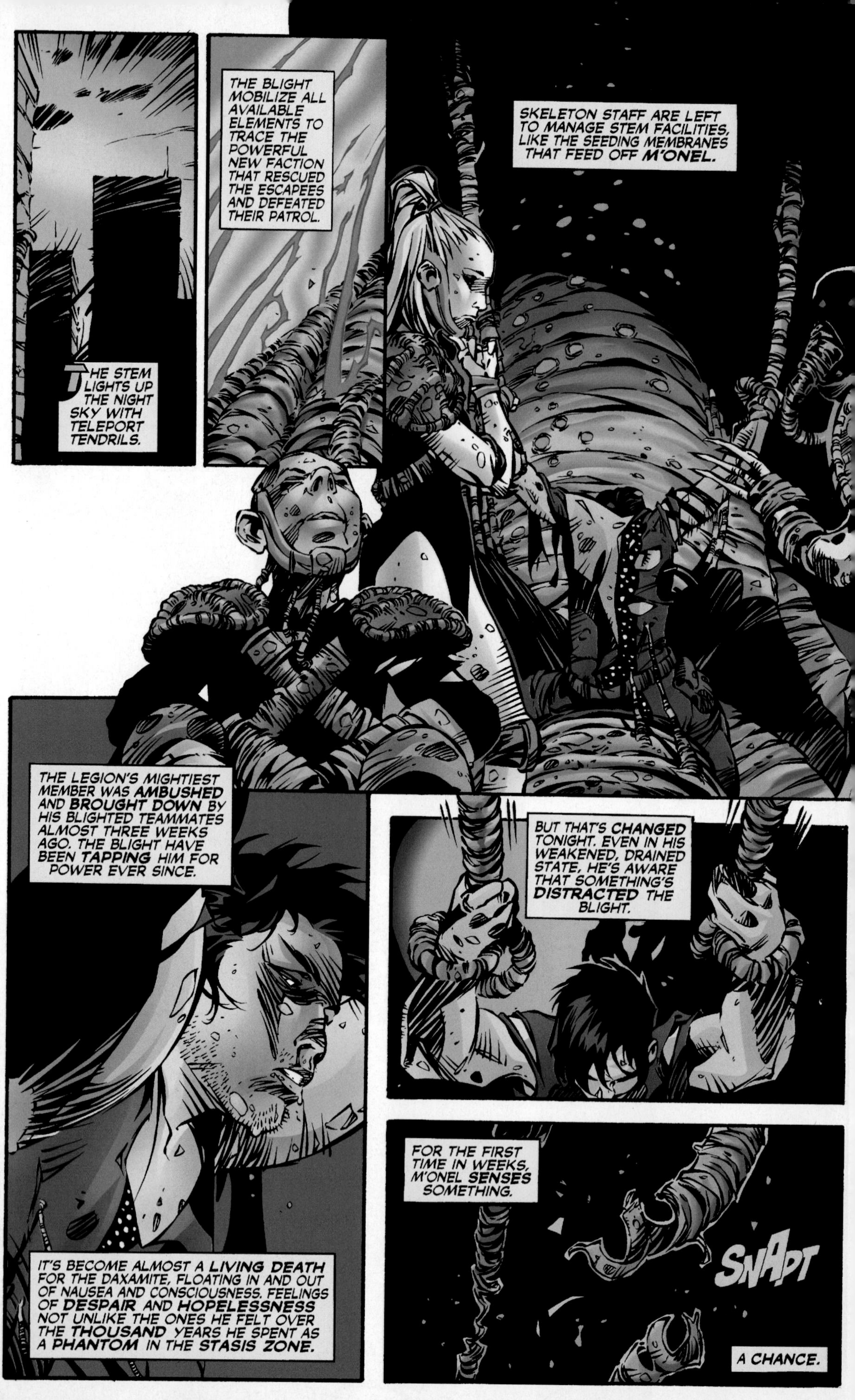
THE STEM LIGHTS UP THE NIGHT SKY WITH TELEPORT TENDRILS.
THE BLIGHT MOBILIZE ALL AVAILABLE ELEMENTS TO TRACE THE POWERFUL NEW FACTION THAT RESCUED THE ESCAPEES AND DEFEATED THEIR PATROL.
SKELETON STAFF ARE LEFT TO MANAGE STEM FACILITIES, LIKE THE SEEDING MEMBRANES THAT FEED OFF M'ONEL.
THE LEGION'S MIGHTIEST MEMBER WAS AMBUSHED AND BROUGHT DOWN BY HIS BLIGHTED TEAMMATES ALMOST THREE WEEKS AGO. THE BLIGHT HAVE BEEN TAPPING HIM FOR POWER EVER SINCE.
IT'S BECOME ALMOST A LIVING DEATH FOR THE DAXAMITE, FLOATING IN AND OUT OF NAUSEA AND CONSCIOUSNESS. FEELINGS OF DESPAIR AND HOPELESSNESS NOT UNLIKE THE ONES HE FELT OVER THE THOUSAND YEARS HE SPENT AS A PHANTOM IN THE STASIS ZONE.
BUT THAT'S CHANGED TONIGHT. EVEN IN HIS WEAKENED, DRAINED STATE, HE'S AWARE THAT SOMETHING'S DISTRACTED THE BLIGHT.
FOR THE FIRST TIME IN WEEKS, M'ONEL SENSES SOMETHING.
SNAPT
A CHANCE.

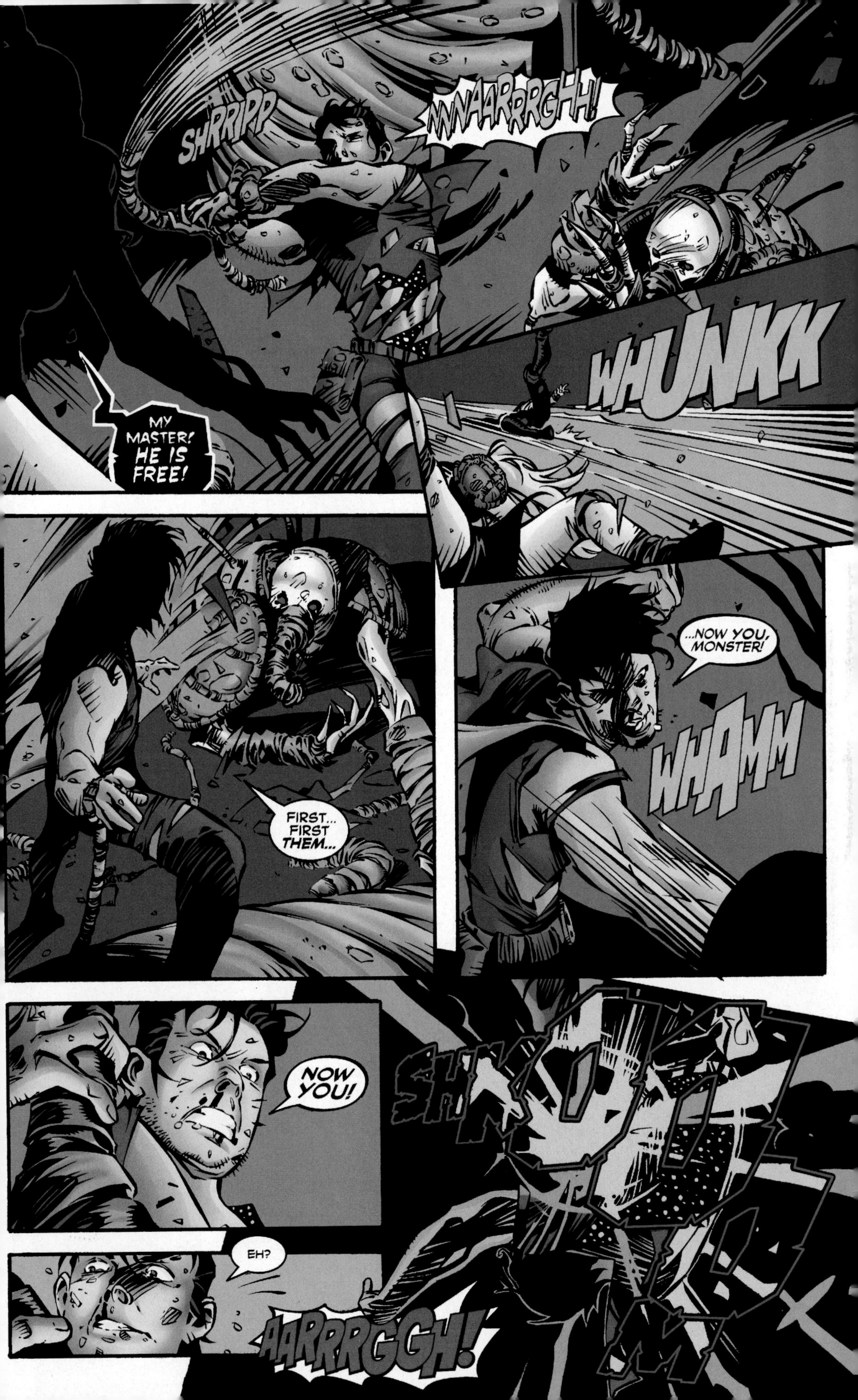
SHRRIPP
NNNAARRRGHH!
WHUNKK
MY MASTER! HE IS FREE!
FIRST... FIRST THEM...
...NOW YOU, MONSTER!
WHAMM
NOW YOU!
EH?
AARRRGGH!

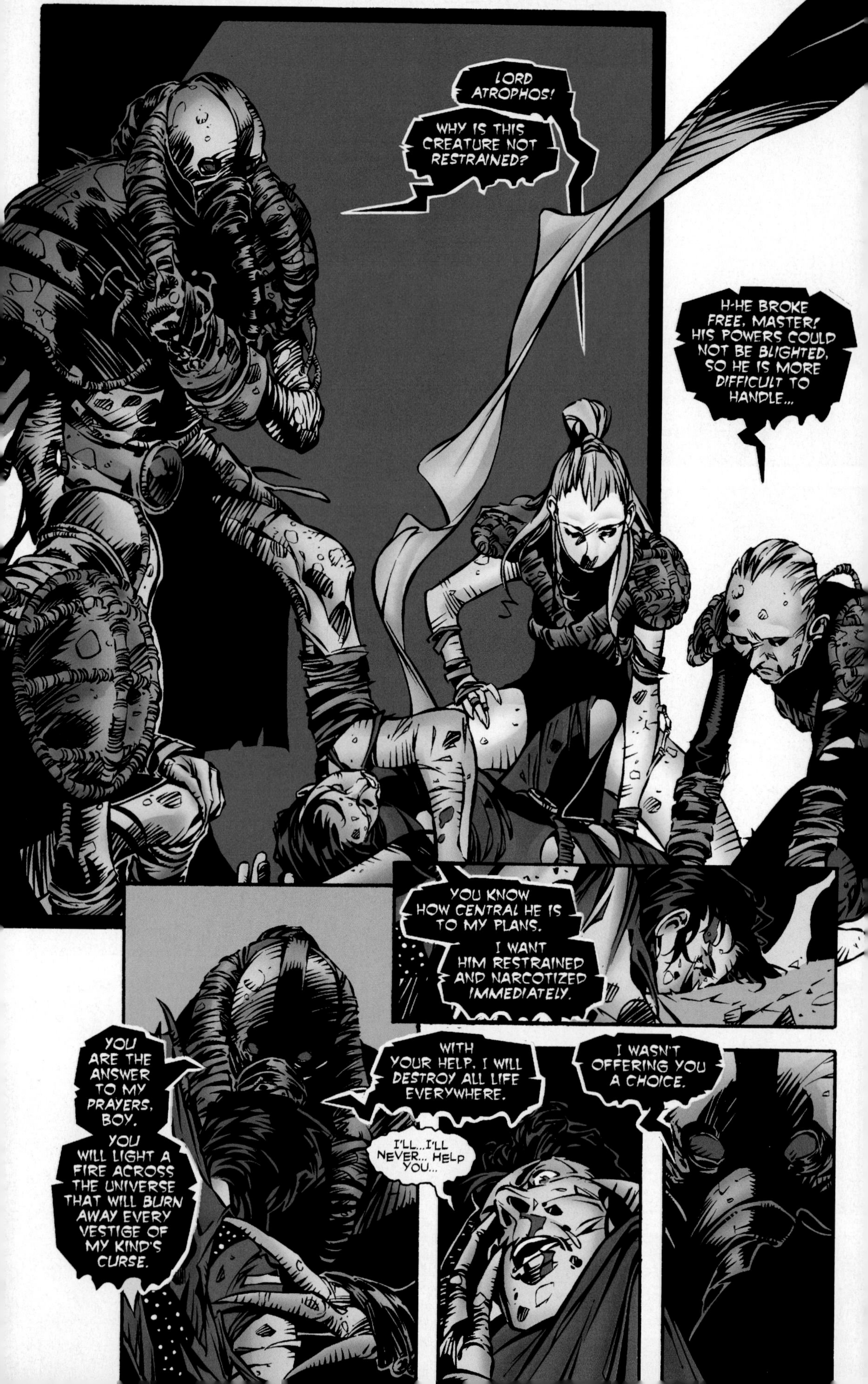
LORD ATROPHOS!
WHY IS THIS CREATURE NOT RESTRAINED?
H-HE BROKE FREE, MASTER! HIS POWERS COULD NOT BE BLIGHTED, SO HE IS MORE DIFFICULT TO HANDLE...
YOU KNOW HOW CENTRAL HE IS TO MY PLANS.
I WANT HIM RESTRAINED AND NARCOTIZED IMMEDIATELY.
YOU ARE THE ANSWER TO MY PRAYERS, BOY.
YOU WILL LIGHT A FIRE ACROSS THE UNIVERSE THAT WILL BURN AWAY EVERY VESTIGE OF MY KIND'S CURSE.
WITH YOUR HELP, I WILL DESTROY ALL LIFE EVERYWHERE.
I'LL...I'LL NEVER... HELP YOU...
I WASN'T OFFERING YOU A CHOICE.

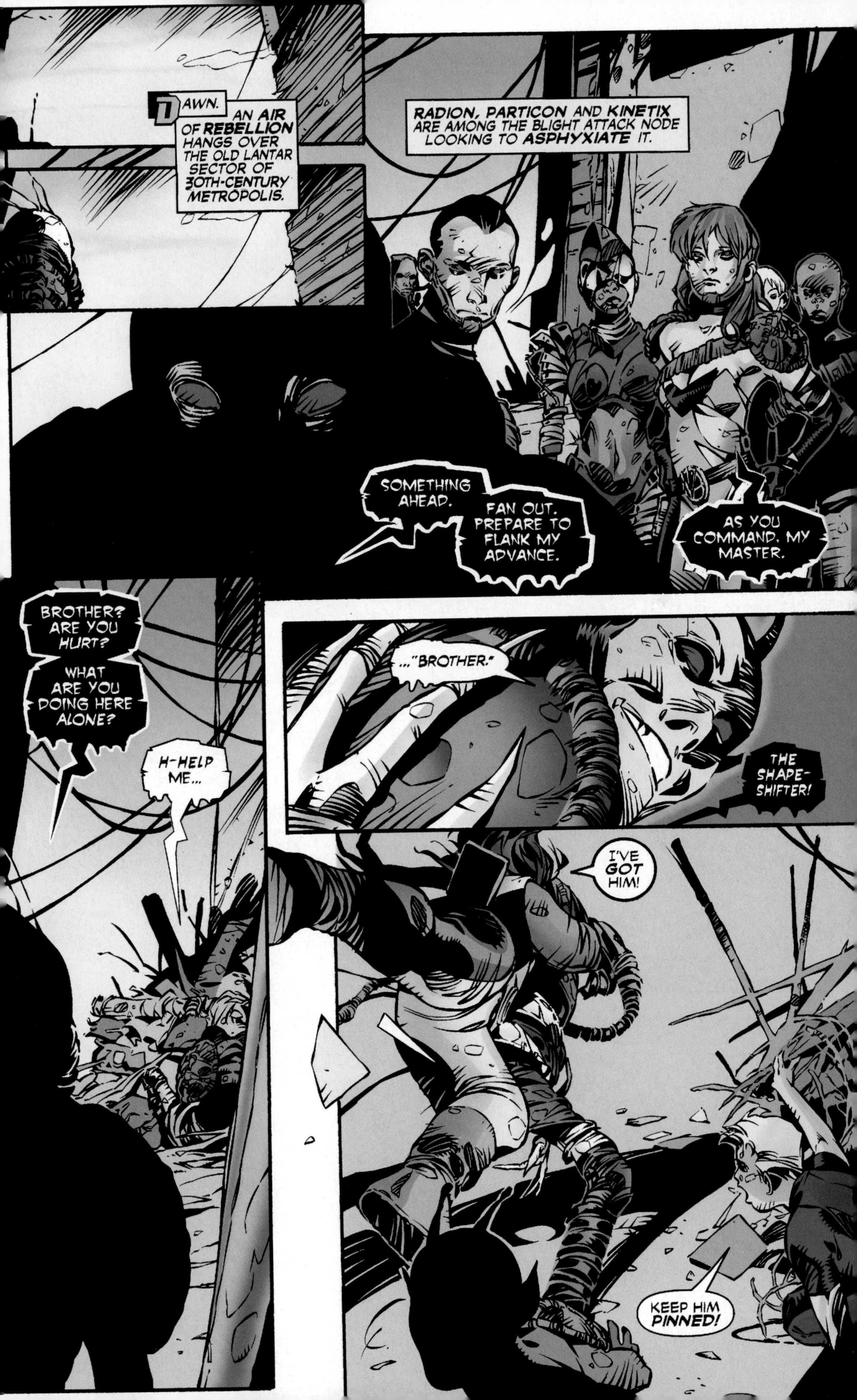
DAWN.
AN AIR OF REBELLION HANGS OVER THE OLD LANTAR SECTOR OF 30TH-CENTURY METROPOLIS.
RADION, PARTICON AND KINETIX ARE AMONG THE BLIGHT ATTACK NODE LOOKING TO ASPHYXIATE IT.
SOMETHING AHEAD.
FAN OUT. PREPARE TO FLANK MY ADVANCE.
AS YOU COMMAND, MY MASTER.
BROTHER? ARE YOU HURT?
WHAT ARE YOU DOING HERE ALONE?
H-HELP ME...
..."BROTHER."
THE SHAPE-SHIFTER!
I'VE GOT HIM!
KEEP HIM PINNED!

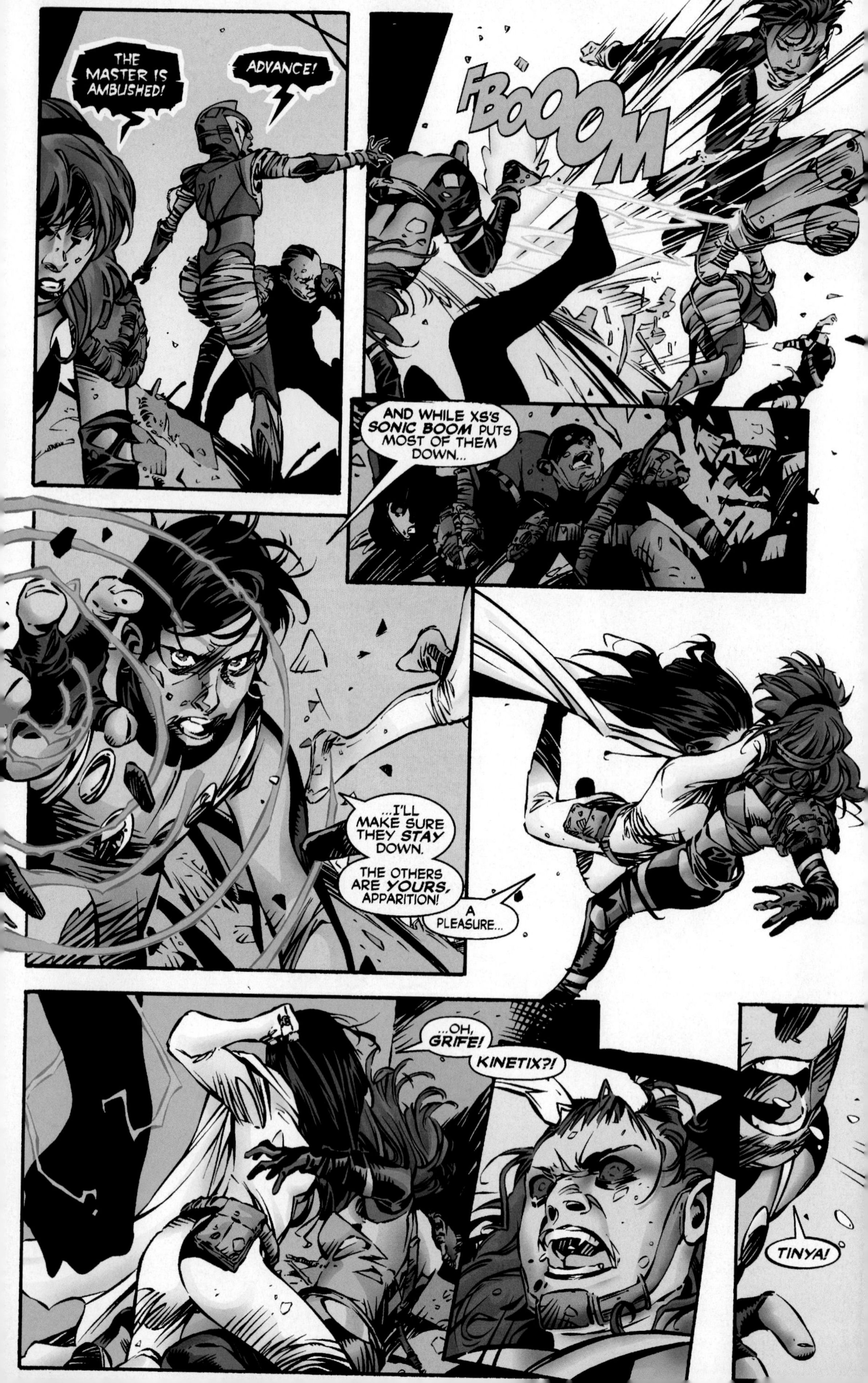

THE MASTER IS AMBUSHED!
ADVANCE!
FBOOOOM
AND WHILE XS'S SONIC BOOM PUTS MOST OF THEM DOWN...
...I'LL MAKE SURE THEY STAY DOWN.
THE OTHERS ARE YOURS, APPARITION!
A PLEASURE...
...OH, GRIFE!
KINETIX?!
TINYA!

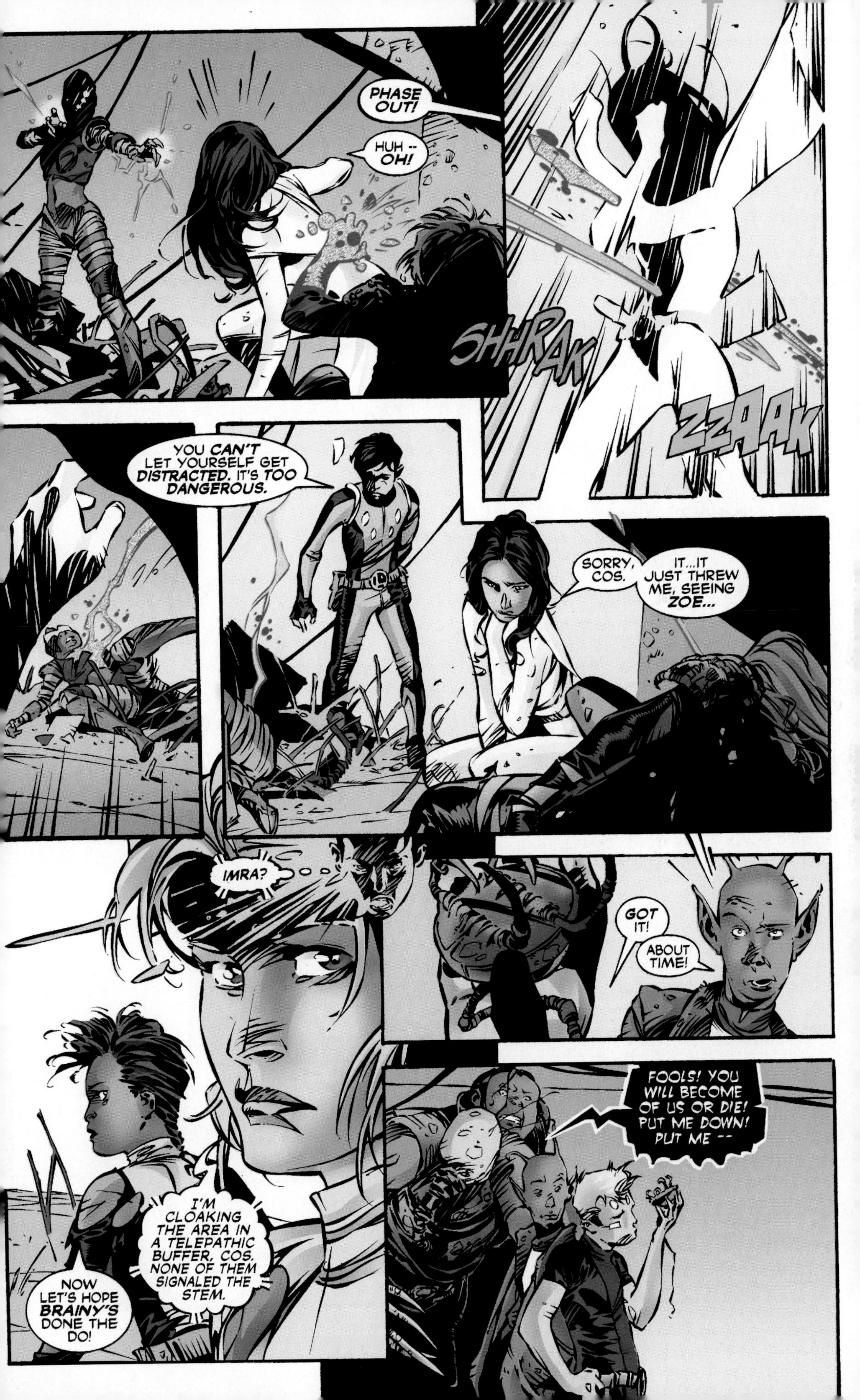
PHASE OUT!
HUH -- OH!
SHHRAK
ZZAAK
YOU CAN'T LET YOURSELF GET DISTRACTED. IT'S TOO DANGEROUS.
SORRY, COS.
IT...IT JUST THREW ME, SEEING ZOE...
IMRA?
GOT IT!
ABOUT TIME!
I'M CLOAKING THE AREA IN A TELEPATHIC BUFFER, COS. NONE OF THEM SIGNALED THE STEM.
NOW LET'S HOPE BRAINY'S DONE THE DO!
FOOLS! YOU WILL BECOME OF US OR DIE! PUT ME DOWN! PUT ME --

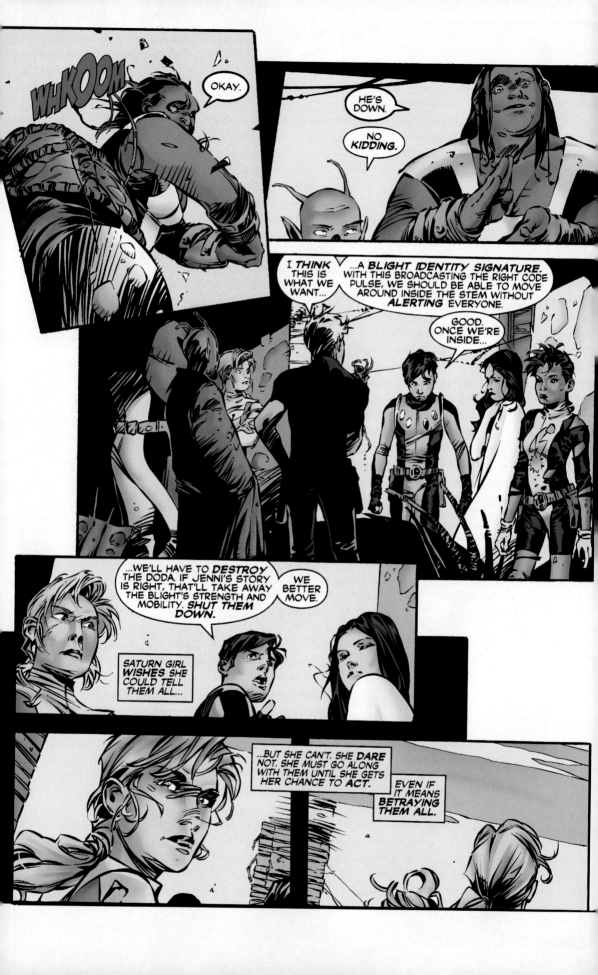

WHKOOM

OKAY.

HE'S DOWN.

NO KIDDING.

I *THINK* THIS IS WHAT WE WANT...

...A *BLIGHT IDENTITY SIGNATURE.* WITH THIS BROADCASTING THE RIGHT CODE PULSE, WE SHOULD BE ABLE TO MOVE AROUND INSIDE THE STEM WITHOUT *ALERTING* EVERYONE.

GOOD. ONCE WE'RE INSIDE...

...WE'LL HAVE TO *DESTROY* THE DODA. IF JENNI'S STORY IS RIGHT, THAT'LL TAKE AWAY THE BLIGHT'S STRENGTH AND MOBILITY. *SHUT THEM DOWN.*

WE BETTER MOVE.

SATURN GIRL *WISHES* SHE COULD TELL THEM ALL...

...BUT SHE CAN'T. SHE *DARE NOT.* SHE MUST GO ALONG WITH THEM UNTIL SHE GETS HER CHANCE TO ACT.

EVEN IF IT MEANS BETRAYING THEM ALL.

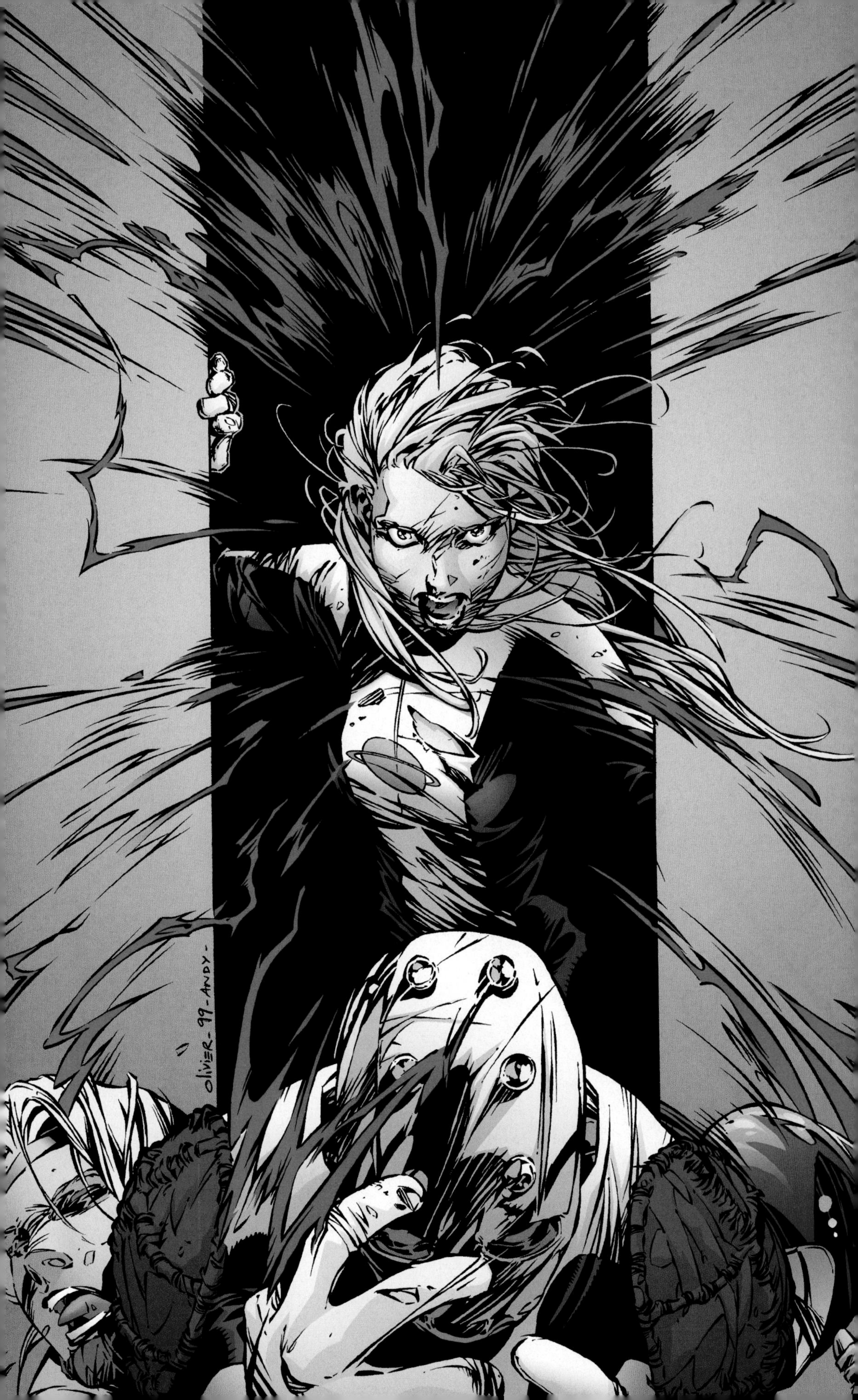
olivier- 99- ANDY-

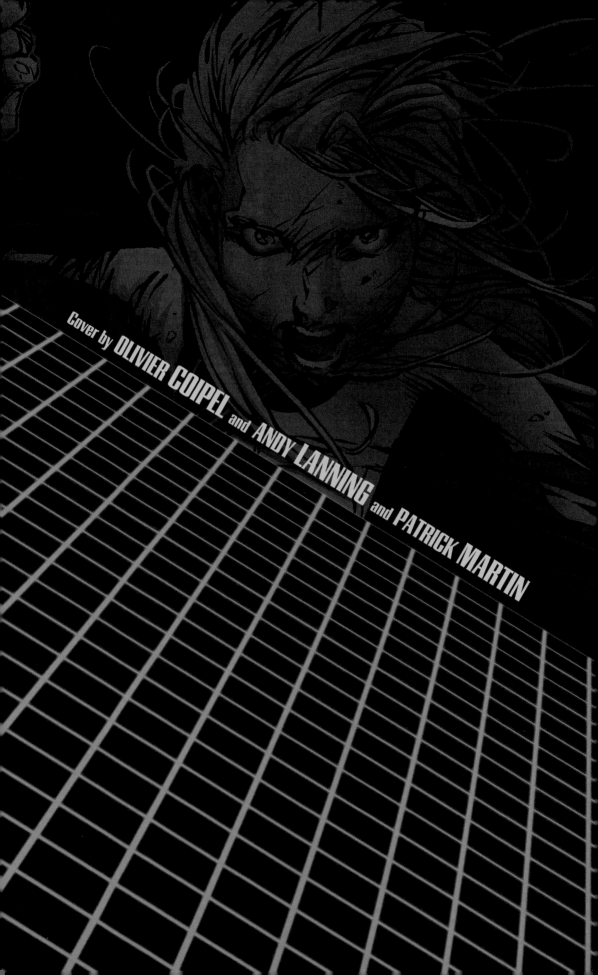

Cover by OLIVIER COIPEL and ANDY LANNING and PATRICK MARTIN

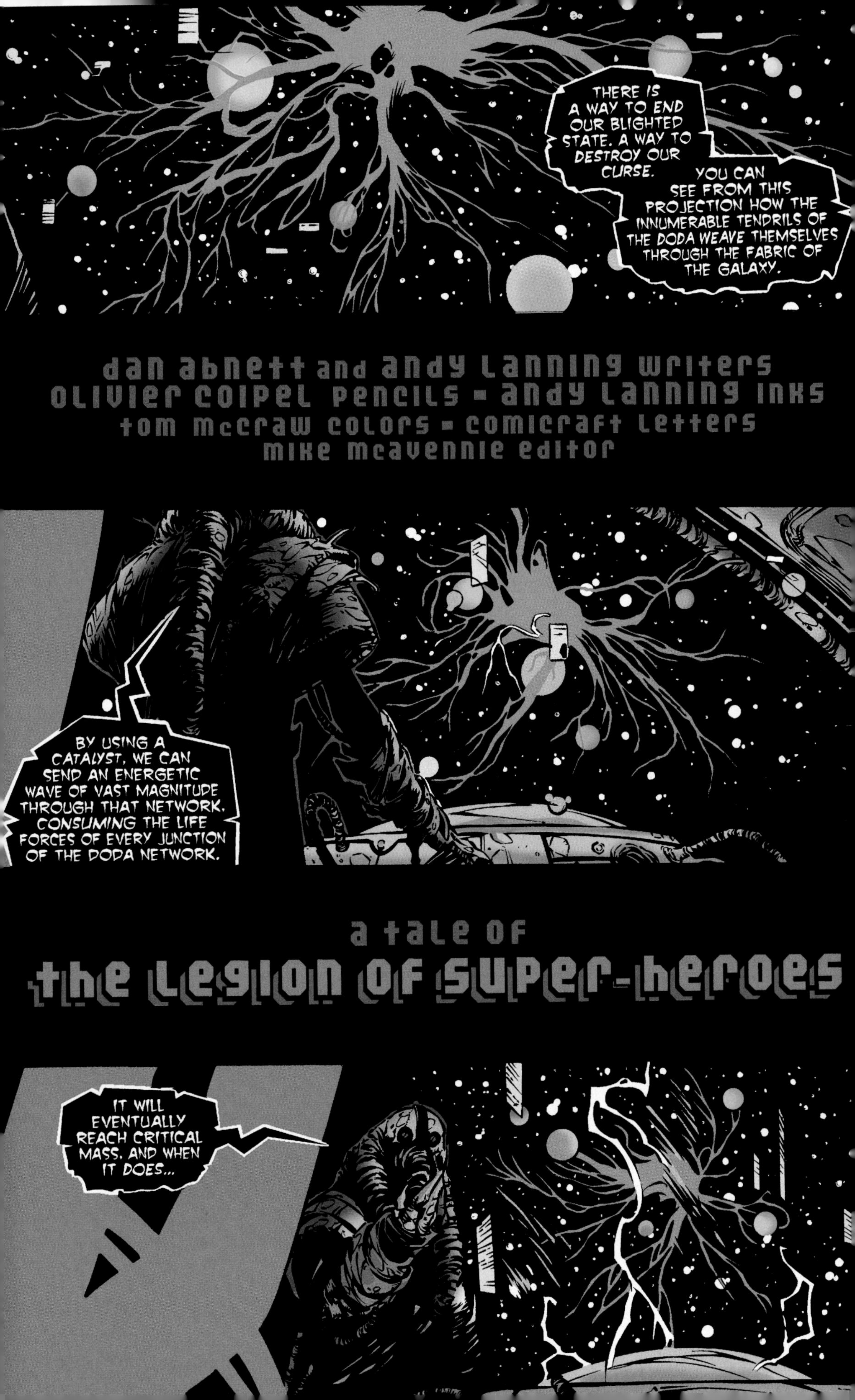
THERE IS A WAY TO END OUR BLIGHTED STATE. A WAY TO DESTROY OUR CURSE.
YOU CAN SEE FROM THIS PROJECTION HOW THE INNUMERABLE TENDRILS OF THE DODA WEAVE THEMSELVES THROUGH THE FABRIC OF THE GALAXY.
dan abnett and andy lanning writers
olivier coipel pencils - andy lanning inks
tom mccraw colors - comicraft letters
mike mcavennie editor
BY USING A CATALYST, WE CAN SEND AN ENERGETIC WAVE OF VAST MAGNITUDE THROUGH THAT NETWORK. CONSUMING THE LIFE FORCES OF EVERY JUNCTION OF THE DODA NETWORK.
a tale of
the legion of super-heroes
IT WILL EVENTUALLY REACH CRITICAL MASS, AND WHEN IT DOES...

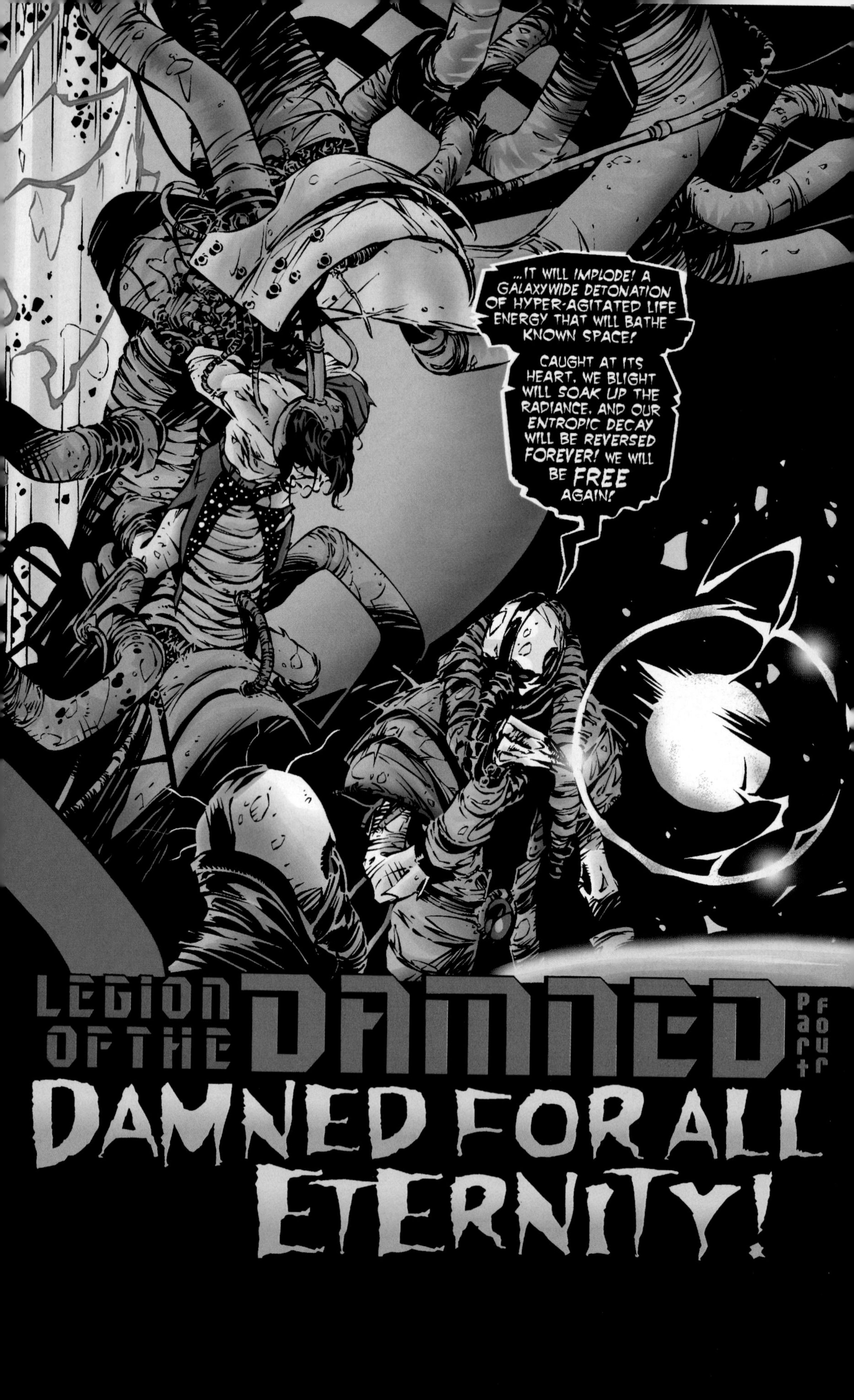

...IT WILL IMPLODE! A GALAXYWIDE DETONATION OF HYPER-AGITATED LIFE ENERGY THAT WILL BATHE KNOWN SPACE!
CAUGHT AT ITS HEART, WE BLIGHT WILL SOAK UP THE RADIANCE, AND OUR ENTROPIC DECAY WILL BE REVERSED FOREVER! WE WILL BE FREE AGAIN!
LEGION OF THE DAMNED part four
DAMNED FOR ALL ETERNITY!

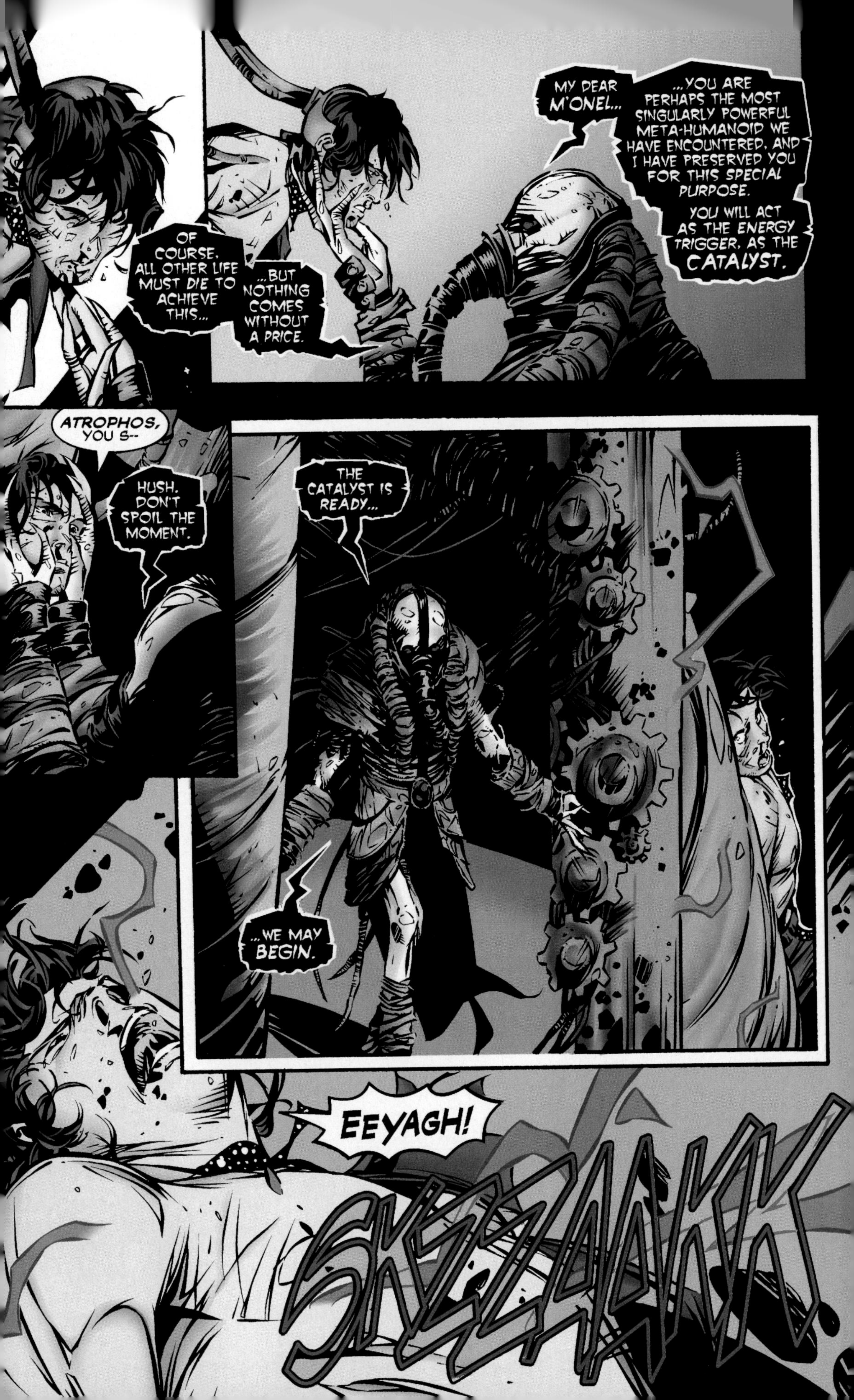
OF COURSE. ALL OTHER LIFE MUST DIE TO ACHIEVE THIS...
...BUT NOTHING COMES WITHOUT A PRICE.
MY DEAR M'ONEL...
...YOU ARE PERHAPS THE MOST SINGULARLY POWERFUL META-HUMANOID WE HAVE ENCOUNTERED, AND I HAVE PRESERVED YOU FOR THIS SPECIAL PURPOSE.
YOU WILL ACT AS THE ENERGY TRIGGER, AS THE CATALYST.
ATROPHOS, YOU S--
HUSH. DON'T SPOIL THE MOMENT.
THE CATALYST IS READY...
...WE MAY BEGIN.
EEYAGH!
SKZZAAKK

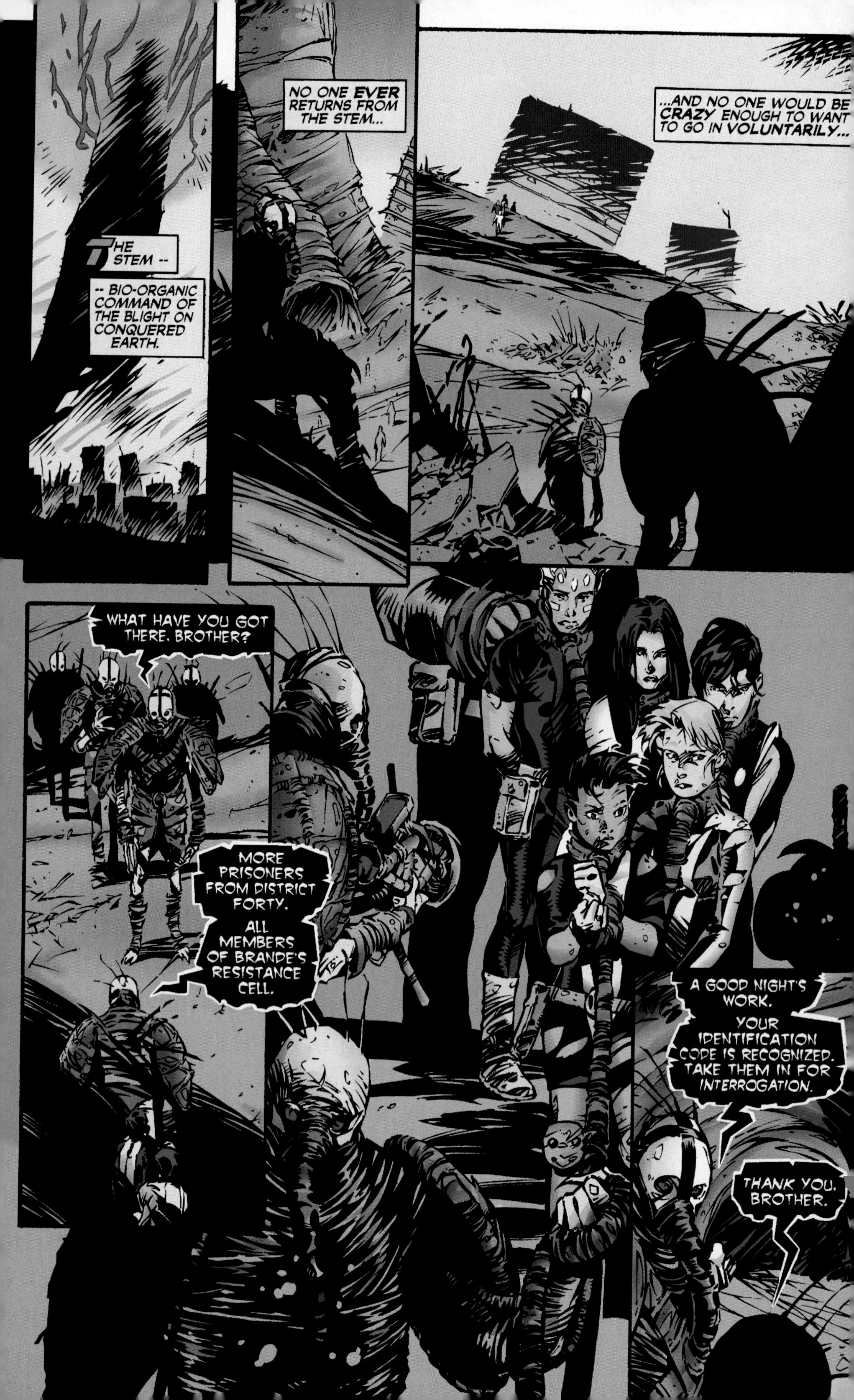
THE STEM --
-- BIO-ORGANIC COMMAND OF THE BLIGHT ON CONQUERED EARTH.
NO ONE EVER RETURNS FROM THE STEM...
...AND NO ONE WOULD BE CRAZY ENOUGH TO WANT TO GO IN VOLUNTARILY...
WHAT HAVE YOU GOT THERE, BROTHER?
MORE PRISONERS FROM DISTRICT FORTY.
ALL MEMBERS OF BRANDE'S RESISTANCE CELL.
A GOOD NIGHT'S WORK.
YOUR IDENTIFICATION CODE IS RECOGNIZED. TAKE THEM IN FOR INTERROGATION.
THANK YOU, BROTHER.

...ESPECIALLY UNDER MY OWN FREE WILL.

QUIET, XS. COMMUNICATE ONLY THROUGH SATURN GIRL'S TELEPATHIC LINK.

NEVER THOUGHT I'D BE COMING BACK HERE...

HEADS UP, GANG. MORE BLIGHT AHEAD.

WHERE TO NOW, SATURN GIRL?

STILL CONCENTRATING, CHAM. IT'S DIFFICULT SEPARATING THE DODA'S EMPATHIC SIGNAL FROM THE BACKGROUND CLUTTER...

WAIT -- I THINK I'VE GOT IT. YES. NOT FAR NOW. DOWN TO THE LEFT, CHAMELE --

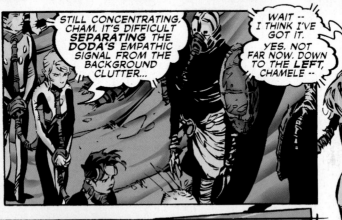

-- UNNHH!

IMRA, WHAT IS IT? WHAT'S THE MATTER?

I CAN HEAR...M'ONEL... IN MY MIND...THEY'RE HURTING HIM...

...FEEDING HIS ENERGIES...INTO THE DODA'S STREAM... TRYING TO SET OFF SOME KIND OF...CHAIN REACTION...

HOLD! THIS ONE IS NOT SUBDUED!

...UHHN... THEY'RE TRYING TO KILL LIFE... ALL LIFE... EVERYWHERE.

NO MORE TIME FOR SUBTLETY...

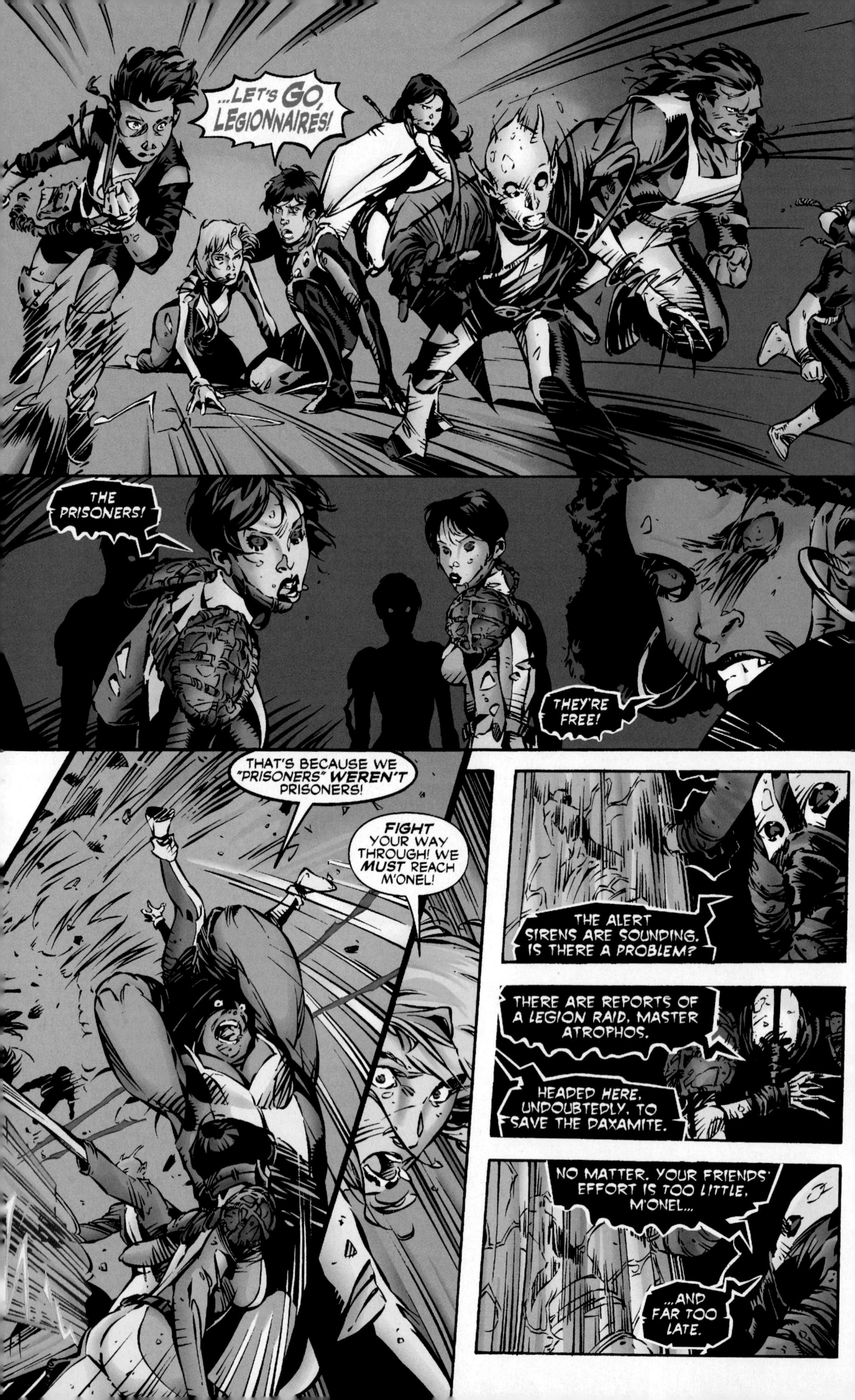
...LET'S GO, LEGIONNAIRES!
THE PRISONERS!
THEY'RE FREE!
THAT'S BECAUSE WE "PRISONERS" WEREN'T PRISONERS!
FIGHT YOUR WAY THROUGH! WE MUST REACH M'ONEL!
THE ALERT SIRENS ARE SOUNDING. IS THERE A PROBLEM?
THERE ARE REPORTS OF A LEGION RAID, MASTER ATROPHOS.
HEADED HERE, UNDOUBTEDLY, TO SAVE THE DAXAMITE.
NO MATTER. YOUR FRIENDS' EFFORT IS TOO LITTLE, M'ONEL...
...AND FAR TOO LATE.

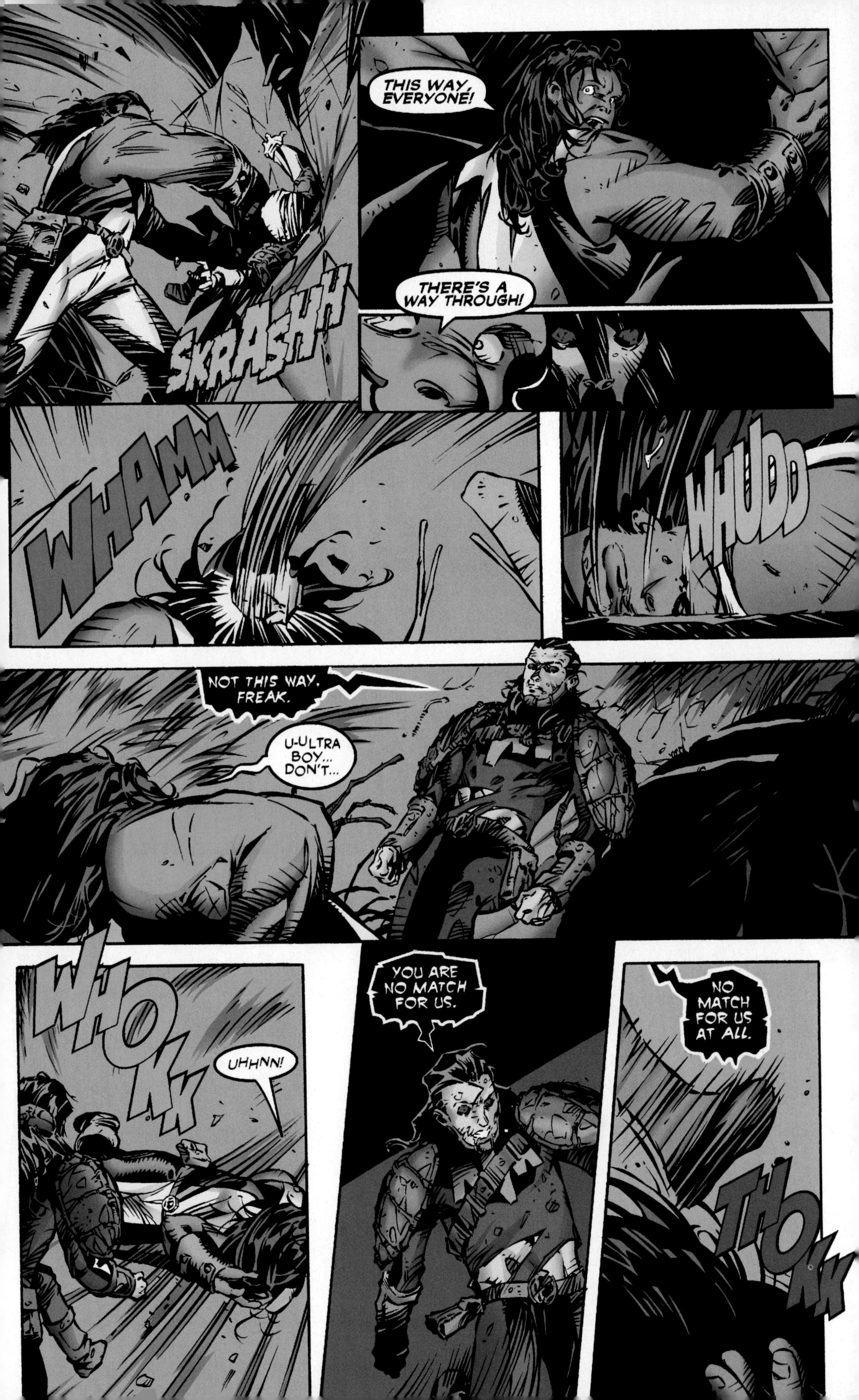

SKRASHH
THIS WAY, EVERYONE!
THERE'S A WAY THROUGH!
WHAMM
WHUDD
NOT THIS WAY. FREAK.
U-ULTRA BOY... DON'T...
WHOKK
UHHNN!
YOU ARE NO MATCH FOR US.
NO MATCH FOR US AT ALL.
THOKK

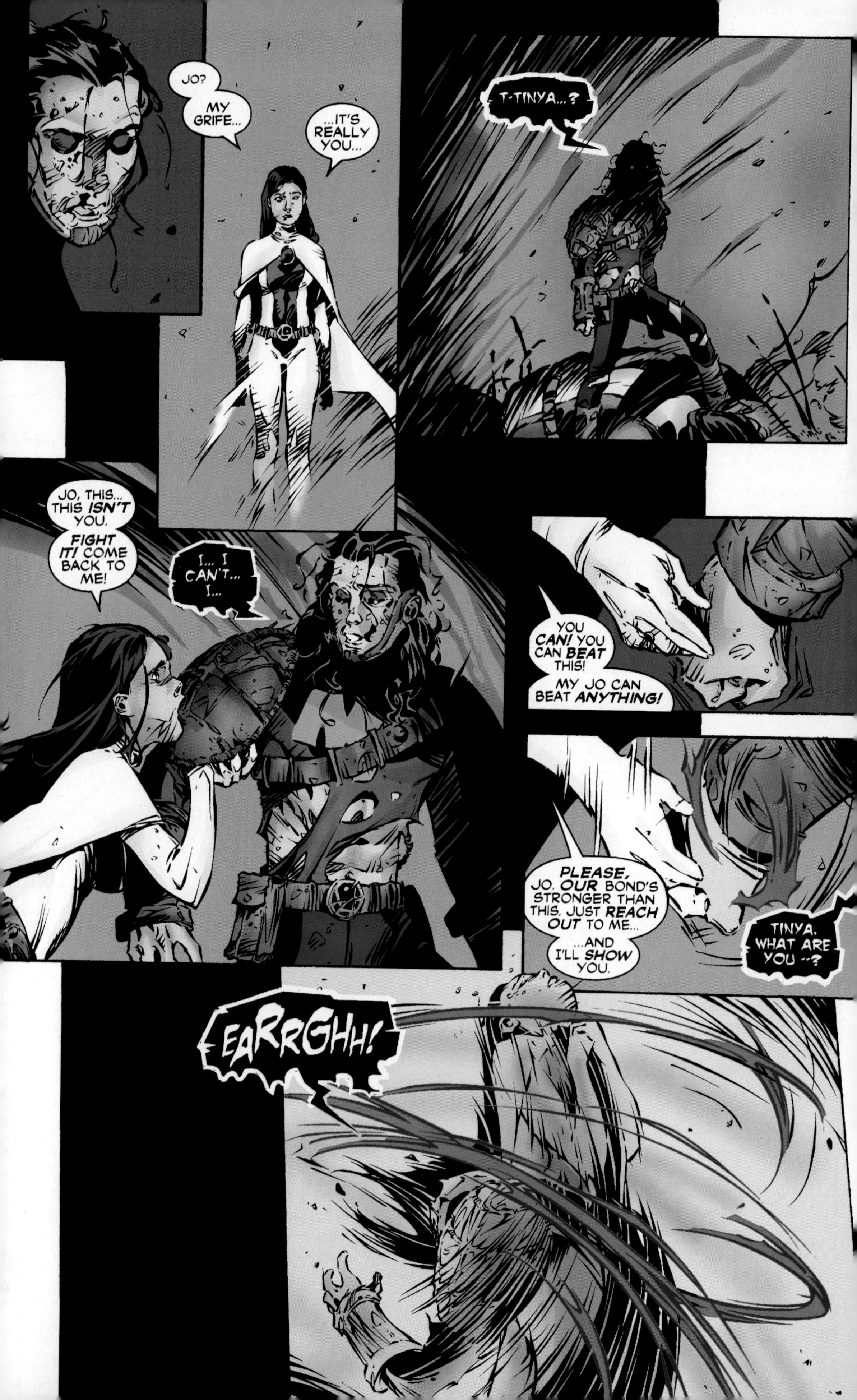

JO?
MY GRIFE...
...IT'S REALLY YOU...
T-TINYA...?
JO, THIS... THIS ISN'T YOU.
FIGHT IT! COME BACK TO ME!
I... I CAN'T... I...
YOU CAN! YOU CAN BEAT THIS!
MY JO CAN BEAT ANYTHING!
PLEASE, JO. OUR BOND'S STRONGER THAN THIS. JUST REACH OUT TO ME...
...AND I'LL SHOW YOU.
TINYA, WHAT ARE YOU --?
EARRGHH!

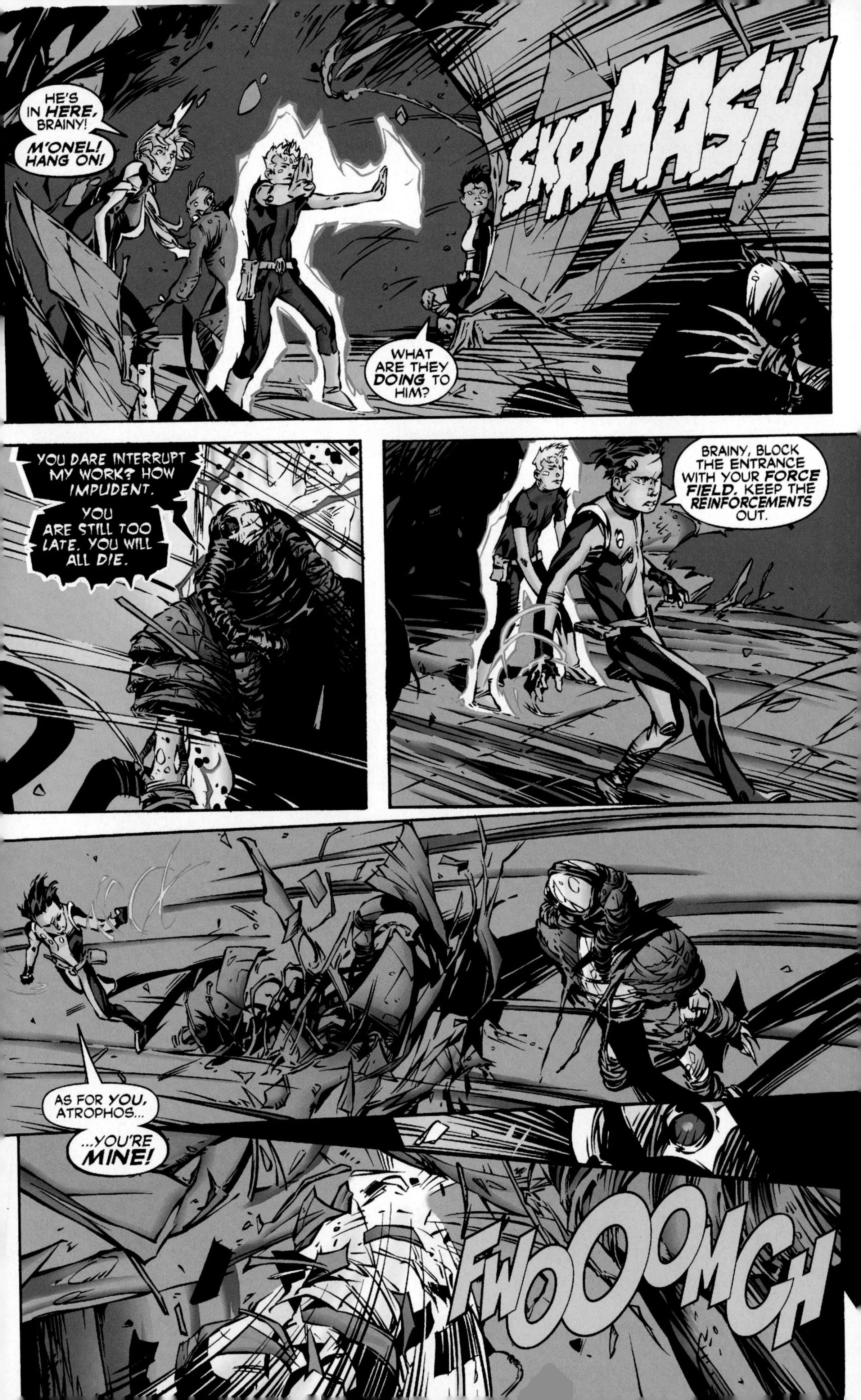

HE'S IN HERE, BRAINY!
M'ONEL! HANG ON!
SKRAASH
WHAT ARE THEY DOING TO HIM?
YOU DARE INTERRUPT MY WORK? HOW IMPUDENT.
YOU ARE STILL TOO LATE. YOU WILL ALL DIE.
BRAINY, BLOCK THE ENTRANCE WITH YOUR FORCE FIELD. KEEP THE REINFORCEMENTS OUT.
AS FOR YOU, ATROPHOS...
...YOU'RE MINE!
FWOOOMCH

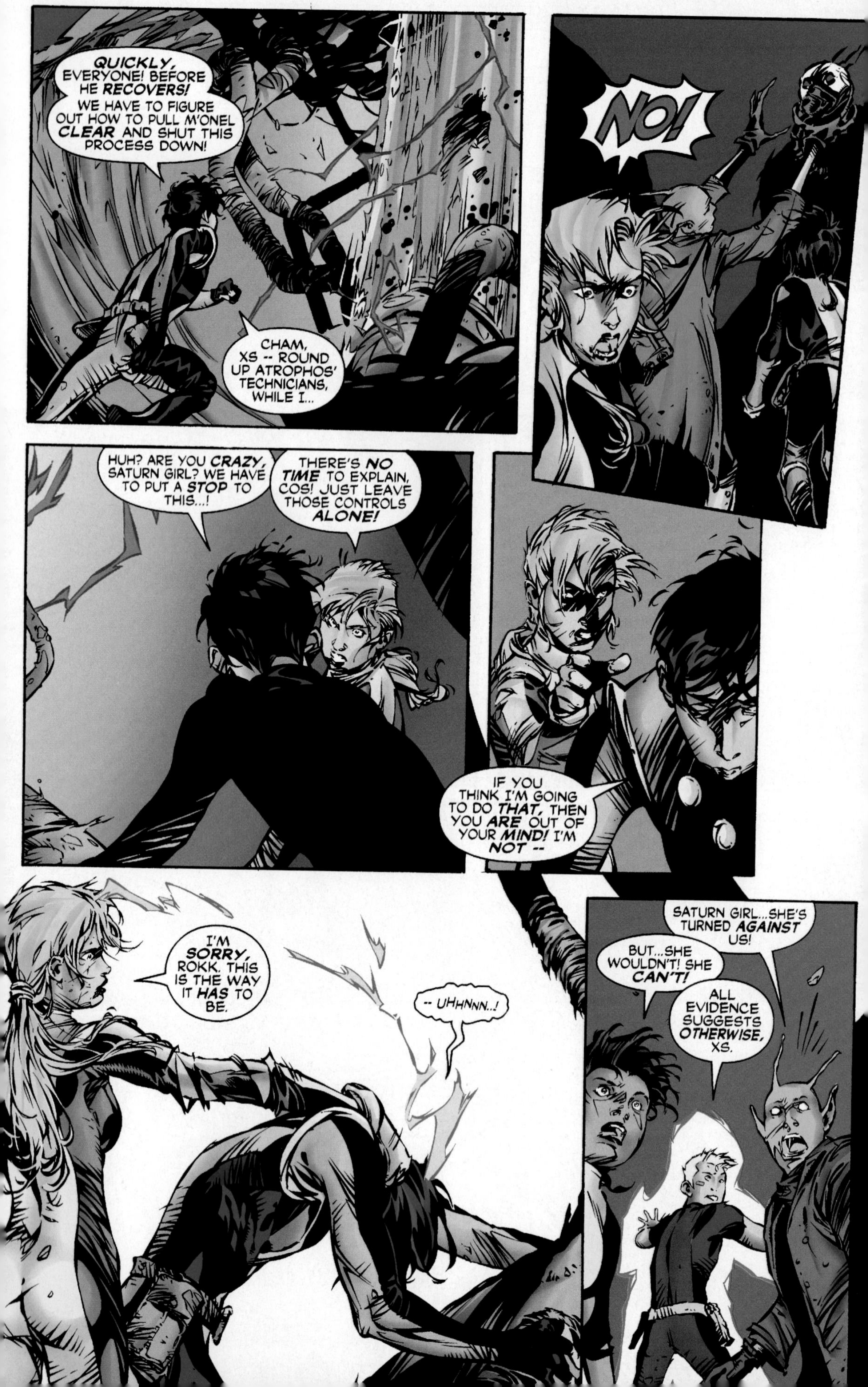
QUICKLY, EVERYONE! BEFORE HE RECOVERS! WE HAVE TO FIGURE OUT HOW TO PULL M'ONEL CLEAR AND SHUT THIS PROCESS DOWN!
CHAM, XS -- ROUND UP ATROPHOS' TECHNICIANS, WHILE I...
NO!
HUH? ARE YOU CRAZY, SATURN GIRL? WE HAVE TO PUT A STOP TO THIS...!
THERE'S NO TIME TO EXPLAIN, COS! JUST LEAVE THOSE CONTROLS ALONE!
IF YOU THINK I'M GOING TO DO THAT, THEN YOU ARE OUT OF YOUR MIND! I'M NOT --
I'M SORRY, ROKK. THIS IS THE WAY IT HAS TO BE.
-- UHHNNN..!
SATURN GIRL...SHE'S TURNED AGAINST US!
BUT...SHE WOULDN'T! SHE CAN'T!
ALL EVIDENCE SUGGESTS OTHERWISE, XS.

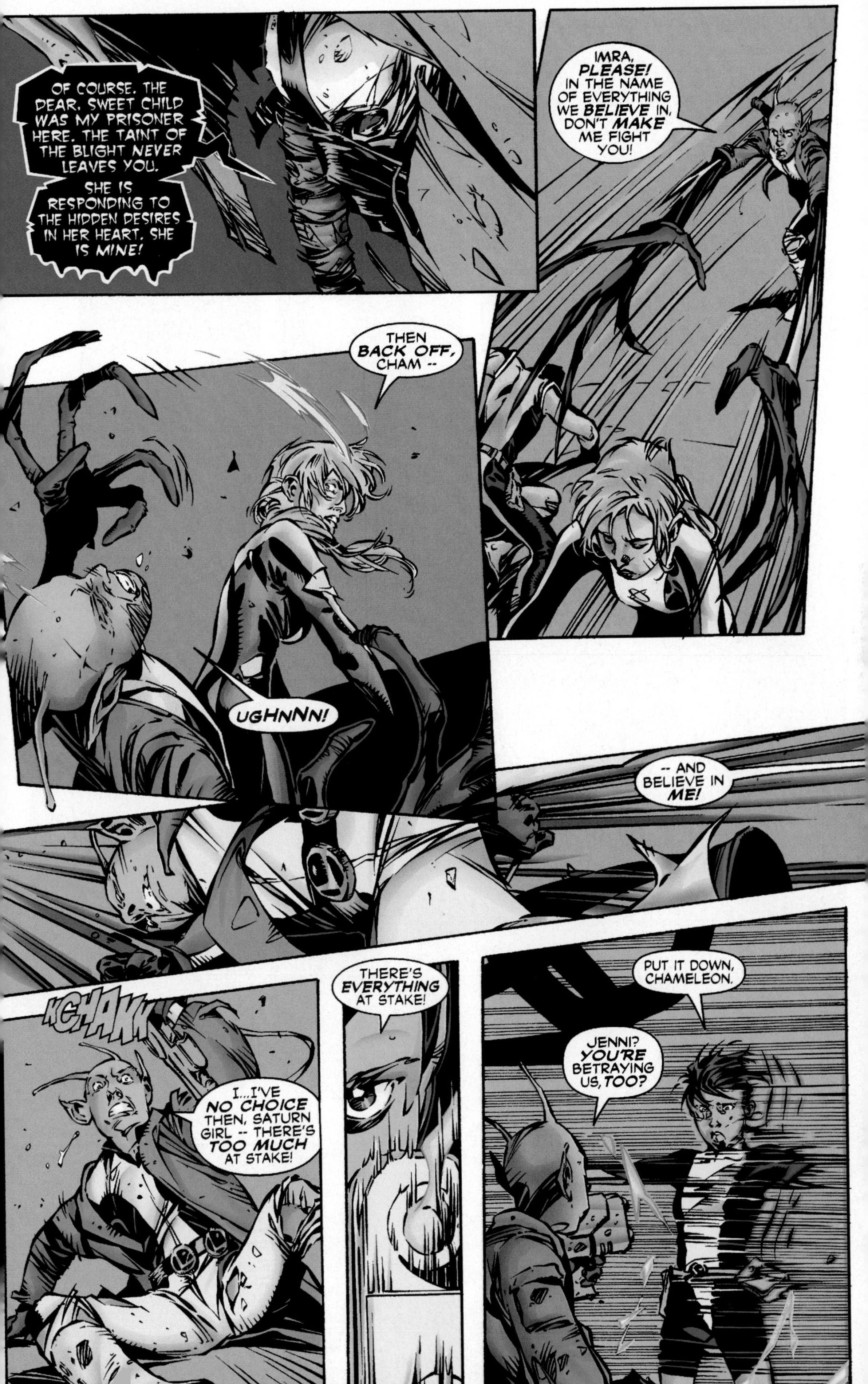
OF COURSE. THE DEAR. SWEET CHILD WAS MY PRISONER HERE. THE TAINT OF THE BLIGHT NEVER LEAVES YOU.
SHE IS RESPONDING TO THE HIDDEN DESIRES IN HER HEART. SHE IS MINE!
IMRA, PLEASE! IN THE NAME OF EVERYTHING WE BELIEVE IN, DON'T MAKE ME FIGHT YOU!
THEN BACK OFF, CHAM --
UGHNNN!
-- AND BELIEVE IN ME!
KCHAKK
I...I'VE NO CHOICE THEN, SATURN GIRL -- THERE'S TOO MUCH AT STAKE!
THERE'S EVERYTHING AT STAKE!
PUT IT DOWN, CHAMELEON.
JENNI? YOU'RE BETRAYING US, TOO?

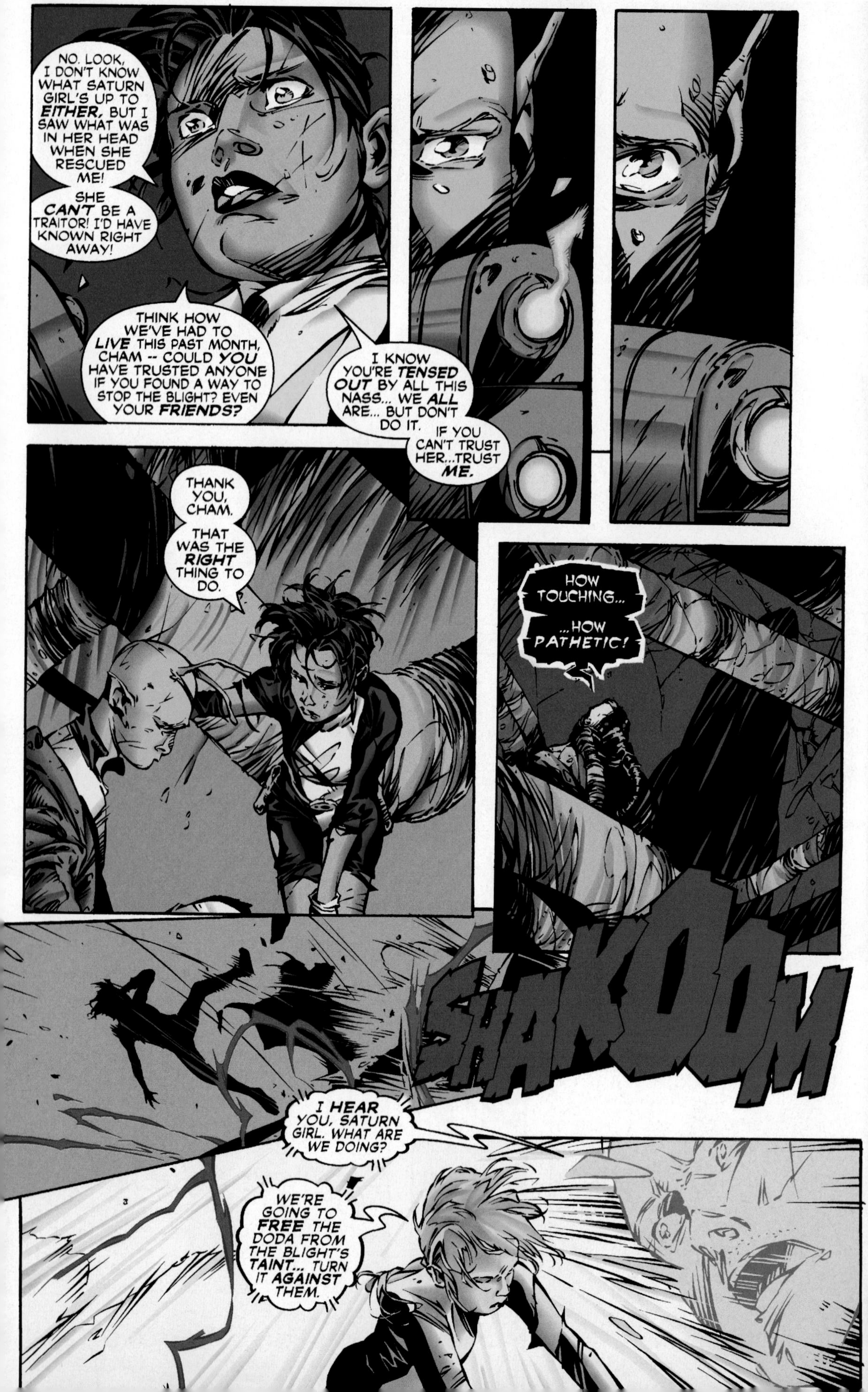

NO. LOOK, I DON'T KNOW WHAT SATURN GIRL'S UP TO EITHER, BUT I SAW WHAT WAS IN HER HEAD WHEN SHE RESCUED ME!
SHE CAN'T BE A TRAITOR! I'D HAVE KNOWN RIGHT AWAY!
THINK HOW WE'VE HAD TO LIVE THIS PAST MONTH, CHAM -- COULD YOU HAVE TRUSTED ANYONE IF YOU FOUND A WAY TO STOP THE BLIGHT? EVEN YOUR FRIENDS?
I KNOW YOU'RE TENSED OUT BY ALL THIS NASS... WE ALL ARE... BUT DON'T DO IT.
IF YOU CAN'T TRUST HER...TRUST ME.
THANK YOU, CHAM.
THAT WAS THE RIGHT THING TO DO.
HOW TOUCHING...
...HOW PATHETIC!
SHAKOOM
I HEAR YOU, SATURN GIRL. WHAT ARE WE DOING?
WE'RE GOING TO FREE THE DODA FROM THE BLIGHT'S TAINT... TURN IT AGAINST THEM.

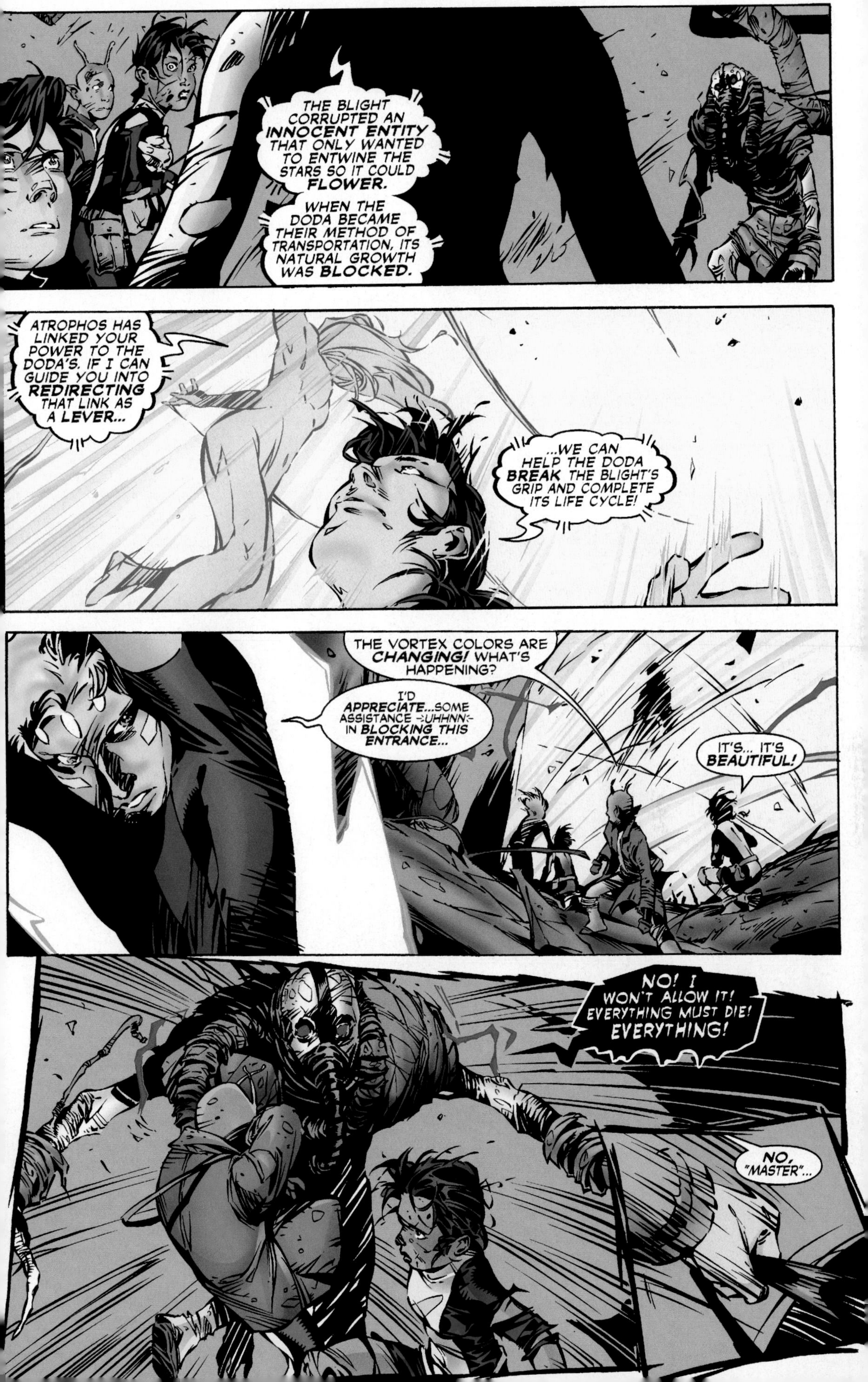
THE BLIGHT CORRUPTED AN INNOCENT ENTITY THAT ONLY WANTED TO ENTWINE THE STARS SO IT COULD FLOWER.
WHEN THE DODA BECAME THEIR METHOD OF TRANSPORTATION, ITS NATURAL GROWTH WAS BLOCKED.
ATROPHOS HAS LINKED YOUR POWER TO THE DODA'S. IF I CAN GUIDE YOU INTO REDIRECTING THAT LINK AS A LEVER...
...WE CAN HELP THE DODA BREAK THE BLIGHT'S GRIP AND COMPLETE ITS LIFE CYCLE!
THE VORTEX COLORS ARE CHANGING! WHAT'S HAPPENING?
I'D APPRECIATE...SOME ASSISTANCE -UHHNN- IN BLOCKING THIS ENTRANCE...
IT'S... IT'S BEAUTIFUL!
NO! I WON'T ALLOW IT! EVERYTHING MUST DIE! EVERYTHING!
NO, "MASTER"...

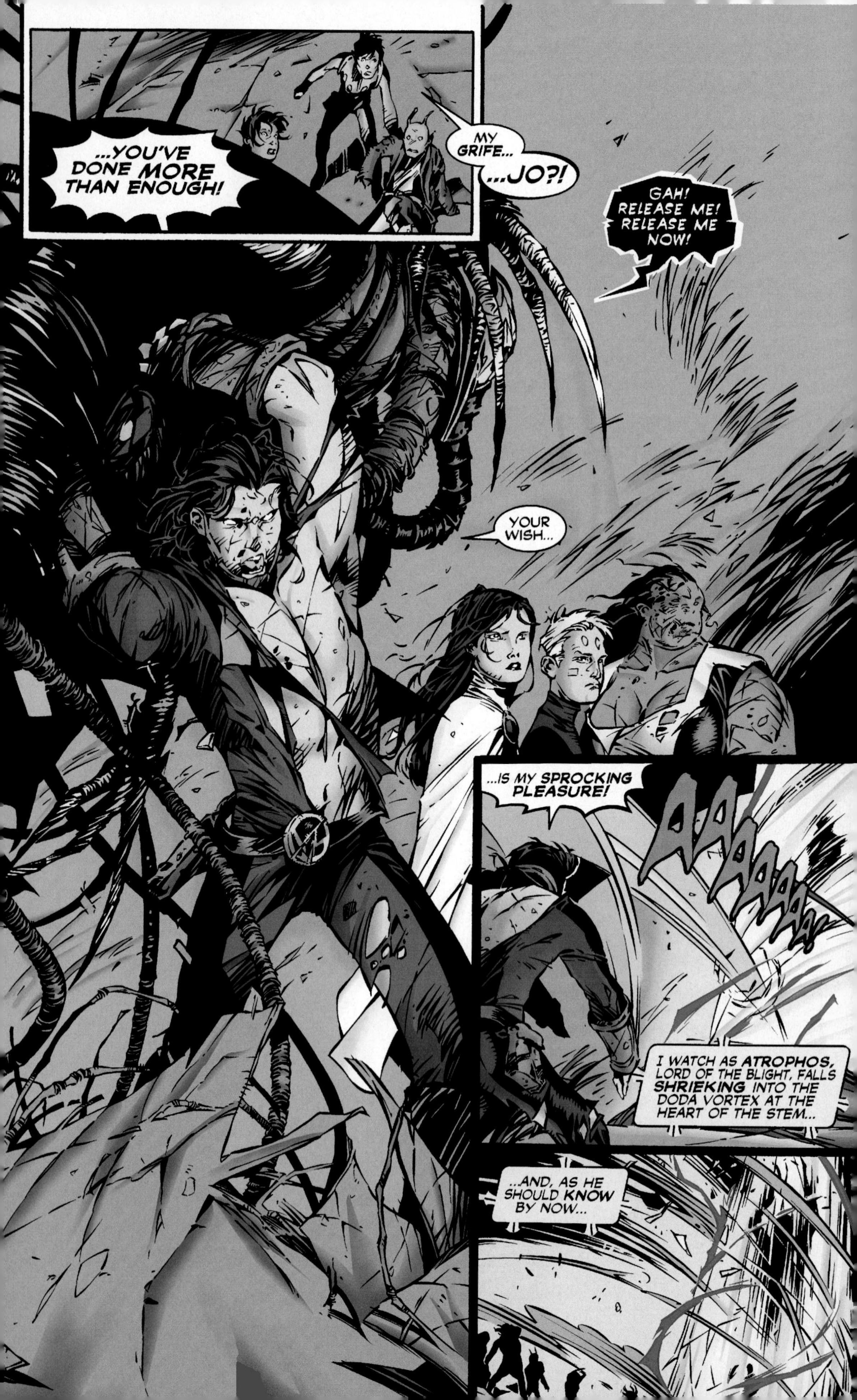
...YOU'VE DONE MORE THAN ENOUGH!
MY GRIFE...
...JO?!
GAH! RELEASE ME! RELEASE ME NOW!
YOUR WISH...
...IS MY SPROCKING PLEASURE!
AAAAAAAA
I WATCH AS ATROPHOS, LORD OF THE BLIGHT, FALLS SHRIEKING INTO THE DODA VORTEX AT THE HEART OF THE STEM...
...AND, AS HE SHOULD KNOW BY NOW...

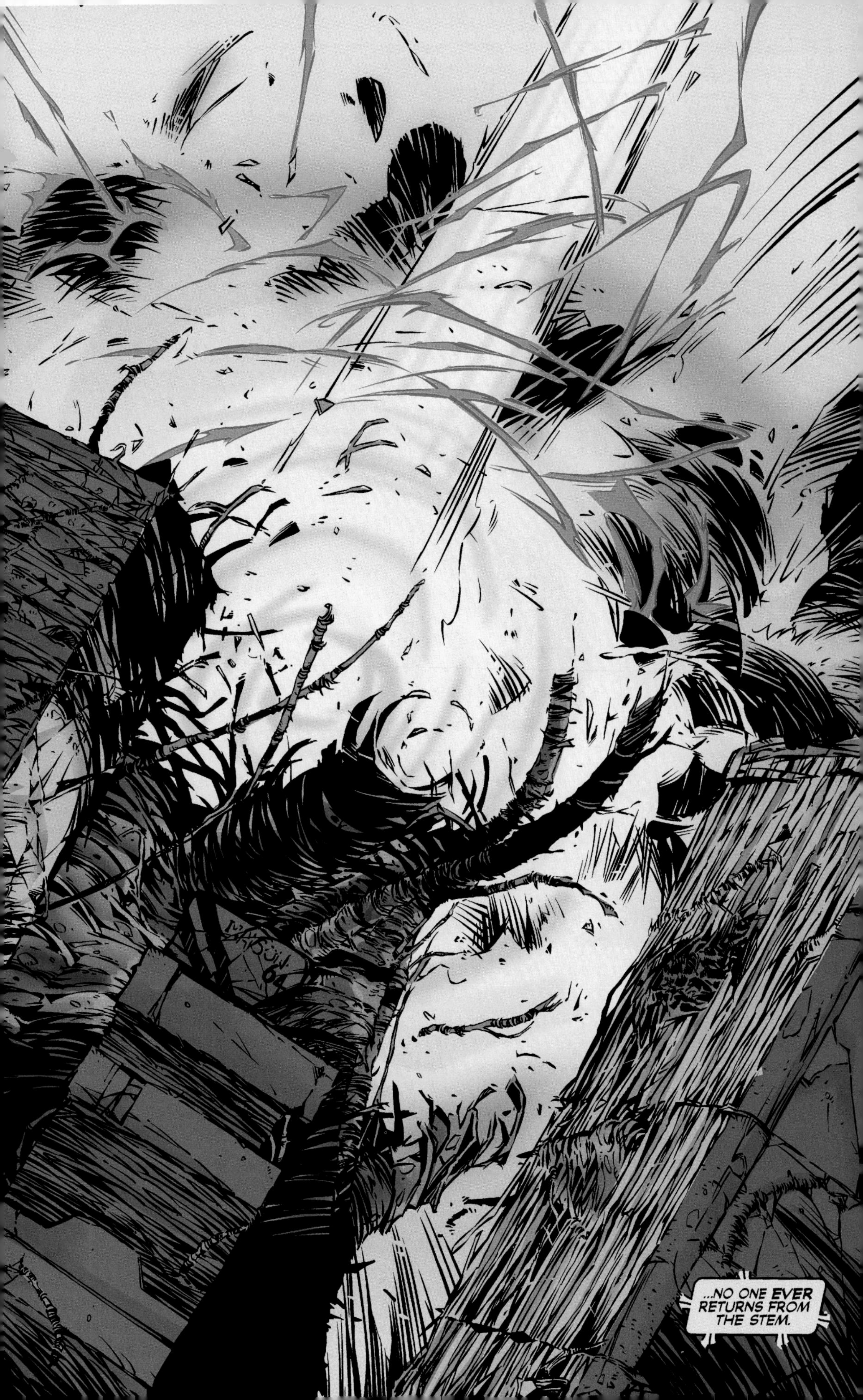
...NO ONE EVER RETURNS FROM THE STEM.

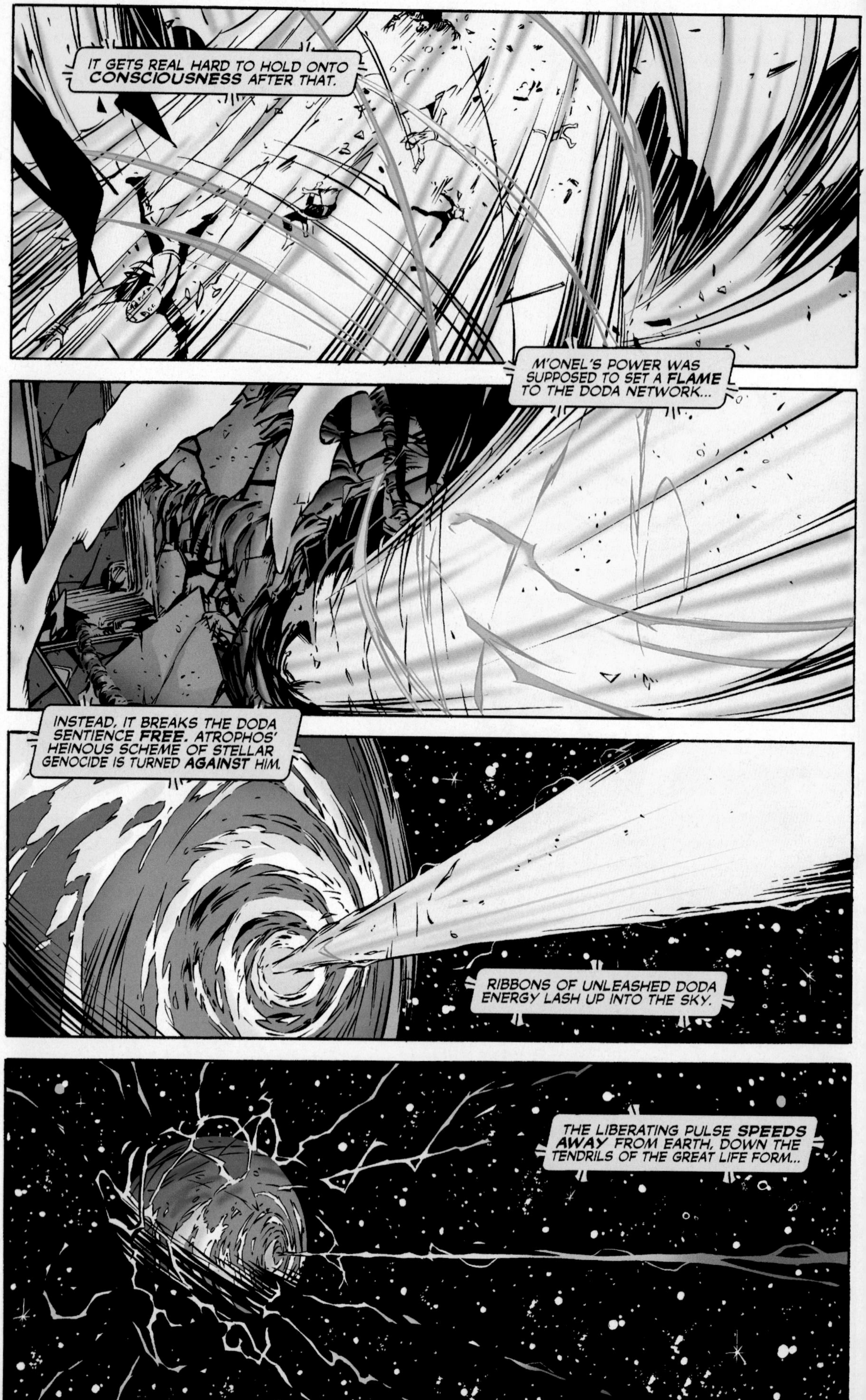
IT GETS REAL HARD TO HOLD ONTO CONSCIOUSNESS AFTER THAT.
M'ONEL'S POWER WAS SUPPOSED TO SET A FLAME TO THE DODA NETWORK...
INSTEAD, IT BREAKS THE DODA SENTIENCE FREE. ATROPHOS' HEINOUS SCHEME OF STELLAR GENOCIDE IS TURNED AGAINST HIM.
RIBBONS OF UNLEASHED DODA ENERGY LASH UP INTO THE SKY.
THE LIBERATING PULSE SPEEDS AWAY FROM EARTH, DOWN THE TENDRILS OF THE GREAT LIFE FORM...

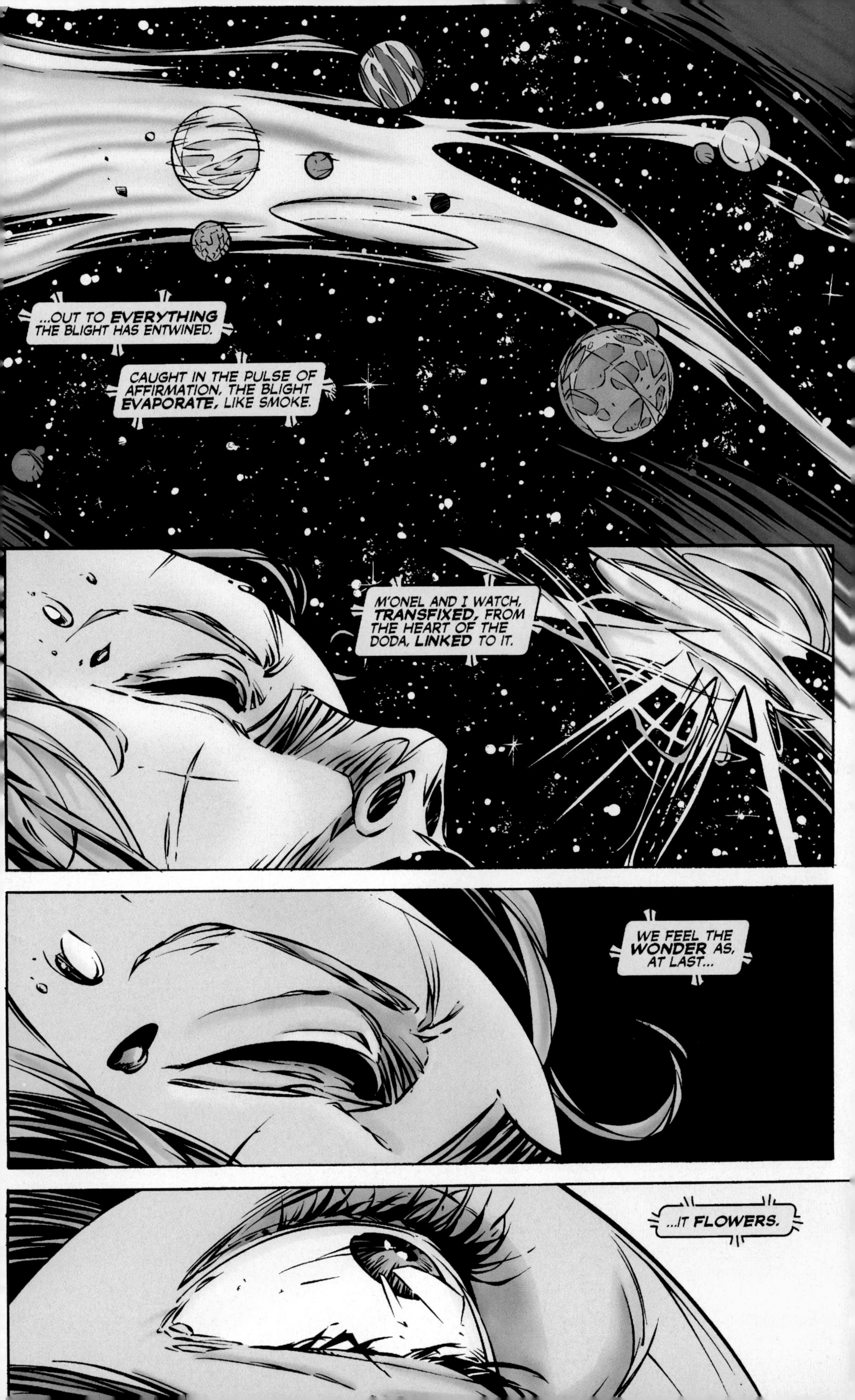
...OUT TO **EVERYTHING** THE BLIGHT HAS ENTWINED.
CAUGHT IN THE PULSE OF AFFIRMATION, THE BLIGHT **EVAPORATE**, LIKE SMOKE.
M'ONEL AND I WATCH, **TRANSFIXED**, FROM THE HEART OF THE DODA, **LINKED** TO IT.
WE FEEL THE **WONDER** AS, AT LAST...
...IT **FLOWERS**.

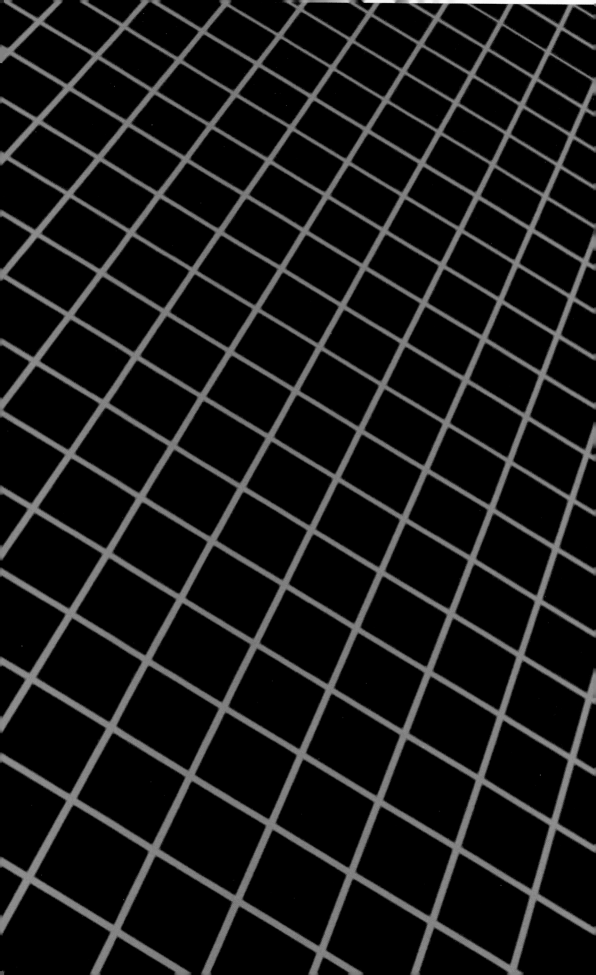

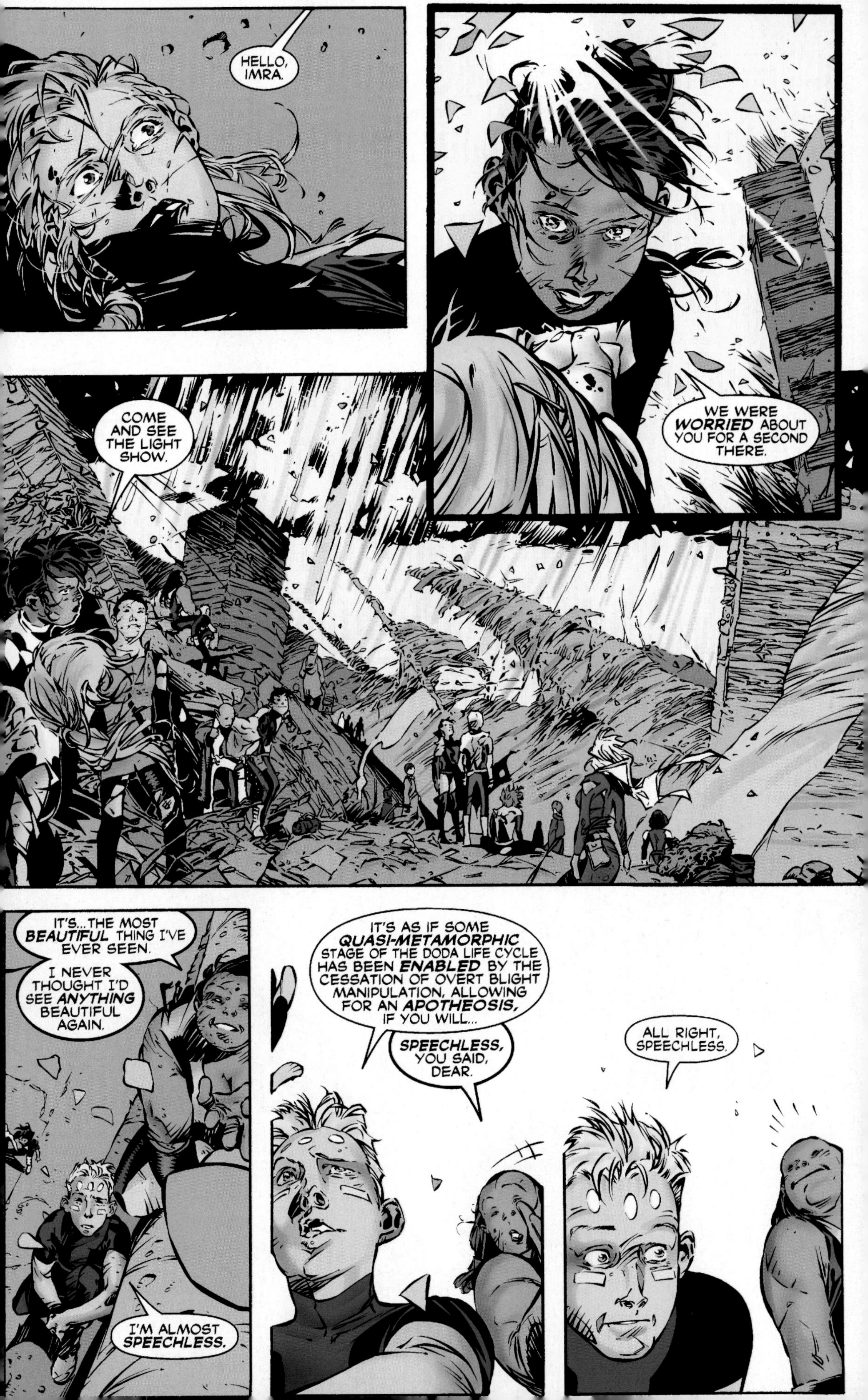
HELLO, IMRA.
WE WERE WORRIED ABOUT YOU FOR A SECOND THERE.
COME AND SEE THE LIGHT SHOW.
IT'S...THE MOST BEAUTIFUL THING I'VE EVER SEEN.
I NEVER THOUGHT I'D SEE ANYTHING BEAUTIFUL AGAIN.
I'M ALMOST SPEECHLESS.
IT'S AS IF SOME QUASI-METAMORPHIC STAGE OF THE DODA LIFE CYCLE HAS BEEN ENABLED BY THE CESSATION OF OVERT BLIGHT MANIPULATION, ALLOWING FOR AN APOTHEOSIS, IF YOU WILL...
SPEECHLESS, YOU SAID, DEAR.
ALL RIGHT, SPEECHLESS.

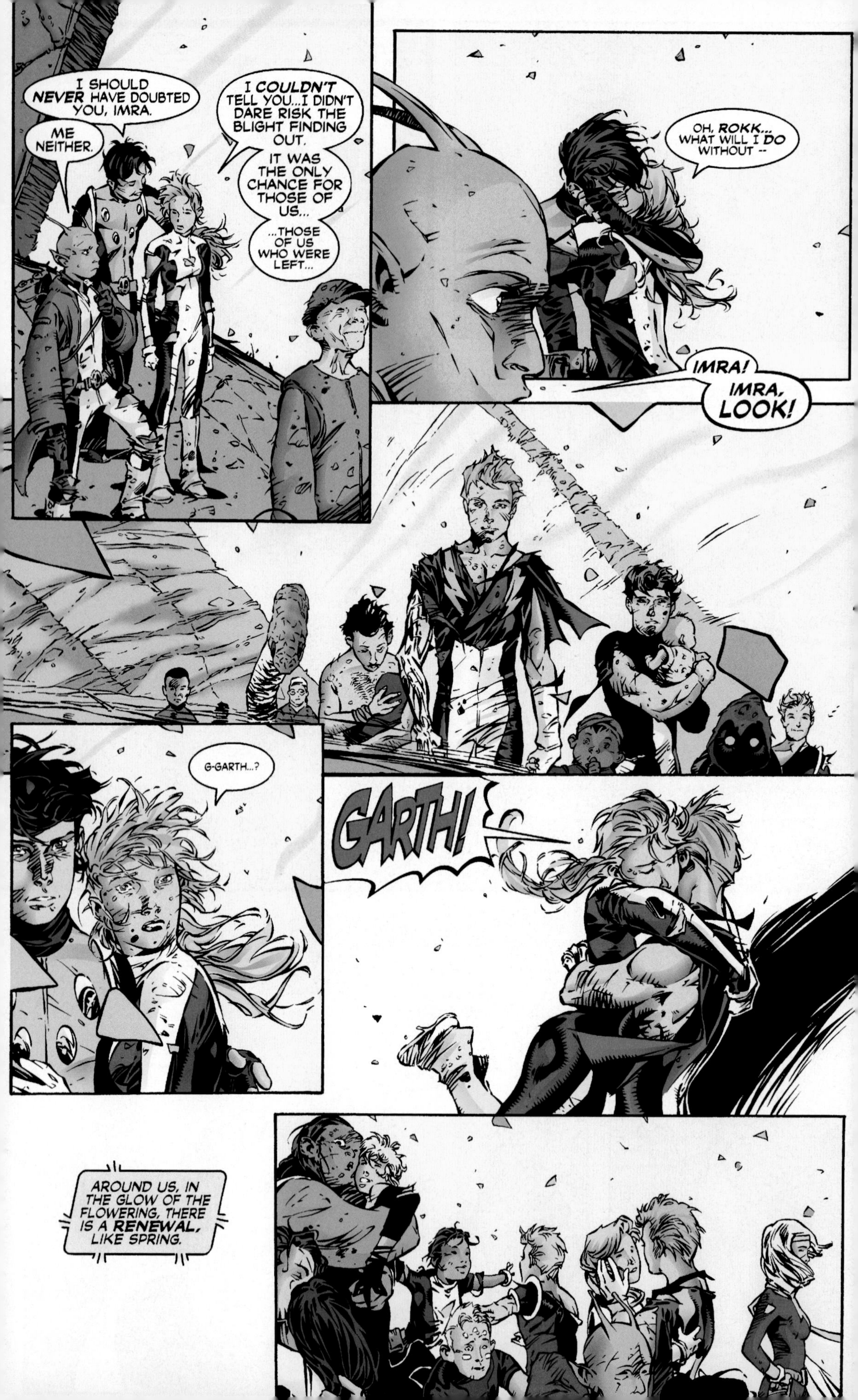
I SHOULD NEVER HAVE DOUBTED YOU, IMRA.
ME NEITHER.
I COULDN'T TELL YOU...I DIDN'T DARE RISK THE BLIGHT FINDING OUT.
IT WAS THE ONLY CHANCE FOR THOSE OF US...
...THOSE OF US WHO WERE LEFT...
OH, ROKK... WHAT WILL I DO WITHOUT --
IMRA! IMRA, LOOK!
G-GARTH...?
GARTH!
AROUND US, IN THE GLOW OF THE FLOWERING, THERE IS A RENEWAL, LIKE SPRING.

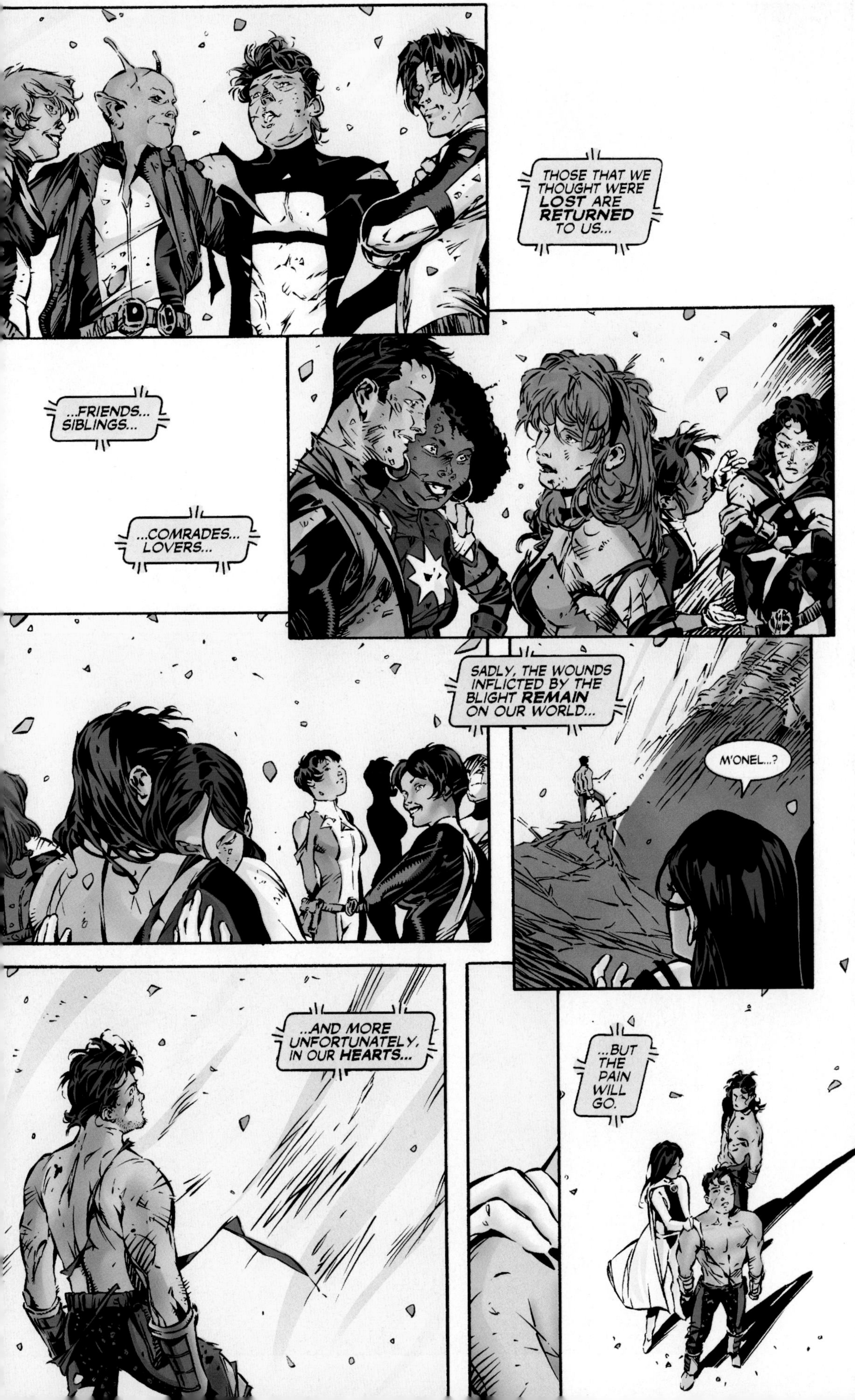
THOSE THAT WE THOUGHT WERE LOST ARE RETURNED TO US...
...FRIENDS... SIBLINGS...
...COMRADES... LOVERS...
SADLY, THE WOUNDS INFLICTED BY THE BLIGHT REMAIN ON OUR WORLD...
M'ONEL...?
...AND MORE UNFORTUNATELY, IN OUR HEARTS...
...BUT THE PAIN WILL GO.

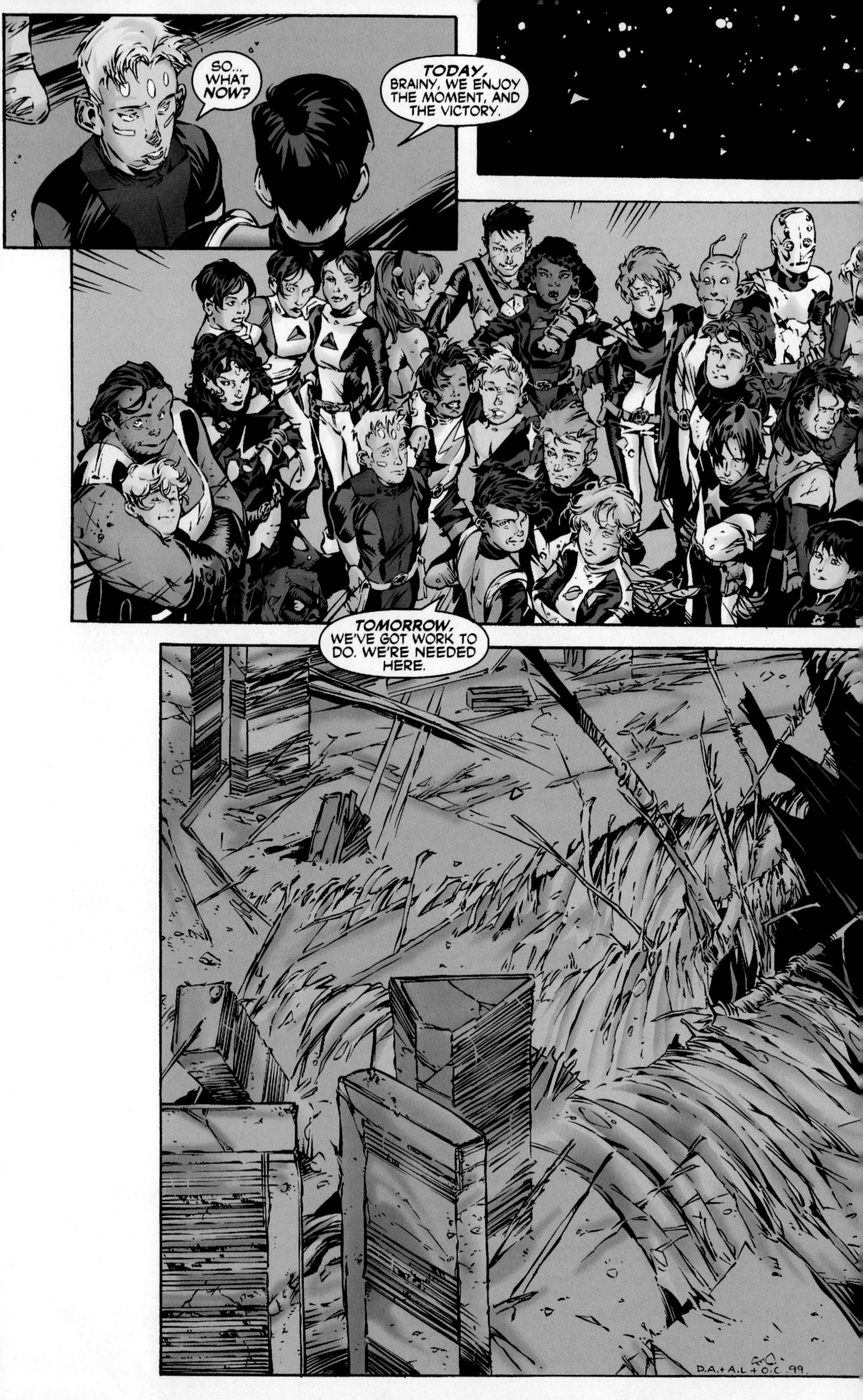
SO... WHAT NOW?
TODAY, BRAINY, WE ENJOY THE MOMENT, AND THE VICTORY.
TOMORROW, WE'VE GOT WORK TO DO. WE'RE NEEDED HERE.
D.A.+A.L+O.C. 99.

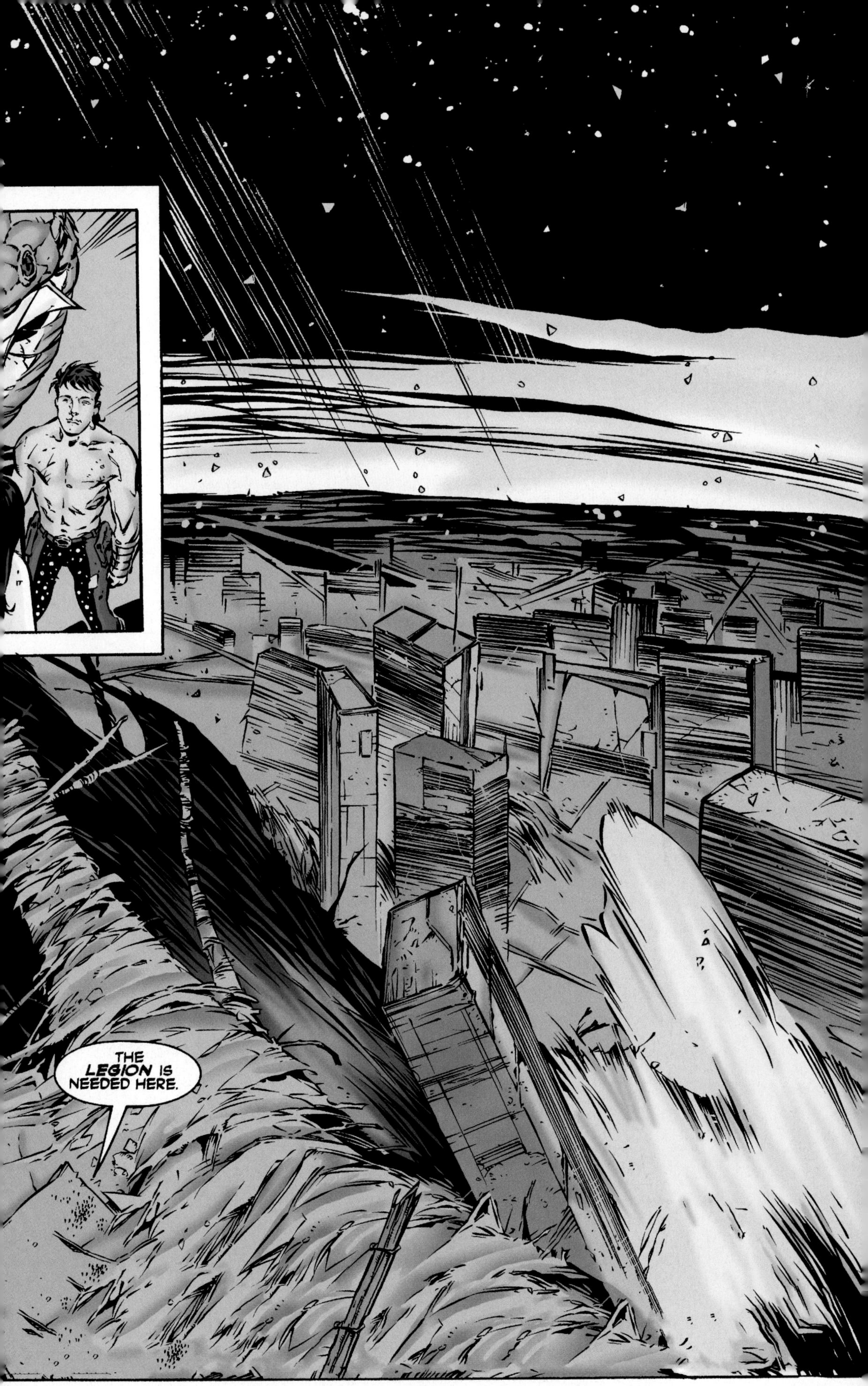
THE *LEGION* IS NEEDED HERE.

THE BLIGHT

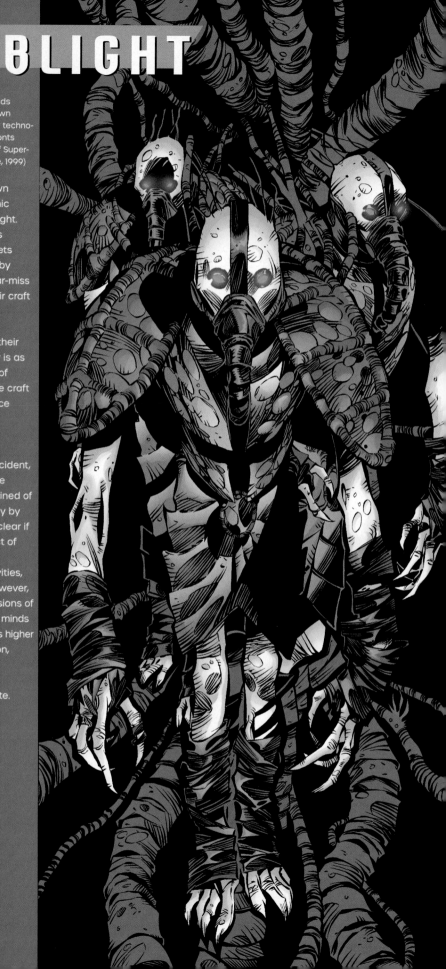

Occupation: Galactic nomads
Base of Operations: Unknown
Biological Type: Apparently techno-biological or organic symbionts
First Appearance: Legion of Super-Heroes Secret Files #2 (June, 1999)

Virtually nothing is known about the techno-organic beings known as the Blight. What little information is available in United Planets archives was gathered by Brainiac 5.1 during a near-miss incident with one of their craft at the Lycidas Stargate.

The level and extent of their technological capability is as unknown as their point of origin or agenda, but the craft and its drive performance clearly indicate a highly advanced standard.

Prior to the near-miss incident, an inhabited moon in the Lycidas system was drained of all life-energy, apparently by the Blight. It remains unclear if this was a deliberate act of violence, some natural by-product of their activities, or even an accident; however, residual psychic impressions of the Blight retained in the minds of the moon's indigenous higher fauna suggest aggression, hostility and malice.

File awaits further update.

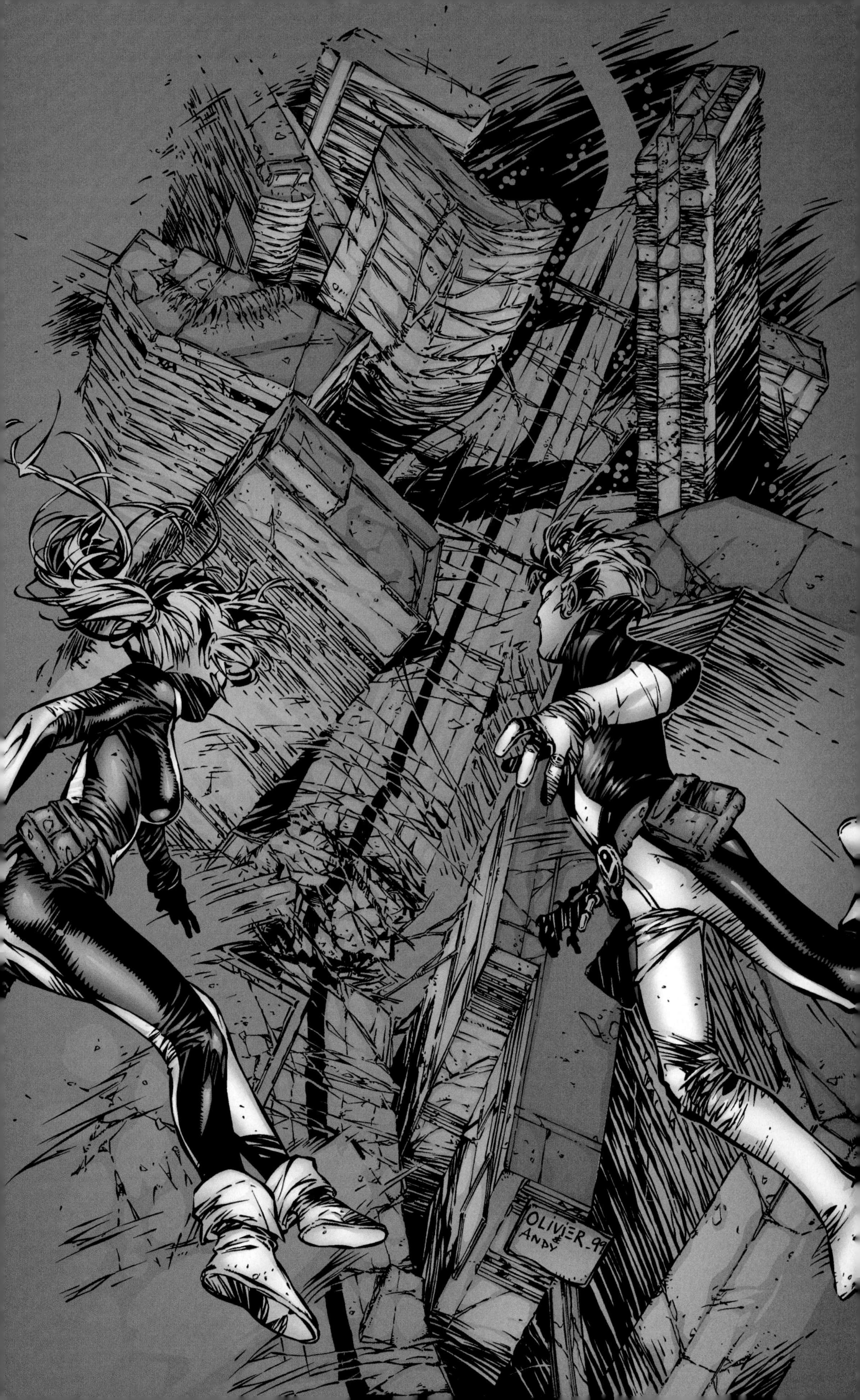
OLIVIER_99
ANDY

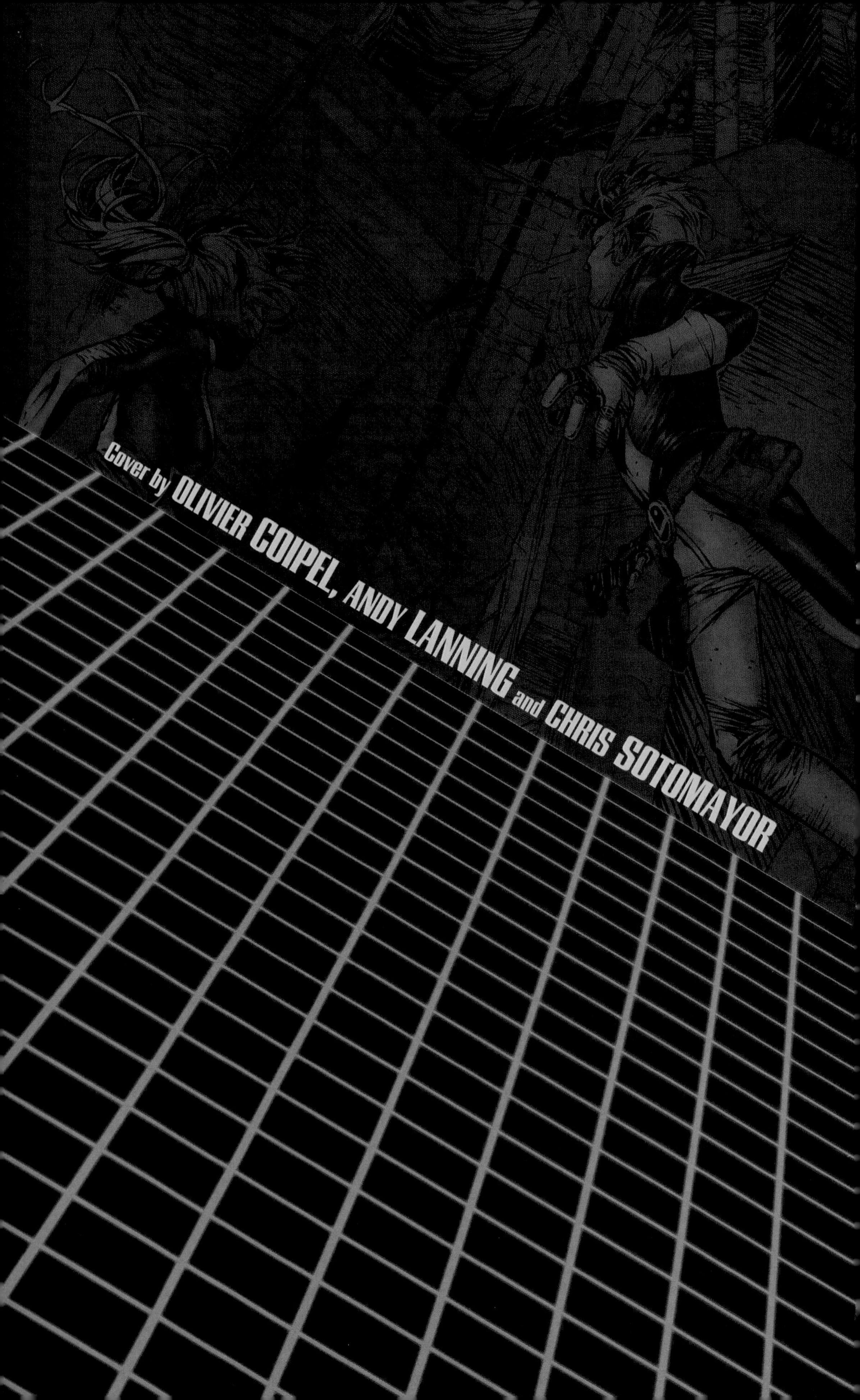
Cover by OLIVIER COIPEL, ANDY LANNING and CHRIS SOTOMAYOR

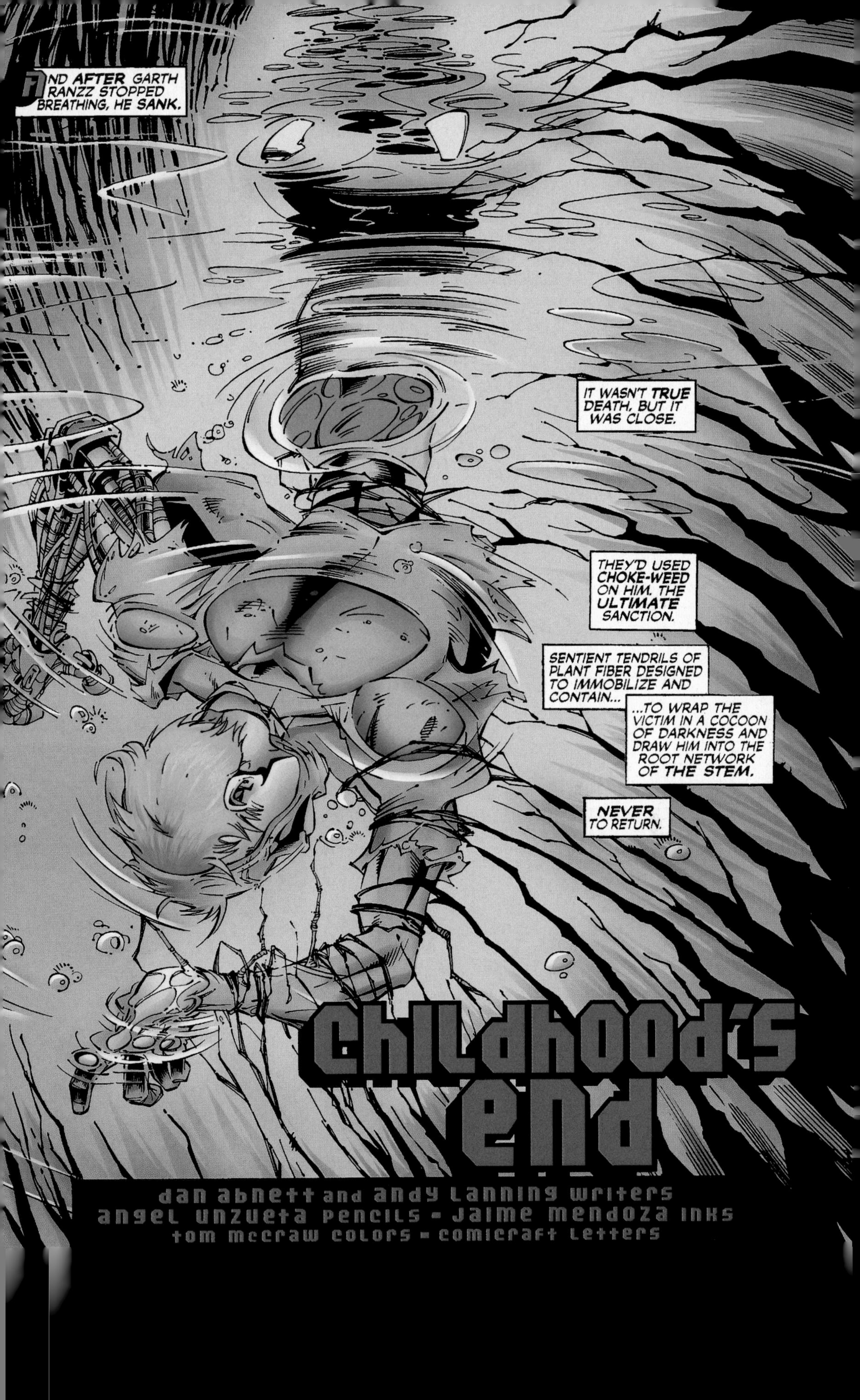
AND AFTER GARTH RANZZ STOPPED BREATHING, HE SANK.
IT WASN'T TRUE DEATH, BUT IT WAS CLOSE.
THEY'D USED CHOKE-WEED ON HIM, THE ULTIMATE SANCTION.
SENTIENT TENDRILS OF PLANT FIBER DESIGNED TO IMMOBILIZE AND CONTAIN...
...TO WRAP THE VICTIM IN A COCOON OF DARKNESS AND DRAW HIM INTO THE ROOT NETWORK OF THE STEM.
NEVER TO RETURN.
CHILDHOOD'S END
DAN ABNETT AND ANDY LANNING WRITERS
ANGEL UNZUETA PENCILS - JAIME MENDOZA INKS
TOM MCCRAW COLORS - COMICRAFT LETTERS

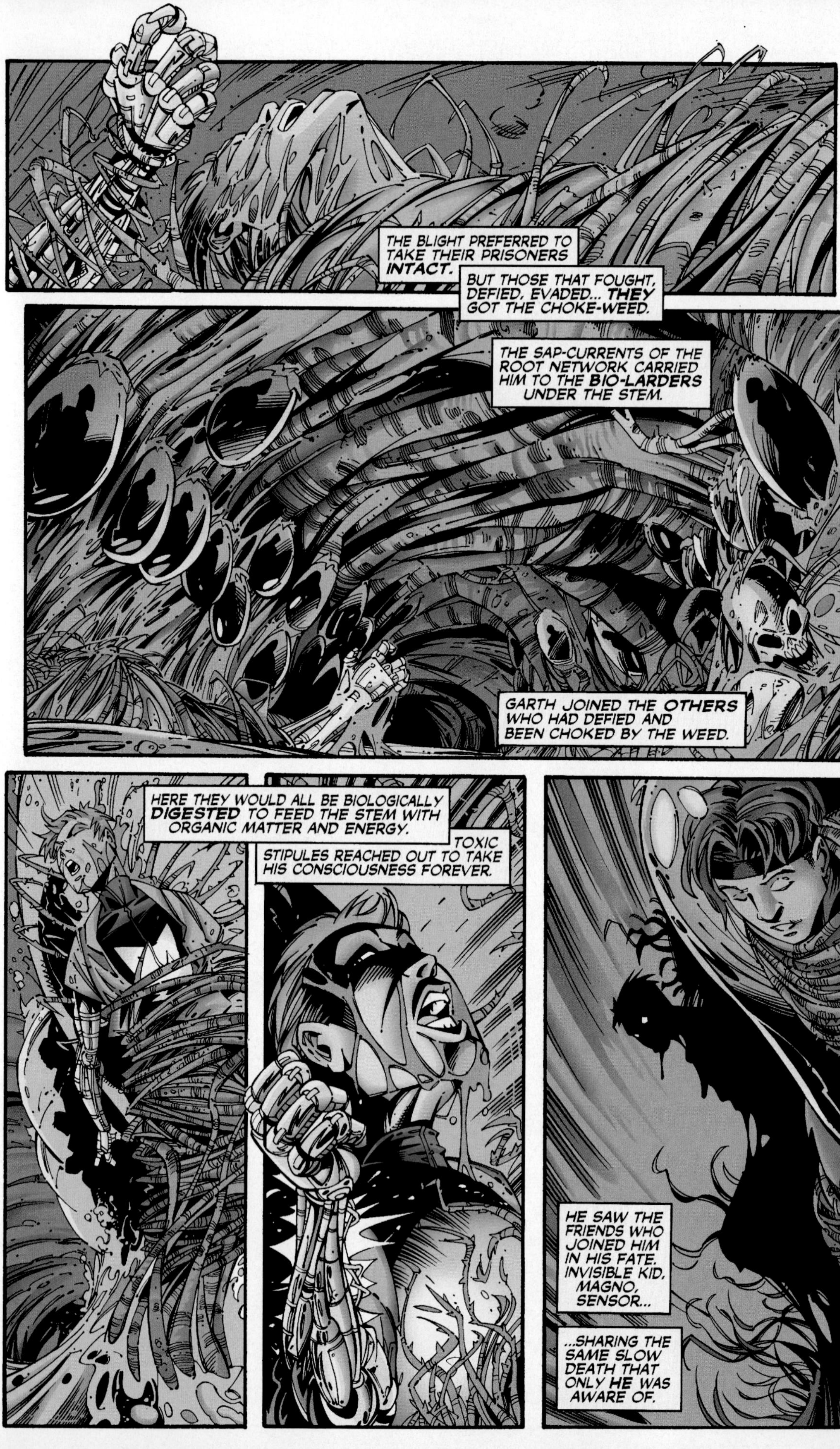

THE BLIGHT PREFERRED TO TAKE THEIR PRISONERS INTACT.
BUT THOSE THAT FOUGHT, DEFIED, EVADED... THEY GOT THE CHOKE-WEED.
THE SAP-CURRENTS OF THE ROOT NETWORK CARRIED HIM TO THE BIO-LARDERS UNDER THE STEM.
GARTH JOINED THE OTHERS WHO HAD DEFIED AND BEEN CHOKED BY THE WEED.
HERE THEY WOULD ALL BE BIOLOGICALLY DIGESTED TO FEED THE STEM WITH ORGANIC MATTER AND ENERGY.
TOXIC STIPULES REACHED OUT TO TAKE HIS CONSCIOUSNESS FOREVER.
HE SAW THE FRIENDS WHO JOINED HIM IN HIS FATE. INVISIBLE KID, MAGNO, SENSOR...
...SHARING THE SAME SLOW DEATH THAT ONLY HE WAS AWARE OF.

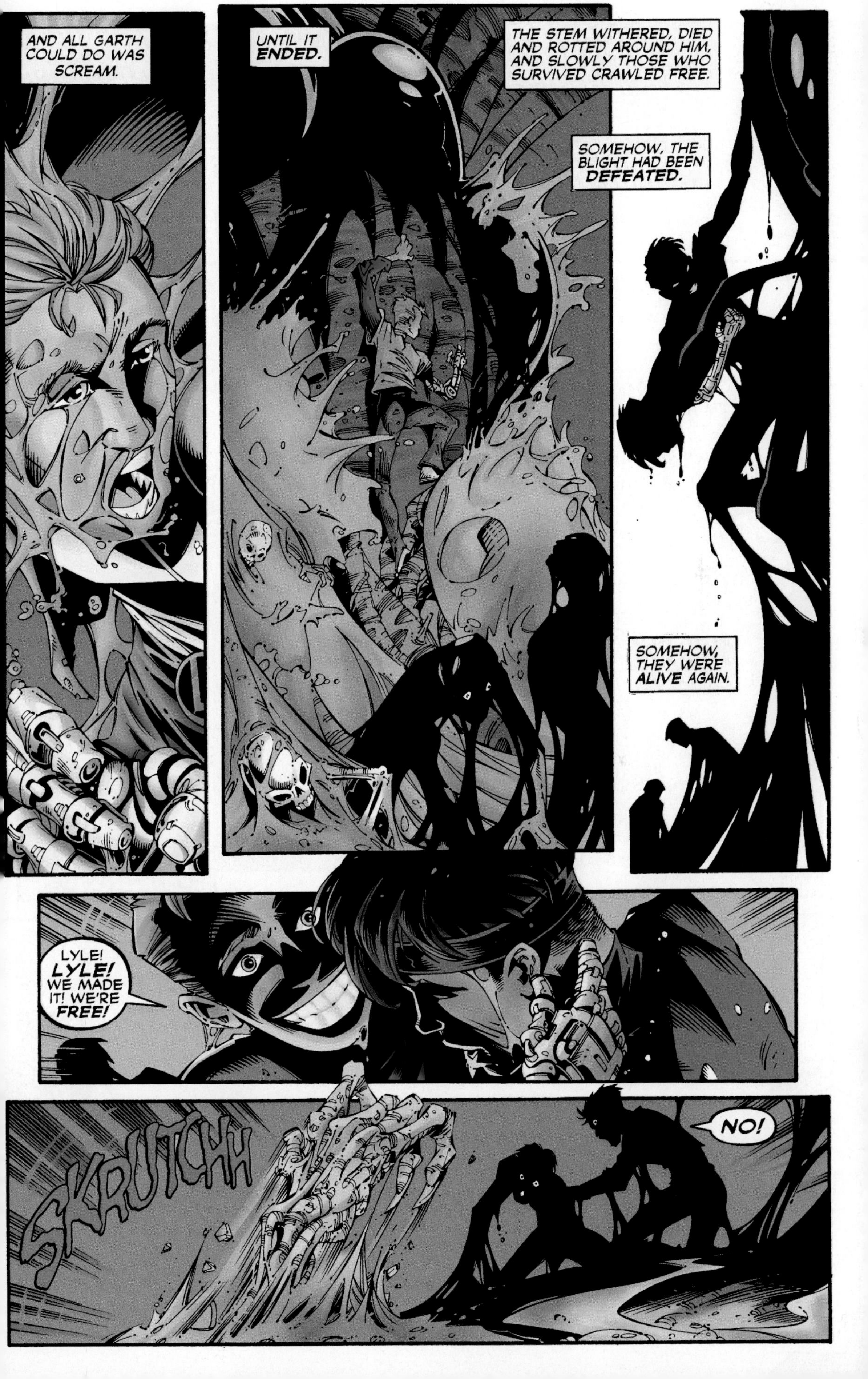
AND ALL GARTH COULD DO WAS SCREAM.
UNTIL IT ENDED.
THE STEM WITHERED, DIED AND ROTTED AROUND HIM, AND SLOWLY THOSE WHO SURVIVED CRAWLED FREE.
SOMEHOW, THE BLIGHT HAD BEEN DEFEATED.
SOMEHOW, THEY WERE ALIVE AGAIN.
LYLE! LYLE! WE MADE IT! WE'RE FREE!
SKRUTCHH
NO!

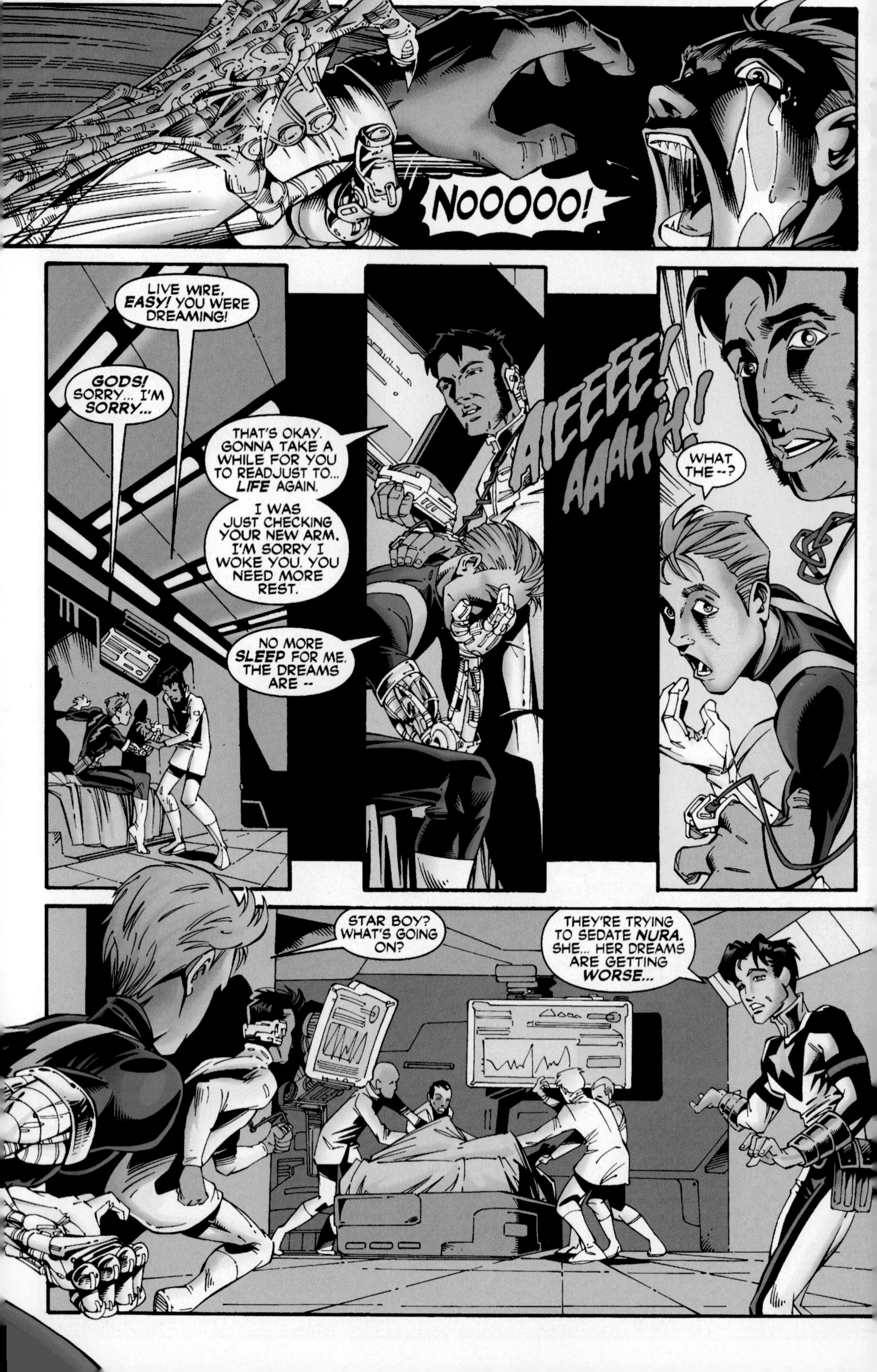
NOOOOO!
LIVE WIRE, EASY! YOU WERE DREAMING!
GODS! SORRY... I'M SORRY...
THAT'S OKAY. GONNA TAKE A WHILE FOR YOU TO READJUST TO... LIFE AGAIN.
I WAS JUST CHECKING YOUR NEW ARM. I'M SORRY I WOKE YOU. YOU NEED MORE REST.
NO MORE SLEEP FOR ME. THE DREAMS ARE --
AIEEEEE! AAAHH!
WHAT THE --?
STAR BOY? WHAT'S GOING ON?
THEY'RE TRYING TO SEDATE NURA. SHE... HER DREAMS ARE GETTING WORSE...

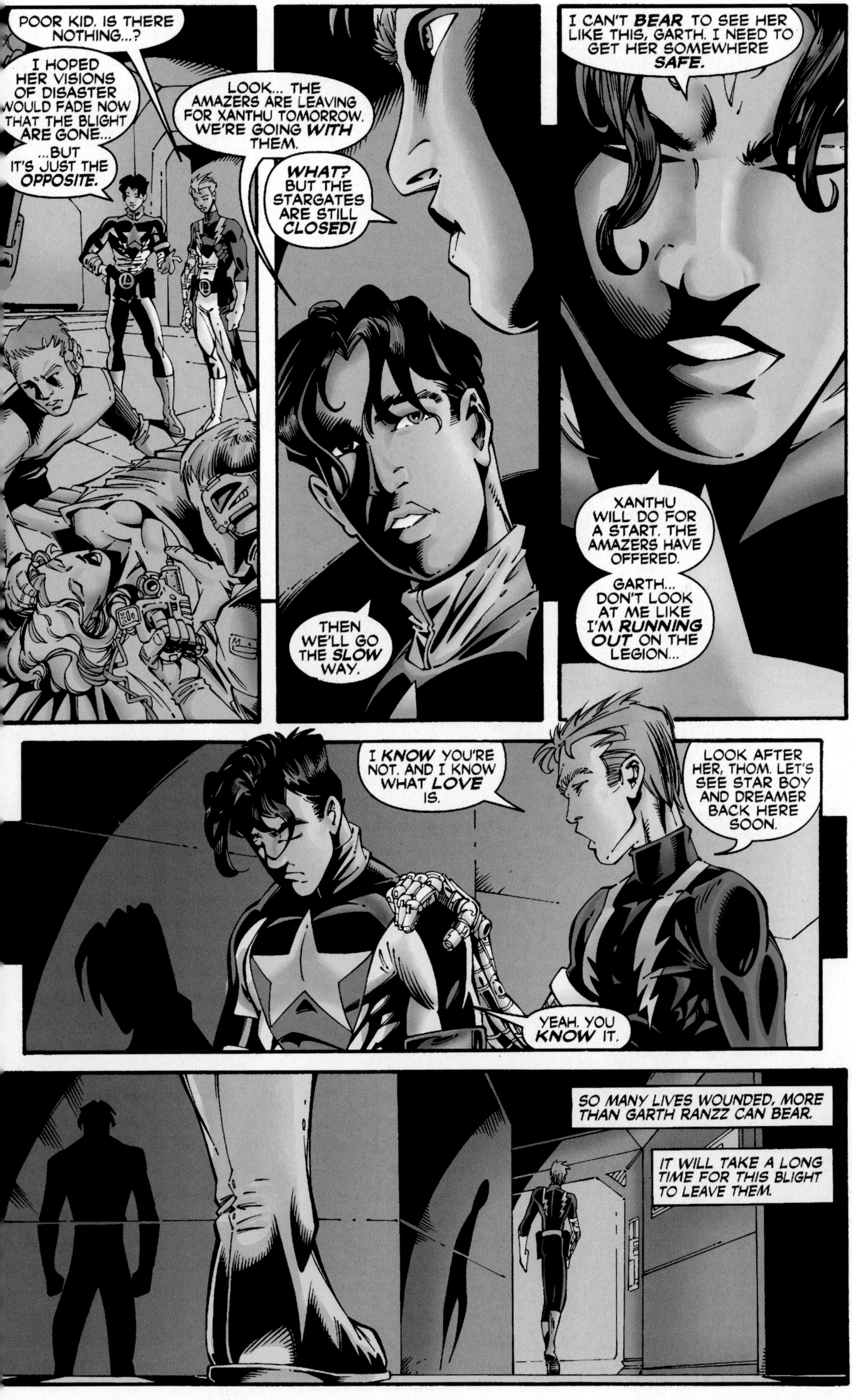
POOR KID. IS THERE NOTHING...?
I HOPED HER VISIONS OF DISASTER WOULD FADE NOW THAT THE BLIGHT ARE GONE...
...BUT IT'S JUST THE OPPOSITE.
LOOK... THE AMAZERS ARE LEAVING FOR XANTHU TOMORROW. WE'RE GOING WITH THEM.
WHAT? BUT THE STARGATES ARE STILL CLOSED!
THEN WE'LL GO THE SLOW WAY.
I CAN'T BEAR TO SEE HER LIKE THIS, GARTH. I NEED TO GET HER SOMEWHERE SAFE.
XANTHU WILL DO FOR A START. THE AMAZERS HAVE OFFERED.
GARTH... DON'T LOOK AT ME LIKE I'M RUNNING OUT ON THE LEGION...
I KNOW YOU'RE NOT. AND I KNOW WHAT LOVE IS.
LOOK AFTER HER, THOM. LET'S SEE STAR BOY AND DREAMER BACK HERE SOON.
YEAH. YOU KNOW IT.
SO MANY LIVES WOUNDED, MORE THAN GARTH RANZZ CAN BEAR.
IT WILL TAKE A LONG TIME FOR THIS BLIGHT TO LEAVE THEM.

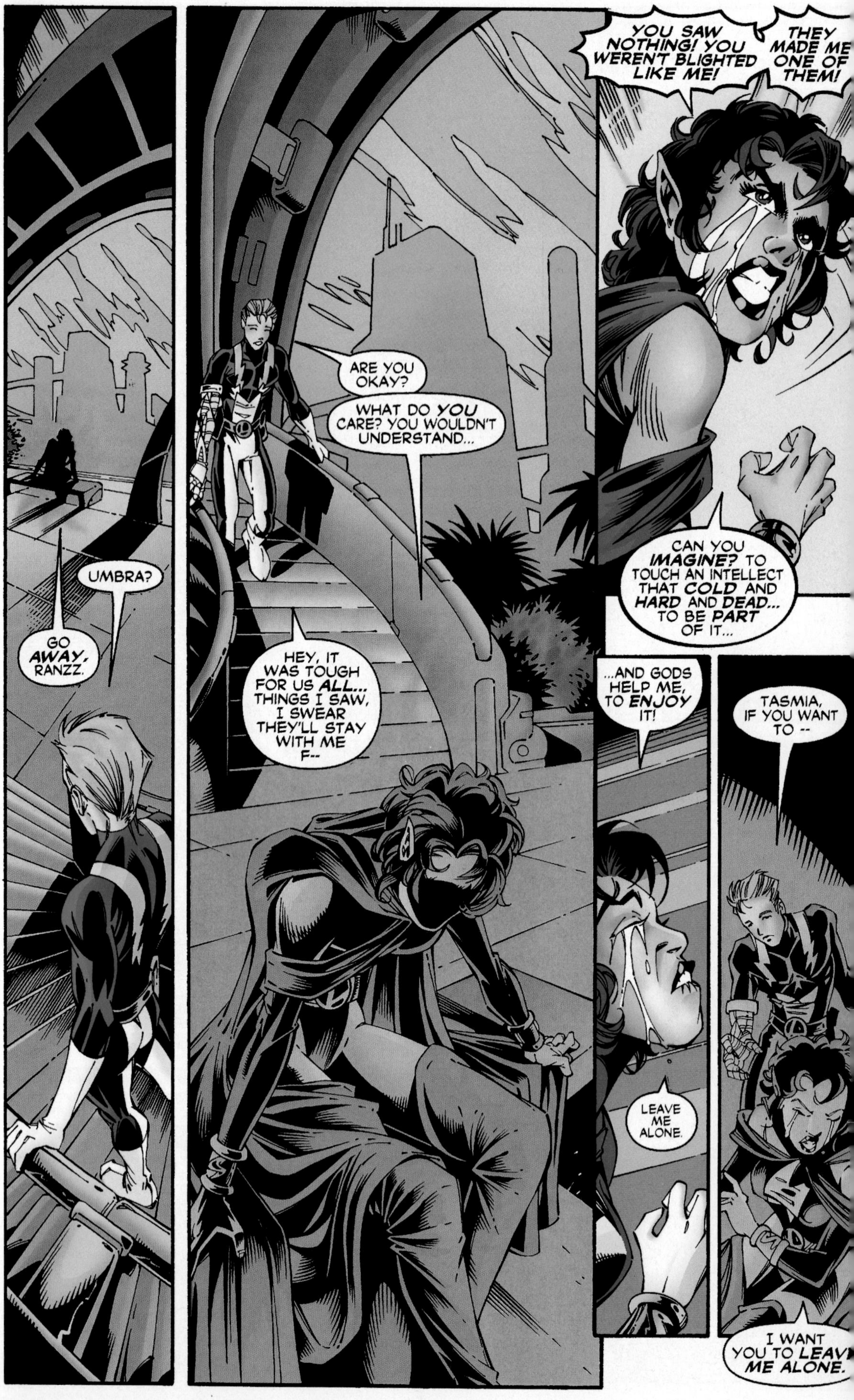

UMBRA?
GO AWAY, RANZZ.
ARE YOU OKAY?
WHAT DO YOU CARE? YOU WOULDN'T UNDERSTAND...
HEY, IT WAS TOUGH FOR US ALL... THINGS I SAW, I SWEAR THEY'LL STAY WITH ME F--
YOU SAW NOTHING! YOU WEREN'T BLIGHTED LIKE ME!
THEY MADE ME ONE OF THEM!
CAN YOU IMAGINE? TO TOUCH AN INTELLECT THAT COLD AND HARD AND DEAD... TO BE PART OF IT...
...AND GODS HELP ME, TO ENJOY IT!
LEAVE ME ALONE.
TASMIA, IF YOU WANT TO --
I WANT YOU TO LEAVE ME ALONE.

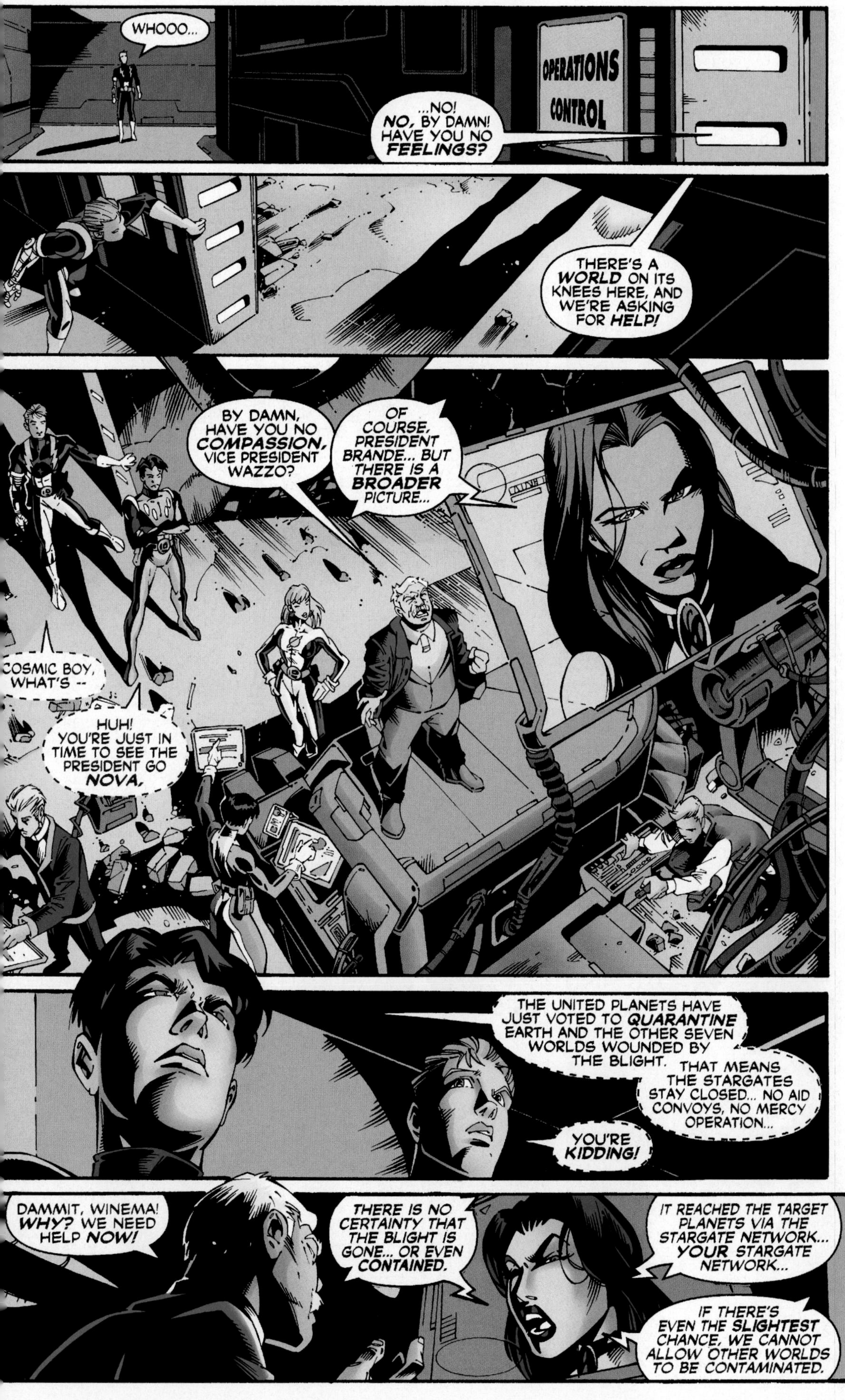
WHOOO...
OPERATIONS CONTROL
...NO! NO, BY DAMN! HAVE YOU NO FEELINGS?
THERE'S A WORLD ON ITS KNEES HERE, AND WE'RE ASKING FOR HELP!
BY DAMN, HAVE YOU NO COMPASSION, VICE PRESIDENT WAZZO?
OF COURSE, PRESIDENT BRANDE... BUT THERE IS A BROADER PICTURE...
COSMIC BOY, WHAT'S --
HUH! YOU'RE JUST IN TIME TO SEE THE PRESIDENT GO NOVA,
THE UNITED PLANETS HAVE JUST VOTED TO QUARANTINE EARTH AND THE OTHER SEVEN WORLDS WOUNDED BY THE BLIGHT.
THAT MEANS THE STARGATES STAY CLOSED... NO AID CONVOYS, NO MERCY OPERATION...
YOU'RE KIDDING!
DAMMIT, WINEMA! WHY? WE NEED HELP NOW!
THERE IS NO CERTAINTY THAT THE BLIGHT IS GONE... OR EVEN CONTAINED.
IT REACHED THE TARGET PLANETS VIA THE STARGATE NETWORK... YOUR STARGATE NETWORK...
IF THERE'S EVEN THE SLIGHTEST CHANCE, WE CANNOT ALLOW OTHER WORLDS TO BE CONTAMINATED.

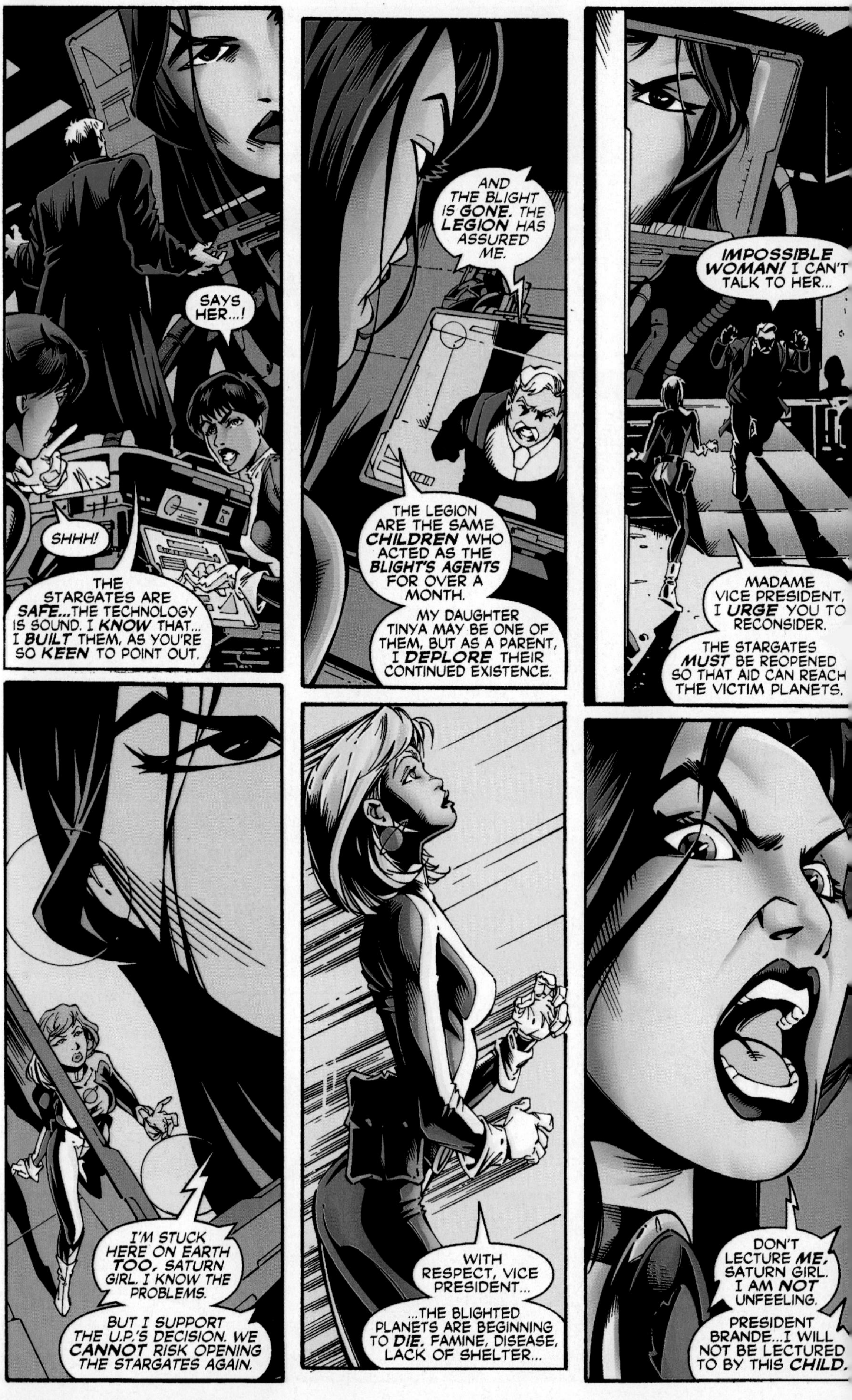
SAYS HER...!
SHHH!
THE STARGATES ARE SAFE...THE TECHNOLOGY IS SOUND. I KNOW THAT... I BUILT THEM, AS YOU'RE SO KEEN TO POINT OUT.
AND THE BLIGHT IS GONE. THE LEGION HAS ASSURED ME.
THE LEGION ARE THE SAME CHILDREN WHO ACTED AS THE BLIGHT'S AGENTS FOR OVER A MONTH.
MY DAUGHTER TINYA MAY BE ONE OF THEM, BUT AS A PARENT, I DEPLORE THEIR CONTINUED EXISTENCE.
IMPOSSIBLE WOMAN! I CAN'T TALK TO HER...
MADAME VICE PRESIDENT, I URGE YOU TO RECONSIDER.
THE STARGATES MUST BE REOPENED SO THAT AID CAN REACH THE VICTIM PLANETS.
I'M STUCK HERE ON EARTH TOO, SATURN GIRL. I KNOW THE PROBLEMS.
BUT I SUPPORT THE U.P.'S DECISION. WE CANNOT RISK OPENING THE STARGATES AGAIN.
WITH RESPECT, VICE PRESIDENT...
...THE BLIGHTED PLANETS ARE BEGINNING TO DIE. FAMINE, DISEASE, LACK OF SHELTER...
DON'T LECTURE ME, SATURN GIRL. I AM NOT UNFEELING.
PRESIDENT BRANDE...I WILL NOT BE LECTURED TO BY THIS CHILD.

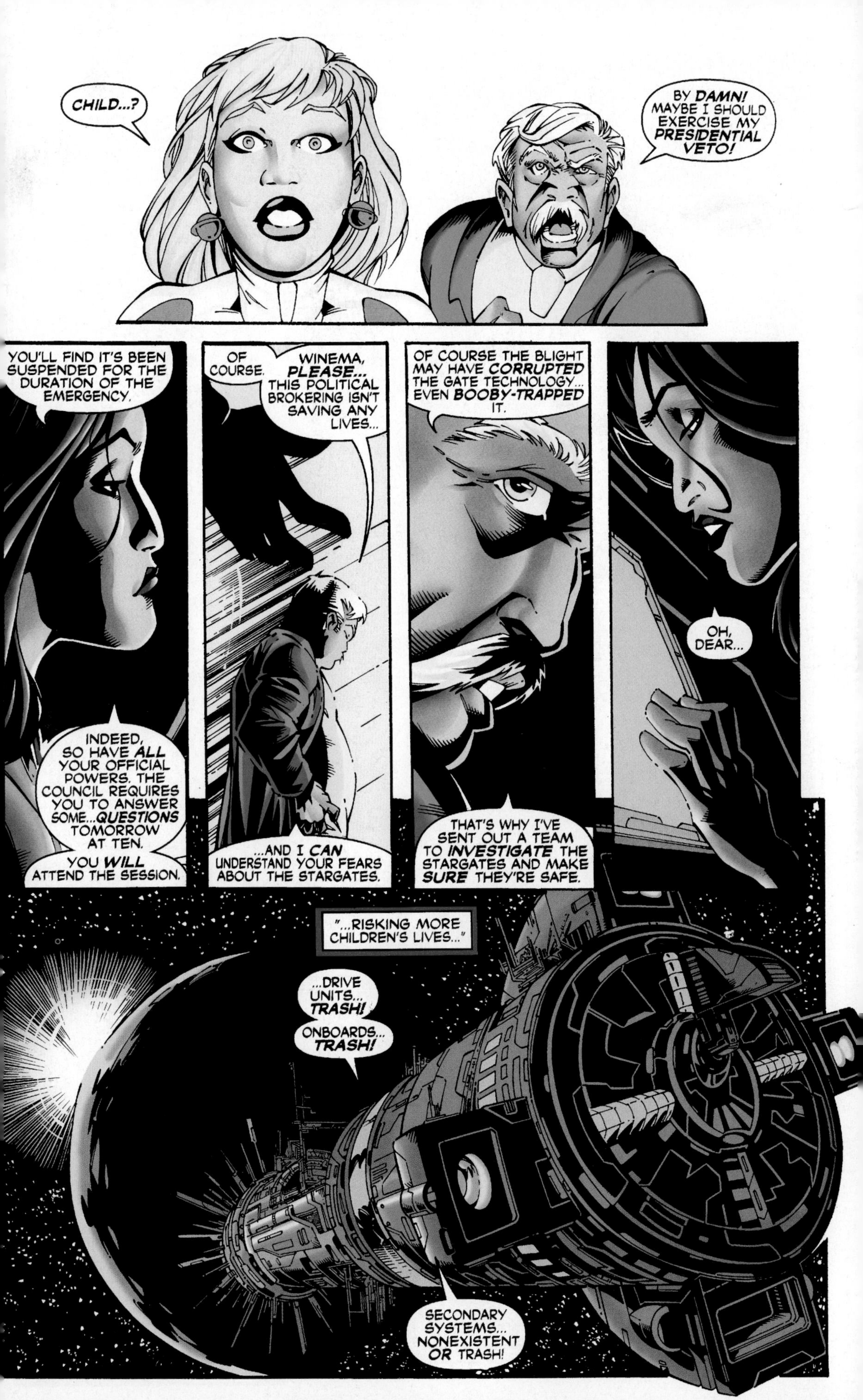
CHILD...?
BY DAMN! MAYBE I SHOULD EXERCISE MY PRESIDENTIAL VETO!
YOU'LL FIND IT'S BEEN SUSPENDED FOR THE DURATION OF THE EMERGENCY.
INDEED, SO HAVE ALL YOUR OFFICIAL POWERS. THE COUNCIL REQUIRES YOU TO ANSWER SOME...QUESTIONS TOMORROW AT TEN.
YOU WILL ATTEND THE SESSION.
OF COURSE.
WINEMA, PLEASE... THIS POLITICAL BROKERING ISN'T SAVING ANY LIVES...
...AND I CAN UNDERSTAND YOUR FEARS ABOUT THE STARGATES.
OF COURSE THE BLIGHT MAY HAVE CORRUPTED THE GATE TECHNOLOGY... EVEN BOOBY-TRAPPED IT.
OH, DEAR...
THAT'S WHY I'VE SENT OUT A TEAM TO INVESTIGATE THE STARGATES AND MAKE SURE THEY'RE SAFE.
"...RISKING MORE CHILDREN'S LIVES..."
...DRIVE UNITS... TRASH!
ONBOARDS... TRASH!
SECONDARY SYSTEMS... NONEXISTENT OR TRASH!

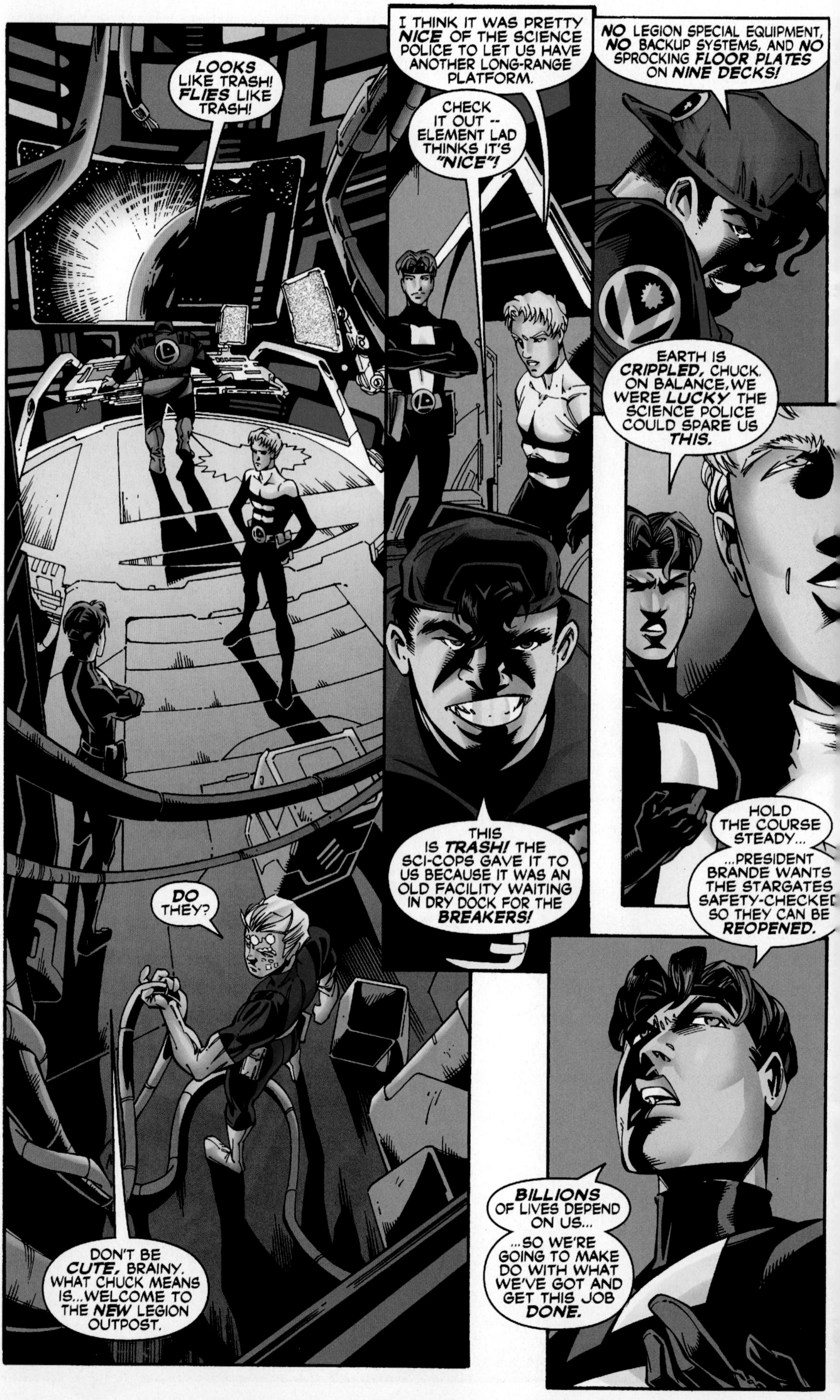

LOOKS LIKE TRASH! FLIES LIKE TRASH!
I THINK IT WAS PRETTY NICE OF THE SCIENCE POLICE TO LET US HAVE ANOTHER LONG-RANGE PLATFORM.
CHECK IT OUT -- ELEMENT LAD THINKS IT'S "NICE"!
THIS IS TRASH! THE SCI-COPS GAVE IT TO US BECAUSE IT WAS AN OLD FACILITY WAITING IN DRY DOCK FOR THE BREAKERS!
NO LEGION SPECIAL EQUIPMENT, NO BACKUP SYSTEMS, AND NO SPROCKING FLOOR PLATES ON NINE DECKS!
EARTH IS CRIPPLED, CHUCK. ON BALANCE, WE WERE LUCKY THE SCIENCE POLICE COULD SPARE US THIS.
HOLD THE COURSE STEADY...
...PRESIDENT BRANDE WANTS THE STARGATES SAFETY-CHECKED SO THEY CAN BE REOPENED.
DO THEY?
DON'T BE CUTE, BRAINY. WHAT CHUCK MEANS IS...WELCOME TO THE NEW LEGION OUTPOST.
BILLIONS OF LIVES DEPEND ON US...
...SO WE'RE GOING TO MAKE DO WITH WHAT WE'VE GOT AND GET THIS JOB DONE.

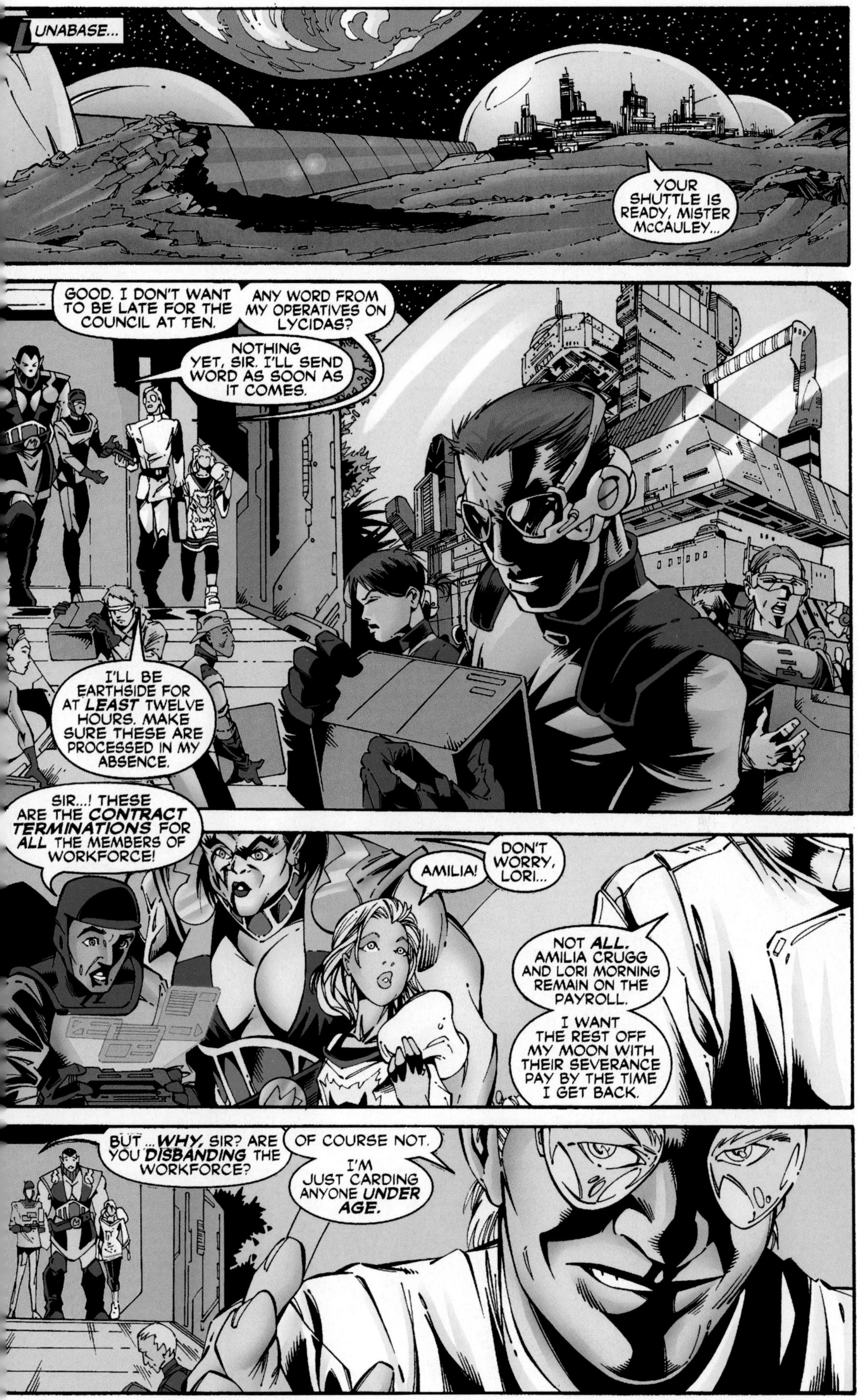
LUNABASE...
YOUR SHUTTLE IS READY, MISTER McCAULEY...
GOOD. I DON'T WANT TO BE LATE FOR THE COUNCIL AT TEN.
ANY WORD FROM MY OPERATIVES ON LYCIDAS?
NOTHING YET, SIR. I'LL SEND WORD AS SOON AS IT COMES.
I'LL BE EARTHSIDE FOR AT LEAST TWELVE HOURS. MAKE SURE THESE ARE PROCESSED IN MY ABSENCE.
SIR...! THESE ARE THE CONTRACT TERMINATIONS FOR ALL THE MEMBERS OF WORKFORCE!
AMILIA!
DON'T WORRY, LORI...
NOT ALL. AMILIA CRUGG AND LORI MORNING REMAIN ON THE PAYROLL.
I WANT THE REST OFF MY MOON WITH THEIR SEVERANCE PAY BY THE TIME I GET BACK.
BUT ...WHY, SIR? ARE YOU DISBANDING THE WORKFORCE?
OF COURSE NOT.
I'M JUST CARDING ANYONE UNDER AGE.

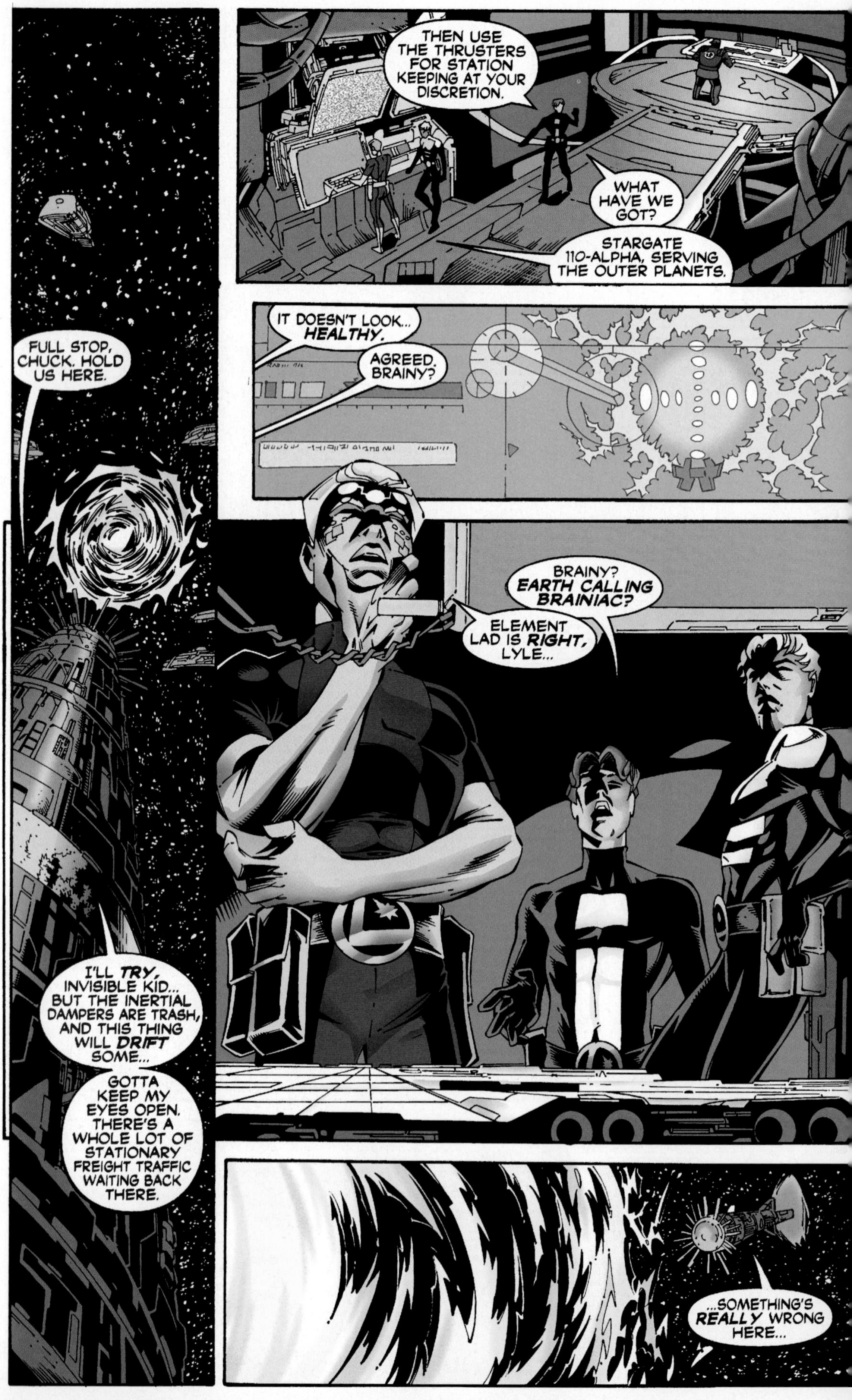
THEN USE THE THRUSTERS FOR STATION KEEPING AT YOUR DISCRETION.
WHAT HAVE WE GOT?
STARGATE 110-ALPHA, SERVING THE OUTER PLANETS.
FULL STOP, CHUCK. HOLD US HERE.
IT DOESN'T LOOK... *HEALTHY.*
AGREED. BRAINY?
BRAINY? *EARTH CALLING BRAINIAC?*
ELEMENT LAD IS *RIGHT,* LYLE...
I'LL *TRY,* INVISIBLE KID... BUT THE INERTIAL DAMPERS ARE TRASH, AND THIS THING WILL *DRIFT* SOME...
GOTTA KEEP MY EYES OPEN. THERE'S A WHOLE LOT OF STATIONARY FREIGHT TRAFFIC WAITING BACK THERE.
...SOMETHING'S *REALLY* WRONG HERE...

UNITED PLANETS HEADQUARTERS, 10:01 A.M....

AMBASSADORS... DELEGATES...

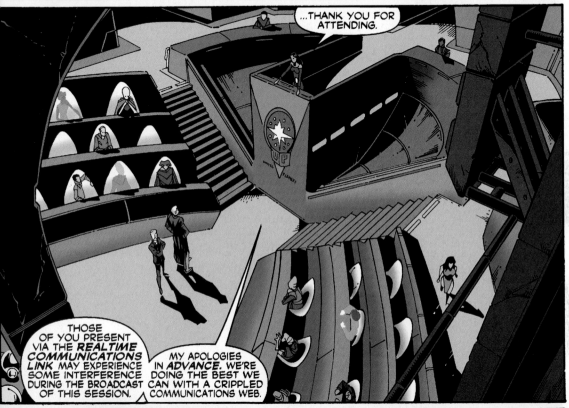

...THANK YOU FOR ATTENDING.

THOSE OF YOU PRESENT VIA THE *REALTIME COMMUNICATIONS LINK* MAY EXPERIENCE SOME INTERFERENCE DURING THE BROADCAST OF THIS SESSION.

MY APOLOGIES IN *ADVANCE.* WE'RE DOING THE BEST WE CAN WITH A CRIPPLED COMMUNICATIONS WEB.

THIS SESSION HAS BEEN CALLED BY A QUORUM OF AMBASSADORS WHO HAVE *URGENT* QUESTIONS TO PUT TO THE PRESIDENT.

I HAVE QUESTIONS OF MY *OWN,* VICE PRESIDENT WAZZO.

THERE WILL BE TIME FOR THOSE *LATER,* MISTER PRESIDENT. IF I MAY *BEGIN...*

CAN YOU CONFIRM THAT THE BLIGHT MENACE REACHED EARTH AND THE OTHER VICTIM PLANETS VIA THE *STARGATE* NETWORK?

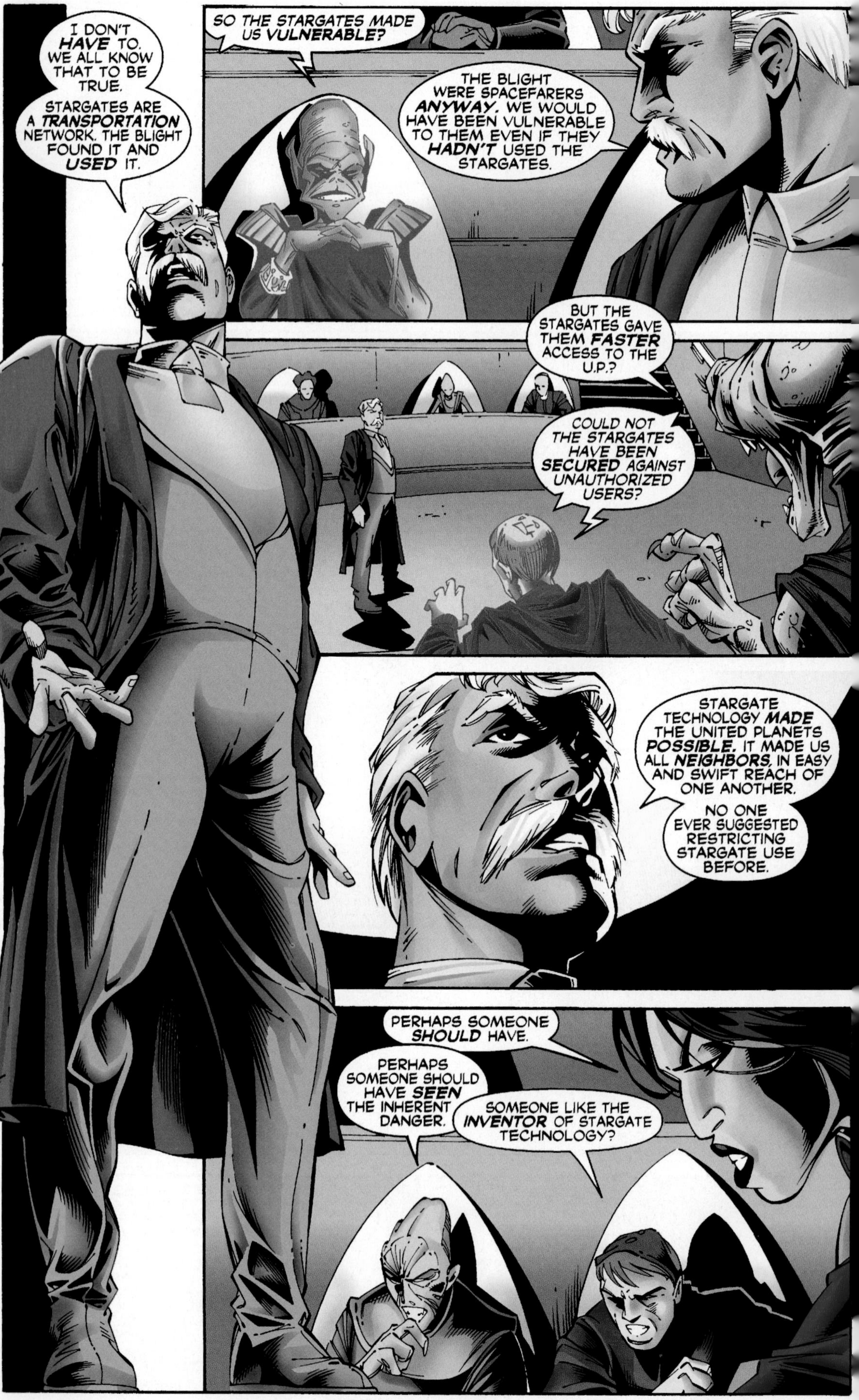
I DON'T HAVE TO. WE ALL KNOW THAT TO BE TRUE.
STARGATES ARE A TRANSPORTATION NETWORK. THE BLIGHT FOUND IT AND USED IT.
SO THE STARGATES MADE US VULNERABLE?
THE BLIGHT WERE SPACEFARERS ANYWAY. WE WOULD HAVE BEEN VULNERABLE TO THEM EVEN IF THEY HADN'T USED THE STARGATES.
BUT THE STARGATES GAVE THEM FASTER ACCESS TO THE U.P.?
COULD NOT THE STARGATES HAVE BEEN SECURED AGAINST UNAUTHORIZED USERS?
STARGATE TECHNOLOGY MADE THE UNITED PLANETS POSSIBLE. IT MADE US ALL NEIGHBORS, IN EASY AND SWIFT REACH OF ONE ANOTHER.
NO ONE EVER SUGGESTED RESTRICTING STARGATE USE BEFORE.
PERHAPS SOMEONE SHOULD HAVE.
PERHAPS SOMEONE SHOULD HAVE SEEN THE INHERENT DANGER.
SOMEONE LIKE THE INVENTOR OF STARGATE TECHNOLOGY?

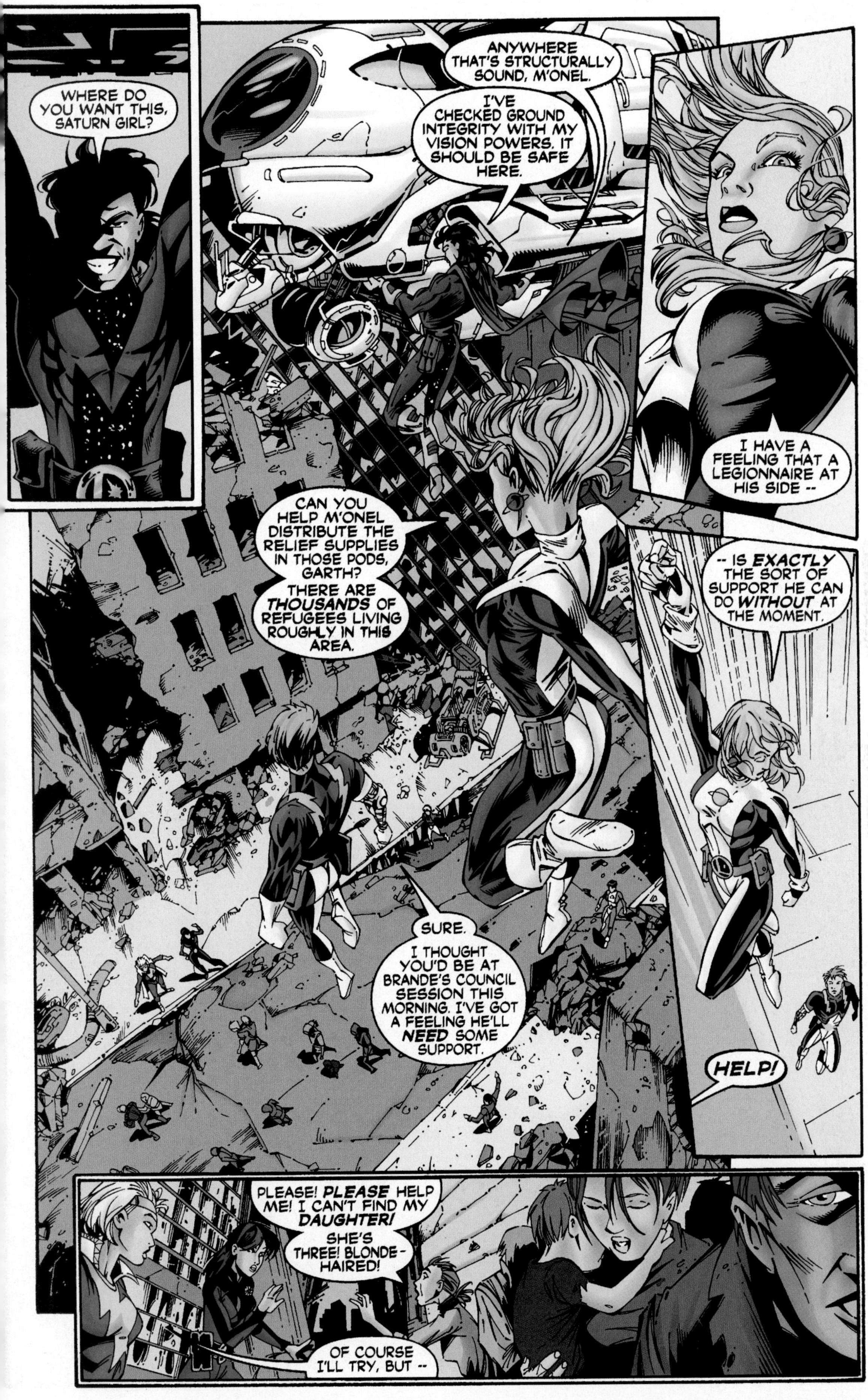
WHERE DO YOU WANT THIS, SATURN GIRL?
ANYWHERE THAT'S STRUCTURALLY SOUND, M'ONEL.
I'VE CHECKED GROUND INTEGRITY WITH MY VISION POWERS. IT SHOULD BE SAFE HERE.
CAN YOU HELP M'ONEL DISTRIBUTE THE RELIEF SUPPLIES IN THOSE PODS, GARTH?
THERE ARE THOUSANDS OF REFUGEES LIVING ROUGHLY IN THIS AREA.
SURE.
I THOUGHT YOU'D BE AT BRANDE'S COUNCIL SESSION THIS MORNING. I'VE GOT A FEELING HE'LL NEED SOME SUPPORT.
I HAVE A FEELING THAT A LEGIONNAIRE AT HIS SIDE --
-- IS EXACTLY THE SORT OF SUPPORT HE CAN DO WITHOUT AT THE MOMENT.
HELP!
PLEASE! PLEASE HELP ME! I CAN'T FIND MY DAUGHTER!
SHE'S THREE! BLONDE-HAIRED!
OF COURSE I'LL TRY, BUT --

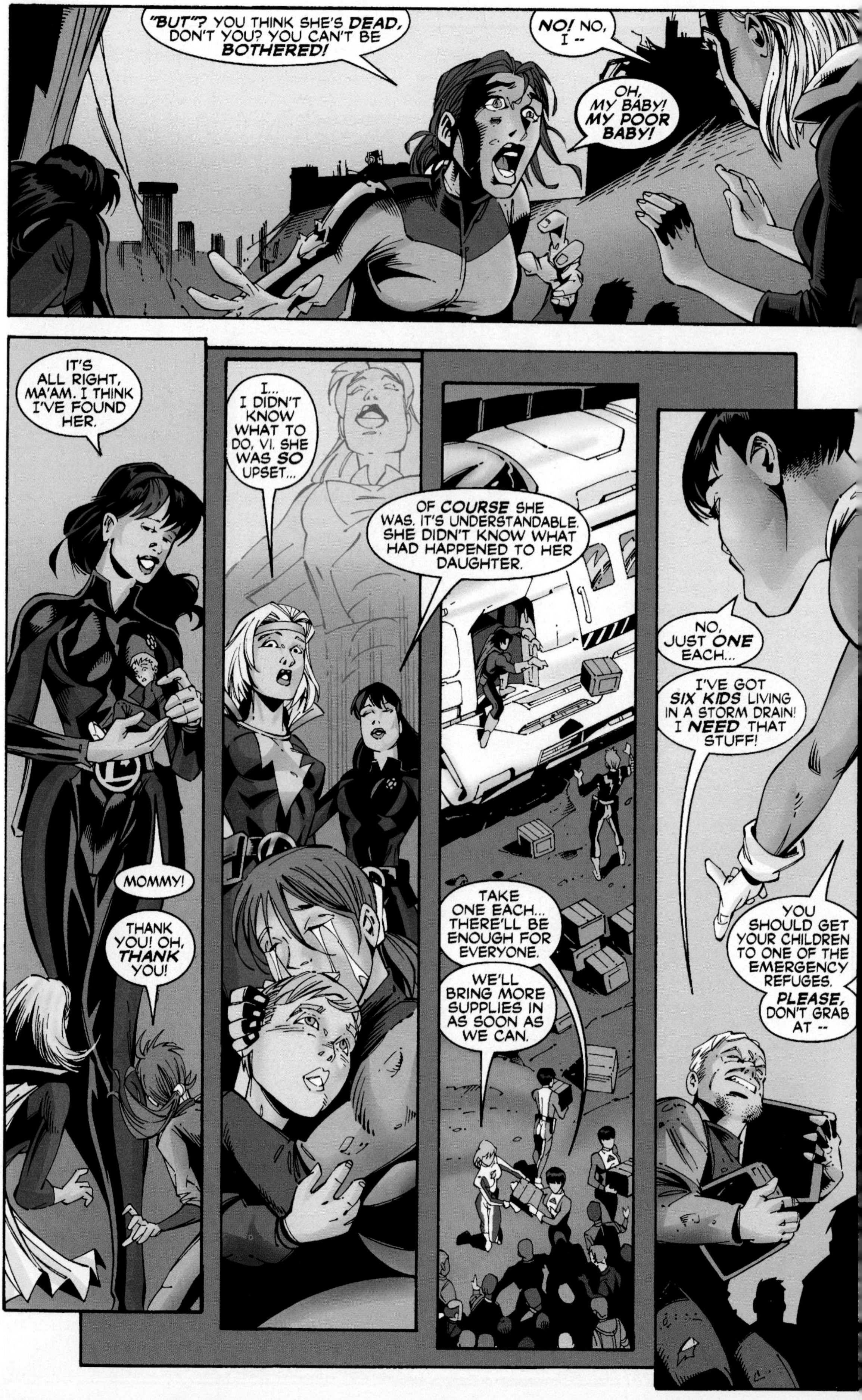
"BUT"? YOU THINK SHE'S DEAD, DON'T YOU? YOU CAN'T BE BOTHERED!
NO! NO, I --
OH, MY BABY! MY POOR BABY!
IT'S ALL RIGHT, MA'AM. I THINK I'VE FOUND HER.
MOMMY!
THANK YOU! OH, THANK YOU!
I... I DIDN'T KNOW WHAT TO DO, VI. SHE WAS SO UPSET...
OF COURSE SHE WAS. IT'S UNDERSTANDABLE. SHE DIDN'T KNOW WHAT HAD HAPPENED TO HER DAUGHTER.
TAKE ONE EACH... THERE'LL BE ENOUGH FOR EVERYONE.
WE'LL BRING MORE SUPPLIES IN AS SOON AS WE CAN.
NO, JUST ONE EACH...
I'VE GOT SIX KIDS LIVING IN A STORM DRAIN! I NEED THAT STUFF!
YOU SHOULD GET YOUR CHILDREN TO ONE OF THE EMERGENCY REFUGES. PLEASE, DON'T GRAB AT --

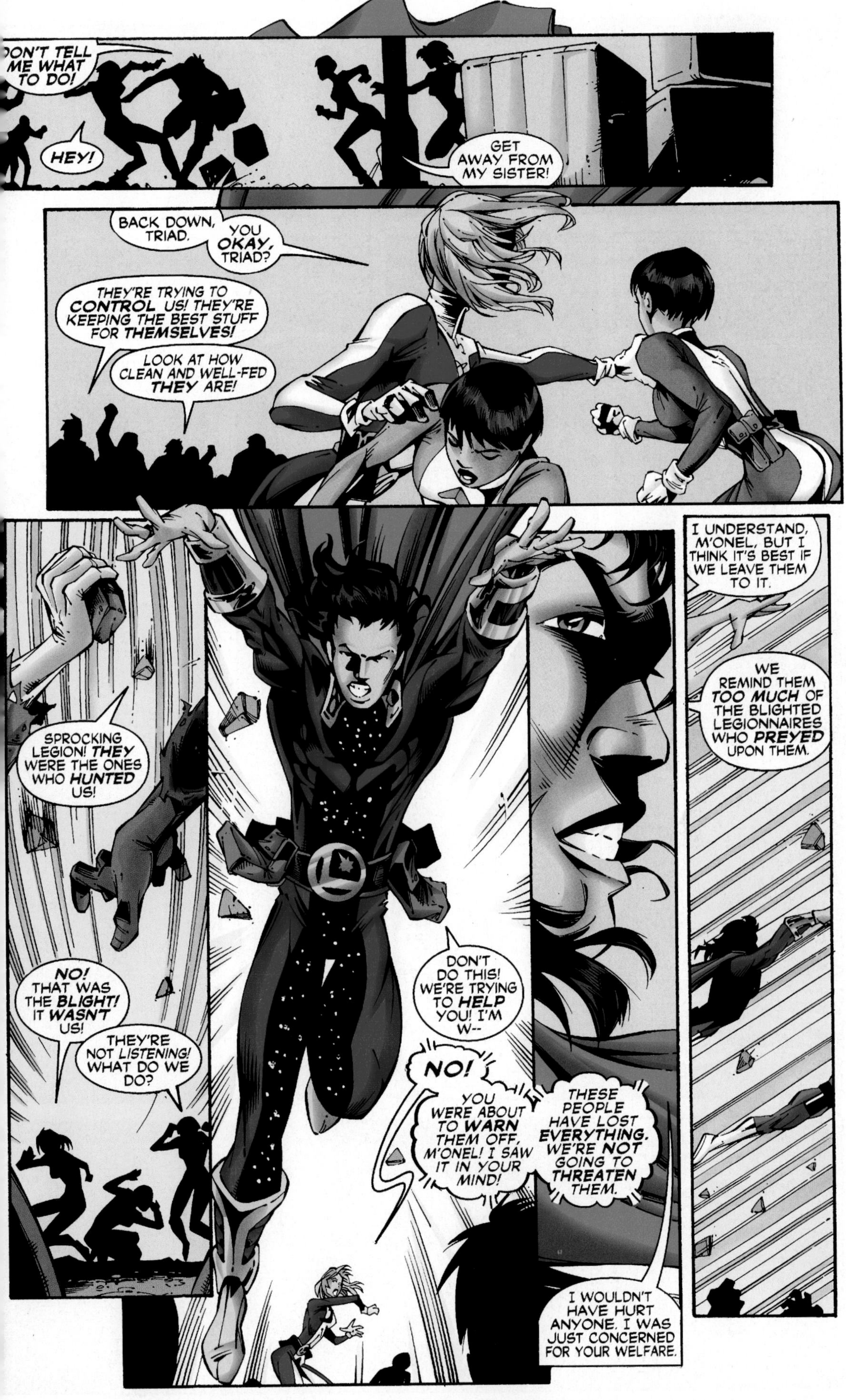
DON'T TELL ME WHAT TO DO!
HEY!
GET AWAY FROM MY SISTER!
BACK DOWN, TRIAD.
YOU OKAY, TRIAD?
THEY'RE TRYING TO CONTROL US! THEY'RE KEEPING THE BEST STUFF FOR THEMSELVES!
LOOK AT HOW CLEAN AND WELL-FED THEY ARE!
SPROCKING LEGION! THEY WERE THE ONES WHO HUNTED US!
NO! THAT WAS THE BLIGHT! IT WASN'T US!
THEY'RE NOT LISTENING! WHAT DO WE DO?
DON'T DO THIS! WE'RE TRYING TO HELP YOU! I'M W--
NO!
YOU WERE ABOUT TO WARN THEM OFF, M'ONEL! I SAW IT IN YOUR MIND!
THESE PEOPLE HAVE LOST EVERYTHING. WE'RE NOT GOING TO THREATEN THEM.
I WOULDN'T HAVE HURT ANYONE. I WAS JUST CONCERNED FOR YOUR WELFARE.
I UNDERSTAND, M'ONEL, BUT I THINK IT'S BEST IF WE LEAVE THEM TO IT.
WE REMIND THEM TOO MUCH OF THE BLIGHTED LEGIONNAIRES WHO PREYED UPON THEM.

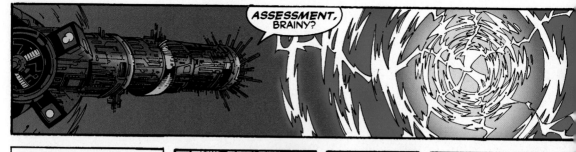

ASSESSMENT, BRAINY?

THE STARGATE IS DEFINITELY UNSTABLE. I CAN'T TELL IF IT'S BEEN DAMAGED BY THE *BLIGHT EFFECT*, OR IF THIS IS SOME KIND OF *DELIBERATE* BLIGHT SABOTAGE.

AND WE NEED TO *OPEN* THE 'GATE TO FIND OUT.

CHUCK, OPEN ME A REALTIME LINK TO THE PRESIDENT'S PERSONAL COMM...

"...WE'LL NEED HIS PERMISSION."

...BY *DAMN*, I DON'T *BELIEVE* THIS! ALL YOU'RE INTERESTED IN IS WHERE TO PLACE THE *BLAME*!

WHERE ARE YOUR *PRIORITIES*? WE *MUST* REOPEN THE STARGATE NETWORK SO THAT *AID* CAN GET THROUGH TO ALL THE BLIGHTED PLANETS! OTHERWISE --

BEEP BEEP

EH?

EXCUSE ME -- I'VE BEEN *WAITING* FOR THIS. MY TEAM IS IN POSITION TO REPORT ON THE SAFETY OF THE STARGATES.

THEY'LL NEED PERMISSION TO OPEN ONE TO COMPLETE THEIR FINAL TESTS.

YOUR TEAM... DON'T YOU *SEE*? YOU'RE RISKING THE LIVES OF *CHILDREN* IN THIS HAZARDOUS ENTERPRISE.

AM I ALONE IN FINDING THE PRESIDENT'S METHODS INCREASINGLY ALARMING?

HE'S MADE THE UNITED PLANETS *VULNERABLE* WITH HIS STARGATES, AND HE CONTINUALLY CHOOSES TO DEFEND US WITH *YOUTHLINGS*.

I *URGE* THE COUNCIL TO VOTE TO *DENY* PERMISSION.

PARDON ME... I HOPE I'M NOT *TOO* LATE...

...BUT I'D LIKE TO PRESENT A *SOLUTION* TO THE PROBLEM AT HAND.

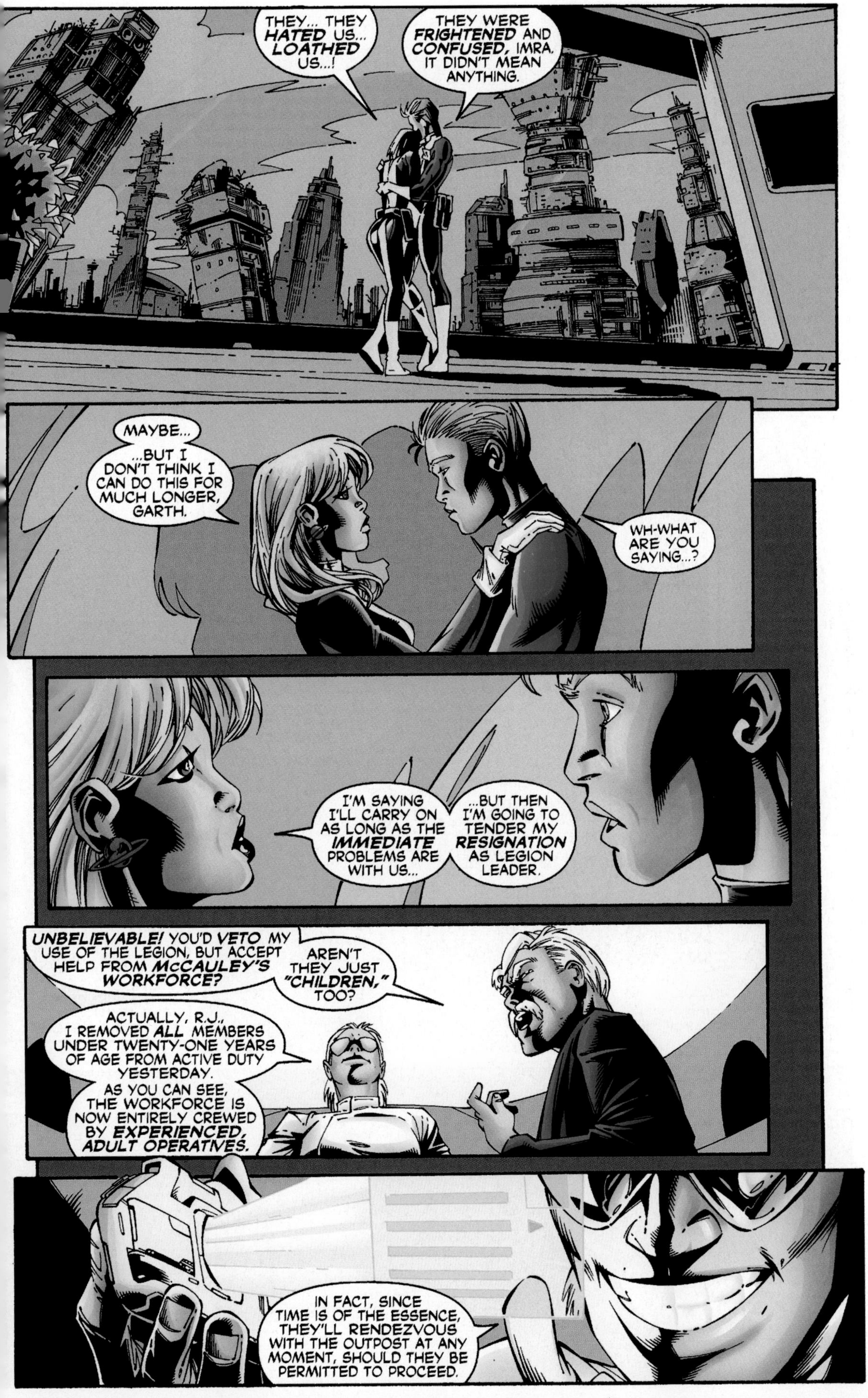
THEY... THEY HATED US... LOATHED US...!
THEY WERE FRIGHTENED AND CONFUSED, IMRA. IT DIDN'T MEAN ANYTHING.
MAYBE...
...BUT I DON'T THINK I CAN DO THIS FOR MUCH LONGER, GARTH.
WH-WHAT ARE YOU SAYING...?
I'M SAYING I'LL CARRY ON AS LONG AS THE IMMEDIATE PROBLEMS ARE WITH US...
...BUT THEN I'M GOING TO TENDER MY RESIGNATION AS LEGION LEADER.
UNBELIEVABLE! YOU'D VETO MY USE OF THE LEGION, BUT ACCEPT HELP FROM McCAULEY'S WORKFORCE?
AREN'T THEY JUST "CHILDREN," TOO?
ACTUALLY, R.J., I REMOVED ALL MEMBERS UNDER TWENTY-ONE YEARS OF AGE FROM ACTIVE DUTY YESTERDAY.
AS YOU CAN SEE, THE WORKFORCE IS NOW ENTIRELY CREWED BY EXPERIENCED, ADULT OPERATIVES.
IN FACT, SINCE TIME IS OF THE ESSENCE, THEY'LL RENDEZVOUS WITH THE OUTPOST AT ANY MOMENT, SHOULD THEY BE PERMITTED TO PROCEED.

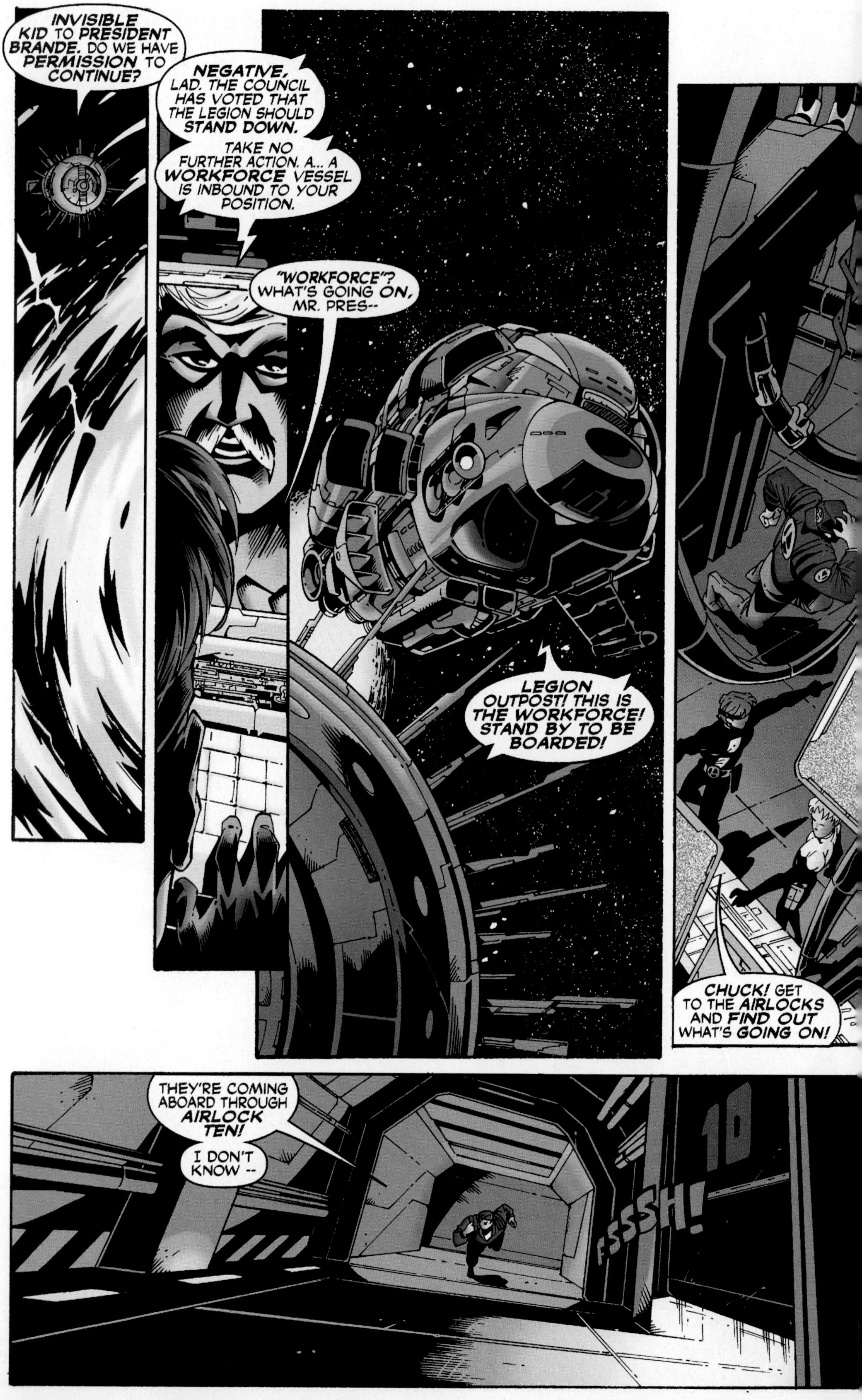
INVISIBLE KID TO PRESIDENT BRANDE. DO WE HAVE PERMISSION TO CONTINUE?
NEGATIVE, LAD. THE COUNCIL HAS VOTED THAT THE LEGION SHOULD STAND DOWN.
TAKE NO FURTHER ACTION. A... A WORKFORCE VESSEL IS INBOUND TO YOUR POSITION.
"WORKFORCE"? WHAT'S GOING ON, MR. PRES--
LEGION OUTPOST! THIS IS THE WORKFORCE! STAND BY TO BE BOARDED!
CHUCK! GET TO THE AIRLOCKS AND FIND OUT WHAT'S GOING ON!
THEY'RE COMING ABOARD THROUGH AIRLOCK TEN!
I DON'T KNOW --
10
FSSSH!

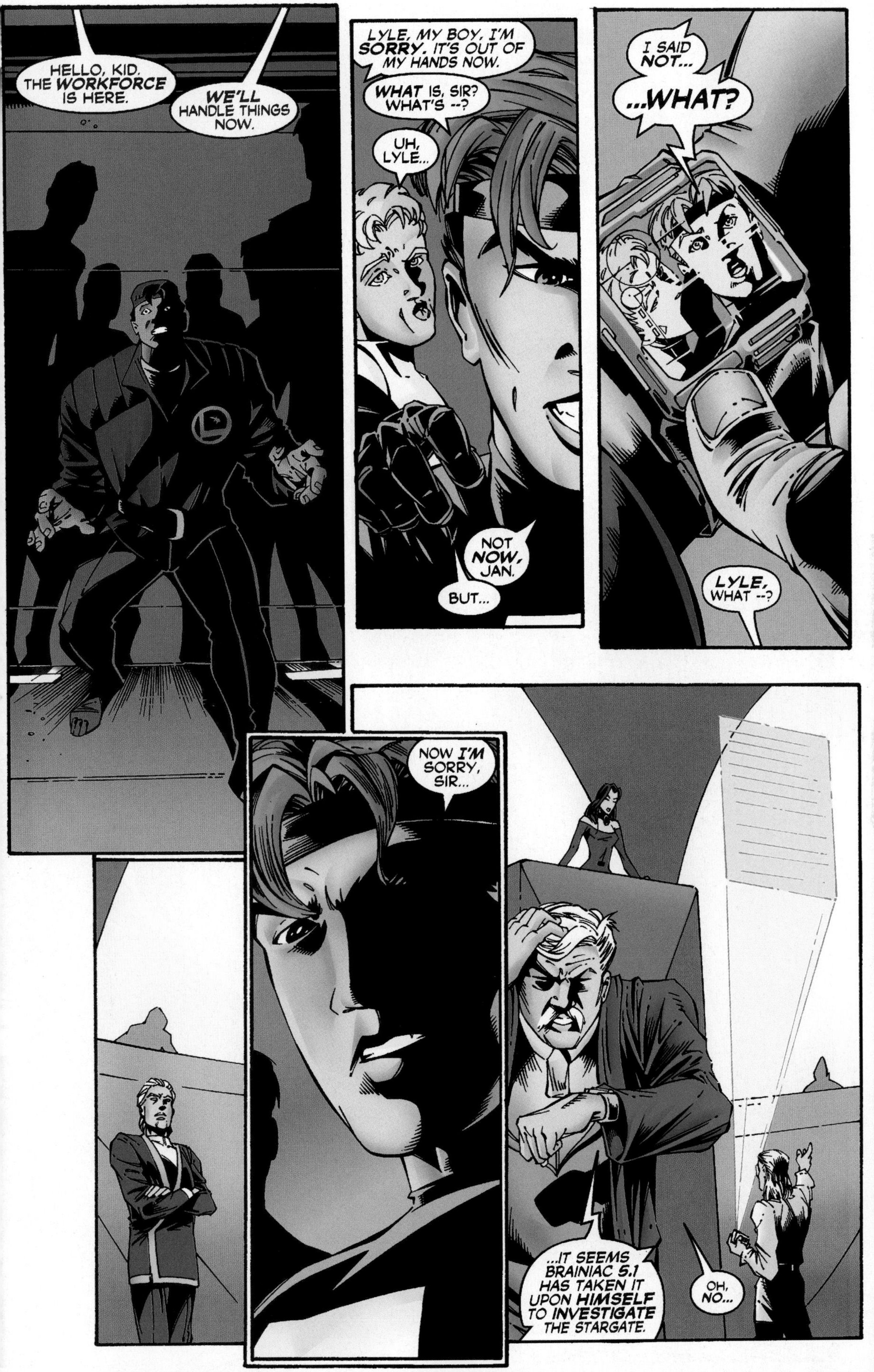
HELLO, KID. THE WORKFORCE IS HERE.
WE'LL HANDLE THINGS NOW.
LYLE, MY BOY, I'M SORRY. IT'S OUT OF MY HANDS NOW.
WHAT IS, SIR? WHAT'S --?
UH, LYLE...
NOT NOW, JAN.
BUT...
I SAID NOT...
...WHAT?
LYLE, WHAT --?
NOW I'M SORRY, SIR...
...IT SEEMS BRAINIAC 5.1 HAS TAKEN IT UPON HIMSELF TO INVESTIGATE THE STARGATE.
OH, NO...

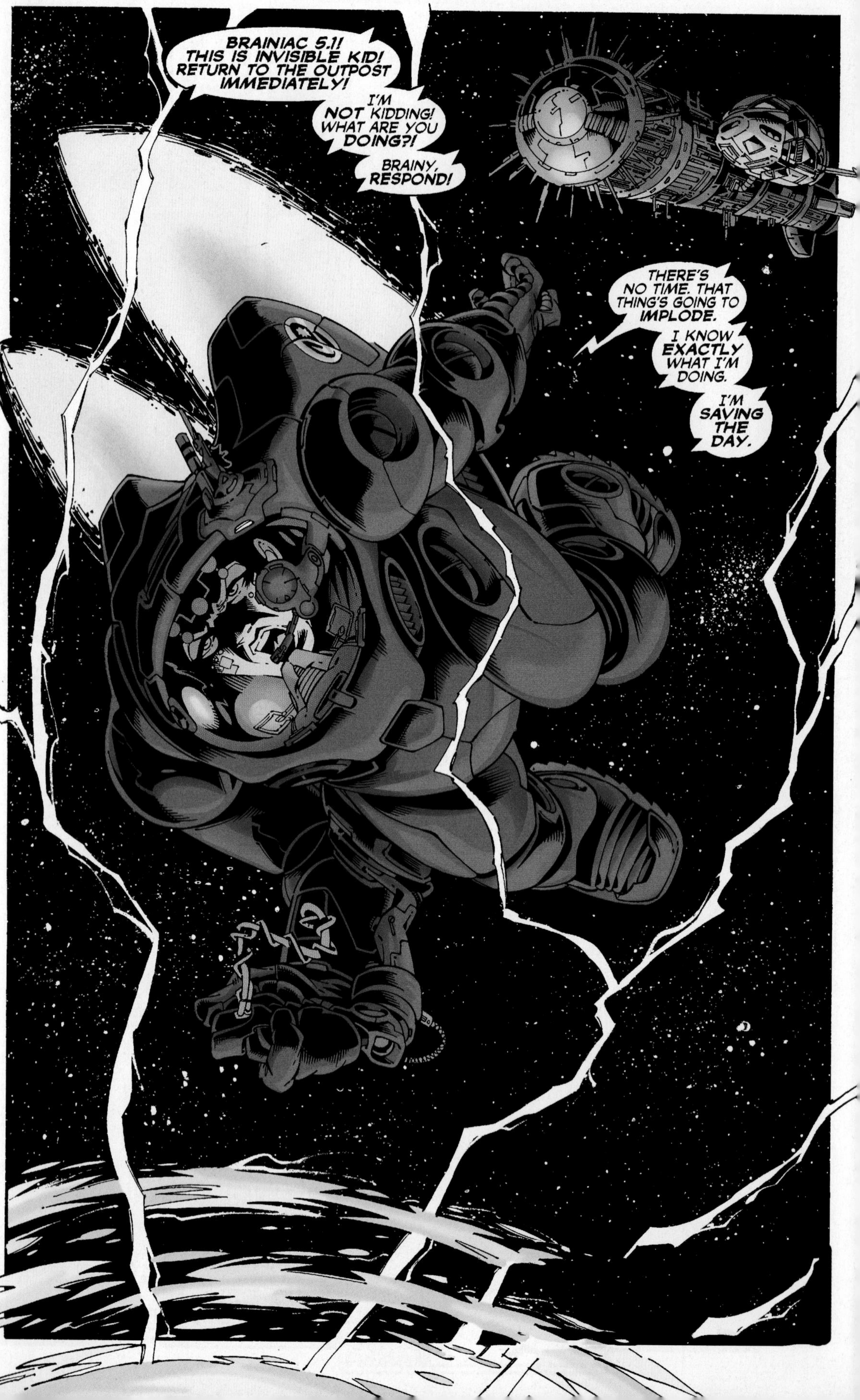
BRAINIAC 5.1! THIS IS INVISIBLE KID! RETURN TO THE OUTPOST IMMEDIATELY!
I'M NOT KIDDING! WHAT ARE YOU DOING?!
BRAINY, RESPOND!
THERE'S NO TIME. THAT THING'S GOING TO IMPLODE.
I KNOW EXACTLY WHAT I'M DOING.
I'M SAVING THE DAY.

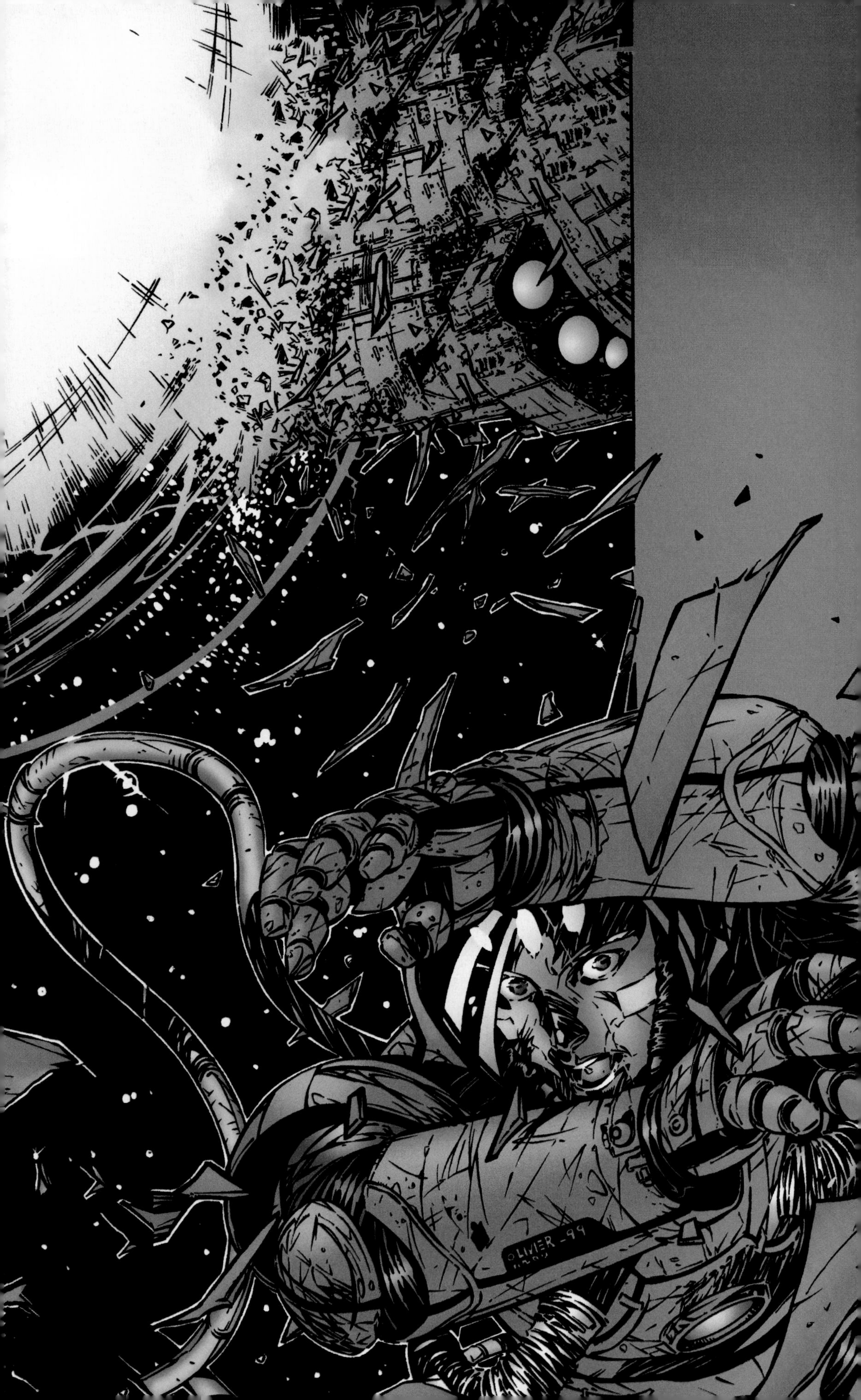
OLIVIER -99

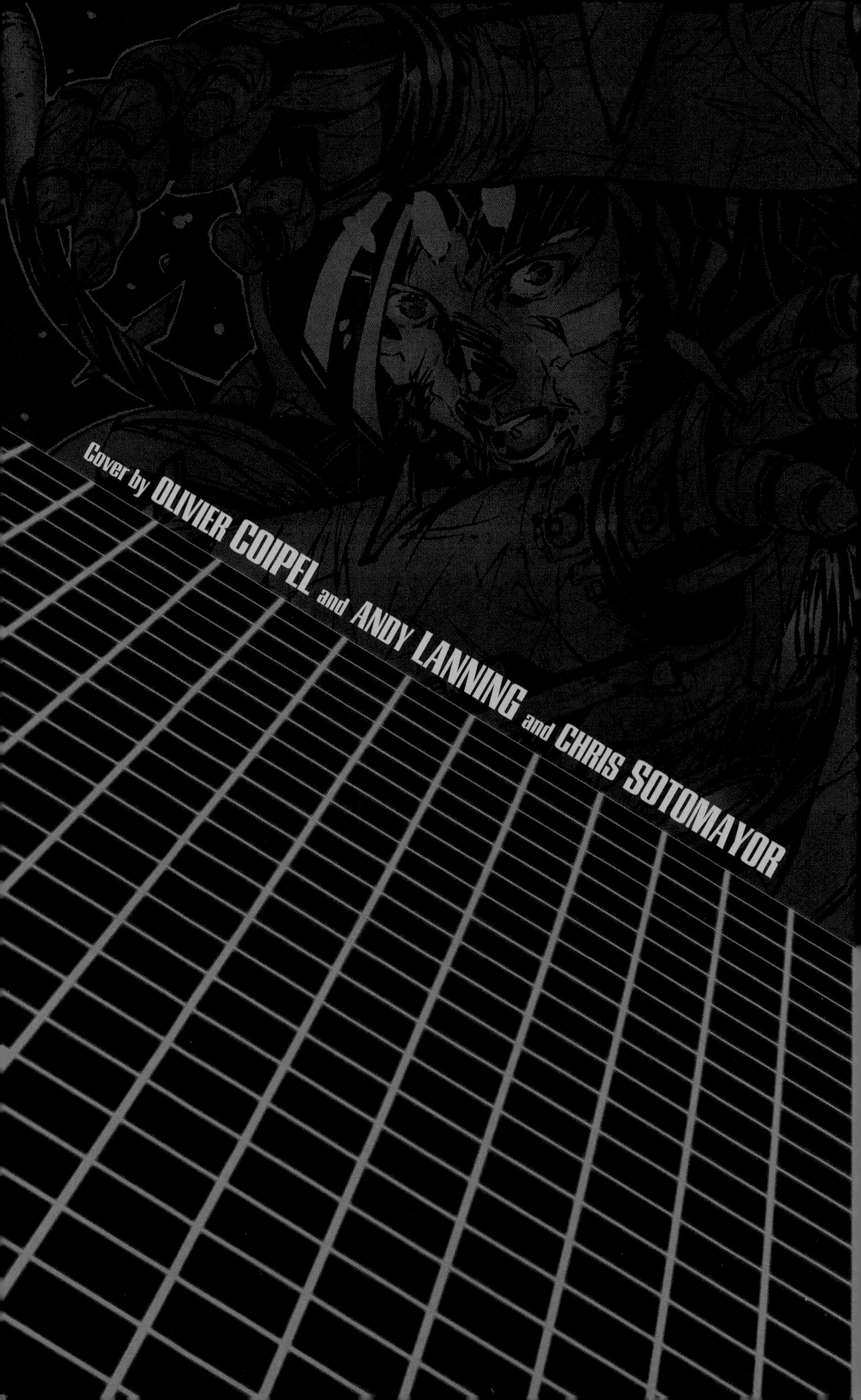
Cover by OLIVIER COIPEL and ANDY LANNING and CHRIS SOTOMAYOR

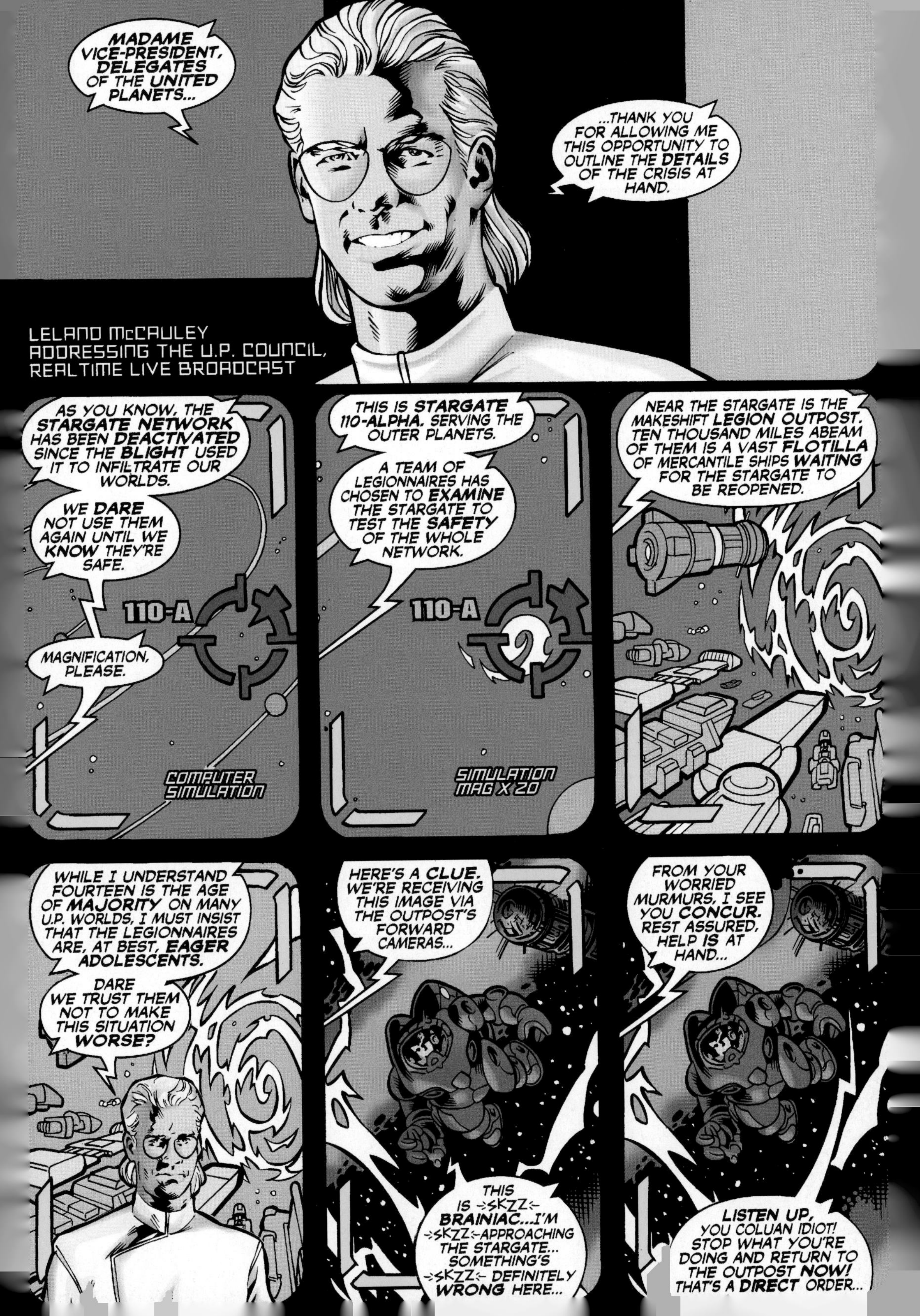

MADAME VICE-PRESIDENT, DELEGATES OF THE UNITED PLANETS...
...THANK YOU FOR ALLOWING ME THIS OPPORTUNITY TO OUTLINE THE DETAILS OF THE CRISIS AT HAND.
LELAND McCAULEY ADDRESSING THE U.P. COUNCIL, REALTIME LIVE BROADCAST
AS YOU KNOW, THE STARGATE NETWORK HAS BEEN DEACTIVATED SINCE THE BLIGHT USED IT TO INFILTRATE OUR WORLDS.
WE DARE NOT USE THEM AGAIN UNTIL WE KNOW THEY'RE SAFE.
MAGNIFICATION, PLEASE.
110-A
COMPUTER SIMULATION
THIS IS STARGATE 110-ALPHA, SERVING THE OUTER PLANETS.
A TEAM OF LEGIONNAIRES HAS CHOSEN TO EXAMINE THE STARGATE TO TEST THE SAFETY OF THE WHOLE NETWORK.
110-A
SIMULATION MAG X 20
NEAR THE STARGATE IS THE MAKESHIFT LEGION OUTPOST. TEN THOUSAND MILES ABEAM OF THEM IS A VAST FLOTILLA OF MERCANTILE SHIPS WAITING FOR THE STARGATE TO BE REOPENED.
WHILE I UNDERSTAND FOURTEEN IS THE AGE OF MAJORITY ON MANY U.P. WORLDS, I MUST INSIST THAT THE LEGIONNAIRES ARE, AT BEST, EAGER ADOLESCENTS.
DARE WE TRUST THEM NOT TO MAKE THIS SITUATION WORSE?
HERE'S A CLUE. WE'RE RECEIVING THIS IMAGE VIA THE OUTPOST'S FORWARD CAMERAS...
THIS IS -SKZZ- BRAINIAC...I'M -SKZZ- APPROACHING THE STARGATE... SOMETHING'S -SKZZ- DEFINITELY WRONG HERE...
FROM YOUR WORRIED MURMURS, I SEE YOU CONCUR. REST ASSURED, HELP IS AT HAND...
LISTEN UP, YOU COLUAN IDIOT! STOP WHAT YOU'RE DOING AND RETURN TO THE OUTPOST NOW! THAT'S A DIRECT ORDER...

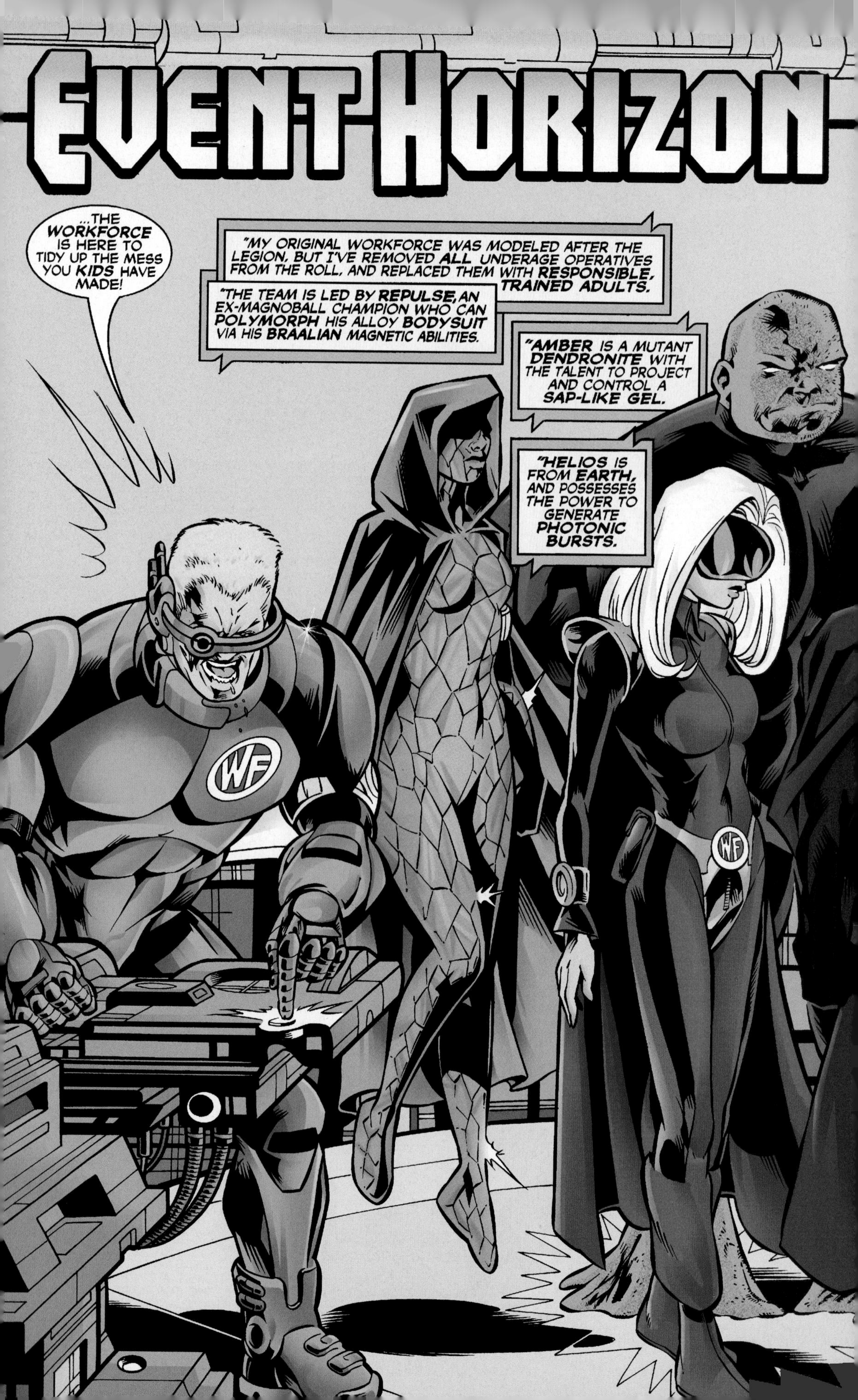
EVENT HORIZON
...THE WORKFORCE IS HERE TO TIDY UP THE MESS YOU KIDS HAVE MADE!
"MY ORIGINAL WORKFORCE WAS MODELED AFTER THE LEGION, BUT I'VE REMOVED ALL UNDERAGE OPERATIVES FROM THE ROLL, AND REPLACED THEM WITH RESPONSIBLE, TRAINED ADULTS.
"THE TEAM IS LED BY REPULSE, AN EX-MAGNOBALL CHAMPION WHO CAN POLYMORPH HIS ALLOY BODYSUIT VIA HIS BRAALIAN MAGNETIC ABILITIES.
"AMBER IS A MUTANT DENDRONITE WITH THE TALENT TO PROJECT AND CONTROL A SAP-LIKE GEL.
"HELIOS IS FROM EARTH, AND POSSESSES THE POWER TO GENERATE PHOTONIC BURSTS.
WF
WF

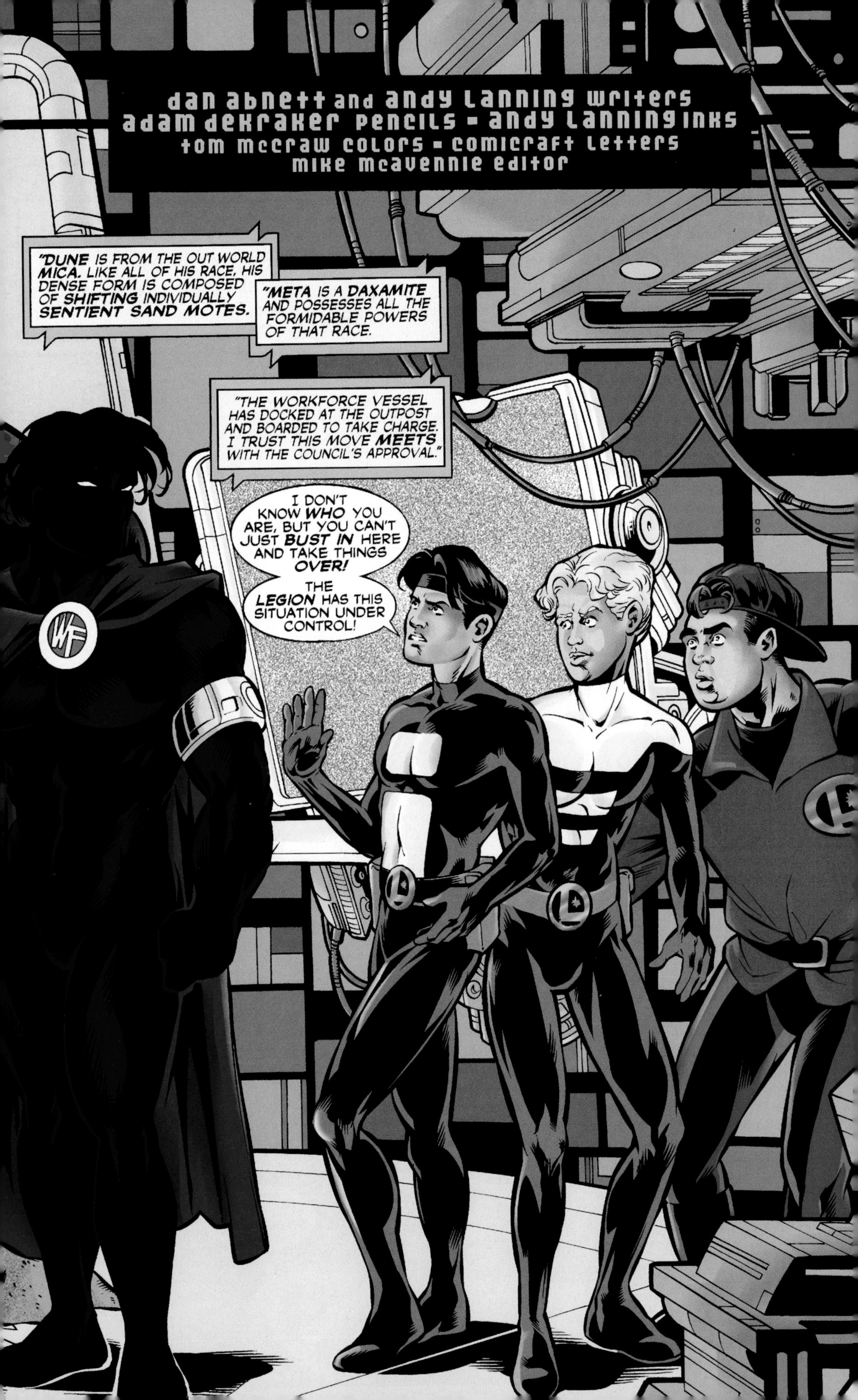
dan abnett and andy lanning writers
adam dekraker pencils - andy lanning inks
tom mccraw colors - comicraft letters
mike mcavennie editor
"DUNE IS FROM THE OUT WORLD MICA. LIKE ALL OF HIS RACE, HIS DENSE FORM IS COMPOSED OF SHIFTING INDIVIDUALLY SENTIENT SAND MOTES.
"META IS A DAXAMITE AND POSSESSES ALL THE FORMIDABLE POWERS OF THAT RACE.
"THE WORKFORCE VESSEL HAS DOCKED AT THE OUTPOST AND BOARDED TO TAKE CHARGE. I TRUST THIS MOVE MEETS WITH THE COUNCIL'S APPROVAL."
I DON'T KNOW WHO YOU ARE, BUT YOU CAN'T JUST BUST IN HERE AND TAKE THINGS OVER!
THE LEGION HAS THIS SITUATION UNDER CONTROL!

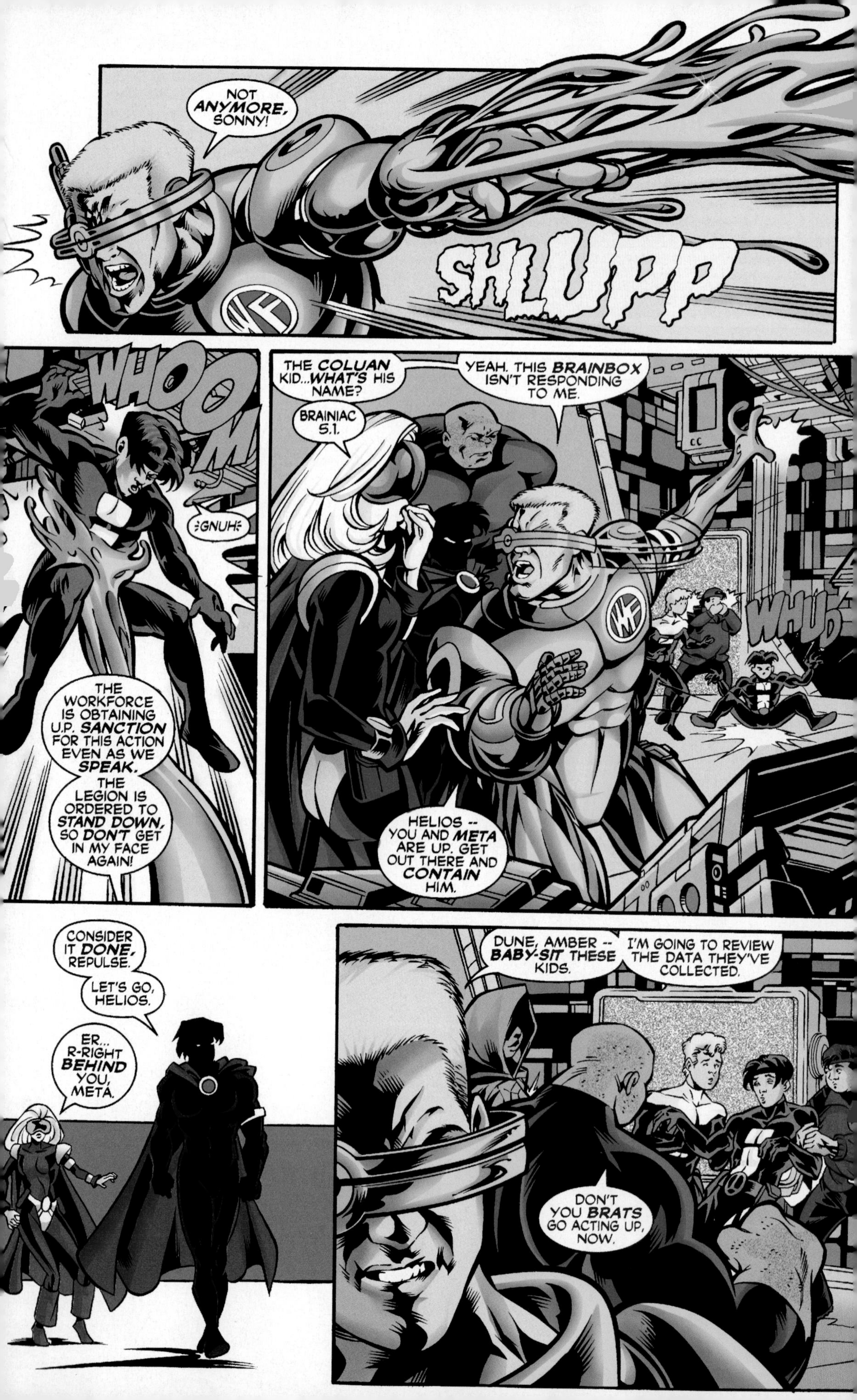
NOT ANYMORE, SONNY!
SHLUPP
WHOOM
GNUH
THE WORKFORCE IS OBTAINING U.P. SANCTION FOR THIS ACTION EVEN AS WE SPEAK.
THE LEGION IS ORDERED TO STAND DOWN, SO DON'T GET IN MY FACE AGAIN!
THE COLUAN KID...WHAT'S HIS NAME?
YEAH. THIS BRAINBOX ISN'T RESPONDING TO ME.
BRAINIAC 5.1.
WHUD
HELIOS -- YOU AND META ARE UP. GET OUT THERE AND CONTAIN HIM.
CONSIDER IT DONE, REPULSE.
LET'S GO, HELIOS.
ER... R-RIGHT BEHIND YOU, META.
DUNE, AMBER -- BABY-SIT THESE KIDS.
I'M GOING TO REVIEW THE DATA THEY'VE COLLECTED.
DON'T YOU BRATS GO ACTING UP, NOW.

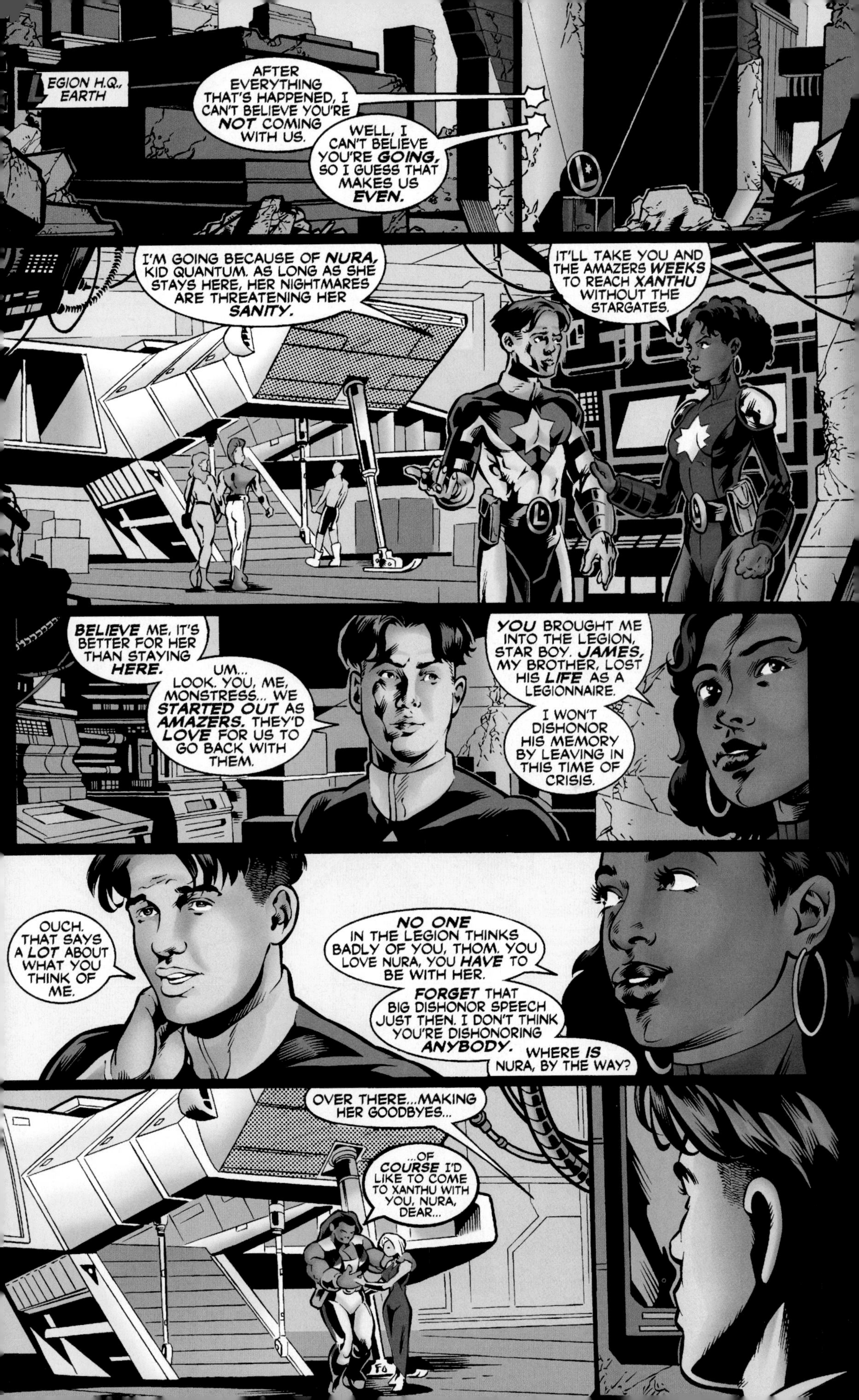
LEGION H.Q., EARTH
AFTER EVERYTHING THAT'S HAPPENED, I CAN'T BELIEVE YOU'RE NOT COMING WITH US.
WELL, I CAN'T BELIEVE YOU'RE GOING, SO I GUESS THAT MAKES US EVEN.
I'M GOING BECAUSE OF NURA, KID QUANTUM. AS LONG AS SHE STAYS HERE, HER NIGHTMARES ARE THREATENING HER SANITY.
IT'LL TAKE YOU AND THE AMAZERS WEEKS TO REACH XANTHU WITHOUT THE STARGATES.
BELIEVE ME, IT'S BETTER FOR HER THAN STAYING HERE.
UM... LOOK. YOU, ME, MONSTRESS... WE STARTED OUT AS AMAZERS. THEY'D LOVE FOR US TO GO BACK WITH THEM.
YOU BROUGHT ME INTO THE LEGION, STAR BOY. JAMES, MY BROTHER, LOST HIS LIFE AS A LEGIONNAIRE.
I WON'T DISHONOR HIS MEMORY BY LEAVING IN THIS TIME OF CRISIS.
OUCH. THAT SAYS A LOT ABOUT WHAT YOU THINK OF ME.
NO ONE IN THE LEGION THINKS BADLY OF YOU, THOM. YOU LOVE NURA, YOU HAVE TO BE WITH HER.
FORGET THAT BIG DISHONOR SPEECH JUST THEN. I DON'T THINK YOU'RE DISHONORING ANYBODY.
WHERE IS NURA, BY THE WAY?
OVER THERE...MAKING HER GOODBYES...
...OF COURSE I'D LIKE TO COME TO XANTHU WITH YOU, NURA, DEAR...

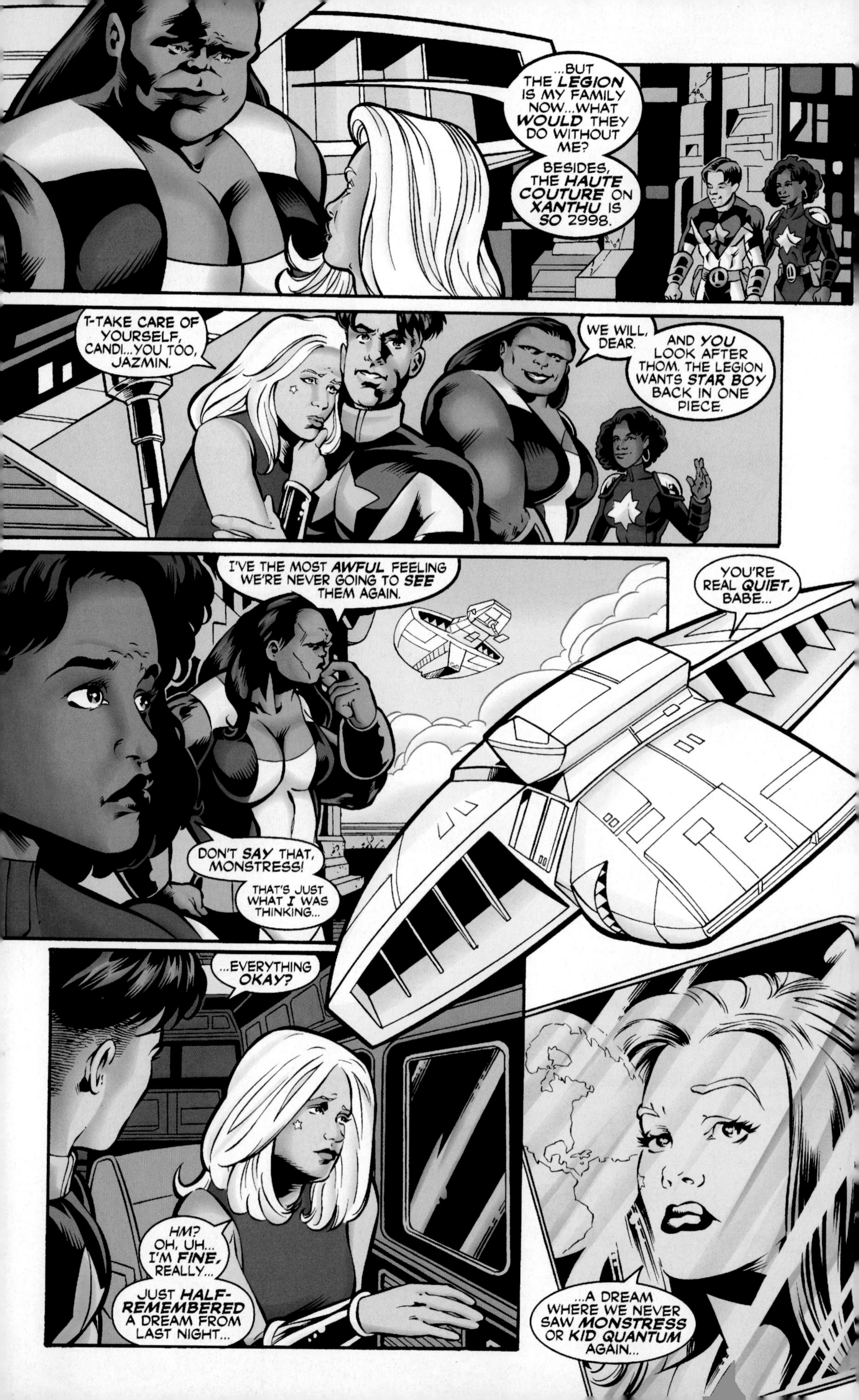

...BUT THE LEGION IS MY FAMILY NOW... WHAT WOULD THEY DO WITHOUT ME?
BESIDES, THE HAUTE COUTURE ON XANTHU IS SO 2998.
T-TAKE CARE OF YOURSELF, CANDI... YOU TOO, JAZMIN.
WE WILL, DEAR.
AND YOU LOOK AFTER THOM. THE LEGION WANTS STAR BOY BACK IN ONE PIECE.
I'VE THE MOST AWFUL FEELING WE'RE NEVER GOING TO SEE THEM AGAIN.
DON'T SAY THAT, MONSTRESS!
THAT'S JUST WHAT I WAS THINKING...
YOU'RE REAL QUIET, BABE...
...EVERYTHING OKAY?
HM? OH, UH... I'M FINE, REALLY...
JUST HALF-REMEMBERED A DREAM FROM LAST NIGHT...
...A DREAM WHERE WE NEVER SAW MONSTRESS OR KID QUANTUM AGAIN...

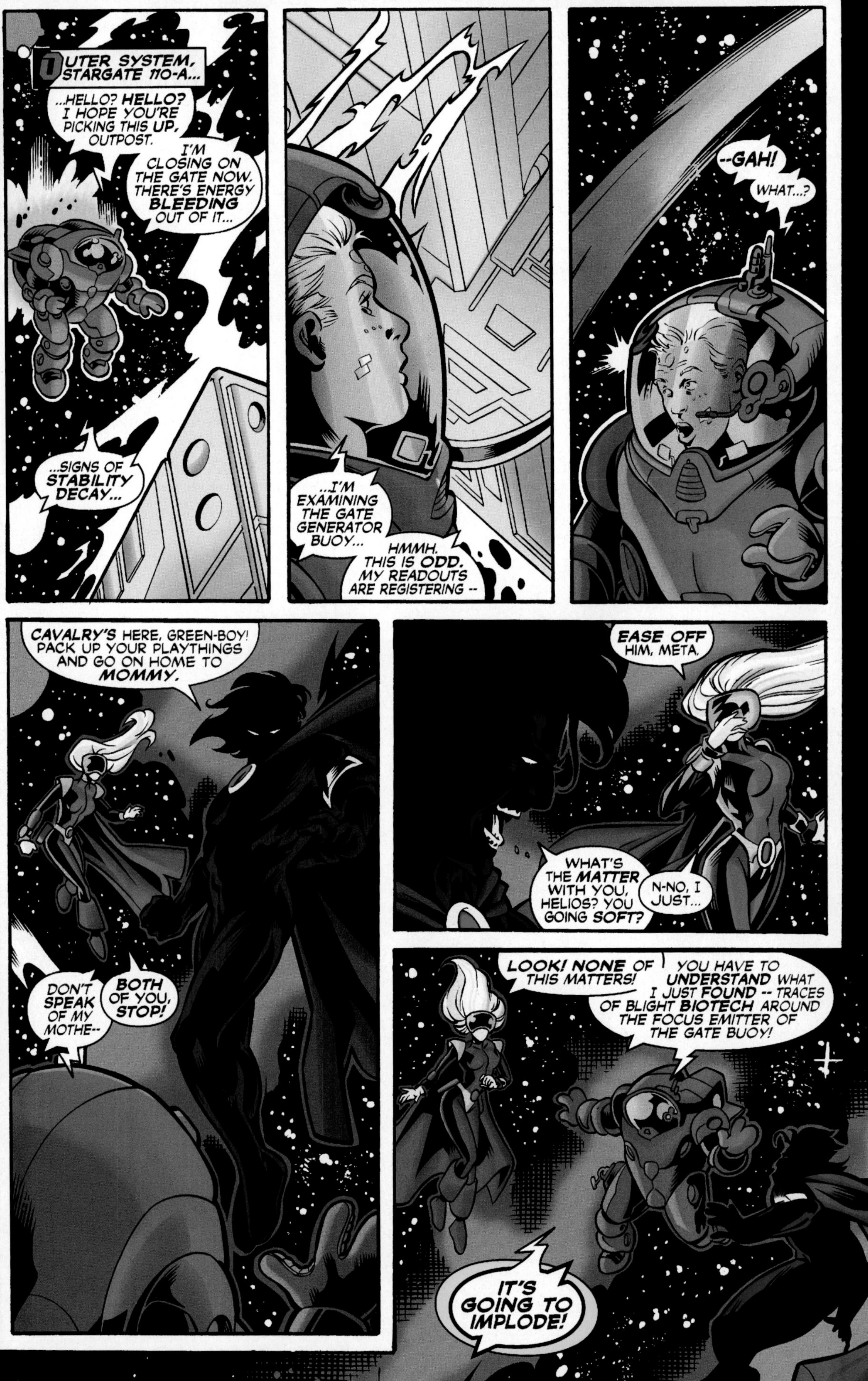
OUTER SYSTEM, STARGATE 110-A...
...HELLO? HELLO? I HOPE YOU'RE PICKING THIS UP, OUTPOST.
I'M CLOSING ON THE GATE NOW. THERE'S ENERGY BLEEDING OUT OF IT...
...SIGNS OF STABILITY DECAY...
...I'M EXAMINING THE GATE GENERATOR BUOY...
HMMH. THIS IS ODD. MY READOUTS ARE REGISTERING --
--GAH!
WHAT...?
CAVALRY'S HERE, GREEN-BOY! PACK UP YOUR PLAYTHINGS AND GO ON HOME TO MOMMY.
EASE OFF HIM, META.
WHAT'S THE MATTER WITH YOU, HELIOS? YOU GOING SOFT?
N-NO, I JUST...
DON'T SPEAK OF MY MOTHE--
BOTH OF YOU, STOP!
LOOK! NONE OF THIS MATTERS!
YOU HAVE TO UNDERSTAND WHAT I JUST FOUND -- TRACES OF BLIGHT BIOTECH AROUND THE FOCUS EMITTER OF THE GATE BUOY!
IT'S GOING TO IMPLODE!

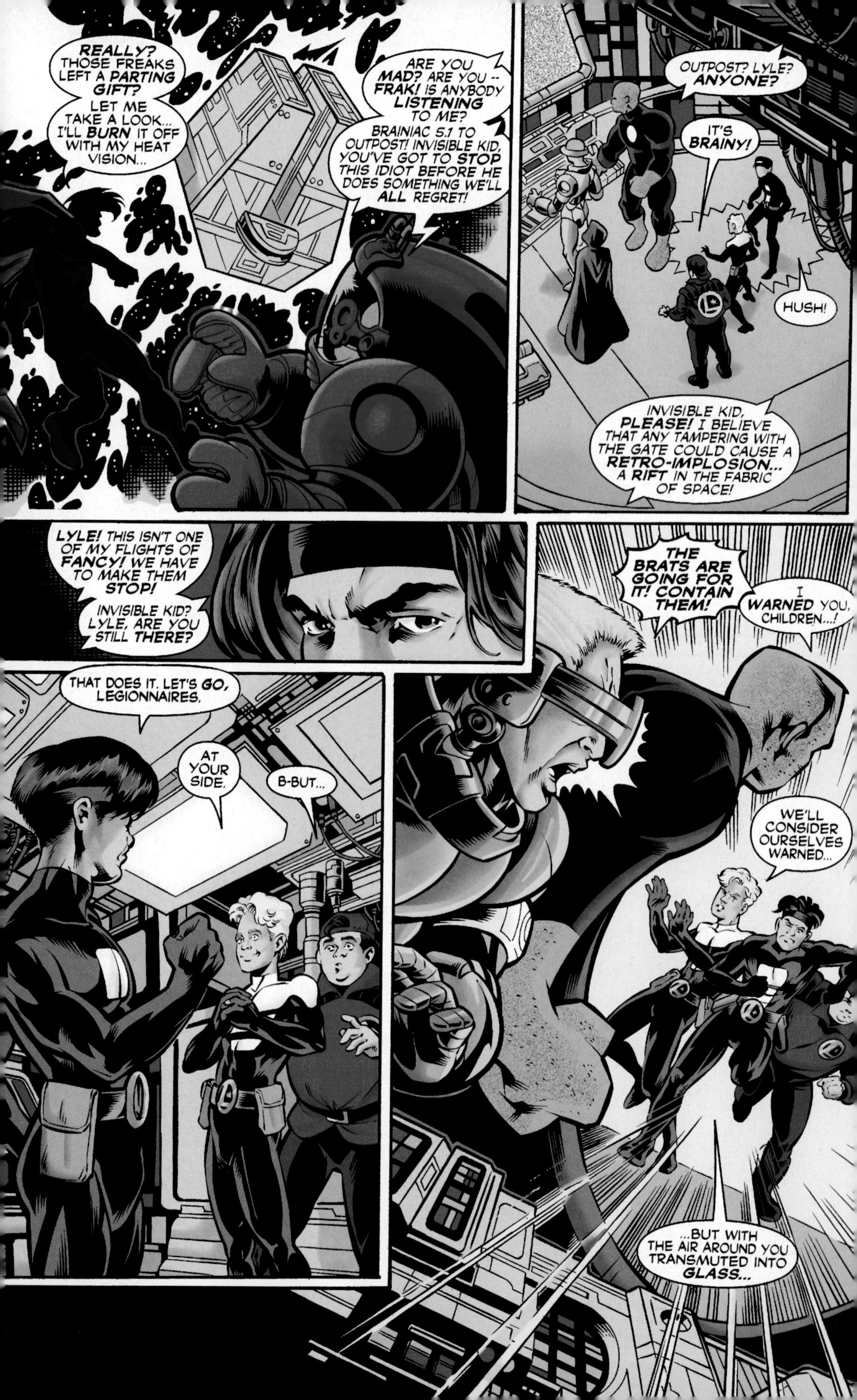
REALLY? THOSE FREAKS LEFT A PARTING GIFT?
LET ME TAKE A LOOK... I'LL BURN IT OFF WITH MY HEAT VISION...
ARE YOU MAD? ARE YOU -- FRAK! IS ANYBODY LISTENING TO ME?
BRAINIAC 5.1 TO OUTPOST! INVISIBLE KID, YOU'VE GOT TO STOP THIS IDIOT BEFORE HE DOES SOMETHING WE'LL ALL REGRET!
OUTPOST? LYLE? ANYONE?
IT'S BRAINY!
HUSH!
INVISIBLE KID, PLEASE! I BELIEVE THAT ANY TAMPERING WITH THE GATE COULD CAUSE A RETRO-IMPLOSION... A RIFT IN THE FABRIC OF SPACE!
LYLE! THIS ISN'T ONE OF MY FLIGHTS OF FANCY! WE HAVE TO MAKE THEM STOP!
INVISIBLE KID? LYLE, ARE YOU STILL THERE?
THE BRATS ARE GOING FOR IT! CONTAIN THEM!
I WARNED YOU, CHILDREN...!
THAT DOES IT. LET'S GO, LEGIONNAIRES.
AT YOUR SIDE.
B-BUT...
WE'LL CONSIDER OURSELVES WARNED...
...BUT WITH THE AIR AROUND YOU TRANSMUTED INTO GLASS...

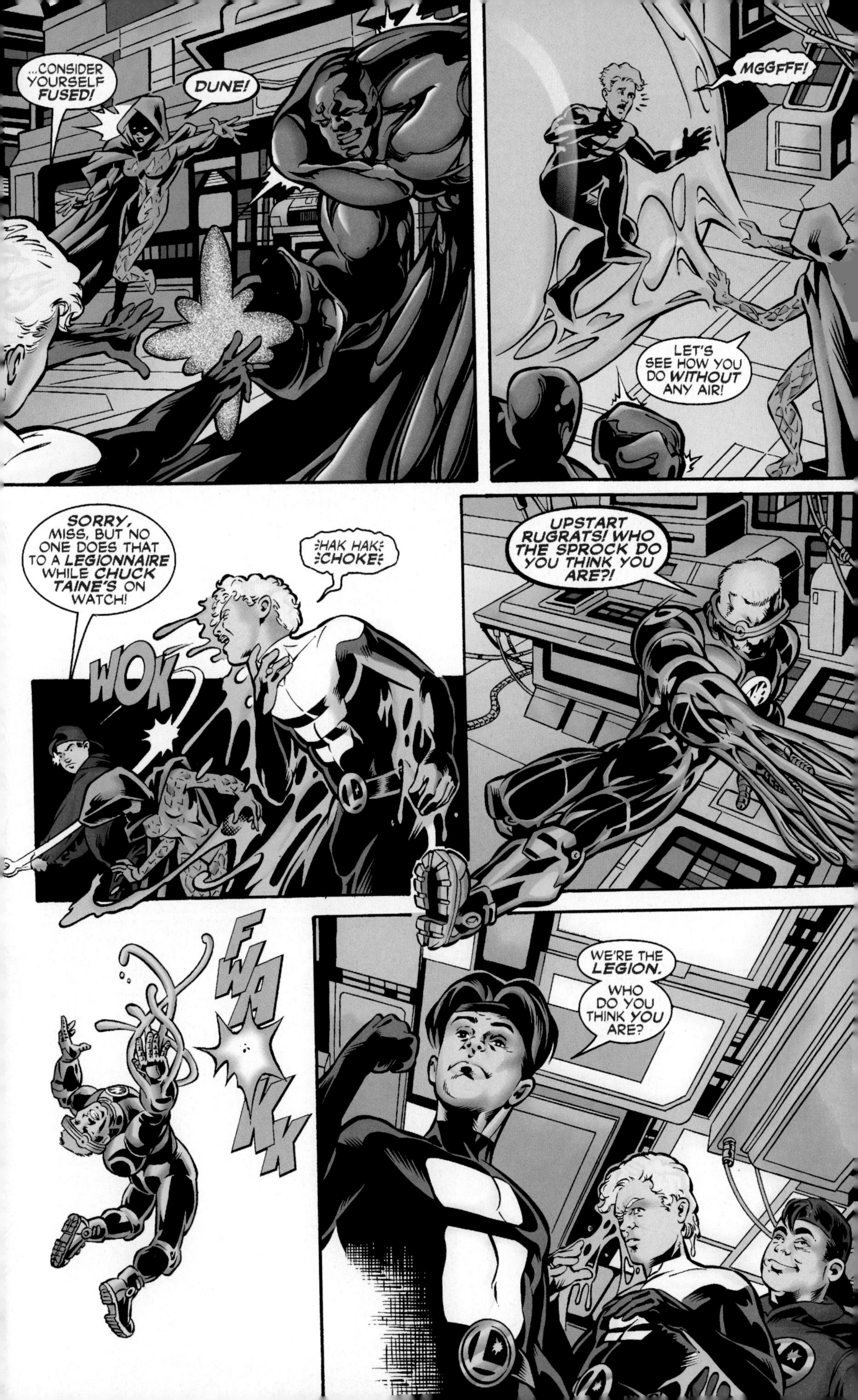
...CONSIDER YOURSELF FUSED!
DUNE!
MGGFFF!
LET'S SEE HOW YOU DO WITHOUT ANY AIR!
SORRY, MISS, BUT NO ONE DOES THAT TO A LEGIONNAIRE WHILE CHUCK TAINE'S ON WATCH!
HAK HAK CHOKE
WOK
UPSTART RUGRATS! WHO THE SPROCK DO YOU THINK YOU ARE?!
FWAKK
WE'RE THE LEGION. WHO DO YOU THINK YOU ARE?

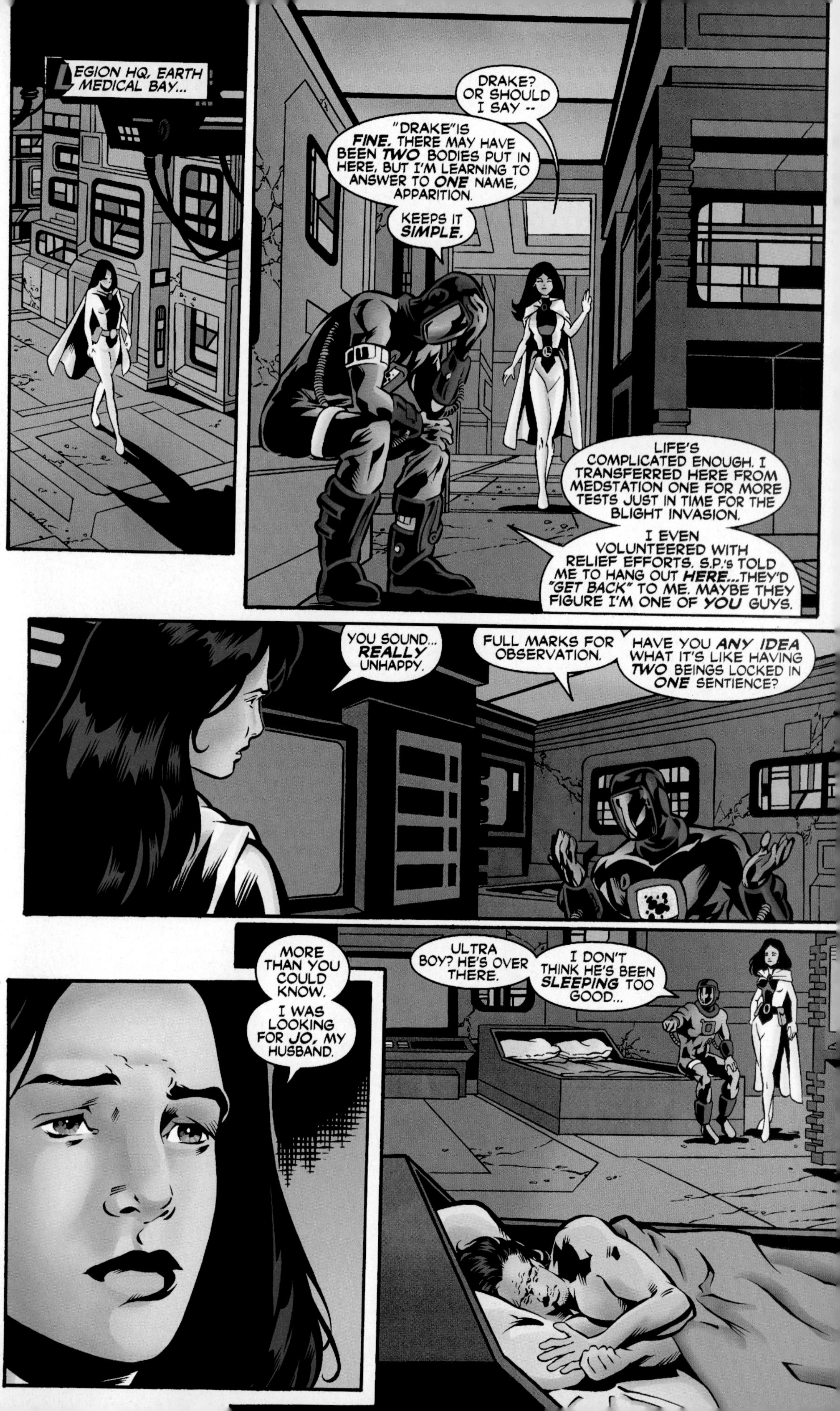
LEGION HQ, EARTH
MEDICAL BAY...
DRAKE? OR SHOULD I SAY --
"DRAKE" IS FINE. THERE MAY HAVE BEEN TWO BODIES PUT IN HERE, BUT I'M LEARNING TO ANSWER TO ONE NAME, APPARITION.
KEEPS IT SIMPLE.
LIFE'S COMPLICATED ENOUGH. I TRANSFERRED HERE FROM MEDSTATION ONE FOR MORE TESTS JUST IN TIME FOR THE BLIGHT INVASION.
I EVEN VOLUNTEERED WITH RELIEF EFFORTS. S.P.'S TOLD ME TO HANG OUT HERE...THEY'D "GET BACK" TO ME. MAYBE THEY FIGURE I'M ONE OF YOU GUYS.
YOU SOUND... REALLY UNHAPPY.
FULL MARKS FOR OBSERVATION.
HAVE YOU ANY IDEA WHAT IT'S LIKE HAVING TWO BEINGS LOCKED IN ONE SENTIENCE?
MORE THAN YOU COULD KNOW.
I WAS LOOKING FOR JO, MY HUSBAND.
ULTRA BOY? HE'S OVER THERE.
I DON'T THINK HE'S BEEN SLEEPING TOO GOOD...

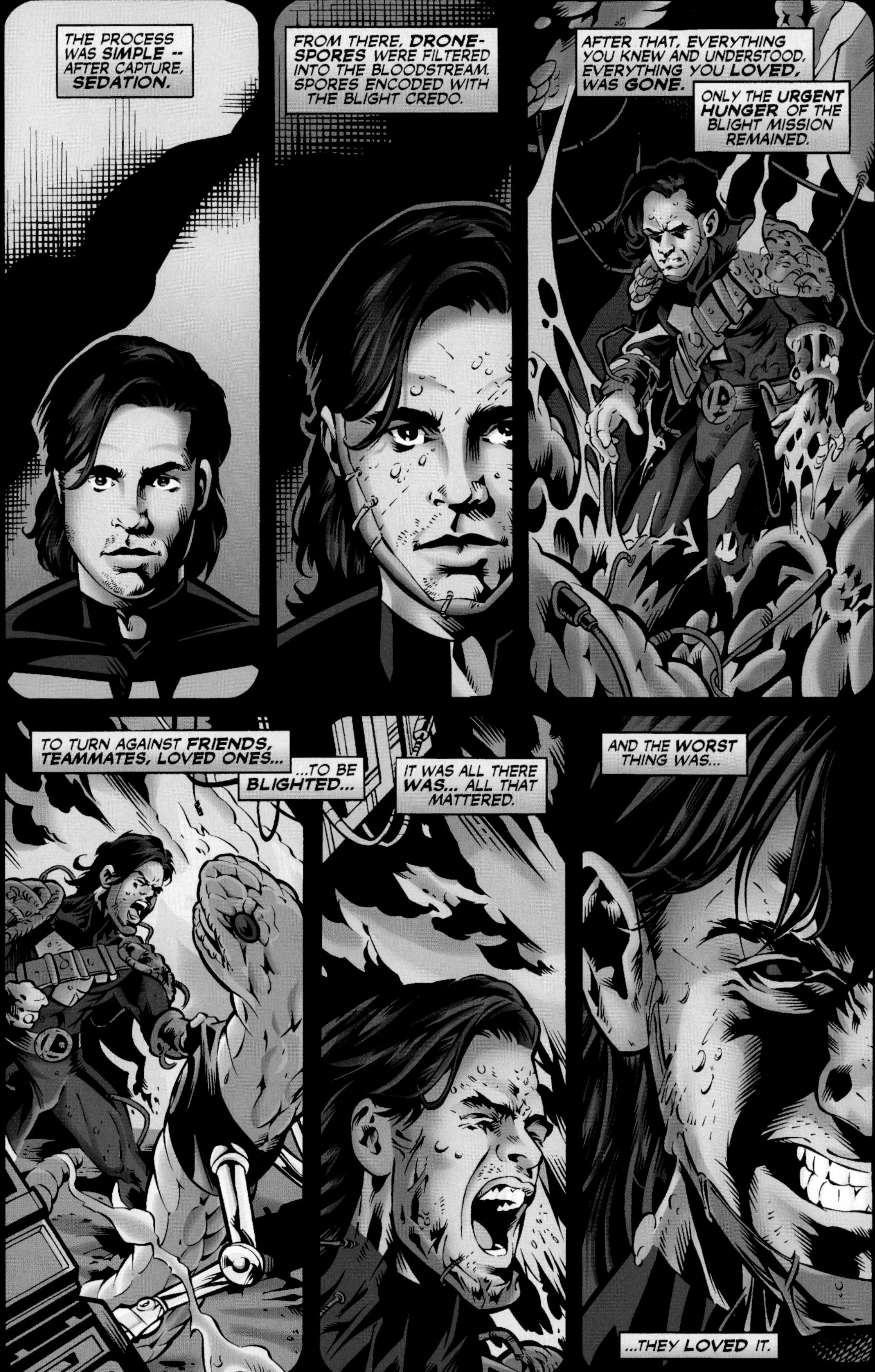
THE PROCESS WAS SIMPLE -- AFTER CAPTURE, SEDATION.
FROM THERE, DRONE-SPORES WERE FILTERED INTO THE BLOODSTREAM. SPORES ENCODED WITH THE BLIGHT CREDO.
AFTER THAT, EVERYTHING YOU KNEW AND UNDERSTOOD, EVERYTHING YOU LOVED, WAS GONE.
ONLY THE URGENT HUNGER OF THE BLIGHT MISSION REMAINED.
TO TURN AGAINST FRIENDS, TEAMMATES, LOVED ONES...
...TO BE BLIGHTED...
IT WAS ALL THERE WAS... ALL THAT MATTERED.
AND THE WORST THING WAS...
...THEY LOVED IT.

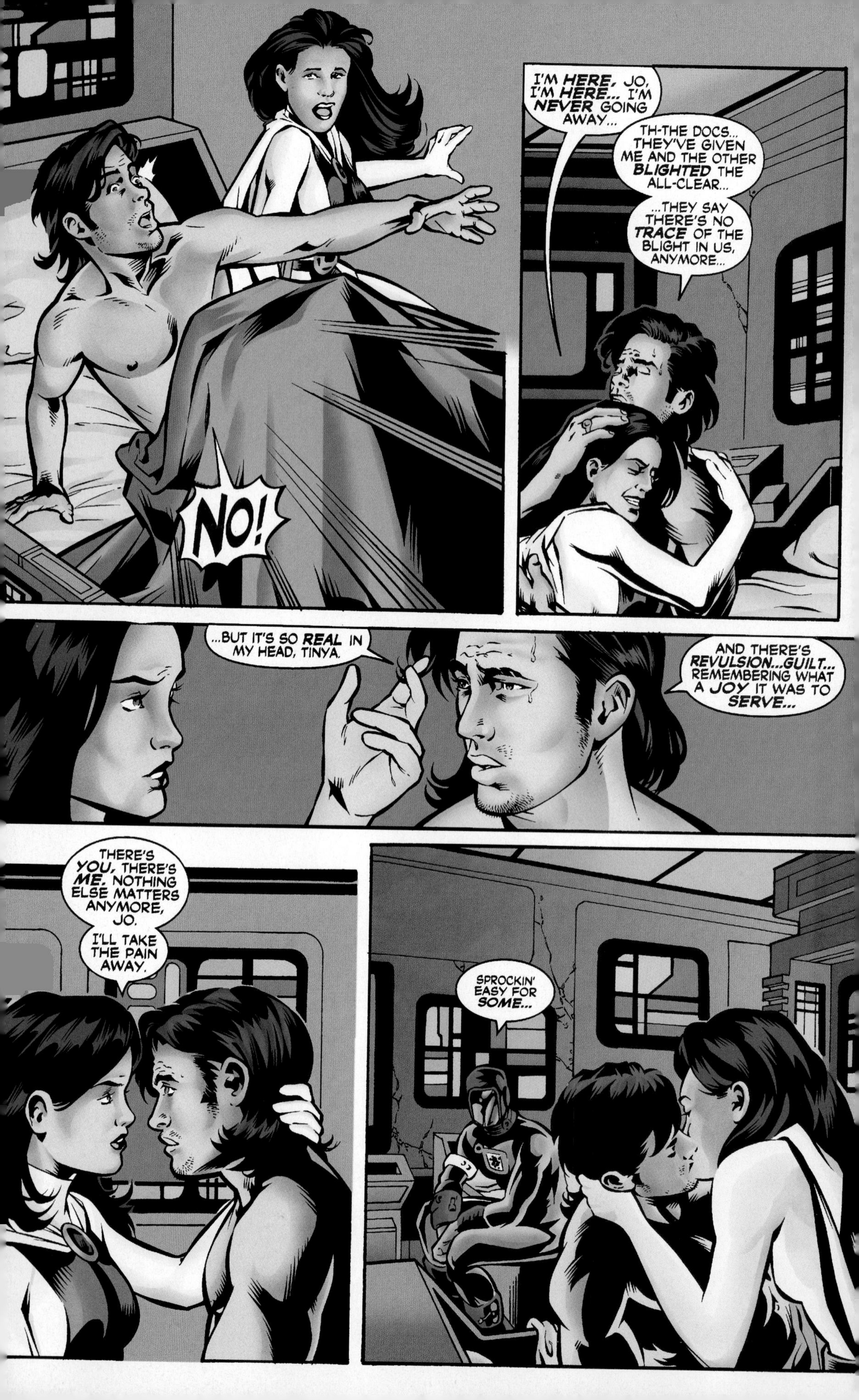
NO!
I'M HERE, JO, I'M HERE... I'M NEVER GOING AWAY...
TH-THE DOCS... THEY'VE GIVEN ME AND THE OTHER BLIGHTED THE ALL-CLEAR...
...THEY SAY THERE'S NO TRACE OF THE BLIGHT IN US, ANYMORE...
...BUT IT'S SO REAL IN MY HEAD, TINYA.
AND THERE'S REVULSION...GUILT... REMEMBERING WHAT A JOY IT WAS TO SERVE...
THERE'S YOU, THERE'S ME. NOTHING ELSE MATTERS ANYMORE, JO.
I'LL TAKE THE PAIN AWAY.
SPROCKIN' EASY FOR SOME...

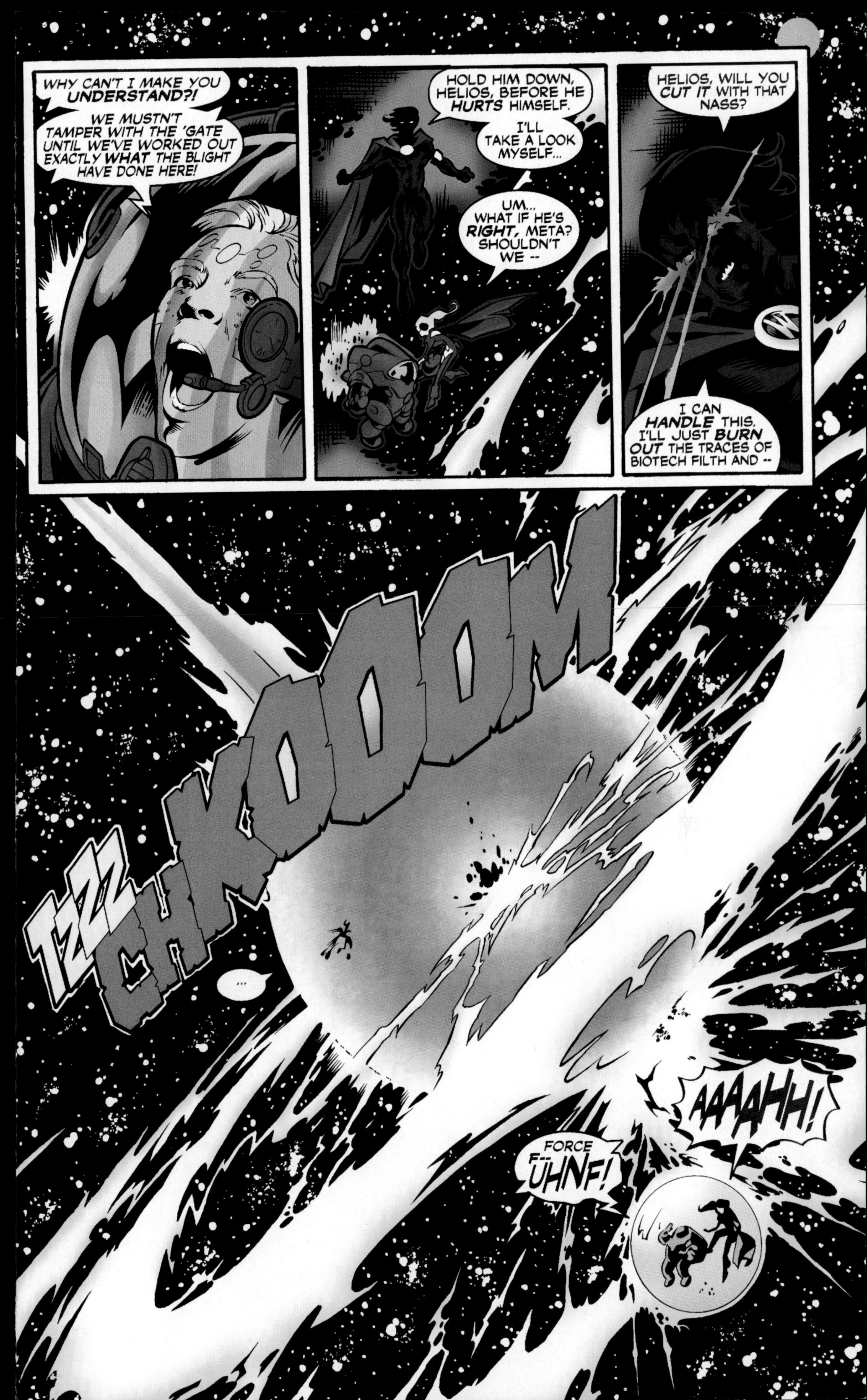
WHY CAN'T I MAKE YOU UNDERSTAND?!
WE MUSTN'T TAMPER WITH THE 'GATE UNTIL WE'VE WORKED OUT EXACTLY WHAT THE BLIGHT HAVE DONE HERE!
HOLD HIM DOWN, HELIOS, BEFORE HE HURTS HIMSELF.
I'LL TAKE A LOOK MYSELF...
UM... WHAT IF HE'S RIGHT, META? SHOULDN'T WE --
HELIOS, WILL YOU CUT IT WITH THAT NASS?
I CAN HANDLE THIS. I'LL JUST BURN OUT THE TRACES OF BIOTECH FILTH AND --
TZZZ CHKOOOM
...
AAAAHH!
FORCE F-- UHNF!

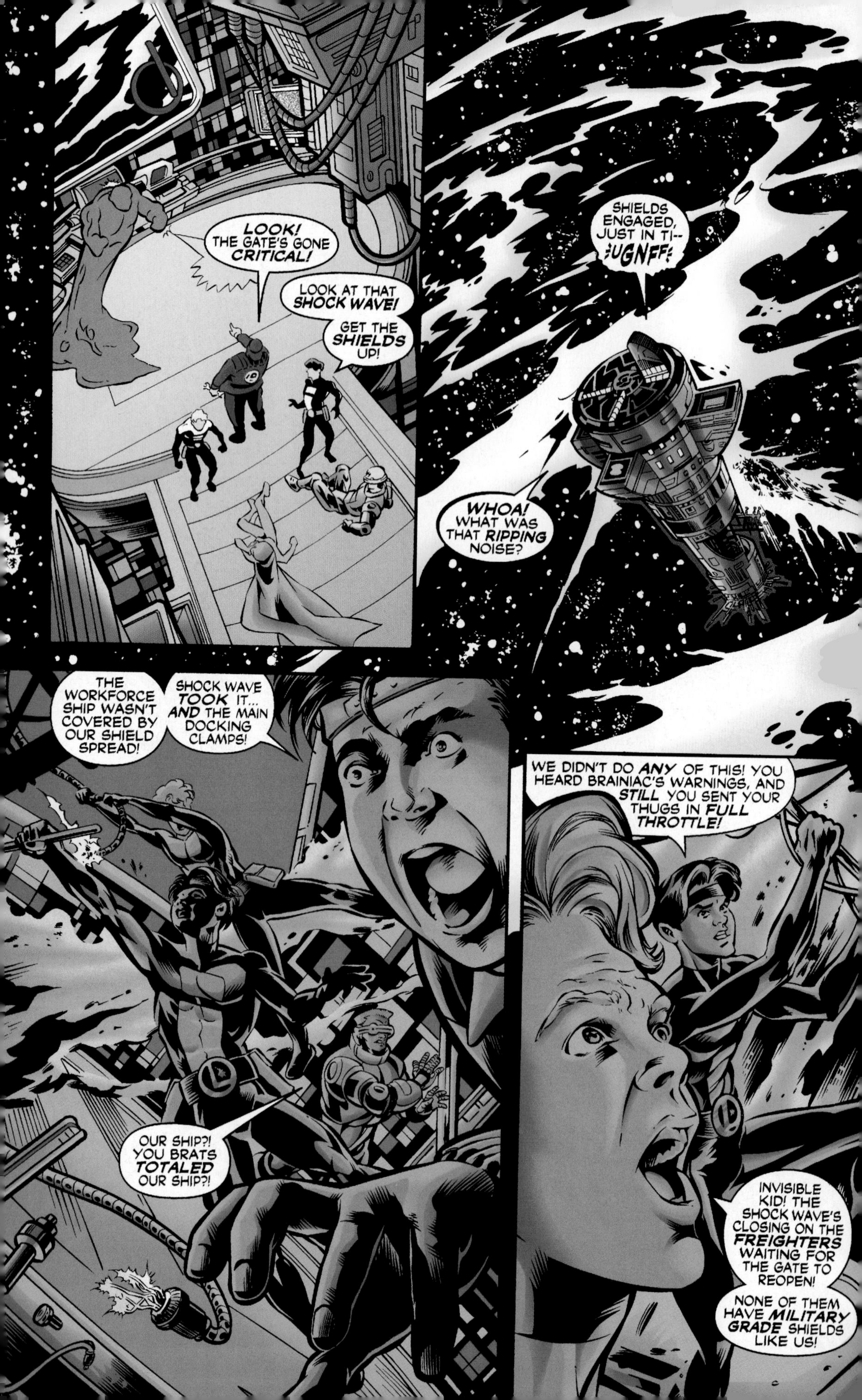
LOOK! THE GATE'S GONE CRITICAL!
LOOK AT THAT SHOCK WAVE!
GET THE SHIELDS UP!
SHIELDS ENGAGED, JUST IN TI-- UGNFF!
WHOA! WHAT WAS THAT RIPPING NOISE?
THE WORKFORCE SHIP WASN'T COVERED BY OUR SHIELD SPREAD!
SHOCK WAVE TOOK IT... AND THE MAIN DOCKING CLAMPS!
OUR SHIP?! YOU BRATS TOTALED OUR SHIP?!
WE DIDN'T DO ANY OF THIS! YOU HEARD BRAINIAC'S WARNINGS, AND STILL YOU SENT YOUR THUGS IN FULL THROTTLE!
INVISIBLE KID! THE SHOCK WAVE'S CLOSING ON THE FREIGHTERS WAITING FOR THE GATE TO REOPEN!
NONE OF THEM HAVE MILITARY GRADE SHIELDS LIKE US!

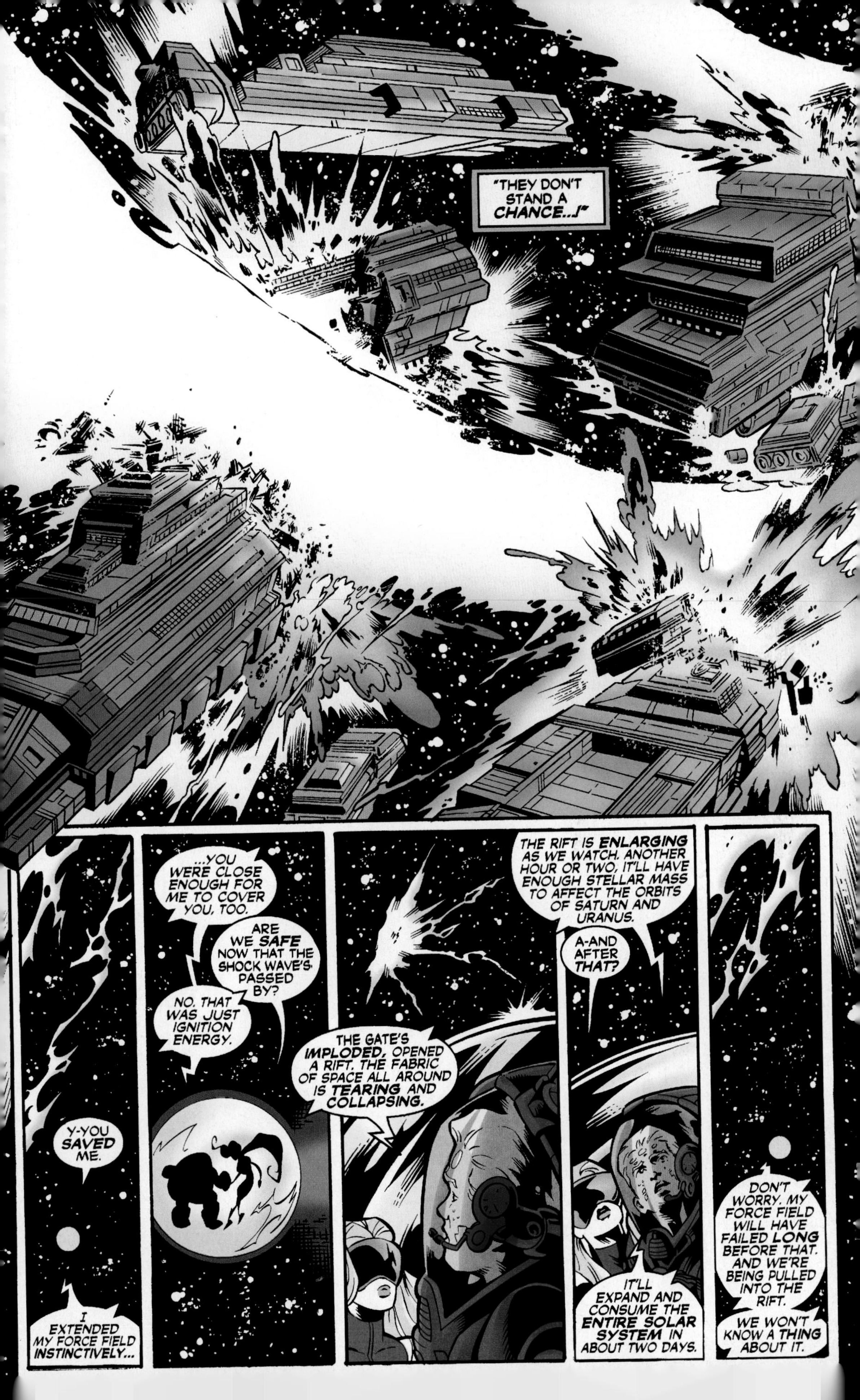
"THEY DON'T STAND A CHANCE...!"
Y-YOU SAVED ME.
I EXTENDED MY FORCE FIELD INSTINCTIVELY...
...YOU WERE CLOSE ENOUGH FOR ME TO COVER YOU, TOO.
ARE WE SAFE NOW THAT THE SHOCK WAVE'S PASSED BY?
NO. THAT WAS JUST IGNITION ENERGY.
THE GATE'S IMPLODED, OPENED A RIFT. THE FABRIC OF SPACE ALL AROUND IS TEARING AND COLLAPSING.
THE RIFT IS ENLARGING AS WE WATCH. ANOTHER HOUR OR TWO, IT'LL HAVE ENOUGH STELLAR MASS TO AFFECT THE ORBITS OF SATURN AND URANUS.
A-AND AFTER THAT?
IT'LL EXPAND AND CONSUME THE ENTIRE SOLAR SYSTEM IN ABOUT TWO DAYS.
DON'T WORRY. MY FORCE FIELD WILL HAVE FAILED LONG BEFORE THAT. AND WE'RE BEING PULLED INTO THE RIFT.
WE WON'T KNOW A THING ABOUT IT.

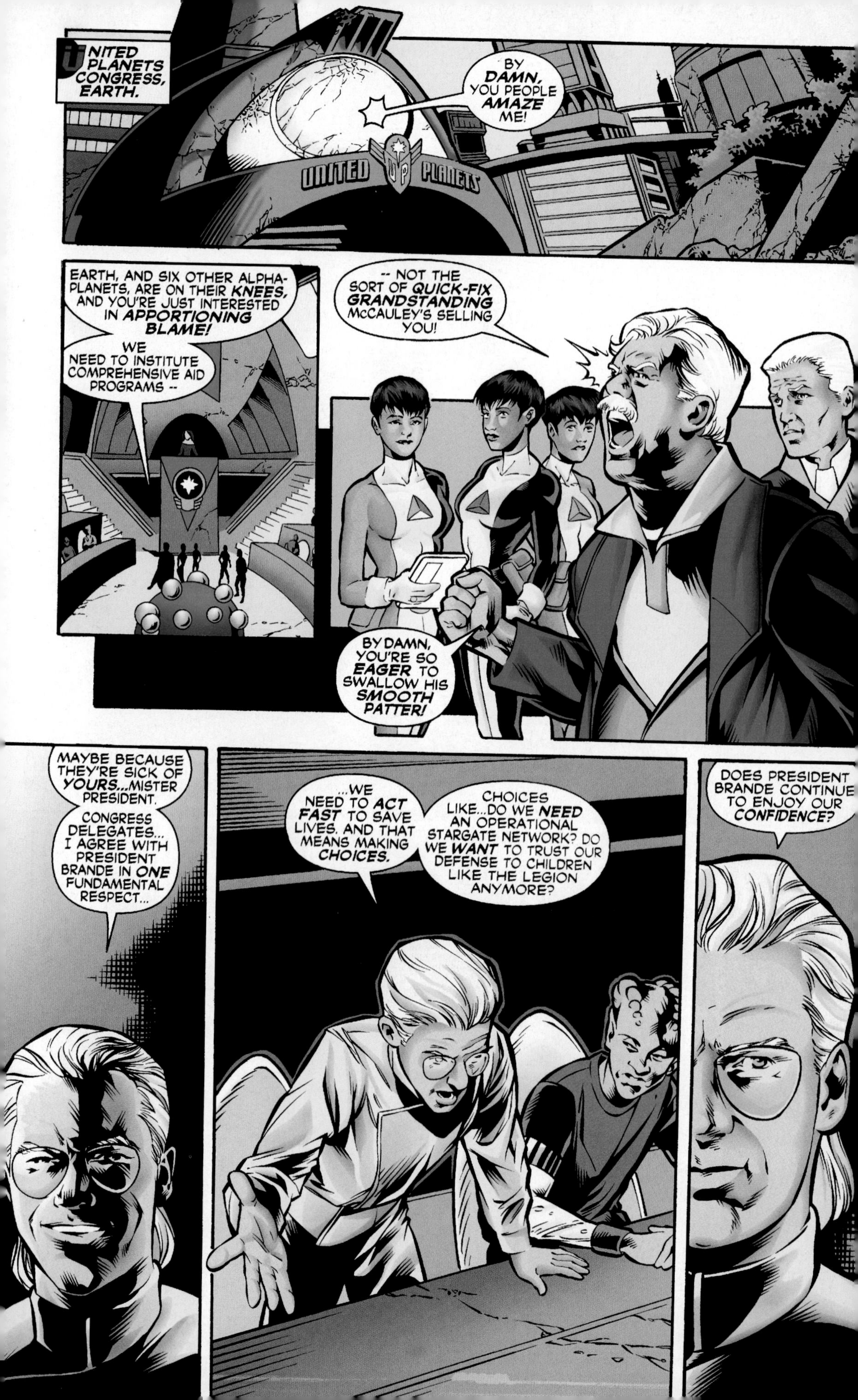
UNITED PLANETS CONGRESS, EARTH.
BY DAMN, YOU PEOPLE AMAZE ME!
UNITED PLANETS
EARTH, AND SIX OTHER ALPHA-PLANETS, ARE ON THEIR KNEES, AND YOU'RE JUST INTERESTED IN APPORTIONING BLAME!
WE NEED TO INSTITUTE COMPREHENSIVE AID PROGRAMS --
-- NOT THE SORT OF QUICK-FIX GRANDSTANDING McCAULEY'S SELLING YOU!
BY DAMN, YOU'RE SO EAGER TO SWALLOW HIS SMOOTH PATTER!
MAYBE BECAUSE THEY'RE SICK OF YOURS...MISTER PRESIDENT.
CONGRESS DELEGATES... I AGREE WITH PRESIDENT BRANDE IN ONE FUNDAMENTAL RESPECT...
...WE NEED TO ACT FAST TO SAVE LIVES. AND THAT MEANS MAKING CHOICES.
CHOICES LIKE...DO WE NEED AN OPERATIONAL STARGATE NETWORK? DO WE WANT TO TRUST OUR DEFENSE TO CHILDREN LIKE THE LEGION ANYMORE?
DOES PRESIDENT BRANDE CONTINUE TO ENJOY OUR CONFIDENCE?

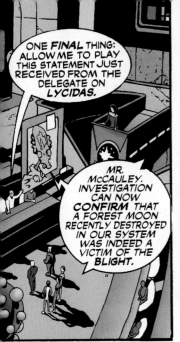

ONE *FINAL* THING: ALLOW ME TO PLAY THIS STATEMENT JUST RECEIVED FROM THE DELEGATE ON *LYCIDAS.*

MR. MCCAULEY. INVESTIGATION CAN NOW *CONFIRM* THAT A FOREST MOON RECENTLY DESTROYED IN OUR SYSTEM WAS INDEED A VICTIM OF THE *BLIGHT.*

THE *BLIGHT* ENCOUNTERED MEMBERS OF THE *LEGION* IN THE STARGATE *BEFORE* THE MOON'S DESTRUCTION.

THERE IS NO DOUBT IN OUR MINDS THAT ALBEIT *UNWITTINGLY,* THE *LEGION* LED THE *BLIGHT* TO EARTH.

FAR BE IT FROM ME TO *"GRANDSTAND,"* BUT I'LL JUST REPEAT THAT...

"...THE LEGION LED THE BLIGHT TO EARTH."

END TRANSMISS

NO... W-WE COULDN'T HAVE...

I'LL...I'LL BE DOUBLE-DAMNED...

VERY *PROBABLY,* MR. PRESIDENT, VERY PROBABLY.

I THINK WE CAN GET RIGHT TO A *VOTE,* DELEGATES.

RE: THE LEGION CONSTITUTION. SECTION ONE, PARAGRAPH TWO...

"...THE LEGION SHALL BE AN INDEPENDENT ORGANIZATION RESPONSIBLE ONLY TO THE PRESIDENT AND COUNCIL OF THE UNITED PLANETS..."

VOTES TO *SUSPEND* THAT CHARTER BASIS?

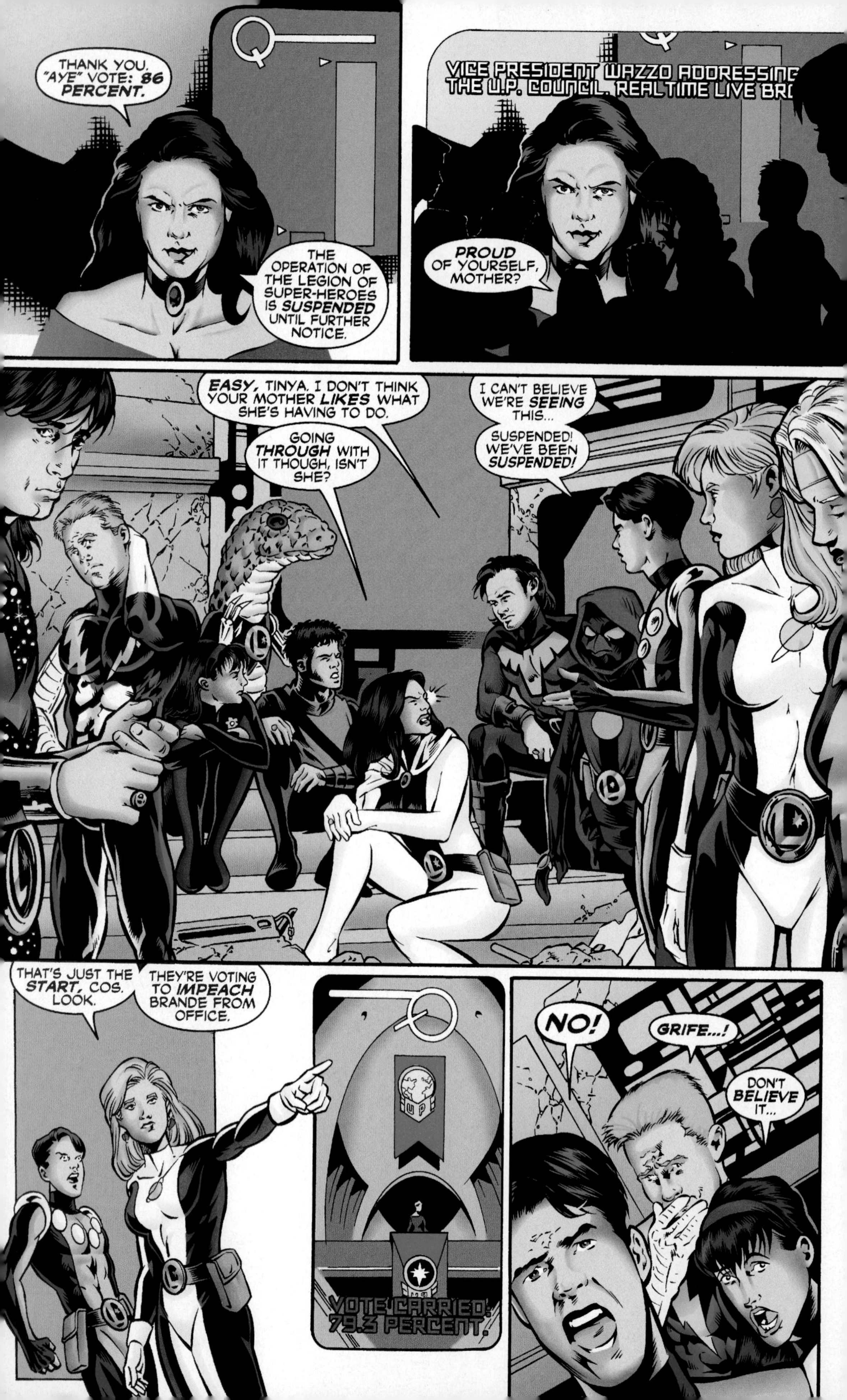
THANK YOU. "AYE" VOTE: 86 PERCENT.
THE OPERATION OF THE LEGION OF SUPER-HEROES IS SUSPENDED UNTIL FURTHER NOTICE.
VICE PRESIDENT WAZZO ADDRESSING THE U.P. COUNCIL, REALTIME LIVE BR
PROUD OF YOURSELF, MOTHER?
EASY, TINYA. I DON'T THINK YOUR MOTHER LIKES WHAT SHE'S HAVING TO DO.
GOING THROUGH WITH IT THOUGH, ISN'T SHE?
I CAN'T BELIEVE WE'RE SEEING THIS...
SUSPENDED! WE'VE BEEN SUSPENDED!
THAT'S JUST THE START, COS. LOOK.
THEY'RE VOTING TO IMPEACH BRANDE FROM OFFICE.
VOTE CARRIED: 79.3 PERCENT.
NO!
GRIFE...!
DON'T BELIEVE IT...

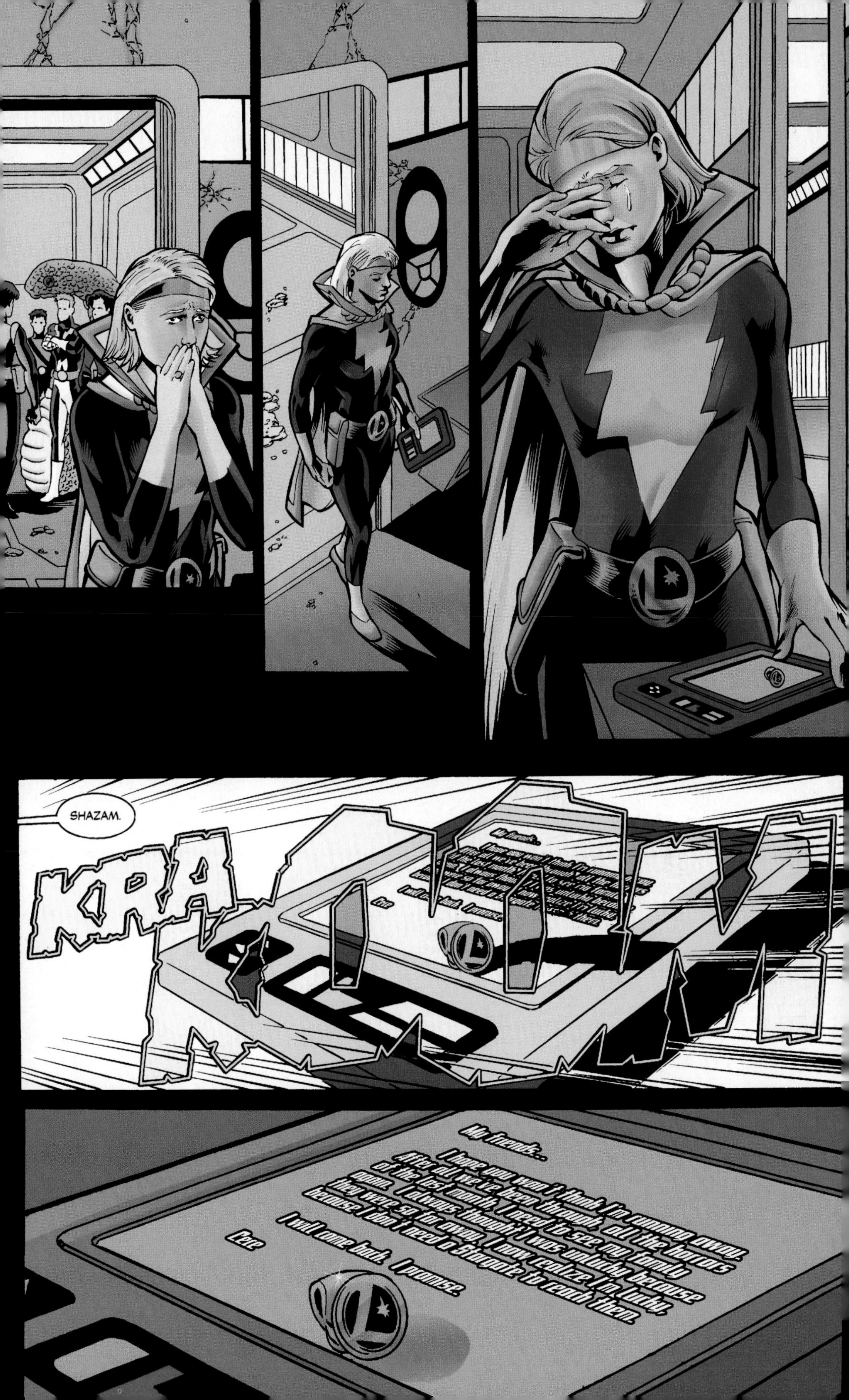
SHAZAM.
KRA
My friends...
I hope you won't think I'm running away. After all we've been through, all the horrors of the last month, I need to see my family again. I always thought I was unlucky because they were so far away. I now realize I'm lucky because I don't need a Stargate to reach them.
I will come back. I promise.
Cece

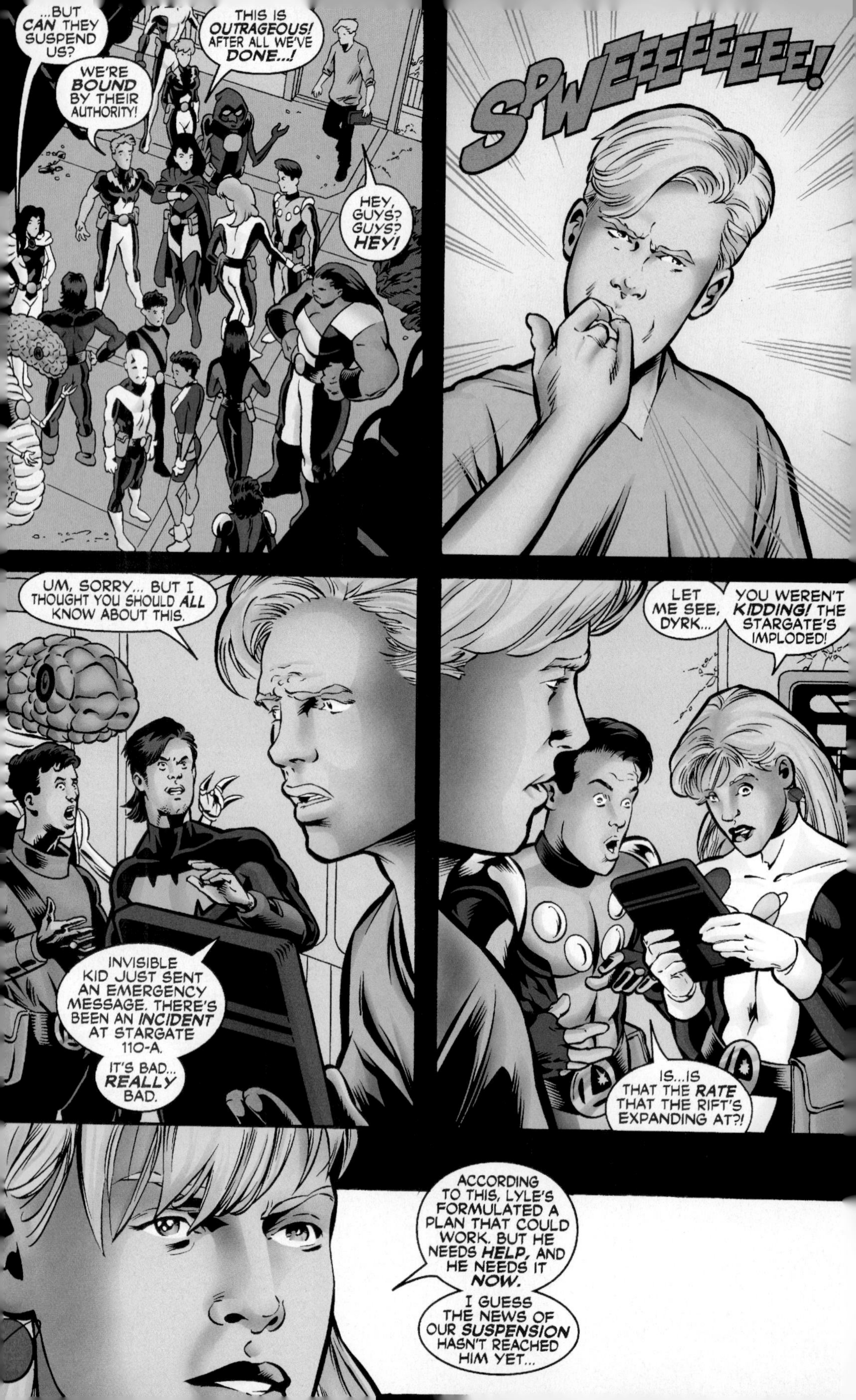
...BUT CAN THEY SUSPEND US?
WE'RE BOUND BY THEIR AUTHORITY!
THIS IS OUTRAGEOUS! AFTER ALL WE'VE DONE...!
HEY, GUYS? GUYS? HEY!
SPWEEEEEEEE!
UM, SORRY... BUT I THOUGHT YOU SHOULD ALL KNOW ABOUT THIS.
INVISIBLE KID JUST SENT AN EMERGENCY MESSAGE. THERE'S BEEN AN INCIDENT AT STARGATE 110-A.
IT'S BAD... REALLY BAD.
LET ME SEE, DYRK...
YOU WEREN'T KIDDING! THE STARGATE'S IMPLODED!
IS...IS THAT THE RATE THAT THE RIFT'S EXPANDING AT?!
ACCORDING TO THIS, LYLE'S FORMULATED A PLAN THAT COULD WORK. BUT HE NEEDS HELP, AND HE NEEDS IT NOW.
I GUESS THE NEWS OF OUR SUSPENSION HASN'T REACHED HIM YET...

IT'S YOUR CALL, IMRA. YOU'RE LEADER.

NOT ANYMORE. THERE'S NO LEGION LEFT TO LEAD.

THEN WHAT DO WE DO?

THE RIGHT THING.

THAT'S WHAT YOU KIDS DO. WHAT YOU'VE ALWAYS DONE.

BUT IF WE DEFY THE COUNCIL VOTE, MR. PRESIDENT, IT COULD MAKE THINGS FAR WORSE FOR YOU...

DON'T WORRY ABOUT ME, BY DAMN! I'M BIG ENOUGH TO LOOK AFTER MYSELF!

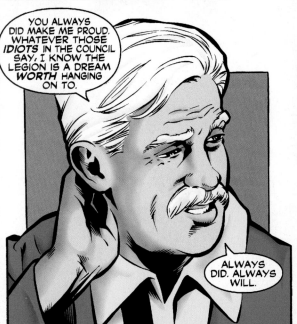

YOU ALWAYS DID MAKE ME PROUD. WHATEVER THOSE IDIOTS IN THE COUNCIL SAY, I KNOW THE LEGION IS A DREAM WORTH HANGING ON TO.

ALWAYS DID. ALWAYS WILL.

HMMM... FROM THE LOOKS OF INVISIBLE KID'S MESSAGE, THAT'S A PRETTY BIG MESS OUT THERE...

EXACTLY. I'M WONDERING WHY WE'RE EVEN ASKING THE QUESTION.

WHO'S WITH ME?

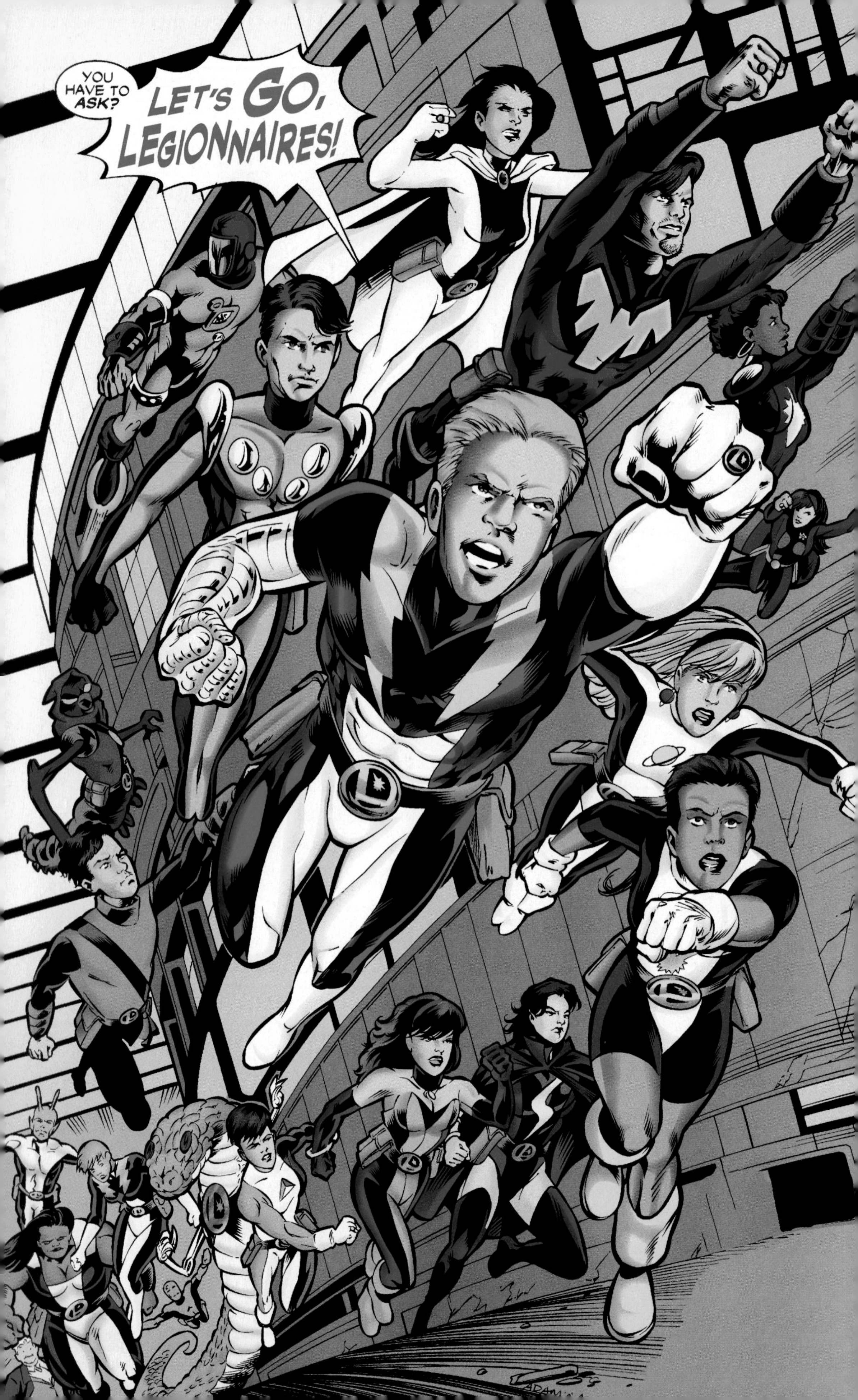
YOU HAVE TO ASK?
LET'S GO, LEGIONNAIRES!

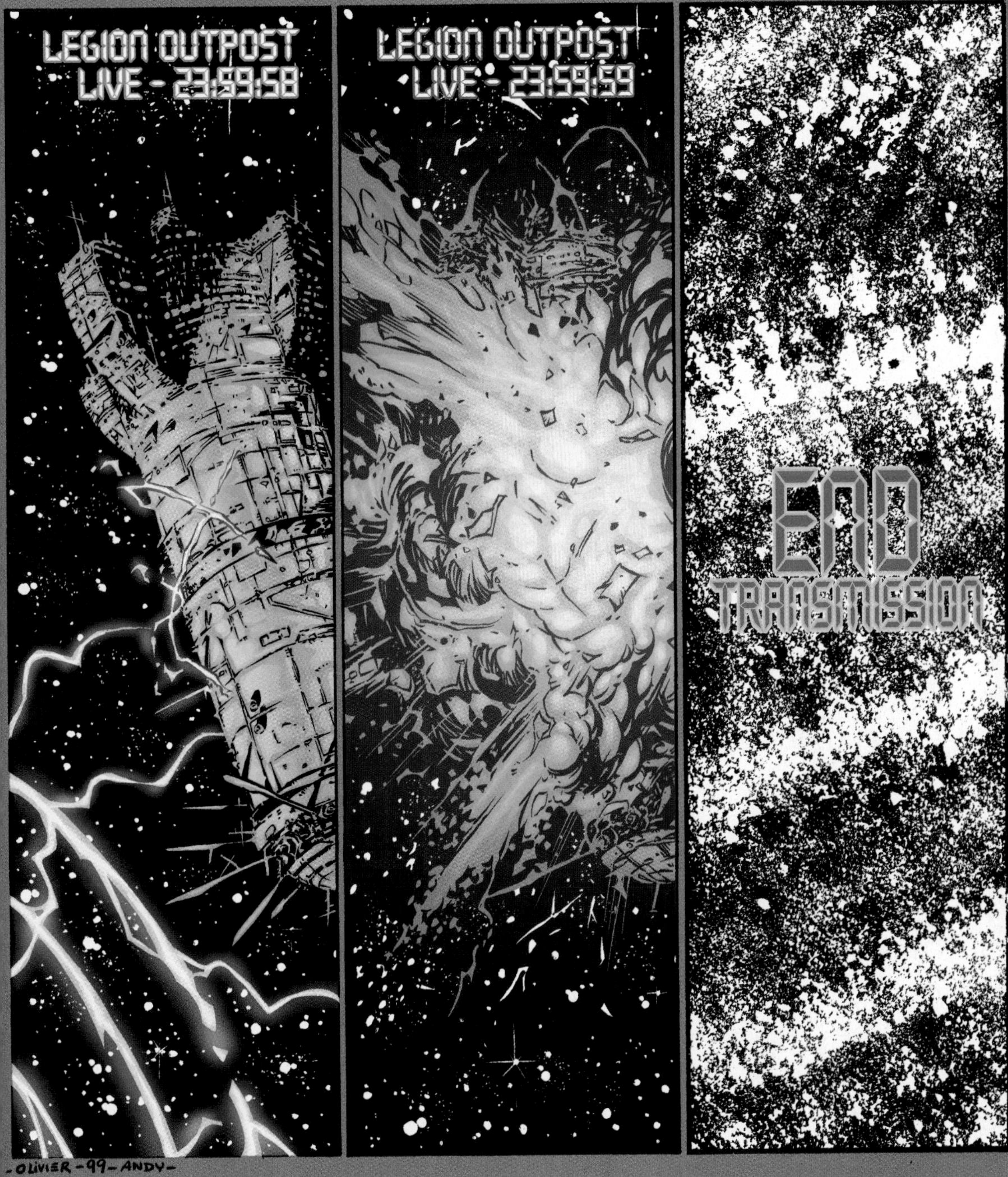
LEGION OUTPOST
LIVE - 23:59:58
LEGION OUTPOST
LIVE - 23:59:59
END
TRANSMISSION
-OLIVIER-99-ANDY-

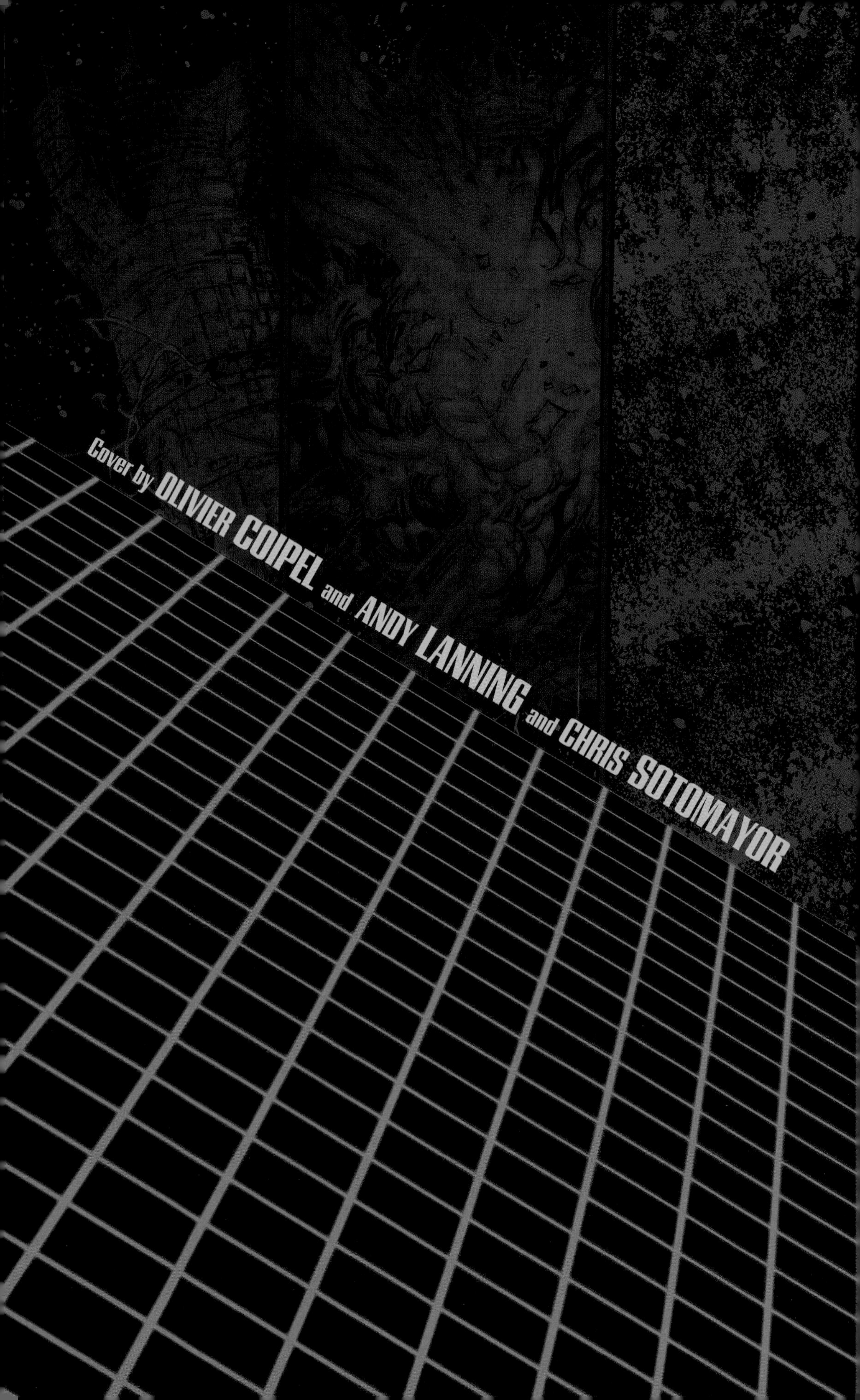

Cover by OLIVIER COIPEL and ANDY LANNING and CHRIS SOTOMAYOR

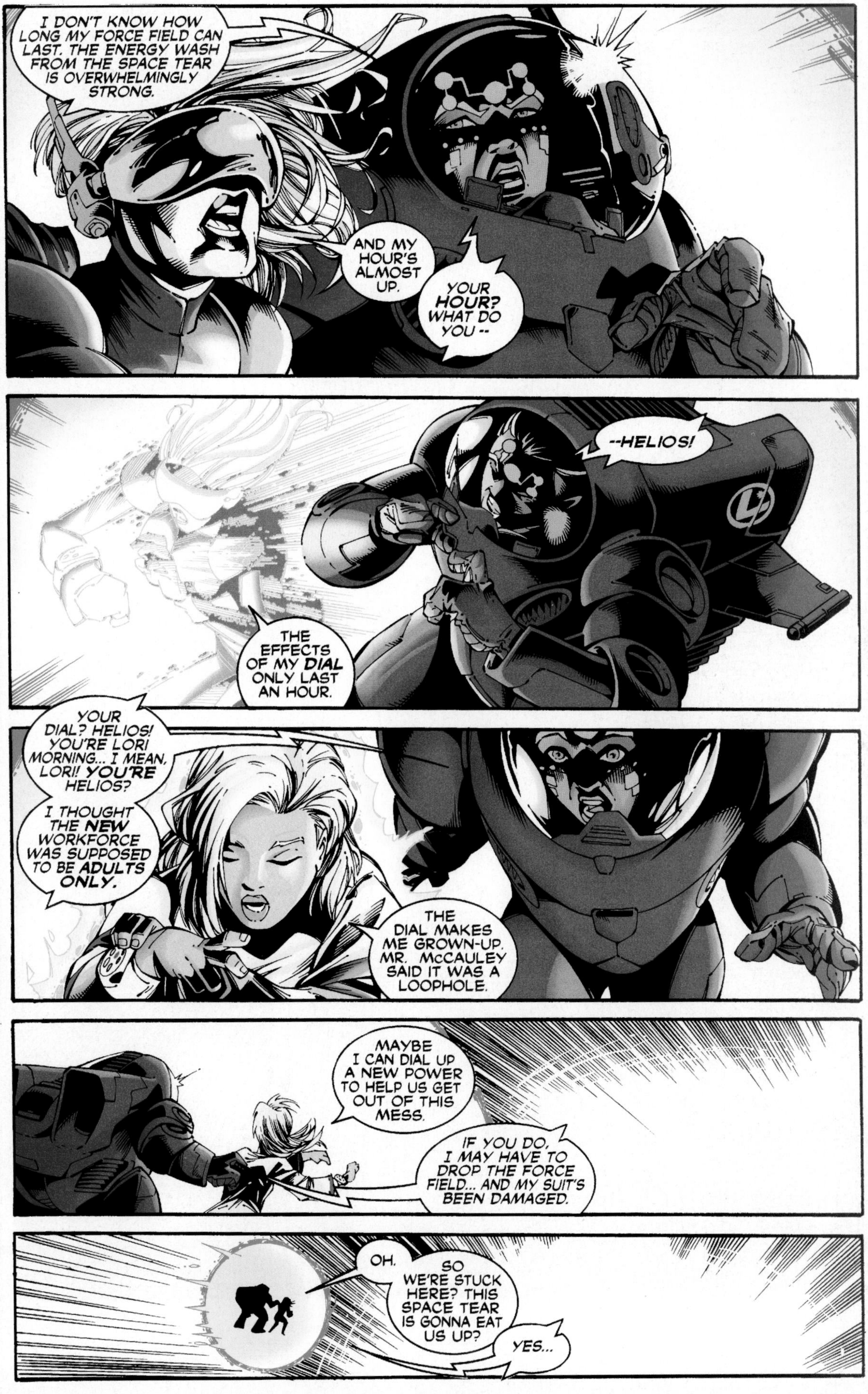
I DON'T KNOW HOW LONG MY FORCE FIELD CAN LAST. THE ENERGY WASH FROM THE SPACE TEAR IS OVERWHELMINGLY STRONG.
AND MY HOUR'S ALMOST UP.
YOUR HOUR? WHAT DO YOU --
--HELIOS!
THE EFFECTS OF MY DIAL ONLY LAST AN HOUR.
YOUR DIAL? HELIOS! YOU'RE LORI MORNING... I MEAN, LORI! YOU'RE HELIOS?
I THOUGHT THE NEW WORKFORCE WAS SUPPOSED TO BE ADULTS ONLY.
THE DIAL MAKES ME GROWN-UP. MR. McCAULEY SAID IT WAS A LOOPHOLE.
MAYBE I CAN DIAL UP A NEW POWER TO HELP US GET OUT OF THIS MESS.
IF YOU DO, I MAY HAVE TO DROP THE FORCE FIELD... AND MY SUIT'S BEEN DAMAGED.
OH.
SO WE'RE STUCK HERE? THIS SPACE TEAR IS GONNA EAT US UP?
YES...

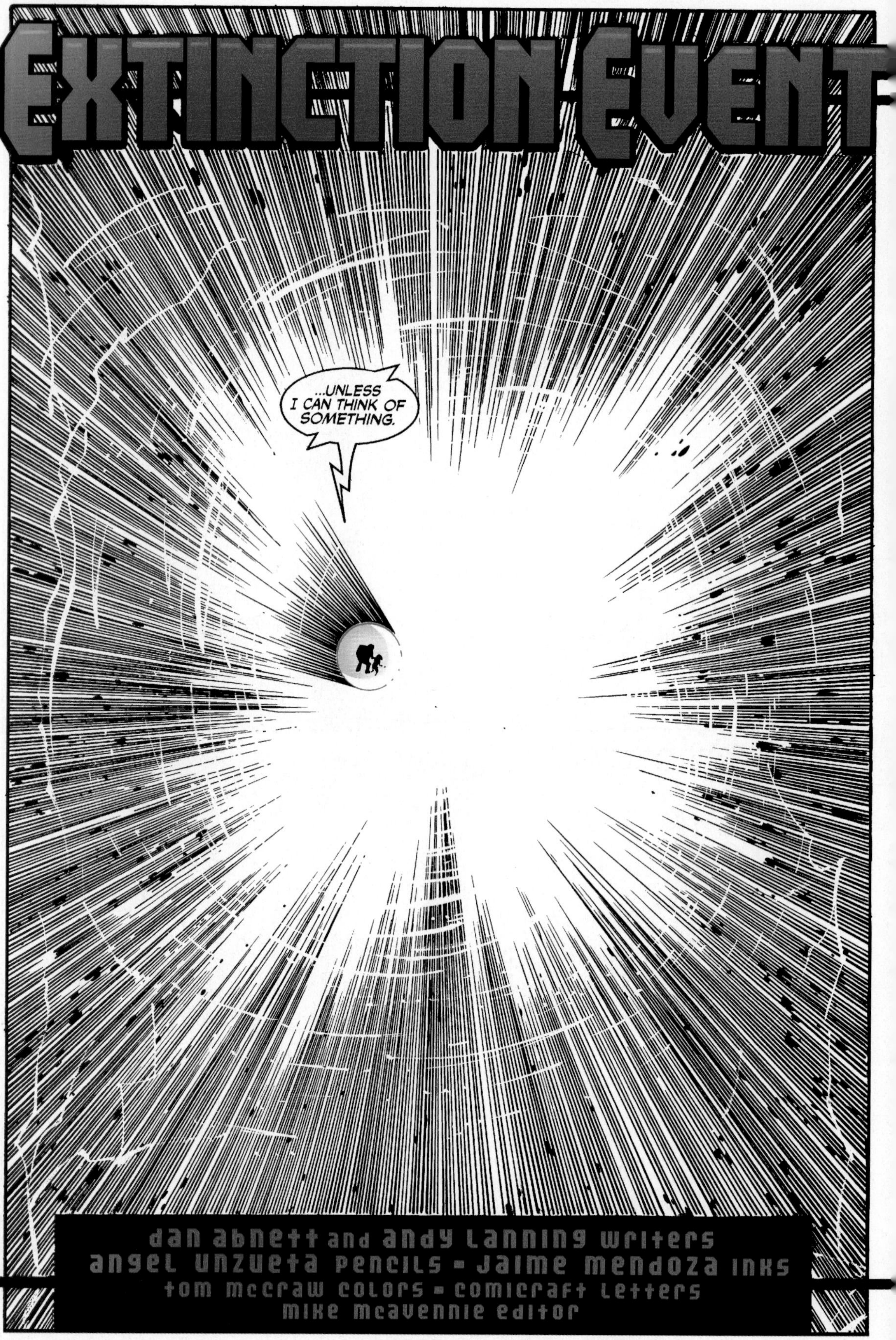
EXTINCTION EVENT
...UNLESS I CAN THINK OF SOMETHING.
dan abnett and andy lanning writers
angel unzueta pencils • jaime mendoza inks
tom mccraw colors • comicraft letters
mike mcavennie editor

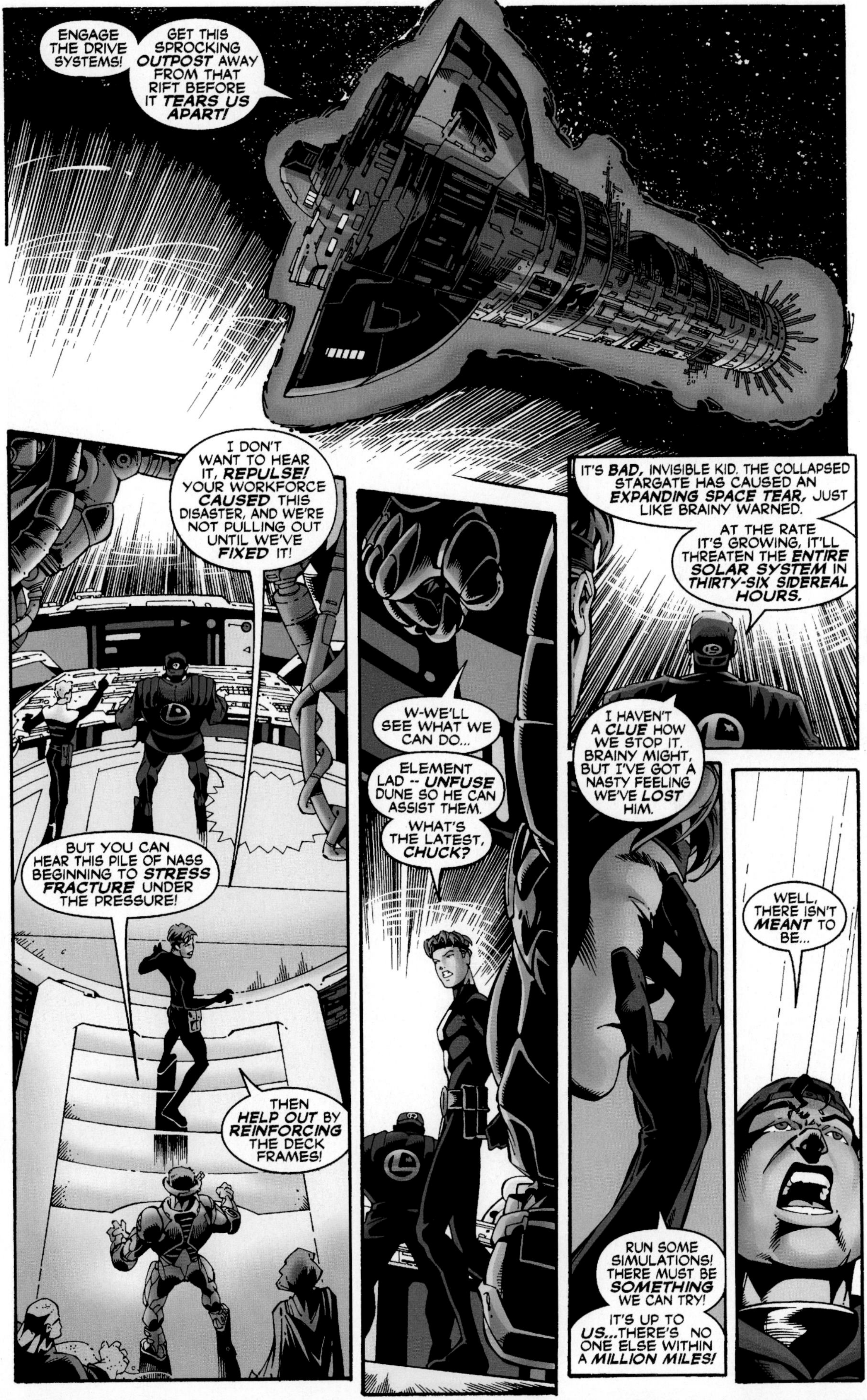
ENGAGE THE DRIVE SYSTEMS!
GET THIS SPROCKING OUTPOST AWAY FROM THAT RIFT BEFORE IT TEARS US APART!
I DON'T WANT TO HEAR IT, REPULSE! YOUR WORKFORCE CAUSED THIS DISASTER, AND WE'RE NOT PULLING OUT UNTIL WE'VE FIXED IT!
BUT YOU CAN HEAR THIS PILE OF NASS BEGINNING TO STRESS FRACTURE UNDER THE PRESSURE!
THEN HELP OUT BY REINFORCING THE DECK FRAMES!
W-WE'LL SEE WHAT WE CAN DO...
ELEMENT LAD -- UNFUSE DUNE SO HE CAN ASSIST THEM.
WHAT'S THE LATEST, CHUCK?
IT'S BAD, INVISIBLE KID. THE COLLAPSED STARGATE HAS CAUSED AN EXPANDING SPACE TEAR, JUST LIKE BRAINY WARNED.
AT THE RATE IT'S GROWING, IT'LL THREATEN THE ENTIRE SOLAR SYSTEM IN THIRTY-SIX SIDEREAL HOURS.
I HAVEN'T A CLUE HOW WE STOP IT. BRAINY MIGHT, BUT I'VE GOT A NASTY FEELING WE'VE LOST HIM.
RUN SOME SIMULATIONS! THERE MUST BE SOMETHING WE CAN TRY!
IT'S UP TO US...THERE'S NO ONE ELSE WITHIN A MILLION MILES!
WELL, THERE ISN'T MEANT TO BE...

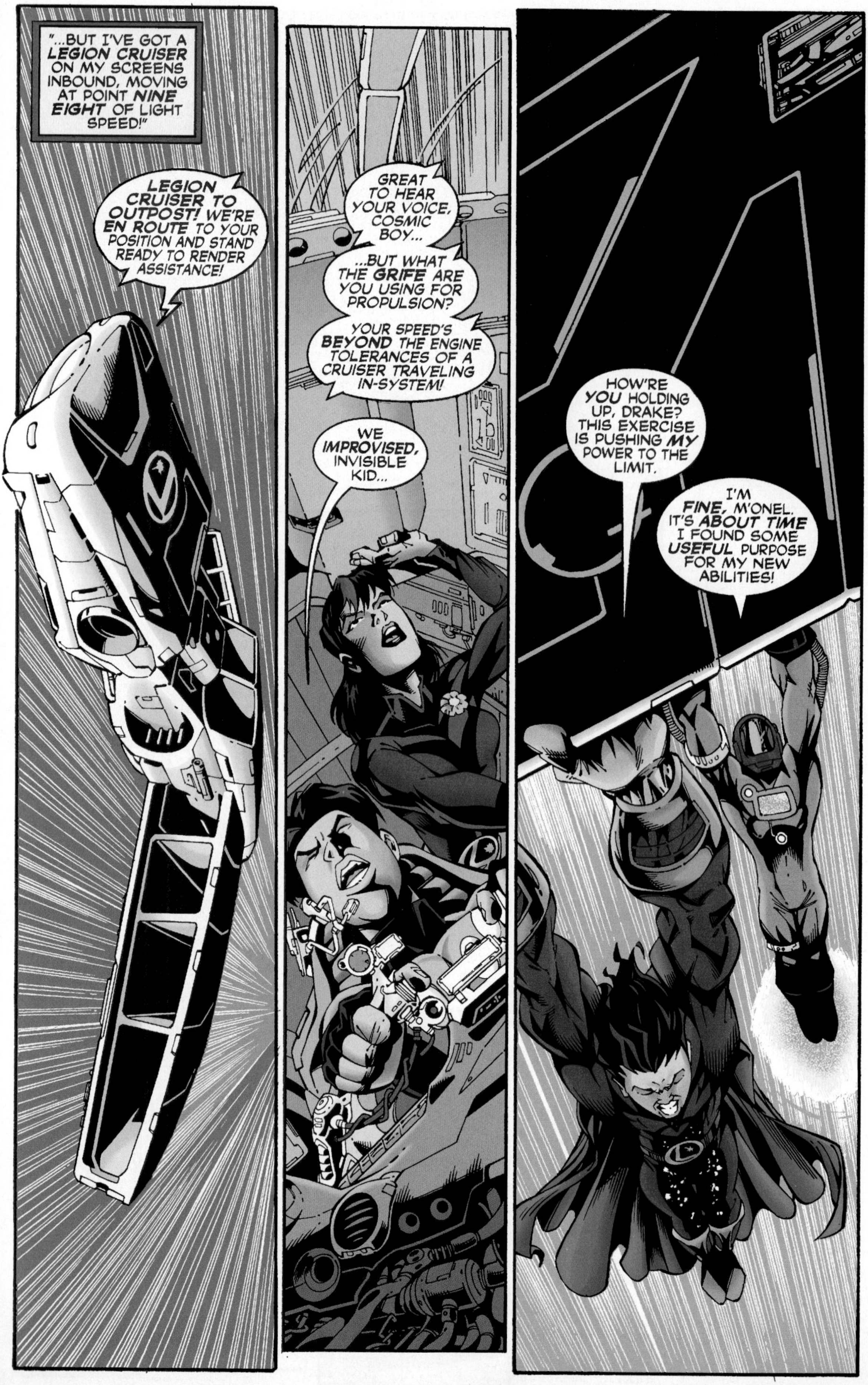
"...BUT I'VE GOT A LEGION CRUISER ON MY SCREENS INBOUND, MOVING AT POINT NINE EIGHT OF LIGHT SPEED!"
LEGION CRUISER TO OUTPOST! WE'RE EN ROUTE TO YOUR POSITION AND STAND READY TO RENDER ASSISTANCE!
GREAT TO HEAR YOUR VOICE, COSMIC BOY...
...BUT WHAT THE GRIFE ARE YOU USING FOR PROPULSION?
YOUR SPEED'S BEYOND THE ENGINE TOLERANCES OF A CRUISER TRAVELING IN-SYSTEM!
WE IMPROVISED, INVISIBLE KID...
HOW'RE YOU HOLDING UP, DRAKE? THIS EXERCISE IS PUSHING MY POWER TO THE LIMIT.
I'M FINE, M'ONEL. IT'S ABOUT TIME I FOUND SOME USEFUL PURPOSE FOR MY NEW ABILITIES!

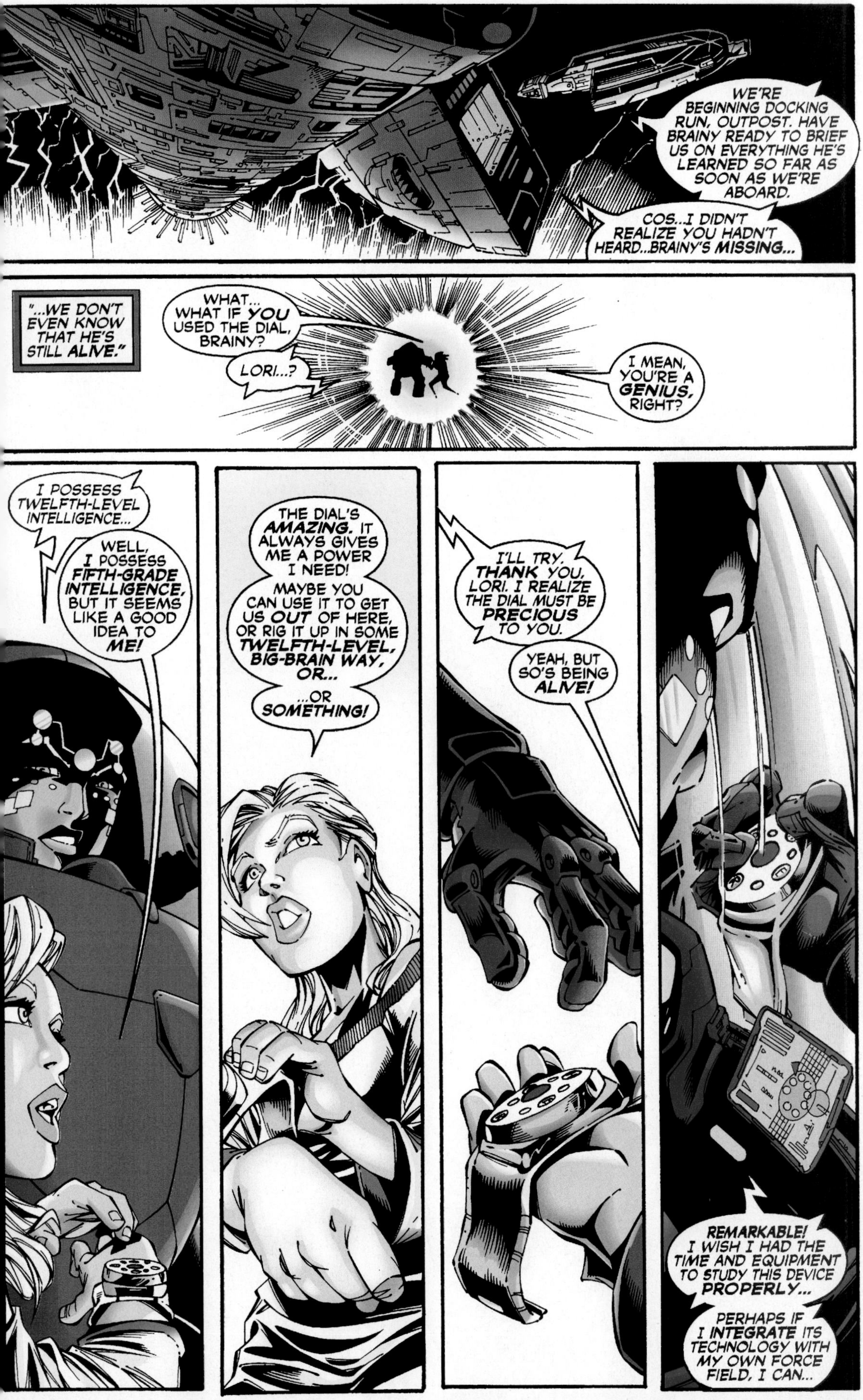

WE'RE BEGINNING DOCKING RUN, OUTPOST. HAVE BRAINY READY TO BRIEF US ON EVERYTHING HE'S LEARNED SO FAR AS SOON AS WE'RE ABOARD.
COS...I DIDN'T REALIZE YOU HADN'T HEARD...BRAINY'S MISSING...
"...WE DON'T EVEN KNOW THAT HE'S STILL ALIVE."
WHAT... WHAT IF YOU USED THE DIAL, BRAINY?
LORI...?
I MEAN, YOU'RE A GENIUS, RIGHT?
I POSSESS TWELFTH-LEVEL INTELLIGENCE...
WELL, I POSSESS FIFTH-GRADE INTELLIGENCE, BUT IT SEEMS LIKE A GOOD IDEA TO ME!
THE DIAL'S AMAZING. IT ALWAYS GIVES ME A POWER I NEED!
MAYBE YOU CAN USE IT TO GET US OUT OF HERE, OR RIG IT UP IN SOME TWELFTH-LEVEL, BIG-BRAIN WAY, OR...
...OR SOMETHING!
I'LL TRY. THANK YOU, LORI. I REALIZE THE DIAL MUST BE PRECIOUS TO YOU.
YEAH, BUT SO'S BEING ALIVE!
REMARKABLE! I WISH I HAD THE TIME AND EQUIPMENT TO STUDY THIS DEVICE PROPERLY...
PERHAPS IF I INTEGRATE ITS TECHNOLOGY WITH MY OWN FORCE FIELD, I CAN...

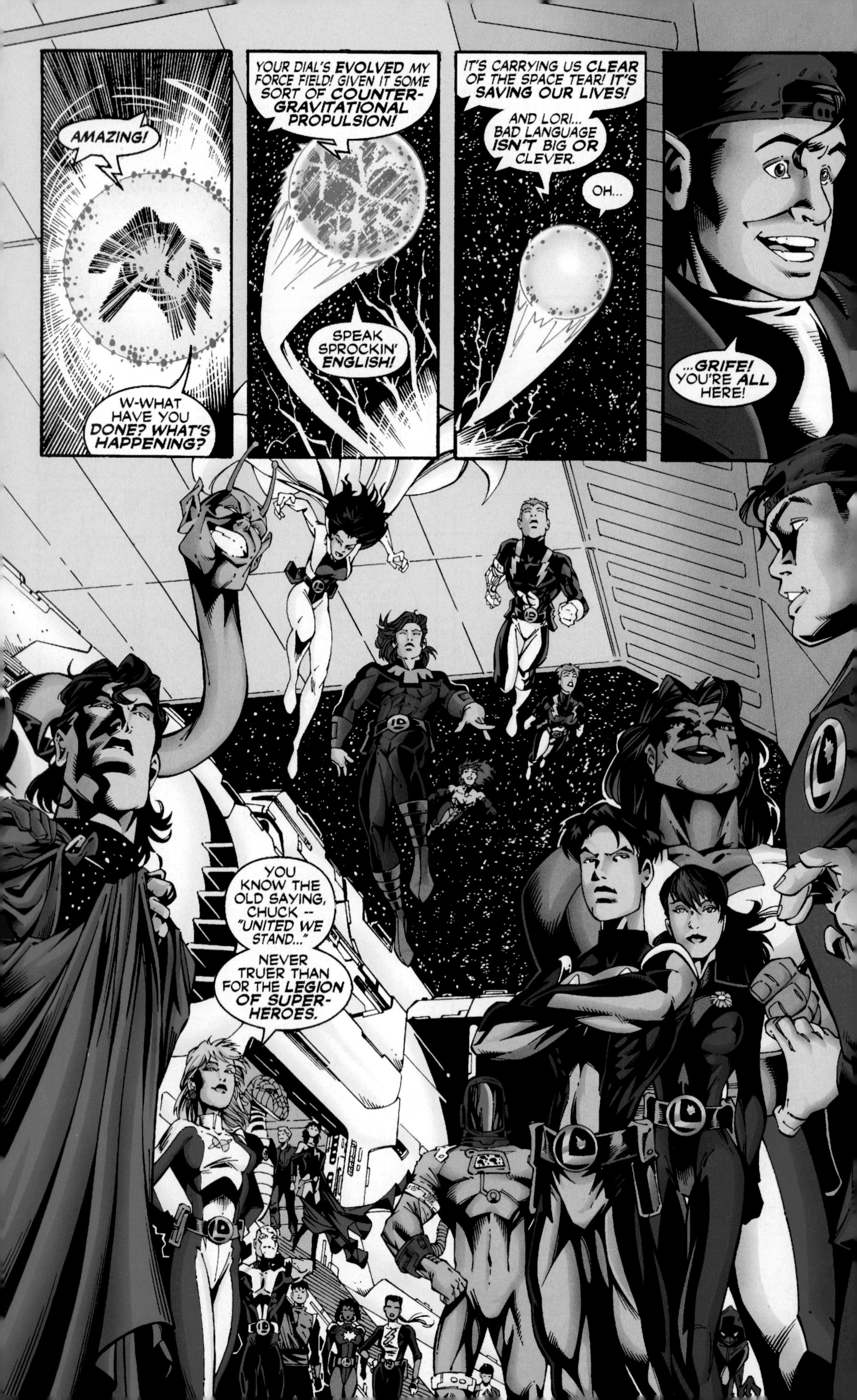
AMAZING!
W-WHAT HAVE YOU DONE? WHAT'S HAPPENING?
YOUR DIAL'S EVOLVED MY FORCE FIELD! GIVEN IT SOME SORT OF COUNTER-GRAVITATIONAL PROPULSION!
SPEAK SPROCKIN' ENGLISH!
IT'S CARRYING US CLEAR OF THE SPACE TEAR! IT'S SAVING OUR LIVES!
AND LORI... BAD LANGUAGE ISN'T BIG OR CLEVER.
OH...
...GRIFE! YOU'RE ALL HERE!
YOU KNOW THE OLD SAYING, CHUCK -- "UNITED WE STAND..."
NEVER TRUER THAN FOR THE LEGION OF SUPER-HEROES.

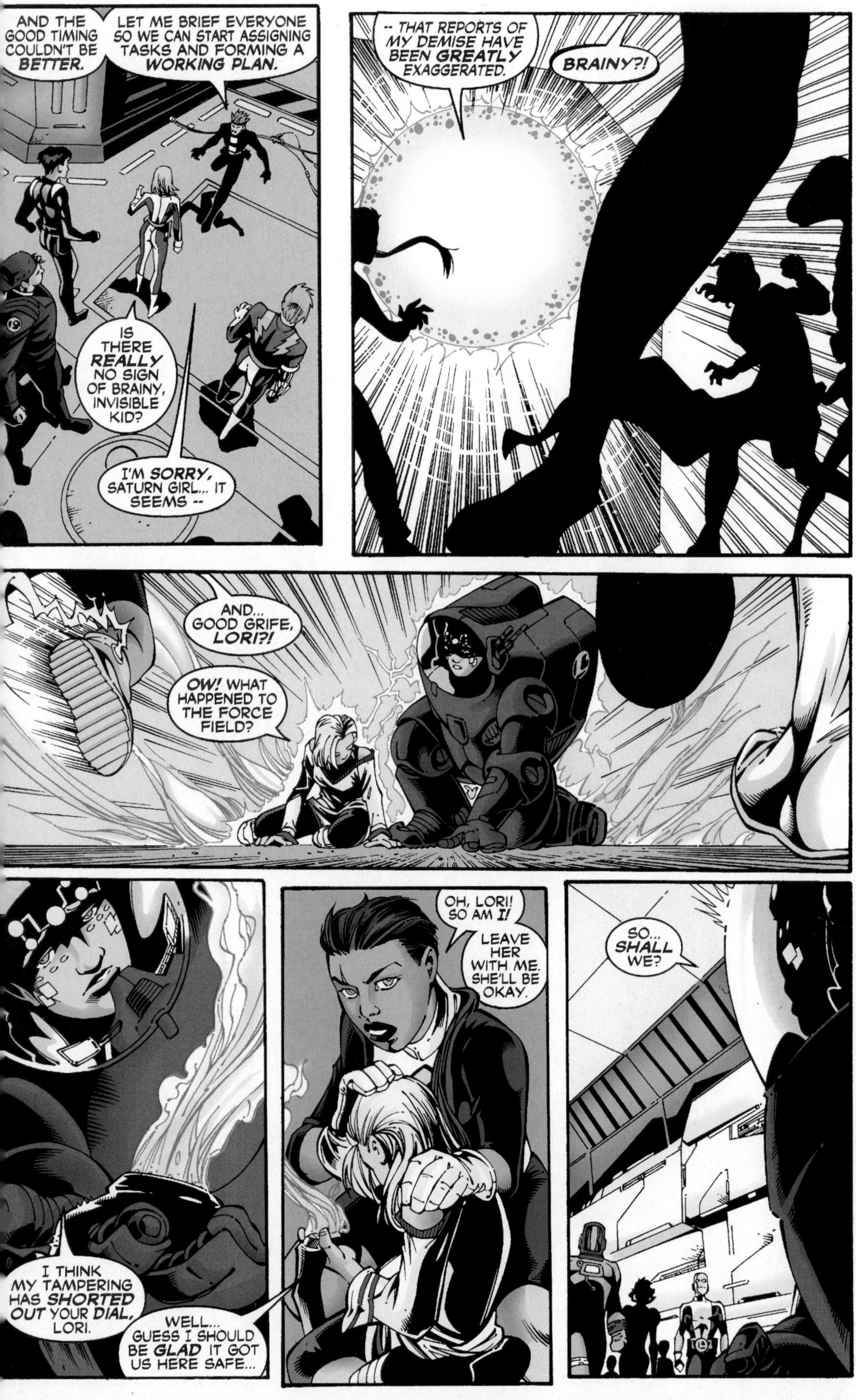
AND THE GOOD TIMING COULDN'T BE BETTER.
LET ME BRIEF EVERYONE SO WE CAN START ASSIGNING TASKS AND FORMING A WORKING PLAN.
IS THERE REALLY NO SIGN OF BRAINY, INVISIBLE KID?
I'M SORRY, SATURN GIRL... IT SEEMS --
-- THAT REPORTS OF MY DEMISE HAVE BEEN GREATLY EXAGGERATED.
BRAINY?!
AND... GOOD GRIFE, LORI?!
OW! WHAT HAPPENED TO THE FORCE FIELD?
I THINK MY TAMPERING HAS SHORTED OUT YOUR DIAL, LORI.
WELL... GUESS I SHOULD BE GLAD IT GOT US HERE SAFE...
OH, LORI! SO AM I!
LEAVE HER WITH ME. SHE'LL BE OKAY.
SO... SHALL WE?

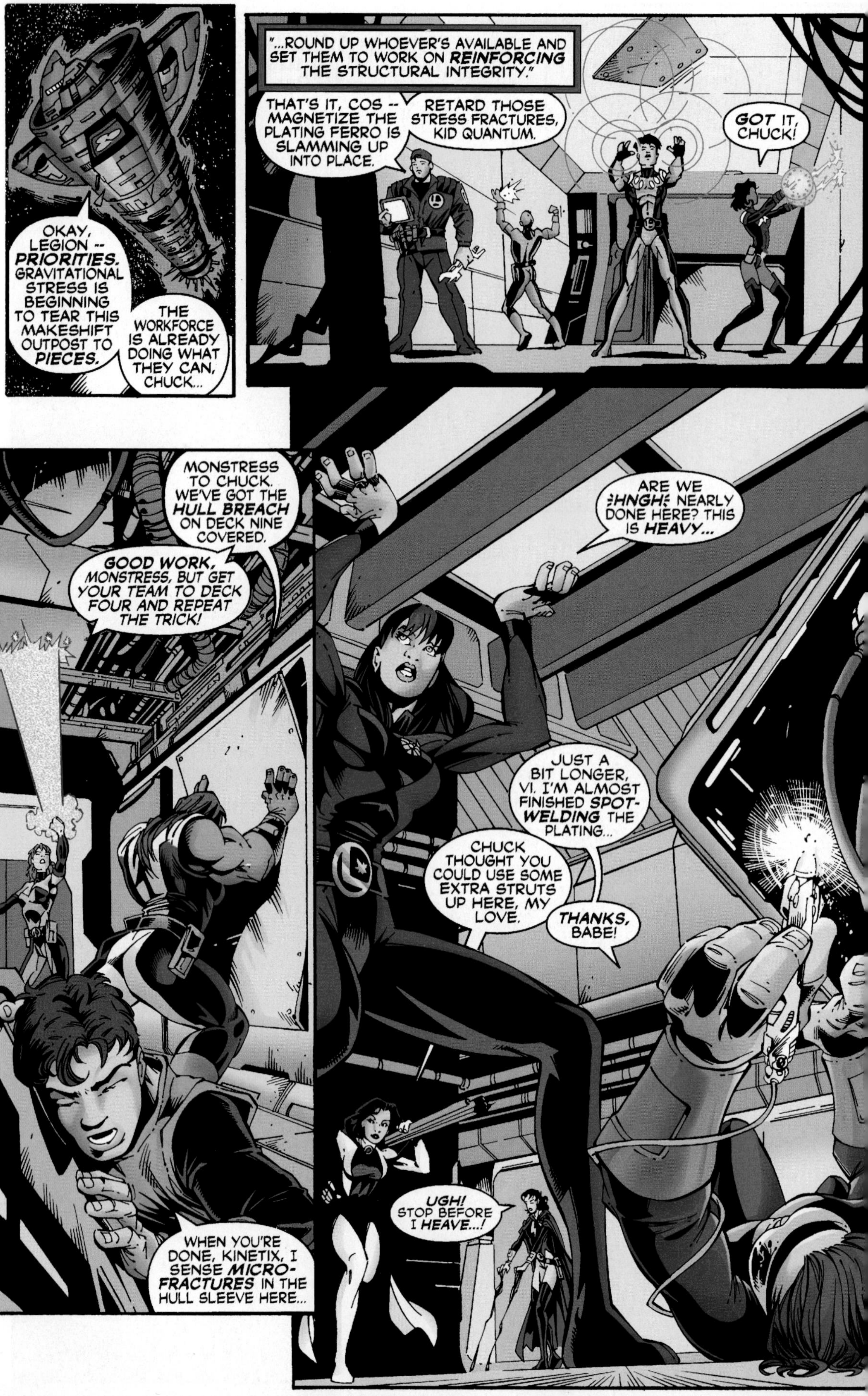

OKAY, LEGION -- PRIORITIES. GRAVITATIONAL STRESS IS BEGINNING TO TEAR THIS MAKESHIFT OUTPOST TO PIECES.
THE WORKFORCE IS ALREADY DOING WHAT THEY CAN, CHUCK...
"...ROUND UP WHOEVER'S AVAILABLE AND SET THEM TO WORK ON REINFORCING THE STRUCTURAL INTEGRITY."
THAT'S IT, COS -- MAGNETIZE THE PLATING FERRO IS SLAMMING UP INTO PLACE.
RETARD THOSE STRESS FRACTURES, KID QUANTUM.
GOT IT, CHUCK!
MONSTRESS TO CHUCK. WE'VE GOT THE HULL BREACH ON DECK NINE COVERED.
GOOD WORK, MONSTRESS, BUT GET YOUR TEAM TO DECK FOUR AND REPEAT THE TRICK!
ARE WE :HNGH: NEARLY DONE HERE? THIS IS HEAVY...
JUST A BIT LONGER, VI. I'M ALMOST FINISHED SPOT-WELDING THE PLATING...
CHUCK THOUGHT YOU COULD USE SOME EXTRA STRUTS UP HERE, MY LOVE.
THANKS, BABE!
WHEN YOU'RE DONE, KINETIX, I SENSE MICRO-FRACTURES IN THE HULL SLEEVE HERE...
UGH! STOP BEFORE I HEAVE...!

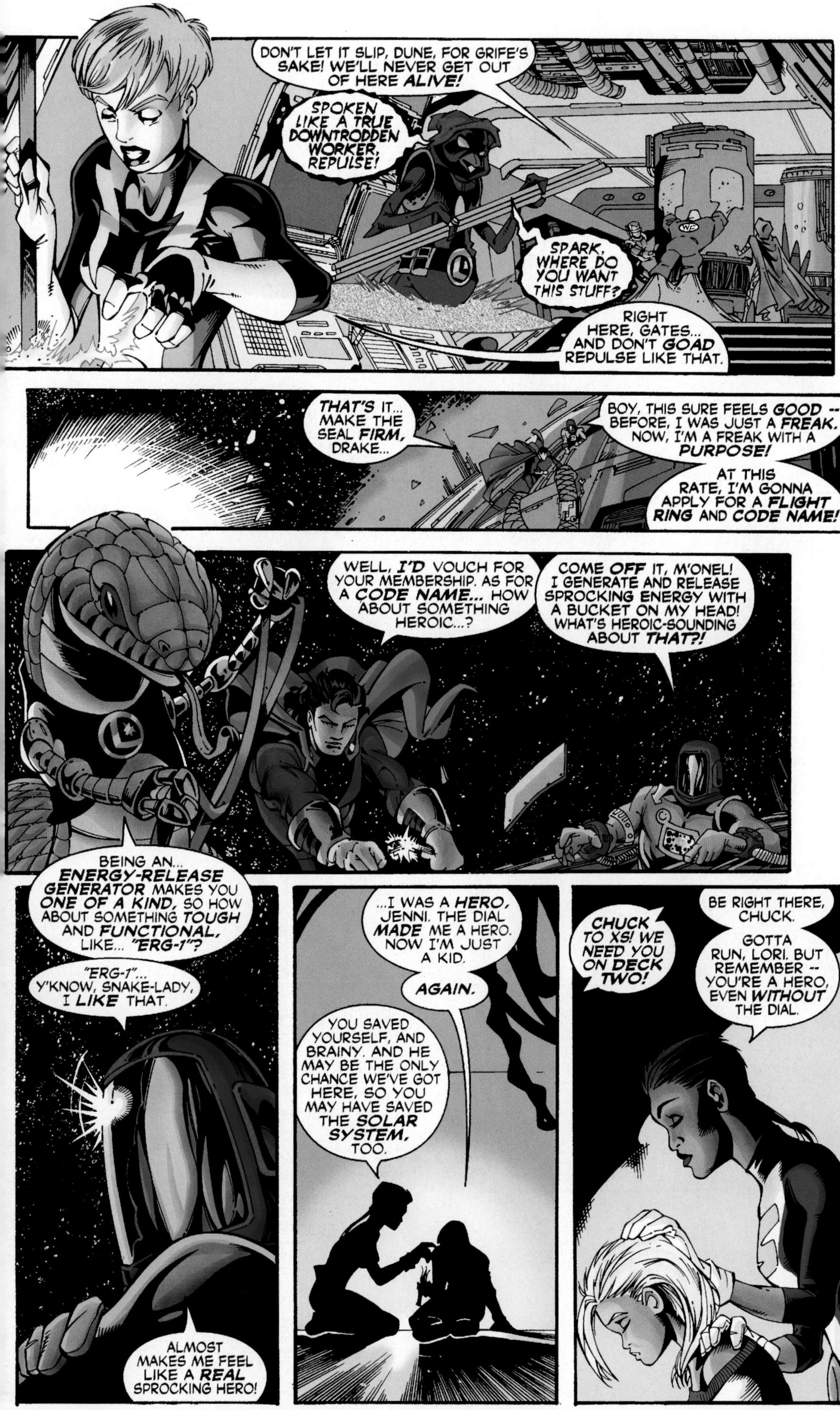

DON'T LET IT SLIP, DUNE, FOR GRIFE'S SAKE! WE'LL NEVER GET OUT OF HERE ALIVE!
SPOKEN LIKE A TRUE DOWNTRODDEN WORKER, REPULSE!
SPARK, WHERE DO YOU WANT THIS STUFF?
RIGHT HERE, GATES... AND DON'T GOAD REPULSE LIKE THAT.
THAT'S IT... MAKE THE SEAL FIRM, DRAKE...
BOY, THIS SURE FEELS GOOD -- BEFORE, I WAS JUST A FREAK. NOW, I'M A FREAK WITH A PURPOSE!
AT THIS RATE, I'M GONNA APPLY FOR A FLIGHT RING AND CODE NAME!
WELL, I'D VOUCH FOR YOUR MEMBERSHIP. AS FOR A CODE NAME... HOW ABOUT SOMETHING HEROIC...?
COME OFF IT, M'ONEL! I GENERATE AND RELEASE SPROCKING ENERGY WITH A BUCKET ON MY HEAD! WHAT'S HEROIC-SOUNDING ABOUT THAT?!
BEING AN... ENERGY-RELEASE GENERATOR MAKES YOU ONE OF A KIND, SO HOW ABOUT SOMETHING TOUGH AND FUNCTIONAL, LIKE... "ERG-1"?
"ERG-1"... Y'KNOW, SNAKE-LADY, I LIKE THAT.
ALMOST MAKES ME FEEL LIKE A REAL SPROCKING HERO!
...I WAS A HERO, JENNI. THE DIAL MADE ME A HERO. NOW I'M JUST A KID.
AGAIN.
YOU SAVED YOURSELF, AND BRAINY. AND HE MAY BE THE ONLY CHANCE WE'VE GOT HERE, SO YOU MAY HAVE SAVED THE SOLAR SYSTEM, TOO.
CHUCK TO XS! WE NEED YOU ON DECK TWO!
BE RIGHT THERE, CHUCK.
GOTTA RUN, LORI. BUT REMEMBER -- YOU'RE A HERO, EVEN WITHOUT THE DIAL.

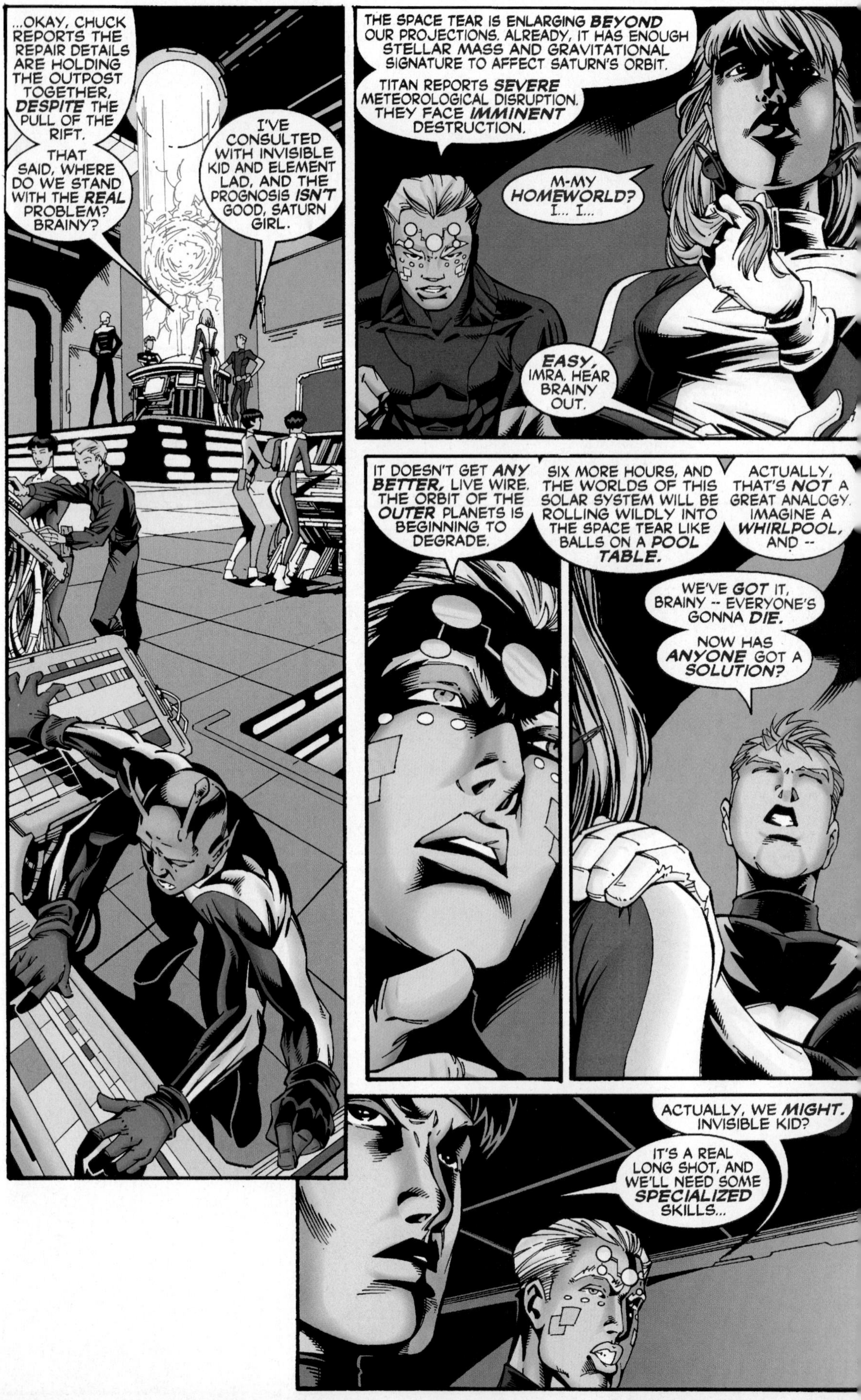
...OKAY, CHUCK REPORTS THE REPAIR DETAILS ARE HOLDING THE OUTPOST TOGETHER, DESPITE THE PULL OF THE RIFT.
THAT SAID, WHERE DO WE STAND WITH THE REAL PROBLEM? BRAINY?
I'VE CONSULTED WITH INVISIBLE KID AND ELEMENT LAD, AND THE PROGNOSIS ISN'T GOOD, SATURN GIRL.
THE SPACE TEAR IS ENLARGING BEYOND OUR PROJECTIONS. ALREADY, IT HAS ENOUGH STELLAR MASS AND GRAVITATIONAL SIGNATURE TO AFFECT SATURN'S ORBIT.
TITAN REPORTS SEVERE METEOROLOGICAL DISRUPTION. THEY FACE IMMINENT DESTRUCTION.
M-MY HOMEWORLD? I... I...
EASY, IMRA. HEAR BRAINY OUT.
IT DOESN'T GET ANY BETTER, LIVE WIRE. THE ORBIT OF THE OUTER PLANETS IS BEGINNING TO DEGRADE.
SIX MORE HOURS, AND THE WORLDS OF THIS SOLAR SYSTEM WILL BE ROLLING WILDLY INTO THE SPACE TEAR LIKE BALLS ON A POOL TABLE.
ACTUALLY, THAT'S NOT A GREAT ANALOGY. IMAGINE A WHIRLPOOL, AND --
WE'VE GOT IT, BRAINY -- EVERYONE'S GONNA DIE.
NOW HAS ANYONE GOT A SOLUTION?
ACTUALLY, WE MIGHT. INVISIBLE KID?
IT'S A REAL LONG SHOT, AND WE'LL NEED SOME SPECIALIZED SKILLS...

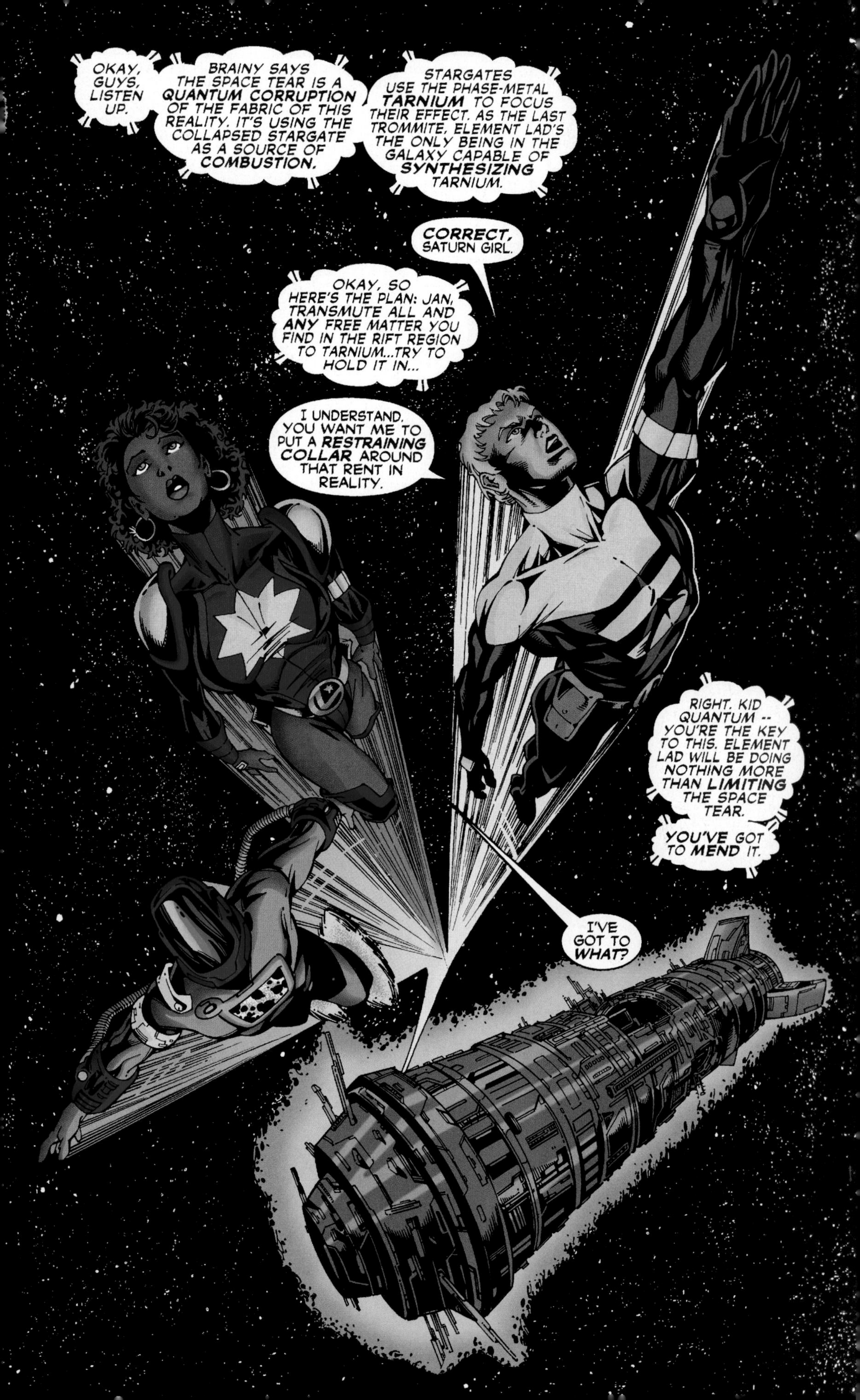
OKAY, GUYS, LISTEN UP.
BRAINY SAYS THE SPACE TEAR IS A QUANTUM CORRUPTION OF THE FABRIC OF THIS REALITY. IT'S USING THE COLLAPSED STARGATE AS A SOURCE OF COMBUSTION.
STARGATES USE THE PHASE-METAL TARNIUM TO FOCUS THEIR EFFECT. AS THE LAST TROMMITE, ELEMENT LAD'S THE ONLY BEING IN THE GALAXY CAPABLE OF SYNTHESIZING TARNIUM.
CORRECT, SATURN GIRL.
OKAY, SO HERE'S THE PLAN: JAN, TRANSMUTE ALL AND ANY FREE MATTER YOU FIND IN THE RIFT REGION TO TARNIUM...TRY TO HOLD IT IN...
I UNDERSTAND. YOU WANT ME TO PUT A RESTRAINING COLLAR AROUND THAT RENT IN REALITY.
RIGHT. KID QUANTUM -- YOU'RE THE KEY TO THIS. ELEMENT LAD WILL BE DOING NOTHING MORE THAN LIMITING THE SPACE TEAR.
YOU'VE GOT TO MEND IT.
I'VE GOT TO WHAT?

YOUR QUANTUM POWERS SHOULD BE ABLE TO *STITCH* THE FABRIC OF TIME-SPACE BACK TOGETHER.

IT WON'T BE EASY, BUT BRAINY AND INVISIBLE KID CAN DIRECT YOU VIA THE OUTPOST SCANNER ARRAY.

O-OKAY... I'LL DO MY BEST...!

PROCEED WITH *CAUTION,* KID QUANTUM. THE INITIAL OUTWASH OF ENERGY FROM THE TEAR *VAPORIZED* A DAXAMITE WORKFORCE MEMBER CALLED META.

WHAT ABOUT *ME,* TITAN-LASS?

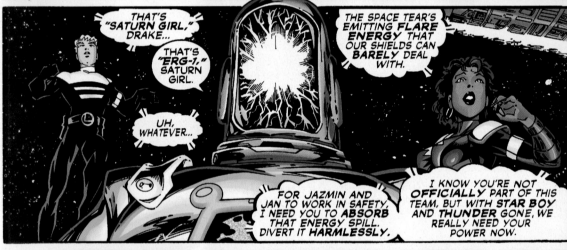

THAT'S "SATURN GIRL," DRAKE...

THAT'S "ERG-1," SATURN GIRL.

UH, WHATEVER...

THE SPACE TEAR'S EMITTING *FLARE ENERGY* THAT OUR SHIELDS CAN *BARELY* DEAL WITH.

FOR JAZMIN AND JAN TO WORK IN SAFETY, I NEED YOU TO *ABSORB* THAT ENERGY SPILL. DIVERT IT *HARMLESSLY.*

I KNOW YOU'RE NOT *OFFICIALLY* PART OF THIS TEAM, BUT WITH *STAR BOY* AND *THUNDER* GONE, WE REALLY NEED YOUR POWER NOW.

YOU *GOT* IT, SATURN GIRL. THANK YOU FOR *NEEDING* A FREAK LIKE ME.

YOU'RE NO FREAK, DRA-- ERG-1.

YOU'RE *LEGION* NOW.

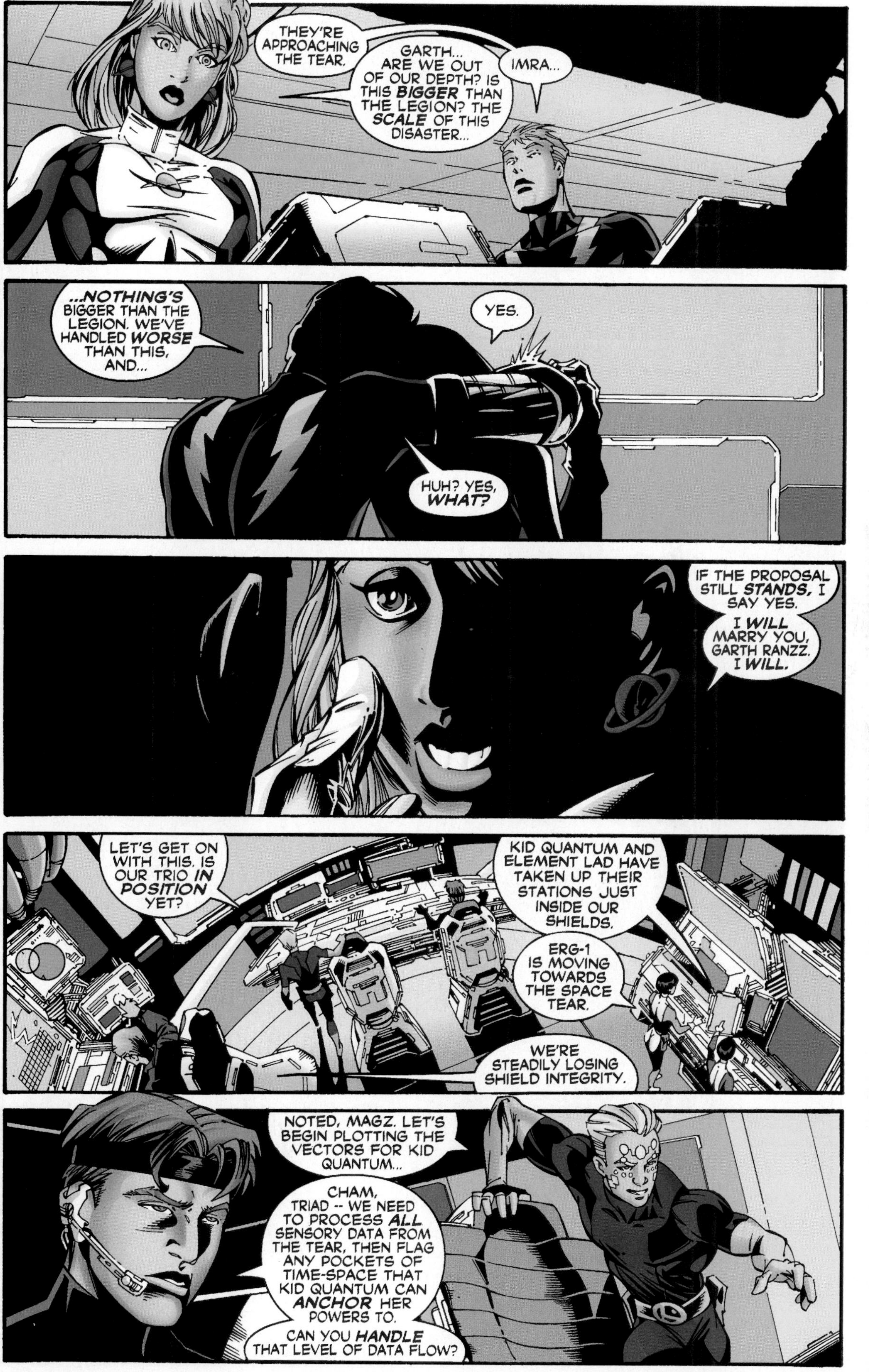

THEY'RE APPROACHING THE TEAR.
GARTH... ARE WE OUT OF OUR DEPTH? IS THIS BIGGER THAN THE LEGION? THE SCALE OF THIS DISASTER...
IMRA...
...NOTHING'S BIGGER THAN THE LEGION. WE'VE HANDLED WORSE THAN THIS, AND...
YES.
HUH? YES, WHAT?
IF THE PROPOSAL STILL STANDS, I SAY YES.
I WILL MARRY YOU, GARTH RANZZ. I WILL.
LET'S GET ON WITH THIS. IS OUR TRIO IN POSITION YET?
KID QUANTUM AND ELEMENT LAD HAVE TAKEN UP THEIR STATIONS JUST INSIDE OUR SHIELDS.
ERG-1 IS MOVING TOWARDS THE SPACE TEAR.
WE'RE STEADILY LOSING SHIELD INTEGRITY.
NOTED, MAGZ. LET'S BEGIN PLOTTING THE VECTORS FOR KID QUANTUM...
CHAM, TRIAD -- WE NEED TO PROCESS ALL SENSORY DATA FROM THE TEAR, THEN FLAG ANY POCKETS OF TIME-SPACE THAT KID QUANTUM CAN ANCHOR HER POWERS TO.
CAN YOU HANDLE THAT LEVEL OF DATA FLOW?

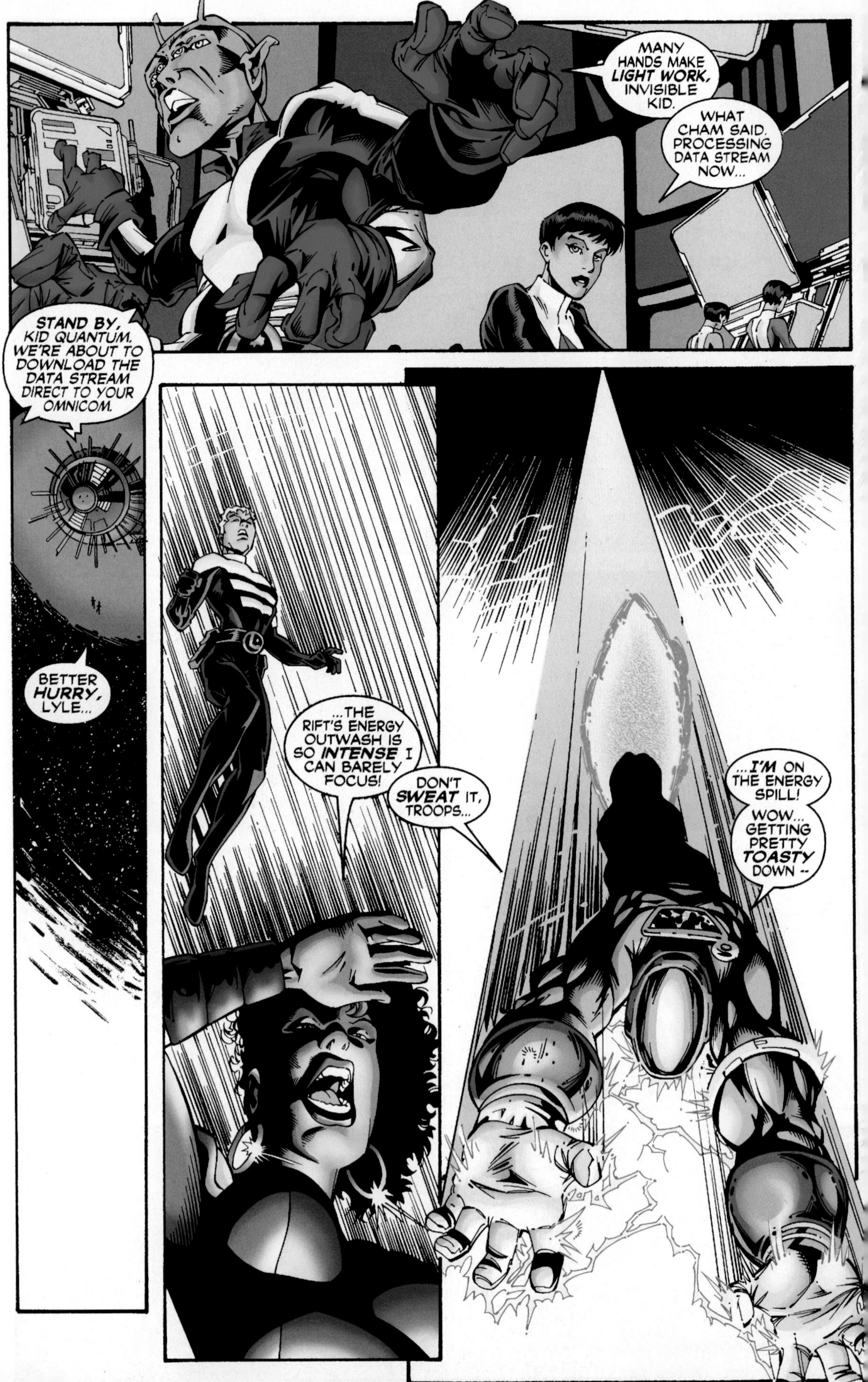
MANY HANDS MAKE LIGHT WORK, INVISIBLE KID.
WHAT CHAM SAID. PROCESSING DATA STREAM NOW...
STAND BY, KID QUANTUM. WE'RE ABOUT TO DOWNLOAD THE DATA STREAM DIRECT TO YOUR OMNICOM.
BETTER HURRY, LYLE...
...THE RIFT'S ENERGY OUTWASH IS SO INTENSE I CAN BARELY FOCUS!
DON'T SWEAT IT, TROOPS...
...I'M ON THE ENERGY SPILL!
WOW... GETTING PRETTY TOASTY DOWN --

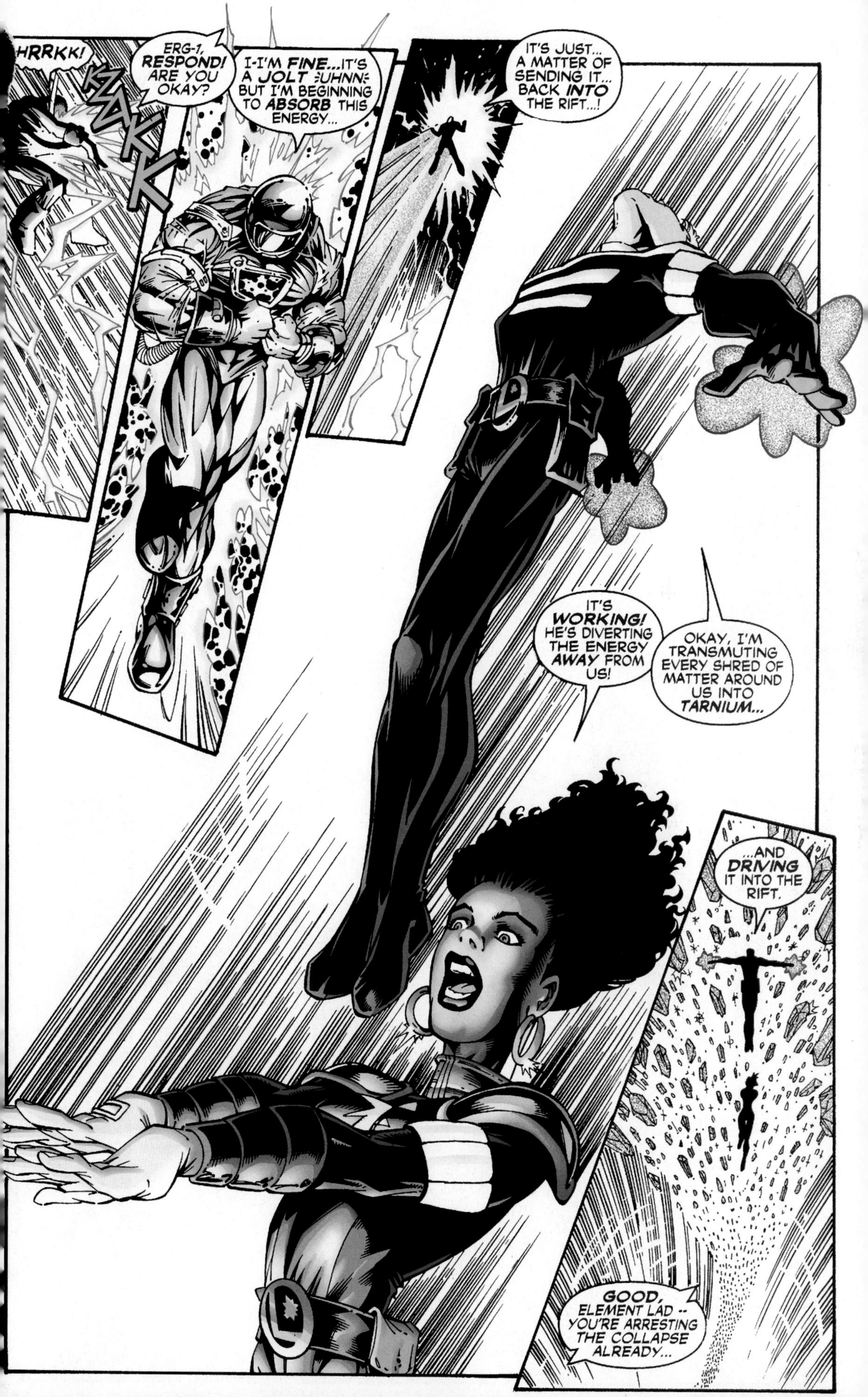
HRRKK!
KZAKK
ERG-1, RESPOND! ARE YOU OKAY?
I-I'M FINE...IT'S A JOLT UHNN BUT I'M BEGINNING TO ABSORB THIS ENERGY...
IT'S JUST... A MATTER OF SENDING IT... BACK INTO THE RIFT...!
IT'S WORKING! HE'S DIVERTING THE ENERGY AWAY FROM US!
OKAY, I'M TRANSMUTING EVERY SHRED OF MATTER AROUND US INTO TARNIUM...
...AND DRIVING IT INTO THE RIFT.
GOOD, ELEMENT LAD -- YOU'RE ARRESTING THE COLLAPSE ALREADY...

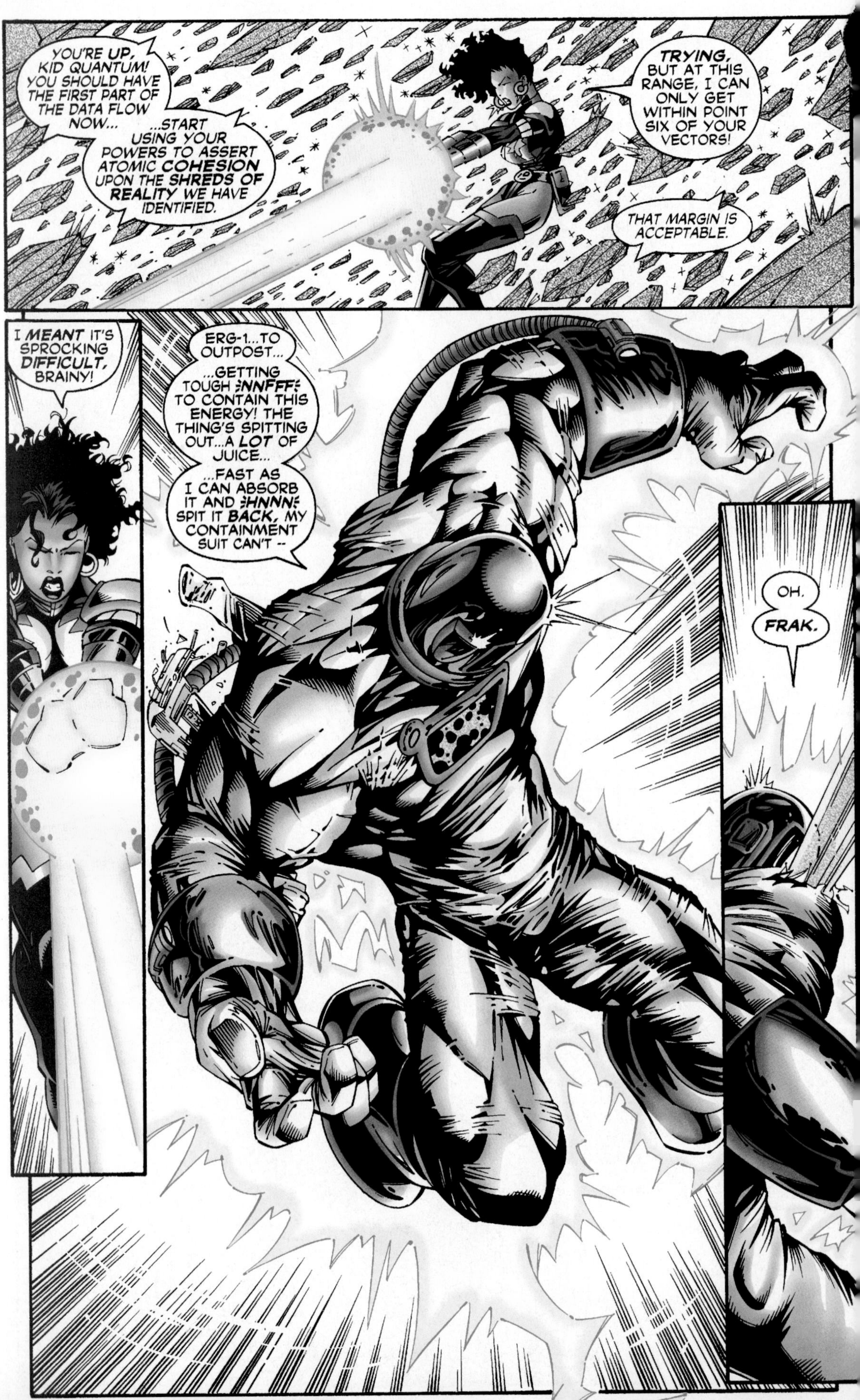
YOU'RE UP, KID QUANTUM! YOU SHOULD HAVE THE FIRST PART OF THE DATA FLOW NOW...
...START USING YOUR POWERS TO ASSERT ATOMIC COHESION UPON THE SHREDS OF REALITY WE HAVE IDENTIFIED.
TRYING, BUT AT THIS RANGE, I CAN ONLY GET WITHIN POINT SIX OF YOUR VECTORS!
THAT MARGIN IS ACCEPTABLE.
I MEANT IT'S SPROCKING DIFFICULT, BRAINY!
ERG-1...TO OUTPOST...
...GETTING TOUGH ‡NNFFF‡ TO CONTAIN THIS ENERGY! THE THING'S SPITTING OUT...A LOT OF JUICE...
...FAST AS I CAN ABSORB IT AND ‡HNNN‡ SPIT IT BACK, MY CONTAINMENT SUIT CAN'T --
OH. FRAK.

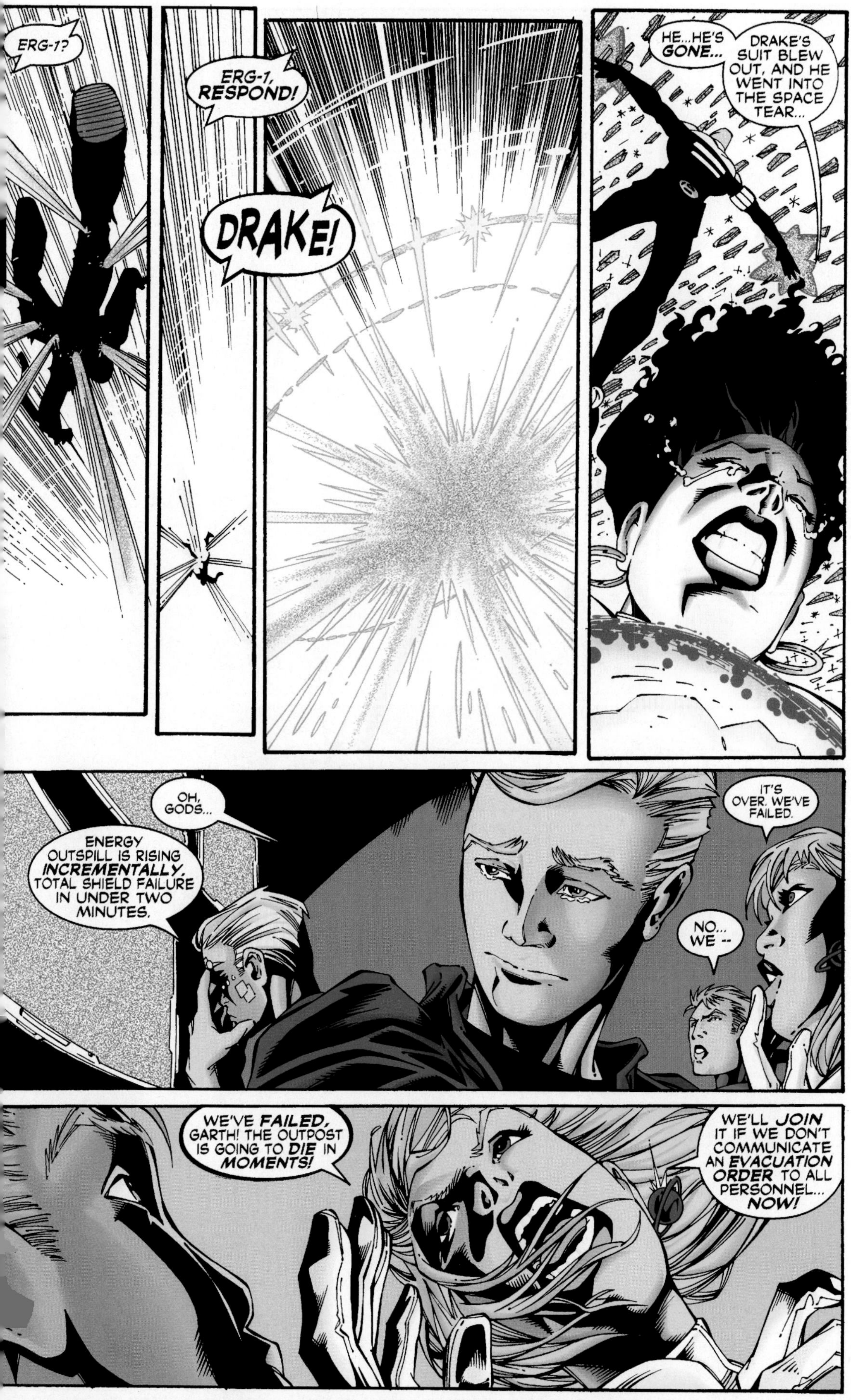
ERG-1?
ERG-1, RESPOND!
DRAKE!
HE...HE'S GONE...
DRAKE'S SUIT BLEW OUT, AND HE WENT INTO THE SPACE TEAR...
OH, GODS...
ENERGY OUTSPILL IS RISING INCREMENTALLY. TOTAL SHIELD FAILURE IN UNDER TWO MINUTES.
IT'S OVER. WE'VE FAILED.
NO... WE --
WE'VE FAILED, GARTH! THE OUTPOST IS GOING TO DIE IN MOMENTS!
WE'LL JOIN IT IF WE DON'T COMMUNICATE AN EVACUATION ORDER TO ALL PERSONNEL... NOW!

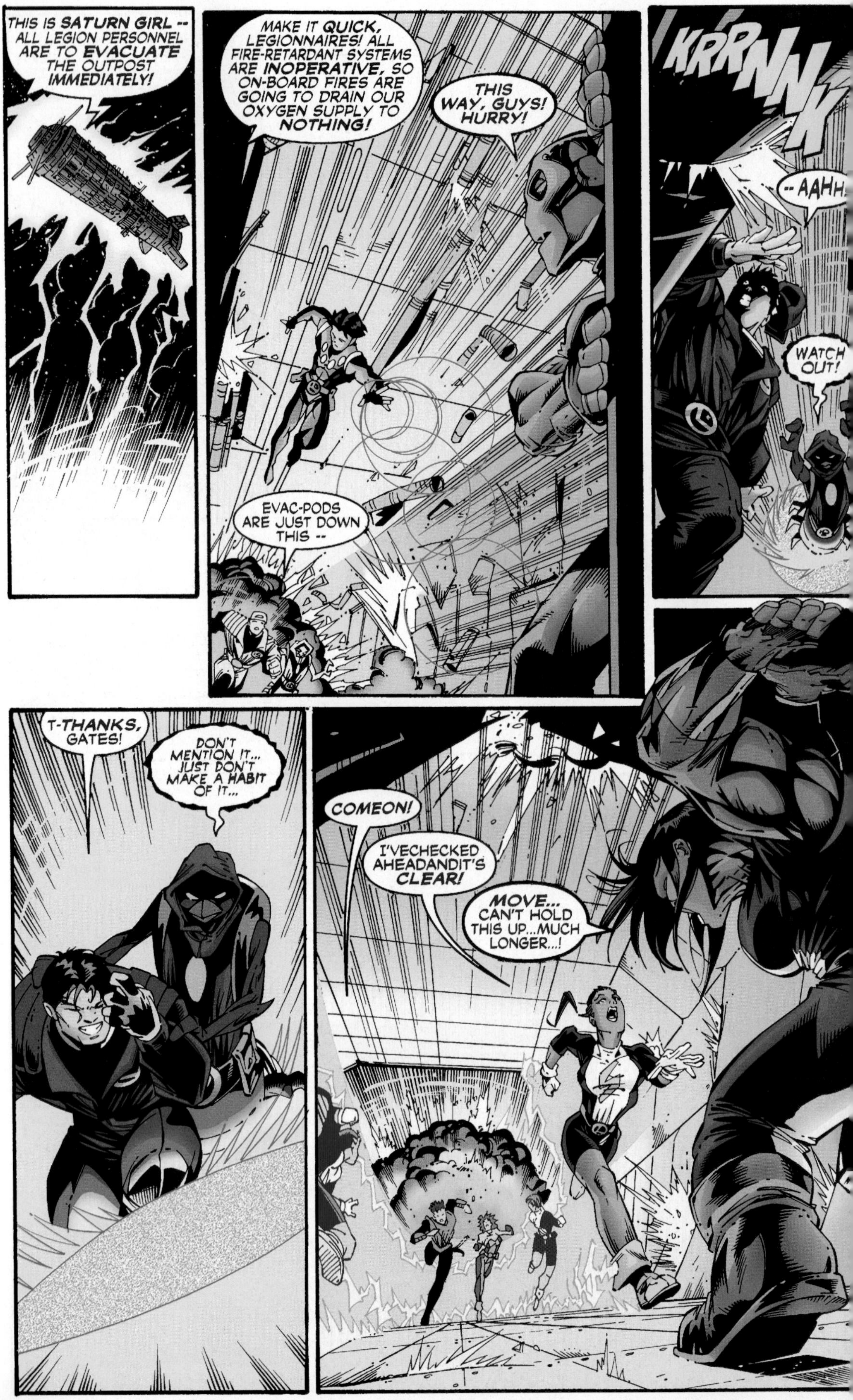
THIS IS SATURN GIRL -- ALL LEGION PERSONNEL ARE TO EVACUATE THE OUTPOST IMMEDIATELY!
MAKE IT QUICK, LEGIONNAIRES! ALL FIRE-RETARDANT SYSTEMS ARE INOPERATIVE, SO ON-BOARD FIRES ARE GOING TO DRAIN OUR OXYGEN SUPPLY TO NOTHING!
THIS WAY, GUYS! HURRY!
EVAC-PODS ARE JUST DOWN THIS --
KRRNNNK
--AAHH
WATCH OUT!
T-THANKS, GATES!
DON'T MENTION IT... JUST DON'T MAKE A HABIT OF IT...
COMEON!
I'VECHECKED AHEADANDIT'S CLEAR!
MOVE... CAN'T HOLD THIS UP...MUCH LONGER...!

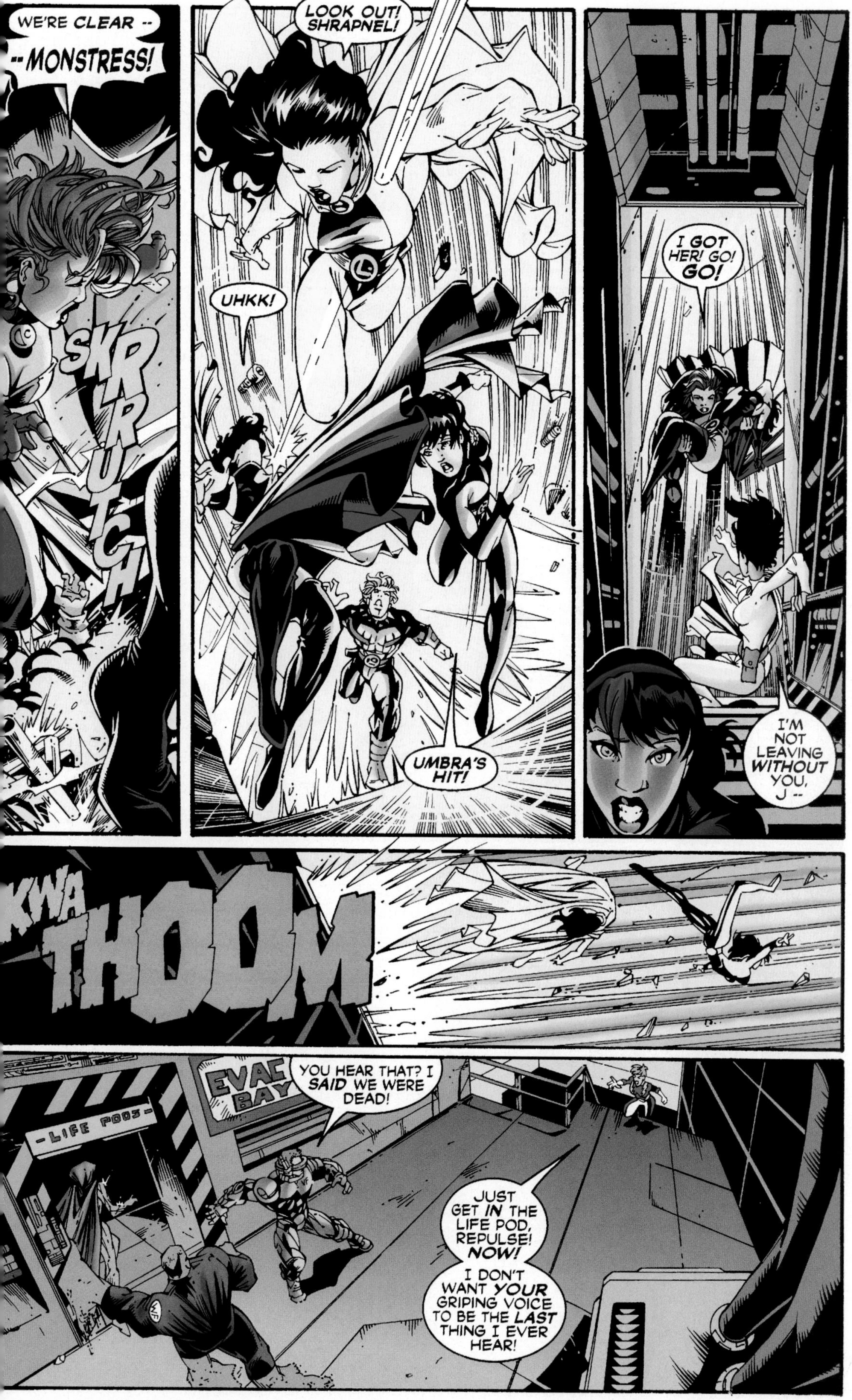

WE'RE CLEAR --
-- MONSTRESS!
SKRRUTCH
LOOK OUT! SHRAPNEL!
UHKK!
UMBRA'S HIT!
I GOT HER! GO! GO!
I'M NOT LEAVING WITHOUT YOU, J --
KWA THOOM
EVAC BAY
LIFE PODS
YOU HEAR THAT? I SAID WE WERE DEAD!
JUST GET IN THE LIFE POD, REPULSE! NOW!
I DON'T WANT YOUR GRIPING VOICE TO BE THE LAST THING I EVER HEAR!

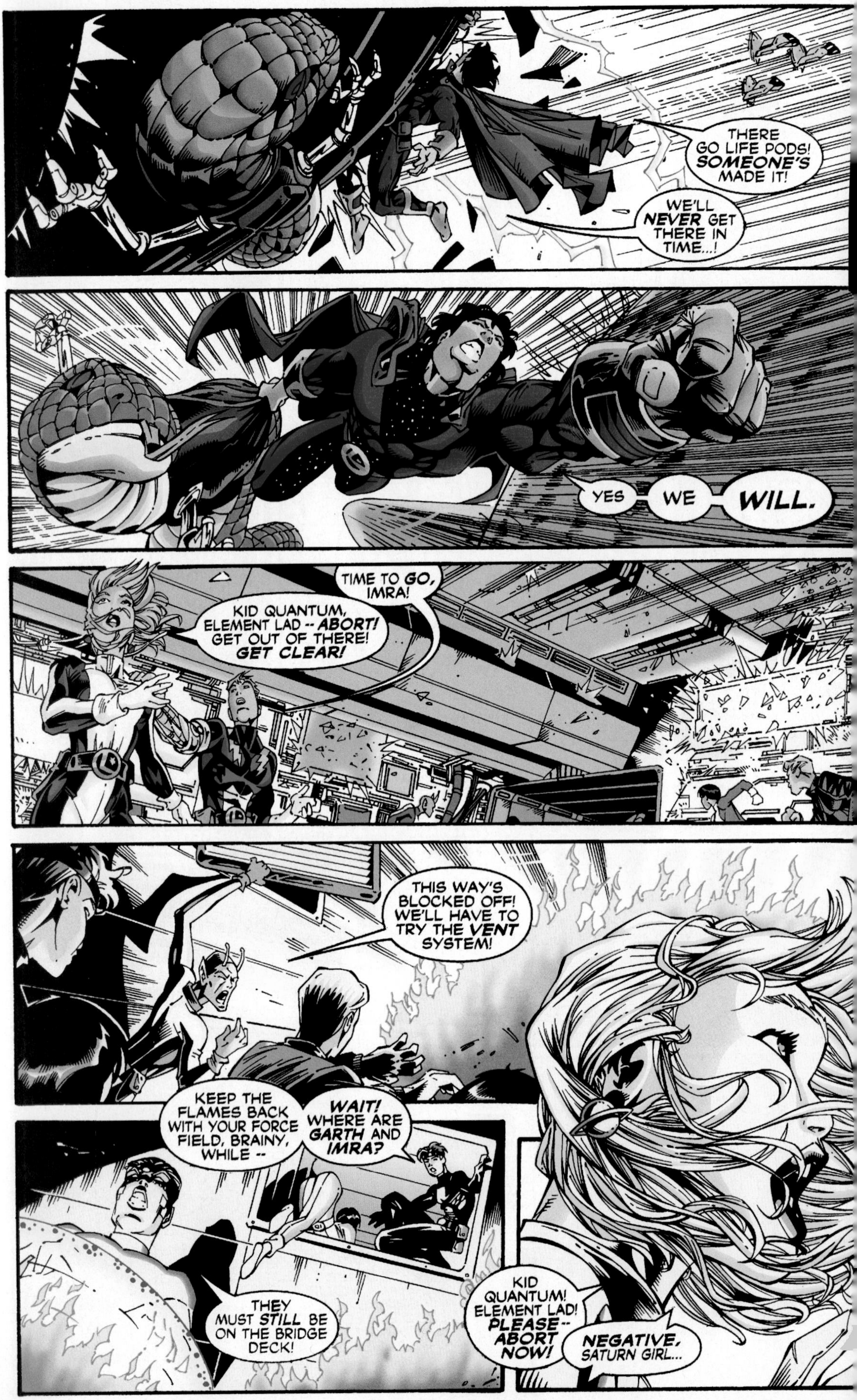
THERE GO LIFE PODS! SOMEONE'S MADE IT!
WE'LL NEVER GET THERE IN TIME...!
YES
WE
WILL.
KID QUANTUM, ELEMENT LAD -- ABORT! GET OUT OF THERE! GET CLEAR!
TIME TO GO, IMRA!
THIS WAY'S BLOCKED OFF! WE'LL HAVE TO TRY THE VENT SYSTEM!
KEEP THE FLAMES BACK WITH YOUR FORCE FIELD, BRAINY, WHILE --
WAIT! WHERE ARE GARTH AND IMRA?
THEY MUST STILL BE ON THE BRIDGE DECK!
KID QUANTUM! ELEMENT LAD! PLEASE-- ABORT NOW!
NEGATIVE, SATURN GIRL...

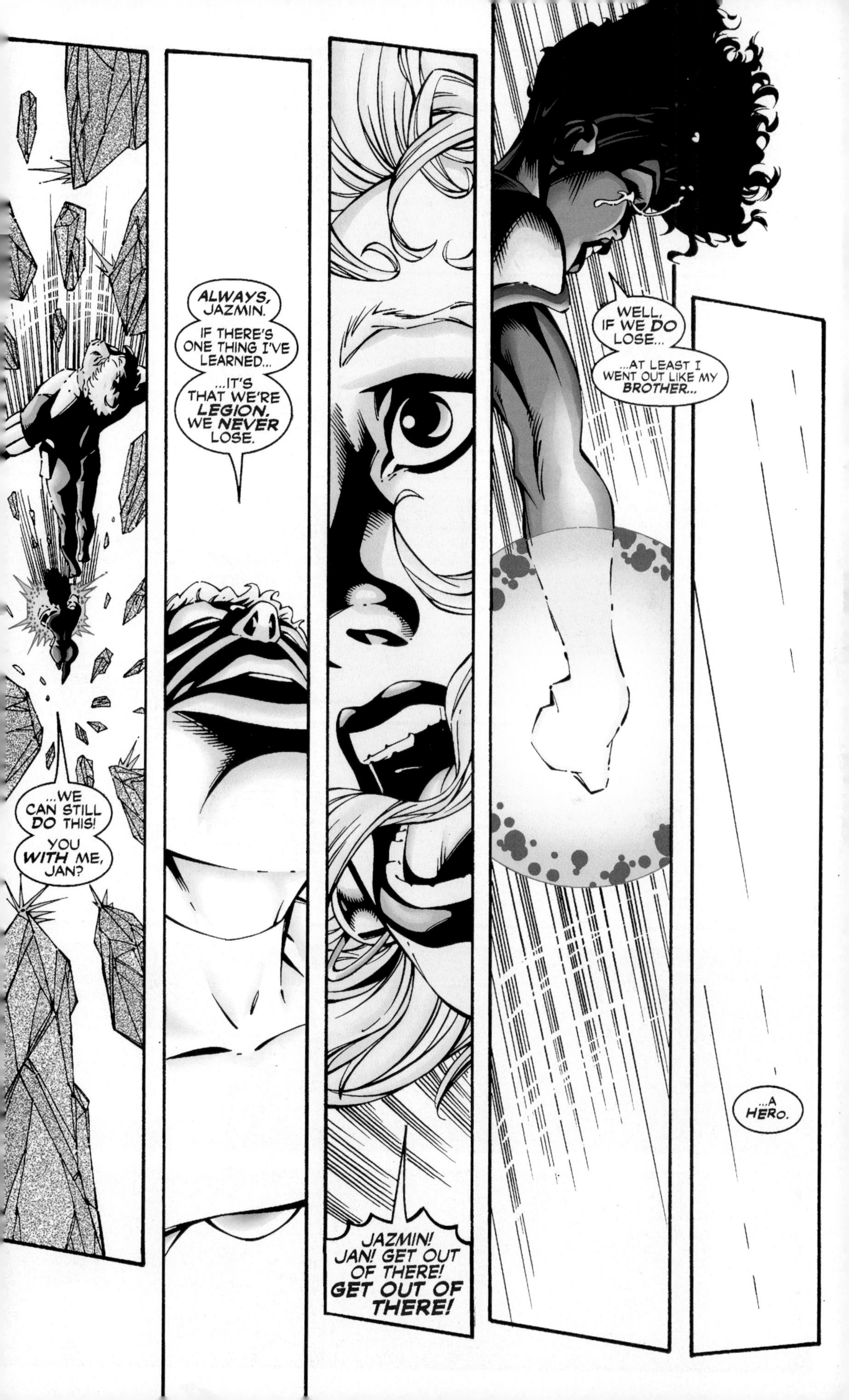
...WE CAN STILL DO THIS!
YOU WITH ME, JAN?
ALWAYS, JAZMIN.
IF THERE'S ONE THING I'VE LEARNED...
...IT'S THAT WE'RE LEGION. WE NEVER LOSE.
JAZMIN! JAN! GET OUT OF THERE! GET OUT OF THERE!
WELL, IF WE DO LOSE...
...AT LEAST I WENT OUT LIKE MY BROTHER...
...A HERO.

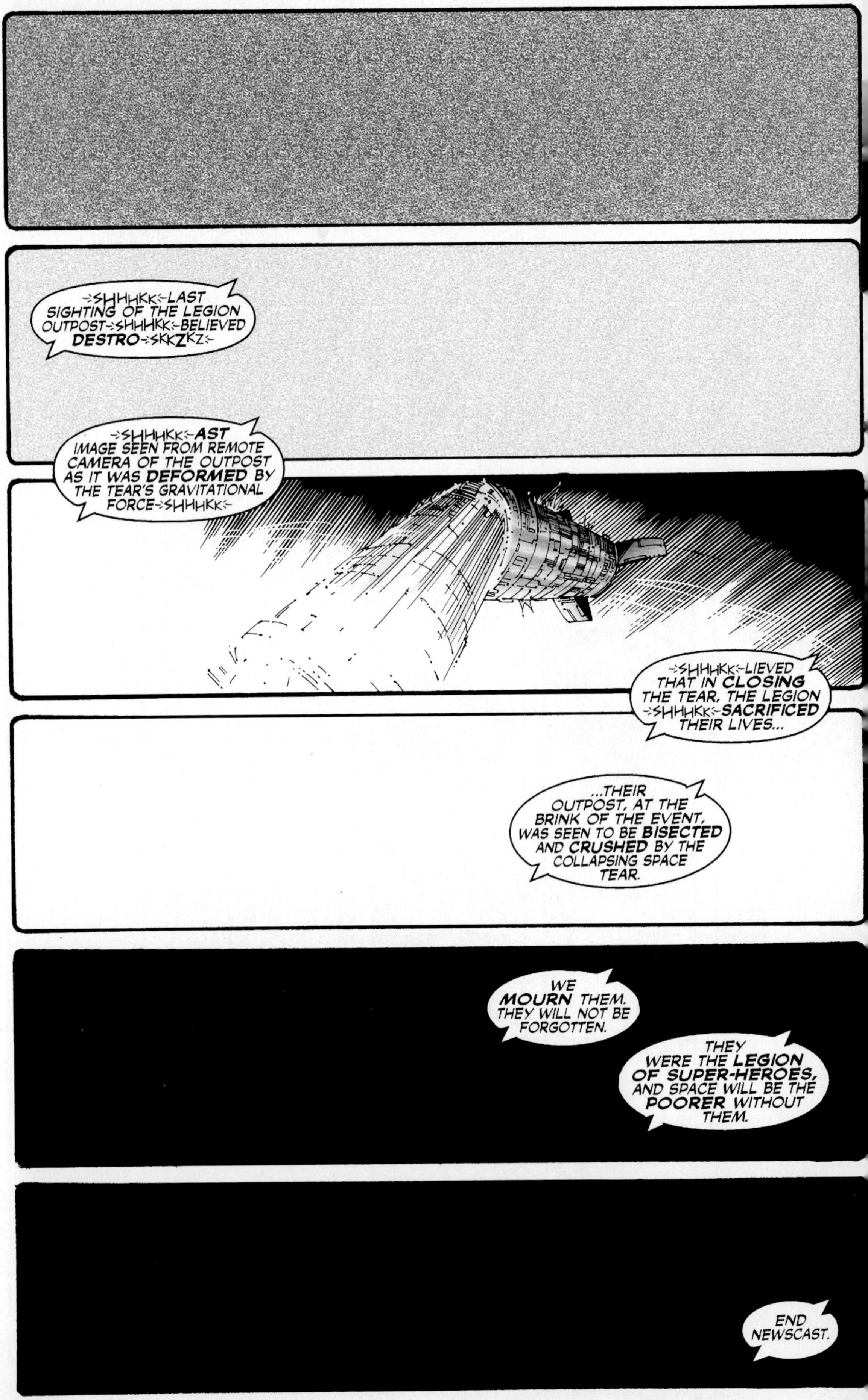

→SHHHKK←LAST SIGHTING OF THE LEGION OUTPOST→SHHHKK←BELIEVED DESTRO→SKKZKZ←
→SHHHKK←AST IMAGE SEEN FROM REMOTE CAMERA OF THE OUTPOST AS IT WAS DEFORMED BY THE TEAR'S GRAVITATIONAL FORCE→SHHHKK←
→SHHHKK←LIEVED THAT IN CLOSING THE TEAR, THE LEGION →SHHHKK←SACRIFICED THEIR LIVES...
...THEIR OUTPOST, AT THE BRINK OF THE EVENT, WAS SEEN TO BE BISECTED AND CRUSHED BY THE COLLAPSING SPACE TEAR.
WE MOURN THEM. THEY WILL NOT BE FORGOTTEN.
THEY WERE THE LEGION OF SUPER-HEROES, AND SPACE WILL BE THE POORER WITHOUT THEM.
END NEWSCAST.

It is my sincere hope that you have enjoyed the collection of stories you now hold in your hands—especially since "Legion of the Damned," the first arc in what I consider to be an amazing run by writers Dan Abnett and Andy Lanning, was born out of... well, necessity.

Sales on LEGION OF SUPER-HEROES and LEGIONNAIRES, not to mention overall interest in the team, were in decline when I assumed the role of editor in late 1997. Numerous reasons were cited. Some claimed the Legion, once among DC Comics' most popular teams and best-selling titles, had been the casualty of retconned DC continuity in the eighties. Others insisted that fast-forwarding the team "five years later" had made the 30th century an uncomfortable, uninviting environment for those not fluent in all bits of Legionnaire business. And there were those who said that "rebooting" the Legion from the events of ZERO HOUR (with which I'm proud to say I was involved as an assistant editor, both on the crossover and the Legion books) was merely a short-term fix that didn't address the longstanding issue that wasn't going away.

Regardless of the reason, fans' "longstanding issue" was consistently clear: this was no longer the "classic" Legion they remembered from the Silver and Bronze Age of Comics.

It was a huge problem, and one that put the talented creators working on LEGION OF SUPER-HEROES and LEGIONNAIRES at that time in a no-win situation. Attempts to change characters or direction incurred the wrath of the readers that supported the reboot. Yet keeping everything status quo was worse. I remember sitting online for a weekly chat where fans would come in and predict upcoming storylines, often with incredible accuracy. Though neither I nor the creators would confirm or deny their prognostications, it was alarming to discover they pretty much knew every step the Legionnaires were about to take *before* they took it.

And so, toward the latter half of 1998, I decided that we had to stop trying to recapture history with a rebooted team that occasionally evoked memories of a Legion that no longer existed, and instead focus on looking forward and producing the Legion the readers wanted.

I got to know Dan Abnett and Andy Lanning while they worked alongside editor Eddie Berganza on RESURRECTION MAN. I loved their work on that series, as well as their appreciation for science fiction; their Marvel UK work was testament to that fact, and I was already familiar with Dan's status as a growing fixture within the *Warhammer* franchise. After working with them on a SUPERGIRL/RESURRECTION MAN crossover and a fill-in story for THE CREEPER, I asked them to pitch a several-issue arc that could run as a miniseries event in LEGION OF SUPER-HEROES and LEGIONNAIRES.

Now, Dan and Andy—"DnA," as they were often called—were not diehard, long-lived Legion fans, but they didn't need to be. Dan was a high-concept storyteller, while Andy made those concepts, no matter how weird and wild, relatable to the characters and the readers. It's what made them such a good writing duo, one of the best and most durable that comics has ever had; they were willing to take chances and shake up the status quo. More so, they recognized the best way to do that with the Legion was to take the team out of its comfort zone: the pristine United Planets.

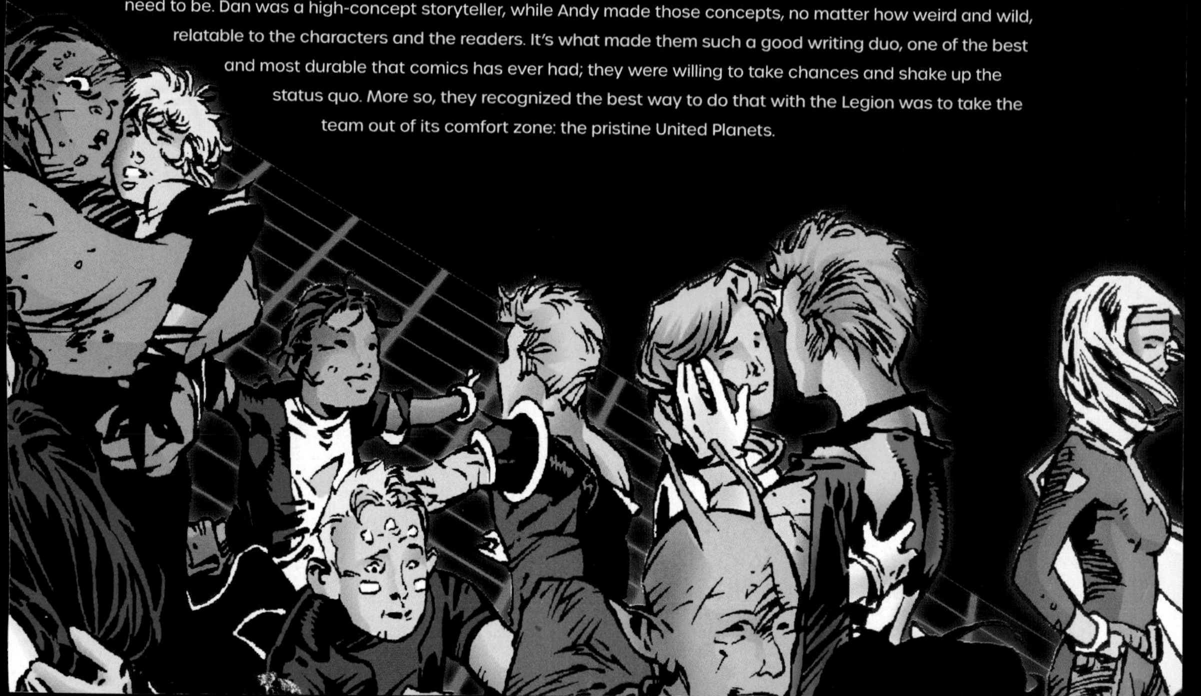

...way to preserve even a semblance of their previous, ...time in a long time, the team's all-too-predictable future ...n science fiction, heroic angst and a monstrous threat

...ssue fill-in, though I had already decided I was going to change the existing creative teams. It was just time for everyone, especially the Legion, to move forward. And once I saw how damn good "Damned" was going to be, I knew the Legion could do so with DnA.

The next step was finding the right artist. That's where I owe my friend, DC VP of Art Direction & Design Mark Chiarello, my eternal gratitude. Mark supported our desire to orchestrate a new future for the Legion, and after reviewing several portfolios together, he showed me some samples from artists he had met in San Diego. A few stood out, but I was immediately blown away by Olivier Coipel's work. His art was like nothing I had seen before in American comics— an assessment immediately shared by British-born Abnett and Lanning.

Abnett and Lanning, Coipel, and Comicraft on letters—it was a severe overhaul of the creative team, except for one: Tom McCraw was there to help me on my very first day as the Legion's assistant editor. He was at the forefront of the team's reboot. And now here he was, not only embracing this bold new venture, but guiding DnA, Olivier and yours truly on how to change everything while remaining true to the essence of the Legion. Tom, if anyone deserves a statue of honor inside Legion HQ, it's you.

How did we do? I remember a lot of hate mail initially. After part one, readers thought we had forever destroyed the Legion, that DnA had no idea what they were doing with the franchise, and that Olivier's art—his earliest comics work, mind you—was "ugly" and "disgusting." By part four, many of those naysayers said the story and art had improved and looked promising. Sales didn't change significantly, but word of mouth, from both fans and professionals, grew. Everyone seemed to like where we were going. At least, until Dan and Andy announced where the Legion was going next. But that's another story.

Nearly 20 years later, Abnett, Lanning and Coipel's "Legion of the Damned" is still an exciting read and a dramatic departure for the Legion of Super-Heroes. From an editorial standpoint, I marvel at how Olivier's art evolves with each chapter, while DnA clearly grow more comfortable writing the Legionnaires with every page. I also think of the minute changes that a more seasoned me would make today—a suggested panel revision here, a tweaked line of dialogue there...it's just the way I'm wired. And though I miss the experience of working with these fantastically talented gentlemen, I will always treasure the time of uncertainty and anxiety that we—and the Legion—went through to achieve it.

MICHAEL McAVENNIE
May 2017